Vivekananda

Vivekananda

The PHILOSOPHER of FREEDOM

GOVIND KRISHNAN V.

ALEPH

ALEPH

ALEPH BOOK COMPANY
An independent publishing firm
promoted by *Rupa Publications India*

First published in India in 2023
by Aleph Book Company
7/16 Ansari Road, Daryaganj
New Delhi 110 002

ISBN: 978-93-90652-92-1

1 3 5 7 9 10 8 6 4 2

Printed in India.

Dedicated to

My parents, Syama and Vijayan, without whose unconditional love, understanding, and support, I am convinced I would have ended up as a lost angry soul. If I ever do anything of use to this world, it is due to them.

and

P. Padmanabhan Nair (Jothi), whose voracious reading in high school took in the philosophical works of Swami Vivekananda, before his brilliant mind was dulled by the fog of mental illness.

CONTENTS

PREFACE

The best antidote to the Sangh's misappropriation of Vivekananda is for more people to read Vivekananda's work. The idea that Vivekananda is not being read enough might sound surprising. After all, there has been a veritable explosion of books written about Vivekananda in recent years. Vivekananda is in the air more than ever. But a peculiar phenomenon that often happens with a historical figure and their work seems to be happening with Vivekananda too. It is that once a text has been referenced often enough in popular consciousness, it becomes like an oft-repeated mantra whose original meaning has been lost, to be replaced by only the sound. Most people have heard about it, many are aware of its contents, and some have even read parts of it, but all this has become foggy and opaque, without real signification.[*]

With a few notable exceptions, the popular literature that has been produced about Vivekananda in the last three decades, especially in English, has been derivative, adulatory, and unoriginal. It is not so much that these books mischaracterize Vivekananda as that they merely rehash known opinions about the monk and his ideas.[†] This contributes to creating the opacity mentioned above. In trying to understand a past thinker's thought, we always approach him with a set of concerns that are uniquely our own. A critical tradition keeps a historical figure alive only by continuously recasting his ideas through the intellectual problems, concerns, and challenges that confront and engage that particular time period. This is precisely what today's discourse on Vivekananda has failed to do. It has failed to make the case for the relevance of Vivekananda's ideas in relation to the issues that preoccupy us today, thus

---

[*]I have borrowed this idea from an unpublished manuscript written by Dr Sayeed Abdul Syed, which he shared with me. As of the writing of this book, the manuscript is scheduled to be published by Permanent Black under the title 'Reflections on B. R. Ambedkar's *Annihilation of Caste*'.

[†]*Vivekananda in India: A Corrective Biography* by Rajgopal Chattopadhyay (1999) and *The Unknown Life of Swami Vivekananda: The Monk as Man* by Shankar (2011) immediately come to mind as two useful contributions to Vivekananda literature. Also deserving mention is *Swami Vivekananda: The Living Vedanta* by Chaturvedi Badrinath (2006). The book paints a psychological profile of Vivekananda from material overlooked by biographers, which is insightful at many points.

consigning him to a pantheon of emblematic national heroes known to us only through empty adulation.

Perhaps nothing has benefited the Sangh in its project of owning the patriot monk's legacy, as much as the gulf between the contemporary Indian intellectual and Vivekananda's work. This is not to suggest that the Indian intelligentsia is at fault for not being enthusiastic readers of Vivekananda. Intellectual fashion changes over time, and the concerns and interests of today's reader are very different from those of earlier generations who read Vivekananda more widely. Globally, religion as a subject is of minimal interest to the modern secular intellectual, whose investment in the episteme of a rational and liberal democracy makes her automatically agnostic towards a domain that is considered occult or 'supernatural'. An unintended consequence of this however, is the de-intellectualization of religion, which leaves the door wide open for fundamentalists to hijack religious traditions for their political ends. The problem is exacerbated in India, because unlike American and European academia, the academia in India has not nurtured the discipline of religious studies. Scholarly attention to religion means that it is perfectly possible for an intellectual in the West to think that Christianity is bunkum and yet be aware of the great tradition of Scholastic Christian philosophy— an awareness that can be deployed against Christian fundamentalism, which is based on literalist, ahistorical, and anti-intellectual readings of the Bible.

It is in this capacity that Vivekananda is a valuable resource to liberals and constitutionalists seeking to combat the tide of Hindutva. Vivekananda stands as a bridge between modernity and a notoriously obscure and hermeneutically difficult textual tradition that is more than three millennia old.[1] This is precisely why Vivekananda is indispensable for Hindus and why getting hold of his legacy allows the Sangh Parivar to make a direct claim on Hinduism itself. But by that very token, given that Vivekananda's interpretation of Hinduism as well as his sociopolitical philosophy is the ideological opposite of the Sangh's, Vivekananda's ideology is one of the most potent weapons one can use to block the inroads Hindutva is making into present day Hinduism and into the public sphere.

But resisting Hindutva is not the only reason for which the liberal intelligentsia would find it useful to turn to Vivekananda.[*] There is the deeper

---

[*] I use the term liberal here to denote those antagonistic to a right-wing ideology and committed to constitutionality. The term is meant to cover a variety of ideological positions within this spectrum, not merely political liberalism.

and more long-term question of democracy itself. If we accept the position that critical rationality is one of the engines that drive democracy forward, then the nature of Indian society and religion's role in it becomes problematic. Organized popular religion often exhibits strong irrational tendencies, and India is a deeply religious country. For democracy to progress, the sphere of critical rationality has to expand to include all phases of public life, and most prevalent notions of religion are resistant, if not hostile to such a process. This is because widely held ideas of religion operate through categories such as the sacred, faith, belief, revelation, and dogma, which, by definition, cannot be interrogated or called into question by reason. The appeal of Vivekananda's thought lies in the fact that he presents the case for rationality from within the domain of religion itself, thus providing an alternative conception of religion that can complement the rational nature of the secular public sphere. What is unique about Vivekananda as a religious thinker is that he went much beyond the claim that religion and reason were compatible. For Vivekananda, religion had to meet the standards of rationality as much as science does. In fact, reason and proof had to be integral components of any authentic search for spiritual truth.

The rise of the Hindutva movement since the demolition of the Babri Masjid in 1992, has been a source of anxiety for everyone who believes in the idea of a secular, pluralist, and tolerant India. Under successive NDA governments, it has become a cause for alarm, as Hindutva's religious bigotry and intolerant ideology receive overt political backing from the ruling Bharatiya Janata Party and covert administrative backing from the government.[2] In the last decade, we have watched as Hindutva morphed from a decentralized but cadre-driven movement controlled by the Sangh Parivar, into an amorphous and diffuse social phenomenon. Various elements of Hindutva thought have become part of the public consciousness, creating a spiral of vigilante violence, attacks on minorities, assaults on freedom of expression, and moral and cultural policing. While these elements still remain largely on the margins of national life, the political forces driving them continue to push them towards the mainstream. Though dispersed, the entirety of the Hindutva project is undergirded by a rigid ideological vision: that of transforming India into a Hindu Rashtra. What exactly would constitute a Hindu Rashtra is a matter of debate, but what cannot be doubted is that whatever form such a political organism would take, it would be defined by majoritarian nationalism and would be the negation of the republic that our founders envisioned. As such, the spread of Hindutva today represents an existential threat to Indian democracy, and the constitutional values which govern it.

If we have to preserve Indian democracy, it is essential that we combat Hindutva in all its phases: political, social, cultural, and intellectual. This book is an effort in the latter direction. There has been a belated but dawning realization in some quarters at least, that it is important to take the fight to Hindutva's home front. Hindutva's basic legitimacy, in fact, its very possibility as a political project, comes from its claim to represent Hinduism. But Hindutva is not coterminous with Hinduism—in fact, there is not even any significant overlap. The former is a distorted, hegemonic, politically charged version of the latter, which in its essence is an open, plural, and intellectually tolerant faith. It is important for those who oppose Hindutva to challenge its proprietary claim to Hinduism and reclaim the religion from its misappropriation by the Sangh Parivar.

This book contests the Rashtriya Swayamsevak Sangh's (RSS) appropriation of Swami Vivekananda, arguably one of the most influential and defining figures of modern Hinduism. I hope to show the reader that Vivekananda was not a Hindu supremacist or even a facile glorifier of Hinduism, as the Sangh portrays him to be. In fact, his religious philosophy, social thought, and ideology are the very anti-thesis of Hindutva. Vivekananda's thought stands in direct opposition to all the fundamental tenets of Hindutva, to its parochial concept of Hinduism, its insular nationalism and cultural conservatism, its authoritarian collectivism and anti-intellectualism. It goes further than that. Vivekananda would have considered Hindutva a perverse inverted mirror image of everything he valued as the true essence of Hinduism: its tolerance for intellectual dissent, acceptance of all faiths as valid paths to God, and the non-normative character of its beliefs and practices. As a liberal and an individualist, he would have found the rigid collectivism of the RSS odious, while as a rationalist he would have found its cultural atavism to be the worst kind of reactionary superstition.

How is it that the RSS has managed to appropriate a figure like Vivekananda who is an ideological foe rather than an ally? There are several reasons for this, though perhaps the simplest explanation is that Vivekananda is hardly read any more. It would seem the more Vivekananda is celebrated as an icon, the less people read the man himself. The critical vacuum around Vivekananda's texts has allowed the RSS to pick up a string of inspirational quotes with a patriotic bend, or those appreciative of Hinduism, and stitch them together to create the popular image of a Vivekananda who can be fit into a Hindu nationalistic frame. This is a Vivekananda whose formidable intellectual reputation can be used to prop up the inadequacies of the conservative Hindu section's world view. A Vivekananda, whose legendary success in conquering the West with Hindu thought, can alleviate the sense of civilizational inferiority that contact with Western colonialism created. Without a powerful counter narrative, the thinking Indian who is presented with such a figure, would find him platitudinous and shallow, not to mention religiously partisan.

There have, of course, been responses to the RSS narrative about Vivekananda. Occasionally, one finds spirited articles in the media which reassert the universal, secular, and rationalist character of Vivekananda's thoughts. One gets the sense that they succeed in clearing the ground a bit, before being swamped again by the incessant propaganda from the right. The other kind of response has been from a section of the academia, broadly influenced by post-critical theory, and seeking to read Vivekananda from a set of concerns different from how he has been read traditionally by liberal left historians. These are postmodern concerns of identity, gender, power, nationalism, representation, and so on.

While these concerns are, for the most part, valid, the critiques launched on their basis leave much to be desired. These examinations of Vivekananda have largely treated his texts in a superficial manner and without a rigorous attempt to understand the totality of his thought, or his philosophical positions. They also tend to be fatally ahistorical and suffer from deep theoretical flaws in the way they endeavour to interpret Vivekananda's ideology. There is also much intellectual confusion, including a lack of clarity regarding how to deal with a figure whose complex perspective shifts continuously with his different but overlapping vantage points: that of philosopher, mystic, populizer, teacher, patriot, monk, and anti-imperialist.

The result has been a series of books and publications which read Vivekananda very differently from traditional historiography. The new perspective sees him as problematic in several aspects. He is viewed as promoting a Hindu masculinity, of being a believer in the superiority of Hinduism, of being sympathetic to the caste system, of marginalizing Muslims and Christians, and, most crucially, of being ideologically oriented towards Hindu nationalism. These postmodern critiques converge towards the Hindutva account of Vivekananda, though what they consider vice is seen as virtue by the latter. Most damaging, in my opinion, has been the tendency to read Vivekananda as a kind of soft Hindutva figure. Far too many commentators have been happy to relinquish Vivekananda to Hindutva without appreciation of the enormous consequences. No one could be happier with this state of affairs than the Sangh.

The debate about Vivekananda today is, thus, complex. Strands of interpretations from these different discourses clash and comingle in such a way that the effect is a lot of white noise. For the average person standing outside these debates, the picture of Vivekananda that emerges from them is a fragmented one, and the effect is one of bewilderment. This often leaves people with the impression that the issue is too problematic to admit of a straightforward answer. The immaculate figure of the humanist Vivekananda starts to appear improbable, and the conviction gains ground that whatever the true picture of Vivekananda is, it must be of a greyish shade.

This book seeks to intervene in this debate, to reinstate the traditional reading of Vivekananda as a universalist and a humanist. It will differ from earlier accounts in two significant aspects. One is that it seeks to incorporate the various concerns which make Vivekananda appear suspect to contemporary critiques. The second is that it does this while looking at Vivekananda through the prism of Hindutva and drawing out the points of opposition. Thus, it hopes to clear the confusions and misapprehensions in the way Vivekananda is received and understood today. The hope that this attempt succeeds is not due to any particularly original or ingenious line of interpretation. It is based rather on the complete unambiguity of Vivekananda's texts. When seen in their proper context, they leave no room for doubt on the issues that we have been discussing.

The book also tries to make Vivekananda accessible to the modern reader. We are so used to the idea of Vivekananda as the modern monk that we are apt to forget that Vivekananda's public life occurred in the late Victorian age and that while his thought anticipated the modern world, its setting is still that of the late nineteenth century. I try to provide a historicization of the key elements of Vivekananda's thought and actions, to provide a framework for the contemporary reader who wants to understand Vivekananda. Though Vivekananda wrote and lectured in almost breathtakingly simple language about abstruse metaphysical concepts, the texts may still present problems to those used to the terms of the current discourse. The book attempts to give the reader a set of conceptual tools through which to approach and understand Vivekananda's life and work.

This book is divided into three sections. The first section mainly explores the contrast and opposition between the beliefs and ideology of Hindutva and those held by Vivekananda. The second section is an exposition of Vivekananda's philosophical position and social thought that flows from the issues discussed in the first section. When the first section argues that Vivekananda is in essence anti-Hindutva, this would be an anachronism if the claim is not explained properly. Vivekananda could not have been against Hindutva in the ordinary sort of way because Hindutva as a political ideology did not yet exist in his time. Vivekananda is anti-Hindutva in the sense that one can call Voltaire anti-fascist—fascism was almost two centuries in the future from Voltaire's time, but its ideology was the extreme antithesis of the political freedom and liberty Voltaire prized and fought for.

The first chapter gives a brief overview of Vivekananda's life and career, including his transformation from Narendranath Dutta to Swami Vivekananda, his journey to the West, and his reception by the Anglo-American world. The second and third chapters introduce the reader to important features of Vivekananda's writing and thinking which have become lost to our public memory. By focusing on these neglected but representative aspects, this segment aims to disrupt the Hindutva narrative about Vivekananda. It explores Vivekananda's views on themes relevant to the Hindutva project: Indian civilization, society, and culture; the nature of the caste system and Brahminism; the history of Islam in India and attitudes towards Islam and Christianity; Hindu mythology, belief, and rituals; individual liberty; attitudes towards the West; and so on.

This is followed by chapters which give historical context to Vivekananda's life and work. The fourth chapter in the book situates Vivekananda's public life in the global context, in fin de siècle Europe and America. It is a time period that sits between two worlds, a Victorian past and the post-World War I world. Unpacking the intellectual and social context of this period which bridges the modern and the pre-modern, is necessary to understand the form, language, and rhetorical strategies through which Vivekananda expressed his ideas. Also surveyed is the cultural and intellectual framework of colonialism within which Vivekananda is operating, as a member of a subject race preaching religion to its imperial masters. I argue that a lack of appreciation of these factors is responsible for the misperception of Vivekananda as having affinities with Hindu nationalism.

The second section goes on to examine how the RSS and the Sangh have used Hindu symbols, rituals, cultural motifs, and issues like Ram Janmabhoomi to push their political agenda. This is contrasted with Vivekananda's treatment of Hinduism. It demonstrates how all the religious paraphernalia that the Sangh has latched on to and defines as the essence of a Hinduism that is under threat from other religions, is completely antithetical to Vivekananda's understanding and exposition of Hinduism. The section ends with an examination of the role Western civilization plays in Vivekananda's and the RSS's respective world views. In the Sangh's xenophobic nativism, the West is the existential other whose cultural influence is to be resisted. The West's civilizational achievements are aggressively rejected and secretly envied. Vivekananda on the other hand, frankly admired the West and thought India had as much to learn from the West as to teach her. Vivekananda's nationalism was superseded by his internationalism and his vision of a universal humanity in which the West and the East could work together.

The third section of the book begins with an exposition of Vivekananda's philosophy of universal religion. Vivekananda's attitude towards other religions was not just one of tolerance, but of acceptance. Vivekananda preached that all religions are equally valid and teach the same truth. They are all valid paths to God, differing only in outward forms. The inability of mankind to realize this has led to war, violence, and squabbles over the externals of religion. Such a view of course, challenges the Sangh's emphasis on the uniqueness of Hinduism as a source of identity for Hindus. But what does the claim that all religions are valid amount to philosophically? The claim would at first glance appear banal and vacuous given the sharply divergent and distinct theologies of each religion. I give an account of how Vivekananda dealt with this particular problem by shifting the essence of religion from theology to mystical experience. I also elucidate the theoretical framework Vivekananda developed to accommodate and relate the varieties of religious experiences with each other and try to demonstrate its coherence. Also explicated is Vivekananda's famous assertion that religion should conform to reason as much as science does. Important consequences flow from this rationalistic conception of religion, and bear upon contemporary debates around religion, democracy, and modernity. Such a conception also offers a solution for the increasing corrosion of the democratic sphere by aggressive assertions of religious faith.

In the closing part of the book, I deal with Vivekananda's position on caste and gender. Vivekananda has been widely considered as an anti-caste reformer. The last two decades or so have seen a flurry of revisionist readings which view Vivekananda as a conservative on the issue of caste. Some have gone further and accused Vivekananda of being actively casteist. I endeavour to show that these are misreadings stemming from a failure to locate Vivekananda within the caste discourse of his day. It is also a result of detaching his statements on these subjects and seeing them in isolation from the overall conceptual structure of his thought. Vivekananda wished to see the death of the caste system and was unwavering in his conviction that all humans are equal in every respect.

The Sangh Parivar has for decades claimed Vivekananda as a kindred spirit, or even an ideological ancestor. They have tried hard to ally the nineteenth-century Hindu reformist's legacy with their own post-colonial project of Hindu majoritarianism. The significance of this for the Sangh's claim of speaking on behalf of Hinduism cannot be overstated. Vivekananda interpreted and defined Hinduism during one of its most important periods of contact with modernity, both for the world and Hindus themselves. As such, many of the modern notions of the religion shared by Hindus and non-Hindus, layperson and academic alike, can be traced back in their original form to Vivekananda's thoughts on the subject. This is why claiming Vivekananda as one of its own gives Hindutva a strong purchase on Hinduism.

But by that very fact, Vivekananda's thought is also the most fertile site to contest Hindutva. The aim in writing this book is not only to reclaim Vivekananda back for liberalism. My hope is that this will be a step towards weaponizing his thought against the Sangh Parivar and Hindutva. Vivekananda's philosophy stands in stark antagonism to almost every issue that the Sangh has made into a cause. To establish that ideologically Vivekananda and the Sangh are arch-enemies would not only place Hindutva proponents in a spot they cannot defend; it would also reveal Hindutva is a distortion of the Hinduism that Vivekananda espoused.

HOW TO READ THIS BOOK

The book tries to address two themes in a comprehensive and rigorous fashion: Vivekananda's ideology and Vivekananda's philosophical thought. While I think most readers would be interested in both these themes, there would be some readers no doubt, who are exclusively interested in one. While I would advise all readers to peruse the book from beginning to end to get a complete picture of Vivekananda, the man and thinker, those with absolutely no interest in abstract philosophy but only in Vivekananda's ideology and the political debates current about him, may choose to skip the first two chapters of the third volume, on Vivekananda's philosophy (chapters 9 and 10). However, they will find the last three chapters, on ethics, gender, and caste (chapters 11, 12, and 13), indispensable. For those who are primarily interested in Vivekananda's thought, I would advise against trying to read the section on his philosophy non-chronologically. The first two volumes contain much material on Vivekananda's views that is a necessary introduction to the more technical philosophy dealt with in Part III. Chapter 4 deals with the overall historical context of America and Europe, where Vivekananda did most of his preaching. Vivekananda's historical context is imperative to understand his work. As such, it is meant to give the reader the right historical tools to read Vivekananda's work. But if any reader finds that they are getting bogged down with details of European history and are not able to relate directly to Vivekananda's life and work, they can move on to chapter 5, which deals with more concrete instances of Vivekananda's historical situation.

PART I

Life, Ideology, and Historical Context

VIVEKANANDA: THE LIFE

On 31 May 1893, a young Hindu monk set sail from Bombay to Japan on the *Peninsular* with tickets purchased through the travel agent Thomas Cook & Son. His ultimate destination was the United States of America, where he hoped to be a delegate at the World's Parliament of Religions. The Parliament was to be part of the World's Fair in Chicago, held to commemorate the four-hundredth anniversary of Columbus's arrival in the New World. In deciding to embark on this voyage, he had broken the injunctions of Hindu orthodoxy against crossing the seas, a rebellion that would become an irritant to him on his return to the homeland. But that was still several years in the future; for that moment, the sanyasi enjoyed the sea voyage and took in the sights each port of call had to offer. He proceeded to Colombo, Penang, Singapore, Hong Kong, Canton, Nagasaki, and finally Kobe. He disembarked at Kobe and travelled to the interior of Japan, visiting Osaka, Kyoto, Tokyo, and Yokohama. Visiting foreign lands for the first time, the monk was visibly delighted. Japan especially impressed him with its energy, industry, and vitality, which he contrasted with what he saw as the dullness and inertia of his own country. From Yokohama, he wrote to a group of friends in Madras: 'I want that a number of our young people should pay a visit to Japan and China every year.... Come, see these people, and go hide your faces in shame. A race of dotards, you lose your caste if you come out! Sitting down these hundreds of years with an ever-increasing load of crystallised superstition on your heads, for hundreds of years spending all your energy upon discussing the touchableness or untouchableness of this food or that, with all humanity crushed out of you by the continuous social tyranny of ages.'[1]

From Yokohama, the sanyasi boarded the *Empress of India*, which took him to Canada. After a rough journey, he got down at Vancouver and travelled through the Canadian Rockies to Winnipeg and then down to Minnesota and Wisconsin. The five-day train journey brought him finally to Chicago where the Parliament of Religions was to be held, but his travails were only starting. A series of misadventures followed over the next month, which pushed the young monk to the brink. For one, he had horrendously underestimated the cost of living in America. With six weeks to go for the Parliament and without any warm clothing or a single acquaintance in the country to turn to for help, he faced the daunting prospect of having to live on the streets in the cold. Add to this the fact that the Parliament only accepted delegates with credentials (he had naively not brought any), and in any case, the time period for registering as a delegate was over! When he went about in public, his Indian attire attracted not only curious stares, but unwanted attention. Strangers heckled him, children played pranks, and once a mob threw stones at him and chased him through the streets of Boston.

How the sanyasi got out of his predicament and found his way to representing Hinduism at the World's Parliament of Religions is a story in itself. It involved a number of serendipitous meetings, some incredible coincidences and the help of many generous American men and women. But finally, on 11 September, the thirty-year-old monk got up to speak to a gathering of thousands at the opening session of the Parliament in Chicago. The first words out of his mouth—Brothers and Sisters of America—were greeted with deafening applause and a standing ovation that lasted for several minutes. At that moment the unknown sanyasi disappeared forever, to be replaced with the persona of Swami Vivekananda.

American newspapers made him a national celebrity and his fame reached India, who found in him a much-needed hero and idol. Vivekananda's brief but powerful address perhaps resonated so much with the listeners because it spoke to the core of the World Parliament's theme: harmony between all the religions of the world. He advocated not merely tolerance, but the universal acceptance of all religions as true; each being different paths to the same God. Though he never spoke about politics, his fiery patriotism had an outsized influence on the first and second generations of the Indian national movement. He inspired figures as diverse in the political spectrum of the national movement as Jawaharlal Nehru, Subhas Chandra Bose, and Mohandas Karamchand Gandhi. Nehru was to say later: 'I can tell you that many of my generation were very powerfully influenced by him…. He was no politician in the ordinary sense of the word and yet he was, I think, one of the great founders—if you like, you may use any other word—of the national modern movement of India, and a great number of people who took more or less an active part in that movement in a later date drew their inspiration from Swami Vivekananda. Directly or indirectly he has powerfully influenced the India of today.'[2]

We find Subhas Chandra Bose echoing almost similar words. But Bose's admiration for Vivekananda and his guru Ramakrishna was much more personal; he credited them with awakening him to the service of the nation.

How shall I express in words my indebtedness to Sri Ramakrishna and Swami Vivekananda? It is under their sacred influence that my life got first awakened.... If Swamiji had been alive today, he would have been my guru, that is to say, I would have accepted him as my Master.... The foundation of the present freedom movement owes its origin to Swamiji's message. If India is to be free, it cannot be a land specially of Hinduism or of Islam—it must be one united land of different religious communities inspired by the ideal of nationalism. [And for that] Indians must accept wholeheartedly the gospel of harmony of religions which is the gospel of Ramakrishna-Vivekananda. ...The harmony of all religions which Ramakrishna Paramahamsa accomplished in his life's endeavour, was the keynote of Swamiji's life. And this ideal again is the bed-rock of the nationalism of Future India. Without this concept of harmony of religions and toleration of all creeds, the spirit of national consciousness could not have been built up in this country of ours full of diversities.[3]

Vivekananda was born Narendranath Dutta in Calcutta on 12 January 1863. He was the eldest son of Vishwanath Dutta, a prominent lawyer, and Bhuvaneshwari Devi. The Duttas were a family of lawyers for generations and very wealthy. Vishwanath Dutta, who practised at the Calcutta High Court, was a man known for his rare refinement and cultured mind, as well as an especially broad outlook on life. He combined in him the best of the three cultures whose currents were mingling and clashing in the Bengal of that time: English liberal education, the Persian literary culture, and the scholarly Sanskritic tradition. As noted by Tapan Raychaudhuri, Vishwanath was a polyglot and a virtuoso of Indian classical music, and held Muslim pirs in high regard while being a practising Hindu. According to one of his sons, he 'read the Bible and the Koran as well as the Bhagavata every day'.[4] Vishwanath Dutta was a representative of the cosmopolitan bhadralok intelligentsia that had formed in Calcutta, which was then the capital of British India, due to contact with Western thought and the modern economic and administrative apparatus of the British Empire. Dutta's parlour[*] would be full of prominent scholars, litterateurs, and other luminaries active in the cultural life of the city, both Hindu and Muslim. Debendranath Tagore (father of Rabindranath Tagore) was an occasional visitor to the Dutta home.

In the lively intellectual debates that happened at these gatherings, the boy Narendranath would often be present. Not content to remain a passive listener,

---

*Dutta seems to have held such informal gatherings in his law office more than his house.

the boy, who by several accounts was not only precocious but possessed of a prodigious memory, would voice his own opinion and interrogate the views expressed by his father's guests. Far from prohibiting this, Vishwanath Dutta seemed to have encouraged Naren (as he was known) to always speak his mind. Later, as Swami Vivekananda, he would say that he learned the importance of thinking independently from his father, an influence that no doubt played a part in Vivekananda's philosophy that nothing should be accepted without first questioning it and then trying to find the truth of it by oneself. He declared again and again before several audiences: 'Do not believe a thing because you read it in a book! Do not believe a thing because another has said it is so! Find out the truth for yourself! That is realization!'[5]

From his mother Bhuvaneshwari Devi, he inherited piety towards the various gods and goddesses of the Hindu pantheon. He would later say that he owed his religious culture to his mother. Narendranath, though possessed of a restless and boisterous nature, often spent long hours in meditation as a child.[6] He was fascinated by asceticism even as a boy, being attracted to wandering mendicants and often boasting to his schoolmates that he would become a sanyasi.[7] But he was not in any way overtly religious, nor did he seem to have observed the daily religious rites that orthodox Hindu households did. Being wealthy, the Duttas could afford to school him at home with private tutors. Once he attained the age for high schooling, Narendranath was sent to the Metropolitan Institute run by the famous educational reformer Ishwar Chandra Vidyasagar.

Naren was a talented singer and Vishwanath Dutta arranged for his son to receive training under reputed masters (ustaads). He learned both Hindu devotional music as well as Urdu and Persian songs. By the time Narendranath became an adult, he could play the tabla and sitar expertly and was recognized as a singer of great talent. Among those favourably impressed by Narendranath's singing was the young Rabindranath Tagore. At a wedding ceremony of the daughter of Rajnarayan Basu, a prominent Bengali writer (and grandfather of Sri Aurobindo), Tagore noticed Narendranath singing in the chorus. Tagore taught three songs he had composed to Narendranath and a few others present there.[8] Narendranath himself is known to have composed a number of Bengali songs, at least three before he was twenty-four years old.[9] He also became interested in musicology. Around the time he was twenty, Narendranath co-compiled an anthology of Bengali songs called *Sangita Kalpataru*. The songs he learned from Rabindranath were included in that anthology. The *Sangita Kalpataru* had a ninety-page preface which discussed the theory of music in relation to various aspects of vocal and instrumental music. The authorship of this treatise on Indian musicology is disputed, but many writers attribute it to Narendranath.[10]

By the mid-1860s, the first feelings of Indian nationalism were stirring in Bengal. The increasingly imperialist British administration portrayed the Bengali 'Babu' as effete and effeminate, in an attempt to stymie their demands on the government for addressing their legitimate interests. The counter-reaction took the form of spreading of physical education among the Bengali middle-class, often led by social reformers of a nationalist bent.[11] Thus gymnasiums and sporting clubs became the frequent haunt of English educated Bengali youth. Narendranath turned out to be prolific in this area as well, reportedly being good at wrestling, swimming, boxing, and lathi play.[12]

Narendranath entered Presidency College in 1880 and registered for a Bachelor's in Arts. However, a bout of malaria forced him to discontinue his studies. He later joined the General Assembly's Institution, established by the famous Scottish missionary Alexander Duff. Later, it would become the Scottish Church College and its alumni would include another legendary national icon—Subhas Chandra Bose. In 1881, for his first year BA examination, then called First Arts (FA), along with English, Sanskrit, Mathematics, and History, Vivekananda studied Western Logic and Psychology as advanced courses. Later, he replaced them with courses in Philosophy. The contact with eighteenth and nineteenth century Western philosophy would be formative for the thought of the future Vivekananda. Interestingly, Vivekananda was drawn to the two opposite poles of modern Western philosophy: British empiricism and German idealism. Of the two, perhaps the more vital influence was that of British philosophy, of both empiricism and political liberalism.

Several accounts from his fellow students survive, most of which attest to Narendranath's remarkable intellectual ability. William Hastie, the then principal of the Scottish Church College reportedly said of his gifted pupil that 'Narendra Nath Dutta is really a genius. I have travelled far and wide, but have never yet come across a lad of his talent and possibilities, even in the German universities amongst philosophy students.'[13] But Narendranath was no dry pedant in the making. Many accounts of contemporaries who knew him then talk of a charismatic personality, of great personal magnetism, sociability, a good humoured and easy nature, an endearing conviviality, as well as a rebellious streak. We have an arresting portrait of the Narendranath of that time from Sir Bajendranath Seal, who would go on to become one of the greatest Indian philosophers of his generation and later the vice-chancellor of Mysore University.

When I first met Vivekananda in 1881, we were fellow-students of Principal William Hastie, scholar, metaphysician, and poet, at the General Assembly's College. He was my senior in age, though I was his senior in the College by one year. Undeniably a gifted youth, sociable, free; and unconventional in manners, a sweet singer, the soul of social circles, a brilliant conversationalist, somewhat bitter and caustic, piercing with the shafts of a keen wit the shows and mummeries of the world, sitting in the scorner's chair but hiding the tenderest of hearts under that garb of cynicism; altogether an inspired Bohemian but possessing what Bohemians lack, an iron will; somewhat peremptory and absolute, speaking with accents of authority and withal possessing a strange power of the eye which could hold his listeners in thrall. This was patent to all.... I saw and recognized in him a high, ardent and pure nature, vibrant and resonant with impassioned sensibilities. He was certainly no sour or cross-grained puritan...he would indulge cynically in unconventional language[*] except when he would spare my innocence. He took an almost morbid delight in shocking conventionality in its tabernacles, respectability in its booths; and in the pursuit of his sport would appear other than he was, puzzling and mystifying those outside his inner circle of friends.[14]

Narendranath's serious engagement with religion started in his college days, but it came not via traditional Hinduism, but the Brahmo Samaj, a religious and social reform movement originally started by Raja Ram Mohan Roy.[†] Like many of the younger generation of the English educated bhadralok, Vivekananda too, had become dissatisfied by the traditional religion with its millions of deities, idol worship, intricate mythology as well as the encrustation of thousands of meaningless rituals that defied explanation. Narendranath felt the need for a rational religion, as had many Western-educated Bengali Hindus for the previous half decade. Narendranath was living in the later phase of what future historians would call the Bengal Renaissance or Indian Renaissance of the nineteenth century, a period of extraordinary cultural, social, and intellectual efflorescence and revitalization that laid the ground for Indian modernity as well as Indian nationalism.

---

[*]The usage 'unconventional language' seems to be a euphemism for either the discussion of taboo topics or the use of profanity.

[†]The Brahmo Samaj was going through a period of schism at this time. What Narendranath joined was the Sadharan Brahmo Samaj, a splinter group of the original or Adhi Brahmo Samaj, which was headed by Debendranath Tagore. Narendranath soon left the Sadharan Brahmo Samaj and joined Keshub Chandra Sen's Bharatvarshiya Brahmo Samaj.

When we think of secular modernity in India, we tend to think of its historical genesis as a Western import and understand its constitutive nature in terms of the historical trajectory that the roots of modernity took in the West—as a secular rational humanism that opposed the dogmas and superstition of religion and church. What has almost been completely forgotten today is that oddly enough, in India, modernity starts with religion. The confrontation and dialectic between progressive rationality, which took reason as an indispensable principle that guides all human endeavours, and a regressive irrationality, which saw tradition as the dogmatic standard for human behaviour, happened in India largely within the domain of religion; rather than between religion and an anti-religious humanism.* The history of the Brahmo Samaj is so central to the Bengal Renaissance that the organization's history forms an axis from which this particular encounter of reason with religion in nineteenth century Bengal can be told.

Brahmo Samaj was founded as Brahma Sabha by Raja Ram Mohan Roy in 1828. Over the course of the century, Brahmo Samaj produced many leaders, the most important of them being Debendranath Tagore and Keshub Chandra Sen. The Brahmo Samaj was both a religious and social reformation organization. Ram Mohan Roy, who died in 1833, has been called both the first 'modern Indian', as well as the father of Indian modernity. Now remembered more as a social reformer and a crusader against the practice of sati, Ram Mohan Roy was much more. In a sense, Ram Mohan Roy formulated the basic synergistic synthesis of Hinduism, Christianity, and Islam as teaching essentially the same core truths—this would become the centrepiece of the Indian form of secularism that played such an important part in the national movement as well as in the post-Independence task of nation building.

◦

Narendranath, was becoming increasingly dissatisfied with the dry rationalistic religion of the Brahmo Samaj. Learning the sceptical philosophy of David Hume, Herbert Spencer, and other philosophers also raised doubts in his mind about the existence of God. He tried for a while to find refuge in Hegel's philosophy by equating the Brahman of the Vedas to the Absolute of Hegel. But this too did not dispel his doubts or quench his spiritual thirst. If God exists, he became convinced, one should be able to see God. Without that, all intutions of and arguments for God's existence were based on second-hand evidence at

---

*This is, of course, a simplification of what intellectual modernity was.

best. With this in mind, the young Narendranath approached Debendranath Tagore. Debendranath Tagore was known for his spiritual nature and ascetic qualities and was popularly known as Maharishi Debendranath Tagore. Thus, Narendranath went to a houseboat where he knew Debendranath was staying. He burst upon Tagore sitting in meditation, who enquired of his guest the reason for the unexpected visitation. 'Sir, have you seen God?' Narendranath asked. Debendranath avoided giving a direct answer. He reportedly told the young Narendranath, 'Son, you have the eyes of a yogi', and then advised him to practise meditation.[15]

Narendranath found the answers he was seeking in the mystic Sri Ramakrishna Paramahamsa, who was the priest of the Kali temple at Dakshineshwar. While the events that occurred in the nearly five years (1881–86) that Narendranath spent as a disciple of Sri Ramakrishna contain too much mystical lore to separate myth from history, it can be reasonably ascertained that if the English Romantic poet William Wordsworth had never picked up his pen, Narendranath might very well not have gone to meet Ramakrishna. William Hastie, the principal of the General Assembly Institution, was teaching Wordsworth's famous poem 'The Excursion' in Narendranath's class. He was reading the opening section which consists of a monologue by a character called the wanderer, who lived in an old cottage. The wanderer speaks thus as he recollects the woman who used to live in the cottage before and who had passed away,

> '...so familiarly
> Do I perceive her manner, and her look,
> And presence; and so deeply do I feel
> Her goodness, that, not seldom, in my walks
> A momentary trance comes over me....'[16]

This reportedly led to a discussion among the students of what exactly the poet had meant to convey by the word 'trance'. Some questioned whether such a state of trance, really existed. To this question William Hastie apparently retorted that if anyone wanted to see a genuine state of trance, they should approach the wonderful mystic who lived in the Kali temple at Dakshineshwar.[17] Not long afterwards, Narendranath paid his first visit to Dakshineshwar to meet Ramakrishna and ask the question he had been asking every holy man: 'Have you seen God?'[18]

During the course of his visit, Narendranath put to Sri Ramakrishna the question that troubled him 'Does God exist?' Ramakrishna answered in the affirmative. Narendranath then asked, 'Have you seen him?' To which

Ramakrishna replied, 'Yes, I have. I have seen God just like I see you, but in a much more intense way.'[19] The answer and the complete self-assurance with which it was given, shocked Narendranath. No one to whom he had asked the question before had answered in the affirmative, and that too, with such conviction. Narendranath proceeded to ask Ramakrishna if he too could see God. Ramakrishna assured him that he could. Narendranath did not know it then, but from that very moment he was Ramakrishna's.*

Narendranath's discipleship of Ramakrishna, the guru–shishya bandhan, was quite unlike the traditional master–disciple relationship to be found in the Indian ascetic traditions (Hinduism, Buddhism, and Jainism), or in the pan-Islamic Sufi tradition of the pir–murid relationship. All these start with the initiate offering unconditional obedience to the master and being initiated into the spiritual life by a mantra, sacred syllables, and so on. In Sri Ramakrishna and Narendranath's case, in the first instance, it was the master who saluted the disciple. As soon as they met, Ramakrishna took Narendranath aside to a private room and to the utter astonishment of the future Swami Vivekananda started talking to him as if to someone he had known for years. In Vivekananda's own reported words, Ramakrishna held his hand and started speaking in this vein with tears of joy gushing down his cheek: 'Ah, you have come so late! How could you be so unkind to keep me waiting so long! My ears are well-nigh burnt by listening to the profane talk of worldly people. Oh, how I yearn to unburden my mind to one who can appreciate my innermost experience.' Then Ramakrishna stood up and addressed Narendranath with folded hands, 'Lord, I know that you are that ancient sage, Nara, the incarnation of Narayana, born on earth to remove the miseries of mankind.'[20]

The future Swami Vivekananda's first impression of his guru, whom he idolized all his life, was that he was a perfect madman. But after observing Ramakrishna's behaviour with his devotees for several hours, he determined that the man was quite normal in his outward behaviour and did not display any signs of mental abnormality. Narendranath came to the conclusion that

---

*This was not the first time that Ramakrishna and Narendranath met. Narendranath sang at a gathering at the house of Surendranath Mitra, one of Ramakrishna's lay devotees. Ramakrishna invited Narendranath to come to Dakshineshwar. But interestingly neither Ramakrishna nor Vivekananda speak of this as their first encounter. It is doubtful whether Narendranath would have taken up this invitation by a stranger. In fact, whenever speaking of his meeting with Ramakrishna, Vivekananda says nothing of an invitation from him. Instead, he says he set out to meet Ramakrishna because he had heard he was a true holy man who could answer his questions about God. This is the reason Hastie's recommendation to his students to go visit Ramakrishna is considered instrumental in taking Narendranath to Sri Ramakrishna.

Ramakrishna was a monomaniac on the subject of God. When he returned home from Dakshineshwar, Narendranath was torn between the idea of Ramakrishna as a saint who had direct experience of God, and Ramakrishna as an eccentric. But Narendranath's doubts as to the spiritual prowess of his soon-to-be guru were put to rest in his subsequent visits to Dakshineshwar. According to him, he had a number of spiritual experiences under the guidance of Ramakrishna. But Narendranath's sceptical nature could not be easily overcome. He spent hours at the library poring over books on the nervous system, especially the spinal cord and brain to see if a state of hypnotism could be invoked by manipulating the nodal points. However, he finally came to the conclusion that he possessed too strong a willpower for his mind to be manipulated without his consent. Narendranath started to receive spiritual training from Ramakrishna. Ramakrishna instructed him in methods of meditation which Narendranath started practising intensely.

Sri Ramakrishna's relationship with the young Narendranath has been the subject of much discussion in the Ramakrishna–Vivekananda literature. There was something both incongruous and fascinating about seeing Narendranath, with his dazzling intellectual prowess and training in the latest philosophical thought of the West, coming under the tutelage of Sri Ramakrishna, who could barely spell his name and whose nature was as simple as that of a child and with a mind almost as completely unanalytical. Narendranath was a rationalist, who found the very idea of a God with a particular form illogical and anthropomorphic, while Sri Ramakrishna was constantly immersed in a world of mystical visions of various forms of gods and goddesses. Schooled as he was in the Brahmo doctrine of a theistic but impersonal God as the only rational view of divinity possible, Narendranath was sceptical of the truth of Ramakrishna's visions and experiences. But as time passed, Narendranath was increasingly drawn into this world. Bajendranath Seal, who saw Narendranath at college regularly during this time, wrote years later: 'I watched with intense interest the transformation that went on under my eyes. The attitude of a young and rampant Vedantist-cum-Hegelian-cum-Revolutionary like myself towards the cult of religious ecstasy and Kali-worship, may be easily imagined; and the spectacle of a born iconoclast and free-thinker like Vivekananda, a creative and dominating intelligence, a tamer of souls, himself caught in the meshes of what appeared to me an uncouth, supernatural mysticism, was a riddle which my philosophy of the Pure Reason could scarcely read at the time.'[21]

Ramakrishna, for his part, treated Narendranath differently from all his other disciples. In fact, he seemed to treat Narendranath more as a peer than as a disciple. He praised his spiritual qualities profusely and constantly in front of his other disciples, devotees, and the many visitors who flocked to Dakshineshwar. He would do this so often and in such superlative terms that it caused Narendranath great embarrassment and he would entreat his guru to stop it. But Ramakrishna would say that he couldn't help it. In other ways also, he would treat Naren as if he were in a distinct class apart from his other disciples. While he asked other disciples to follow dietary discipline and avoid the company of young women in social situations, he did not expect the same of Narendranath. Ramakrishna, when questioned about this attitude occasionally, would answer that Naren's was such a high spiritual nature that nothing could defile him and no temptation overcome him.

There are two important landmarks in the evolution of Narendranath's spiritual views in the nearly five years he spent under Ramakrishna's tutelage before the latter's death. As a member of the Brahmo Samaj, Narendranath believed in a theistic but formless God. He didn't believe in the different deities of the Hindu pantheon and he would not worship images. Ramakrishna, on the other hand, was dedicated to the worship of Goddess Kali. Ramakrishna was also an Advaitist. The Hindu scriptures teach that the highest reality is even higher than the personal God (Ishvara); an impersonal absolute reality called Brahman. Unlike the Brahmo Samaj's formless God who had many attributes like love, goodness, mercy, and so on, the Absolute Brahman of the Vedas was beyond all dualities, without any limiting attributes and even beyond the distinction of subject and object. Brahman cannot be worshipped, but only experienced in a state akin to the Buddhist nirvana, where the person loses all sense of 'I' and a separate selfhood.* In that state, one realizes that the plurality of the world is an illusion, and all that exists is Brahman. The universe and all its creatures are one with Brahman. Narendranath used to scoff at the Advaitic idea that ultimately all that exists is God.

But Narendranath's ideas would change dramatically. According to Vivekananda's later account, Ramakrishna caused him to have a mystical experience where he caught a glimpse of the Advaitic state. This experience, he says, lasted for days. After coming out of that state, according to Vivekananda, he could no longer deny the reality of what was described in the scriptures. Not a man given to half measures, Narendranath now swung to the other extreme. If he was a firm believer in the theism of a formless personal God, now he became

---

*I am referring here to the popular understanding of the Buddhist nirvana. The exact nature of nirvana is a contested issue within Buddhism with different schools of philosophy holding different positions.

almost a fanatic Advaitin. He declared all notions of a personal anthropomorphic God to be incompatible with the highest reason; even the idea of a formless but loving God. He continuously argued with Ramakrishna who tried to convince him that Kali and other forms of God existed. When Ramakrishna spoke of his own direct experience of the Goddess in meditation, Vivekananda argued that there was no proof that his experience was real since Western science had shown how the brain creates hallucinations from imaginations.

The second landmark was Narendranath's acceptance of the reality of Kali, as the manifestation of the impersonal Brahman in a feminine aspect. This came about after, and perhaps even as a result of, a drastic upheaval in the fortunes of the Dutta family. Narendranath's father, Vishwanath Dutta, died suddenly. When his family went through the records of his financial assets, they were shocked to learn that he was under a massive amount of debt. As the moneylenders came calling, the family, which had been immensely rich through generations, found itself practically destitute. Things were at such a pass that they had difficulty arranging three square meals a day. Swami Saradananda, a brother disciple of Vivekananda recollected Narendranath as saying of the darkest hours of his life in these words:

> Even before the period of mourning was over, I had to go about in search of a job. Starving and barefooted, I wandered from office to office under the scorching noonday sun with an application in hand…. But everywhere the door was slammed in my face. This first contact with the reality of life convinced me that unselfish sympathy was a rarity in the world—there was no place in it for the weak, the poor and the destitute. I noticed that those who only a few days ago would have been proud to have helped me in any way, now turned their face against me, though they had enough and to spare. Seeing all this, the world sometimes seemed to me the handiwork of the devil.[22]

Narendranath vacillated between faith and doubt during this period. Sometimes, he would doubt whether the Absolute Brahman he believed in actually existed. At the same time, he also started to feel the need for the grace of a personal God. He emerged from his spiritual crisis with a deeply ecstatic spiritual experience of the Goddess Kali at the Dakshineshwar temple.

> 'How I used to hate Kali!' the future Swami Vivekananda would say, 'And all Her ways! That was the ground of my six years' fight—that I would not accept Her. But I had to accept Her at last! Ramakrishna Paramahamsa dedicated me to Her, and now I believe that She guides me in everything

I do, and does with me what She will…. Yet I fought so long! I loved him, you see, and that was what held me. I saw his marvellous purity…. I felt his wonderful love…. His greatness had not dawned on me then. All that came afterwards when I had given in. At that time I thought him a brain-sick baby, always seeing visions and the rest. I hated it. And then I, too, had to accept Her!'[23]

Sri Ramakrishna was overjoyed that Narendranath had come to accept Kali. Within six months of that however, Ramakrishna fell ill. He was diagnosed with cancer of the throat. To care for him, his disciples shifted him from Dakshineshwar to a house in Calcutta.* The young set of disciples who were to become sanyasis and later form the Ramakrishna Mission, nursed him there. Narendranath automatically assumed the position of leader, and started organizing Ramakrishna's medical treatment. Ramakrishna ailed for one whole year before passing away. According to the traditional narrative given by the monastic disciples of Sri Ramakrishna, during this period, Narendranath achieved the ultimate spiritual experience he was thirsting for—complete absorption in the supreme reality of Brahman, the transcendental Absolute.[24] Vivekananda, who was normally very reticent in talking about his putative mystical experiences, also spoke of this experience on a few rare occasions in later years.

Ironically, it was when Sri Ramakrishna lay dying that his fame as a saint and holy man reached its apex. The result was a veritable crowd of visitors who flocked to the Calcutta house and tried to see Ramakrishna. In spite of the terrible agony he endured when he spoke, Ramakrishna continued to give spiritual instructions till almost the very end. In his last days, however, he could barely speak and communicated through writing using his extremely rudimentary knowledge of the Bengali script. According to Mahendranath Gupta, Ramakrishna's first biographer, one day Ramakrishna handed over a piece of paper in which he had written: 'Naren will teach.' Characteristically, Narendranath reportedly replied, 'I will do nothing of that sort.' Ramakrishna supposedly replied, 'Your very bones will make you do it.'[25]

A few days before he passed away, Ramakrishna initiated twelve youngsters, including Narendranath, into sanyas. Ramakrishna made it clear that Narendranath was his spiritual heir and tasked him with taking care of his brother disciples as their leader. He died on 16 August 1886. Narendranath was then twenty-three years old. He had decided to follow his guru's inspiration and

---

*First a house in Shyampukur, and later in Cossipore.

become a monk, a sanyasi, renouncing his poverty-stricken family when they most needed him. In later years, Vivekananda was often wracked by guilt at his decision to abandon his widowed mother and siblings when they expected him, as a graduate and the eldest son, to become the breadwinner and take care of the family. But he reasoned that it was done for the greater good and he had sacrificed the happiness of a few people for the spiritual welfare of the many. For whether it was due to Ramakrishna's prophecies about his future, or from an inner conviction born from the dynamism of his personality, Narendranath, now Swami Vivekananda, believed that he had a mission to accomplish in his life. That of, to use his own words, broadcasting to the world, the life-giving spiritual ideas of his master.

Vivekananda and the other disciples of Sri Ramakrishna rented a house at Baranagar in Calcutta, where they lived together and spent their time in spiritual practice. Two years after his guru's passing, Vivekananda started travelling to different places in India as an itinerant monk. From 1888 to 1893, he travelled all over India, from the Himalayas in the north to Kanyakumari in the south. His experiences travelling through the length and breadth of India were probably the most formative experiences to have shaped his outlook after his discipleship of Sri Ramakrishna. Vivekananda started with Varanasi, going on to Ayodhya, Lucknow, Agra, and Vrindavan. He stayed for some time in Vaidyanath and Allahabad and then moved on to Ghazipur where he stayed for a fairly long duration. In 1890, he returned to Calcutta. After staying at the Baranagar math for some time, he decided to go to the Himalayas. In 1891, he descended from the Himalayas and reached Delhi where he took in the sights of the city. Then he headed west to present-day Rajasthan and Gujarat. His journey through Rajasthan and Gujarat brought him into contact with cultural milieus quite unknown to Bengalis at the time. Few people from Bengal travelled this far West.

Vivekananda made a life-long friend in Ajith Singh, the maharaja of Khetri. Khetri was a small kingdom but was one of the most advanced and progressive in Rajasthan. Vivekananda stayed for almost five months in Khetri, by far the longest he would stay at one single place during his journey through India. Ajith Singh would come to Vivekananda's aid at several crucial moments in the monk's life. Ajith Singh is also credited with teaching Vivekananda how to tie a turban in the Rajasthani style. Vivekananda learned the basic technique and then tried several variations on it. It was to become part of his wardrobe and he wore it on several occasions: most notably during his first journey to America. Vivekananda then travelled to Mahabaleshwar and Pune in Maharashtra and then onwards to Bombay. While travelling in a train in Bombay, Vivekananda met Bal Gangadhar Tilak, the nationalist leader. On Tilak's invitation he stayed for a few days at his home, before heading to Goa.[26]

During all these travels, Vivekananda came into contact with a rich cross-section of Indian society. He met, interacted, and stayed with hundreds of people, from almost all strata of society: orthodox Hindu scholars, Muslims, 'untouchable' castes, maharajas, diwans, the professional classes, merchants, students, and so on. During his travel, the monk took no money with him, travelling by foot or bullock cart and by train when some stranger was kind enough to buy him a ticket. He got his food by begging and also undertook extreme ascetic practices. He often spent days meditating in forests and caves without food and sleep. In many of the places he visited, he left behind disciples. A lot of people found in the young, erudite monk, with his unconventional views and excellent command over English, a fascinating personality as well a deep spiritual nature. Often, small crowds would gather in the villages and towns he halted in, and ask him to deliver spiritual discourses. But he would not stay in any one place too long and refused to accept money or gifts that were offered him. He would set off again to the next destination that occupied his mind, carrying only a kamandalu (water pot), his walking staff, and his begging bowl.[27]

In 1892, Vivekananda set his sights on South India, reaching Bangalore by the middle of the year. From there he journeyed to Mysore, where he was received cordially by Chamrajendra Wodeyar, the king of Mysore. It would appear that it is from the Maharaja of Mysore that the suggestion first came that Vivekananda should represent Hinduism at the World Parliament of Religions, scheduled to be held the next year in Chicago.[*] The suggestion planted a seed in Vivekananda's mind that would grow over the course of almost a year. The same idea was suggested to him later by others as well, like the raja of Ramnad. From Mysore, Vivekananda went through Kerala, travelling mainly by foot through Thrissur, Ernakulam, and Travancore. Through Nagercoil, he reached the last bit of Indian land at Kanyakumari.[28]

Through his travels over the past years, his experience and knowledge of India had increased by several scales of magnitude. Places, traditions, practices, and cultures that he had earlier only heard of or read about in books, he now

---

*Accounts of this incident vary.

encountered as tangible living realities. But he also soaked in the suffering of the masses: the poverty, social ostracism, and untouchability, and the brutally hard and short life that was the lot of the majority of the nearly 300 million people in the country.[29] Records of conversations from those who met him in this period show that the young monk, whose temperamental nature often swung between agony and ecstasy, went through periods of intense anguish at the suffering he saw all around him. At Kanyakumari, he swam out to the sea and sat on a rock for three days meditating on the future of India.

From there Vivekananda, turned northwards and proceeded to present-day Tamil Nadu. The thought of attending the World's Parliament of Religions was still in Vivekananda's mind, though it had yet to become a firm resolve. But more than delivering a spiritual message at the Parliament, what Vivekananda really considered as his mission in going to America was to seek help from Americans to import industrial and agricultural technology to help India make material progress.[30] In the beginning of 1893, he travelled to Madurai, Rameshwaram, Pondicherry, and Madras. It is in Madras that he made his greatest impact before his journey to America. Vivekananda impressed several notable personages in the city, as well as a band of youngsters, who became devoted to his cause of regenerating India. Some of them would continue his work even after his death in 1902. He became quite well-known in the literary circles of Madras, delivering lectures both at the Triplicane Literary Society and the Theosophical Society. One of his lectures was reported by the *Madurai Mail* with the headline 'A Bengali Sadhu on Hindu Religion and Sociology'.[31] In Madras too, people who had heard of the upcoming Chicago Parliament urged Vivekananda to go to America. Vivekananda, who was still unsure as to whether he should undertake the American adventure or not, demurred.

Around this time, Vivekananda received an invitation to visit the princely state of Hyderabad. The fame of the Bengali monk had spread so far among the elite classes of South India that he was greeted at the railway station by a crowd of around 500 people, which included prominent members of the Muslim aristocracy.[32] He met Asif Jah Mahboob Ali Khan, the nawab of Hyderabad, who, upon hearing of Vivekananda's desire to attend the Parliament of Religions, offered to give Rs 1,000 to finance his journey. But Vivekananda abstained from accepting the offer at the time. When he returned to Madras, however, things began moving with greater speed. His disciples had managed to collect Rs 4,000. Vivekananda himself was now sure that something great awaited him in America. But before he could sail, Ajith Singh importuned Vivekananda to visit him in Khetri and bless his newly born son. Vivekananda couldn't refuse his friend. The result was that Vivekananda sailed to America from Bombay, rather than Madras. And this might have been for the best, for as we saw earlier, Vivekananda transferred from the *Peninsular* to the *Empress of India* at Japan. En route to Vancouver on the *Empress*, he met Jamshetji Tata, an encounter which would have some interesting consequences. Then, on the train from Vancouver to Chicago he met a lady from Boston named Kate Sanborn. That meeting would change Vivekananda's destiny.

⌣

Vivekananda took on several disciples in the West, who took monastic vows. The most prominent among them was an Irish woman living in London, Margaret Noble. Vivekananda considered her his spiritual daughter and gave her the monastic name of Sister Nivedita. Less remembered now, she was a significant actor in India's political and cultural life in the first decade of the twentieth century. She gave financial and logistical help to the nascent nationalist movement and maintained direct contact with young revolutionaries, including the Anushilan Samiti, the revolutionary organization led by Aurobindo and Barindra Ghosh. She also financially supported the research of Indian scientist Jagadish Chandra Bose, who could not find funding for his experiments for a long stretch of his career.

Writing about her master's journey to the Parliament of Religions, after Vivekananda's death, Nivedita wrote:

> To their unbounded faith it never occurred, that they, [his disciples in Madras] were demanding what was, humanly speaking, impossible. They thought Vivekananda had only to appear and he would be given his chance. The Swami himself was as simple in the ways of the world than these his disciples; and when he was once sure that he was divinely called to make the attempt, he could see no difficulties in the way. Nothing could have been more typical of the unorganisedness (sic) of Hinduism itself than this going forth of its representative unannounced, and without formal credentials, to enter the strongly guarded doors of the world's wealth and power.[33]

As we have seen, Vivekananda arrived six weeks before the Parliament of Religions was to open and was left stranded in Chicago. Vivekananda would later say in a speech: 'The money I had with me was little, and it was soon spent. Winter approached, and I had only thin summer clothes. I did not know what to do in that cold, dreary climate, for if I went to beg in the streets, the result would have been that I would have been sent to jail. There I was with the last few dollars in my pocket. I sent a wire to my friends in Madras.'[34]

Vivekananda asked his disciples in Madras to send more money urgently to finance his stay. The wire read, 'Starving. All money spent. Send money to return at least'.[35] Vivekananda would later call this telegram, with the idea of returning to India, 'a moment of weakness'.[36] It seems that he did not seriously contemplate just returning to India, though it looked impossible that he could become a delegate at the parliament. He had trust that divine providence would open a way. And if not, he was determined to at least make a go of it and try to succeed in America by some other means.

Divine or not, it was definitely providential that during his five-day train journey from Canada to Chicago, Vivekananda decided to walk over to the observation room in the train, as it was passing through the Lake District of Minnesota. Many people were milling about here, including Parsi merchants, Filipino women, and Japanese delegates on their way to the Chicago Fair.[37] They were all taking in the beauty of the scenery. A particularly friendly middle-aged woman, who was chatting with everyone, soon struck up a conversation with Vivekananda. On parting, she invited everyone in the room to visit her if they ever came to Boston, saying that she would introduce them to some really cultured and artistic people.[38] This woman was Kate Sanborn and she lived in a small village near Metcalf, near Boston. Vivekananda had no idea if the woman would remember him. But in any case, he had heard that the cost of living was much cheaper in Boston and the lady's hospitality was the only avenue open to him. So, after several days, he took a train from Chicago, Illinois to Boston, the capital of Massachusetts. From a hotel in Boston, he telegraphed Sanborn.

Kate Sanborn, as it happened, was a well-known author and educationist. An important part of the New York literary establishment, she had started supporting herself through her writing from the age of seventeen. A woman with an independent spirit, she wrote books, essays, and journalistic columns. When the idea that women lacked a sense of humour became a topic of discussion in the literary circles of America, Sanborn set out to research humorous writing by female authors and published an anthology, which became a bestseller; many of her later books were widely acclaimed as well. Her work is marked by humour and an easy conversational style, whose wit often lay in gentle ridicule usually directed at her own authorial persona. In 1888, Sanborn became interested in agriculture and decided to become a farmer. She brought an abandoned farm near Boston, and thus moved to rural New England (a region in the northeast of the United States, perhaps most familiar to Indians through the nature poetry of Robert Frost).* Fortunately for Vivekananda, she remembered their chance meeting on the train only too well and gladly agreed to be his hostess.

In a book she published the very next year, she recounted the impression Vivekananda left on her when she talked to him on the train.

> But most of all I was impressed by the monk—a magnificent specimen of manhood, six feet two (Vivekananda's height was probably 5'8", but he looked considerably taller in his turban), as handsome as Salvini† at his best, with a lordly, imposing stride, as if he ruled the universe, and soft, dark eyes that could flash fire when roused, or dance with merriment if the conversation amused him.... He spoke better English than I did, was conversant with ancient and modern literature, would quote easily and naturally from Shakespeare or Longfellow, or Tennyson, Darwin, Müller, Tyndall; could repeat pages of our Bible, was familiar with and tolerant with all creeds. He was an education, an illumination, a revelation![39]

With her connections to the literary and artistic world and her cosmopolitan personality, Kate Sanborn herself was an oddity in rural Metcalf. One can imagine the sensation when Vivekananda, dressed in colourful Indian attire, alighted at the railway station. We do have a description from Kate Sanborn:

> As the cars stopped, even the piercing whistle had a derisive sound, and I trembled at the effect he might produce on the crowd gathered for the mail. But he was received in breathless silence. He was such a surprise! If he had looked regal but bizarre among a group collected from all nations, he was simply amazing at the platform at Gooseville. His luggage was so considerable in amount that the train was ten minutes late at the next stopping place. He had brought almost a Bodleian Library‡ of books with him recondite and rare, heavy in either sense.... He never minded the stares and grins that were evident to me.[40]

Kate Sanborn soon introduced Vivekananda to a number of her acquaintances, who came down from Boston and New York to meet the 'Hindoo monk'.[41] Most, no doubt, were drawn by the exotic nature of such a specimen, but to their credit, they were an open minded and friendly people. As a cross-cultural

---

*Kate Sanborn lived in two farms in a small village near Metcalf, one after another. When Vivekananda met her, she had just moved to the second farm, named 'Breezy Meadows'.

†The reference is possibly to the character 'Salvini' in the opera *Adelson e Salvini* by Vincenso Bellini.

‡The Bodleian Library is the library of records at Oxford University.

encounter, there were insurmountable barriers, leading to some bizarre and even surreal exchanges but nonetheless, at least some of the people Vivekananda encountered responded genuinely to his ideas. On her side, one of the most colourful characters Kate Sanborn introduced Vivekananda to was her cousin Franklin Sanborn—journalist, writer, biographer, and former outlaw. Franklin was deeply sceptical of Vivekananda's claims to be a genuine Hindu yogi and visited his cousin's farm with the full expectation of meeting a crank or a Buddhist passing off as a Hindu. But on talking to Vivekananda, Franklin Sanborn was completely converted. He appreciated the significance of Vivekananda's spiritual message, something which Kate Sanborn could not.

The fact is that while Vivekananda can correctly claim to be the first Hindu spiritual missionary to America, he would not have been able to succeed had the intellectual ground not been prepared for him by two groups of people. One was the Theosophists led by Annie Besant, and the other, and far more important, were the group of writers and thinkers known as the American Transcendentalists. This group consisted, among others, of the poet Ralph Waldo Emerson, the writer Henry David Thoreau, and, at least through literary influence, the poet Walt Whitman. Transcendentalism took root, was nourished, and grew to bear fruit on the soil of New England (consisting of the states of Massachusetts, Connecticut, Maine, New Hampshire, Rhode Island, and Vermont). Transcendentalism was directly influenced by Indian religious thought, especially the Bhagavad Gita, which both Thoreau and Emerson read. Thoreau, in his masterpiece *Walden*, a book describing his experiment of living a solitary life in a small cabin in the woods in Walden Pond, wrote: 'In the morning I bathe my intellect in the stupendous and cosmogonal philosophy of the Bhagavat Geeta, since whose composition years of the gods have elapsed, and in comparison with which our modern world and its literature seem puny and trivial; and I doubt if that philosophy is not to be referred to a previous state of existence, so remote is its sublimity from our conceptions.'[42]

Transcendentalism also had significant similarities to the Vedanta which Vivekananda preached. It included a belief in spiritual or transcendental truth beyond sense perception, the innate goodness of man and the idea that any person can reach spiritual truth through intuition and looking within herself. While the Transcendentalist movement eventually influenced the whole of American letters, its influence remained particularly strong in New England, its place of birth. And Boston and the nearby Harvard University (which Emerson and Thoreau attended), were at the heart of the Transcendentalist movement. Vivekananda could not have asked for a place where his informal talks on Vedanta would be better received and the excitement of the presence of a real Hindu monk would spread rapidly among the literati and intelligentsia.

Franklin Sanborn opened more doors for Vivekananda in this direction because he was one of the last of the Transcendentalist writers and was friends in his youth with both Emerson and Thoreau. He was also a celebrity for his role in an important incident in American history. Franklin and five other men dubbed 'The Secret Six' helped finance a raid on a United States armoury by the abolitionist John Brown in a bid to seize the arms and start a slave rebellion in the southern states. Though the raid failed, it was one of the reasons that led to the South deciding to secede and the outbreak of the Civil War of 1861–65. Franklin took Vivekananda to Boston and arranged for him to give several talks at various places and forums, from small churches in Salem to the important American Association of Sociology in Saratoga Springs in the neighbouring state of New York. The *Boston Evening Transcript* on 24 August reported the arrival in the city of 'Swami Vere Kananda [*sic*]…in the company of Mr. FB Sanborn'.[43] There were only eighteen days left to 11 September, when the Parliament of Religions would open.

Vivekananda's ticket to the Parliament of Religions would prove to be Professor John Henry Wright of Harvard, a friend of the Sanborns. Wright, in his early forties, was a professor of Greek at Harvard and a scholar of formidable reputation known for his work on the history of Athens. He also had an interest in eastern civilizations and had studied Sanskrit for two years at a German university. It has not been established how Wright came to know about the Hindu monk, whether he heard of Vivekananda directly from the Sanborns or through another channel. In any case, he invited Vivekananda to come and spend a long weekend with his family at a seaside resort 65 kilometres from Boston, where they were vacationing. Vivekananda accepted and what followed were three days of intense discussion on religion, philosophy, and history between the monk and the professor.

In fact, Vivekananda met him just at the point when he would enter the mature phase of his career and cement his place as one of the great American classical scholars of his generation. The next year, Professor Wright would be elected president of the American Philological Association and become the dean of the School of Arts and Sciences at Harvard the year after. Academically, he would go on to translate into English selections from dozens of Greek writers including poets like Homer and Sappho, philosophers like Plato and Xenophon, dramatists like Sophocles and Euripides, and historians like Thucydides and

Herodotus. At the peak of his career, he would edit and supervise the publication of an encyclopaedic work on world history, *A History of All Nations from the Earliest Times*, in twenty-four volumes.

To say that the scholarly Professor Wright was impressed by Vivekananda would be an understatement. They became lifelong friends and, in their correspondence, Vivekananda would address him by the nickname Adhyapakji (Hindi for 'respected teacher'). The question of Vivekananda attending the Parliament of Religions came up and Vivekananda bewailed his lack of credentials. The professor reportedly exclaimed, 'To ask you Swami, for credentials, is like asking the sun to state its right to shine.'[44] Wright assured him that he would use his academic connections to make sure that Vivekananda could attend the Parliament and that the committee of the Parliament would be willing to make an exception in his case regarding the date of registration. The professor immediately wrote to the chairman of the committee for the selection of delegates, saying of the thirty-year-old Vivekananda, 'Here is a man who is more learned than all our learned professors put together.'[45] On 2 September, Vivekananda, who was then lecturing in Saratoga Springs, received a letter of invitation to be a delegate at the Parliament of Religions.

Realizing that Vivekananda had little money with him, Professor Wright presented him with the train fare to Chicago.[46] He also gave him a letter of introduction to the committee in charge of the 'Oriental' delegates, who would take care of his accommodation in Chicago. All should have proceeded smoothly, but the sanyasi had to go through a final trial by fire before he could deliver his famous Chicago speeches. Vivekananda, it seems, arrived in Chicago on the evening of 9 September.[*] To his consternation, he had lost the address of the place where he was supposed to present himself. He tried asking passers-by for instructions, but unfortunately, he was in the German part of the city and couldn't make himself understood. He had no money for a hotel and night was coming on. Finally, he decided to go to the freight section of the railway station; he spent the night inside a goods train.[†] The next morning, on 10 September, hungry, unshaven and wearing a rumpled saffron robe, Vivekananda walked through the city, till he reached the English-

---

[*]Though this is usually the date assigned by most biographers, Mary Louise Burke, who did extensive archival research on Vivekananda's activities in the West, states that it could also have been the evening of 8 September.

[†]Most accounts state that Vivekananda spent the night in an abandoned box in the freight section. But Mary Louise Burke convincingly argues that he probably spent the night in a boxcar; that is a goods train, and not a box.

speaking parts. He had arrived at one of the poshest areas in Chicago. He went from door to door asking for food and directions. But he was turned away by liveried servants, or snubbed or even abused by the residents. He walked down the street as far as his tired legs would carry him, and finally exhausted, he sat down on the street pavement. The Parliament was to open on the morning of the next day. Vivekananda had no idea what to do. He was completely new to Western society and had no idea of public telephones or phone books. He sat there, resigning himself to God's will. Suddenly the door of the nearby house opened, and a tall, regal woman stepped out. She took in the monk's exotic costume and worn-out state in a glance and asked him, 'Sir, are you a delegate to the Parliament of Religions? Do you need help?'[47]

Again, this coincidental meeting proved helpful in more ways than one. The lady was Mrs George Hale, and she invited him into her house and provided him with breakfast. Then she had him driven to the office of the chairman of the general committee of the Parliament of Religions. There, Vivekananda presented the letters of introduction given by Professor Wright and was able to register as a delegate. In time, he became extremely close to the Hale family, which consisted of Mr and Mrs George Hale, their two daughters Mary and Harriet, and their nieces Isabelle and Harriet McKindley. After the Parliament, the Hale home would become Vivekananda's headquarters of operation from where he toured various cities and towns across America. Through the Hales, he would meet several important people who would both assist and finance his work and the establishment of the Ramakrishna Mission in India and the construction of the Belur Math in Calcutta and the Almora Math in the Himalayas. And personally, of all the various families at whose homes Vivekananda would stay during his years in America, the Hale family would become the closest to his heart. A good portion of his correspondence was directed to the Hale family, especially Mary Hale. He called all of them by nicknames: Father Pope and Mother Church for Mr and Mrs Hale, and 'babies' for the daughters and nieces. 'You are all so kind, the whole family, to me,' he wrote them from India in 1898, 'I must have belonged to you in the past as we Hindus say.'[48] Towards the end of his life, his health wrecked by unrelenting travel and work, and mentally preparing for death, Vivekananda would write to Mary Hale: 'All blessings on you and the sisters and Mother. Mary, you have been always the sweetest notes in my jarring and clashing life.'[49]

Our national imagination is used to the story of a masterful Vivekananda, confidently striding on to the stage at the Chicago Parliament and delivering his opening address. The truth is slightly different. Vivekananda, who was seated alongside dozens of distinguished and eminent personages from all over the world, from erudite Catholic bishops to representatives of Buddhism and Shintoism from Sri Lanka and Japan, was facing an audience of 6,000 highly educated people,[*] and was extremely nervous. He knew some of the Indian delegates: Annie Besant of the Theosophical Society, Pratap Chandra Majumdar of the Brahmo Samaj, and Virchand Gandhi representing the Jains. Vivekananda kept postponing his opportunity to speak every time his turn came up; the chairman started to think he was not going to speak at all.

Vivekananda recounts:

Imagine a hall below and a huge gallery above, packed with six or seven thousand men and women representing the best culture of the country, and on the platform learned men of all nations of the earth. And I who never spoke in public[†] in my life to address this august assemblage! ...Of course, my heart was fluttering and my tongue nearly dried up; I was so nervous and could not venture to speak in the morning.... They were all prepared and came with ready-made speeches. I was a fool and had none, but bowed down to Devi Saraswati and stepped up, and Dr Barrows introduced me. I made a short speech. I addressed the assembly as 'Sisters and Brothers of America', a deafening applause of two minutes followed, and then I proceeded; and when it was finished, I sat down, almost exhausted with emotion. The next day all the papers announced that my speech was the hit of the day, and I became known to the whole of America.[50]

As part of the project of demythologizing Vivekananda, the received story about the events at Chicago has recently been questioned. Questions have been raised about whether Vivekananda really received as much success in America as it has been made out, whether his opening of the five words quoted above were indeed greeted by instantaneous and inexplicable applause, and even whether his Chicago address really preached the doctrine of a universal religion.

---

[*]The size of the audience is given in the first volume of *World Parliament of Religions* by John Henry Barrows.

[†]Vivekananda had spoken in public in India a few times before. The largest crowd he addressed was probably a group of students in a Hyderabad college. But all these were closed-door meetings. It was the first time that Vivekananda was addressing a public audience.

According to Vivekananda's own account, his five opening words were greeted by instantaneous applause which lasted for two minutes.[*] Many newspapers in Chicago and outside reported the contents of Vivekananda's speech with his opening lines included. Mrs S. K. Blodgett, a woman from Los Angeles who was among the spectators, later recollected the reaction of the crowd when Vivekananda spoke for the first time. 'I was at the Parliament of Religions in Chicago in 1893' she said, 'When that young man got up and said, "Sisters and Brothers of America", seven thousand people rose to their feet as a tribute to something they knew not what. When it was over, I saw scores of women walking over the benches to get near him, and I said to myself, "Well, my lad, if you can resist that onslaught, you are indeed a God!"'[51]

How much of an impact did Vivekananda's speeches at the Chicago Parliament, really make on the American public? The question is not difficult to answer because there exists a large number of newspaper reports, pen portraits, memoirs, and reminiscences, all of which the enquirer can draw upon. Except for the orthodox Christian papers which criticized Vivekananda on various grounds (usually that he was too universal, not the other way around),[†] most newspapers in their general report on the Parliament of Religions spoke of Vivekananda in appreciative, glowing, and even superlative terms. He was, by majority opinion, the most successful speaker at the parliament. There are some recurrent themes that were part of a majority of the reports. The young monk was invariably described as handsome, sometimes as exceptionally so;[‡] as

---

[*]The historian Amiya P. Sen has questioned whether Vivekananda really did address the audience as 'Sisters and Brothers of America'. He argues: 'While the official history of the Parliament notes how "a peal of applause that lasted for several minutes" followed Vivekananda's opening words, a contemporary publication titled *A Chorus of Faith as Heard in the Parliament of Religions* (Chicago, Unity Publishing Co, 1893) altogether omits such a reference.' See 'On the anniversary of Vivekananda's Chicago speeches, time to remember what he said—and didn't', *Scroll.in*, 11 September 2019.

Sen has been rather hasty in coming to his conclusion based on the book he cites. The introduction to *A Chorus of Faith* makes it clear that it is a selection of 115 extracts from 115 speeches, and does not aim to reproduce all these speeches in full. Worse, the authors have taken the reports from the local newspapers. The introduction also states: 'This little book will not take the place of the larger two-volume history of the Parliament edited by Dr. John Henry Barrows.' The history by John Barrows is the official history of the Parliament and includes the address 'Sisters and Brothers of America'.

[†]The Orthodox Christian newspapers criticized Vivekananda on the grounds that Hinduism was not what he claimed it to be and could not be given an equal place as Christianity, as well for his comments that the Christian missionary efforts to India were largely a failure.

[‡]For example, *Chicago Times* reported on 12 September, 'The face and dress that received the most notice, especially from the ladies, was that of Swami Vivekananda, a young man exceptionally

extremely charismatic, as greatly learned, and as a powerful, even mesmerizing speaker. Many newspapers remarked on his 'brilliant intellect' and his mastery of the English language. More rarely, papers which ventured to make that sort of judgement, would describe him as truly spiritual or as possessed of some deep intangible wisdom. Many interviews of Vivekananda appeared in the Chicago as well as Boston newspapers in the months following the parliament. They reveal the sanyasi, even in a completely foreign setting, as self-confident and at ease with the interviewer, witty, with a great sense of humour and with absolutely no airs about him.

An enterprising reporter for the *Boston Evening Transcript* gained access to the tent in which the delegates were hosted during the parliament. He interviewed Vivekananda and wrote: 'Vivekananda's address before the parliament was broad as the heavens above us, embracing the best in all religions, as the ultimate universal religion—charity to all mankind, good works for the love of God, not for fear of punishment or hope of reward. He is a great favourite at the parliament, from the grandeur of his sentiments and his appearance as well. If he merely crosses the platform he is applauded, and this marked approval of thousands he accepts in a childlike spirit of gratification, without a trace of conceit.'[52]

Vivekananda's speeches were apparently such a hit that the organizers used to keep him for last, so the audience would not leave till all the delegates in a session had spoken. The *Northampton Daily Herald* of 11 April 1894 ran a piece recalling the Parliament of Religions held six months earlier: 'At the Parliament of Religions, Vivekananda was not allowed to speak until the close of the programme, the purpose being to make the people stay until the end of the session. On a warm day when some prosy professor talked too long, and people would leave the hall by hundreds, it only needed the announcement that Vivekananda would give a short address before the benediction was pronounced to hold the vast audience intact, and thousands would wait for hours to hear a fifteen minutes talk from this remarkable man.'[53] Among other reports to the same effect, the *Boston Evening Transcript* reported, '[T]he four thousand fanning people in the Hall of Columbus would sit smiling and expectant,

---

handsome and with features that would command attention anywhere. His dress was bright orange, and he wore a long coat and regulation turban of that colour.... Prof. Wright of Harvard is quoted as saying that he is one of the best educated men in the world.' The London *Woman's Herald* of 26 October described Vivekananda as '[T]he popular Hindu monk, whose physiognomy bore the most striking resemblance to the classic face of the Buddha.' See *The Complete Works of Swami Vivekananda* and *Vivekananda in the West: New Discoveries*.

waiting for an hour or two of other men's speeches, to listen to Vivekananda for fifteen minutes.'[54]

It was an age of unprecedented prosperity for the upper middle class, and the women of that class were expected to be educated and take part in cultural and intellectual life. Religion was an area in which women took a more active interest than men. Consequently, most of Vivekananda's admirers, supporters and even co-workers were women. The enthusiasm of the ladies of Chicago for Vivekananda was often commented upon. One particular newspaper wrote of the parliament, 'Ladies, ladies, ladies packing every place—filling every corner, they patiently waited and waited while the papers that separated them from Vivekananda were read.'[55] American newspapers continuously highlighted how women were drawn to Vivekananda, with the underlying suggestion being that it was not spiritual enthusiasm alone but the monk's good looks and charisma that attracted them to his talks.

However, more intellectually serious publications and observers were bowled over by the sanyasi from India. The greatest stamp of approval perhaps came from *The Critic*, a celebrated New York-based magazine of literature and culture. New York was at that time the literary and artistic centre of America. Chicago, which was a rapidly growing industrial metropolis was, however, a cultural backwater as far as New York was concerned. However, in the 1880s the artistic and literary scene in Chicago acquired a new vitality and even gave rise to a movement in American literature called 'New Realism'. Lucy Munroe, *The Critic*'s Chicago correspondent, who over the next two decades brought national attention to Chicago's artistic and literary scene, wrote:

> But the most impressive figures of the Parliament were the Buddhist priest, H. Dharmapala of Ceylon, and the Hindoo monk, Swami Vivekananda.... But eloquent as were many of the brief speeches at this meeting...no one expressed so well the spirit of the Parliament, its limitations and its finest influence, as did the Hindoo monk. I copy his address in full, but I can only suggest its effect upon the audience, for he is an orator by divine right, and his strong intelligent face in its picturesque setting of yellow and orange was hardly less interesting than these earnest words and the rich, rhythmical utterance he gave them.[56]

Other delegates from India spoke at the parliament and some were warmly applauded. They included Pratap Chandra Majumdar, Chakravarthi, and Nagarkar.[57] Except the fact that he spoke extempore (as did a few others like Dharmapala the Buddhist monk from Ceylon), the text of Vivekananda's

Chicago speeches do not show anything extraordinary. They are eloquent, sincere, and heartfelt. But there are other speeches too, which possess these qualities as we read them. However, none of them created the stir that Vivekananda's did. In a *Scroll* article from 2019, historian Amiya P. Sen claimed that Vivekananda had preached only pluralism and not universal religion. He argues that there was nothing revolutionary about Vivekananda's message, and so we have to account for the 'Vivekananda effect' in other terms. 'In hindsight, Vivekananda's popularity at Chicago may be attributed to several factors. First, there was undoubtedly the charisma of the man himself. Second, some of his statements fed into the contemporary American psyche. His point about the perfectibility of man proved attractive to a young nation, greatly attuned to notions of success and power. Similarly, his critique of doctrinal Christianity came at a time when the American mind was growing disenchanted with it.'[58]

What is being missed in such a line of thinking is that these were not papers presented at an academic conference, or printed in an anthology, where people paid minute attention to the argument or the prose style. This was oration. We live in age where a 'great speech' is an artefact of the past. For most of civilized human history, from at least the early city states of Greece, speeches were powerful agents of social as well as political change. But unlike a text, which is an enduring entity, a speech is an event. It is not what is said, nor even the way it is said, but the totality of what transpires between a speaker and audience that constitute the import of a speech. It is at this level that a speech becomes capable of conveying insight, truth, or even altering the consciousness of the listener at a cognitive level.

Among those who were profoundly moved by Vivekananda's speeches and his message of universality at the parliament, was a poet, Harriet Monroe.[*] Though forgotten today, Monroe's place in creating the modern English poetic tradition is significant. Nearly three decades later, in 1912, Monroe would find and edit the avant-garde magazine *Poetry*, the most prestigious poetry magazine in the world today. *Poetry* created a much-needed space for the emerging movement of modernist poetry as well as the work of other young poets, now famous, which went against conventional literary norms. It was *Poetry* that published the modernist masterpiece and T. S. Eliot's first poem 'The Love Song of J. Alfred Prufrock'. Ezra Pound, the father of the modernist

---

*Harriet Monroe had written the official poem of the Chicago Fair, the 'Columbian Ode' to great appreciation.

movement in English poetry, and Eliot's mentor, was a collaborator of Monroe, publishing many of his own poems in *Poetry* and introducing Monroe to many young modernist poets, whose work she published. *Poetry* also promoted the work of a struggling Robert Frost and introduced the work of Rabindranath Tagore to the Western world, a year before Tagore won the Nobel Prize. Thus, in Monroe, there was an intellect of the first order fused with the aesthetic sensibilities of the poet.

Years later, Monroe wrote about witnessing the Parliament of Religions. After describing the foreign delegates, Monroe writes: 'It was the last of these, Swami Vivekananda, the magnificent, who stole the whole show and captured the town. Others of the foreign group spoke well.... But the handsome monk in the orange robe gave us in perfect English a masterpiece. His personality, dominant, magnetic, his voice rich as a bronze bell; the controlled fervour of his feeling; the beauty of his message to the Western world he was facing for the first time—these combined to give us a rare and perfect moment of supreme emotion. It was human eloquence at its highest pitch.'[59]

As she continues, she muses in an almost melancholic vein, giving us an example of how strangely and powerfully external events and things can impact the sensibilities of a poet. 'One cannot repeat a perfect moment—the futility of trying to has been almost a superstition with me. Thus I made no effort to hear Vivekananda speak again,* during that autumn and winter when he was making converts by the score to his hope of uniting East and West in a world religion above the tumult of controversy.'[60]

Vivekananda's Chicago speeches were also to have an unexpected impact on American intellectual history. At the end of the nineteenth century, academic philosophy in both America and Britain was dominated by the idealist school. (Idealism is the philosophy which holds that the mind, consciousness, or spirit is the fundamental entity that constitutes reality). The greatest American idealist was the celebrated Josiah Royce, professor of philosophy at Harvard. But the tide of philosophical fashion changed in the post-war Anglo-American world. Philosophy became more closely allied to science and logic. In the twentieth century, idealism was banished from the philosophical scene and replaced with realism and materialism. One of the few philosophers who kept the idealist tradition alive in the twentieth century was William Ernst Hocking, a student of Josiah Royce, who took his work on idealism forward.

---

*Harriet Monroe and Lucy Monroe were sisters. Unlike her sister, Lucy heard Vivekananda speak more than once and also reported on it.

As a twenty-year-old, Hocking, who had lost his belief in Christianity and had almost become a convinced materialist, turned up at the Chicago Fair a week after the Parliament of Religions started, and wandered into the plenary session. This turned out to be a transformative experience, one which he described as 'religious' and that set him back on track to a belief in the reality of the spirit and ultimately his philosophical journey towards Idealism. When he walked in, Vivekananda happened to be on stage, delivering a paper on Hinduism.

Hocking wrote in his autobiography about listening to Vivekananda speak:

He spoke not as arguing from a tradition, or from a book, but as from an experience and certitude of his own. I do not recall the steps of his address. But there was a passage toward the end, in which I can still hear the ring of his voice, and feel the silence of the crowd—almost as if shocked. The audience was well-mixed, but could be taken as one in assuming that there had been a 'Fall of man' resulting in a state of 'original sin', such that 'All men have sinned and come short of the glory of God.' But what is the speaker saying? I hear his emphatic rebuke: 'Call men sinners? It is a SIN to call men sinners!' ...Through the silence I felt something like a gasp running through the hall as the audience waited for the affirmation which must follow this blow. What his following words were I cannot recall with the same verbal clarity: they carried the message that in all men there is that divine essence, undivided and eternal reality is One, and that One, which is Brahman, constitutes the central being of each one of us.[61]

Vivekananda's exact words which Hocking could not recall were these: 'Children of immortal bliss—what a sweet, what a hopeful name! Allow me to call you, brethren, by that sweet name—heirs of immortal bliss—yea, the Hindu refuses to call you sinners. Ye are the Children of God, the sharers of immortal bliss, holy and perfect beings. Ye divinities on earth—sinners! It is a sin to call a man so; it is a standing libel on human nature.'[62] Hocking continued:

For me, this doctrine was a startling departure from anything which my scientific psychology could then recognize. One must live with these ideas and consider how one's inner experience could entertain them. But what I could feel and understand was that this man was speaking from what he knew, not from what he had been told. He was well aware of the books; but he was more immediately aware of his own experience and his own status in the world; and what he said would have to be taken into account in any final world-view. I began to realize that Spencer could not be allowed the last word. And furthermore, that this religious experience of mine, which Spencer would dismiss as a psychological flurry, was very akin to the grounds of Vivekananda's own certitude.[63]

Vivekananda stayed in America for almost four years, giving lectures and speeches in various cities and towns throughout the country. Freed from the limitations of time imposed at the Parliament's sessions, he would usually give lectures that lasted one or two hours. This gave him the opportunity to expound the Vedanta philosophy, especially the Advaita Vedanta, at length and give a basic exposition of its philosophical concepts. What was unusual about Vivekananda, compared to earlier Vedantic commentators in the tradition of classical Indian philosophy (seventh to sixteenth century), is that he tried to apply abstract Vedantic principles to problems of history, society, human relationships, and the various intellectual questions, both religious and secular, that were posed in his time. In between, he visited England twice for lecturing, in the summer of 1895 and 1896. He also took a continental tour in 1896, visiting France, Switzerland, Germany, and the Netherlands. While he was appreciated in London and lectured at important forums and was heard by people of varied classes, including members of the aristocracy, he did not create the sensation that he did in America. It was America that truly celebrated him, giving him the epithet 'the cyclonic Hindu', partly a reference to his uninterrupted lecturing from town to town and city to city at a breathtaking pace. In little over a year, Vivekananda toured Chicago, Wisconsin, Minnesota, Iowa, Tennessee, Michigan, Ohio, Massachusetts, New Hampshire, New York, Baltimore, and Washington. Many of these lectures charged a modest fee for entrance. At others, especially at lectures held at Unitarian churches, the lectures were free, but many people donated money for the work Vivekananda wanted to carry out in India. The money Vivekananda made this way was sent to his brother disciples to start a newspaper, publish tracts, organize events, and so forth. He also held private classes for small groups of people who wanted to learn raja yoga* and study the Vedanta philosophy.

In 1897, he returned to India via Italy. He stopped at Sri Lanka and addressed the Hindus in Ceylon, before reaching India in January. He realized his aim of setting up an organization for spiritual and social work, naming it the Ramakrishna Mission. With money earned from lecture tours and donations from his American friends, maths were set up in Belur in Calcutta, in Madras,

---

*Not to be confused with hatha yoga, which consists of physical exercises and which is what is today commonly denoted by the word 'yoga'.

and, a few years later, in Almora in the Himalayas. During this period, he gave several public addresses to crowds numbering in the hundreds and thousands, but at a less 'cyclonic' pace than in America. Though he spoke several times about the Vedanta philosophy, the thrust of most of his lectures in India was towards nation building, reviving Hinduism, reforming Hindu society by abolishing untouchability and caste privileges, educating women and the masses, and other similar projects. He spent just about two-and-a-half years in India before embarking on his second voyage to the West in 1899. This time the visit would be shorter, lasting just one-and-a-half years. The idea was both to continue preaching and ensure that the organizations for the spread of Vedanta that he had founded in America and England were put on a solid footing. He visited Britain first and after a series of lectures there sailed to New York. He lectured for a year in America. He travelled less this time, mainly staying for months in New York, Chicago, California, and Michigan.

In 1900, he left to attend the Paris Congress of Religions. After spending almost two months in Paris, he travelled with a group of friends on the famous Orient Express through Eastern Europe to Constantinople (now Istanbul) in Turkey, then ruled by the Ottoman Empire. On the way, he stayed at Vienna, Belgrade, Budapest, and a few other cities. He delivered a few lectures in Paris and Constantinople and though we know their themes, no records of them are known to exist. From Constantinople, Vivekananda went to Athens, and to Egypt where the group travelled for ten days, seeing the Sphinx and the Pyramids.[64] At Egypt, he suddenly parted company from his group of friends, announcing that he wanted to return to India. Sailing through the Gulf of Suez, he embarked at Bombay. He had not written to anyone in India informing them of his arrival. On 9 December 1900, his brother monks at Belur Math in Calcutta, were having a late dinner, when Vivekananda, whom they assumed to be somewhere in Europe, strolled in saying that he was ravenous. Returning home after travelling for a year, Vivekananda found the gates of the math locked and jumped the gate without waiting for anyone. He had less than nineteen months to live.[65]

᠊

Though Vivekananda's success in America is undoubtable, the fact remains that unlike the French writer Alexis de Tocqueville, who toured America in the 1830s and wrote a historically enduring critique of it,[*] Vivekananda's visit

---

[*]*Democracy in America* published in 1835 and 1845 in two volumes.

in the 1890s is little more than a footnote in American history and is nearly completely absent from the country's cultural memory. This has raised the question in recent times whether Vivekananda's success was more celebrity and fanfare, a kind of cultural sensation, than a true introduction of Vedantic ideas into the intellectual life of America. There are a complex set of reasons why Vivekananda's name has disappeared from American historical consciousness, the greatest being drastic changes in the intellectual climate and attitudes towards religion and intellectual alliances in the twentieth century. At the same time, Vivekananda's star in his own country has grown to gigantic proportions, and at least part of it is predicated on the idea that Vivekananda won recognition and respect for Indian thought from the intellectual luminaries of the West, which had colonized the Indian nation.

Part of the reason Vivekananda's impact on the thinking of America and Great Britain at the turn of the nineteenth century is not so apparent today is that the names he was associated with in his campaign to spread Vedantic thought in the West are no longer prominent in our intellectual and cultural memory. The reason for this primarily was that Vivekananda was active in the West at the very end of a long epoch in history. Within twenty years of Vivekananda's final visit to the West, the modern age would start. When we deal historically with past epochs, the figures who dominate the scene towards the very end of that time usually tend not to do so well. Whether it is intellectual, cultural, or political, the very last representatives of an epoch do not usually represent its ripest fruit as much as the culmination of the great ideas, sensibilities, and forces that shaped the epoch. The great innovations, the most original contributions, the most consequential developments, are found not in the very beginning or end of a period, but in the years that lie between. And when dealing with an age foreign to us, these are the elements that interest us and we give prominence to the personalities associated with such salient events and ideas. We are less interested in those who polished and gave the final touches to the products of that age, whether they are artistic, literary, intellectual, or political. But that is of course a historical evaluation completely at odds with that of the contemporaries of these men and women. They were considered the great minds of the age and held in the highest esteem, being valuable conduits of new ideas to the thought current of the period and playing a large role in shaping public consciousness.

At that level, Vivekananda interacted with and espoused his ideas to some of the finest minds in America and Europe. In his own immediate field of activity, Indian philosophy, Vivekananda met Max Müller, then the greatest living Indologist, at Oxford in 1896. Past his seventies, Müller was now at the pinnacle of a brilliant career and had just been honoured by being appointed to the privy council of the British monarch. The study of Sanskrit literature had begun under the British in the late eighteenth century and British scholars were the pioneering explorers of what was till then virgin territory. But by around the middle of the nineteenth century, Germany became the centre of Indological scholarship. Müller, who was German born, studied philology and ancient languages including Sanskrit, in German universities. Max Müller studied under the great German romantic philosopher Frederick Schelling, friend and later bitter rival of Hegel. Müller began his career in the translation of ancient Sanskrit texts by translating the Upanishads for Shelling. Though he remained a Lutheran Christian, Müller was deeply influenced by the Vedanta philosophy and his Lutheranism was shot through with a pantheism completely foreign to the Protestant tradition.

At their meeting, Vivekananda was deeply impressed by Müller, not only for his scholarship and intellect, but by his humaneness, calling the professor 'a Vedantist of Vedantists'. Müller, who had heard of Sri Ramakrishna from his Brahmo Samaj connections, was thrilled to meet a direct disciple of the great mystic. Müller would later write to Vivekananda, 'As for your beloved master of blessed memory, Bhagaban Sri Ram Krishna, how can I ever tell you what he is to me, I love and worship him with my whole heart. To think of him makes my eyes fill with tears of gladness that I was permitted to hear of him.'[66] Three months later, Max Müller published an article on Sri Ramakrishna Paramahamsa in one of the most important literary journals of the time, *The Nineteenth Century*, edited by John Knowles; this introduced Sri Ramakrishna to the Western world. Müller requested Vivekananda for first-hand information about Ramakrishna's discourses, which Vivekananda forwarded to him. With few alterations, the material Vivekananda sent him became the core of a book Max Müller published in 1898 titled *Ramakrishna: His Life and Sayings.** The book did much to spread the name of the mystic among the Anglo-American intelligentsia.

The other great Indologist Vivekananda came into contact with was Paul Deussen, whom Vivekananda met in Germany. Deussen, a generation younger than Max Müller, was a college mate and lifelong friend of the philosopher Friedrich Nietzsche, whom he had introduced to Vedantic thought.[67] While Vivekananda admired Max Müller as someone who was Vedantist in spirit, he

---

*Müller acknowledges his debt to Vivekananda for the material.

did not agree with Müller's understanding of Vedanta in many parts, which he found Eurocentric. In Deussen Vivekananda found someone who accepted the Vedanta philosophy fully (though Deussen understood Vedanta through the lens of Schopenhauer's philosophy) and with whom he could have scintillating discussions on the philosophy's finer points. Deussen would visit India a decade after Vivekananda's death.

Vivekananda had a keen interest in the sciences, especially physics and chemistry. We do not know how much technical knowledge he had of these subjects, but his oeuvre indicates a sound conceptual grasp of the state of knowledge of the fundamental sciences of his time. An incident recorded in a biography shows him giving out a reading list of Chemistry textbooks to an enquirer at a social gathering. In the West, especially in America, Vivekananda had the chance to interact and hold discussions with several prominent scientists of the age. It was an age in which the relation between science and metaphysics engaged many scientists and philosophers. The most prominent men of science Vivekananda met and talked with included Lord Kelvin, who discovered the second law of thermodynamics, and William Von Helmholtz, who revolutionized ophthalmology by inventing an instrument that allowed doctors to see the inside of the eye (ophthalmoscope). Both physician and theoretical physicist, Helmholtz made important contributions to the study of conservation of energy and was the doctoral advisor of the great Max Planck, whose discovery of the 'quanta' of energy would initiate the quantum revolution in physics.

Perhaps the most interesting and almost certainly the most extraordinary mind Vivekananda encountered in the West was Nikola Tesla, the electrical inventor and scientist. Today the name Tesla is famous because the futuristic automobile and electronic company Tesla, currently headed by Elon Musk, was named in tribute to Nikola Tesla. Tesla was a prolific inventor most known for his invention of the first commercially usable AC motor as well as for his lifelong rivalry with Thomas Alva Edison. The lighting at the Chicago Fair of 1893 (of which the Parliament of Religions was a part), was run on an AC electric power system designed by Tesla in the first such use of AC current for lighting in the world.

Vivekananda ran into Tesla quite unexpectedly in New York, as so often happened in high society in those days, during the winter of 1896. Vivekananda was attending a play called *Iziel* which he called a 'Frenchified life of the Buddha'. It starred the French actress Sarah Bernhardt, who in her long career spanning sixty years (1860–1920), counted among her ardent admirers Sigmund Freud, Mark Twain, and Oscar Wilde. Vivekananda was by this time so well known that Bernhardt recognized him from the stage and sought an audience after the play ended. They were joined by a few acquaintances of Bernhardt, which included Nikola Tesla. There followed a long discussion between the scientist and the monk on matters physical and metaphysical. Tesla apparently was extremely interested by the cyclical theory of the universe in Vedantic cosmology and the ideas of akasha (ether) and prana (force). The issue is too technical to be discussed here, but Vivekananda interpreted matter and force as a manifestation in the physical universe of the underlying spiritual substance called akasha and spiritual force called prana. For some time, he had been speculating based on Vedantic ideas that matter and force can be reduced to energy. Tesla thought he could prove that matter and force can be converted to potential energy.[68] He invited Vivekananda over to his home and promised to demonstrate the proof to him. But as it turned out, when Vivekananda visited him, Tesla found that he was unable to derive such an equation. Nine years later, in 1905, Albert Einstein proved that matter (mass) and energy are interconvertible in his famous equation $E=mc^2$.[*] (In quantum physics, which describes the world of atoms, there is no quantity called force.)

Vivekananda had a predilection for making speculations, some of which turned out to be eerily true in the future. (And like all those who made bold speculations, he made many that turned out to be wrong.) Whether such occasions were sheer coincidence, whether he arrived at his conclusions through some process of intuitive thinking, or whether it was a combination of both, it is impossible to tell. For instance, Vivekananda makes this most curious statement during a speech sometime in the 1890s:

> For practical purposes, let us talk in the language of modern science. But I must ask you to bear in mind that, as there is religious superstition, so also there is a superstition in the matter of science…. As soon as a great scientist's name, like Darwin or Huxley, is cited, we follow blindly. It is the fashion of the day. Ninety-nine per cent of what we call scientific knowledge is mere theories…. True science asks us to be cautious. Just as

---

*Tesla was however, not pleased with Einstein's results and if Vivekananda were alive, neither would he be. The energy mass equivalence is part of the theory of relativity, whose conclusions Tesla rejected. Vivekananda was looking for a physical theory where everything in the universe is reducible to a primal entity. While it was possible to imagine such a scenario within the framework of Newtonian physics, the possibility disappeared altogether when Newtonian physics was replaced by the theory of relativity and quantum mechanics.

we should be careful with the priests, so we should be with the scientists. Begin with disbelief. Analyse, test, prove everything, and then take it. Some of the most current beliefs of modern science have not been proved. Even in such a science as mathematics, the vast majority of its theories are only working hypotheses. With the advent of greater knowledge they will be thrown away.[69]

The last sentence is particularly astonishing, given the period in which it was delivered. The late nineteenth century was a time when different theories of physics were clashing. There were problems that remained to be ironed out, but no one envisaged a fundamental reorganization of even the sub-domains of the field, let alone the complete restructuring of the field of physics two decades later by the theory of relativity; and in another decade by quantum mechanics. The physicist Albert Michelson said famously that physics as a subject was dead and all that was left was to make measurements to greater degrees of accuracy.* Even Max Planck, who in 1900 introduced the idea of quantized energy, thought of his innovation as more of a mathematical trick rather than a discovery so fundamental that it would bring the whole edifice of classical physics crashing down. Vivekananda's comments on mathematics strike one at first glance as being almost outlandish. But if we take a closer look at the history of the subject, we find that after set theory was developed in the 1870s and was adopted as the foundational theory of mathematics, it led to problems which culminated in a crisis in the foundations of mathematics in the early twentieth century. This led to the idea that mathematics and set theory required rigorous meta-mathematical proof of the kind mathematicians had not sought before. To solve these problems, various programmes were initiated by mathematicians (David Hilbert, Bertrand Russell, Gottlob Frege, and others) to give formal proofs for mathematical statements starting from a set of logical or mathematic axioms. The programme did not completely succeed and research in the area continues to this day.

Another example is his prediction about the future of European civilization. Vivekananda was perspicacious enough to notice the building of huge armaments and the increasing military presence in various European countries. He once referred to Europe as 'a vast military camp'.[70] His political, social, and historical knowledge of Europe was unusually deep and sharp. In a memoir of his European travels in 1900, he wrote:

---

*This comment is famously, but erroneously, attributed to Lord Kelvin.

In the present times a huge wave of nationalism is sweeping over Europe, where people speaking the same tongue, professing the same religion, and belonging to the same race want to unite together. Wherever such union is being effectively accomplished, there is great power being manifested; and where this is impossible, death is inevitable. After the death of the present Austrian Emperor, (Francis Joseph II died in 1916) Germany will surely try to absorb the German-speaking portion of the Austrian Empire—and Russia and others are sure to oppose her; so there is the possibility of a dreadful war. The present Emperor being very old, that catastrophe may take place very early. The German Emperor is nowadays an ally of the Sultan of Turkey; and when Germany will attempt to seize Austrian territory, Turkey, which is Russia's enemy, will certainly offer some resistance to Russia; so the German Emperor is very friendly towards Turkey.[71]

This is not exactly how World War I played out, but it was one of the plausible scenarios which an acute observer of the time could envisage. He is also reported to have said in 1895, 'Europe is on the edge of a volcano. Unless the fires are extinguished by a flood of spirituality, it will blow up.'[72]

On his return to India in 1897, the second public speech Vivekananda delivered was in Paramakudi. In it Vivekananda predicted:

The whole of Western civilisation will crumble to pieces in the next fifty years if there is no spiritual foundation. It is hopeless and perfectly useless to attempt to govern mankind with the sword. You will find that the very centres from which such ideas as government by force sprang up are the very first centres to degrade and degenerate and crumble to pieces. Europe, the centre of the manifestation of material energy, will crumble into dust within fifty years if she is not mindful to change her position, to shift her ground and make spirituality the basis of her life.[73]

World War II ended exactly forty-eight years from when Vivekananda spoke these words, leaving almost all of Europe in a shambles; with cities destroyed, the economy almost irreparably damaged and tens of millions of people dead. In fact, if it was not for the economic assistance poured in by the United States through the Marshall Plan, post-war European prosperity would not have been possible. The point here is not that Vivekananda discerned the possibility of a European war. Not only were there many observers who did this throughout the two decades at the turn of the century, but political circles in European capitals were always talking about the inevitability of war.

However, no one anticipated a conflict that would reshape the very basis of Western civilization.* Apart from the communists who dreamt of a revolution by the European proletariat, no one considered it possible that the European political order and its increasingly integrated economies would head towards self-destruction in a mere fifty years.

We have more than one account of Vivekananda thinking that there would be a world-changing revolution in Russia. According to his disciple Christina Greenstidel, he told a group of friends and devotees out of the blue, 'The next great upheaval which is to bring about a new epoch will come from Russia or China. I can't quite see which, but it will be either Russia or China.'[74] The Russian revolution took place in 1917. But the intriguing thing here again is that for almost everyone, Russia was the last place where a revolution could take place. Both conservatives and liberals considered Tsarist Russia to be too autocratic, the economy too industrially backward, and the peasants too poor for the traditional monarchical order to be threatened. Other than Russian socialist revolutionaries, very few in the European Marxist and other socialist movements thought Russia was ripe for revolution.

After Tesla, the most original mind Vivekananda encountered in the West was probably William James, brother of the novelist Henry James. Today, William James is considered the most important philosopher who was active in the late nineteenth century in the Anglo-American world.† Vivekananda was invited by Harvard University to speak at the university's Graduate Philosophical Society in 1896. The society later published the lecture as a pamphlet with an introduction written by the dean of Harvard's school of theology.[75] The late Eugene Taylor, a William James scholar at Harvard, wrote of Vivekananda's lecture in his 2011 book on James's philosophy, 'These ideas were of particular interest to the philosophers at Harvard, who were concerned with...issues of monism and pluralism.... Of greatest interest was Vivekananda's definition of psychology. By it, he meant the spiritual evolution of consciousness, not simply the description of sense data and its analysis by the mind.'[76] Vivekananda was reportedly informally offered the chair of Oriental philosophy by the Harvard

---

*Militarily, European generals expected short wars of the kind that took place during the Napoleonic era. Neither European politicians nor military men were prepared for 'total war' that would pit the whole resources of countries against each other. And the eventual destruction of the European political order, including the Asian and African colonial empires, following World War II, was a possibility few could have imagined between 1890 and 1910.

†I have omitted John Dewey, because while Dewey had indeed started publishing towards the end of nineteenth century, his major works appeared only in the next century.

philosophy department, an offer he turned down.

Among the audience were William James and Josiah Royce (the idealist philosopher mentioned earlier). In the discussions they had, both the philosophers were impressed by Vivekananda's exposition of Vedanta. James was both an academic psychologist as well as a philosopher. In his ground-breaking 1890 book *The Principles of Psychology*, he introduced the influential and now ubiquitous concept of a 'stream of thought'. In philosophy, he was one of the pioneers of the philosophy of 'Pragmatism'. Since Plato, the philosophical question of 'What is the criterion for saying something is true'?' has been a dominant theme in Western philosophy. So far, there had been two competing theories trying to explain what truth consists of. Pragmatism introduced a third theory of truth,* which gave an explanation of truth by tying it to its usefulness.

William James and Vivekananda struck up a friendship; they would meet again at least twice, once in America and another time in Paris. James was deeply impressed by Vivekananda's personality, writing to a common friend that Vivekananda 'was an honour to humanity'.[77] When James met Vivekananda, he was starting to turn his attention to the psychology of religion. A year after their meeting, in 1897, he published *The Will to Believe*, in which he tried to reconcile science and religion. In 1898, he published *Human Immortality: Two Supposed Objections to the Doctrine*, where he defended the possibility of the immortality of the human soul. Of the possible influence of Vivekananda on William James's ideas of religion, Eugene Taylor writes, 'James also had numerous encounters with Eastern Meditation teachers.... Vivekananda seems particularly important because his ideas appear frequently in James's writings... he made numerous references to him at various times in his writings...(he) made extensive references to Vivekananda in his *Pragmatism* (1907).'[78]

⌣

Around a year after his return to India from his first tour of the West, Vivekananda's health began deteriorating. He suffered from severe diabetes, diseases of the liver and kidney and eventually heart problems. The long years of living on the road in India, dependent on the charity of others for food and days of starving, followed by years of arduous travel and non-stop work was taking its toll. Vivekananda lived in an age before antibiotics, when contracting tuberculosis was a death sentence. A severe infection, even if it did not kill you,

---

*The pragmatic concept of truth originated with the work of Charles Sanders Pierce and was taken forward by Pierce and William James, and later John Dewey.

could worsen your health for years. Vivekananda suffered bouts of both malaria and dengue. Travel itself was much more primitive and far more uncomfortable than we can visualize today. Prolonged and continuous travel could do great cumulative damage to one's health, especially if it was already impaired.

Vivekananda took several medical opinions and treatments, and they often helped him recover from spells of illness which forced him to take rest. But the moment he was better, he would plunge himself into frenetic work again. It would seem that while the medical opinion he took showed his condition as potentially serious, no one seemed to have considered him at grave or immediate risk. But by 1898, Vivekananda started to become increasingly convinced that he was a dying man. He carried out his work with even greater urgency because he felt he had only a few years to finish it. From his correspondence of those years, he appears quite unaffected by his bad health, or even his personal belief that he had only a few years left to live. He spoke of it only infrequently and his friends, disciples, and brother disciples did not take these occasional pronouncements of impending death seriously.

But a careful examination of Vivekananda's actions from 1900 onwards shows that he was convinced that the end of his life was near. He got the Ramakrishna Math registered as a trust and registered the land in the name of all the extant disciples of Sri Ramakrishna, excluding himself. He resigned the presidentship of the Ramakrishna Mission and handed it over to his brother disciple Swami Brahmananda. Vivekananda's was a conflicted nature with several powerful but opposite forces seeking balance in his personality. Vivekananda swung between action and meditative contemplation, between zest for life and the need to escape what he considered its illusory nature. In the last two years of his life, the quieter contemplative part of his nature came to the fore. He hardly undertook any speaking engagements or journeys. The last one year of his life was mostly spent in seclusion in the Belur Math, where his constant companions were a dog and sheep he had adopted. An American friend who visited the math during that time recounted Vivekananda telling her, 'I will not live to see forty.'[79]

His emotions during this period, as expressed in his numerous letters, are characterized by an increasingly devotional attitude, a sense of growing detachment from life, and a wish to be liberated by death from the finiteness of earthly existence. His sense of anxiety that he would not be able to finish the spiritual mission Sri Ramakrishna had entrusted to him in his youth, completely left him. He left it to the will of the Goddess Kali, whom he worshipped in the form of the Mother Goddess. A most interesting letter from this phase of his life is one written to his friend Josephine MacLeod, on 18 April 1900. In the letter, Vivekananda painted a picture of his state of mind, as he was travelling on a boat on a river in East Bengal:

My dear Joe,

Just now I received yours and Mrs Bull's welcome letter. ...Work is always difficult; pray for me Joe that my works stop forever, and my whole soul be absorbed in Mother. Her works, She knows...I am well, very well mentally. I feel the rest of the soul more than that of the body. The battles are lost and won, I have bundled my things and am waiting for the great deliverer. 'Shiva, O Shiva, carry my boat to the other shore.' After all, Joe, I am only the boy who used to listen with rapt wonderment to the wonderful words of Ramakrishna under the Banyan at Dakshineswar. That is my true nature; works and activities, doing good and so forth are all superimpositions. Now I again hear his voice; the same old voice thrilling my soul. Bonds are breaking—love dying, work becoming tasteless—the glamour is off life. Only the voice of the Master calling.—'I come Lord, I come.'

...Yes, I come. Nirvana is before me. I feel it at times—the same infinite ocean of peace, without a ripple, a breath.

I am glad I was born, glad I suffered so, glad I did make big blunders, glad to enter peace. I leave none bound, I take no bonds. Whether this body will fall and release me or I enter into freedom in the body, the old man is gone, gone for ever, never to come back again! The guide, the Guru, the leader, the teacher has passed away; the boy, the student, the servant is left behind....

The sweetest moments of my life have been when I was drifting: I am drifting again—with the bright warm sun ahead and masses of vegetation around—and in the heat everything is so still, so calm—and I am drifting languidly—in the warm heart of the river! I dare not make a splash with my hands or feet—for fear of breaking the marvellous stillness, stillness that makes you feel sure it is an illusion!

Behind my work was ambition, behind my love was personality, behind my purity was fear, behind my guidance the thirst of power! Now they are vanishing, and I drift. I come! Mother, I come! In Thy warm bosom, floating wheresoever Thou takest me, in the voiceless, in the strange, in the wonderland, I come—a spectator, no more an actor.

Oh, it is so calm! My thoughts seem to come from a great, great distance in the interior of my own heart. They seem like rains, distant whispers, and peace is upon every thing, sweet, sweet peace—like that one feels for a few moments just before falling into sleep, when things are seen and felt like shadows—without fear, without love, without emotion. Peace that one feels alone, surrounded with statues and pictures—I come! Lord, I come!

The world is, but not beautiful nor ugly, but as sensations without exciting any emotion. Oh, Joe, the blessedness of it! Everything is good and beautiful; for things are all losing their relative proportions to me—my body among the first. Om That Existence!...

Yours faithfully,

Vivekananda.[80]

Vivekananda got his wish for final peace in the summer of 1902. He was active throughout the day in Belur Math. He took a class on Sanskrit grammar for the young monks in the math. He gave instructions for a religious function to be held the next day. In the evening, he entered the meditation room, and in an unusual act, bolted the door and closed all the windows. He meditated inside alone for an hour. Afterwards, he went and lay down in his room. He died within half an hour; he was six months shy of reaching forty years of age. The day, coincidentally, was the Fourth of July—the American day of independence.

VIVEKANANDA AND HINDUTVA

The date 9/11 will forever be associated with the images millions across the world watched on their television screens—the twin towers of the World Trade Centre in New York crumbling as two airplanes crashed into them. On 11 September 2001, members of the Al-Qaeda, an Islamist terrorist organization, hijacked four passenger planes and crashed them into prominent American landmarks with the intention of creating as many mass casualties as possible. The stated aims of Osama-bin-Laden, the leader of the Al-Qaeda, were political—American support for Israeli occupation of Palestine, the Chechnyan war, conflict in Somalia and Libya, and sanctions imposed on Iraq—but religion played its part in Al-Qaeda's campaign, where it recruited mujahideen by portraying Islam as a religion in eternal war against infidel religions.[*] There are several ironies and coincidences in the events surrounding the terror attack that occurred that day which killed 2,977 innocent men and women. For one, Mohammad Atta, the leader of the attack who piloted the first plane that demolished the WTC skyscraper, was an architect by training whose PhD research was on the preservation of heritage buildings in Aleppo. A strange coincidence which was underreported by the media was that the plan of flying hijacked commercial airplanes in a suicide terror attack on American soil first appeared in the plot of Tom Clancy's bestselling thriller *Debt of Honour*. Something hardly reported is the fact that in a combination of coincidence and deep irony, Vivekananda delivered his famous Chicago speech for religious tolerance exactly 118 years ago on 11 September 1893.

The Parliament of Religions held in Chicago in 1893, represented a moment of great optimism, which was the acme of a nineteenth century largely free of major wars in the West and of increasing religious tolerance.[†] While there were quite a number of delegates who spoke of peace between all religions at the Parliament, and some who spoke of the equality of different faiths, Vivekananda

---

[*]For Al-Qaeda's theological literature, see *The Al Qaeda Reader: The Essential Texts of Osama Bin Laden's Terrorist Organization*, ed. Raymond Ibrahim, New York: Doubleday, 2007.
[†]The Napoleanic Wars, which ended in 1815, were the last major wars that involved the big European nations.

might have been the only one to dwell upon the violence that religion had created in the world. Vivekananda extolled the wonders of spiritual truths, but he was a rarity among religious preachers in that he constantly pointed out that the religious enterprise, by its very nature, inherently carried within it the possibility of fanaticism and violence. Given that the 11 September attack took place on the 118th anniversary of Vivekananda's Chicago speech, the conclusion of his speech seems all the more a historical irony. Vivekananda closed his address to the Parliament with the following words:

> Sectarianism, bigotry and its terrible descendent fanaticism, have possessed long this beautiful earth. It has filled the earth with violence, drenched it often and often with human gore, destroyed civilisation and sent whole nations into despair. Had it not been for these horrible demons, human society would be far more advanced than it is now. But its time has come, and I fervently believe that the bell that tolled this morning in honour of the representatives of the different religions of the earth, in this parliament assembled, is the death-knell to all fanaticism, that it is the death-knell to all persecution with the sword or the pen, and to all uncharitable feelings between brethren wending their way to the same goal.[1]

It was not only what transpired on 9/11 that would prove Vivekananda's 'fervent belief' and hope was too optimistic. That hope was already being belied in India.

⤳

At that very moment, the bigotry and fanaticism that Vivekananda warned against was haunting his homeland, igniting deeply buried religious passions and extinguishing lives in its wake. Barely a month after Vivekananda set sail from Bombay, Hindu–Muslim clashes over the killing of cows started in the North-Western Provinces in Azimgarh during Bakrid. In a few months, they would claim more than a hundred lives in the North-Western Provinces, Bihar, and Bombay Presidency. At the root of what the British called the 'cow row', were gauraksha sabhas or cow protection societies. Formed a decade earlier in the Central Provinces, they soon spread to Bihar, Punjab, and central North India, all places with substantial Muslim populations.[2] Vivekananda's voyage to America coincided with an upswing in the belligerence of gauraksha sabhas, which would eventually result in communal riots. A year before, the British government had increased Indian representatives in legislative councils. Sensing opportunity, gauraksha sabhas began to demand for a legal ban on cow slaughter, while conducting shrill public campaigns around protecting the mother cow. The situation has many parallels to what is happening today in India in the name of cow protection.

Around Bakrid, rumours started spreading in Azimgarh that the Muslims planned to sacrifice more cows than usual for the festival. The British attempted to scotch this rumour but things still got out of hand. Roaming bands of Hindus took to the streets, forcibly stopping Bakrid sacrifices. This led to thirty to forty Hindu–Muslim clashes. In Prabhas Pathan, Gujarat, Muslims are said to have destroyed temples during Muharram and killed Hindus.

The news of the riots spread across the fragile communal fabric of the British administered subcontinent, causing more riots in Rangoon, Burma. In Bombay, gaurakshak sabhas had been particularly militant. As news of the clashes in Azimgarh and Rangoon reached Bombay, members of gaurakshak sabhas took to the streets, holding massive demonstrations and calling for a ban on cattle slaughter throughout India. When the news of the killings of Hindus in Gujarat reached Bombay, the atmosphere became more tense and Hindus held meetings where they accused the British administration of being partial to Muslims. Muslims held counter meetings where they accused the provincial authorities of favouring Hindus. The communal tinderbox was set afire when the police fired at an irate Muslim mob at the city's Jama Masjid. Three days of Hindu–Muslim riots followed; the worst Bombay had ever seen. For the next two days, Hindu and Muslim gangs roamed the streets, destroying, looting, and plundering. In all, eighty people lost their lives.

Vivekananda returned from America four years later as a celebrity and a national hero. By the time he reached his hometown of Calcutta in February 1897, he had been feted all across the country for his success at representing India and Hinduism to the West. To get a sense of how radically the fortunes of the itinerant monk had changed, one needs only look at the reception he was given when he arrived in India, disembarking at modern day Tamil Nadu. When Vivekananda reached the princely state of Ramnad, he was welcomed by the Rajah himself, who greeted him by prostrating at his feet. Vivekananda was carried around in a carriage in a ceremonial procession, and the Rajah himself pulled the carriage. At Madras, an estimated 10,000 people turned out to hear him speak and excitement reached such a fever pitch that he had to address the crowd in the streets, standing on the driver's seat of a carriage box. He was treated as a holy man and people came in droves for his blessings. A rumour spread that Vivekananda was an incarnation of Sambandar Swami (a Shaiva saint) and women from all over the city turned up to seek his blessings and worship him. His experience on reaching Calcutta was similar. He was driven from Sealdah station to Ripon College in a carriage. A group of enthusiastic youngsters unyoked the horses and pulled the carriage themselves all the way.

Two weeks after his arrival in Calcutta, Vivekananda had his only recorded encounter with a member of a cow protection committee, a man who, in a sense, was the ancestor of modern day gaurakshaks or cow vigilantes. Their conversation was taken down by Vivekananda's disciple Sharat Chandra Chakravarty, and gives us valuable insight into what Vivekananda thought of cow protection and its positioning with regard to Hinduism. It is probable that Vivekananda never knew about the cow riots which shook north India and Bombay in his absence. This was not merely because the public sphere in India was extremely fragmented and information travelled slowly. The fact is that lives came cheap in British India; a hundred deaths might not even have invited public attention. A disastrous famine had been raging since the previous year, claiming over 9 lakh lives. It would go on to claim a million lives and affect a population of nearly 70 million. Famines were a routine part of life in British administered India. An estimated 30 to 60 million people died in India in the last quarter of the nineteenth century from famine. Sharat Chandra, who describes the member of the gaurakshak sabha as an 'enthusiastic preacher', narrates the following conversation, which can be found in the sixth volume of *The Complete Works of Swami Vivekananda*.

At the announcement of this preacher of cow-protection Swamiji came out to the parlour room. The preacher saluted Swamiji and presented him with a picture of the mother-cow. Swamiji took that in his hand and, making it over to one standing by, commenced the following conversation with the preacher:

Vivekananda: What is the object of your society?

Gau rakshak: We protect the mother-cows of our country from the hands of the butcher. Cow-infirmaries have been founded in some places where the diseased, decrepit mother-cows or those bought from the butchers are provided for.

Vivekananda: That is very good indeed. What is the source of your income?

Gau rakshak: The work of the society is carried on only by gifts kindly made by great men like you.

Vivekananda: What amount of money have you now laid by?

Gau rakshak: The Marwari traders' community are the special supporters of this work. They have given a big amount for this good cause.

Vivekananda: A terrible famine has now broken out in Central India. The Indian Government has published a death-roll of nine lakhs of starved people. Has your society done anything to render help in this time of famine?

Gau rakshak: We do not help during famine or other distresses. This society has been established only for the protection of mother-cows.[3]

The preacher was unmoved by Vivekananda's exhortation that it was his duty to help his fellow brothers and sisters who were facing death. He replied, apparently without any sense of irony, that the famine-stricken people were suffering because of their past karma and nothing could be done for them. The reply apparently infuriated Vivekananda, who told the gaurakshak bluntly that he had no sympathy to spare for societies which would not lift a finger to help human beings but wasted piles of food on birds and beasts. Vivekananda further countered that if one were to appeal to the principle of karma, then the cows were falling into the butcher's hand because of their own karma, and it was useless to do anything for them.

This retort flummoxed the preacher. 'Yes, what you say is true, but the Shastras say that the cow is our mother.' Vivekananda's reply sums up his thoughts. 'Yes, that the cow is our mother, I understand: who else could give birth to *such* accomplished children?'[4]

Between May 2015 and December 2018, at least thirty-six Muslims in India have been lynched for transporting cows or over rumours of eating beef.[5] Hundreds of Muslims and Dalits have been attacked by vigilante gaurakshak groups. Two states have banned the consumption of beef altogether, while others have instituted severe restrictions on cattle slaughter.[6] Instead of arresting the vigilantes, the police have often arrested the victims or lent active assistance to the vigilantes.[7] The Rajasthan, Haryana, and Uttarakhand governments (the former during the BJP's tenure) announced that they will officially recognize gaurakshaks by issuing them with identification cards.[8] The State has clearly shown that its might is behind those who take up cow protection and its coercive powers are behind aiding that agenda. All this is done behind a thin screen of constitutionality. The laws that the State invokes to ban cattle slaughter, and to set up official gaurakshak groups and committees, are animal husbandry provisions and directive principles of state policy. On paper, there is nothing about religion or Hinduism. Or about the cow being sacred.

But in public discourse, the holiness of the cow to Hinduism is central to how the Rashtriya Swayamsewak Sangh (RSS), the Vishwa Hindu Parishad (VHP), the Bajrang Dal, and other Sangh Parivar groups have sought to justify and mobilize support for the cause.[9] Those who eat beef are accused of hurting the sentiments of the Hindu community. Implicit in this claim is the idea that cow worship is an integral and inviolable part of the Hindu religion and tradition. Oddly enough, the nomenclature of 'hurt religious sentiments' has found its way into the national conversation from the legal lexicon, from a badly worded provision created by the British to guard against hate speech.* This provision has been deliberately misconstrued in the public imagination to push the idea that religious groups have an inherent right to demand that other people respect their feelings, customs, traditions, and so on. But this is not the case. In a democracy like India, and the way our founding fathers envisaged it, every citizen has the fundamental right of expression to criticize, and even ridicule, religions. Religions, on the other hand, are not recognized as legal entities and have no rights under the Constitution. Rights inhere in individual citizens, and religious beliefs enter the picture only as private beliefs possessed by citizens.

Vivekananda's ridicule of the gaurakshak was not merely incidental. He disagreed vehemently with the two key assumptions behind cow protectionism. The idea that one should not do things that ran afoul of the feelings of a religious community; and the claim that Hinduism forbade the slaughter of cows. As to the former, Vivekananda was antagonistic not merely to such special privileges organized religions claimed—he was critical of organized religion itself. He was also keenly aware that religious identity was always exercised in opposition to an 'other'. In a speech to an audience in San Francisco, he put his views on the matter in characteristically unambiguous fashion:

If you want to be religious, enter not the gate of any organised religion. They do a hundred times more evil than good, because they stop the growth of each one's individual development. Study everything, but keep your own seat firm. If you take my advice, do not put your neck into the trap. The moment they try to put their noose on you, get your neck out and go somewhere else. As the bee culling honey from many flowers remains free, not bound by any flower, be not bound. Enter not the door of any organised religion. Religion is only between you and your God, and no third person must come between you. Think what these organised

---

*Section 295(a) of the Indian Penal Code which punishes 'deliberate and malicious acts, intended to outrage religious feelings of any class by insulting its religion or religious beliefs'.

religions have done! What Napoleon was more terrible than those religious persecutions? If you and I organise, we begin to hate every person. It is better not to love, if loving only means hating others. That is not love. That is hell! If loving your own people means hating everybody else, it is the quintessence of selfishness and brutality, and the effect is that it will make you brutes.[10]

As for the prohibition on eating beef, in his public and his personal life, Vivekananda treated the Hindu custom with indifference at best. Thus, we find him in London at the beginning of the new century, treating the brother of his disciple Margaret Noble to a beef steak dinner (as narrated by Mary Louise Burke in the fifth volume of *Swami Vivekananda in the West: New Discoveries*).[11] Vivekananda thought of the taboo against beef eating as a mere cultural custom, and as with all cultural taboos, he regarded it with disdain. So, he was often not merely dismissive, but went out of his way to provoke orthodoxy on the question of beef and meat eating. As mentioned by historian D. N. Jha in *The Myth of the Holy Cow*, he would point out that the early Vedas show Brahmins eating beef.[12] Before his journey to America, when he arrived in Travancore (now Thiruvananthapuram) in his journey through India, he met with some orthodox Brahmins. In the course of the conversation, they asked him which age he considered the most glorious age of Hinduism. In Swami Nikhilananda's biography of Vivekananda, the monk is quoted as saying 'The Vedic age...when five brahmins used to polish off one cow.'[13]

It was not merely that historically Hindus had consumed beef. Religious beliefs evolve over time. And it would be certainly possible to hold that while the prohibition against cow slaughter entered the Hindu tradition at a particular point in history, it should now be a universal religious prohibition for practising Hindus.* But it is significant that Vivekananda held categorically that neither the prohibition on cow slaughter nor the worship of cows are a part of the essential structure of Hinduism. For him, this flowed not only from Hindu theology proper, but also from his philosophy of religion per se. As far as Hindu theology goes, matters are rather straightforward. The major scriptures, the principal Upanishads, the Bhagavad Gita, the Ramayana, and the Mahabharata etc., contain no injunctions against killing cows on religious grounds. Those injunctions which exist in the two great epics were not usually on religious grounds. As noted by Jha, the Vedas often recommend cow slaughter as a social custom or for ritual purposes.[14] Vivekananda once told an audience, 'You will

---

*Today, many Hindus eat beef, especially in South India.

be surprised to know that according to ancient Hindu rites and rituals, a man cannot be a good Hindu who does not eat beef.'[15] On another occasion, he talked about the ritual necessity of eating beef in early Hinduism, 'There was a time in this very India when, without eating beef, no Brahmin could remain a Brahmin; you read in the Vedas how, when a Sannyasin, a king, or a great man came into a house, the best bullock was killed.'[16] Both these instances are mentioned in the third volume of *The Complete Works of Swami Vivekananda*.

It is important to note here that for Vivekananda, it was not merely a contingent question of whether this particular practice had scriptural sanction. Admittedly, the lack of any scriptural injunction, unlike in Islam where there is an explicit Quranic injunction against eating pork, made the task of brushing aside the issue of beef eating in Hinduism rather easy. But even if Hindu scriptures like the Bhagavad Gita had prohibited it, it is doubtful whether Vivekananda would have countenanced a taboo which he found arbitrary and superstitious. Vivekananda's teachings on religion, and in fact of Hinduism itself, did not recognize the authority of any scriptures in any usual sense. Scriptures and religious books were only signposts and aids on the way to true religion. According to Vivekananda, 'Religion is not in books, nor in theories, nor in dogmas, nor in talking, not even in reasoning. It is being and becoming.'[17] Historically, he felt this applied particularly to Hinduism because of the latitude it permitted its adherents on the matter of theological belief. 'The Hindu religion does not consist in struggles and attempts to believe a certain doctrine or dogma, but in realising—not in believing, but in being and becoming.'[18] Religious texts did not exist as closed entities that laid down immutable laws. They stood in a nexus with reason; for Vivekananda held that religions had to meet the tests of reason as much as any other secular discipline. Vivekananda's whole view of religion necessarily precluded the elevation into law of any kind of rule. At its most fundamental, Vivekananda preached and understood the goal of religion to be human freedom and an uncompromising search for truth. Such an enterprise had necessarily to be free of rules and regulations; it could only be guided by the principles of freedom and knowledge.

⁓

The RSS and the Sangh Parivar claim Vivekananda as an inspiration; Vivekananda is most important in the Sangh's pantheon of cultural figures. However, Vivekananda had no influence on the RSS in its formative years when it developed its political ideology of Hindutva, or in the years immediately following Independence.[19] The Sangh's public adulation of Vivekananda seems to have begun in the sixties. He was presented as both a patriot and a glorifier of Indian culture and Hinduism. The Sangh tried to create greater recognition for a more Hinduized, nationalistic Vivekananda. A watershed was the movement led by the RSS and the VHP to install a Vivekananda memorial in Kanyakumari. The Tamil Nadu government was not keen, so the RSS was able to build a movement out of the Vivekananda memorial, making it into a national cause.[20] They distributed lakhs of leaflets with quotations from Vivekananda, in the process impressing on people's minds an association between Vivekananda and the Sangh. Having garnered support from across India, the RSS eventually got the memorial as well as a Vivekananda Kendra built.

This allowed the RSS and its Sangh affiliates to forge an association in the popular mind between them and the figure of Vivekananda, giving the RSS's claim of representing Hinduism legitimacy. Vivekananda was already part of the national consciousness in the sixties. With their tireless efforts to further iconize his image, the Sangh not only took credit for doing something for Hinduism, but also gained the legitimacy of association with one of modern Hinduism's most revered and admired figures. (In the sixties, the RSS was a political outcast, never having recovered from the shadow of the ban imposed on it after the assassination of Mohandas Karamchand Gandhi.) In the late seventies, the RSS joined with other opposition parties and organizations to protest the Emergency imposed by Indira Gandhi. After the Emergency was lifted, it was able to shed its outcast image and enter the mainstream. The eighties onwards have been a period of intense groundwork for the RSS, which intensified the activities of various Sangh Parivar organizations like the VHP, the Bajrang Dal, and the Vanvasi Kalyan Ashram. Besides specifically political programmes, the Sangh also began spreading its political ideology, which it called 'Hindutva', at the grassroots level, through organizing and promoting Hindu religious and cultural events.[21] It is in the background of the Sangh's religious and cultural outreach that Vivekananda became an important figure for the Sangh and its ideological aims.

Today, Vivekananda's pictures adorn numerous RSS public meetings; usually the iconic picture of the sanyasi in flowing orange robes and turban, standing with his hands crossed and head held high.* The RSS organizes regular commemorative events, conferences, meetings, and symposiums on Vivekananda. Embedding Vivekananda in the public narrative of Hindutva has allowed the Sangh to create the impression that Vivekananda, the man

---

*This picture was taken during Vivekananda's first visit to America.

and the thinker, is an ideological predecessor and an ally. This perception has been reinforced by the lack of powerful counter narratives which challenge the Sangh's appropriation and by the deification of Vivekananda in popular consciousness. Vivekananda's thoughts and ideas are rarely discussed, even by those who valorize him. Even in academia, there have been very few critical discussions of his key texts, philosophical ideas, and ideological leanings. This ensures that Vivekananda remains just an emblem that admirers across the political spectrum pay homage to. This lack of a critical discourse around Vivekananda has allowed the Sangh to create the impression of a kinship between Vivekananda's thought and their own Hindutva ideology, merely by juxtaposing Vivekananda's persona with its cultural and religious activities.

Over the decades the Sangh has been trying with increasing success to convert Vivekananda into a mascot of Hindutva. But what exactly is Hindutva and how does it relate to the teachings of the nineteenth century monk?

WHAT IS HINDUTVA?

The word 'Hindutva' as denoting a political project entered public discourse twenty-one years after Vivekananda's death. Its populizer was a man named Vinayak Damodar Savarkar. A Marathi Brahmin from near Nasik, Savarkar was an Indian nationalist revolutionary who operated from England in the first decade of the twentieth century. Savarkar was arrested by the British after his fellow revolutionary Madan Lal Dhingra assassinated the political aide-de-camp to Britain's India secretary. Transported to the cellular jail in the Andaman and Nicobar Islands, Savarkar would spend the early years of India's freedom struggle in exile. Savarkar did not witness the transformation in Indian society and polity brought about by Gandhi's Non-cooperation Movement and the Khilafat Movement firsthand. But the ideology of Hindu cultural nationalism he developed during this time would be hugely influential in shaping the minds of many who did. Hindu nationalism crystallized in reaction to the Khilafat movement, which mobilized Muslims across India to oppose the deposition of Turkey's caliph. It was also a response to a series of Hindu–Muslim riots which followed in the wake of the Khilafat movement. Savarkar wrote the book *Hindutva: Who is a Hindu?* in 1923, where he set forth his vision of ethnic Hindu nationalism, which he termed 'Hindutva'. The book would become the foundational text of Hindu nationalism, and its broad contours would determine the development of Hindutva ideology into the decades after Independence. The Rashtriya Swayamsevak Sangh (RSS) founded in 1926 by another Marathi Brahmin, Keshav Baliram Hedgewar, would carry on the political legacy of Hindutva. Savarkar's writings would deeply influence and mould the thinking and life of Hedgewar, who was inspired by the book as well as Savarkar's personal influence to start the RSS. Savarkar's ideas would also have an impact on the writing of the RSS's greatest ideologue and its second head, M. S. Golwalkar.[22]

Savarkar defines Hindutva as the totality of the historical and cultural experience of the Hindu race and the Hindu nation. For Savarkar, Hindutva is a term which encompasses more than the Hindu religion; it is a monolith that fuses in itself what he calls 'Hindu culture', the 'history of the Hindu race', and the socio-religious fabric of Hinduism.[23] Two major issues regarding the claims of Savarkar and his ideological heirs in the Sangh Parivar, have been about the relationship of Hindutva and Hinduism on the one hand, and about the coherence of categories like Hindu culture, race, and nation on the other. Proponents of Hindutva have always taken care to distinguish Hindutva and Hinduism in public discourse, both for polemical purposes, like Savarkar, and for strategic reasons, like the RSS. Today's RSS, when accused of promoting a communal identity in spreading Hindutva, often takes recourse to differentiating Hindutva from Hinduism and casting the former in a nationalist idiom more acceptable to secular discourse. But what is clear from perusing the writings of Hindutva ideologues like Savarkar, Golwalkar, and Deendayal Upadhyaya, is that such a distinction in no way takes away the fundamental dependence of Hindutva upon Hinduism for its meaning and legitimacy. Though the precise definition of what constitutes Hindutva or its equivalent varies in the literature, Hindutva always derives its force from its association with Hindu religion.

The second issue is that there seems to be no uniform features of culture, ethnicity, or social practices through which one can locate a Hindu identity in these spheres.[24] Hindu religion and its society are far too diverse, plural, and open-ended to impose the kind of regularity required for Savarkar's political purposes. The arguments Savarkar gives in *Hindutva* for this purpose are in any case not convincing; they consist of little more than emotional appeals to early twentieth century sources of Hindu identity, obfuscated argumentation, and blanket assertions. But what is quite clear are the ingredients that make up the Hindutva package. The template for Hindu nationalism that Savarkar produced has persisted to this day, though with modifications and alterations along the way.

According to Savarkar, India is the land of the Hindu race, who are a people united by common blood. He claims that a single continuous Hindu civilization existed from the Vedic ages onwards, which was always aware that the Hindu people constituted a nation. The Aryans, claims Savarkar, first developed a sense of nationality in the Vedic ages. They also developed a national culture, a 'Sanskriti', which evolved over the millennia but which he claims retained an essential character. According to Savarkar, 'Everyone who is a Hindu inherits this Sanskriti* and owes his Spiritual being to it.'[25] This essential Hindu Sanskriti is the real culture of Hindu civilization and of the Indian nation. Hindutva is the basis of the Indian nation. To be a member of the Indian nation fully, Savarkar requires that a person inherits and possesses this Sanskriti.

What is this Sanskriti and who qualifies on its account to be a member of the India that Savarkar imagines? In *Hindutva*, Savarkar sets out what he means by Sanskriti concretely. It consists, he says, of Hindu rituals and festivals, of Hindu jurisprudence and customs, of places of pilgrimage and sacraments. It also includes a common Hindu religious literature and arts and Hindu cultural heroes. The Hindu, by his very birth, reveres all this. So do the Sikhs and Jains, who Savarkar says, for cultural purposes, can be considered Hindus. Christians and Muslims, however, present a huge problem for Hindutva and its concept of a nation. For Savarkar, Christians and Muslims are an alien other; the cultural reference points of the Semitic traditions lie outside India and their religious traditions are too different from Hinduism to be brought under the umbrella of Hindutva.

Christianity and Islam are foreign presences within the national organism which are to be assimilated into a hegemonic Hindu culture. If they do not allow themselves to be assimilated, the loyalty of these minority communities to the nation will always remain suspect.

> Look at the Mohammedans. Mecca is to them a sterner reality than Delhi or Agra. Some of them do not make any secret of being bound to sacrifice all India if that be to the glory of Islam or could save the city of their prophet. Look at the Jews. Neither centuries of prosperity nor sense of gratitude for the shelter they found, can make them more attached or even equally attached to the several countries they inhabit. Their love is, and necessarily must be divided between the land of their birth and the land of their Prophets.... Take the case of America...the Negro citizen there sympathise more with their brethren in Africa than with their countrymen.[26]

---

*In Golwalkar, the roughly equivalent ideological term is 'Samskara', while it is 'Bharatiya' in Deendayal Upadhyaya.

M. S. Golwalkar was more forthright in *We or Our Nationhood Defined*, a book he published in 1939, a year before he became the sarsanghchalak (head) of the RSS.

> There are only two courses open to these foreign elements...either to merge themselves in the national race and adopt its culture or to live at its mercy so long as the national race may allow them to do so and quit the country at the sweet will of the national race. That is the only sound view on the minorities' problem...foreign races in Hindustan must either adopt the Hindu culture and language, must learn to respect and hold in reverence Hindu religion, must entertain no idea but those of the glorification of the Hindu race and culture, i.e., of the Hindu nation and must lose their separate existence to merge in the Hindu race, or may stay in the country, wholly subordinated to the Hindu Nation, claiming nothing, deserving no privileges, far less any preferential treatment—not even citizen's rights.[27]

Savarkar and his followers understand Indian history and society through the lens of an enduring clash of civilizations between Hindus on one hand and Muslims and Christians on the other. The most seminal event in this history is the conquest of India by Muslim invaders. Savarkar writes that it started a war which was 'brought to conclusion only when the Marathas took the battle to the Mughals and restored Hindu pride'. It is the Islamic conquest with which begins the decline of India and Muslim kings, by holding the Hindu race in slavery, prepared the way for the British conquest. For Savarkar, and for much of the Sangh, every Muslim is a Hindu who has been converted by the force of arms. To date, for the RSS and the Sangh Parivar, the presence of Christianity and Islam is a reminder of foreign invasions and rules of the past which they believe oppressed Hindus and fatally disrupted the organic unity of Indian civilization and retarded its growth. For the Sangh, conversion out of Hinduism is considered an existential threat to the religion itself. Thus the Vanvasi Kalyan Ashram has been working from almost Independence to counter Christian proselytizing in tribal areas and bring converted adivasis into the fold of Hinduism through 'ghar wapsi' programmes. The Sangh has aggressively pushed for and helped the enactment of legislation that bans religious conversion by 'force'. On the ground, this translates to various administrative and social hurdles placed before Hindus who want to convert to Christianity and Islam. It also tends to criminalize proselytizing, especially by Christian groups,[28] even though the right to spread one's religion is a fundamental right guaranteed under the Indian Constitution.

It is now close to a hundred years since Savarkar penned *Hindutva*. Yet it is astonishing how the fundamental elements of his thought still exert its influence on contemporary India through the politics of Hindutva. Apart from the religious polarization and 'othering' of Christians and Muslims that we are witnessing, many other concrete forms that Hindutva is taking today have its echoes in Savarkar's ideology. These include the current Hindutva discourse on Vedas, science, Indian culture, Sanskrit, and Hindu mythology. They have taken more extreme and concrete forms than the theoretical deliberations of Savarkar, but its seeds are easily found in the latter.

In his writing, Savarkar uncritically valorizes Indian, or Hindu, civilization. Indian civilization is not only glorious, but also essentially perfect. Every historical, social, and cultural development since the Vedic age has been necessitated by political or material need. The Hindu race has never committed a mistake, its glories are all magnificent triumphs, its perceived mistakes all historical requirements. Thus, even the old Hindu prohibition of losing caste if you travel overseas, finds a reason and justification in Savarkar's telling of Indian history. India's civilizational greatness is not only the greatest the world has seen, it is all encompassing. 'Verily whatever could be found in the world can be found here too. And if anything is not found here it could be found nowhere.'[29]

The only aberrations in the course of India's civilizational progress are the Muslim invasions and the British conquests. Even the caste system, the most iniquitous of all social evils, came from outside the Hindu fold. While the RSS today blames Muslim invasions for creating the caste system,[30] Savarkar traces the origin of the caste system to the impact of Buddhism. Savarkar's attitude towards Buddhism itself is double edged. While he acknowledges and even pays respect to the spiritual greatness of Buddha and Buddhism, he holds the doctrine of ahimsa responsible for weakening India's martial vigour and paving the way for the invasions of the Huns, Shakyas, and Tartars. These are not necessarily contradictory positions, but it is worth noting that in his castigation of the alleged military weakness that Buddhism produced, he often strays into denigrating the principles of Buddhism which he professes to admire. He lays the blame on the 'opiates of universalism and non-violence'[31] and the 'mealy-mouthed formulas of ahimsa'.[32]

A cornerstone of Savarkar's exposition of Hindu nationalism is veneration for Vedic civilization. Worshipping the civilization of the ancient Aryans is not merely an expression of Savarkar's personal admiration. It is a norm that every member of the Hindu Rashtra should believe in to fully participate in the life of the Indian race and nation. The Vedic civilization is not only hallowed, but is also the oldest in the world, surpassing all other nations in antiquity. This supposed ancientness is a central source of identity for the Sangh Parivar's conception of Indian civilization and culture and for its claims to superiority over all other world civilizations. But the character and nature of this civilization as expounded by the Sangh is rarely historical but part of a myth-making project. Savarkar's views in regard to Vedic civilization too are decidedly ahistorical and closer to the mythical.

> Certain it is that long before the ancient Egyptians and Babylonians had built their magnificent civilization, the holy waters on the Indus were daily witnessing the lucid and curling columns of the scented sacrificial smokes and the valleys resounding with the chant of Vedic hymns.... Hindu would be the name that this land and the people who inhabited it bore from time so immemorial that even the Vedic name Sindhu is but a later and secondary form of it.... The word Hindu dates its antiquity from a period so remoter than the first (Sindhu), that even mythology fails to penetrate—to trace it to its source.[33]

It hardly needs stating that all available historical evidence date the Egyptian and Babylonian civilizations to several centuries before the Vedic age and that the origins of the word Hindu lie in first millennium BCE Persian and Greek and not in a pre-Vedic remote past.[34] The word was used by Persians and Greeks to refer to the people who lived beyond the Sindhu (Indus).[35]

Another key element of Savarkar's vision of Hindutva is Sanskrit. Sanskrit is not only a perfect language, it is also the mother tongue of the Hindus and the national language of India. All the languages spoken in India, including the Dravidian languages, are descended from Sanskrit according to Savarkar. The language which has retained most of Sanskrit's essence is Hindi, and hence it should be promoted as India's national language. Along with veneration for Sanskrit comes veneration for the earliest literature in the language as well as in the world, the Vedas. The Vedas are a primordial part of the history and identity of the Hindu race and an essential constituent of Hindu ethnicity. Similarly, historical and mythical figures, forefathers and patriarchs are fountains of authority and cultural authenticity.

Throughout his tract on Hindutva, Savarkar does not sharply distinguish between mythology and history. This obscurantism is leveraged for the project of Hindu nationalism. This is particularly the case when it comes to characters in Hindu mythology. He treats mythological characters as real or quasi-real. Thus, Ramayana's account of Ram crossing to Sri Lanka becomes a seminal event in the nation's history.

> At last the great mission which the Sindhus had undertaken of founding a nation and a country, reached its geographical limit when the valorous Prince of Ayodhya made a triumphant entry in Ceylon and actually brought the whole land from the Himalayas to the Seas under one sovereign sway. The day when the Horse of Victory returned to Ayodhya...the great white Umbrella of Sovereignty was unfurled over the Imperial throne of Ramachandra the brave, Ramachandra the good, and a loving allegiance to him was sworn, not only by Princes of Aryan blood, but Hanuman, Sugriva, Bibhishana from the south—that day was the real birth-day of the Hindu people. It was truly our national day: for Aryans and Anaryans knitting themselves into a people were born as nation.[36]

THE RSS'S APPROPRIATION OF VIVEKANANDA

For Vivekananda, to confuse myth for history would be an intellectual disaster where one loses sight of truth and falls into superstition. Mythology was an entirely different entity from history, which was based on evidence and fact. He did not view Hindu mythology as in any way an exception to this. Even in a time period where research into India's past was in its infancy and there was nothing definite to say about the historicity of Puranic characters one way or another, Vivekananda boldly doubted the historical veracity of the Puranas and its divine personages. For example, he cast doubt more than once on whether Krishna ever really existed. For example, on a discourse on the Gita he gave at the Alambazar Math in Calcutta to some disciples, he took up the question of the historicity of the events and persons described in the scriptures.

> Much doubt exists about the personality of Krishna.... It is human nature to build round the real character of a great man all sorts of imaginary superhuman attributes. As regards Krishna the same must have happened, but it seems quite probable that he was a king.... Bearing on the subject of the Kurukshetra War, no special evidence in support of it can be adduced.... Another thing: how could there be so much discussion about Jnana, Bhakti, and Yoga on the battle-field, where the huge army stood in

battle array ready to fight, just waiting for the last signal? And was any shorthand writer present there to note down every word spoken between Krishna and Arjuna, in the din and turmoil of the battle-field?[37]

Vivekananda did not consider that those who follow Hinduism had to believe in the literal truth of its sacred myths. In fact, he would say again and again, to take mythology literally is to get stuck in a crude stage of spiritual growth. Mythology had an important place in religion, but it had to be understood as allegory, as literary and symbolic illustrations of the abstract principles of spirituality. There was no contradiction in worshipping the gods of Hinduism's lore as forms of divinity, while recognizing the non-historical and mythological character of their depiction in scriptures.

Vivekananda's thought on all themes important to Hindutva nationalism—Hindu identity, the nature of Hinduism, the place of minorities in India—stand in stark opposition to the thought of the RSS's icons like Savarkar, Golwalkar, and Hedgewar. As a result, the RSS does not project Vivekananda as an ideological forerunner to the Savarkar–Golwalkar brand of hardline Hindutva. It is difficult to put Vivekananda, the central theme of whose thought was universal religious tolerance, in the same box with Hindutva ideologues who were openly and deeply hostile to Islam and Christianity. The RSS and other Sangh outfits do not generally discuss Vivekananda's work, choosing only to make use of the symbolic value of invoking his name and image for their events, activities, and organizations. On the occasions that writers associated with the RSS have ventured to write on Vivekananda, they proceed by ignoring or underemphasizing the universal and non-denominational aspects of his work. Instead, a nationalistic, culturally conservative, and Hinduized Vivekananda is presented. This is achieved through cherry picking writings and utterances that appear to bear idiomatic similarities to certain aspects of Hindutva when they are lifted out of their original contexts. This is followed by attributing to Vivekananda on this basis, beliefs and ideological positions he never held.

For example, RSS ideologue P. Parameswaran in his writings on Vivekananda, presents Vivekananda as a figure who was predominantly concerned with the preservation of 'Indian values'.[38] Parameswaran bemoans how Indian youngsters have fallen away from these values in their lifestyle. The younger generation, especially the Indian diaspora in the US, is turning away from 'Indian cultural values' and leading a degenerate lifestyle (marked, among other things, by sexual liberty), forgetting their cultural heritage. Parameswaran claims that Vivekananda was proud of Hindutva. According to Parameswaran, Vivekananda believed that a thousand years of slavery had made the Hindu community lose its pride and had caused it to become divided. The task that Vivekananda saw before him was to organize and mobilize the disunited Hindus.

From the RSS's account, Vivekananda emerges as an advocate of Hindu exceptionalism. It is claimed Vivekananda preached that Indians were an extraordinary nation. India had been considered a holy land, a 'punyabhoomi', from ancient times. Vivekananda's patriotism was rooted in and was a continuation of this older ethno-religious tradition, cast in new nationalist terms. According to this narrative, Vivekananda firmly believed that India and Hindus had a special destiny in the world, a destiny that stemmed from the knowledge contained in the Vedas and the Upanishads.[39]

In the Sangh's version, Vivekananda was not only a cultural conservative whose primary concern was the perpetuation of Indian cultural values; he was also a champion of the universal relevance and inherent superiority of those values. He was an evangelist for Hindu spirituality, whose patriotism was based on 'extraordinary pride in Indian culture.'[40] Particularly, he laid emphasis on the Upanishads, the final portions of the Vedas. In Parameswaran's rendering of Vivekananda's thought, Vivekananda criticized the West and its consumer culture.[41] Parameswaran writes that consumer culture is built on an incomplete philosophy of life. 'This is what western modernity has shown the world for two centuries. Swept in its seductive net, India is today ready to forget its own roots and is eager to imitate the western model.... Humanity's longevity requires a different philosophy of life. This is what Swamiji meant by Upanishadic darshana.... Swamiji instructed that the national regeneration had to be based on Vedanta, and the Upanishadic message should be the warp and woof of the national life. It was his firm belief that such a new India would be a model and guide for the whole world.'[42]

According to the RSS's story about Vivekananda, the greatness of Hinduism was an ever-present theme with him. India's destiny was the spiritual conquest of the world through the export of Hindu spirituality. Vivekananda thought Hindu tradition and culture offered solutions to the modern world's problems. In fact, the West would go to destruction without Indian spirituality. Vivekananda wanted Indians to teach the West our spiritual traditions and secure for India the position of spiritual teacher to the West forever. Only the Upanishadic message, Vivekananda believed, could save the West from its destructive materialism.

While it is true that Vivekananda wanted to spread the message of the Upanishads throughout the world and believed that Advaita Vedanta gave philosophical answers to intellectual challenges that religion faced from modern scepticism, the RSS narrative about Vivekananda does not come close to even being a caricature. But the matter doesn't end there. We have to take note of what the RSS passes off under the umbrella terms of 'Indian culture' and 'Hindu spirituality', which it attributes to Vivekananda.

THE RSS WORLD VIEW

Mohan Bhagwat, who became RSS's chief in 2009, stated in February 2019, that 'Ram' and 'Gau Mata' are the basis of Hindu culture. 'We revere Ram. Gau mata and Ram form the basis of the Hindu culture. Every Indian must feel that the Ram temple in Ayodhya should be built at its original place. If it comes up there, the identity of Hinduism will be established in the world,' he said. 'Muslims are free to follow their method of worship but they must feel that we belong to the same country and culture and that our ancestors were the same.'[43]

The RSS often uses Hindu and Indian culture in an interchangeable manner in different contexts, since it is to their advantage to conflate these two terms. But when 'Bharatiya Sanskriti' or 'Indian culture' is used as a standalone concept without religious connotations, it serves as a catch-all bag into which every kind of conservative social norm can be thrown. After the horrific Delhi gang rape in 2012, Mohan Bhagwat grabbed headlines by saying that rapes happen only in India and not Bharat.[44] The media reported him as saying: 'Rapes take place in cities and not in villages. Women should refrain from venturing out with men other than their relatives. Such incidents happen due to the influence of Western culture and women wearing less clothes.'[45] The same sentiment was expressed by RSS leader Indresh Kumar who blamed sexual assault in India on people celebrating Valentine's Day. 'Love is pure, but the western culture has changed it into passion, which has somehow manifested into a business. The reason behind rape, divorce is this western culture.'[46] Other organizations in the Sangh Parivar have promoted the same line.

While the RSS's primitive social conservatism is packaged as Bharatiya Sanskriti, social freedoms are clumped together under the oppositional 'other' of Western culture. Indian culture is always besieged by the influences of the liberal West which threatens to destroy it. Other Sangh Parivar organizations have diligently promoted the same discourse, while its more hardline members like the Bajrang Dal have systematically terrorized the population for decades through moral and cultural policing, most infamously in Mangalore and other parts of coastal and northern Karnataka.[47] A statement made to the media by Ashok Singhal, former president of the VHP, is typical of the organization's views. 'This western model is alarming. What is happening is we have imbibed the US. We have lost all the values we had in cities.' He attacked live-in-relationships and said: 'It is not only foreign to our culture, but also hostile.'[48]

The RSS supports a number of educational organizations across the country, some of them even named after Vivekananda. They all oppose the present secular educational system which is seen as Western and liberal. For example, the then head of Vidya Bharati Akhil Bharatiya Shiksha Sansthan, Ramendra Rai said, 'Your child may speak English today, but he will leave you alone in the street when you are old. English might give their children good careers but only Indian education will make them respectful of family values.... It is only when the children start talking back to them that parents regret having put them in schools that are run on the principles of western culture.'[49]

The common thread running through all these different expressions of the Sangh's world view is the need for social control of the individual. Social authority exercised through the family, through cultural norms, religious tradition, and societal diktats have to control individual choice and agency. The Sangh's opposition to modernity is embedded in a deeply held fear of individualism and personal liberty. The rejection of individual liberty is reflected in the organizational structure of the RSS and other Sangh organizations. It follows the leader principle, which vests all authority in one individual as the sole leader of the organization. The RSS sarsanghchalak's authority regarding its functioning is absolute and his orders are carried out without question down the chain of command. The entire organizational hierarchy functions the same way with absolute authority being delegated downwards and those lower in the hierarchy sworn to obey functionaries in higher positions unquestioningly.[50]

However, the RSS and the Sangh Parivar are more than just a conservative movement constantly battling the spread of liberal values in society. They are a revivalist movement, hoping to bring back an imagined golden past of Hindu society. The Vedas and Vedic culture occupy a hallowed place in this project of cultural revival. The RSS has always laid less emphasis on capturing the institutions of State power than on changing the social polity along the lines it envisages.[51] While details of the Bharatiya Sanskriti and Vedic culture it wants to spread in Indian society have never been spelled out by Sangh thinkers and ideologues in detail, the kind of thing that meets with the RSS's approval is apparent enough.

For example, in 2014, three young men in search of ancient Vedic literature made an astonishing historical discovery. They located an entire lost tradition of the Rig Veda in a village in Rajasthan. An entire recension of the Rig Veda, which was thought lost to history, was found in the village of Banswada. The three men found hundreds of manuscripts covering the entire Rig Veda, with its oldest parts going back to 1468 BCE. With money sourced from well-wishers the entire manuscript collection is being digitized so it can be preserved for the future.[52] It hardly bears mentioning that this is an extremely significant achievement from the point of view of historical research. But after this point, their project deviated from traditional historical conservation efforts.

Two members of the group have decided to dedicate several years to learning how to recite the Rig Veda in the rediscovered tradition and open several Veda Vidyalayas. These Vidyalayas would teach the correct ritual practices of the Rig Veda to youngsters and children. The long-term aim of their project is to revive the Vedic way of life and the rituals that regulate it, in the entire Ganga–Yamuna region.

An article on the website of the *Organiser*, the mouthpiece of the RSS, describes these efforts in glowing terms.

> When we say 'Ours is a traditional society', or 'Indian civilization is a 5000 year old living civilization', seldom do we realize the full import of these statements that we are making; and seldom do we realize the responsibility that it puts on our shoulders. Indian civilization, whose fountainhead are Vedas, is not a 'traditional' and 'living civilization' just because we have a set of old books with us, but because we still pass these Vedas from one generation to another through oral transmission, from father to son and from Guru to Shishya. Not on paper or palm-leaves but Vedas are preserved in the memory of such Pandits. Whole set of complex rituals are preserved through their practitioners. It's through such transmission that the Vedic corpus and rituals have survived and reached us through thousands of years. In other words, every traditional Vedpathee we see in a Ved-Vidyalaya today is the newest addition to an unbroken chain at least three thousand years old. We have the Vedic corpus till we have these 'keepers' among us, and if by any misfortune they cease to exist, so do these traditions, so do the Vedas.[53]

The Rajasthan based project of reviving the Vedic lifestyle states its aims as the following:

> Veda is to be lived, not merely studied, keeping this in mind, prachaara (propagation) of Sanskrta Bhaashaa (Sanskrit language), Vaidika Principles, Vaidika Education and Vaidika Lifestyle. To inspire and motivate people to uphold the Vaidika traditions of Sandhyopaasanam, Shrauta Karma, Gopaalanam and to help such people in overcoming the challenges they face.

Gosamvardhana (Cow rearing) (sic) and to make Gau (cow) an important factor in the Economy of the Nation. To promote the idea of Svadeshi, especially Veshabhooshaa (dress), Bhaashaa (language) and thoughts.[54]

For this purpose, the group has been training Vaidikas (priests), teaching children, conducting camps where Vedic yajnas are taught, conducting programmes that promote 'Vaidika culture' among people; and so on. The idea is to bring back life as lived during the Vedic age in as literal a form as possible. People will be encouraged to live their daily lives according to the specific Vedic rituals that govern household duties. The minutiae of a person's life, from waking to sleeping will be regulated by the performance of rituals prescribed for that purpose in the Rig Veda. An article about the project gives a hint of the level of detail specified by the rituals.

> Another scholar, possibly local, has written the entire paddhati, or ritual performance manual. [A] Sutra would merely state that an...oblation would have to be given to the accompaniment of a specific...hymn from the Rig Veda. The Bhashya would further elaborate how the oblation is to be given, the specific implement to use and more details on the (hymn) to pronounce. The paddhati would elaborate on how the implement is to be cleansed, with what material, if it is to be whisked with the darbha grass, how many times. Essentially, the paddhati is purely for the practitioner, intended as a guide to choreograph every thought and action of each individual involved in the ritual.[55]

VIVEKANANDA ON LIBERTY: SOCIAL AND SPIRITUAL

As we saw in the first chapter, after the World Parliament of Religions concluded in Chicago, Vivekananda spent almost four years in the West. Most of it was spent in the United States where he gave public lectures on the Vedanta philosophy. Leading the life of an itinerant lecturer, Vivekananda stayed at the homes of friends and admirers he made along the way. The monk freely participated in the social life of the cities he found himself in, while remaining committed to his vows of poverty and celibacy.* Thus we find him at high society

---

*Vivekananda initially accepted money for his lectures, arranged through a lecture bureau. But he soon broke off his engagement with the bureau and his lectures were henceforth offered free of charge generally. He took donations from friends and well-wishers, from which a modest amount went for his living expenses; the rest going for what would eventually become the Ramakrishna Mission.

dinners, literary salons, musicals, parties, the opera, plays, and even at séances, which had become something of a fad in America in those days. All this gave him an excellent vantage point from which to observe the foreign society he found himself in. And he was a keen observer, as revealed in countless letters he sent to correspondents in India, reporting on America and Western society.

More often than not Vivekananda's hosts were women. American women were probably more liberated and confident in their destinies than their counterparts in Europe at that time; and their independence, zest, and education deeply impressed the monk from India. After a year in the country, Vivekananda wrote to a friend in India of his impressions of American women and American society.

Nowadays, however, American girls don't want to marry. During the Civil War a large number of men were killed and women began to do all kinds of work. Since then, they have not wanted to give up the rights they have acquired. They earn their own living and therefore they say, 'There is no use in marrying. If we truly fall in love, then we shall marry; otherwise we shall earn and meet our own expenses....' In this country there are rivers of wealth and waves of beauty, and an abundance of knowledge everywhere. The country is very healthy; they know how to enjoy this earth.... In America the best blood strains of Europe have blended, and therefore the American women are very beautiful. And how they take care of their beauty! Can a woman retain her beauty if she gives birth to children every hour from her tenth year on?[*] Damn nonsense! What a terrible sin! Even the most beautiful woman of our country will look like a black owl here.... Many of the American women are very well educated and put many a learned professor to shame; nor do they care for anyone's opinion. And as regards their virtues: what kindness, what noble thought and action! Just think, if a man of this country were to visit India, nobody would even touch him;[†] yet here I am allowed to do as I please in the houses of the best families—like their own son. I am like a child; their women shop for me, run errands for me. For example, I have just written to a girl for information about the machine,[‡] which she will gather carefully and send on to me. Again, a phonograph was sent

---

[*]Vivekananda was, and remained, a life-long opponent of the then prevalent custom of child marriage in India.

[†]Upper-caste Hindus considered the touch of foreigners to be polluting. As 'mlechchhas', people of the West had no caste.

[‡]A sewing machine.

for the Maharajah of Khetri: the girls managed the whole affair very well. Lord! Lord! It is the difference between heaven and hell. [Compared to India] 'They are the goddess Lakshmi in beauty and the goddess Saraswati in talents and accomplishments.' ...I say, can you send out some men and women to see the world? Only then will the country wake up—not through the reading of books.[56]

Vivekananda was already critical of the Indian religious orthodoxy when he travelled the country as a wandering monk for several years. He was shocked by the depredations of the caste system, the social iniquities, the ubiquitous poverty, and the indifference of the Indian elite to the condition of the masses. In America, he encountered an alternative model of social organization and he was tremendously impressed by its strengths. From the perspective of the conditions prevalent in India, American society was egalitarian, dynamic, socially progressive, and intellectually vibrant. Before his Chicago speech, Vivekananda had visited a women's penitentiary and was struck by the humane approach to reforming the inmates. The contrast with the way the oppressed classes were treated in India, depressed him. Analysing the material success of America, Vivekananda came to regard two features as essential factors in that success: organizational ability and individual liberty. He was to speak strongly of the necessity of both these for India throughout his life. Barely a month after the above letter, Vivekananda wrote again from New York, this time to his disciple Alasingha Perumal in Madras, an orthodox Vaishnava who was a graduate of the Madras Presidency College and the principal of Pachaiyappa's school.

'Liberty is the first condition of growth,' he wrote as he instructed his disciple on how to build up an organization to propagate spiritual ideals. 'Just as man must have liberty to think and speak, so he must have liberty in food, dress, and marriage, and in every other thing, so long as he does not injure others.' He makes clear that he is not talking in a vacuum. It is not the ideal principle of liberty, but its concrete application to Indian social conditions that occupied the monk's mind. And what he had seen in America had shown him that social growth and progress can only be predicated on freedom for the individual to express her full potentiality. 'There cannot be any growth without liberty. Our ancestors freed religious thought, and we have a wonderful religion. But they put a heavy chain on the feet of society, and our society is, in a word, horrid, diabolical. In the West, society always had freedom, and look at them,' he wrote. He goes on to dismiss the disdain that the Hindu orthodoxy of his day showed towards the material progress of Western civilization. It was a matter of sour grapes, he wrote. He questioned the use of a spiritual conception which was not able to provide for the basic material well-being of the people and held them down in social oppression in order that a few thousand people in India could become spiritual.

Bread! Bread! I do not believe in a God, who cannot give me bread here, giving me eternal bliss in heaven! Pooh! India is to be raised, the poor are to be fed, education is to be spread, and the evil of priestcraft is to be removed. No priestcraft, no social tyranny! More bread, more opportunity for everybody! Our young fools organize meetings to get more power from the English. They only laugh. None deserves liberty who is not ready to give liberty. Suppose the English give over to you all the power. Why, the powers that be then, will hold the people down, and let them not have it. Slaves want power to make slaves.[57]

Vivekananda traced the oppressive social structures in India to the work of priests. The Brahmins had made themselves masters of Indian society through much of its history, and had invented all sorts of rules that kept the lower castes, women, and the individual human being oppressed. The tyranny of the orthodoxy the Brahmins created was manifested most strongly in the caste system. The worst evil that the caste system created was that its restrictions crushed individuality, it took away the personal agency of people, whether they belonged to the oppressed or oppressor castes. The remedy Vivekananda proposed was to reassert the liberty of the individual against all kinds of social sanctions. He warned Westerners that even socialism, an idea which enjoyed intellectual currency in America and Europe at that time, while inspired by the noblest motives, would nonetheless lead in the end to social tyranny. 'Freedom is the watchword. Be free! A free body, a free mind, and a free soul! That is what I have felt all my life; I would rather be doing evil freely than be doing good under bondage.'[58]

Vivekananda was neither an iconoclast, nor an anarchist. He valued what spiritual tradition, scriptures, and the accumulated wisdom of humanity had to offer the individual. He considered the Upanishads (the philosophical part of the Vedas) to contain the grandest truths of existence ever discovered by man and the Buddha to have preached the highest morality ever conceived. But all these were valuable only if man received them freely and accepted these truths after examining them with her own discriminative faculty. No one should be coerced to accept them or live according to anything other than the dictates of her own conscience. He even saw his vow of sanyas as the embracing of spiritual freedom free from all the regulations and authority exercised by formal religion. He averred often that the sanyasi stands on the head of the Vedas.

While living in New York, Vivekananda once discussed the question of how much man should bend to the demands of society, with his American friend Mary Hale. Mary had written a letter reprimanding Vivekananda for stating his religious views too frankly during his long sojourn in New York and causing offence to the feelings of many, often leading to heated exchanges. She advised him to accommodate himself more to expected forms of behavior in genteel society. Vivekananda wrote back: 'The duty of the ordinary man is to obey the commands of his "God", society; but the children of light never do so. This is an eternal law. One accommodates himself to surroundings and social opinion and gets all good things from society, the giver of all good to such. The other stands alone and draws society up towards him.'[59] Vivekananda goes on to make clear that he sees social liberty and spiritual liberty as two sides of the same coin. They were both expressions of the same principle of freedom, which for Vivekananda was the ultimate goal of human existence.

> Liberty, Mukti, is all my religion, and everything that tries to curb it, I will avoid by fight or flight. Pooh! I try to pacify the priests!... Come out if you can of this network of foolishness they call this world. Then I will call you indeed brave and free. If you cannot, cheer those that dare dash this false God, society, to the ground and trample on its unmitigated hypocrisy; if you cannot cheer them, pray, be silent, but do not try to drag them down again into the mire with such false nonsense as compromise.... What! Measure my soul according to what the bond-slaves of the world say?—Pooh! Sister, you do not know the Sannyasin. 'He stands on the heads of the Vedas!' say the Vedas, because he is free from churches and sects and religions and prophets and books and all of that ilk![60]

SCRIPTURES, RITUALS, AND THE GODS

Vivekananda's attitude towards the scriptures, holy men, and sacred sites of Hinduism was informed by the same principle of freedom discussed above. They were means to achieve spiritual realization; not ends in themselves. He constantly reiterated that real religion was not to be found in books. Drawing upon the Vedantic tradition of Hinduism, Vivekananda emphasized that Hinduism did not recognize the authority of any books, not even the Vedas. The Vedas were guides which the Hindus believed contained spiritual laws discovered by ancient seers. They are guides to spiritual realization, not a prescriptive set of rules for living. The fact that the Vedas say something is not a reason for that something to be considered true. Its truth has to be ascertained on its own merit. 'Vedanta* does not believe in any of these teachings. First, it does not believe in a book—that is the difficulty to start with. It denies the authority of any book over any other book. It denies emphatically that any one book can contain all the truths about God, soul, the ultimate reality. Those of you who have read the Upanishads remember that they say again and again, "Not by the reading of books can we realize the Self,"' he told a San Francisco audience around the same time he wrote to Mary Hale, in a lecture titled 'Is Vedanta the future religion?'[61]

According to Vivekananda, Hinduism teaches that scriptures are not sources of normative authority. Vivekananda looked upon the sacred scriptures as texts to be treated critically, not sacrosanct objects which should be worshipped blindly. This allowed him to treat scriptures as historical objects and negotiate their contents using reason. The way he described the Vedas to an American audience was typical of his attitude. 'These Hindu scriptures, the Vedas, are a vast mass of accumulation—some of them crude—until you come to where religion is taught, only the spiritual.'[62] (That is, the Upanishads).

He would freely criticize the scriptures where he felt they did not agree with reason, or when he found they advocated socially unjust practices. In a letter to Singaravelu Mudaliar, a disciple, he criticized the Vyasa sutras, which are traditionally considered to be Vyasa's commentary on the Vedas, as exclusionary.[†] 'Read the Gita and the Sutras of Vyasa, or get someone to read them to you. In the Gita, the way is laid open to all men and women, to all caste and colour, but Vyasa tries to put meanings upon the Vedas to cheat the poor Shudras. Is God a nervous fool like you that the flow of His river of mercy would be dammed up by a piece of meat? If such be He, His value is not a pie!'[63] He also mocked the religious orthodoxy's puritanism. He would quote the scriptures against the conservative pretensions of the traditionalists. Referring to the Vaishnavites who prohibited taking meat and alcohol on religious grounds, he said, as noted in the fifth volume of his *Complete Works*, 'Instances are found in the Ramayana and the Mahabharata of the drinking

---

*When Vivekananda talked of Vedanta, he did not refer only to the philosophical tradition of that name, whose prime expositor is traditionally considered to be Shankara. He included in the word the entire mystical tradition of Hinduism which testified to the experience of the oneness of all reality as the ultimate spiritual experience.

†Mudaliar's story is an interesting one. He was a professor at Madras Christian College who was an unorthodox freethinker and agnostic. After coming into contact with Vivekananda, he became a convert to Vedanta, gave up his job and family, and lived as an ascetic in search of spiritual truth.

of wine and the taking of meat by Rama and Krishna, whom they worship as God. Sita Devi vows meat, rice, and a thousand jars of wine to the river-goddess, Ganga.'[64]

Vivekananda rued that the upper-caste Hindu society of his day was completely indifferent to the oppressive and deprived conditions in which the lower classes and castes lived. He was irked by the attitude among contemporary Hindus that morality consisted of following the injunctions of the scriptures, and which countenanced apathy towards the sufferings of the poor and the marginalized. Such tradition-bound religiosity struck Vivekananda as nothing but selfishness and hypocrisy cloaked in the garment of religion. During a talk with his disciple Sharat Chandra Chakravarty in 1899 on the importance of doing humanitarian work, Vivekananda told him bluntly 'Throw aside your scriptures in the Ganga and teach the people first the means of procuring their food and clothing, and then you will find time to read to them the scriptures.'[65]

An inward-looking religiosity which focused too much on rituals and ceremonies showed, according to Vivekananda, not only an absence of real spirituality, but given the social conditions that prevailed in India, a lack of basic human empathy. Spending extravagant amounts of money on religious activities when India was not free of poverty and people suffered from want of basic needs, seemed to Vivekananda nothing less than blasphemy against humanity and God. Following in the footsteps of his Advaitic predecessor Shankaracharya, Vivekananda eschewed rituals and ceremonials as useless in the pursuit of religion. He saw ritualism as a bane on Hinduism and as representative of a superstitious, intellectually regressive mindset.

From America, he wrote a letter to his brother disciples (the disciples of Sri Ramakrishna Paramahamsa), part of which is reproduced below from the sixth volume of his *Complete Works*.

Those into whose heads nothing but that sort of silliness [ritualism] enters are called imbecile. Those whose heads have a tendency to be troubled day and night over such questions as whether the bell should ring on the right or on the left, whether the sandal-paste mark should be put on the head or anywhere else, whether the light should be waved twice or four times—simply deserve the name of wretches, and it is owing to that sort of notion that we are the outcasts of Fortune, kicked and spurned at, while the people of the West are masters of the whole world.... There is an ocean of difference between idleness and renunciation. If you want any good to come, just throw your ceremonials overboard and worship the Living God, the Man—god—every being that wears a human form—

God in His universal as well as individual aspect. The universal aspect of God means this world, and worshipping it means serving it—this indeed is work, not indulging in ceremonials. Neither is it work to cogitate as to whether the rice-plate should be placed in front of the God for ten minutes or for half an hour—that is called lunacy. Millions of rupees have been spent only that the temple doors at Varanasi or Vrindaban may play at opening and shutting all day long! Now the Lord is having His toilet, now He is taking His meals, now He is busy on something else we know not what. ...And all this, while the Living God is dying for want of food, for want of education![66]

ON INDIA'S DECLINE

Vivekananda's constant concern about the upper classes' apathy towards the masses, was not an isolated matter. It was an essential theme in an array of factors he understood to be involved in the degeneration of India. The Sangh promotes the idea that the fall of Indian civilization began with the foreign invasions by Muslims and continued through the 'foreign rule' of the Mughals and the British. Vivekananda had a completely different view on why India declined from its position as a leading civilization of the ancient world. According to him, foreign invasions were only external causes. The real cause for India's fall was internal and lay within herself.

Vivekananda's efforts for India's national regeneration had two aspects. One was to instill confidence, self-worth, and pride in a people who had lost all these under British colonialism. The other was to sharply criticize and oppose the attitudes and tendencies which led Indians to their fall from civilizational greatness to social and cultural degradation and economic destitution. People who portray Vivekananda as an uncritical or dogmatic glorifier of India and Indian values, exaggerate the former aspect while completely ignoring the latter. Vivekananda saw India as potentially great, with an ancient past whose philosophical and spiritual achievements were unparalleled and could be an inspiration for the future. But he also saw with stark clarity the mistakes of the past as well as the present; and he had no compunctions in laying the blame squarely at the feet of Indians and Indian civilization.

During a lecture on the Vedanta philosophy delivered in Lahore in 1897 on his return from the West, Vivekananda contrasted the condition of the American lower classes with those of India. While in America, he had seen the self-confidence that economic and social opportunity gave the poor, in India, they were sunk in a state of debasement.

> Aye, in this country of ours, the very birthplace of the Vedanta, our masses have been hypnotized for ages into that state. To touch them is pollution, to sit with them is pollution! Hopeless they are born, hopeless they must remain! And the result is that they have been sinking, sinking, sinking, and have come to the last stage to which a human being can come. For what country is there in the world where man has to sleep with the cattle; and for this, blame nobody else; do not commit the mistake of the ignorant. The effect is here, and the cause is here, too. We are to blame. Stand up, be bold, and take the blame on your own shoulders. Do not go about throwing mud at others; for all the faults you suffer from, you are the sole and only cause.[67]

Some months earlier, Vivekananda wrote to Sarala Ghosal (later Devi Chaudhurani), editor of the Bengali magazine *Bharati*, and Rabindranath Tagore's niece, from Darjeeling. (Tagore was then unknown nationally and would remain so till a decade after Vivekananda's death.) Sarala Devi was one of India's early feminists and had written a tribute to Vivekananda's success in the West in *Bharati*. The letter was intended as an acknowledgment and expression of gratitude, and went on to discuss the problem of national regeneration that occupied the Indian intelligentsia of the day. After outlining the material limitations India faced on the path of growth, Vivekananda's pen alighted on what he considered a historical flaw in the national character; and which was as much an impediment to progress as the lack of material goods and resources. 'We have brains, but no hands. We have the doctrine of Vedanta, but we have not the power to reduce it into practice. In our books there is the doctrine of universal equality; but in work we make great distinctions. It was in India that unselfish and disinterested work of the most exalted type was preached; but in practice we are awfully cruel, awfully heartless—unable to think of anything besides our own mass-of-flesh bodies.'[68]

This difference between ideal and practice is essential to understanding Vivekananda's views on Indian civilization. Vivekananda was an idealist in his historical thinking. The power of ideas in human history loomed large in the horizon of his intellectual understanding. He saw each civilization as attempting to work out a central truth or idea within the material conditions it was situated in. When Vivekananda talked about the spiritual greatness of ancient India, its intellectual boldness and philosophical brilliance, its tolerance for other faiths and spirit of renunciation; he was speaking of the ideals that the thinkers of ancient India tried to realize in society. He did not see the attempt as in any way less than successful. But he was too perspicacious a thinker not to realize that the maximum expression that these civilizational themes could find in society was still necessarily circumscribed by the material limitations and the power inequalities that confronted ancient societies. Vivekananda recognized a line of progress, however meandering, from the early tribal societies (like that of the Vedic Aryans or the Mayans), through the urban societies of classical antiquity and the middle-ages, to the modern era.[*] He saw that with the beginning of democratic movements in the West a new era was dawning in world history, one which could potentially empower the common man by dismantling the dominance of kings, priests, and feudal overlords.[69] For this very reason, unlike Hindutva thinkers, Vivekananda did not preach an ancient golden age of pristine purity that he wanted India to return to. What he exhorted Indians of his time to do was to take inspiration from the success of the past to transcend their enslaved colonial condition, and to revive those civilizational principles in the national life. But that meant in no way that the future he envisaged for India was an imitation of the past or the kind of Vedic cultural revival that Hindu traditionalists like Dayanand Saraswati (1824–83) had attempted. Vivekananda had no interest in reviving a past way of life (in fact, he would have likely considered any such enterprise regressive); what he wanted to revive was abstract spiritual and philosophical principles.

Vivekananda professed that India's degradation was because of falling away from applying its ideals. After the classical age, (or even during it), while lip service was paid to the spiritual ideals of egalitarianism and universal humanity, in practice, the masses were ground underfoot by the Brahmins and the Kshatriyas, by the priests and the kings. 'The mass of Brahmin and Kshatriya tyranny has recoiled upon their own heads with compound interest; and a thousand years of slavery and degradation is what the inexorable law of Karma is visiting upon them,' he wrote.[70] While the West uplifted the masses by giving them education and rights, the Indian elites continued their oppressive rule, so that the country failed morally in the most reprehensible way.[†] And there was also direct cause and effect. The empowered masses of Europe built the material wealth and power of their nations, which was precisely what was being used to colonize India. Above all, it was the spirit of conservatism and

---

[*]I realize that this is a reading with which many scholars of Vivekananda might take issue.
[†]Vivekananda was, of course, not imagining that the European elite uplifted the masses out of the goodness of their heart. He correctly traced the empowerment of the European people back to the Renaissance.

superiority that caused India to turn inward upon itself, isolating itself from the thought currents of the world and putting itself for centuries under the dark shadow of insularity, superstition, hypocrisy, and inertia. 'No man, no nation, my son, can hate others and live. India's doom was sealed the very day they invented the word "mlechchha" and stopped from communion with others,'[71] Vivekananda wrote to a disciple.

The historical result was that India was immersed in what Vivekananda called by the Sanskrit term 'tamas'. Tamas can be tranalated into English as inertia, but the word means more than that. It conveys a host of meanings including inactivity, spiritual and moral degradation, and lack of a positive will to life. While the West made progress along material lines as well as in the creation of a more just and egalitarian society, India stagnated at a certain point of its historical evolution,[*] mired in caste, social inequality, and intellectual retrogression. The European conquest of India was, to Vivekananda, an external factor, acting on the ground prepared for it by internal weakness. It worsened the crisis by plunging India into political slavery. But the deeper cause was the lack of empathy and internal divisions which permeated Indian society. Vivekananda touched on this in a letter to the same disciple, two months later.

> And it is jealousy and want of combination which cause and perpetuate slavery (in India). You cannot feel the truth of this remark until you come out of India. The secret of Westerners' success is this power of combination, the basis of which is mutual trust and appreciation. The weaker and more cowardly a nation is, so much the more is this sin visible.... But, my son, you ought not to expect anything from a slavish race. The case is almost desperate no doubt, but let me put the case before you all. Can you put life into this dead mass—dead to almost all moral aspiration, dead to all future possibilities—and always ready to spring upon those that would try to do good to them? Can you take the position of a physician who tries to pour medicine down the throat of a kicking and refractory child?[72]

VIVEKANANDA'S ATTITUDE TOWARDS HINDUISM

The history of a civilization and the history of its dominant religion must necessarily overlap. Vivekananda's idea of a decline in Indian national life reflected

---

[*]Vivekananda's literature doesn't give an exact period where he envisaged the regress of Indian civilization had started, though he does remark that it perhaps started a few centuries before the Muslim conquest.

in his views on Hinduism and its evolution. Vivekananda, unlike Hindutva's key thinkers, nowhere expresses the idea that Indians had a sense of political nationality before the arrival of the British. He, however, seems to have extended the notion of nationality to include the cultural substratum on which political nationalism and the idea of a nation takes root, and it is in this sense that he talks of the Indian nation and its life since the Vedic ages. There is no doubt of the fact that Vivekananda held Hinduism in the very highest esteem as a religion. He was proud to be a Hindu in an age when Western colonial discourse held Hinduism in contempt. He self-identified with the tradition of its spiritual gurus and part of his life mission was to regenerate Hinduism and give Hindus self-confidence. He was passionate about this cause and often exalted the spiritual greatness of the ideals of Hinduism in the most lyrical manner.

But that is where the similarity of the historical Vivekananda with the Sangh's picture of Vivekananda ends. For what is nowadays widely forgotten or ignored, is that Vivekananda was also a sharp and at times even harsh critic of contemporary Hinduism. What Vivekananda valued was what he considered the essence of Hinduism, which was constituted by the experiences of a line of spiritual mystics over the centuries; and the Vedanta philosophy expounded in the Upanishads, the metaphysical portion of the Vedas. Following the tradition of Vedantists like Shankara, Vivekananda considered the rituals and ceremonials of Hinduism to be devoid of any spiritual value.[73] Worse, an obsession with ritualism had, in his view, led to the moral decay of Hinduism. This ritualism, fused with notions of purity and those of caste, drew forth Vivekananda's unalloyed scorn and anger.

When he disembarked in Tamil Nadu after his first visit to the West, he received a welcome from the Hindus of Shivaganga. In his address to them, he remarked:

> Think of the last six hundred or seven hundred years of degradation when grown-up men by hundreds have been discussing for years whether we should drink a glass of water with the right hand or the left, whether the hand should be washed three times or four times, whether we should gargle five or six times. What can you expect from men who pass their lives in discussing such momentous questions as these and writing most learned philosophies on them! We are neither Vedantists, most of us now, nor Pauranikas, nor Tantrikas, we are just 'Don't touchists'. Our religion is in the kitchen. Our God is the cooking-pot, and our religion is, 'Don't touch me. I am holy.' If this goes on for another century every one of us will be in a lunatic asylum.[74]

The idea that the modern Hindus's religion was in the kitchen was one that Vivekananda expressed several times as a rebuke to disciples and devotees, especially when he encountered narrowness of the mind and conservative attitudes. In a letter to Alasingha, he exclaimed, 'You (Hindus), have no religion, your God is the kitchen, your Bible the cooking-pots.'[75] In an interview given to the *Madras Times* on his return from the West, Vivekananda made the same kind of remark about the Hindu religion having got into the kitchen. 'The present Hinduism is a degradation,' he added.[76]

Vivekananda's criticisms of Hindus and Hinduism were in the nature of an internal critique required for course correction rather than as an external attack on the religion. But the uncompromising nature of that critique and its comprehensiveness give lie to the notion that Vivekananda was an uncritical singer of paeans to Hinduism, let alone a Hindu supremacist. Vivekananda did not feel that he was confined to the framework of Hinduism and his independence as a thinker ensured that he could stand outside it and critique Hinduism, as he would any other religious system. While Vivekananda exalted the unique egalitarianism of the Advaita philosophy (the most significant school of Vedanta), he never lost sight of the fact that Hindu society had by and large failed to translate it into social egalitarianism. In fact, the hierarchical caste bound society of India was a mutilation of the principles of the Vedanta. Three weeks before he addressed the Chicago Parliament of Religions on Hinduism, Vivekananda wrote to a correspondent: 'No religion on earth preaches the dignity of humanity in such a lofty strain as Hinduism, and no religion on earth treads upon the necks of the poor and the low in such a fashion as Hinduism.'[77]

While Vivekananda held out the Upanishadic figures of Maitreyi and Gargi as examples of how early Hinduism allowed women the same rights as men to preach religion, he was perfectly clear that this was an aspirational ideal, not a historical account of the status of women throughout the history of Hinduism. He was unsparing in his criticism of Hinduism's treatment of women. For example, during a conversation with Sharat Chandra Chakravarty in 1901, a year before his death, Vivekananda talked about his plans to establish a math for women (something completely unheard of then) on the banks of the Ganga. Chakravarty objected to this innovation; there were, he said, no maths for women even in ancient India. The Buddhists had started maths for women and lot of corruption had resulted from this, he went on. Vivekananda responded: 'It is very difficult to understand why in this country so much difference is made between men and women, whereas the Vedanta declares that one and the same conscious Self is present in all beings. You always criticize the women, but say what have you done for their uplift? Writing down Smritis[*] etc., and binding them by hard rules, the men have turned the women into mere manufacturing machines!'[78]

The Sangh tries to present Vivekananda as an upholder of 'Indian values' and 'Indian culture'. Neither of these terms or anything approximating them find a single mention in Vivekananda's oeuvre. Of course, cultural conservatism of the kind that the Sangh parks under the umbrella of Indian values, could only have drawn the monk's contempt, if one were to look at his attitude towards social conservatism in his own time. His consistent criticism of Indian society for not treating women as equal, for oppressing the powerless and the lower castes, showed that he found Indian society patriarchal, feudal, and casteist. And while a lot of progress has been made from Vivekananda's time, these conditions are to a substantial degree unchanged even today and are part and parcel of the Sangh's social and cultural conservatism. Even in the case of high culture, of art and literature, Vivekananda was not a singer of praises for everything Indian. It was only for Indian philosophy that Vivekananda claimed an inherent superiority of insight into the nature of reality. While the Sanskrit epics and the hymns of the Rig Veda drew his appreciation and he considered Indians to be a naturally poetic race, he felt Indians were deficient in many areas of high culture (as was the case with any country) and could learn a lot from the world outside. Even before his visit to America, he would write:

That the Hindus, absorbed in the ideal, lacked in realistic observation is evident.... Take painting and sculpture. What do you see in the Hindu paintings? All sorts of grotesque and unnatural figures. What do you see in a Hindu temple? A Chaturbhanga Narayana or some such thing. But take into consideration any Italian picture or Grecian statue—what a study of nature you find in them! A gentleman for twenty years sat burning a candle in his hand, in order to paint a lady carrying a candle in her hand.[79]

VIVEKANANDA AND RSS ON CASTE

The biggest difference between the Hindutva idea of India and that of Vivekananda's is their opposing views on the reasons for India's material

---

[*]Smritis are Hindu scriptures whose authority is secondary to that of the Shrutis, viz. the Vedas.

destitution and loss of greatness. For the Sangh and Hindutva thinkers like Savarkar, it is the British and Muslim conquests which veered India off her natural path and was primarily responsible for all her ills. For Vivekananda, in the final analysis, it was the Indians themselves who were responsible. While Vivekananda identified a number of factors as being jointly responsible for India's decline, the most prominent cause was the oppression of the lower castes and classes by the kings, nobility, priests, and upper castes. During his journey of triumph though India after his return from the West, Vivekananda was felicitated by the Hindus of Kumbakonam, in Tamil Nadu. Vivekananda delivered a speech on the occasion on 'The Mission of the Vedanta'. During the speech, he spoke on the question of India's present condition.

> The Hindu is a man of introspection; he wants to see things in and through himself, through the subjective vision. I, therefore, ask myself: Who is responsible? And the answer comes every time: Not the English; no, they are not responsible; it is we who are responsible for all our misery and all our degradation, and we alone are responsible. Our aristocratic ancestors went on treading the common masses of our country underfoot, till they became helpless, till under this torment the poor, poor people nearly forgot that they were human beings. They have been compelled to be merely hewers of wood and drawers of water for centuries, so much so, that they are made to believe that they are born as slaves, born as hewers of wood and drawers of water. With all our boasted education of modern times, if anybody says a kind word for them, I often find our men shrink at once from the duty of lifting them up, these poor downtrodden people.[80]

Central to the oppression of the masses by the elite class was the caste system. Since its inception, the RSS has had an ambiguous relationship with the question of caste. On the one hand, since at least Golwalkar, the RSS has professed a social egalitarianism that aims in the long term to eliminate caste difference among Hindus. Whether this goal would mean the elimination of the caste system itself is not clear. But the gradual erosion of caste-based divisions is paramount to the RSS since it is an essential condition for its aim of consolidating the Hindu community. But this egalitarian commitment stands in stark contrast with the brahminical milieu of the RSS leadership. The early leadership of the RSS including the organization's founder Hedgewar, were largely Maharashtrian Brahmins. Almost all senior RSS leaders to this day are Brahmins. This has drawn accusations from critics of the RSS that it is an ideologically brahminical organization. Such a claim is difficult to assess because the term 'brahminical' has been used so widely and loosely that its exact provenance is not clear. But what is obvious is that the RSS's attitudes towards several questions are predicated on an upper-caste world view.

This is most apparent today when it comes to the question of reservations for socio-economically backward castes. The RSS has long been an opponent of such reservations. Its objection is not that the system is ineffective in meeting its desired objectives, but rather that it divides Hindus by fostering a divisive, identarian caste-based politics.[81] In the run up to the Bihar state elections in 2015, RSS chief Mohan Bhagwat caused quite a controversy with his demand that the government take another look at the reservation policy.[82] The RSS's conservatism on the question of caste also comes across in its apologetics on behalf of Hindu society. While the RSS admits the caste system was oppressive, it is reluctant to criticize the Hindu concept of the varnashrama dharma which gave quasi-scriptural sanction to the caste system. The RSS defends an idealized varna system that existed in India's golden past which served a useful social purpose and was not socially oppressive. In the RSS's view, it was the system's corruption which led to upper caste dominance and while this is regrettable, it is also natural.

Golwalkar, RSS's greatest ideologue, wrote about the genesis of the caste system in his *Bunch of Thoughts* published in 1966.

The other main feature that distinguished our society was the Varna Vyavastha. But today it is being dubbed 'casteism' and scoffed at. Our people have come to feel that the mere mention of Varna Vyavastha is something derogatory. They often mistake the social order implied in it for social discrimination. The feeling of inequality, of high and low, which has crept into the Varna system, is comparatively of recent origin. The perversion was given a further fillip by the scheming Britisher in line with his 'divide and rule' policy. But in its original form, the distinctions in that social order did not imply any discrimination such as big and small, high and low, among its constituents.... Society was conceived of as the fourfold manifestation of the Almighty to be worshipped by all, each in his own way and according to his capacity. If a Brahman became great by imparting knowledge, a Kshatriya was hailed as equally great for destroying the enemy. No less important was the Vaishya who fed and sustained society through agriculture and trade or the Shudra who served society through his art and craft. Together and by their mutual interdependence in a spirit of identity, they constituted the social order.[83]

In a lecture given in 1974 at Pune, Golwalkar's successor as RSS chief, Balasaheb Deoras spoke on the theme of 'Social equality and Hindu consolidation'. If Golwalkar's thought is the ideological foundation of the RSS, then the organizational shape of the modern RSS is the work of Deoras. Deoras in his lecture took a less rigid, but essentially similar position on caste as Golwalkar did.

> It is said that there was no Varna Vyavastha in olden times. Later on it was felt that some system was necessary to ensure the proper and steady progress of society. The leaders of society at that time thought that the society could progress only if four kinds of functions were properly and efficiently executed. Hence the society was classified into four groups depending upon the specific propensities and aptitudes of individuals and groups of individuals. Thus, the Varna system was evolved. Any system entails classification. However, this system did not envisage any differences in the status of the people belonging to the different groups. Classification is one thing and class-discrimination is another.... On the other hand, the whole society was visualized as a single living entity, personified into a magnificent figure with 'a thousand heads, a thousand eyes and a thousand feet'.* Such a glorious concept does not permit the perverse and ridiculous notion that the thighs are superior to the feet, the hands are superior to the thighs, or the head is superior to the hands. The idea is that all these limbs are equally essential for the proper functioning of society. The sense of high and low that we witness today had no place in that concept of one corporate living social entity. To imagine otherwise would be to do grave injustice to those people. The idea is that all these limbs are equally essential for the proper functioning of society.[84]

Vivekananda spent considerable time and effort thinking about the question of caste and what role Hinduism played in perpetuating the wicked social system. His conclusion was that it was not Hindu religion that was responsible for caste but Hindu society. Caste was a social system that had taken on religious overtones, not a religious belief which led to the creation of a social system. Caste was not part of the primary corpus of Hindu scriptures, (the Vedas, the Upanishads, and the Bhagavad Gita) which were the repository of spiritual laws

---

*This is a reference to the Purusha Sukta verse of the Rig Veda. The verse describes the process of creation where the gods cut up the cosmic person and throw his body parts to the ground. The Brahmins came out of the mouth of the cosmic person, the Kshatriyas from the arms, Vaishyas from the thighs, and the Shudras from the feet.

discovered by a long tradition of mystics (rishis). Rather, notions of caste appear in the secondary scriptures and texts that regulate social law, like the *Manusmriti* and the *Dharmashastras*. These texts, Vivekananda argued, had nothing to do with the religion proper since they did not concern themselves with any of the foundational questions of Hindu theology, metaphysics, eschatology, or soteriology. They do not address religious questions about the nature of God, the soul, of salvation, human destiny, divine justice, and so one. Instead, the scriptures which lay down caste regulations are concerned with legislating and ordering social relations and activities. They can be compared for example with the canon law of the Catholic Church. To compare them with the Islamic sharia would be less exact, for the reason that though all the schools of sharia too sought to adjudicate on social matters, sharia claimed divine authority on the basis of the Quran and Hadiths and had to justify all its juridical precepts in reference to the former, which formed the primary scriptural authority in Islam. The *Dharmashastras* on the other hand, do not usually refer to the Vedas to justify the rules and edicts they lay down. In fact, as Vivekananda argued, they could not, because the Vedas were not concerned with social arrangements. For Vivekananda, these texts were the production of Brahmins and priests, who attempted to consolidate all power in their hands.

Vivekananda did not ever mount a defence of an idealized early caste system. But neither did he think that the caste system was a unique iniquity for which Indian civilization bore greater moral responsibility than other nations. In all ancient civilizations, the Mesopotamian, Egyptian, Babylonian, Greek, or Roman, stratified societies and systems of slavery were developed by the kings and priests. In the case of Hindu society, he unequivocally blamed the machinations of the Brahmins for the ruinous caste system.

> So long as man thinks he has to cower before a supernatural being, so long there will be priests to claim rights and privileges and to make men cower before them, while these poor men will continue to ask some priest to act as interceder for them…. Priestcraft and tyranny go hand in hand. Why was it invented? Because some strong men in old times got people into their hands and said, you must obey us or we will destroy you. That was the long and short of it. It is the idea of the thunderer who kills everyone who does not obey him.[85]

While Hindutva thinkers posit a golden period in Vedic history where the varna system functioned in a benign manner, Vivekananda considered caste to be unjust and exploitative even in ancient times.* He did not mince words when he spoke about the effects of the varna system; he wrote the following in the article 'Modern India', which appeared in the Bengali magazine *Udbodhan* (Ramakrishna Mission's second official publication) in 1899:

> By this very qualitative caste-system which obtained in India in ancient days the Shudra class was kept down, bound hand and foot. In the first place scarcely any opportunity was given to the Shudra for the accumulation of wealth, or the earning of proper knowledge and education; to add to this disadvantage, if ever a man of extraordinary parts and genius were born of the Shudra class, the influential higher sections of the society forthwith showered titular honours on him and lifted him up to their own circle. His wealth and the power of his wisdom were employed for the benefit of an alien caste and his own caste-people reaped no benefit of his attainment.[86]

Unlike Hindutva figures, Vivekananda was not willing to overlook the enormous culpability of the upper castes of Hindu society for the condition of the poor and lower castes. While he criticized the aristocracy and the zamindars, his ire was especially directed at the Brahmins who stood at the top of the social and religious hierarchy. He held them responsible more than any other section for the degeneration and decline of Hindu religion as well as society. The Brahmins had misused religion, arrogated all kinds of privileges for themselves, and created tyrannical social regulations that crushed humanity. And in the British ruled modern India of his own time, Brahmins continued to perpetuate the same social injustices even as the current of modernization ran against them. 'You have Brahmanas here (in India)...they are bringing the country down to the verge of ruin by their awful tyranny, and consequently what they have naturally is vanishing away by degrees,' he told a disciple, Priya Nath Sinha, during a conversation.[87]

In 'Modern India', Vivekananda made a prediction about the future of Brahmin domination. He often urged the upper castes to dedicate themselves to uplifting the distressed masses as a way to redeem their privilege of birth and the sins of their ancestors. If they continued to set their faces against the forces of progress and attempted to hold on to their privileges, Vivekananda warned that they would perish in the counter-reaction that was sure to arise.

---

*A few times, Vivekananda did talk about an original varna system that classified people on their individual qualities. But he seemed to speak of this as a philosophical idea (this formulation of varna is the one used in the Gita), rather than something that was ever practised socially.

If the current state of affairs goes on running in this course, then it is a question of most serious reflection, no doubt, how long more will the priestly class continue on India's soil…in obedience to the inevitable law of nature, the Brahmin caste is erecting with its own hands its own sepulchre; and this is what ought to be. It is good and appropriate that every caste of high birth and privileged nobility should make it its principal duty to raise its own funeral pyre with its own hands.[88]

Like so many political moderates of the pre-Bengal partition era, Vivekananda considered British rule of India to be a mixed blessing. While the political domination and economic exploitation were odious, he believed that British rule also brought several benefits that could potentially save India.[89] Vivekananda thought that the introduction of economic competition under British rule was slowly but surely prying apart the rigid caste and feudal structures which had constituted Indian society for over a millennia. Modern education, though confined to upper castes at that point of time, could eventually emancipate the lower classes and castes. Modern scientific ideas were corroding the claims of religious orthodoxy and thus indirectly diluting their claim to social privileges.

But the apathy of the upper classes towards the destitute multitude troubled him, even as he tried to work out his plans for national regeneration and educating the poor with the help of some among the upper castes. The extent to which Vivekananda thought a recalcitrant upper class and its social system stood in the way of India's progress is made apparent in an angry diatribe he wrote in 1899. In a published report of his travel abroad which he wrote on the ship carrying him to America for a second time, he wrote in sharp anger of the selfishness of the upper classes/castes:

However much you may parade your descent from Aryan ancestors and sing the glories of ancient India day and night, and however much you may be strutting in the pride of your birth, you, the upper classes of India—do you think you are alive? You are but mummies ten thousand years old! It is among those whom your ancestors despised as 'walking carrions' that the little of vitality there is still in India, is to be found; and it is you who are the real 'walking corpses'…. In this world of Maya, you are the real illusions, the mystery, the real mirage in the desert, you, the upper classes of India! You represent the past tense, with all its varieties of form jumbled into one. That one still seems to see you at the present time, is nothing but a nightmare brought on by indigestion. You are the void, the unsubstantial non-entities of the future. Denizens of the Dreamland.

Why are you loitering any longer? Fleshless and bloodless skeletons of the dead body of past India that you are—why do you not quickly reduce yourselves into dust and disappear in the air? Aye, in your bony fingers are some priceless rings of jewel treasured up by your ancestors and within the embrace of your stinking corpse are preserved a good many ancient treasure-chests. So long you have not had the opportunity to hand them over. Now under the British rule in these days of free education and enlightenment, pass them on to your heirs, aye, do it as quickly as you can. You merge yourselves in the void and disappear and let New India arise in your place.[90]

In the task of building a 'New India', Vivekananda believed two things to be of vital importance: to raise the masses out of poverty and to give them education. For both these purposes, his efforts to mobilize resources from India and outside did not bear fruit. Vivekananda did not develop concrete plans for alleviating India's poverty or educating its people. But he was a tireless and extremely powerful advocate of these ideas and influenced several people, to take up the cause, including the industrialist Jamshetji Tata who would attempt to set up a science institute, which would eventually take form as the Indian Institute for Science (IISc). Even if he never worked out concrete plans, Vivekananda was impressively clear-sighted even at the turn of the nineteenth century, on what social justice in relation to caste discrimination consisted of. It is interesting to note the contrast of the RSS's opposition to educational and economic reservations for depressed castes with Vivekananda's observations on the principle of positive discrimination. Addressing a Hindu audience at Kumbakonam in Tamil Nadu, he said:

> I also find that all sorts of most demoniacal and brutal arguments, culled from the crude ideas of hereditary transmission and other such gibberish from the Western world, are brought forward in order to brutalize and tyrannize over the poor, all the more.... Aye, Brahmanas, if the Brahmana has more aptitude for learning on the ground of heredity than the Pariah, spend no more money on the Brahmana's education, but spend all on the Pariah. Give to the weak, for there all the gift is needed. If the Brahmana is born clever, he can educate himself without help. If the others are not born clever, let them have all the teaching and the teachers they want. This is justice and reason as I understand it.[91]

CHRISTIANITY AND ISLAM

'We have taken up the Cross. Thou hast laid it upon us,
and grant us strength that we bear it unto death. Amen.'

—Letter from Vivekananda to Pramadadas Mitra[1]

In the latter half of the nineteenth century, Hindu society was troubled by Christian missionaries converting the lower castes, and Christianity, especially in its missionary form, came increasingly to be viewed as both an imperialistic and an alien presence. Reaction from Hindu revivalists like Swami Dayanand Saraswati (1824–83) took the form of invective and denigration of Christian beliefs and of Jesus Christ. In America, Vivekananda was often questioned on the Hindu attitude towards the Christian faith.

Responding to an audience in America, Vivekananda once proclaimed: 'We want missionaries of Christ. Let such come to India by the hundreds and thousands. Bring Christ's life to us and let it permeate the very core of society. Let him be preached in every village and corner of India.'[2] Vivekananda was not talking about the Anglo-American missionary enterprise which sought to convert 'heathen souls' to the Christian religion. He had in mind the God intoxicated religion of the renunciate Christ, who as he was often fond of saying, had not a place on earth to lay his head.

Following in the footsteps of his guru Sri Ramakrishna Paramahamsa, Vivekananda developed a deep devotion to Christ, whom, along with Buddha, he revered as the greatest men to have walked the earth. And he was as good as his word. On his return to India, he arranged public receptions for Dr Barrows, a Christian preacher he had met at the Parliament of Religions. He wrote to newspapers entreating Hindus to welcome Barrows and his teaching. Vivekananda wrote in the *Indian Mirror*:

Moreover, he comes to us in the sacred name of religion, in the name of one of the great teachers of mankind, and I am sure his exposition of the system of the Prophet of Nazareth would be extremely liberal and elevating. The Christ power this man intends to bring to India is not the intolerant, dominant, superior, with heart full of contempt for everything else but its own self, but of a brother who craves for a brother's place as a co-worker of the various powers, already working in India.[3]

For Vivekananda, Christianity formed a beautiful part of the fabric of the universal religious experience of mankind. He often used the analogy of music, of a grand orchestra which comprised the universal harmony of all religions. And in this orchestra, the religion of Christ sounded a cadence which he not only related to personally but which was an integral part of his spiritual life. Vivekananda's personal relationship with Christianity extended beyond his devotion to the figures of the Christ and the Virgin Mary. It took in the entire history of Christendom, the early churches of Rome, the medieval monasteries with their ascetic monks, the Gothic architecture of European churches, the beauty of the Catholic mass and the sacrament, the spiritual giants among Catholic saints, the millennia of spiritual seeking by layman and priest, novice and monk. The presence or reminder of any of these could bring forth from him an outpouring of intense emotion, or a mood of spiritual contemplation.

To a woman who was surprised on seeing his devotion to Christ, the leader of a religion different from his own, he responded: 'Madame, had I lived in Palestine in the days of Jesus of Nazareth, I would have washed his feet, not with tears, but with my heart's blood.'[4] In a lecture delivered on 'Christ the messenger' to a Los Angeles audience, he tried to give a picture of the spiritual power he thought was manifested in Jesus.

> The three years of his ministry were like one compressed, concentrated age, which it has taken nineteen hundred years to unfold, and who knows how much longer it will yet take! Little men like you and me are simply the recipients of just a little energy. A few minutes, a few hours, a few years at best, are enough to spend it all, to stretch it out, as it were, to its fullest strength, and then we are gone forever. But mark this giant that came; centuries and ages pass, yet the energy that he left upon the world is not yet stretched, nor yet expended to its full. It goes on adding new vigour as the ages roll on.[5]

Ramakrishna had considered Christ to be a divine incarnation, and while Vivekananda was apt to consider the historical Jesus an enlightened soul, his faith in Christ as a form of the one all-powerful God accompanied him throughout his life and sustained him. We have already recorded the trials and misfortunes through which Vivekananda passed in his attempt to become a delegate at the World's Parliament of Religions. As late as three weeks before the start of the Parliament, Vivekananda had no idea of how to get in touch with the Parliament's organizers, or how to convince them to overlook his lack of credentials and the expiry of the deadline for registering as a delegate. As was the sanyasi's wont, he had given it all up to God's will. With little money, and no conceivable prospects of fulfilling his mission, he still trusted in the divine will to protect him. 'I am here amongst the children of the Son of Mary, and Lord Jesus will help me,' he wrote to a disciple.[6]

It is not just that Vivekananda embraced Christianity within his catholic spiritual vision. Christianity also played a role in moulding Vivekananda's spiritual life. We saw how for five years he travelled the length of the country, by foot and train, eating only food that was offered to him as alms. He carried no money and no possessions. His only travelling companions were a kamandalu, a walking staff, and two books meant as spiritual guides. One was the Bhagavad Gita, the other was *The Imitation of Christ*.

The Imitation of Christ is a book of Christian mysticism, believed to be authored by Thomas à Kempis, a medieval Christian monk. Its impact on Vivekananda was profound. During his years at the Baranagar math, he used the book as a source for instructions for the sanyasis to follow in their spiritual practice. At around the same time, he translated the book into Bengali for a Bengali periodical, rendering the name as 'Ishanusarana'. The depth of the impression the book left on Vivekananda's mind can be gleaned from his preface to the translation:

The Imitation of Christ is a cherished treasure of the Christian world. This great book was written by a Roman Catholic monk. 'Written', perhaps, is not the proper word. It would be more appropriate to say that each letter of the book is marked deep with the heart's blood of the great soul who had renounced all for his love of Christ. That great soul whose words, living and burning, have cast such a spell for the last four hundred years over the hearts of myriads of men and women; whose influence today remains as strong as ever and is destined to endure for all time to come; before whose genius and Sadhana (spiritual effort) hundreds of crowned heads have bent down in reverence; and before whose matchless purity the jarring sects of Christendom, whose name is legion, have sunk their differences of centuries in common veneration to a common principle—that great soul, strange to say, has not thought fit to put his name to a book such as this. Yet there is nothing strange here after all, for why should he? Is it possible for one who totally renounced all earthly joys and despised the desire for the bauble fame as so much dirt and filth—is it possible for such a soul to care for that paltry thing, a mere author's name?...

All wise men think alike. The reader, while reading this book, will hear the echo of the Bhagavad-Gita over and over again. Like the Bhagavad-Gita it says, 'Give up all Dharmas and follow Me'. The spirit of humility, the panting of the distressed soul, the best expression of Dasya Bhakti (devotion as a servant) will be found imprinted on every line of this great book and the reader's heart will be profoundly stirred by the author's thoughts of burning renunciation, marvellous surrender, and deep sense of dependence on the will of God. To those of my countrymen, who under the influence of blind bigotry may seek to belittle this book because it is the work of a Christian...the teachings of Siddha Purushas (perfected souls) have a probative force.... If in ancient times Greek astronomers like Yavanacharya could have been so highly esteemed by our Aryan ancestors, then it is incredible that this work of the lion of devotees will fail to be appreciated by my countrymen.[7]

Vivekananda also seemed to have had a deep interest in Christian theology and church history, topics which are often arcane even for devout lay Christians. During his wanderings through India in search of spiritual knowledge, Vivekananda reached Belgaum (today in Karnataka) towards the end of 1892. From there he decided to go to Goa, then a Portuguese colony, where there were rumoured to be old Latin texts and religious literature which were not to be found anywhere else in India. A friend from Belgaum arranged an introduction to a Sanskrit scholar who lived in Margao, Goa. Through him, Vivekananda came into contact with a Christian lawyer who, impressed with Vivekananda's knowledge and interest in the Christian scriptures, made arrangements for Vivekananda to stay in the Rachol seminary, and study the manuscripts in the library.[8] The seminary at Rachol was first established as a college by Jesuits in 1610. It passed into diocesan hands and was turned into a seminary after the Portuguese authorities expelled the Jesuits from Goa in the mid eighteenth century. Vivekananda was presumably interested in the Latin texts the Jesuit scholars had left behind. He spent three days reading manuscripts in the library and discussing theology with the professors and students at the seminary. His stay generated such excitement that word spread soon and clergymen from all over Goa came to see Vivekananda and converse with him during the remainder of his time there. Swami Vivekananda's visit to Rachol seminary is still remembered there: Vivekananda's portrait is mounted prominently at the Rachol library.[9] On the hundred and twenty-fifth anniversary of Vivekananda's

Chicago speech, the Rachol seminary organized a lecture to commemorate the event.[10]

A peek into Vivekananda's erudition in Christian history is given in an account by Emma Calvé, the most famous French operatic singer of the Belle Époque. Calve accompanied Vivekananda and a group of friends as they travelled through Europe. Having taken in Germany, Switzerland, and Rome, the company reached Istanbul. In Istanbul, Vivekananda met and held long theological discussions with Père Hyacinthe, a famous French theologian and former Catholic monk. After leaving the priesthood, he had taken up the name of Loyson. Emma Calvé wrote in her memoirs, 'It was interesting to see that the Swami was able to give the exact text of a document, the date of a Church Council, when Father Loyson himself was not certain.'[11]

In America, many of Vivekananda's lectures were held in Unitarian churches. Thus, he not only befriended many clergymen but often joined in worship at churches. But it was not Protestantism, but Roman Catholicism, with its grand architecture, rituals, art, and iconography which really called forth his devotion and excited his spiritual imagination. The Roman Catholic Church has produced many great saints, he would say, 'St Francis of Assisi, Ignatius Loyola, St Teresa, the two Catherines and many others.'[12] While most of his time was spent preaching in Protestant America and England, he encountered Catholicism during his short European travels. The unfortunate consequence of this from the point of view of the historian is that we have only a sketchy picture of Vivekananda's devotional experiences with Christianity. But we do find him in Cologne attending mass at a cathedral, enthralled by its magnificent Gothic architecture, its rich art treasures, and magnificent tapestry. From there he journeyed to the Alps, whose snow-clad beauty left a deep impression on him. Chancing upon a mountain chapel, he picked up flowers saying, 'Do let us offer some flowers at the feet of the Virgin.' Apprehensive that he might not be allowed inside the church, he handed the flowers to a woman friend. He asked her to place it before the icon of the Virgin 'as a sign of my gratitude', averring, 'for she also is the Mother'.[13] The last refers to the conception of God in the feminine form, as the mother of the universe; Vivekananda worshipped Kali in that form.

It was Rome that called forth his reverence of ancient Christendom most. Accompanied by the singer Emma Calvé and other friends he spent several days in Rome. As a biography of Vivekananda written by his disciples reports: 'He walked through its early catacombs, he visited the splendid palaces, churches and basilicas of its medieval period. Impressed with the immense Vatican, its chapels, its magnificent Renaissance art treasures: he pondered over the wonderful organizing genius and missionary spirit of Christianity.... Many times, he spoke touchingly of the child Christ.' During their tour, when one of his companions complained about the vast expense of the Catholic Church when millions were starving, Vivekananda was quick to rise to the defence of the Church. 'What! Can one offer too much to God! Through all this pomp the people are brought to an understanding of the power of a character like Christ, who, though himself possessed of nothing, has by the supreme character of his personality inspired to such an extent the artistic imagination of mankind.'[14]

Vivekananda also found affinities between the rituals of the Roman Catholic Church and those of Hinduism, seeing in both similar methods to invoke a sense of the divine presence. Both religions worshipped divinity in its female form. After his return to India from his first visit to the West, Vivekananda was worshipping at the temple of Kshir Bhavani, when he claimed to have a vision of the Goddess in which he heard her speak to him. Later, when he was staying near the Dal Lake in Kashmir, that vision inspired a mood of ecstatic revelation, where Vivekananda says he underwent a profound experience of God in her aspect of terror and destruction. He penned the poem 'Kali the Mother' in this state.

> The flash of lurid light
> Reveals on every side
> A thousand, thousand shades
> Of Death begrimed and black—
> Scattering plagues and sorrows,
> Dancing mad with joy,
> Come, Mother, come!
> For Terror is Thy name,
> Death is in Thy breath,
> And every shaking step
> Destroys a world for e'er.
>
> Thou 'Time', the All-Destroyer!
> Come, O Mother, come!
> Who dares misery love,
> And hug the form of Death,
> Dance in Destruction's dance,
> To him the Mother comes.[15]

He saw a reflection of the same experience in the esoteric mysticism of Christianity—behind the meditation of the Western mystic on skull and bones was the same universal aspect of the worship of the terrible aspect of God.[16]

But above all, the most significant part of Vivekananda's relationship with Christianity was his love and devotion for Christ and the Virgin Mary. For Vivekananda, praying to the Virgin was no different from praying to Kali, and his devotion could both inspire and elevate others, sometimes evoking a palpable atmosphere of spirituality. An arresting account is given by Constance Towne, who met Vivekananda as a twenty-four-year-old young woman in New York. Constance, who held liberal religious views outside the fold of her Catholic faith, developed a deep friendship with Vivekananda. In an account written approximately forty years after their meeting, she recalled:

> How liberal he was, how understanding of others' point of view! He went to Mass with me at St Leo's Church, the little one on Twenty-eight Street, where all was beauty and the old priest Father Ducey, such an artist. There he knelt at high noon at the canon of the Mass. A ray of light falling from the stained glass window—blue, red and gold—lit his white turban and outlined his beautiful profile against the marble walls. A great, gorgeous spot of living fire his orange robe made on the marble pavement, and the dear face was rapt in prayer. As the bell rang at the consecration and all heads were bowed in adoration of the presence of Christ on the altar, his hand touched mine, and he whispered 'It is the same God and Lord we both worship.'[17]

A visceral hatred for Muslims has marked the Hindutva movement from its very beginnings in the early twentieth century. The roots of Hindutva can be traced further back to the latter half of the nineteenth century, to organizations like the Arya Samaj and various Hindu sabhas, which were antagonistic in general to Muslims and Islam. (The All India Muslim League was formed only in 1906). These organizations, active during Vivekananda's time, were a distinctively colonial phenomenon. Thus, Islamophobia is a relatively recent phenomenon in the history of the subcontinent. And though it continues in a particularly virile form in the present, it has gone through a series of transformations over time in response to changing political situations.

Islamophobia in the West, however, has had a much longer history, going back to the Crusades, and its form and the stereotypes it operates on has shown a surprising continuity from the Middle Ages into the twenty-first century. In the contemporary West, when Islamophobes portray Islam as an essentially anti-women faith, they are employing a trope that has roots in medieval Christendom. One of the most common ways in which this trope is employed by the right-wing as well as mainstream Western media is to invoke Prophet Muhammad's polygamy and the Quran's rule of permitting men four wives.* Those who attempt to defend Islam point out that the Quran has to be seen in its historical context. In sixth century Arabia, polygamy was rampant; the Prophet's proscription was to limit the number of wives a man could take. The Quran granted rights to women which were far in advance of what they enjoyed at that time, and to a degree no other Semitic religion did.

It is interesting to see the same debate played out towards the end of the Victorian age, with Vivekananda defending Islam against Western interlocutors. A group of Vivekananda's Western friends were travelling with him in India when the conversation turned to Islam. Vivekananda was discoursing on the early struggles of the Prophet, when a woman present in the group objected, saying he 'advocated polygamy'. A disciple recounts the exchange, which bears much similarity to the debate about Islam today in the West. 'Vivekananda explained that what Mohammed did was to limit a man to four wives: polygamy in a far worse form was practiced in Arabia. "He taught that women have no souls," said another with an edge to her voice. This called forth an explanation regarding the place of women in Mohammedanism. The Americans who listened were somewhat chagrined to find that the Moslem woman had certain rights not enjoyed by the so called free American woman.'[18]

Vivekananda did not have the same depth of personal devotion towards Islam that he had towards Christianity. But he held Islam in respect, considered the prophet a spiritual revolutionary, and admired Islam for its sense of equality. Admonishing an American audience about Christian pretensions to universal brotherhood, Vivekananda once said:

> Mohammed by his life showed that amongst Mohammedans there should be perfect equality and brotherhood. There was no question of race, caste, creed, colour, or sex. The Sultan of Turkey may buy a Negro from the mart of Africa, and bring him in chains to Turkey; but should he become a Mohammedan and have sufficient merit and abilities, he might even

---

*See for example Peter Allen, 'France's interior minister targets immigrants who practise polygamy', *The Telegraph*, 8 August 2010; 'Polygamy stokes France's Muslim debate?', *Indian Express*, 26 April 2010; Engy Abdelkader, 'American Muslim Sister-Wives? Polygamy in the American Muslim Community', *HuffPost*, 17 December 2011.

marry the daughter of the Sultan. Compare this with the way in which the Negroes and the American Indians are treated in this country! And what do Hindus do? If one of your missionaries chance to touch the food of an orthodox person, he would throw it away. Notwithstanding our grand philosophy, you note our weakness in practice; but there you see the greatness of the Mohammedan beyond other races, showing itself in equality, perfect equality regardless of race or colour.[19]

The quality of fostering a universal brotherhood of believers, of realizing a spirit of equality amongst them—Vivekananda considered this a unique achievement of Islam. He was quite clear that equality was not something that Hinduism, with its iniquitous caste system, had ever achieved.[20] He told a group of Western disciples: 'Mohammedanism is the only religion that has completely broken down the idea of the priest. The leader of the prayer stands with his back to the people, and only the reading of the Koran may take place from the pulpit.'[21]

While Vivekananda admired Catholic saints of the past, he did not encounter anyone during his travels in the West, who personally impressed him as having attained a state of spiritual enlightenment. This is not really surprising since mysticism and monasticism had been in decline in Christendom since the sixteenth century and had all but disappeared in the nineteenth. The industrial revolution and other facets of modernity, as well as the confluence of the Protestant work ethic and capitalism,[22] made for a form of religion focused on faith and 'good works' rather than one engaged in contemplation and reflection. In India, however, social conditions as well as religious tradition fostered religious mendicants, monks, and mystics in both Hinduism and Islam and in them, behind the outward difference in religious dress, Vivekananda saw the same spiritual phenomena. At Allahabad for instance, he came into contact with a Muslim saint. Vivekananda described the saint as, 'every line and curve of whose face showed that he was a Paramahamsa (One who has attained the highest state of spiritual enlightenment).'[23]

We have no reliable account of Vivekananda praying in mosques;[24] this could have been due to lack of opportunity. With the extent of segregation between Hindus and Muslims in nineteenth-century India, Vivekananda's contacts with Muslims were sporadic. In Europe, while he did travel to the Ottoman Empire, his interactions there were largely restricted to Western (Christian) immigrants and travellers. But there are accounts of several visits to dargahs in India, and he made a study out of the Quran. He saw the Quran as another important episode in the spiritual unfolding of humanity, carrying the universal message of the brotherhood of man and the oneness of God. He also thought it valuable for its particularity, for its own unique religious character. During his wandering days, Vivekananda was hosted in Alwar by a maulvi, a high school teacher of Urdu and Persian. During a discussion on religion, he remarked to the maulvi, 'There is one thing very remarkable about the Quran. Even to this day, it exists as it was found eleven hundred years ago. It retains its pristine purity and is free from interpolations.'[25] Vivekananda was a man of remarkable intellect and his biographers, including Swami Nikhilananda, credit him with a prodigious memory. So, it is not surprising that he discoursed on the Quran too when the occasion demanded. As he proceeded south, he came to the kingdom of Mysore where he was received by the maharaja and asked to stay as a royal guest. As news of his erudition and spiritual knowledge spread, Abdul Rahman Saheb, a state councillor came to Vivekananda for spiritual discourse. Abdul Rahman posed several doubts on the Quran, which the monk helped clear.[26]

Nineteenth-century India, especially in its second half, witnessed an almost total absence of a community or civic life where Hindus and Muslims met and interacted with each other. The period was a long interregnum between the decline and end of the Mughal dynasty (even the symbolic emperor Bahadur Shah Zafar was deposed by the British in 1857), with its mixed courts, administrative apparatus, and cultural institutions, and the mass public sphere which took shape because of the national movement beginning in early twentieth century. Without a robust common civic or political life, social attitudes hardened, with most upper-caste Hindus, now placing Muslims increasingly within the schema of ritual pollution associated with orthodox Hindu social practices. Except for a miniscule cosmopolitan minority influenced by English university education and British institutions, Hindu society at large followed several social taboos which regulated contact with Muslims. Hindus would not eat food touched or cooked by Muslims and would not share meals with them; the more orthodox considered even the touch of Muslims to be polluting.

In his youth, Vivekananda, as a member of the cosmopolitan Bengali intelligentsia, with its more relaxed attitude towards questions of religion and caste, did not follow these discriminative practices. But after he became a sanyasi and took the monastic name of Swami Vivekananda, his field of action increasingly moved into traditional Hindu society. In his mission to spread spirituality and Vedanta, his associations, acquaintances, and social milieu were all located in upper-caste Hindu society. But Vivekananda uncompromisingly refused to sanction or follow discriminatory practices against the lower castes and Muslims. He stayed in the houses of Dalits and Muslims, shared food with them, and fraternized with them without any restrictions.[27] To the recriminations of the orthodox and to implied threats of losing social legitimacy, he responded with superb disdain.

During his wandering days, when upper-caste Hindus asked him if he ate food cooked by non-Hindus, he replied that he took food from everyone, including Muslims.[28] We have many accounts of him staying at the homes of Muslims he became acquainted with during his travels. Travelling through Rajasthan, he spent weeks meditating in a cave near Mount Abu. A Muslim vakil (pleader) in a nearby princely state chanced upon Vivekananda and started visiting him frequently. He developed a deep attachment to the sanyasi, and as the rainy season was approaching, the vakil invited Vivekananda to abandon the cave and live in his home. Vivekananda accepted and moved into the vakil's bungalow. Since he was a Muslim and Vivekananda a Hindu ascetic, the vakil assured him that he would make separate arrangements for his food. Vivekananda brushed the offer aside.

Through the vakil, Vivekananda made the acquaintance of many state officers of various princely states in the region. The private secretary to the maharaja of Khetri, Munshi Jaganmohanlal, visited Vivekananda while he was living in the vakil's house. Seeing the unorthodox social situation before him, Jaganmohanlal commented, 'Well Swamiji, you are a Hindu monk. How is it that you are living with a Muslim? Your food may now and then be touched by him.' The question apparently drew Vivekananda's ire, for he responded, 'Sir, what do you mean? I am a sanyasi. I am above all your social conventions. I can dine even with a Bhangi. I am not afraid of God, for He sanctions it; I am not afraid of the scriptures for they allow it: but I am afraid of you people and your society.'[29] To see how ahead Vivekananda was of his times, it is instructive to look at how Gandhi wrestled with Hindu notions of Muslim impurity at the beginning of the national movement. Almost thirty years after the above incident, during the launch of the Khilafat movement, Gandhi had to appease Hindu anxieties about inter-dining with Muslims in order to garner their support.* He wrote in *Young India*, 'In order that we may help them (Muslims) on the Khilafat issue, there is absolutely no need to drink water from the same glass, sit together at meals or give sons and daughters in marriage.' As evidence, he recounted how when he stayed with a maulvi in Lucknow,

---

*In his personal life, Gandhi did not follow any restrictions on interacting with Muslims. Many of his close associates during his days in South Africa were Muslims and he led a close communal life with them, different in no aspect from his life with his fellow religionists.

the maulana 'sent for a Brahmin cook for me.... He is a non-vegetarian but he did not let me catch even a glimpse of meat in his house.'[30]

After his return from his first visit to the West, we find Vivekananda in Ambala, where he held long talks on scripture with the local Muslim community. He also visited a Hindu–Muslim school there, a representation of something in which he had a keen interest: promoting the fraternization of the two communities. Further in his Punjab journey, we find the now famous monk in Rawalpindi, trying to broker peace between the Arya Samajis and the Muslims, with reportedly some degree of success. Later, during a pilgrimage to Amarnath, he again had to encounter the prejudices of the orthodox. Vivekananda was besieged by orthodox monks seeking discussion and instruction. Though impressed by the young sanyasi's knowledge, they could not understand his liberal views on religion and his sympathy for Islam.[31] They also objected to his Western disciples staying among them, which became a source of friction. Ironically, the state official who was in charge of arranging the pilgrimage was a Muslim tehsildar. Vivekananda gave daily talks which were attended by the tehsildar and his subordinates. Attracted by Vivekananda's religious discourse and personality, the tehsildar asked for spiritual initiation from the monk, and Vivekananda obliged gladly.

Vivekananda believed in the common humanity of man and was completely indifferent to religious identity. This was based in part on the ideas of liberal English philosophers he studied and admired: John Locke, David Hume, and Herbert Spencer. But its wellspring issued from an even deeper source: the teachings of Sri Ramakrishna and his own spiritual experience that every human soul is a manifestation of the divine.* We can see Vivekananda give concrete form to this deeply held conviction during a visit to Kashmir. After having worshipped at the temple of Kshir Bhavani there, he passed through an intense phase of devotion to the Goddess. In their journey through Kashmir, Vivekananda and the friends and disciples who accompanied him travelled and lived in house boats. At Srinagar, moved by devotional rapture, Vivekananda wanted to carry out a then prevalent ritual—the worship of the Goddess Uma in the form of a girl child. It was a mode of worship frequently practised by Ramakrishna Paramahamsa. The ritual had a two-fold significance. It was symbolic, seeing the child as a pure representation of divinity manifesting as the female principle. This is part of the tradition of Shakti worship. But at

---

*For example, Vivekananda supposedly underwent spiritual experiences when meditating under a tree at Bodh Gaya. This included an experience of the unity of all living beings.

the Advaitic level, it was also a literal act of worshipping the god in man, of outwardly recognizing the essential identity of the human soul with the transcendental God. Traditionally, an upper-caste Hindu girl is chosen as the object of such worship. In Srinagar, Vivekananda instead chose the four-year-old daughter of his Muslim boatman.[32] He worshipped the child ceremoniously as the visible representation of the Goddess Uma.

Another interesting encounter Vivekananda had after his return from the West was with a man named Mohammed Sarfaraz Hussain. Hussain was already attracted to the Advaitic philosophy, though unfortunately we have no information about the man or the philosophic influences that acted on him before he met Vivekananda. But if one were to speculate, it is pertinent to note here that the Sufi mystical tradition in Islam has striking parallels to Advaita, something religious scholars have commented on copiously.* Sarfaraz Hussain was immensely impressed by Vivekananda and asked to become his disciple. Vivekananda initiated Hussain and he took on the name of Swami Mohammedananda. The disciple's admiration for his master's spirituality was limitless, and went to the extent of considering him an avatar of the monotheistic God or Ishvara. At Nainital, Hussain told Vivekananda, 'If in after-times any claim you as an avatara, a special Incarnation of the Godhead, remember that I, a Mohammedan, am the first.'[33]

Since the Bharatiya Janata Party (BJP) government came to power at the Centre in 2014, there has been a steady move to erase or marginalize the history of the Mughals and other Muslim rulers in India. In 2016, various BJP functionaries floated the idea of renaming Akbar Road in New Delhi as Maharana Pratap Road.[34] While the road eventually retained the name of the Mughal emperor, these demands reflect the extent to which today's BJP is under the grip of the Sangh Parivar's ideology. For the RSS and its affiliated Hindutva organizations, Indian history is the story of the triumph of the Hindu race or civilization, which moves away from its natural course and goes into terminal decline with the invasion of Islamic rulers and the British. While

---

*See R. C. Zaehner, *Hindu and Muslim Mysticism*; Supriya Gandhi, 'The Persian Writings on Vedanta Attributed to Banwalidas Wali', *Indian Journal of Philosophy*, Vol. 48, 2019, pp. 79–99; Rachelle Syed, 'Vedanta in Muslim Dress: Revisited and Reimagined', *Journal of Dharma Studies*, Vol. 2, 2019, No. 1, pp. 1–12; Gopal Stavig, 'Congruences between Indian and Islamic Philosophy', *Annals of the Bhandarkar Oriental Research Institute*, Vol. 81, No. ¼, 2000, pp. 213–26.

most contemporary historians[*] agree that the Mughals and many other Islamic dynasties ruled as Indians and not foreigners, the Sangh perceives the entirety of the Mughal rule as the continual oppression of Hindus by their Muslim rulers. While the Mughals are the villains in this historical narrative, figures like Shivaji and Maharana Pratap, who contested their territorial power, emerge in this historical narrative as heroes at the vanguard of a Hindu resistance. There is no gainsaying that this is both bad and motivated history. But it has been a central motif of Hindutva and the RSS since its inception. And now the political programme of erasing India's Islamic history is getting the open administrative backing of the government.

In 2017, the Maharashtra education board decided to delete most of the chapters on Mughal history in school textbooks, confining the material to a few brief paragraphs. Instead, the textbooks focused on Shivaji and the Marathas. As of the writing of this book, eleven out of the thirteen chapters of the seventh standard textbook entitled 'Medieval India' focus on Shivaji and the Marathas.[35] The Taj Mahal, the iconic symbol of Mughal rule, has become a frequent target for the right wing. In the same year, the Uttar Pradesh official tourism guide omitted the Taj Mahal from its pages. When questions were asked in the media, then BJP MLA Sangeet Som questioned why Taj Mahal was part of India's historical heritage at all and proclaimed that Mughal history would be erased from India. He said, 'Many people got hurt when Agra's Taj Mahal was removed from the list of historical monuments. What kind of history are you talking about? The same history in which the person who built the Taj Mahal imprisoned his father? The same history in which the man who built the Taj Mahal planned to annihilate all Hindus from Uttar Pradesh and India? If such people continue to have a place in history, it is very unfortunate and I guarantee you that this history will be changed.'[36] He continued, 'Whether it is Babar, Akbar or Aurangzeb, the government is working to erase them from history.' In response to the controversy the comments generated, BJP spokesperson G. V. L. Narasimha Rao defended Som, saying, 'As far as the Muslim Mughal rule in this country is concerned, that period can only be described as exploitative, barbaric and a period of incomparable intolerance which harmed Indian civilization and traditions immensely.'[37]

In 2018, the Uttar Pradesh government changed the name of Allahabad to Prayagraj, and Faizabad to Ayodhya. Both the cities were established during

---

*See Romila Thapar, *A History of India* (Volumes 1 and 2); John F. Richards: *The New Cambridge History of India: The Mughal Empire*; Abraham Eraly, *The Mughal World: The Life in India's Last Golden Age.*

Mughal rule. This led to proposals from several BJP-ruled states to change the names of other places. Former Gujarat Chief Minister Vijay Rupani proposed that Ahmedabad should be renamed Karnavati. The BJP–Shiv Sena ruled Maharashtra government considered whether to change the names of Aurangabad and Osmanabad to Sambhajinagar and Dharashiv respectively. The BJP reportedly also wants to change the name of Hyderabad to Bhagyanagar. Sangeet Som explained the policy, 'BJP is just trying to bring back the culture of India, which was deliberately changed by the Muslim rulers to end Hindutva. Therefore, BJP is working just to safeguard and retain the Indian culture back by renaming the cities with their original names.'[38]

These ideas of the degradation of the Hindus through Muslim rule and the fantasy of reclaiming the nation for Hindus has its roots in Hindutva's ideological preceptors, especially Savarkar and Golwalkar. For Golwalkar, the Muslims had ruled by force and used that power to harass Hindus and attack their religion and way of life. The only solution by which India could achieve true nationality was for the Muslims to return to the mother faith. In the book Bunch of Thoughts, Golwalkar addresses the 'question of Muslims'.

> They had come here as invaders. They were conceiving themselves as conquerors and rulers here for the last twelve hundred years. That complex was still in their mind. History has recorded that their antagonism was not merely political…it was so deep-rooted that whatever we believed in, the Muslim was wholly hostile to it. If we worship in the temple, he would desecrate it. If we carry on bhajans and car festivals, that would irritate him. If we worship cow (sic), he would like to eat it. If we glorify woman as a symbol of sacred motherhood, he would like to molest her. He was tooth and nail opposed to our way of life in all aspects-religious, cultural, social, etc. He had imbibed that hostility to the very core.

If the Muslim invaders originally consisted of only a small army from central Asia, how could a sizable portion of India have become Muslim? Why did millions leave Hinduism and embrace Islam? Golwalkar's answer is that every converted Muslim abandoned Hinduism because of forced conversions, coercion, deceit, or the lure of material benefit.

> Everybody knows that only a handful of Muslims came here as enemies and invaders. So also, only a few foreign Christian missionaries came here. Now the Muslims and Christians have enormously grown in number. They did not grow just by multiplication as in the case of fishes. They converted the local population.… Now, how did the converts leave their ancestral

home? Was it out of their own sweet will and out of conviction of the superiority of those faiths? Well, history does not record a single notable instance of that sort. On the contrary, history tells us that the reason was the fear of death or coercion or the various temptations of power, position, etc., or the desire to please the powers that be by adopting their ways and customs and finally even taking to their faiths. There was a lot of deception also. A piece of beef or a loaf used to be thrown into the water tank of a village and the villagers ignorant of what had happened, used to take the water as usual. On the next morning the missionary or the moulvi would come and declare that since they had used the polluted water they had all lost their religion and the only way left for them was to join his fold! In this way, whole villages have been converted to Islam in the North....[39]

What did Vivekananda think about the centuries of Muslim rule in India? A perusal of Vivekananda's writings and speeches and of the accounts of people who knew him, shows that his views on Islamic rule in India were the exact opposite of those held by the Sangh and its ideological gurus. In a lecture he gave in India titled 'The Future of India', he speaks about the effect of Muslim rule. 'Even to the Mohammedan Rule we owe that great blessing, the destruction of exclusive privilege. That Rule was, after all, not all bad; nothing is all bad, and nothing is all good. The Mohammedan conquest of India came as a salvation to the downtrodden, to the poor. That is why one-fifth of our people have become Mohammedans. It was not the sword that did it all. It would be the height of madness to think it was all the work of sword and fire.'[40]

While Vivekananda believed that the early invasions saw forced conversions, he did not believe that Islam spread throughout the Indian subcontinent by force of arms. Rather, the oppressed condition of the lower castes who were denied all freedoms made Islam, with its more egalitarian social order, a welcome home for those who wished to escape the tyranny of the caste system.[*] The Muslim conquerors, especially the Mughal dynasty, ruled India not as colonizers, but as rulers who identified with the country and its people, carrying out administration like any other native dynasty.[41]

---

[*]Such a view of early Islamic society in India, within the context of a caste-divided Hindu society, finds support in the view of Marshall G. S. Hodgson. In his unparalleled work on the history of Islamic civilization, *The Venture of Islam*, he writes about the period of the Delhi Sultanate: 'In both Europe and India, Islam represented a socially flexible allegiance which the most vigorous persons locally could adopt; and though they might be barred from rising within their own communities, as Muslims they could rise almost indefinitely.' See *Volume 2: The Expansion of Islam in the Middle Periods*), Chicago: University of Chicago Press, 1977, p. 278.

Vivekananda's attitude towards India's Islamic past was not one of mere toleration. He saw the Muslim contribution as an essential part of the fabric of national life. A history enthusiast, Vivekananda was fascinated by Mughal architecture, by its art and poetry, but above all by the Mughals themselves. His disciple Sister Nivedita recounted that the greatness of the Mughals was a theme that never wearied the sanyasi.[42] Though a rationalist by conviction, Vivekananda was a romantic at heart, and his exquisite imagination had full play in the presence of the past. He would be absorbed by ancient ruins, palaces, paintings, and sculpture, and his companions could expect to be treated to a rhapsody of historical reconstruction. Vivekananda's vivid imagination and erudition combined to paint a panoramic picture of the lives, events, and personages whose genius had left its imprint on rock and stone. All phases of India's history exercised his passion, but it seems he was especially captivated by the allure of the Mughal period. He is known to have visited Akbar's palace and the dargah of the Muslim saint Moinuddin Chishti in Ajmer, Akbar's tomb in Sikandra, the Taj Mahal in Agra, and the Mughal monuments and ruins in Delhi.

Enchanted by the Taj Mahal, Vivekananda described it as: 'A dimness, and again a dimness, and then a grave.'[43] Vivekananda first visited the Taj Mahal in 1892. The beauty of the monument apparently overpowered him. He told a companion: 'Every square inch of this wondrous edifice is worth a whole day's patient observation, and it requires at least six months to make a real study of it.'[44] Before Vivekananda reached Agra, he was in Lucknow, where he had visited the palaces, monuments, and gardens built by the nawab of Oudh. He visited the monuments again in 1898 with his Western friends, disciples, and brother monks, marvelling at the glory of the nawab's court. The party, which was travelling to Nainital in the Himalayas, then proceeded to Delhi, where they spent a day admiring the Mughal monuments. Vivekananda was enthralled by the splendour of the Mughal dynasty and spoke of it fervently to those who accompanied him. One of them recollected: 'He vivified the past before us. Indeed, we forgot the present in the past and lived with dead emperors and mighty kings of old.'[45]

Nivedita wrote about the experience of travelling with Vivekananda and hearing him bring to life India's past for his Western disciples. The Mughals were a frequent topic for Vivekananda's perorations and Akbar a special object of the sanyasi's admiration. It would seem that in Vivekananda's eyes, except for perhaps Ashoka, Akbar was the greatest monarch who had reigned in India. In Akbar, he saw a marvellous combination of temporal power and spirituality, of valour and piety, of cultivation and tolerance. Particularly impressive was Akbar's religious pluralism and the emperor's idea of a universal religion, a notion that found an echo in Vivekananda's own philosophy. 'Oftener still, it was Akbar of whom he would tell, almost with tears in his voice, and a passion easier to understand,' Nivedita writes.[46] Vivekananda estimated Akbar's character so highly that he used to remark that Akbar was a soul aspiring for enlightenment in his last birth, but who had missed the goal.

His admiration was not confined to the most famous of the Mughals. Babur, Humayun, Jahangir, Noor Jahan, Shah Jahan, all elicited praise and appreciation. About Shah Jahan, he exclaimed: 'Ah! He was the glory of his line! A feeling for, and discrimination for beauty that are unparalleled in history. And an artist himself! I have seen a manuscript illustrated by his hand.'[47] According to Vivekananda, Mughal emperors were anything but non-Indian.

We have a first-hand account of Vivekananda's impassioned perorations on the Mughals from Christine Greenfield, a German-born American disciple. She accompanied him, Nivedita, and others on a journey from Calcutta to the Himalayas. During the journey, Vivekananda entertained his Western friends with a narration of Mughal history. It is worth reading Christine's account of Vivekananda's fascination with the Mughals in her own words.

> The Moguls seemed to have cast a spell over Swami Vivekananda. He depicted this period of Indian history with such dramatic intensity, that the idea often came to us that he was telling the story of his own past.... We saw Babar, the twelve-year-old king of Ferghana, influenced by his Mongol grandmother, and living a hard rough life with his mother.... The time came when we saw his men booted and spurred, crossing the great mountain passes and descending on the plains of India. Although an alien and invader, as Emperor of India, he identified himself with the country, and began at once to make roads, plant trees, dig wells, build cities.
>
> After his death the kingdom fell into other hands and Babur's heir, Humayun, became a fugitive. In the deserts of the Sind, with only a handful of followers he fled from place to place, in danger of his life. Here he met the exquisite young Mohammedan girl Hamida, married her, and shared with her his most unhappy fate. ...And in the deserts of Sind was born, her only son, later to become the emperor Akbar....
>
> Humayun regained his empire, but he was not to enjoy it long: for in the forty eighth year of his age he met with a fatal accident at his palace in Delhi and died, leaving his throne to his only son Akbar, then little more than thirteen years old. From that time, until his death at the age of sixty-

three Akbar was the undisputed master of India. ...Mohammedan though he was, he listened to teachers of all religions—listened and questioned. ... In later years he conceived the idea of establishing a new religion of which he was to be the head—the Divine Religion, to include Hindus, Christians, and Parsees as well as Mohammedans. ...His genius as an administrator enabled him to pass on a united empire to his son Salim, later known as Emperor Jehangir. Under this 'Magnificent son of Akbar' the Mogul court reached a splendor before which all previous ideas of luxury paled.

Now appears the fascinating figure of Nur Jehan, the Light of the World, Empress of Jehangir, and for twenty years the virtual ruler of India. ...To her great gifts of wisdom and tact were due the stability, prosperity and the power of the empire, in no small degree. It was during the supremacy of Nur Jehan that the new style of architecture was introduced, a feminine type of architecture in which the virile red-sandstones of Akbar's buildings was supplanted by white marble inlaid with precious and semi-precious stones.[48]

The natural consequence of Vivekananda's regard for Islam and appreciation of Islam's contributions to India, was an idea of India in which Muslims were as much a part of the national life as Hindus. Vivekananda's idea of nationhood stands as a polar opposite to that of the RSS and the Sangh, who conceive of Muslims as second-class citizens, who have to accommodate themselves within a Hindu national ethos. While Savarkar and Golwalkar blamed India's civilizational decline on foreign conquests by Muslims and Christians, Vivekananda blamed the Indians themselves. For Vivekananda, India's decline started before the Islamic conquest, with the ossification of the caste system, an increasing insularity of intellectual life, unremitting orthodoxy, and restrictions of social freedoms.* He understood and appreciated the piety of Muslims and saw them as integral to the fabric of Indian civilization.

A biography compiled by his disciples and friends narrates the experiences of Vivekananda's wandering days as related by him. 'It had been his pleasure then to reach some village compound at dusk and watch the cows' home coming. The piety of the Hindu on the banks of the Ganga, and the piety of the Mussalman kneeling in prayer at the appointed hours, were in his eyes equally Indian and of equal worth...the Vedic chanting by Brahmana children in the temple courtyards of Varanasi and the South; the Muslim's kneeling in

---

*A recent historian who shares a similar view is Abraham Eraly. See *The First Spring: The Golden Age of India*, Delhi: Penguin Books, 2011.

prayer wherever the time of prayer might find him; the spirit of equality and fraternity observed among the followers of the prophet—all these, the Swami would say, were facets of the culture of his land.'[49]

Sociological thought of that time was not developed enough to differentiate Hindu and Muslim societies into further sub-identities. Hindu and Muslim people were thought of as two monolithic civilizations, often overlapping and mingling, but having their own distinct and defining characteristics. In so far as Vivekananda could imagine a future Indian nation, he could do so mostly in civilizational terms, rather than political ones. He did not, and could not, put it in the notions of citizenship, rights, and secularism that we employ today. But that did not mean he was any less committed to a vision of India where Hindus and Muslims lived under equal conditions. When he did visualize India's nationhood, Muslims were an integral and important part of India's nation building process. Vivekananda believed that a spiritual revolution based on the oneness of all beings, should be the basis of India's moral, social, and material regeneration. The philosophical foundation of such a spiritual revolution was envisaged as Advaitic, but it was by no means to be an exclusively Hindu affair. He welcomed Muslims to join it as equal partners. Vivekananda wrote in a letter to Sarfaraz Hussain towards the middle of 1898:

> Whether we call it Vedantism or any ism, the truth is that Advaitism is the last word of religion and thought and the only position from which one can look upon all religions and sects with love. I believe it is the religion of the future enlightened humanity. The Hindus may get the credit of arriving at it earlier than other races, they being an older race than either the Hebrew or the Arab; yet practical Advaitism, which looks upon and behaves to all mankind as one's own soul, was never developed among the Hindus universally.
>
> On the other hand, my experience is that if ever any religion approached to this equality in an appreciable manner, it is Islam and Islam alone.
>
> Therefore I am firmly persuaded that without the help of practical Islam, theories of Vedantism, however fine and wonderful they may be, are entirely valueless to the vast mass of mankind. We want to lead mankind to the place where there is neither the Vedas, nor the Bible, nor the Koran; yet this has to be done by harmonising the Vedas, the Bible and the Koran. Mankind ought to be taught that religions are but the varied expressions of THE RELIGION, which is Oneness, so that each may choose that path that suits him best.

For our own motherland a junction of the two great systems, Hinduism and Islam—Vedanta brain and Islam body—is the only hope.

I see in my mind's eye the future perfect India rising out of this chaos and strife, glorious and invincible, with Vedanta brain and Islam body.[50]

To the contemporary reader, Vivekananda's metaphor of Hindu brain and Islamic body might sound patronizing, but this would be to misunderstand the sense and context in which he is using these terms. Vivekananda's original contribution to Advaita, and his point of departure from the earlier tradition, was precisely in developing what he called 'Practical Vedanta'. He delivered several lectures on this theme, and it was central to his writing and speeches on many occasions.

Vivekananda prized Advaita Vedanta because he believed it provided an unparalleled philosophical foundation for a universal and egalitarian ethics. But he held at the same time that for the most part, the Advaitic insight had remained purely theoretical. Hinduism and Indian civilization had failed to convert abstract philosophy into concrete action, to work out the egalitarian principles into real forms of social equality. From a certain standpoint, Vivekananda's life's work can be seen as an attempt, whether we judge it as successful or not, to resolve the problem of transforming the contemplative moral principles discovered by religion into a practical programme of social justice and uplift. For Vivekananda, a religion which was concerned solely with the spiritual enlightenment of a select few while setting aside the well-being of the majority of humankind, was at best a very limited endeavour, at worst a travesty of the human spirit. Intellectual philosophy and practical action were the opposite balancing poles of the spiritual enterprise, each powerless to function without the other. It is in this sense that Vivekananda extorts Hussain for the combination of a Hindu brain and Islamic body. The gesture towards Islam is not gratuitous, but a hard thought-out recognition of the religion's history and character. It stems from the understanding that the Quran is perhaps unique among the world's sacred texts in the emphasis it places on social equality and justice.[*]

---

*For the egalitarian ideas of early Islam see Karen Armstrong, *Islam: A Short History* and Reza Aslan, *No god but God: The Origins, Evolution, and Future of Islam.*

THE WEST: HISTORICAL CONTEXT

The contemporary reader who comes to Vivekananda's writings and speeches (collected and published by the Ramakrishna Mission as *The Complete Works of Swami Vivekananda* in nine volumes) may not find them immediately accessible. More than a century separates Vivekananda's output from us. Today's reader might not at first glance find an unambiguously universal, liberal rationalist in Vivekananda. They would find him contradicting himself in places, occasionally saying things that sound extremely regressive to us, and often talking within a framework whose assumptions are unacceptable for a progressive discourse.

This is because, however visionary and ahead of his times a thinker might be, he is still talking to his contemporaries. He has to talk in their language, because otherwise he would not be understood at all. In moments of insight, an original thinker transcends the limitations of his age and speaks to all humanity; but in the ordinary course even the most prophetic of thinkers is bound by the knowledge economy, concepts, and power structures of his age. These factors are part of the concrete historical situation of the thinker, which has to be taken fully into account if one is to understand his life and thought.

This chapter explores the historical context of Vivekananda's public life, less than nine years at the turn of the nineteenth century (1893 to 1902).

When author Hindol Sengupta named his 2016 book on Vivekananda *The Modern Monk*, it was a title that resonated with our deeply entrenched conception of the sanyasi. It is in many ways an accurate epithet. Vivekananda speaks to us through values that we recognize as distinctly modern: liberty, reason, scientific temperament, individualism, universal humanism, and patriotism. In his intellectual efforts, Vivekananda stands as an interlocutor between ancient Hinduism and modernity. Almost all twentieth century Hindu spiritual gurus, including the highly original revolutionary turned ascetic Aurobindo, have drawn from the conceptual framework that Vivekananda created.[*]

But we have grown so used to the idea of Vivekananda as the modern monk, that we tend to forget that he actually lived in the Victorian era. Vivekananda lived

---

[*]Swami Shivananda, Ramana Maharshi, Swami Chinmayananda, and Nisgaradutta Maharaj are some prominent examples.

from 1863 to 1902, and died just short of forty, having outlived Queen Victoria by only six months. Because of the general perception that Vivekananda shares with us the quality of being 'modern', our collective imagination is disposed to place him in the same historical space as Gandhi, Tagore,* and other early figures of modern India. But the less than two decades that separate Vivekananda's final years from the India of anti-Rowlatt Act protests and Jallianwala Bagh (1919), is in many ways a bridge across two completely different worlds: the post-World War I world and the pre-modern nineteenth century. For all that his thinking anticipated dominant themes of the future, we have to take firm cognizance of the fact that Vivekananda's life and work are situated in the second half of the nineteenth century. A failure to realize this crucial fact has I believe, contributed enormously to recent misreadings of Vivekananda.

One way to refresh our historical memory is to place Vivekananda along with some of the great personages and events from the short stretch of time during which the monk lived and worked. It bears remembering that the legendary Victorian poets Lord Alfred Tennyson and Robert Browning were still alive and publishing when Vivekananda undertook his famous tour of India as an itinerant monk. Tennyson, whose poetry continued to appear till his death, died just two months before Vivekananda's famous meditation on the rock at Kanyakumari, and less than a year before his Chicago Address. *The Adventures of Huckleberry Finn* and *Anna Karenina* were published when Vivekananda (then Narendranath Dutta) was a teenager, and both Mark Twain and Leo Tolstoy outlived Vivekananda by almost eight years. Richard Wagner composed his masterpiece *Parsifal* when Vivekananda was studying in Calcutta University.

The posthumously famous nineteenth-century philosopher Frederick Nietzsche published his final works in 1888, five years before Vivekananda's first visit to the West. Nietzsche passed away just two years before Vivekananda did. Friedrich Engels was still alive when Vivekananda landed on American soil. Oscar Wilde's famous play *The Importance of Being Ernest* premiered in London in 1895, the same year that Vivekananda visited the city for a series of lectures on Vedanta. H. G. Wells's classic science fiction novel *The Time Machine* was also published at the same time. Vivekananda's visits to the West were also contemporaneous with the publication of the Sherlock Holmes novels, in which Arthur Conan Doyle created the quintessential private detective for posterity.† And turning from fictional to real crime, it

---

*Tagore was Vivekananda's contemporary by birth, being actually two years older than the monk. But he did not rise to national prominence till after he received the Nobel Prize in Literature in 1913.
†The first in the four Sherlock Holmes novels, *A Study in Scarlet*, was published in 1887, while

had been only five years since London recovered from the scare of the serial murders by Jack the Ripper.

A marker of the historical remoteness of the period of Vivekananda's activities in the United States is how recently that country had emerged from the shadows of the North–South conflict. Less than thirty years separates the end of the American Civil War from the America which held the World Parliament of Religions in 1893. The famous abolitionist and author of *Uncle Tom's Cabin* Harriet Beecher Stowe was still alive and literarily active when Vivekananda began his career in America. In the five years preceding Vivekananda's arrival, newspaper obituaries were just drawing the curtain on the public lives of the last of the great figures of the Civil War. Union General William Sherman, who captured Atlanta in the Civil War, died in 1891, having recently refused a proposal to nominate him as the Republican candidate for president. Two years earlier, Confederate President Jefferson Davis had published his memoirs. He died that same year in New Orleans, to almost unprecedented public mourning in the southern States. The memory of the Civil War was kept alive in the 1880s by a series of books and memoirs by former participants. Legendary Confederate General P. T. Beauregard, whose fame had spread to the North because of his post-war support of Black civil rights and suffrage, died just about six months before Vivekananda arrived in the United States.

In locating Vivekananda's historical position, it is certainly also relevant to note that when Vivekananda left the Baranagar monastery and started his spiritual quest as a wandering sanyasi, only three decades had gone by since the revolt of 1857 and the replacement of the East India Company's rule with that of the British government. Or that Vivekananda's life ended just three years before the partition of Bengal (1905) and the first nationalist mass movement, the Swadeshi Movement, it inspired. India's historical context is an important factor in understanding many facets of Vivekananda's thought, but for reasons I will explain, this chapter choses to focus on the historical context of the West. Though Vivekananda divided the nine years of his public life almost evenly between India and the West,[*] approximately 80 per cent of his literary output in the form of writing, public speeches, and lectures was delivered in America and Great Britain. And importantly, his focus in his speeches in India tended to be more (though by no means exclusively) on themes of nation building, reforming and reviving Hinduism, or addressing

---

the fourth one, *The Hound of Baskervilles*, was published in 1900.

[*]There was a short time spent in Sri Lanka also. He delivered two speeches in Sri Lanka at Colombo and Jaffna.

India's material and social problems. The dominant themes of his philosophy, including the vaunted Vedanta and that of a universal and scientific religion, were mostly expressed in the Anglo-American world. More significantly, they were articulated in response to late Victorian intellectual trends, anxieties, and problems. The particular form that Vivekananda's philosophical thought took, was one that was formed by the encounter of certain prominent strands of nineteenth-century European thought with the Indian Vedantic philosophy. The larger setting for this encounter was the novel phenomenon of sociocultural and economic modernity which was developing in the West.

Thus, it is not only the intellectual conditions of the West that we need to know to interpret Vivekananda correctly, but also its social and cultural conditions. While Vivekananda lectured more in America than Great Britain, the Victorian era still remains the most appropriate interpretative paradigm to use. British colonialism and American industry combined to form what has been called Anglobalization,* a process of global trade similar to the globalization of the twenty-first century but predicated on the political structures of British imperialism. As the centre of the process that was connecting the world together through trade, commerce, and the exchange of ideas, British intellectual, social, and cultural attitudes widely influenced American society and its institutions. Vivekananda also travelled widely in Europe, though speaking engagements were rare. He spoke at the Paris Congress of Religions in 1900, but we have only second-hand and very fragmentary accounts of what he said there. The more significant point here is that Europe, especially central and Western Europe, formed, as it were, an outer sphere of influence on the Victorian world through its sociopolitical structures and intellectual activity. Great Britain and Europe were also being shaped by a common historical process of transformation, which prefigured modernity and made the second half of the nineteenth century unprecedented in Europe's previous history. To get a complete picture of the environment in which Vivekananda was active, it is thus useful to consider the American and European situation as a whole.

AMERICA AND EUROPE AT THE TURN OF THE NINETEENTH CENTURY

One helpful way to imagine how the influence of these forces constitutes Vivekananda's context, would be to think of them as making up two concentric circles, with America and Great Britain in the centre, and Continental Europe

---

*The term was coined by the American historian Niall Ferguson.

forming the outer circle. But what exactly made up this context? What was the West which Vivekananda went to at the end of the nineteenth century like?

It is not an easy question to answer. What was happening in Europe was both so extraordinary and so varied a process that to capture it in a brief frame is exceedingly difficult. One way to put it is that the Victorians confronted a new world so completely different from anything that had gone before in the continent and the world's history that the experience of change was vertiginous. The tremendous transformation that took place from the middle of the nineteenth century onwards was the culmination of forces of technological, social, cultural, and political changes that had been gathering from the Renaissance of the sixteenth century onwards. But in spite of dramatic innovations in science, technology, and trade, the industrial revolution of the eighteenth century, and the French Revolution, there was still a broad continuity in the sociocultural, religious, and political institutions of Europe, going back to the medieval age.* The nature, meaning, and relationships of these institutions were constantly changing, often in ways perceived as cataclysmic by the people, but the old institutions still defined European life till mid-nineteenth century.†

This state of affairs, the basic continuity of the historical experience of over a millennium, started changing rapidly in Great Britain from the beginning of the mid-Victorian age (1850–75), and in much of western and northern Europe after the political revolutions of 1848. As the mid-Victorian age progressed, the relics of Europe's feudal past which had been facing gradual attrition, crumbled completely. Serfdom disappeared from Europe, even from backward countries like Russia, which abolished it in 1861. Guilds, which were professional trade associations that dominated the commercial life of Europe, were swept away by industrialization and often banned by law. Centuries of discriminatory laws that barred Jews and other religious minorities from universities, officialdom, and various other professions were repealed. The separation of the sexes into two separate spheres, the public sphere for men and the domestic sphere for women, came to an end as women started to gain increasing access to the public sphere. Religion, which dominated all aspects of life till fifty years before, was now in decline. It was not that there was a rise in non-believers, but that religion no longer regulated every facet of social and personal life. Christian theology no longer defined the intellectual, moral, and legal horizons of European existence.

---

*The great exception to this was the Reformation.
†The crucial landmark here is the 1848 Revolution in France.

Along with the increasing secularization of society, a technological and economic revolution was changing life for Europeans in ways they could not have dreamt of. Railway networks and the telegraph not only made travel and communication exponentially faster than ever before, they also changed the very way in which people experienced reality. The scope and pace of the transformation can be seen in the growth of railways. In 1850, only 2,390 kilometres of railway tracks had been laid in Great Britain. By 1875, this figure had increased almost tenfold to 23,368 kilometres. In the same period France and Germany increased their rail networks almost fifty and sixty times respectively, to 19,357 kilometres and 27,910 kilometres. The Russian empire, the most underdeveloped among the great Western powers, had only 27 kilometres of railway track in 1850. In 1875, a tremendous push towards modernization resulted in a 19,029-kilometre-long railway network being built to connect its vast lands.[1] After 1850, there was also a rapid increase in steel and iron production. Great Britain almost tripled its output during this time to 6 million and 200,000 metric tons.[2]

These were more than technological innovations to the people who lived through the social changes they wrought. 'To them, these technologies seemed to erase the primeval boundaries of human experience, and to usher in a kind of Millennial era, a New Age, in which humankind had definitively broken its chains and was able, as it became proverbial to say, to "annihilate time and space". Even the most important inventions of the 19th century that were not simply applications of steam or electrical power, such as the recording technologies of the photograph and the phonograph, contributed to this because they made the past available to the present and the present to the future.'[3] On the other hand, along with this, came a heady sense of command over nature, of using science and technology to master nature for human progress. This vision was articulated as early as the seventeenth century by the British thinker Francis Bacon in his book *Novum Organum*, but it took till the middle of the Victorian age for it to be grounded in concrete technological developments, and to be shared by the larger educated classes of America and Europe. This sense of both social and technological progress, of a bright optimism of Western science conquering the world for humankind, was a dominant factor in Vivekananda's milieu when he was active in the West.[*] He was both influenced by it and

---

*In the last quarter of the nineteenth century, even as the middle and upper classes experienced an optimism based on technological and social progress, intellectuals of the late Victorian age, especially in Europe, were becoming disillusioned with the idea of 'progress' and displayed an increasingly pessimistic outlook.

reacted against it, but perhaps most significantly, like most other thinkers of the age, it was an integral element he had to contend with in his attempts to analyse human reality.

The face of American and European towns and cities were also undergoing drastic changes as a result of industrialization and the commercial revolution. Urbanization increased at a blinding pace, along with large scale migration from villages to the cities. London, the first world city, tripled its population in over three decades, reaching a population of 3.18 million by 1860. It was nearly double that by the end of the Victorian era. Perhaps the most extreme case of urbanization was Chicago. At the beginning of this period, in 1850, Chicago had less than 30,000 residents. When Vivekananda arrived there to attend the World Parliament of Religions, Chicago housed more than a million people. Technological and scientific improvements played an important part in this transformation of the urban fabric of America and Europe. Improved methods of sanitation, hygiene and town planning changed crowded cities from cesspools of dirt, disease, and squalor to something resembling our modern metropolises.* Epidemics, especially cholera, which frequently brought mass death to towns and cities of old Europe, almost became a thing of the past. By the time Vivekananda reached the West, many of its cities had taken on the architectural landmarks that we now know them for. For example, in the last quarter of the century Paris underwent a large scale and ambitious reconstruction into its present form and acquired the iconic Eiffel Tower in 1889. Vienna underwent a similar urban renewal, constructing its famous Ringstrasse in 1865.

All these changes spread across the political, social, and cultural dimensions of American and European experience. While every particular manifestation was singular and unique, in their totality they represented a revolutionary transformation that occurs rarely in the course of human history. It was a tectonic shift in the fundamental material basis of civilization as well as in the cultural life expressed on that basis. The industrial revolution was only one of the axes of this shift, but it was a defining axis; so much so that we speak of the history of the human species as divided into the pre-agricultural, agricultural, and industrial age. There are three important points we have to keep in mind when considering the nature of the transformation the Victorian era experienced.

---

*The poor quarters of these cities, like London's East End, continued to languish in terrible conditions well into the twentieth century.

The first is that there were at least three distinct revolutions happening almost simultaneously—in the political, economic, and cultural orders respectively. These are the rise of the nation state, the rise of industrial capitalism, and the rise of modernity. All three were preceded by the scientific revolution of the seventeenth century, and it can be argued that the scientific revolution contributed in differing degrees to the revolutions that were to follow in the nineteenth. The second point is that all the three revolutions that took on more tangible and visible forms in the latter half of the nineteenth century, were processes that started much further back. According to the individual historian's predilection, the emergence of capitalism, of the nation state, and modernity, can each be placed from the late eighteenth century to as early as the seventeenth century. But not many would doubt that all these unique phenomena came together in their historically evolved forms in the middle of the Victorian age, creating the civilizational template for what was to follow in the twentieth century. The final point that bears remembering is that the totality of the civilizational transformation which these political, economic, and social revolutions wrought, was not confined to the West alone. During the Victorian age, it was being exported all around the globe, through European imperialism. These political and socio-economic structures—nation states, capitalism, and modernity—would come to define life in the twentieth century.*

The challenge in understanding the Victorian era is to understand both this continuity and the difference. Vivekananda's thought is relevant to us today to the extent that it tries to offer solutions to certain foundational problems relating to religion and modernity, which arose during the Victorian age, but continue to exert their influence today. At the same time, to interpret Vivekananda correctly, in order to understand the setting in which he spoke, we have to be aware of how these defining structures, even while they display a continuity with our own contemporary existence, aligned themselves with very different forms of political, social, and cultural life in the nineteenth century.

While Vivekananda can be considered purely as a philosopher, it is not a straightforward matter to extract his social and political ideology from the tenets of his philosophy. In fact, a less than careful reading of Vivekananda can even create confusion as to what the exact purport of his philosophy is. The problem is not that Vivekananda's writings and speeches are complex or obscure. Even Vivekananda's worst detractors would admit that he is the soul of

---

*The Soviet Union and the Eastern Bloc did not share in capitalism or even the individual centric ethos of modernity. In that sense our unipolar globalized twenty-first century is closer to Vivekananda's time both economically and socially.

simplicity itself. The problem is a peculiar one, or rather one that arises from a combination of rather unique circumstances. In the first place, Vivekananda was not a systematic philosopher. This is not to imply that he was in any way unsystematic in his thinking or fell short of the required intellectual rigour. What this means is that he did not construct a formal system of philosophy, unlike say his Advaitic predecessor Shankara.* He did not write formal treatises on philosophy explicating his system or addressing contentious points. Rather his philosophy was propounded mainly in speeches to an educated, but lay audience. His interlocutors not being philosophers themselves, this had the effect that Vivekananda never had to address demands for formal or technical clarity.

But the larger interpretative problem is that impromptu lectures delivered without notes are a poor vehicle for articulating a system of metaphysics. It is not a format that allows for laying down formal definitions, for the use of technical terms, or for developing a philosophical point at great length. This necessarily leaves many gaps in developing a detailed picture of Vivekananda's philosophical system. However, the careful reader faces little difficulty in developing at least a broad outline of it. The real difficulty, and where one might get misled, is that Vivekananda in his oration spoke of a broad range of topics, often mixing the purely philosophical with social and historical issues that were of interest to his audience. A casual reading might lead one astray here, for this aspect of the matter calls for a critical approach that is at least implicitly exegetical.

But for the reader seeking to infer Vivekananda's political ideology, to read him without a sense of historical context, is to get stuck in an interpretative

---

*There is a continuing debate among Indologists on to what extent, if at all, Vivekananda was an original philosopher and what the relationship of his philosophy with Advaita Vedanta was. In assessing the place of Vivekananda as a Vedantic thinker, two opposite set of demands seem to be made of him. One set of commentators, like Paul Hacker, set the terms of the debate merely in terms of faithfulness, asking to what extent Vivekananda faithfully represented Advaita to the world. To me, this approach seems misguided as it allows no room for Vivekananda to innovate as a thinker within that tradition but seeks to restrict his role to merely representing that tradition as it existed before him to the West. No continuing philosophical or spiritual tradition is frozen in time as a definitive object—such a tradition would be dead, like Greek Stoicism or Gnosticism. In seeking to represent Advaita, Vivekananda sought to represent a living tradition, a tradition whose signifiers were altered by the very act of his interpreting it, as the latest link in a long chain of such interpreters. The other approach points to the opposite extreme, deflating any claim to originality on Vivekananda's behalf, by demonstrating that he did not make any formal innovations to the Advaitic system, unlike many of Shankara's successors. I think that this is to take too restricted a view of what counts as innovation. Vivekananda's originality in interpreting Advaita did not lie in technical philosophy but in reorienting the tradition around elements which were underemphasized before.

quagmire.* To reiterate, the required historical awareness is to properly grasp the aspects of both continuity and difference. The seeds of the modern world lay in the Victorian age. Many of the defining features of modern life which grew out of the revolutions of the nineteenth century, like secularism, democracy, individual rights, nationalism, and many other political and sociocultural phenomena, were already anticipated in the Victorian era. When speaking on subjects as diverse as metaphysics and ethics to women's rights and the destiny of India, these developments formed part of the imperceptible background in relationship to which Vivekananda's views were articulated. The ideological bent of Vivekananda's views can only be understood through these relationships. In order to do that, we must necessarily bring into view those features of modernity relevant to the particular opinions we are trying to understand. The grave danger here, and it is one into which more than one recent commentator has fallen, is to assume that these features existed in the same shape and form in Vivekananda's time as they are present to us today. Such uncritical assumptions end up greatly distorting the meaning of Vivekananda's utterances. In the late Victorian age, modernity and its various elements were in an incipient state, and vastly different in nature and scope from what they would evolve into in the twentieth century.

To take a hypothetical example, if one were reading a comment by Vivekananda on democracy, it is important to understand that the very meaning of the word 'democracy' differed in the late nineteenth century from the one it has for us now. America was the only existing democracy in the world. Europe was ruled by non-Constitutional monarchies, though their absolutism was tempered by increasingly assertive parliaments. But it was only a very small minority who thought that the increasing role the electorate played in influencing the governments of their countries would lead to the replacement of monarchies with democracies (an eventuality that might never have come to pass but for the World Wars). Indeed, it was far from clear whether democracy was a universally viable system of government at all. In so far as the word meant anything more than a political arrangement free from kingship, such meanings were more in the nature of the hopes and aspirations of a minority based on the American experiment. It lacked the concrete associations of equality, liberty, and individual rights the term now encompasses. In our hypothetical example, suppose Vivekananda were to express himself in a way that is not very supportive

---

*This might strike some readers as an exaggeration but there are a number of additional complicating factors, a major one being Vivekananda's predilection for saying the exact opposite of what he said on one occasion, on another.

of democracy. It would be a serious error to conclude from this that Vivekananda is 'anti-democratic'. While this example is purely imaginary, a host of recent commentators have read similar assertions by Vivekananda on other issues, and rushed to judge his views as reactionary or conservative in terms of the ideological issue they were examining. Such readings are historically anachronistic and come from simplistically assuming that many modern institutional values had the same normative meaning in the late Victorian age.

Understanding the radically transformational nature of the Victorian age is not just necessary to understand Vivekananda's milieu and situate him properly at the end of the period. The changes we have talked about did not merely constitute the context in which Vivekananda expressed his views; they formed one part of a civilizational encounter. This civilizational encounter has been characterized as one between the West and the East, with Vivekananda being the representative of the latter. Such a characterization has come both from adulatory as well as critical literature. For the former, the essence of the matter is the West discovering the spiritual wisdom of the East through Vivekananda; for the latter, the questions revolve around how Vivekananda represented or misrepresented Hinduism to the West. What has received almost no attention is the fact that as an encounter, this was a two-way street. The social, intellectual, economic, and political transformations that were shaping the West also exerted considerable influence on Vivekananda as an Indian subject, and as a thinker.

The British empire's rule over India brought many of the nascent structures of modernity developing in the nineteenth century West, to India. British colonialism introduced to India modern universities, natural sciences, modern government, technology such as railways and the telegraph, a centralized bureaucracy, and Enlightenment ideas of political liberty, social justice, and nationalism. Above all, it created a cultural modernity, which combined with capitalistic modes of commerce and production to call into question the traditional social order. All these forces were playing out in the backdrop of the idea of India as a nation and as the basic political unit, a conception which developed in the decades after the British government took over India's administration from the East India Company.

In coming to the West, Vivekananda encountered in their original form and setting, the forces whose distant influence was shaping India and presenting it with profound challenges in many spheres of her existence. Vivekananda was a keen enough observer to realize that the Anglobalization that the world was witnessing, in spite of its exploitative imperialistic nature, was binding the people of the world together and that the emerging structures of modernity (though he would not have called them that) would shape the future world order. This awareness coloured almost the entire range of his thought, (except the purely metaphysical and spiritual core), even the parts that dealt specifically with India and Hindu society and religion. In thinking through and attempting to find solutions to the various challenges India faced, Vivekananda thought and spoke in relationship to the dynamic of forces that were shaping the world at the turn of the century. 'Even in politics and sociology, problems that were only national twenty years ago can no more be solved on national grounds only. They are assuming huge proportions, gigantic shapes. They can only be solved when looked at in the broader light of international grounds. International organizations, international combinations, international laws are the cry of the day,' Vivekananda said.[4] To understand the political, social, and intellectual landscape of the West is thus essential also in understanding Vivekananda's thinking as a whole, especially as he brought it to bear on contemporary social and political issues.

How did this landscape appear to the Victorians themselves? The most common attitude among Victorians towards their own reality was that theirs was an age of universal human progress and prosperity. The notion of progress was understood broadly as consisting of two different but often overlapping processes. One was the use of scientific knowledge and the resources of the nation state to address social issues like the living conditions of the poor, the state of prostitutes, illiteracy, child labour, slavery, etc., features of social existence that for millennia had been considered unalterable. The other was the result of the increasing influence of liberalism, the ideological child of the Enlightenment and the French Revolution. The rise of liberalism led to wide ranging political and social reform, especially increased guarantee of civil rights to citizens.

A number of cultural assumptions wove themselves around this idea of progress. A central assumption was a historical self-understanding of their own era as one appointed to take humanity on the path of material improvement and universal progress. The idea of progress was tied closely to the advance of science and reason, both seen as the vanguard in a fight against ignorance and ancient superstitions that has held humanity back. In many quarters, the hope, indeed often a complacent certainty of material and social progress, took on an almost millenarian tone. The combination of liberalism, industrial capitalism, and science and technology was widely seen to have ushered in a new age in the annals of humankind. And in the last quarter of the nineteenth century, Europe and America felt that they were standing on the threshold of an age of even greater things. All human problems seemed capable of a potential solution in the triumphal march of progress. And the torchbearer of this progress was the West.

Such attitudes slid, especially in the last quarter of the nineteenth century, into cultural assumptions about the superiority of Western civilization and culture. In its milder form, it took the shape of a belief in a historically contingent civilizational superiority that the West had achieved and whose fruits it was called upon to share with the rest of humanity. The West thus, had a 'civilizing mission' in Asia and Africa, to shed the light of reason and progress on those less fortunate cultures. Towards the end of the century, the perceived inferiority of non-Western civilizations took on racial overtones, and there was a proliferation of pseudo-scientific theories like eugenics which sought to give a rational explanation for racial superiority. From this perspective, the difference in technology and economic and military power between the Western nations and others, were not a matter of historical achievement, and in principle reversible, but expressed an essential difference in inherent capabilities. Both these viewpoints undergird the project of Western colonialism, providing rationalization and intellectual support.

These ideas about universal human progress, as well as the West's special role in it, were shared by most of the audiences Vivekananda spoke to in America and Great Britain, as well as by many of his intellectual interlocutors. These cultural and intellectual attitudes were part of the dialogue Vivekananda carried out with his listeners. They set the broad terms for the conversation and it was essential to Vivekananda's project that he disrupt them and set his own terms for delivering his message. This was particularly so when it came to assumptions of Western superiority. As we will see in the next chapter, much of the fiery assertion of Indian and Hindu civilizational superiority over the West which Vivekananda made on occasion, and which form the tenuous basis for his appropriation by Hindutva today, was aimed at levelling the discursive playing field by negating deeply embedded ideas of Indian inferiority and Western superiority.

What made Vivekananda's situation unique and perhaps less easily identifiable is that he had to depend completely upon his own resources to combat imperialistic cultural notions about Asia, India, and Hinduism. There was no broader tradition of anti-imperialistic discourse in the West he could readily draw upon. The main discontents with the dominant idea of progress which was predicated on liberalism, laissez-faire capitalism, and colonialism, were the old European conservatives and the socialists. While it might be expected that Vivekananda would find a natural ally against narratives of cultural imperialism among socialist thinkers, this was not so. The socialist case against imperialism would be developed in detail much later and in terms that were purely economic rather than cultural or civilizational. (As late as 1897, the great socialist thinker Eduard Bernstein wrote a defence of colonialism based on socialist principles, casually referring in the process to the colonized natives as 'savages'.)* The singularity of Vivekananda's terms of reference in his attempts to combat colonial stereotypes about India and Hinduism has had the unfortunate consequence that it shares in no other discourse but that of Hindu nationalism which later appropriated them. This has meant that it is not easy to tell them apart at first glance, and a contemporary reader who approaches Vivekananda with the suspicion that he is complicit in the Hindutva project, might find her suspicions strengthened if she does not take the trouble to read him with a minimum extent of detail and care.

HOW THE NEW WEST SHAPED ITSELF (1850–90)

While the uses imperialism and racism put the notion of progress to is important to understand, it is equally important not to dismiss the entire impulse as counterfeit. While it is true that the Victorians were naive in retrospect to expect history to move in a linear line of progress and failed to acknowledge the oppressive nature of colonialism and the class inequalities produced by the precursor to capitalism, we are able to say this only with the benefit of historical hindsight. Irrespective of whether modernity represents progress or not, its building blocks were laid in the Victorian age. And in so far as the project of modernity was understood in its infancy as offering a true prospect of historical improvement and distribution of justice, the Victorians were sincere in their assessment of themselves as engaged in an enterprise aimed at human progress.

This is reflected most in that the period we are concerned with was an age of reform. This was true of the entire West but was particularly felt in America and Great Britain. In 1867, Great Britain introduced the Second Reform Act, which increased the number of those eligible to vote to a significant number of adult males. While this was far from the intention of its creators, the Reform Act laid the groundwork for democracy in Britain. While the parliamentary party system had existed in Britain for centuries, it thus far represented little

---

*For a brief history of how socialist thinking about colonialism developed in the nineteenth century and beyond, see Gregory Claeys, 'Socialism and Empire', *Imperial Sceptics: British Critics of Empire, 1850–1920*, Cambridge: Cambridge University Press, 2010.

more than a check on the absolute authority of the monarch exercised by the elite sections of society. In the eighteenth century the first industrial revolution changed the very nature of agrarian society and set in motion a commercial revolution (often called commercial capitalism to distinguish it from the later industrial capitalism) that made the dimensions of economic and military activity far more complex than anything experienced heretofore. Within such a context, the parliamentary system and the central bureaucracy evolved into something more than it was before: into specialized extensions of the autocratic state necessary to legislate on and administer an immensely complex polity and economy, a task which was now far beyond the capacities of a single man (the monarch) and his immediate administrative entourage.

The expansion of the state to include independent legislative bodies and a semi-independent administrative apparatus, while novel phenomena, did not in itself presage a development of democratic tendencies. A centralized and relatively independent bureaucracy had existed in ancient China for millennia. But, to borrow and modify an immortal phrase, the spectre of republicanism was haunting Europe. At the broadest structural level, all the eventful political changes of the first half of the nineteenth century in Europe, including the Napoleonic Wars, can be understood as a struggle for supremacy between the old aristocratic order and the legacy of political liberty that flowed from the French Revolution (1789). This took the form of a battle between authoritarianism and revolutionary radicalism in politics and society, and the idea of the divine right of kings and constitutional republicanism on the ideological field. The concerted efforts of European monarchies to maintain the status quo of pre-revolutionary Europe with its absolutist state structure, failed by the mid-century. After a series of revolutions in Europe starting with the revolution in 1848 which overthrew the absolute monarchy in France, a new political compromise was worked out throughout the European nations. The curtain fell over the ancient regime. This compromise saw a significant realignment of political and social forces and the emergence of a new synthesis, which would determine the dynamic of how the defining structures of a nascent modernity would arise and evolve in the second part of the century.

At the beginning of the mid-Victorian age (approximately 1850s to 1860s), except for Russia, conservatives across Europe were forced to come to terms with constitutionalism and parliaments. A new kind of State was coming into being. The old regimes of Europe understood that the demand for people's role in government was backed by social and economic forces too powerful to ignore. Fearful of popular uprisings which would overthrow the monarchy, the establishment's strategy became one of co-opting the populace's demands for democratic reforms and turning them away from the hands of the revolutionaries. For the next six decades, until World War I, this strategy broadly worked. But as increasing concessions were made to political and civil reforms, the nature of the polities and states itself changed to produce hybrids of monarchies and modern government.

By 1870, the three major European powers, Great Britain, France, and Germany, were all constitutional monarchies with powerful parliaments and a ministerial system of government.[*] Ministerial and parliamentary power switched between conservative and liberal parties, who implemented or promoted policies that broadly represented the class interests of the gentry and the middle classes respectively. It is easy to imagine the whole trajectory of increasing democratization that marked the second half of the nineteenth century, as a battle of attrition where liberals pressed reform on conservatives who wished to maintain the status quo. But the picture is not so simple. Liberals were not always pro-reform, and neither were conservatives uniformly against reform. The spirit of the times, with its clash of profound ideas and overwhelming change did not allow people to act from fixed ideological positions. For example, it was the conservative English politician Benjamin Disraeli who enacted the Second Reform Act. Similarly, the extremely conservative chancellor of Germany Otto von Bismarck introduced extensive social security policies and ruled in the latter part of his career in an informal coalition with liberal parliamentarians.

What broadly united all political actors was a shared sense of the possibility of progress. The idea of progress, or at least some measure of it, was shared by conservatives, liberals, radicals, and socialists alike.[†] Thus, the period was simultaneously one of confidence and uncertainty. There was deep social anxiety among both the upper classes and sections of the middle class as ancient verities and traditions crumbled. But the feeling of uncertainty also inhabited the consensus about progress in the political, intellectual, and social spheres. The uncertainty was not always felt to be negative; it could and did generate an exciting sense of possibilities. In essence, the uncertainty accrued from the fact that men (it was almost exclusively men) of different ideologies saw different

---

[*]Among these three great powers of Europe, Germany's parliament was comparatively weak and could not control the monarchy effectively.

[†]The socialist position on progress was different from that of the liberals. While they decried that the changes happening in the Victorian age indicated progress, they saw bourgeois democracy as an improvement on the feudal state, which would create the necessary conditions for a future socialist revolution.

solutions to the fundamental problem of how progress was to be achieved. This is not a novel condition for us. Such uncertainty is a basic feature of the modernity we live in. But for the Victorians, emerging from a pre-modern past where religious and social myths created a universal reality, it was a unique experience. The second source of uncertainty was that even within an ideological orientation, say liberalism, socialism, or evangelical Christianity, there was no consensus on what specific form the solutions they offered to the fundamental challenges of the age would take. In other words, no thinking individual knew how things would turn out. Only the cheeriest optimist could be sure that the future would resemble the present even in the broadest possible ways.

This intellectual atmosphere of uncertainty is reflected in the form of Vivekananda's own thinking. It was typical of his philosophy as well as a reflection of the Victorian uncertainty about the future that he usually refused to offer tangible solutions to the very social and political issues that he was most concerned with. He saw that the future remained unknown and that pressing problems of both national and global existence were being shaped by powerful, diverse, and conflicting historical forces whose end result was almost impossible to predict. Contemporary thinkers who put forward ways in which such problems were to be solved invariably predicated these solutions on the triumph of one set of forces or tendencies. Such institutional solutions also overlapped with the implications of particular ideological orientations. Vivekananda on the other hand, refused to favour any particular direction in the cross-currents of ideological and historical potencies that constituted society at the turn of the century. I have mentioned that Vivekananda was an idealist in his historical thinking. In respect to social issues too, he preferred to analyse the deeper moral and spiritual forces he saw working beneath the more perceptible manifestations of social and political life.

This reticence to vigorously advocate institutional and theoretical solutions has led to accusations of apathy or even sympathy with anti-reformist tendencies. For example, the fact that Vivekananda did not make a frontal assault on social ills like child marriage and the caste system in his public speeches has led some to accuse Vivekananda of being ambivalent or even conservative on these issues.[5] (Vivekananda attacked caste privileges in his speeches but did not attack the existence of the caste system itself openly. I examine this issue in detail in Chapter 13.) The fact that Vivekananda was deeply opposed to both child marriage and the caste system in his thought and life, but did not vociferously campaign against them publicly, has to be seen against his similar quiescence on almost the entire range of sociopolitical issues associated with his thought. This is true equally of positions with which he is unquestioningly identified, like nationalism. For someone whom the leaders of the Indian Independence movement like Gandhi, Nehru, and Subhas Bose regarded as a key inspiration behind the national movement, it almost defies belief that there is not even a single statement in favour of Indian political autonomy in Vivekananda's work. The work of the Indian National Congress finds not more than a few mentions in his entire oeuvre, though Vivekananda had shared the stage with Dadabhai Naoroji in Britain and had met Tilak in India. Yet, it would be extremely foolhardy to conclude from this that Vivekananda would not have supported political independence for India.* The fact is that whether it was Indian independence or child marriage, there can be no doubt what his views were. But being a public campaigner for the political causes he supported never attracted him. As a spiritual preacher, his role, as he saw it, was to elucidate the abstract moral ideals and spiritual principles at issue in these causes (for example liberty, ignorance, idealism, materialism, empathy, justice, and so on) and allow for people to make the right choices by themselves. His attitude was also an expression of an acute intellectual awareness of the unsteady balance of forces that marked the age, of the Victorian sense of uncertainty.

In spite of such persisting uncertainty about long-term ends, a broad consensus emerged on several fronts at the start of the mid-Victorian age. If we take the year 1850 as the starting point for a fundamental transformation which set the West on a trajectory towards the modern world, we see that these transformations stemmed from a series of watershed events. As monarchies with constitutions and parliaments replaced absolute monarchies across Europe, there ensued a realignment between various sections of society, their ideological commitments and the political order. The first and most far reaching in the immediate term was the accommodation of conservative politics and the old order to economic and political liberalism. Conservative politics had its social bases among the aristocracy, the landed gentry, and the upper classes, who had their economic interests tied to the land and an agrarian economy. Increasing industrialization and free trade had over several decades favoured a shift in balance of economic and social power towards the mercantile classes and the bourgeois. However, this process was resisted by powerful aristocratic interests until the middle of the century.

---

*Vivekananda's most famous disciple, Sister Nivedita became actively involved in the national movement.

In the 1850s, starting with France under Louis-Napoléon Bonaparte, conservative politics started encouraging free trade and entrepreneurship. The idea was that economic growth would make for political stability by reducing the base of economic discontent which had launched popular revolutions in the past. The shift in conservative politics that started with France spread over Europe in the next decade, with the result that there now emerged a near universal consensus on capitalism, as opposed to the protectionist economic measures favoured by the landed gentry and the artisan class. As the legal and institutional obstacles to free trade from mercantilist interests disappeared, (Britain abolished import duties on corn in 1847 in a major victory for liberals), capitalism finally became the dominant economic ideology of the Western world.

In the decades leading up to Vivekananda's career in the West, the economic forces unleashed by the State's unencumbered support for capitalistic policies, brought about a fundamental structural shift in social relations. While the aristocrats and upper classes continued to maintain privileges (increasingly in the nature of social legitimacy than legal ones), power within the overall system shifted decisively and dramatically towards the middle classes. This had multiple effects across the entire sociopolitical complex, most markedly in Western Europe. For one, the drive for sociopolitical and administrative reform now increasingly coincided with and was driven by the political aspirations of the economically dominant middle class. Secondly, it replaced the cultural values of old Europe which were tied to religion and tradition, with those of the rising middle class. For over a millennium, the cultural loyalties of European people consisted of variations on religious, feudal, and monarchical themes. These now shifted towards an entirely new configuration, determined by the social needs of a newly evolving economic framework, which was based on free trade, expanding markets, and industrialization. The emergence of the professional classes and the petit bourgeois, introduced a baseline of social values closely linked to their economic functions, hard work, thrift, efficiency, civic sense, etc. These values undergird the evolution of a larger system of moral values and social norms. Every section of society, to some extent, shared in this developing value system, and increasing social mobility led to a diffusion of this new cultural ethos across all classes.[6]

In locating Vivekananda, it is important not only to determine his position in historical time, but also in social space. Society in both Britain and (though to a lesser extent) America was stratified by class. Vivekananda's milieu was largely what is termed 'polite society', formed from the upper middle class and the gentry. These were the kind of people who found themselves dissatisfied with traditional Christianity and were interested in a more liberal non-denominational form of spirituality. They turned up enthusiastically at Vivekananda's lectures, attended classes on raja yoga, and formed a network of supporters and friends who helped further his mission of spreading the message of Vedanta. They constituted Vivekananda's immediate social circle, serving as a conduit for his ideas to the West and reversely as channels for his understanding of the West. Vivekananda's social location is an important factor to take into account when considering many of his comments on European and American society. They often reflected social mores and beliefs that were ingrained in the polite society he moved in. At the same time, this social location was the vantage point from which Vivekananda saw Western society. It formed the locus of his experiential and theoretical knowledge of America and Europe; and it thus offered a very partial and at times even erroneous perspective of the condition of marginalized sections within Victorian society and the Anglobalized world: the working class, black people, Native Americans, the Islamic world, etc. It also insulated him from contact with and hence knowledge of avant-garde social elements and political dissidents on the margins of European society—sexual libertines, radical feminists, Marxists, anarchists, and others—who would come to play an increasingly important role in the political discourse of the West from the second decade of the twentieth century.

Vivekananda's contacts sometimes strayed beyond his accustomed social class, and included business magnates like John D. Rockefeller, rich society hostesses, and celebrities and, at the other end of the class ladder, middle class men and women who sometimes attended his lectures and classes. The Victorian value system that developed fully towards the last quarter of the century permeated all sections of society, but its norms took on different forms according to whether it was articulated among the working class, lower middle class, polite society, or the aristocracy. Vivekananda internalized some of these norms, while rejecting others outright. But most social norms remain invisible to those influenced by them, leaving residual traces behind in a fossilized form in their words, concepts, and in the everyday notions they held, for future historians to dig out. Even when Vivekananda's thinking disagreed with the majority of Victorian social assumptions and their ideological implications, he had to use the same language and concepts as his contemporaries, at least to mark his point of departure.

Growing economic might led to demands for greater bourgeois representation in European parliaments and the American Congress, which succeeded to varying degrees. In Britain, for example, while parliament continued to be dominated by the upper classes for most of this period, rich upper middle-class individuals increasingly became members of the House of Commons. Workers had started to organize into unions, though unionizing was illegal in most countries till the last quarter of the century. While the working classes did not acquire representation, they made their voice felt politically through strikes, riots, and working-class movements. As the social power shifted from the aristocracy and upper classes to the middle classes, and the working classes started to become more visible, the nature of the State itself underwent a transformational change. Till the middle of the nineteenth century,[*] all across Europe, Asia, and the Islamic world, the state as an entity was a monopoly of elite power. Reinforced by religious theories of the divine right of kings to rule with absolute authority over the subjects, the state did not need to seek an independent reason for its existence or the power it exercised over the population. Of course, the king had to rule for the good of his subjects, but this was an abstract principle which remained at the level of ethical discourse about kingship, rather than as an enforceable political principle.

The undiluted power of the state, which has been a universal feature of human existence since the formation of agricultural societies, was altered drastically in Europe after 1850. As agrarian social patterns were replaced by those of industrial society, the state was no longer able to base its political legitimacy on the support of a small, but powerful, elite. It had to increasingly justify itself in terms of public good, broadly construed as representing all sections of society even when class hierarchy was explicitly recognized. Governments started becoming self-consciously committed to public good and invested in actively pursuing policies that were aimed at increasing the welfare of the polity, which was increasingly understood through the concept of nationhood.

The decreasing hold of the 'divine right' theory of absolutism was directly linked to a decline in the power of organized religion in the Victorian age. The church and the state were inextricably intertwined in Europe, with the former providing the latter with ideological support through Christianity, and the latter sharing its power with the church. Throughout its history, the Western nations were constituted as theological states to an extent which was unprecedented in most contemporary civilizations. In contrast, however much influence the ulama in the Islamic world, the Brahmin priests in Hindu kingdoms, the Confucian

---

[*]The process started from the late eighteenth century itself, but the nature of the state did not undergo a full-blown transformation till the 1850s.

establishment in China, or the Shinto/Buddhist religious orders in Japan exerted on state policy, they could never intrude into the political–military domain, which remained the exclusive preserve of the state. But the changes brought about by the Renaissance and Reformation turned things around in the West, so that by the Victorian age, the relationship between the West and the rest of the world in this matter had reversed. While in the Middle East, Asia, and Latin America, the state largely retained a denominational religious character, European nation states increasingly divested themselves of their involvement with religious orders. Of course, the majority Christian denomination remained the official state religion throughout Europe and America, but the implications of this for heretical Christian sects, Jews, and other non-Christians became far less consequential as the Victorian age progressed.

A few years before Queen Victoria ascended the throne, a law banning non-Anglicans, Catholics, and other religious dissenters from holding public office was repealed by the British Parliament.* But other kinds of restrictions continued to curtail the civic rights of religious minorities. One of the most far-reaching restrictions was on access to university education. In the early Victorian age, Oxford refused to admit religious dissenters, while Cambridge refused to grant them degrees; the contentious issue dragged on. The first major victory for the dissenters was in 1854 when Oxford allowed non-Anglicans to take bachelor's degrees. The issue was contested for two decades between reformers and the church with gradual progress for the cause of the dissenters over the years. It was only in 1871 that religious non-conformists were allowed equal admissions and rights in both universities.[7]

In the 1850s and especially the 1860s, Jews were granted legal formal equality with Christians across much of Europe. Britain elected its first Jewish member of parliament (MP) in 1857. In the early 1860s the south German states of Baden and Bavaria granted full voting rights to Jews in both parliamentary and state elections. These legal changes become part of the Constitution of the German nation when it was formed between 1867 and 1871, at the same time that the Austro-Hungarian Empire emancipated its Jewish population. Similar processes took place in the Low Countries and Italy during this time.[8]

All these changes represented the withdrawal of the state from religion, which increasingly developed a secular character. This secularism was not merely a passive process of disentangling the state from religious authority.

---

*In practice, most dissenters occupied public posts as long as they were willing to accommodate themselves to Anglican requirements or misrepresent their religion. But many conscientious dissenters refused to do so.

In the latter part of the nineteenth century, many European states proactively pursued an ideological commitment to secularism. The Third Republic of France systematically assaulted the Catholic establishment while the German state in its zeal for secularization went so far as to persecute Catholics in authoritarian ways. Across the West, including Britain where the Anglican Church was officially the national church, state policies purposively accelerated the cultural secularization of the public sphere. One of the main arenas where this ideological conflict between traditional religion and the modern state played out was in education.

For centuries, school education had been the responsibility of the lower clergy. Parish schools imparted elementary education which was strongly centred on the Bible, while priests played an important role as instructors in secondary schools. Till the middle of the century, school children grew up with a predominantly Christian world view imparted through education. Education was a crucial factor in the development of the modern secular nation state. Citizens indoctrinated with a religious world view no longer served the interests of the emerging nation state, the economic interests which supported it, or the liberal philosophy that drove its ideology. Subjects, whose primary loyalty was towards a king backed by the religious legitimacy of the church, were being transformed into citizens who were increasingly loyal to the abstract idea of a territorial 'nation'. The state's need for reducing the power of the religious establishment, in education as well as other domains of public life, aligned with the economic imperatives of a capitalist economy. The Christian religious establishment espoused religious values which lent ideological support to a traditional social order which could not accommodate the social and cultural patterns required for expanding capitalism. This order was hierarchical, restrictive, static, and exclusionary—all modes of social life that impeded the open society that capitalism needed in order to maximize economic productivity and efficiency. It placed restrictions on people's freedom of movement and employment, tended to exclude women and religious minorities from public life and civic spaces, and distributed resources based on social rank rather than ability. This was in direct conflict with capitalism's tendency to increase productivity by maximizing labour participation, allowing migration of people across professions, and to create a social order where economic class rather than birth determined an individual's place in society. As with so many other changes that occurred during the Victorian age, secularization and the retreat of religion from public life was driven by a confluence of political, economic, and ideological factors.

The developments of the mid to late Victorian age which have been outlined here form the general historical background against which one has to understand and interpret Vivekananda. But if one were to read Vivekananda very closely and aim at getting as accurate a sense of his views, attitudes, and thought processes as possible, we need to locate him a bit more precisely within the long stretch of the latter nineteenth century. Vivekananda's public career was in the closing decade of the Victorian age and it occupies a most interesting place at roughly the junction of two momentous ages in history—the Victorian age, when modernity started developing within the political and cultural framework of the old European order, and the post-World War I period when the old European order crumbled, and modernity took hold.

World War I shattered the nineteenth century political formations of Europe's monarchies and empires to replace them with modern nation states, many of which were full-fledged democracies. Germany, which was ruled by a powerful monarchy, became a republic. The Russian empire broke apart and Tsarist Russia became a communist dictatorship. The Austro-Hungarian Empire devolved into the independent nations of Austria and Hungary and the rule of the Hapsburg dynasty came to an end. The Ottoman Empire broke apart into several independent nation states and Turkey became a republic, replacing the sultanate. Great Britain under King George V now transitioned to a complete constitutional monarchy, with the king having no more than a symbolic role. France, the other major European power, had been a republic from 1870 onwards.

With the disappearance of the old European order, the social and cultural values associated with that order also dissipated, to be replaced by those that we tend to identify as characteristically belonging to the twentieth century. When we look back at Vivekananda from our present historical location, the year 1914 forms a dividing line beyond which the terrain of the past becomes unfamiliar. Yet, he is not so far in the past that we can consider him a representative nineteenth century figure like say, Karl Marx or Alfred Tennyson. An easy misunderstanding one can arrive at is that Vivekananda lived in an age of transition between the Victorian age and the post-war modern world. But this is not the case. Vivekananda's career occurred in the dying years of the Victorian age, coming to end less than two years into the twentieth century (1893–1902). It was a period when the historical currents that defined the past and the future ebbed and flowed across the imaginary boundary line separating them. Victorian social and cultural patterns continued to shape many areas of life while being relatively absent in others. Several of the elements that combined to form the life patterns of the post-war decades were already present in the 1890s. These elements did not have the same scope or arouse the same set of expectations, but even at that time, they were hazy indicators of the tremendous changes to come.

In many ways, the World's Parliament of Religions that Vivekananda attended in Chicago in 1893 was symbolic of the changes that were already transforming the United States. It was held as part of the World's Colombian Exposition, an international fair organized on a gigantic scale to mark the four-hundredth anniversary of Columbus's arrival in the New World. Apart from 27 million visitors from all over the world, the fair attracted a galaxy of famous personages. Hellen Keller and her teacher Anne Sullivan, Alexander Graham Bell, Nikola Tesla (whose acquaintance Vivekananda made later), Harry Houdini, and innumerable minor celebrities thronged the exposition. (On the less savoury side, the fair was also visited by America's first known serial killer H. H. Holmes). With its 200-odd buildings constructed in a Neoclassical style and spread over 690 acres, hundreds of displays of the latest technological marvels, and pavilions showcasing massive artillery and military equipment, the exhibition was meant to awe and astonish the visitor. The Ferris wheel debuted at the Colombian Fair as did the world's first moving walkway. Other technological exhibits included the first fully electrical kitchen with an electrical dishwasher, phosphorescent lamps, Thomas Edison's phonographs, and an early prototype of an aerosol spray. The most impressive was the electrical display. The fair itself was lit by around 90,000 electric lamps and was meant to showcase the new AC current system being promoted by Westinghouse Electric which used Tesla's design, and had outbid General Electric's DC lighting system which used Edison's design. An electricity building housed the latest in electrical gizmos: Edison's kinetoscope (an early motion picture device), a seismograph, search lights, an electric car, switchboards, transformers, and appliances like fans and radiators. The sense of grandeur and the wonder of technology were meant to celebrate the material and technological progress of the age. But it also had a more purely national dimension, symbolizing to the world that the United States was a modern nation, ready to take its place on the international stage.

In the two decades leading up to Vivekananda's arrival in America, the country had gone through a fundamental transformation, stemming from the changed post-Civil War conditions. The first landmark in this transformation was the completion of the transcontinental railroad in 1869 which connected the East Coast and the West Coast. This allowed for a national market and a pricing system to emerge. This enabled commerce on a scale unseen before and provided America with the single largest market in the world leading to the rapid expansion of American agriculture and industry. America started transforming from a primarily agrarian country to a modern industrialized nation like the great European powers. By the 1890s, American manufacturing had grown to such an extent that it produced more goods than Britain, Germany, and France put together.[9] The US was emerging as an economic rival to Great Britain and many people were already predicting a future when America would overtake Britain as the dominant global economic and military power.

The 1890s, when Vivekananda was active in the West, particularly saw the emergence and wider incorporations of the kinds of technology and life patterns that were to become more prominent and routine in the modern age after World War I. This period saw a new thrust of rapid urbanization in the West, especially Europe, with construction of underground railways, electric tramlines, and installation of electric grids for domestic and commercial power. The use of motorized cars by people in the 1890s, though on a very small scale, made the vehicle part of the urban landscape. Many urban households came to have electric lighting and use telephones. In 1888, the Kodak film camera revolutionized photography by placing the camera in the hands of anyone who could press a button. This not only made photography a more ubiquitous part of urban life but allowed people to capture and chronicle casual moments of their lives. On the social level, settled patterns of middle-class life emerged that continued into the twentieth century.

But in spite of this, there were fundamental and sharp differences between society at the end of the nineteenth century and in the decade following World War I. They consisted of mainly the emergence of mass culture, mass media, and consumer culture. These were accompanied by the collapse of the Victorian code of proper social behaviour. To recognize the absence or presence of these factors in Vivekananda's milieu is crucial if an artificial continuity is not to be assumed with the beginnings of twentieth century modernity. Such a view would completely distort the sense and intent of many statements and claims made by Vivekananda.

In spite of the enormous destruction caused by World War I, American industry and business financed a European recovery which ushered in a commercial revolution across the Western world in the post-war era. America led the automobile revolution and automobiles became an integral part of American life. By 1921, there were 9 million cars on American roads. Department stores increasingly replaced neighbourhood shops and family-run trades and created a mass market for ready-made goods. Clothes were increasingly bought off the rack and as demand for mass produced apparel increased, prices fell, making clothing affordable for lower sections of society. The stratified class distinctions and social boundaries of the late Victorian age were diluted considerably as even salesgirls and clerks started dressing fashionably. Brand names acquired great importance and became markers of a common identity built around consumption which cut across class, race, and geographical barriers.[10]

Even with the appearance of new means of communication and an exponential growth of newspapers and periodicals, the public sphere in the late Victorian age remained fragmented. The popularization of the radio after the war, however, went a long way towards the creation of a universal mass public sphere. Broadcasting stations appeared in all major cities in Europe and America. In 1921, the first radio report of a sporting event was broadcasted in America. Information which earlier took weeks to disseminate, could now spread across a nation in a matter of days. The radio brought the world into the home.

Along with the creation of a truly universal public sphere through mass media, national mass cultures evolved concurrently. In America, for instance, as spectator sports became increasingly popular, traditions started to be built around them that became part of the fabric of a national consciousness. Sports like college football and boxing became widespread and took on the role of cultural institutions while baseball became part of the national culture. There was an explosion in movies in the 1920s, which created new forms of popular culture. Hollywood stars like Charlie Chaplin, Greta Garbo, and Joan Crawford became household names. A mass culture in which everyone participated was created as people increasingly took part in the same forms of leisure and entertainment, watched the same advertisements, heard the same radio programmes, and shopped at the same department chains. It is important to realize when thinking of Vivekananda as operating in the West near the beginning of the twentieth century, that all these features of the post-war world with which we are familiar, were absent in his time.

All these created a culture of hedonism where people sought pleasure unabashedly. This had significant consequences for both sexuality and constructions of gender. Sex was no longer considered a taboo subject and became more openly discussed, both in social situations and in the mass media. In the Victorian age, women were deified as pure beings untainted by lust, but in practice treated as social inferiors. Victorian notions of the respectable woman were based on effectively erasing women's sexuality and erecting social protocols of interaction with men that precluded the possibility of premarital sex. The decade of the World War had changed this social discourse completely so that by the twenties, young men and women no longer met solely at the girl's residence with a chaperone. With the increasing use of automobiles and the opening of modern avenues of entertainment like movie theatres, dating shifted to public spaces. Open display of public affection, which would have been socially unimaginable two decades ago, increasingly became the norm even among the middle classes.

These social factors are important considerations to take into account when dealing with some of Vivekananda's comments on women. Vivekananda's views on women and women's rights were very advanced for the age he lived in, even if one were to compare him to Victorian men and women of letters such as Marx, Nietzsche, Schopenhauer, Beatrice Webb, Anne Nathan Mayer, and so on. He believed in the complete equality of men and women as regards their abilities and potential. Indeed, it was a tenet of his faith, flowing directly from the Advaitic philosophy of the unity of the individual Self (Atman) and God (Brahman). After spending a little over a year in America, Vivekananda wrote to his fellow disciples in September 1894 of his admiration of the modern American woman. 'I am really struck with wonder to see the women here. How gracious the Divine Mother is on them! Most wonderful women, these! They are about to corner the men, who have been nearly worsted in the competition. It is all through Thy grace, O Mother! ...I shall not rest till I root out this distinction of sex. Is there any sex-distinction in the Atman (Self)? Out with the differentiation between man and woman.'[11] Vivekananda supported voting rights for women, which was a radical position for the time, given that the suffrage movement was still to gain steam.[12] And even when it did, it was opposed by the majority of public intellectuals, including many women active in promoting women's rights.

In spite of his pro-woman views, in the article 'Modern India', we find him writing: 'The present writer has, to some extent, personal experience of Western society.... We have not the least sympathy with those who, never having lived in Western society and, therefore, utterly ignorant of the rules and prohibitions regarding the association of men and women that obtain there, and which act as safeguards to preserve the purity of the Western women, allow a free rein to the unrestricted intermingling of men and women in our society.'[13] Passages like these have been picked up by the uncritical and biased to portray Vivekananda as a promoter of patriarchal values. Indeed, if this passage were to be written today, it would be nothing short of the most blatant sexism and moral policing. But the fact is that it was written in 1899 and the question of what this says of Vivekananda's attitude towards the relationship of the sexes can only be understood by placing Vivekananda within the gender discourse of the late Victorian age.

It is a truism that while a person can be completely committed to certain principles of equality or justice, even if that person is in advance of her times, it would be almost impossible for her to completely see through or free herself from all the social forms of life that subvert those very principles. While Vivekananda held the most progressive views on the equality of men and women and practised them consistently in his life, his ideas on gender roles were still circumscribed by the framework of the Victorian understanding of gender, shared by both the men and women of the late nineteenth century.

It does not follow from his comments cited above that Vivekananda was a doctrinaire advocate of regulating social intercourse between men and women, like a lot of Indian conservatives were in his time and continue to be today. His rejection of 'unregulated mixing' was based upon the idea of protecting the 'purity' of women. It was a centrepiece of the Victorian construction of the idea of the respectable woman, whose standing in society was based on confining her sexuality within the confines of marriage. But here, we must remember that people never bring ideas of gender, race, class, or other forms of social emancipation and equality to the table completely a priori. These ideas are to a significant extent also drawn from one's experience of the possibilities of being-in-the-world disclosed, or at least indicated, by the subject of emancipation. In other words, the historical limits of the life possibilities available to an oppressed class also determine the horizon of emancipatory possibilities imagined both by members of that class as well as outsiders who are invested in their rights. This is why many opinions of leaders who are the vanguard of progress, look tame or even reactionary in the future.

Vivekananda's ideas and impressions of the liberated modern woman were based on his encounter with young American women drawn mainly from the upper middle class and polite society. Many of them, like Mary Hale, Harriet Hale, Isabelle McKindley, Harriet McKindley, Alberta Sturges, Margaret Noble (a British woman who later became Sister Nivedita), and Josephine MacLeod became intimate friends and regular correspondents. These women were highly educated, intelligent, and prescribed to then current liberal notions of women's liberty and equality. Nonetheless, they all thought and acted broadly within the sexual mores of the late Victorian age, where single women received men only at their residence, and would be seen in public spaces with single men only if accompanied by a chaperone. It is doubtful if Vivekananda ever came into contact with women who questioned these sexual boundaries. Women who held such opinions or acted on them existed only on the periphery of Anglo-American society; being associated more with the Bohemian avant-garde art circles of Paris and Vienna. Even the lower classes of the late Victorian age aspired towards emerging norms of middle-class morality and respectability, with traditionally more sexually open spaces like alehouses and pubs being frequented only by men at the time.[14]

If the comments we are examining were made even twenty years later, they would fall in the conservative spectrum. But if Vivekananda had been alive and visited the West after World War I, he would have encountered a culture that by Victorian standards was licentious. And he would have had the benefit of encountering and hearing the voices of women who, staying within the mainstream of society, rebelled against the sexual and gender boundaries imposed on them, such as the 'flappers' in the 1920s. It is important to realize that Vivekananda was no prude. While he could not transcend the Victorian gender discourse on 'purity' of women in spite of his belief in gender equality, he did not subscribe, as most Victorians did, to the opposite side of that ideological construction, to the moral condemnation of the woman who strayed. There were varying social penalties for an 'impure' woman, depending on the degree and severity of the transgression. As the very opposite image of the pure respectable woman, stood the 'fallen woman', the prostitute, who was the incarnation of sexual impurity. The two ideas were interdependent, functioning as the two ends of an ideological pole. To enforce norms of respectability on middle-class women, the prostitute had to be condemned and ostracized out of society.

It is true that the Victorian age was an age of reform and charity organizations tried to rehabilitate prostitutes. But this was done through a patronizing rhetoric of 'saving' the woman from sin and moral corruption. The prostitute might deserve sympathy and even help in the eyes of the Victorians, but she was still held to have committed a terrible sin for which she needed to seek religious and social absolution. Vivekananda on the other hand showed genuine empathy for prostitutes and their conditions without bringing in moral judgments or seeing their actions as forms of sexual depravity. There are many instances in his writings where he sets his face against prevalent social attitudes to prostitution. For example, in a letter dated 1896, he wrote from London to a friend in New York: 'At twenty years of age I was the most unsympathetic, uncompromising fanatic; I would not walk on the footpath on the theatre side of the streets in Calcutta. At thirty-three, I can live in the same house with prostitutes and never would think of saying a word of reproach to them.'[15] We will take a deeper look at Vivekananda's attitude towards women in the twelfth chapter. But here, it would suffice to say that no proper sense can be made of Vivekananda's views on the subject without a correct appreciation of his historical background and social location.

This is also true with regard to Vivekananda's comments on other religions, including Islam and Christianity. Vivekananda could be as critical of religion as a social institution as he could be an expounder of what he considered its sublime philosophical truths. Vivekananda believed that religion had always been monopolized by priests and kings and had throughout history been the source of oppression and violence. Hence, he often not only criticized religion in general, but also the actions and attitudes of particular religions. It is important to note that throughout his work, there is far more criticism of his own religion, Hinduism, than of others. When criticisms of other faiths do occur, it is necessary for the biographer or historian to assess whether they are the products of attempts at objective judgment or of religious prejudice. And if prejudice is involved, to examine if they are the result of ideology, wrong assumptions, or ignorance.

For example, in a speech delivered in a Universalist Church in California in 1900, Vivekananda said: 'In this line the Mohammedans were the best off; every step forward was made with the sword—the Koran in the one hand and the sword in the other: "Take the Koran, or you must die; there is no alternative!" You know from history how phenomenal was their success; for six hundred years nothing could resist them, and then there came a time when they had to cry halt.'[16] At first glance, this might come off as part of the kind of anti-Muslim rhetoric we are so familiar with in India today, which portrays Muslims as religious fanatics who conquered India, demolished temples, and converted entire populations by force.

In trying to understand the intent behind such criticism, it is important that we do not read the past in terms of our present. Today, Christianity and Islam are minority religions in a Hindu majority India, whose governing structure is that of a secular democratic republic. In Vivekananda's time however, Christianity was the religion of the ruling Britishers, and a crucial ideological component of Western imperialism, which had conquered half of Asia and most of Africa. Through the Ottoman Empire, with its vast territories and vassalages that stretched across Asia, the Balkans, Eastern Europe, and the Middle East, Islam was a power on the world stage. In India, with no meaningful representation for Indians in the British administration the dynamics of a majority and minority between the Hindu and Muslim communities was still to develop in a significant measure.

The title of the lecture in question was 'The Way to the Realisation of a Universal Religion'. It is in the context of the need for a universal religion that Vivekananda touches upon the problem of religious fanaticism and the use of violence to spread religion. It was a particularly apposite theme for the audience he was addressing. Colonial conquest was justified in American society as a means to spread the Christian religion. Before speaking of Islam, Vivekananda pointed out the absurdity and violence behind such attitudes held by even educated Christians:

> Just hear what one of the best preachers in New York says: he preaches that the Filipinos should be conquered because that is the only way to teach Christianity to them! They are already Catholics; but he wants to make them Presbyterians, and for this, he is ready to lay all this terrible sin of bloodshed upon his race. How terrible! And this man is one of the greatest preachers of this country, one of the best informed men. Think of the state of the world when a man like that is not ashamed to stand up and utter such arrant nonsense; and think of the state of the world when an audience cheers him! Is this civilization?[17]

Vivekananda never criticized Christianity, the religion. He had only kind and generous words to offer the religion of Christ. The criticisms that he did make were always aimed at the hypocrisy of the West; at the use of Christianity as a tool in its colonial domination of Asia and Africa and in the cultural hegemony it sought to impose on subject civilizations. And he always spoke from the experiential position of a colonized subject. After criticizing the New York Presbyterian preacher, Vivekananda comments on the religious violence of the Islamic conquest. But he leaves his audience in no doubt that he is criticizing an aspect of Islamic history, not indicting the religion itself. He brings up the subject of Islam again with the audience with these words:

> Christian people hate no religion in the world so much as Mohammedanism. They think it is the very worst form of religion that ever existed. As soon as a man becomes a Mohammedan, the whole of Islam receives him as a brother with open arms, without making any distinction, which no other religion does. If one of your American Indians becomes a Mohammedan, the Sultan of Turkey would have no objection to dine with him. If he has brains, no position is barred to him. In this country, I have never

yet seen a church where the white man and the negro can kneel side by side to pray. Just think of that: Islam makes its followers all equal—so, that, you see, is the peculiar excellence of Mohammedanism.[18]

Last but not least, we have to take into account the knowledge economy of the Victorian age within which Vivekananda is situated. Vivekananda's earlier comment about Islam refers to the Arab conquests which began in the seventh century. Muhammad's heirs, starting with Abu-Bakr, led a series of military campaigns which conquered the Iranian Sasanian Empire and large parts of the Byzantine Empire. In a century, the Arabs had conquered the Levant, Egypt, Persia, Mesopotamia, the Sindh in India, the Maghreb region in Africa, and the Iberian Peninsula in Europe. The speed of the Islamic expansion was faster than anything the world had seen, to be outdone only by the Mongol conquests of the thirteenth century.

The idea that the population of these regions was converted to Islam by force is erroneous. But this was not known in Vivekananda's time. As an English university educated Bengali of his generation, Vivekananda's knowledge of the history of the Arab conquests and of the Islamic Caliphate came from European, particularly British, historiography, just as our knowledge of that period still does. But the European historians of the later Victorian age put together the speed of the Arab conquests and the massive shift in the conquered population to Islam, to infer that the one caused the other. It was assumed by European historians who wrote on the period that the Islamic expansion of the sixth to twelfth centuries followed up territorial annexation with forced or coerced conversions on a massive scale. It is probably only from the 1920s to the 1930s that the earliest studies of Islamic civilization, that were mainly based on original Arabic and Persian sources, appeared in Europe. These studies provided a different picture of the spread of Islam in the Middle East and the West and showed that the Arabs did not initially seek to convert the non-Muslim (dhimmi) population. This picture was filled in by succeeding generations of historians so that we know today that by and large, the Islamization of these areas took place through gradual cultural accretion and proselytization, rather than force.[19] But as far as Vivekananda knew then, he was relying on credible, mainstream history.

The greatest gulf separating Vivekananda's time from the post-war world two decades away, was the very warp and woof of knowledge and thought. The early twentieth century saw important revolutions in several areas of knowledge that not only changed what we knew about vital aspects of human existence, but the very way we thought about being human. Sigmund Freud's theory of psychosexual development revolutionized the way human sexuality would be thought of hence. Sociology as a major academic discipline was first established with the Chicago school of sociology (1915 to 1935) in the University of Chicago. The emergence of sociology had a ripple effect through several fields; most importantly history, political science, and economics. Approaches to historical and sociological thinking in the Victorian age were completely superseded by the impact of the discipline of sociology. Modern art as seen in Futurism, Cubism, Dadaism, and Surrealism challenged the very understanding of the aesthetic and the beautiful as understood since the dawn of civilization. Victorians understood the physical world to be governed by precise physical laws in a mechanistic fashion. By the 1920s, quantum physics dismantled this orderly picture, substituting in its stead randomness, paradoxical, and mysterious looking subatomic phenomena and counter-intuitive concepts. Thus, the mechanistic philosophy which informed much of the thought of Victorian thinkers, including Vivekananda, when they drew upon analogies from science to understand society, politics, and history had been largely supplanted.

PART II

Hinduism, the Sangh, and the West

HINDOOS, AMERICANS,
AND ENGLISHMEN

Over the years, I have had a number of conversations about the nature of Vivekananda's thought and whether, and to what extent, he has been appropriated and misrepresented by Hindutva. These discussions often follow a pattern. Most people I talk to have not read Vivekananda and assume that he is a somewhat orthodox Hindu thinker or even a soft Hindutva figure. These opinions may change when I present them with a fuller picture of Vivekananda's life and thought and draw out the oppositions with the positions of the Sangh. But I find that many people are still not completely convinced and are left with a sense that 'there is no smoke without fire'. These conversations ultimately come around to the question of how, if Vivekananda was as liberal as all that, the Sangh managed to appropriate him so successfully in the first place. This is a reasonable question, and it is a question that I think any contemporary intellectual biography of Vivekananda should address.

The reason the Sangh has been able to appropriate Vivekananda is the same as why some contemporary academics have misread Vivekananda as a Hindu supremacist or as someone with a strong belief in the superiority of Hinduism over other religions. Vivekananda often spoke in America and Great Britain of the East, India, and Hinduism as being spiritually more evolved than the West. For example, at an address delivered at Wimbledon in London, Vivekananda remarked:

People who are capable of seeing only the gross external aspect of things can perceive in the Indian nation only a conquered and suffering people, a race of dreamers and philosophers. They seem to be incapable of perceiving that in the spiritual realm India conquers the world. ...What may be that force which causes this afflicted and suffering people, the Hindu, and the Jewish too (the two races from which have originated all the great religions of the world) to survive, when other nations perish? The cause can only be their spiritual force. The Hindus are still living though silent, the Jews are more numerous today than when they lived in Palestine.

The philosophy of India percolates throughout the whole civilised world, modifying and permeating as it goes.[1]

He spoke of the wisdom and glories of India's rishis and seers in terms that may appear hyperbolic to us today. He attacked the materialism of the West while extolling the spiritual wealth of India. In a letter written to Mary Hale in 1897, Vivekananda writes:

> On metaphysical lines no nation on earth can hold a candle to the Hindus; and curiously all the fellows that come over here from Christian lands have that one antiquated foolishness of an argument that because the Christians are powerful and rich and the Hindus are not, so Christianity must be better than Hinduism. To which the Hindus very aptly retort that, that is the very reason why Hinduism is a religion and Christianity is not because, in this beastly world it is blackguardism and that alone which prospers, virtue always suffers. It seems, however advanced the Western nations are in scientific culture, they are mere babies in metaphysical and spiritual education.[2]

In many of his speeches Vivekananda did not make a verbal distinction between Hindu and Indian spirituality, and between the Hindu 'race' and Indians. This is a particularly suspicious formulation for contemporary readers because the binary of a materialistic West and a spiritual India has been played upon by the Sangh ceaselessly to promote its brand of pseudo-nationalism.[*] And once Indian spirituality has been deliberately conflated with Hinduism, the way is open to fuse nationalism and Hinduism.

While this part of Vivekananda's discourse has formed the basis for a crop of academics to suspect Vivekananda of Hindu chauvinism, and for the Sangh to claim him as a champion of Hindu exceptionalism, a different set of statements and assertions made by the monk has recently elicited the charge that far from being the social reformer he is widely known as, he was a social and cultural conservative, a figure whose attitudes aligned more closely with Hindu orthodoxy; represented by figures such as Bal Gangadhar Tilak. Tilak famously opposed the legislative prohibition of child marriage among Hindus, seeing it as interference by the government in the religious affairs of the Hindu

---

*See, for example, 'Book Launch Of "Culture During Crisis" By Dr. Subramanian Swamy And Ms Jaya Jaitly', available <https://indiaeducationdiary.in/book-launch-of-culture-during-crisis-by-dr-subramanian-swamy-and-ms-jaya-jaitly>.

community.* While Vivekananda's writings, speeches, and correspondence are filled with vehement denunciations of child marriage, the oppressed state of women in Hindu society, caste discrimination, lack of social freedom, and other ills, there are indeed a small number of comments where he seems to be rationalizing these customs, or at least their historical genesis. The charge of social and religious orthodoxy is sustained only by selectively focusing on these statements to the exclusion of most of what Vivekananda said on these subjects. This is neither sound methodology nor objective. At the same time, those who understand Vivekananda as a liberal and socially progressive figure need to offer an explanation for these seeming contradictions in Vivekananda's viewpoint.

Both these lines of interpretation, one characterizing Vivekananda as a Hindu chauvinist and the other as a conservative, are misreadings. They occur not so much from historical anachronism as a complete lack of attention to Vivekananda's social and political situation. A careful reading of *The Complete Works of Swami Vivekananda* in itself reveals the rough contours of the sociopolitical context he was working within and which forms the setting within which to properly evaluate his assertions. But a deeper study, as attempted in this chapter, of the social geography and the network of interactions within which Vivekananda operated will serve to make the situation clearer.

To understand the civilizational claims Vivekananda made for Hinduism, and his reasons for making them, we need to acquaint ourselves with the colonial narrative surrounding Hinduism in the nineteenth century and the ideas that held currency in that period. The British understood India as a dominantly Hindu civilization and Vivekananda occupied a peculiar position—a colonized subject who preached religion to the colonizer. British and European imperialism worked not only by force of arms, but by creating a narrative about the subject race and its civilization.

This narrative, which operated through all the instrumentalities of the empire, created a cultural hegemony by othering the East, Hindus, and India as savage, pagan, sensual, barbarous, idolatrous, effeminate, irrational, and primitive in contrast to the civilized, rational, masculine, and scientific West. Social evils like the caste system, poverty, attitudes towards women, infant marriage, sati, and religious superstitions, were often recruited to the cause of the colonial cultural narrative.

---

*Tilak was apparently personally opposed to child marriage. But he considered it an internal matter of reform for the Hindu community, rather than an object of government action.

Stereotypes, false beliefs, and ignorance about India and Hinduism informed the audiences Vivekananda lectured to in the West, determined their attitude towards him and set the stage for his perorations. The situation is complicated by the fact that religion was part of the story in a big way. For the West, Christianity was both a source of self-definition and a cultural narrative that served imperialist hegemony. The term 'civilization and light', originally part of the eighteenth century reaction against the Catholic Church, had been appropriated by both evangelical Christianity and imperialism. Western prosperity was adduced as a testament to the truth of Christianity and both the empire and Christianity were self-invested with a mission to civilize and enlighten the peoples of Asia and Africa.

The binary of the spiritual East and the materialistic West were not simply stereotypes floating in the air that Vivekananda latched on to. They came about because Vivekananda boldly contested bigoted assumptions about the superiority of Western civilization and turned the colonial narrative on its head. It was an act of resistance, of clearing the ground, of creating the very possibility that he could address his colonial interlocutors as equals. And this was by no means an easy task. To challenge the cultural assumptions and identities of a civilization on its home ground, that too from the position of the 'other', required considerable intellectual ability, force of personality, and mental dexterity. Vivekananda had all of these and used them with considerable skill to create the conditions necessary to deliver his message.*

THE COLONIAL DISCOURSE ABOUT INDIA AND HINDUISM

The first civilizational encounter of the British with India did not start with the racist, bigoted, and self-serving assumptions that would come to define them later. Early British imperial policy in India was driven by the idea that the empire could be best administered by understanding the people's languages, history, and culture. A group of Orientalist scholars, many of them civil servants of the East India Company, delved deeply into the languages and literatures of India, especially Sanskrit. The most significant contribution came from the British judge Sir William Jones, whose philological research into Sanskrit established that Sanskrit had a common origin with European languages, all of them having descended from an ancient common language, which is now

---

*The last four paragraphs appeared in a slightly modified form in 'Hindu not Hindutva', *Fountain Ink*, 6 October 2014.

termed Proto-Indo-Aryan. It also led to the theory that Indians and Europeans were descended from a common race of nomadic horsemen called the Aryans who migrated to different continents from an original home, whose location was the subject of much debate during the nineteenth century. Most scholars today identify it with the Central Asian steppes.

The idea of the common descent of Europeans and Indians went some way in creating a sense of commonality, even kinship, with a people that Europeans found exotic, bewildering, and backward. This led to a respect, even veneration among Orientalist scholars for the ancient civilizational achievements of India. Rather than seeing India as a society that had yet to reach a state of civilization, the Orientalists began perceiving India as a great civilization that had collapsed, like the Romans, and was in a state of decay. As an Aryan language much older than even classical Greek, the literature of Sanskrit attracted much scholarly interest. William Jones founded the Asiatic Society in Calcutta in 1783, with the support of then governor general of Bengal, Warren Hastings. Till Jones's death, the Asiatic society was an important centre for spreading his ideas about the importance of Hindu learning and of the considerable importance of Sanskrit among the Aryan languages. The society collected and published thousands of manuscripts in Sanskrit and other Indian languages, stimulating widespread philological, linguistic, literary, and philosophical enquiries among both European and Indian scholars.[3]

The British also established Fort William College in Calcutta in 1800, initially with the aim of training British recruits of the East India Company. Later it became a centre of research into Indian languages, whose scholars standardized non-classical Indian languages, codifying, compiling, and producing dictionaries and formal grammar books. The college also employed famous Sanskritists like Henry Thomas Colebrooke and John Gilchrist. It offered courses in Arabic, Persian, and Urdu, popularizing the literature of these languages. The work emanating from Fort William inspired the emergence of modern regional literature in many languages, including Bengali. The scholarship produced at the college eventually contributed to the intellectual ferment of the Bengal Renaissance.[4]

However, as the nineteenth century progressed, there occurred a decisive shift in the attitude of the British which was to have very detrimental consequences for the future of the Empire in India. Brian Pennington, in his historical study of the colonial construction of Hinduism writes: 'Sometime between 1789 and 1832, the British perception of Hindu religious traditions underwent a seismic shift. Sir William Jones had complained in 1789 that

Hindu mythology confronted the historian with a virtually impenetrable "cloud of fables," but by 1832 utilitarians and missionaries were rejecting…Jones's abiding appreciation for [their] antiquity and beauty…. Their many differences notwithstanding, Protestant evangelicals and utilitarians a generation after Jones were united against the Orientalists he represented in their insistence that, beneath a veil of confusion and contradiction, Hindu traditions operated with clear, regular, and sinister principles that demanded disclosure.'[5]

One of the first and most significant events of this shift was the appearance of utilitarian philosopher James Mill's book *The History of British India*. First published in 1819 and immensely popular, the book became highly influential in shaping colonial policy towards India. It also moulded educated opinion in Britain about Indians, Hindus, and Hinduism. An enlarged and revised fifth edition was published as late as 1858, just five years before Vivekananda's birth. Despite Mill's serious scholarship, the whole book was enveloped in extreme racism, prejudice, and cultural superiority. Mill wrote: 'Whenever indeed we seek to ascertain the definite and precise ideas of the Hindus in religion, the subject eludes our grasp. All is loose, vague, wavering, obscure, and inconsistent. Their expressions point at one time to one meaning, and another time to another meaning; and their wild fictions…seem rather the playsome whimsies of monkeys in human shape than the serious asseverations of a being who dignifies himself with the name of the rational.'[6] Theodore Koditschek, a prominent historian specializing in the history of the British Empire in the nineteenth century, called Mill's work part of the 'British assault on Indian history'. Koditschek writes, 'Mill's *History* became, in fact, a tract for the times. Its arrogant indictment of Indian civilization corresponded all too well with the needs of an imperial power whose rapidly expanding might and influence had made it the dominant force in the subcontinent.'[7]

The British read Indian civilization and culture as predominantly Hindu. The construction of the 'Indian' in the British mind was usually synonymous with Hindu. The reasons for this are not completely clear, and require further historical research, but one can speculate that part of the reason is that Europe had had encounters with Islam since the Middle Ages and also shared roots with it due to a common Abrahamic religious tradition. Hinduism on the other hand was far more exotic and 'other'. The outcome of this was that everything that was alien, bewildering and difficult about Indians, or offended British sensibilities, was usually given Hindu roots. Mill, who had never even set foot in India, wrote confidently, 'under the glossing exterior of the Hindu, lies a general disposition to deceit and perfidy'. He wrote that, 'the same insincerity, mendacity, and perfidy; the same indifference to the feelings of others; the same prostitution and venality' were the conspicuous characteristics of both the Hindus and the Muslims.[8] 'The Muslims, however, were perfuse, when possessed of wealth, and devoted to pleasure; the Hindus almost always penurious and ascetic'; and 'in truth, the Hindoo like the eunuch, excels in the qualities of a slave'.[9] Other epithets liberally applied by the philosopher-historian to the Hindus included 'dissembling', 'mendacious', and 'treacherous'; in his opinion, the Hindus possessed these qualities to 'an excess which surpasses even the usual measure of uncultivated society'.[10]

Racial attitudes continued to harden as the century progressed, taking a turn for the worse after the revolt of 1857.[11] As the rule of India passed from the British East India Company to the British government in 1858, what can be called the era of imperialism proper, took birth. As Brian Pennington puts it: 'With the British established as clear overlords through violence and coercion, ruling ideologies that took for granted the superiority of British blood and culture over their Indian counterparts also gained ascendency.'[12] Fearful of the possibility of another revolt, British imperial policy and practice embraced the need for controlling the Indian population. It was thus underpinned by a racial ideology which envisaged Europeans, especially Anglo-Saxons, as a master race equipped to rule and Indians as an inferior one incapable of self-administration. This narrative, which was enacted through the various institutions and structures of the colonial state, resonated with a discourse of very different origins—of British and American Christian missionaries working in India.

The British administration in India did not encourage missionary activity or the attempt to convert Hindus to Christianity. They were even chary about it. But at the level of social discourse, the imperialistic narrative of racial and civilizational superiority over Hindus, blended with and strengthened the missionary discourse of the superiority of Christianity over Hinduism. The social position that British missionaries occupied in India at the time, clubbed with a British-owned English press that was sympathetic to their views, meant they wielded enormous power in shaping public discourse. Missionaries occupied important positions—as educationalists in the most important colleges, as scholars, as administrators of charities and of hospitals. While they made extremely important contributions in all these fields, they were also driven by the vision of converting India to a Christian country and saving the souls of millions of heathens. Their success in this endeavour fell far short of the expectations of the missionary enterprise, with mass conversions being confined to relatively few areas. But this did not deter these zealous men, whose continued quest for Christianizing India was driven by the Christian theological conviction that accepting Christ as the redeemer was essential for the salvation of the soul after death. This quest took the form of a continued assault on Hinduism as a religion. As a result, many Hindu intellectuals found themselves in the position of apologists for their religion, having to justify the beliefs and practices of Hinduism in an unequal dialogue where the terms of discussion were set by British Christians.

All this was filtered through deep Protestant and Western prejudices about Hindus and Indians. In the hands of crude and bigoted men, the missionary effort became grossly abusive and vituperative.* But even in the hands of the learned and sophisticated, and amidst the most civilized discussions, Christian commentary on Hinduism was more often than not deeply insulting and disparaging. For example, William Hastie, the erudite principal of General Assembly's Institution who sent Vivekananda to meet Ramakrishna Paramahamsa, published a treatise on Hinduism around the same time. Titled *Hindu Idolatry and English Enlightenment: Six Letters Addressed to Educated Hindus Containing a Practical Discussion of Hinduism*, it concluded that Hinduism was 'groundless superstition'.[13] It is worth noting here that for a fervent Protestant like Hastie, even Catholics were idolaters for worshipping saints and relics. William Hastie wrote that the Hindu practice of worshipping idols led to 'senseless mummeries, loathsome impurities…every conceivable form of licentiousness, falsehood, injustice, cruelty, robbery, murder…. Its sublimest spiritual states have been but the reflex of physiological conditions in disease.'[14] It is important to note here that Hastie was no bigot. He was beloved by his Indian students and Vivekananda spoke fondly of him. He was also a trained philosopher who went on to produce the first English translation of Immanuel Kant's astronomical treatise *Universal Natural History and Theory of the Heavens*. It was simply that in the colonial discourse of the day, such treatment of Hinduism was normalized.

The Anglo-American missionary enterprise in India was more than a century old when Vivekananda went to America. The first influential British missionary to arrive in India was William Carey, who had an illustrious career as a scholar

---

*Dayanand Saraswati reacted against this by attacking Christianity and constructing a rational form of Hinduism that would be immune to Christian critique. But this required going back to an imagined golden age of Vedic Hinduism, a notion introduced first by British Orientalists. Dayanand Saraswati's version of Vedic Hinduism, as propagated by the Arya Samaj, however, was very different from contemporary Hinduism. It abandoned idol and temple worship and many other components most Hindus think of as essential to their religious practice.

and social reformer. Arriving in Calcutta in 1793, he later moved to Serampore in Bengal and established a university there. He played an important role in the movement to end sati. He served as a professor at Fort William and produced a translation of the Ramayana from Sanskrit into English. But in spite of this deep engagement with Indian society and its literary traditions, in his reports back to Britain, Carey painted Hinduism in the dreariest light. Many followed in Carey's footsteps in the course of a century. Missionary polemic not only posed the challenge of self-justification to Hinduism in India, but throughout the nineteenth century, missionary reports were the main source of information about Hinduism and India for the Western public. These reports, sent by evangelical missionaries to their sponsors in Britain and America, and which were later published in Christian literature, formed the basis on which the English-speaking world constructed the image of Hindus and India.[15]

The construction of Hindus, the Orient, and Africa was also an exercise in the construction of Western self-identity. The Hinduism that emerged through missionary eyes was filtered through both their experiences as proselytizers and through Christian theological prejudices and dogma. 'Missionary reports from India also reflected the experience of foreigners in a land whose native inhabitants and British rulers often resented their presence.... Plagued with anxieties and fears about their own health, regularly reminded of colleagues who had lost their lives or reason, uncertain of their own social location, and preaching to crowds whose reactions ranged from indifference to amusement to hostility, missionaries found expression for their darker misgivings in their production of what is surely part of their speckled legacy: a fabricated Hinduism crazed by blood-lust and devoted to the service of devils,' writes Pennington.[16]

One of Carey's close associates at Serampore was journalist-turned-missionary William Ward, who became probably the single most influential reporter on India to the West. William Ward was a close observer of the life, manners, and practices of Hindus. His writings were filled with vivid detail, giving them a sense of authenticity which added to their wide appeal.[*] But Ward interpreted Hindu India through the lens of an imagination fuelled by racial and religious prejudice, with the result that the Hinduism he constructed was a phantasmagoria of the fears, hidden obsessions, and anxieties that lurked in the unconscious of Protestant Christendom. Ward raised his voice against sati and called for its elimination, just like Indian reformers such as Raja Ram Mohan Roy

---

*Ward published a massive, four-volume book *Account of the Writings, Religion, and Manners of the Hindoos between 1807 and 1811*. In 1815 he published a slightly abridged version of two volumes titled *A View of the History, Literature and Mythology of the Hindoos*.

and many British orientalists. The latter opposed sati because they considered it an aberration and a regionally restricted practice that was unrepresentative of Hinduism and had no sanction in the scriptures. For Ward, however, sati was a manifestation of the violence against women inherent in Hinduism. He characterized sati as uniquely violent in the world's cultural history, writing that 'nothing equal to it exists in the whole work of human cruelty'.[17] Ward informed his readers that sati, infanticide, and human sacrifice were practices essential to the Hindu faith. Ward cited many alleged instances of Hindu practices which he said showed the uniquely violent nature of Hinduism. For example, Ward claimed that religious suicide was common and that devotees sacrificed themselves to deities ritually. Infanticide too was a practice that had religious sanction. He claimed many Hindu women left sick babies hanging in baskets on trees unattended through the night to expiate evil spirits. But in the morning only tiny skeletons were left by the ants and birds.[18]

In a volume of his writing exclusively dedicated to Hinduism as a religion[*], Ward reviewed the pernicious social effects of Hindu beliefs. They included adultery, ingratitude, flattery, lying, murder, greed, and gambling. For Ward, the defining characteristics of Hindu religious practice were violence and eroticism. He concluded that 'there is not a vestige of real morality in the whole of the Hindoo system; but…it adds an overwhelming force to the evil influences to which men are exposed, and raises into a horrid flame all the impure and diabolical passions which rage in the human heart.'[19]

Extracts and images from Ward's writing continued to appear in the English-speaking world as late as the 1857 revolt. Ward's ideas did not just influence laymen, but also policymakers, administrators, and intellectuals in the Anglo-American world. Ward's writings were a major source for James Mill's book on the history of India. Another event which suggests his lasting impact is an address delivered to the British Parliament in 1793 by William Wilberforce, the most prominent British anti-slavery crusader, who also happened to be an evangelist. He told the House of Commons that 'to all who have made it their business to study the nature of idolatrous worship in general, I scarcely need remark, that in its superstitious rites, there has commonly been found to be a natural alliance between obscenity and cruelty; and of the Hindoo

---

[*]Brian Pennington comments on Ward's *A View of the History, Literature and Mythology of the Hindus* that the major flaws in the final product come primarily not from factual errors, 'but from a selective highlighting of certain sensational events, his uncritical reliance on hearsay, and his generalisations about Hindu ritual on the basis of his observations of local Bengali practices.' See *Was Hinduism Invented?*, p. 90.

superstitions it may truly be affirmed, that they are scarcely less bloody than lascivious.'[20]

An interesting non-Indian counterpoint is provided by the contemporary Catholic French missionary Abbé J. A. Dubois. Dubois shared with Protestant missionaries their horror at the idol worship of Hindus and deep antipathy to Hindu social customs in general. But he had a far more sympathetic view of Hindus and Hinduism. After more than three decades of work in India, he returned to France convinced that it was not possible to convert the majority of Hindus to Christianity. He published a book on Hindu religion and social life in French. He then engaged in a series of exchanges with Protestant missionaries, objecting to the way they represented India and Hindus to the West. He wrote that evangelical proselytization would not work because in the eyes of Protestants Hindus were 'nothing but barbarians, without a spark of virtue'.[21] In an appendix to his book *Vindication of the Hindoos, both Males and Females*, he attacked Ward, expressing sadness that 'a peaceful and submissive people have been made the target of malevolence'.[22] He rebuked the Protestants for filling India with Bibles when what the people urgently needed was food and clothing. He refuted Protestant allegations of the dishonesty and moral turpitude of Hindus, defended their character, and dismissed these claims as simply lies meant to attract public attention and generate money for the evangelical mission.

There are several similarities between Vivekananda's own views on Anglo-American missionary activity and that of Abbé Dubois. Vivekananda did not question the right of the missionaries to try and spread their religion. But he objected to their vilification of Hinduism and their tendency to exaggerate social evils for ulterior motives. More than anything he felt that if America and Britain wanted to really help India, the money poured into missionary efforts would be much better spent providing material resources to her poverty-stricken people.

AMERICA AND HINDOOS

Hardly six months after his speech in Chicago, Vivekananda was lecturing in Detroit. He wrote to the Hale sisters of Chicago from there, commenting on the absurdities that were said and written about him in America. 'The funniest thing said about me here was in one of the papers which said, "The cyclonic Hindu has come and is a guest with Mr. Palmer. Mr. Palmer has become a Hindu and is going to India; only he insists that two reforms should be carried out: firstly that the Car of Jagannath should be drawn by Percherons (a breed of horse)* raised in Mr. Palmer's Loghouse Farm, and secondly that the Jersey cow be admitted into the pantheon of Hindu sacred cows.'"[23]

What the unnamed newspaper wrote about Vivekananda was of course absurd, as were many things Vivekananda had to respond to. He was often asked by audiences why Hindu women threw their babies to the crocodiles in the Ganga. An American newspaper reported that Vivekananda once responded to this question by saying that he too had been thrown into the river as a baby but because he was a fat baby and difficult to chew, the crocodiles returned him. He was frequently asked why devotees threw themselves under the wheels of Jagannath's ratha, chariot, to die (the term juggernaut in English derives from this myth). Many newspapers reported that Vivekananda was a raja, maybe on the basis of the colourful clothes he wore. Others described him as a Brahmin high priest. (Vivekananda was neither a priest nor Brahmin). Other American responses to Vivekananda were more in the realm of the abusive than the humorous; during the early period of his stay in America, in many newspaper reports and meetings he attended, he was referred to as a heathen or pagan.

Let us take a look at what impressions, ideas, and notions American audiences shared about Hindus and India before Vivekananda initiated what was fundamentally an intercultural dialogue. Consisting of the educated upper and middle classes, these Americans would have drawn their first ideas of India at school. Samuel Augustus Mitchell, whose geography textbook was the most circulated in America before 1900, used race as the primary category of analysis for the different societies of the world. Titled *A System of Modern Geography* and first published in 1844, it described the human race as 'differing greatly from each other in colour, form, and features'. Mitchell argued that these physical characteristics primarily defined race. The primary race categories the textbook identified were European, Asiatic, African, American (American Indian), and Malay. The textbook made it explicit that there was a hierarchy among these races; Europeans, at the top of this race hierarchy, were the noblest race in the world. Mitchell instructed students that the European race 'excels all others in learning and the arts and includes the most powerful nations of ancient and modern times. The most valuable institutions of society and the most important useful inventions have originated with the people of this race.' The textbook was mostly read by common school students who were almost exclusively white and Protestant.[24]

---

*My insertion.

As part of the exercises included in the textbook, students were asked to identify which racial category they belonged to. This kind of racial discourse was not unique to Mitchell's textbook, but was representative of the kind of educational material that gave American students an idea of the world and peoples outside the United States. These schoolbooks classified societies based on how far they were perceived to have become civilized, and generally placed 'savage' societies at the bottom of the race ladder. These were societies that were yet to develop material civilization. Higher up were the 'half-civilized' societies. In his study of how Hinduism and Hindus were represented in America in the eighteenth and nineteenth centuries, Michael J. Altman describes how this category was conceived. 'These societies had established laws and religion, could read and write, and had some commerce. But they also treated their women as slaves, and were "very jealous of strangers".'[25] Most Asian countries, including India, fell under this category. At the top of the hierarchy came societies that were deemed to have obtained civilization. The penultimate category was that of 'civilized societies'. The defining characteristics of being civilized were knowledge of science, printing, and technology and the humane treatment of women. The societies that were included in the group were largely East European and South European. These were Christian countries which were not Protestant, and mainly followed either the Catholic or the Greek Orthodox Church and were described as people who continued to believe in superstitions. They also oppressed the poorer sections of society. At the apex of the civilizational ladder stood the 'enlightened societies'. This mainly comprised the United States and Western European countries. The enlightened societies were described as having advanced science and art to its zenith, of having raised women to 'their proper station in society, as equals with, and companions for the male sex',[26] and having developed political systems which allowed freedom to citizens. White American school students were hence made aware from a very young age that they were part of the most superior race, civilization, and religion.

Other textbooks of the period like Roswell Smith's *Geography on the Productive System* and Samuel Goodrich's *A System of School Geography* followed the same pattern. Another textbook by Goodrich for younger children called *Peter Parley's Geography for Beginners* begins its section on India thus: 'I shall now tell you of a people, who may be regarded as the most interesting of all the inhabitants of Asia, I mean the Hindoos...the Hindoos, in personal appearance, in disposition, in character, and in religion, are a distinct and peculiar nation.'[27] India and 'Hindoos' were represented as exotic and different from Americans to school children at the precise age when they were forming their self-identity. 'American children needed to learn they were white, Protestant, and enlightened before they encountered others in the pages of schoolbooks. When they encountered India, they could identify Hindoos as brown, half-civilized, pagan, and inferior to themselves in all three categories. While these differences could be the engine for missionary outreach, they also buttressed children's self-understanding as white Protestant Americans,' writes Michael J. Altman.[28]

The caste system was given similar treatment through an ethno-religious, nationalist lens. The condemnation of the institution was packaged into the ideological project of valorizing a free, Protestant, and civilized America in contradistinction to a Hindu India of opposite qualities. The textbooks *The Tales of Peter Parley about Asia* and *Lights and Shadows of Asiatic History* are two examples of this. Even at a time when most southern states in America kept millions of African Americans as chattel slaves, Americans conceived of themselves as a uniquely free society by virtue of its democracy and the absence of institutionalized classes as in Europe. Thus, American society was considered civilized and non-hierarchical in nature. Protestantism was held to have played a fundamental role in the development of both political and social freedom in America. The majority of Americans at that time were migrants from Britain. As such they defined their Protestantism in opposition to both Catholicism and the Anglican Church. Freedom of individual conscience was one of the foundational issues on which reformed Christianity had split from Catholicism. Protestants thus saw Catholicism, which held individual belief in abeyance to church decreed dogma, as religion under the bondage of authority. In rejecting many non-Biblical practices like the worship of icons, saints, relics, and so on that had accrued to the Catholic tradition over the centuries from various pagan cultures, Protestantism considered that it was rejecting superstition.

As recently migrated Protestants trying to build their own traditions of national self-identity, they identified themselves against what they saw as an authority worshipping, hierarchical, superstitious, and idolatrous Catholicism. It was easy for religious Americans to imagine that it was a Protestant ethic of freedom from authority, superstition, and hierarchy that provided the philosophical and moral force to American democracy, progress, and society. The Hindu caste system was represented as a product of the superstitious idolatry of Hindu religion. In fact, comparisons between Hinduism and Catholicism were often explicitly drawn on this basis. Belief in the caste system was presented as essential to the Hindu faith analogous to the manner in which a belief in the incarnation of Christ is essential to most forms of Christianity or belief in the oneness of God (Tawhid) is to Islam. Hindus were supposed to believe in the four-fold division of society into four hierarchical castes because it was God's dispensation. Here, blind belief in religious authority, translated, just as with Europe's Catholic countries, into a hierarchical society without freedom, though one which was far more religiously perverse and socially unjust. The caste system was a sign of not just an uncivilized society but of an inferior and superstitious religious faith.

An example of school instruction where all the defining differences of science, religion, and civilization come together in the representation of Hinduism, is provided in a school textbook of the time authored by Salem Town and Nelson M. Halbrook. In their *The Progressive Third Reader*, first published in 1857, a chapter called 'The Theory of Rain' depicts India and Hindus through a story. The story is about a fictional dialogue between the famous Scottish missionary to India, Alexander Duff and an Indian youth. Alexander Duff was, interestingly enough, the founder of the General Assembly's Institution, where a young Narendranath Dutta had studied. In the story, Duff is talking to a young Hindu man who is simply named 'Hindoo'. The discussion is about where rain comes from. 'Hindoo' says that rain comes from the trunk of Indira's elephant; his guru has told him that thus it is written in the scriptures. Duff then proceeds to demonstrate the scientific principles behind cloud formation to the young man. He uses several examples like a pot of water boiling with the lid on it, to explain how water vapour rises and forms clouds. The man's eyes are opened by Duff's explanation. He exclaims: 'Ah, our Shastra must be false! Our Shastra must be either not from God, or God must have written lies!'[29] With that, Hindoo was on the path to becoming Christian and rational.

Where did these textbooks prescribed for American school children get their material on India from? It came, not surprisingly, from American evangelical and missionary literature. The reach of such literature was much greater in America than in Britain, which had witnessed a great Protestant religious revival in the beginning of the nineteenth century (Second Great Awakening: 1795–1835) and consequently remained a more traditionally Protestant society than their English cousins. Though at first American missionary literature usually reproduced the accounts of British missionaries in India, it likely underwent a transformation as it was filtered through the lens of an ethnocentric American Protestantism. As Altman points out in *Heathen, Hindoo, Hindu*, the positing of the Hindu as a defining civilizational and religious 'other' for national self-determination was a distinctly American phenomenon.[*]

Some of the earliest depictions of Hindus to become popular in America were the reports of the East India Company chaplain Claudius Buchanan. 'Buchanan presented Hindoo religion as a bloody, violent, superstitious, and backward religious system that needed to be overcome by the bright light of the gospel. Buchanan presented this image of Hindoo religion to Americans through a piece of Indian religious culture that dominated their imaginations for the rest of the century: the Juggernaut.'[30] Juggernaut is the anglicized name of Jagannath, the deity at the Jagannath temple in Puri in Odisha. The wide circulation of this term and the story associated with it received in America can be seen in the fact that the word is used today in modern English to describe a force that is merciless, destructive, and unstoppable. Even when Vivekananda arrived in America in 1893, 'Juggernaut' was the image most commonly associated with Hinduism. The oft-repeated myth that the deity's devotees killed themselves by throwing themselves under his chariot originated with Buchanan's reports from Puri where he is supposed to have spent a week during the annual procession of the deity. Buchanan wrote that during the procession of Jagannath, (Ratha Yatra) he saw devotees throwing themselves under the giant chariot and getting crushed to death. He described the idol itself as bloody and claimed that the Hindus believed that Jagannath was pleased with every new sacrifice. Along with Buchanan, other American missionaries equated Hinduism with bloodthirstiness and violence. For them, practices like hook-swinging which drew blood were the essence of Hinduism as a religion.

Buchanan not only painted Hinduism as a religion of violence, he also cast it in Biblical terms as the antithesis of Christianity. According to him, 'Juggernaut' was the 'chief seat of Moloch on the whole earth'.[31] (Moloch is the Biblical name of a Canonite God associated with child sacrifice). He described Puri as another Golgotha (the place of Jesus's crucifixion) filled with skulls. He also compared the scene of the Jagannath festival to the valley of 'Hinnon' from the Old Testament where children are sacrificed to false Gods.[32]

Other than violence, Buchanan also introduced a theme with which Hinduism was to be associated in the Anglo-American and, to an extent, the European mind throughout the century—sexual perversity. Victorian moral norms and taboos prevented Buchanan, and other missionaries and travellers

---

*On the other side of the coin, it is only in America (other than Germany) that Hindu philosophy exercised a distinct cultural influence. The American transcendentalists of the nineteenth century, including Ralph Waldo Emerson and Henry David Thoreau were directly, or indirectly, inspired by the philosophy of the Upanishads and the Bhagavad Gita.

who followed in his wake, to explicitly describe the wanton licentiousness that they alleged went on in Hindu temples, but they gave the most tantalizing and dark hints. He describes the exterior of the Puri Jagannath temple thus: 'As other temples are usually adorned with figures emblematical of their religion; representations (numerous and various) of that vice, which constitutes the essence of his worship. The walls and gates are covered with indecent emblems, in massive and durable sculpture.'[33] During the ratha yatra Buchannan reported that he witnessed a priest pronounce 'obscene stanzas' and 'a boy of about twelve years was then brought forth to attempt something yet more lascivious...the child perfected the praise of his idol with such ardent expression and gesture, that the god was pleased...and the multitude emitting a sensual yell of delight, urged the car along.'[34] After that an 'aged minister of the idol then stood up, and with a long rod in his hand, which he moved with indecent action, completed the variety of this disgusting exhibition.' Buchanan wrote that he 'felt a consciousness of doing wrong in witnessing it'. The noise made by the Hindu worshippers drew his comments in several articles he published. In one, he described the sounds made by the women devotees as 'a kind of hissing applause'. He wrote that they 'emitted a sound like that of whistling, with their lips circular, and the tongue vibrating: as if a serpent would speak by their organs, uttering human sounds', and compared it to the hissing sound of Satan's assembly in Milton's *Paradise Lost*.[35]

After Buchanan's accounts first appeared, American missionaries started travelling to India. The myth of the Juggernaut and his fanatic Hindu devotees became a staple theme of the missionary depiction of Hinduism in America. The motif of violence as a defining element of Hinduism was built upon by American missionaries. Apart from the depravities of the Jagannath festival, early reports from American missionaries dwelt on other bloody aspects like sacrifice of roosters and lambs, and the practice of hook-swinging. These practices were not only portrayed in lurid language as violent and bloody, but as constituting the essence of Hinduism. In the report of an early American missionary in Bombay, describing how roosters were sacrificed to the goddess of wealth 'Luxumee', the devotees are said to apply the blood of the dead animal to their foreheads. In another account, the same missionary offered the image of scores of sheep being sacrificed to the idol in minute detail, including the opening up of the sheep's belly and the removal of the liver. All these elements were painted as ritualistic norms of Hinduism. The idea of violence and sacrifice as an interlinked concept in Hinduism was extended to other social ills, which have been described more neutrally by contemporary social observers and reformers as products of institutional oppression. Sati for example was called 'female sacrifice', evoking the human sacrifices of pre-Abrahamic pagan religions condemned in the Old Testament. From exaggeration and distortion, sometimes the missionary reports passed into speculative fantasy. Human sacrifice was often hinted at or even claimed to occur, furthering the violence–sacrifice equation. For example, an American missionary report from Bombay narrated: 'there is good evidence that human sacrifices, within a few years past, and within a few miles of Bombay, have been repeatedly made on various occasions to local deities.'[36]

Along with blood and violence, American missionaries followed Buchanan's lead in establishing sexual licentiousness as one of the defining characteristics of Hinduism. The earliest American missionaries, who settled in Bombay, condemned the dancing that accompanied Hindu festivals as obscene and erotic. They thundered in their writings against 'those parts of the Hindoo system, which recommend and enforce impurity, licentiousness, and indecency, by annual exhibitions.'[37]

All these cultural tropes about Hindus and Indians which were introduced in America through missionary literature became stereotypes that acquired larger circulation in American society over time. We have already noted how by the mid-nineteenth century they formed the source for depictions of Hindus and Hinduism in school textbooks. They also influenced public figures, men of letters, and the educated public. In 1854, Caleb William Wright published *India and Its Inhabitants*, an immensely popular book on his travels in India. It was based on a series of lectures given by Wright, who had returned to America as an India expert. While Americans were getting used to reading about India, it was a rare thing to be able hear an eyewitness account of the country and its strange customs. Wright's lectures were enthusiastically attended not just by the masses but also by eminent personalities. His travelogue was endorsed by twenty prominent academicians including former and then presidents of Yale, Princeton, and Rutgers University.[38]

Wright was not a missionary and his aim in visiting India was not to convert Indians to Christianity. He was a traveller who was attracted by the lure of adventure and knowledge of a new and strange land. But the missionary discourse about Hinduism provided him with a readymade framework to interpret his experiences of India. While he writes about both the Hindus and Muslims he encountered in India, he saw Indian civilization as Hindu in character. And India's myriad problems, in the form he understood them, are traced back to the nature of Hindu society, which in turn is traced back to the nature of Hinduism, using the same line of reasoning employed for decades by British and American missionaries.

As he introduces his readers to the Hindu people, Wright uses an anecdote to illustrate a trait which he takes to be of the most general character of the 'mind of the Hindu'. 'An English gentleman devised various plans of introducing improvements. Among others, he wished to substitute wheelbarrows for the baskets in which the natives carried burdens on their heads. He caused several of these useful articles to be constructed, and labored with much assiduity to introduce them among his workmen. In his presence, they used them with apparent cheerfulness, and even admitted that they were far preferable to the baskets. The gentleman was delighted with his success. On one occasion, however, having been absent a few hours, on returning somewhat unexpectedly, he was surprised to find all his labourers carrying the wheelbarrows filled with earth on their heads.' Wright concluded from this apocryphal story that: 'Their unyielding attachment to ancient customs is the natural result of their religious belief. Any change, however slight, in the mode of labor or business, is a violation of religious duty. It is evident, therefore, that the comforts and improvements of civilised life can never be introduced among the Hindus until they become convinced of the falsity of their Shasters [sic] and the foolishness of their traditions. The first step in the process of reform and improvement is to renounce that system of religion which for thousands of years has held them in the most cruel bondage.'[39]

The influence of missionary literature in setting the terms of Wright's depiction of Hindus can be seen in the way he linked together several observations using the same cultural narratives that Christian missionaries produced about Hindus and Hindu civilization. The position of women in Hindu society is a case in point. Wright linked exaggerated accounts of female infanticide as well as the position of women in Hindu society to the falsity of pagan Hinduism. He wrote about female infanticide:

> So little valued is the life of female infants, within the domains of Paganism, that great numbers are put to death, solely to avoid the trouble and expense of feeding and clothing them. The singular custom formerly prevailed in the northern part of Hindustan, whenever a female child was born, of carrying her to the market-place, and there, holding up the child in one hand, and a knife in the other, proclaiming, that if any person wanted to rear her for a wife, they might then take her; if none appeared to accept of her, she was immediately destroyed. The consequence of this course, was, that the men of the tribe became much more numerous than the women; and hence arose the custom of appropriating several husbands

to one wife—a custom that still prevails in some of the southern as well as the northern tribes of Hindustan; among the Rajpoot tribes in the north-west part of that country nearly all the female children are put to death immediately after birth; consequently the men are obliged to procure their wives from other tribes.[40]

Both Hindu and Muslim women that Wright encountered in his travels in India lived in a state of oppression under their husbands, not because of social conditions, but because of the diktats of their false religions. Christianity, by contrast, had liberated women and given them an equal place in society, a fact that was one more testament to the inherent truth and justice of Christianity. Christianity was the only religion that could form a natural basis for a morality and a moral order in society. 'But the degradation of woman under the fell influence of false religions is not yet fully seen. She is her husband's slave, and with unquestioning servility, must yield to his behest, on penalty of torture, separation, or death. Nor is this a mere accident of her condition. The religion of her country decrees it—the sacred books demand it. The Koran, and the Hindu Shasters, whose doctrines sway the mind, and determine the practice, of more than two hundred millions of the human family, make woman infinitely man's inferior, the mere pander to his passions, the abject drudge, owing him unconditional submission.'[41]

The next link in the chain that equated social injustice with religious belief, equated religious belief with rationality. While female infanticide, polygamy, and the status of women in Hindu society showed the cruelty or immorality of the Hindu religion, the nature of this cruelty was not merely a moral failing; it proceeded from irrationality. Wright wrote in his travelogue: 'From time immemorial, Hindu mothers have thrown their infant children into the Ganges, to be devoured by alligators; not because they were destitute of maternal affection, but because a mother's love was overpowered by her fears of the wrath of some offended deity.'[42] The Hindu man or woman was not immoral by nature but acted that way because they were in thrall to a religion that was superstitious and cruel, because it was irrational. Christianity could redeem Hindus because it was rational, and hence humane.

Wright commented in length on the character of the Indian woman, who was unexposed to the rational and civilizing influence of Christianity. 'We have now cursorily glanced at the character of woman, as unaffected by the refining and elevating influences of Christianity. We have seen her trodden down as the mire of the streets by him whom Heaven created to be her protector and comforter.... We have seen her lost to self-respect, dead to instinctive affection, ignorant of the rights with which her Maker has invested her, unacquainted with her relations to eternity, indulgent to the wildest passions of depraved nature, and plunged far down the abyss of unnatural crime.'[43]

Paradoxically, even as Indian women were portrayed as victims of an uncivilized society as well as a superstitious religion, the character of Indian women was implicated in some of the very evils of which she was usually deemed the victim. Thus, Indian women were represented in literature and reports about India as callous, sexually profligate, immoral, ignorant, and without self-control. This reflected the double standards of the Protestant Christian discourse around American national identity. Its sense of civilizational superiority came partly from claiming an enlightened position for Western women. Even taken at face value, it was a dishonest claim. Women's emancipation, in so far as it had progressed in America or the West in general, was not a Protestant, let alone a Christian achievement. It was the legacy of the free thinker, the non-sectarian, and religious dissident, of the intellectual forces of a broadly anti-Christian modernity, which had to achieve rights for women mostly in the face of opposition from established religion. The double standard was reflected in the fact that in spite of professing the principle of women's equality, evangelical and missionary discourse operated with a tribal conception of women's honour as constitutive of the honour and prestige of the race. This value system was deployed most sharply in the project of civilizational hegemony in constructing the Hindu 'other'. The emancipated, morally pure, and chaste American woman was held up in contrast to the oppressed, sexually impure, and corrupted Indian or Hindu woman. The latter qualities went to indirectly affirm the superiority of a rational, Protestant, and materially superior American nation in comparison to an irrational, heathen, poverty-ridden India.

REPRESENTING HINDUISM AND INDIA TO THE WEST

The orthodox Protestant depiction of Hindu women is a particularly important point to bear in mind when dealing with many of the statements Vivekananda made in America and Britain about Indian women and their position in society. Today, when we read Vivekananda's speeches that touch on these issues in passing, we read them in isolation, divorcing them from their social context. In these speeches, while we do find many assertions of the inferior role women occupied in Indian society, we do not find, on the whole, an unmitigated condemnation of Indian society in regard to the treatment of women. On the other hand, Vivekananda is often defensive about the status of women in

Indian society. He refutes claims that Indian women are uniquely oppressed compared to other societies or that child marriage and female infanticide plague them. This was not because Vivekananda did not recognize that women were oppressed in India or did not disapprove stridently of child marriage. That he did is made abundantly clear in his recorded conversations with friends and disciples, and in his correspondence.

Less than three months after his speech at the Parliament of Religions, he wrote to Hari Pada Mitra contrasting the condition of American and Indian women. In the letter, written in Bengali, he touches upon the problem of child marriage as well. 'Few (American) women are married before twenty or twenty-five, and they are as free as the birds in the air. They go to market, school, and college, earn money, and do all kinds of work. Those who are well-to-do devote themselves to doing good to the poor. And what are we doing? We are very regular in marrying our girls at eleven years of age lest they should become corrupt and immoral.... Can you better the condition of your women? Then there will be hope for your well-being. Otherwise you will remain as backward as you are now.'[44] In another letter written a year later to Manmathanath Bhattacharya, Vivekananda even forges the same kind of link between the fate of Indian civilization and its treatment of women that Christian missionaries often did. He also states that it was a terrible mistake for the Hindu community to oppose the British government's efforts to bring a law banning child marriage. The law in question was the Age of Consent Act (1891) which criminalized sexual intercourse with a girl below the age of twelve. While Hindu social reformers supported the law and campaigned to bring it into being, orthodox Hindus opposed the reform as an interference in their religion. The country saw prolonged protests from the orthodox faction, in Calcutta, Bombay, Madras, and other regional centres. Vivekananda's views were in line with that of reformers like Justice Mahadev Ranade, and diametrically opposed to that of conservatives like Bal Gangadhar Tilak.

> You will have to stop this shameful business of marrying off nine-year-old girls. That is the root of all sins. It is a very great sin, my boy. Consider further what a terrible thing it was that when the government wanted to pass a law stopping early marriage, our worthless people raised a tremendous howl! If we don't stop it ourselves, the government will naturally intervene, and that is just what it wants to do.... O Lord, is there any punishment unless there has been a sin? It is all the fruit of Karma. If ours were not a terribly sinful nation, then why should it have been booted and beaten for seven hundred years?[45]

Vivekananda's assertions in the West defending Indian society against charges of oppressing women, child marriage, and occasionally the caste system, arose in discursive friction with hegemonizing Protestant American (and sometimes British) cultural narratives about India and Hinduism, woven around these very themes. The space did not exist in such a context for Vivekananda to present a neutral critique of Indian society. The picture of Indian society that was commonly shared by his audience, and critics (mostly orthodox Protestant clergymen), was deeply distorted along the lines described before. Any attempt by Vivekananda to criticize Indian society for its social ills would have been immediately assimilated within this discursive field of Protestant American civilizational superiority. To talk to his cultural interrogators as their equal, Vivekananda had to go on the offensive, employing a variety of rhetorical strategies. When presented with the cultural assumption that India was half-civilized because of the way it treated its women, Vivekananda had no option but to dispute what was being presented as fact. What he was disputing was exaggerated and distorted ideas of women's enslavement in India, which went to serve a Western imperialist agenda. In the same way, in several places Vivekananda stresses the 'purity' of Indian women. Taken without context, this may come off as an ideological obsession with the sexual purity of the nation's women, a thread that runs through many kinds of reactionary nationalisms, including Hindutva. But these assertions were made against the prevalent nineteenth-century Protestant narrative of Hindu women as sexually immoral and depraved.

A lot of recent scholarly attention has focused on the question of how Vivekananda represented Hinduism and India to the West, in the sense in which we understand representation now, in terms of how certain identities are represented in literature, art, or mass media. But this is the wrong question to ask and the analyses that have been produced on the basis of posing this question are consequently flawed, whether they see Vivekananda's efforts in a negative or positive light. This is because, to raise the question of representation is to assume, even if tacitly, that the power relationship between Vivekananda and his listeners was such that conditions for objective representation existed. This was manifestly not the case. For representation in the usual sense to occur, a certain level of neutrality from the receivers of the representation towards the object of representation needs to exist. This was not the case of the American and British audiences Vivekananda spoke to about India and Hinduism. The audience as subjects were already embroiled in a power dynamic with the object of representation, where the former's self-constitution in terms of nationality, race, and religion was crucially dependent on maintaining a power hierarchy with the latter. What Vivekananda attempted to do was to disrupt this power hierarchy sufficiently to create the conditions where some kind of representation would become possible. He had to try and strike a balance between giving a faithful account of conditions in India and contesting the Western cultural narrative about these conditions.

The possibility of representation also assumes a capacity on the part of the audience to receive knowledge about the object of representation. This is always severely lacking in the early stages of the encounter between two cultures which have little in common with each other nor are linked together through the mutual influence of a third culture. This fact has to be recognized if we are not to fall into the mistake of thinking that Vivekananda was constructing monolithic narratives about India and Hinduism when he talked about 'the Hindu mind', 'the character of the Hindu race', 'the soul of India', etc. (Such essentializing expressions were the standard fare of Victorian thinkers.) Equally many of his statements about Hinduism or India may appear to us as exaggerations or misrepresentations. But what is at work here is the limited space for accurate intercultural representation, which is only opened up during civilizational encounters such as the kind that took place between the West and India at the end of the nineteenth century. An illustrative example can be provided by how Vivekananda encountered the same difficulties when talking about aspects of Islam to Western audiences. As we have seen before, Vivekananda has used Islam as a foil against the West occasionally to point out the hypocrisies of Christianity's assumptions about itself. Thus, as discussed earlier, he averred on more than one occasion that Islam was the only religion which had succeeded in achieving equality among its followers. While it is perfectly correct that in many ways Islam went much beyond other ancient religious traditions in building an egalitarian society, Vivekananda's characterization of universal mutual acceptance among Muslims is highly misleading if it was to be taken at face value. It ignores the centuries of Sunni–Shia conflict, which included not only persecution but often bloody massacres. If the currently fashionable approach to reading Vivekananda on Hinduism were to be applied to this statement, the critic would accuse him of erasing the history of internecine violence within Islam to falsely construct the narrative of a Muslim people historically united in mutual affection. Of course, such a reading is patently absurd because Vivekananda is not a Muslim and had no investment in the construction of a Muslim identity.

But nonetheless, Vivekananda does make the claim of a universal egalitarianism for Islam. Why? For the same reason he made similar claims for Hinduism or India. The inter-cultural space in both instances was too narrow and did not allow for more accurate and nuanced representations. To talk of the sectarian violence that had marred the history of Islamic civilization at various points in history would only have served to feed into American conceptions of Islam as a violent religion. What Vivekananda could do in such a context was only to disrupt this conception. Only when such conceptions had been replaced with a fairer picture of the history of Islam would it be possible to introduce nuances, modifications, and differentiations to this picture. And because Americans' knowledge of Islam was limited and they knew and understood Islam only as a monolithic entity, Vivekananda could only use the same conception as his point of departure if he hoped to be understood. This is the same phenomena which, mutatis mutandis, occurred when Vivekananda spoke about Hinduism and India. But as he spoke of Hinduism far more and in innumerably varied contexts, this phenomenon of cultural incommensurability took on several complex forms. To try and give any kind of taxonomy of these forms would be tedious. It should be enough to say that the various forms bear enough similarity for the phenomena to be easily recognized and taken into account in interpreting Vivekananda's text.

To take another example, when Vivekananda undertook once in a speech to give an explanation of the genesis of child marriage in Indian society, he defended it as a logical custom within the material conditions that existed in ancient Indian society. There are a few things to keep in mind when we try to understand a statement of this kind. (Vivekananda likewise offered the occasional defence for lack of freedom of marriage among Indians, the evolution of the caste system, and some other social ills when speaking in the West.) Firstly, Vivekananda was not, in these instances, defending child marriage or the caste system or trying to rationalize them away as Hindu conservatives did. What he was trying to do was substitute historical explanations for the evangelical inspired moral explanations which indicted Indian civilization on the basis of these social ills.

A parallel can be drawn with the kind of explanation modern historians give for the rise of absolutism in Chinese and Islamic civilizations. The trope of the Oriental despot was a popular one in Victorian times, especially in the case of Islamic countries. European absolutism was seen as civilized and less oppressive in contrast, as the powers of the monarch were circumscribed by parliaments, estates, the nobility, or similar bodies. European monarchs were less given to acts of wanton and brutal cruelty compared to the Sultans of the

East or Chinese royalty, who wielded truly absolute power. The emperor of the Safavid empire in Iran, for example, was always accompanied in public by an executioner to carry out the ruler's orders.[46] 'Oriental despotism' was used by writers and thinkers of the Victorian age to indict the Chinese, Turks, and Arabs as an inherently cruel people. In the twentieth century, historians have foregone this moralistic approach and now tend to understand absolutism as a political institution necessary for structural reasons. In the Islamic lands from the Nile to the Amu Darya, the tribal nature of society needed a cohesive force from outside to hold it together. Absolute power vested in a single ruler who could stand apart from various tribal allegiances, was the logical solution found to the problem of erecting political institutions that could govern a society divided on lines of tribal affiliations.[47] To say this is not to deny the oppression inherent in these forms of absolutism, but to historicize it within the horizon of political possibilities which were available to Islamic civilizations. This is precisely what is at work in Vivekananda's occasional explanations for Hindu social ills as necessary historical developments.

THE WORLD'S PARLIAMENT OF RELIGIONS

As seen above, the narrative about Hinduism that American missionaries circulated in America from the second quarter of the nineteenth century onwards informed the representation of India in the American school curriculum well into the last quarter of the century. After the middle of the century both Europe and America underwent drastic changes that took them rapidly along the path to modernity. One of the consequent effects as noted before was an increasing secularization of the public sphere and state institutions and the decreasing hold of traditional religion. This was accelerated by the transformation America underwent through rapid urbanization and industrial capitalism. By the time Vivekananda arrived in America in 1893, atheism, which would have been socially unacceptable in the mid-century, no longer raised eyebrows. To be sure, most people continued to be staunch Christians and religion continued to have an outsized influence on their lives. But the nature of these religious commitments themselves had undergone significant changes. The rise of unitarianism and liberal Christianity, as well as the introduction of Darwin's theory of evolution and materialistic philosophies, influenced the stream of religious consciousness. Among the upper classes and polite society, religious dogmatism was weakened by the challenge of science and the need was strongly felt for a rational form of religion. This consequently produced a more open orientation towards other faiths. While Christianity was still regarded as the one true religion, more and more liberal clergymen and believers came to believe that all religions had some measure of truth in them.

This was the atmosphere in which the World Parliament of Religions was held in Chicago in 1893. It was the first and perhaps biggest interfaith conference held in the modern world. The stated intention of its organizers was to create a forum for religious harmony united by universal religious principles. The president of the Congress, Charles Bonney opened the Parliament with the words: 'This day the sun of a new era of religious peace and progress rises over the world, dispelling the dark clouds of sectarian strife. This day a new flower blooms in the gardens of religious thought, filling the air with its exquisite perfume. This day a new fraternity is born into the world of religious progress, to aid the upbuilding of the kingdom of God in the hearts of men.'[48] The delegations at the Parliament were truly international, though they excluded many ethnicities including native Americans. There were papers presented by Muslims, Hindus, Taoists, Buddhists, Shintoists, Jews, Jains, Confucians, and Zoroastrians. Americans, Europeans, Russians, Turks, Japanese, Chinese, and people from the Indian subcontinent, all spoke at the Parliament.

But the outward liberalism and universalism of the Parliament, was undercut by an agenda to showcase Western and Christian supremacy. Richard Hughes Seager, who studied the East–West encounter in the Parliament of Religions, notes that in spite of its ecumenical tendencies, a dominant strain in the proceedings of the Parliament was an ethnocentric Western triumphalism and the belief in the superiority of Christianity among the majority of the Protestant delegates.[49] To be sure, there were many Christian delegates who were broadminded and liberal like President Bonney. But the majority occupied a range of positions from Christian exceptionalism to extreme religious bigotry, which believed that every religion except Christianity was false and salvation was possible only through converting to Christianity. It is notable that most of the delegates from the other religions represented at the Parliament, especially those from Asia, did not hold to similar exclusive views of their own religion.

Many American and British missionaries who worked or were working in India presented papers on Hinduism. Even the friendliest of them, who often expressed profound admiration for the philosophical thought of Hinduism, nonetheless came across as patronizing. For example, the Reverend T. E. Slater, who had come from Bangalore, after comments that were extremely sympathetic and in parts even admiring of Hinduism, went on to say that the Indian religion was a foreshadowing of the Christian gospel. He said 'Brahminical Hinduism may be regarded as a preparation for the Gospel.... It should be borne in mind however throughout, that this foreshadowing relation between Hinduism and Christianity is ancient rather than modern, that these "foreshadowings" of the gospel are unsuspected by the masses of the people...the whole enquiry becomes clear only after we realize that Hinduism has been a keen and pathetic search after a salvation to be wrought by man, rather than a restful satisfaction in the redemption designed and offered by God.'[50]

On the other extreme, perhaps the most chauvinistic of the Christian delegates was the Boston priest, Reverend Joseph Cook (who interestingly had travelled to India and once met Sri Ramakrishna Paramahamsa). For Cook, the rise of modern science made it imperative that religion should conform to the scientific spirit, and the only religion that was capable of doing that in his opinion was Christianity. He started his address to the Parliament by quoting Shakespeare's famous lines on Lady Macbeth trying to wash away the invisible stains of blood on her hand after the murder of King Duncan. Drawing an allegory to sin, he asked 'I turn to Mohammedanism, can you wash away our red right hand? I turn to Confucianism and Buddhism and Brahmanism (Hinduism). Can you wash our red, right hands?'[51] The question was, of course, purely rhetorical. Cook answered it himself—only Christianity was able to offer mankind salvation. And other religions were true only as so far as they approximated Christianity. 'I turn to every faith on earth other than Christianity, and I find every such faith a Torso [sic]. But if its lines were completed it would be a full statue corresponding in expression with Christianity.... It is a certainty and a strategic certainty that, there is no religion in heaven and among men that effectively provides for the peace of the soul by its harmonisation with itself, its God and its record of sin.'[52] Evangelical missionary George Pentecost attacked the lack of morality of Hinduism and claimed that Indian temples housed 'hundreds of priestesses who were known as immoral and profligate' and who were 'prostitutes because they were priestesses and priestesses because they were prostitutes'.[53]

Interestingly, even some American newspapers criticized the Christian speakers. On 23 September 1893, *Every Saturday*, a local Chicago newspaper, wrote in its editorial that some of the comments by the Christian delegates were downright bigoted and barbaric:

The utterances of many of the Christian speakers at the religious congress tend to make one feel as though civility and charity were not characteristics of the Christian religion. In as much as this is a Christian country and that it is the host of the occasion, some of the bigoted and ill-bred remarks of men such as Joseph Cook, are to say the least, an insult to every guest from abroad. Our friends from the Orient, the followers of Confucius, Buddha, Mohammad and other religious leaders, will get a very erroneous impression of what Christianity pretends to be...if they judge by the barbarism and bigotry of some of its false prophets.[54]

On the same day, the *Springfield Journal* also criticized Reverend Cook, saying: 'It is a sad commentary on professed Christians that all the intolerance thus far exhibited in the Parliament of Religions has come from them and not from the "heathen" for whom they are wont to express so much scorn. These scholarly foreigners were invited here to express their views and are entitled to the fullest courtesy. They should be protected from the insults of the Joseph Cooks and other opinionated bigots.'[55]

This was the overall climate in which Vivekananda delivered his lectures and speeches. Though attitudes had shifted considerably by the end of the century compared to mid-century, there were still strong undercurrents of the missionary stereotypes about Hinduism and India. The audiences that Vivekananda addressed were informed to different degrees by these discursive currents. He was also often attacked by clergymen who resented the ideas he was spreading since they undercut the exclusivity of Christianity. It bears repetition that all of Vivekananda's speeches were delivered extempore. *The Complete Works* mostly don't give any details of the context of a speech except for information regarding the place and date in some cases. We know from reports that Vivekananda spoke in all kinds of places and before various kinds of audiences: churches, clubs, opera houses, ladies' societies, lecture platforms, universities, private saloons, in front of religious and literary societies, and in many other formal and informal settings. The audience varied with these settings, in areas of interest, their knowledge about India, their class and professional composition, and so on. It also varied with geography. We know from Vivekananda's comments that he considered audiences in different American cities to have distinct natures. His extempore speeches were dynamic affairs where both the content and expression changed according to the reaction of the audience. This social context, which explains many sections of the speech, is completely exorcized when we read his words as pure text.

For example, we have this report from the *Detroit Free Press* on a lecture delivered in the city by Vivekananda on 11 March 1893. 'The Hon. T. W. Palmer, in introducing the distinguished visitor (Vivekananda), referred to the old tale of the shield that was copper on one side and silver on the other and the contest which ensued.... Vive Kananda [*sic*], from the Christian standpoint, said Mr. Palmer, was a pagan. It would be pleasant to hear from a gentleman who spoke about the copper side of the shield.'[56] While most of Palmer's comments were well intentioned, the reference to Christianity as the silver side of the shield and Hinduism as the copper side, was infinitely patronizing and the reference to Vivekananda as a pagan while introducing him to the audience was of course, deeply denigrating. The topic of the speech was that of Christianity in India. Palmer's comments probably set the tone for a lot of what followed in Vivekananda's oration. Vivekananda's speech critiqued the usefulness of missionary efforts in India and went on to challenge Christian claims to superiority in a civil, but sarcastic exposition. If the text is read without the introductory comments by Mr Palmer, parts of it might read as just expressing unprovoked spleen. And with most of Vivekananda's speeches, such social context is missing.

Palmer, a former US senator, was not ill-disposed towards non-Christian religions. In fact, he had a fairly liberal attitude towards other religious denominations by the standards of the time. He was not only a personal friend of Vivekananda, but Vivekananda stayed as Palmer's guest throughout his time in Detroit.[57] In this light, Palmer's comments reflected the casual bias against non-Christians that was part of the fabric of American society at the turn of the nineteenth century. From those who were not friends, but actually hostile, Vivekananda received vitriolic attacks. The Presbyterian press attacked Vivekananda and heathenism viciously. One particularly nasty number was headlined 'The Honest Hindoo', ironically insinuating that Vivekananda was in fact, a lying Hindu and dedicating the contents of the article to showing that Vivekananda's claims were the product of mendaciousness.[58] Vivekananda's audiences were not completely immune to this discourse and Vivekananda often had to address this, either through polemical rhetoric or a wide-ranging defence which was as ambiguous as the sweeping and wild nature of the allegations it responded to. All these elements in the text have a completely different complexion if set apart from their immediate social context. Vivekananda many times spoke at events where he was only one of the invited speakers. His speech was preceded by comments by other speakers of which we have no account. This included combative clergymen whose attitudes ran the whole spectrum from biased to bigoted. Vivekananda's speeches, in so far as it also had to respond to such attacks, has to be understood in that context.

To state it as a general and, one would think, commonly understood principle of interpretation, isolated utterances within extempore speeches which develop in response to a dynamic social situation cannot be treated as expressions of categorical ideological positions. The fact that so many present-day interpreters of Vivekananda have fallen prey to such an extremely simple fallacy raises questions not only about intellectual competency, but also of bias.

WAS VIVEKANANDA ANTI-CHRISTIAN?

In 2010, the Central Bureau of Investigation (CBI) arrested a man named Swami Aseemanand from an ashram in Haridwar for allegedly planning the Samjhauta Express blasts, the Mecca Masjid blasts, the Ajmer Sharif blasts, and other terror attacks on civilians.[59] In all, 119 people were reported dead in these terror attacks. During his time in prison as an undertrial, Aseemanand gave judicial confessions stating that he was part of the terror conspiracies. In an interview given to a *Caravan* magazine journalist from prison, Aseemanand claimed that top RSS functionaries, including current RSS chief Mohan Bhagwat, gave tacit approval to the plot.[60] Later, Aseemanand retracted the judicial confessions and also claimed the interview had been fabricated. He was acquitted of all charges by 2018. Several media organizations raised doubts about the correctness of the acquittals.[61] In his youth, Aseemanand associated with the Ramakrishna Mission, before turning to the RSS. Then he worked for a decade with the RSS's tribal affairs organization, the Vanavasi Kalyan Ashram, where he worked among tribal people to convert them to Hinduism. Many organizations and the media have alleged that he played a major role in the violent attacks on Christians and their places of worship in Gujarat in the late nineties.[62]

In a strange twist of irony, Aseemanand was born in the same village as Sri Ramakrishna Paramahamsa, in Kamarpukur in the Hooghly district of Bengal. He was greatly influenced by Vivekananda. According to the *Caravan* article, as a young man, Aseemanand believed in the Ramakrishna Mission's view that all religions are equal and understood Vivekananda as a preacher of religious tolerance. His views on both accounts were changed by an RSS worker who convinced him that the Ramakrishna Mission was misrepresenting Vivekananda's views. In the *Caravan* article, he is quoted as saying that one particular line from Vivekananda dominated his thinking regarding the monk's message: 'Every man going out of the Hindu pale, is not only a man less, but an enemy the more.' '"I got a huge shock after reading this," Aseemanand said. "In the days that followed, I gave this a lot of thought. It is not in my limited capacity to realise or fully analyse Vivekananda's teachings, but since he has said it, I will follow it all my life." He never visited the Ramakrishna Mission again.'[63]

The line occurs in an interview Vivekananda gave to *Prabuddha Bharata*. The interviewer asked Vivekananda if those who had converted out of Hinduism (predominantly to Christianity) should be allowed to return to Hinduism if they wanted to. In that time, the Hindu orthodoxy did not encourage conversions into Hinduism, even in the case of those who had been Hindus before. By taking up another religion, they had lost their caste. Vivekananda replied that such people as wished to return should certainly be taken back, and that over the long run the Hindu population would decrease if reconversion were not permitted. He refers to the history of Farishta to say that at the time of early Muslim rule, Hindus numbered at 600 million. The population in Vivekananda's time was numbered at around 300 million. 'And then every man going out of the Hindu pale is not only a man less, but an enemy the more.'[64]

In Vivekananda's entire corpus, there is not another line that refers to anything remotely like enmity between Hindus and people belonging to other religions. It is filled with hundreds of instances where he calls not only for religious toleration but asserts that all religions express the same fundamental truth. The previously-mentioned statement is a complete anomaly. Neither is the issue of conversion out of Hinduism, a marginal, let alone dominant concern in Vivekananda's work or in his recorded conversations with other people. The statement that so influenced Aseemanand's thinking is a singular anomaly in Vivekananda's entire oeuvre. While Vivekananda criticized Christian missionaries, he mainly did so only in America, and usually in response to queries or claims about the success of the missionary enterprise from his audience. There is not a single instance when he disputed the right of Christians to spread their own religion in India. His objections, which were moral, were chiefly: the crying need of India was food not religion, and Indians would be better served if the millions of dollars spent on the missionary enterprise were instead directed to the supply of material want; it was objectionable that in order to gain converts to Christianity, missionaries should resort to abusing and attacking Hinduism and the Hindus; since all religions expressed the same essential truth, conversion from one religion to other was superfluous. An individual's religious sensibilities were moulded by the concrete historical tradition in which they were located. It could do great spiritual harm to them to dislocate them from it. Vivekananda followed this principle in his own ministry in the West, teaching only abstract philosophical and spiritual principles and asking people to work it out within their own religious traditions.

Vivekananda also empathized with the, largely lower caste, people who had converted to Islam in the past and were converting to Christianity in his time. He stated several times that it was a natural result of the oppression they faced within a casteist Hindu society. During his wandering days, Vivekananda visited Kerala and was shocked by the severity of the caste discrimination and Brahminical domination there. From Bombay, he wrote to a friend in the kingdom of Khetri in 1892, about how people from the lower castes were converting to Christianity. 'And come and see what they, the Padris, are doing here in the Dakshin (south). They are converting the lower classes by lakhs; and in Travancore, the most priestridden country in India—where every bit of land is owned by the Brahmins...nearly one-fourth has become Christian! And I cannot blame them; what part have they in David and what in Jesse? When, when, O Lord shall man be brother to man?'[65]

It takes a particularly fanatic and frighteningly narrow mind to take up the one line that smacks of intolerance in nine volumes of material whose one predominant theme is religious tolerance, and build an understanding of Vivekananda on that line. While this is not surprising to see in extreme right-wing circles, critics from the liberal–left spectrum have not been wanting, who lighted upon this single passage and declared that Vivekananda was promoting an ideologically doctrinaire enmity towards other religions. The intellectual parallelism is troubling.

In this connection it is apposite to mention Jyotirmaya Sharma's *Cosmic Love and Human Apathy: Swami Vivekananda's Restatement of Religion*. Published in 2013, the book makes the same assertion regarding this particular quote but situates it as part of a larger network of arguments which presents the case that Vivekananda is the ideological progenitor of Hindutva. In so far as the book forms part of the existing conversation about Vivekananda that is being engaged with here and that it presents a unique point of view not shared by any other commentator, it requires mention.* However, the book is deeply intellectually dishonest, and works only on the assumption that most of its readers would not have read too much of Vivekananda. Its most central claim, from which most of the other arguments follow, is that Vivekananda sidelined and denied dualistic conceptions of a personal god, bhakti, and mystical experiences. The claim is laughable and patently untrue. In fact, one wonders if any biography of Vivekananda exists that is not replete with stories of his personal devotion to Kali and his own mystical experiences of personal deities

---

*There have been critics who have alleged similarities between Vivekananda's thought and Hindutva, or even that he anticipated some of its aspects. But as far as I know, Sharma is the only one to claim that Vivekananda incubated the Hindutva project and the only one to dedicate a book to proving that argument.

of the Hindu pantheon. The book is full of distortions and cherry picking and Sharma makes things out of whole cloth by claiming that Vivekananda discriminated against certain forms of Hinduism, because they had low-caste and tribal origins. Sharma writes, 'To bring about the unlikely synthesis in India between a projected European society and an Indian religion, the non-Sanskritic, bhakti, tantric, tribal, folk, low-caste, vernacular and all other non-elite and politically marginal perspectives had to be sidelined and discredited.'[66] There is not a single line in the Vivekananda corpus that can be given such an interpretation without the reader importing meanings into it and *Cosmic Love and Human Apathy* does not include any quotes from Vivekananda to prove this original and quite extraordinary claim.[*]

But how do we explain this statement from Vivekananda? The first principle one could apply is the general one in biographical studies that when highly uncharacteristic remarks of a subject are reported in newspaper interviews, one should treat their accuracy with scepticism. This is especially so with a period as far back in the past as Vivekananda's, where reporting standards and journalistic rigour were less developed. But on the whole, I am inclined to think that Vivekananda did make these remarks, or at any rate something akin to them. For one, the interview was published in the *Prabuddha Bharata*, a magazine of the Ramakrishna Mission, so his words being misreported seems unlikely. To understand why Vivekananda would say something like this and the scope of its meaning, we have to look at the Christian missionary dynamic with Hinduism as well as with Vivekananda and the Ramakrishna Mission.

In 1897, just after Vivekananda returned from America, a polemical book was published simultaneously in Madras and London by British missionaries against Vivekananda's alleged success in the West and the resurgence of Vedanta thought. Published by the Christian Literary Society for India, it was titled *Swami Vivekananda and his Guru*. The tract was not exceptional in any way in that it was quite typical of the attacks on Vivekananda and the Ramakrishna Mission that had started appearing since as early as 1894 when Vivekananda's initial success in America became known in India.[†] Christian literature of this kind was quite expansive, and to my knowledge no critical survey has been done of it in the area of Vivekananda–Ramakrishna studies. The book started out with deeply personal and even slanderous attacks on both Ramakrishna Paramahamsa and Vivekananda.

*Readers who are familiar with *Cosmic Love and Human Apathy* may like to read my review of the book for an extensive critique: 'Hindu, not Hindutva', in *Fountain Ink*, October 2014.
†The Ramakrishna Mission was formed in 1897 by Vivekananda.

A section in the book titled 'The Swami's Guru: Bhagawan Sri Ramakrishna Paramahamsa "Deva"', begins with mocking the title that Vivekananda and his fellow disciples addressed their guru by. The tract helpfully explains to its reader, '"Deva", allied to "theos" and "deus", God is like the "divus" of the Roman Emperors who were deified after death. According to the Swami, the latest accession to the already well-stocked Hindu pantheon must at once have taken his place among the "dii majorus", (the greater gods) if not as Rama Krishna "optimus maximus."'[67] The book then goes on to give a short sketch of the life of Sri Ramakrishna, culminating with his bhakti towards Kali.

> It is curious that Ramakrishna should have selected for his 'mother' the most blood-thirsty deity of the Hindu pantheon. She is frequently presented as a black woman, with four arms. In one hand she has a weapon, in another the head of the giant she has slain…. For earrings she has two dead bodies; she wears a necklace of skulls; her only clothing is a girdle made of dead men's hands. Kali, it might be added was the protectress of that noble fraternity the Thugs, and the divinity who especially delighted in human sacrifices…. Professor Max Müller says 'Nothing, I believe is so hideous as the popular worship of Kali in India.'[68]

The book then attempts to dispute that Ramakrishna was a saintly character in a none too edifying manner. It implies that Ramakrishna's practice of yoga had deranged him mentally and that he had a most corrupting influence on Keshub Chandra Sen, the head of the Brahmo Samaj. It then contends that Sri Ramakrishna, not being a proper scholar by Hindu definitions, was not qualified to teach the Vedanta. Consequently, Vivekananda himself had no right to teach the Vedanta and that his pretensions to be a qualified exponent were fake. The book ends the section on Ramakrishna by concluding that: 'In plain language, "Bhagavan Sri Ramakrishna Paramahamsa Deva", the latest addition to the Hindu pantheon was a half-crazy ascetic, unlearned, but with some poetic talent and personal magnetic influence.'[69]

The next section, titled 'Swami Vivekananda's pretensions to be a Sanysasin', consisted almost entirely of personal attacks on the person of Vivekananda, which strike one as petty even by the standards of the bile that Christian missionaries regularly threw at Hinduism and its representatives at the time. It claimed that Vivekananda's motives for taking up sanyasa had nothing to do with renunciation. Rather, Vivekananda chose this path to avoid doing the hard work of earning a living. 'It is not strange that now and then Indian graduates should be induced to join this "noble army of martyrs" (ascetic mendicants).

The market value of a second class BA, as a teacher in Calcutta, is not high. Ramakrishna's temple, as already mentioned, is pleasantly situated in a garden on the banks of the Hugly.... Instead of the drudgery of teaching, the Babu might at Dakshineshwar enjoy...ease and dignity.'[70]

The book was meant to appeal to British people who might have gained a favourable impression of Vivekananda and Vedanta, and moderate Hindus who saw in the Ramakrishna movement a resurgent Hinduism which was capable of holding its own against Western science and Christianity. In order to do the latter, Christian missionaries often attempted to discredit Vivekananda's credentials as a sanyasi using what they took to be normative Hindu beliefs and laws. In that spirit, the rest of the section on Vivekananda was spent in a demonstration of how Vivekananda was not a genuine sanyasi because he did not follow the laws laid down by Manu and in other scriptures regarding sanyasa. Then, a broader appeal is made in trying to show that Vivekananda lived a life of luxury in the West, thus violating the rules of asceticism and poverty essential to sanyasa.

It accused Vivekananda of eating beef while in the West (in spite of his liberal attitude towards meat eating, there is no evidence that Vivekananda ever consumed beef) and strongly suggested that the monk entertained himself with wine and whisky when abroad. Vivekananda, it was alleged, had broken all the rules of sanyasa and wallowed in the lap of luxury in the West: frequenting first-class hotels, while presenting himself as a renunciate. The section ends with the quote: The Sannyasiship a fraud. 'The Sunday Times speaks of the Swami as "savouring of anything but the popular idea of asceticism." He is sleek and has apparently been living on "the fat of the land". How does the life he led in America and England comport with his profession? How much punya (religious merit) will accrue therefrom to his supporters? India's "great and peerless legislator, the divine Manu" being the judge, the Swami's sannyasiship is a mockery. There is no objection to an Indian, if he can afford it, living in a New York Fifth Avenue Hotel; but to make at the same time, pretensions to sannyasiship, is what is condemned.'[71]

In order to persuade orthodox Hindu readers, the book even brought Vivekananda's caste into the picture. Vivekananda was from the Kayastha caste and there was some controversy over whether Kayasthas were Kshatriyas or Shudras. (This was only a matter for the caste-obsessed Hindu orthodoxy, for the Kayasthas were a powerful feudal caste and for all practical purposes were very high up in the social hierarchy of Bengal.) The book quoted Hindu texts to the effect that Shudras are not allowed to study the Vedas, and that Vivekananda had no right to be a sanyasi. This was one of the attacks Vivekananda had faced from orthodox Brahmins who were opposed to his egalitarian ideas. In a speech in Madras after returning from his first trip to the West, Vivekananda responded that he would be glad if they called him a Shudra but it would not repay even a small amount of the tyranny his ancestors had imposed on the community.[72]

We do not know if Vivekananda ever saw this particular book, but he surely came across other productions of a similar kind. Vivekananda's correspondence is replete with his responses to complaints by his brother monks of scurrilous attacks by the Christian press, in which he would always advise them to ignore such attacks and move on. It might be supposed that a man who has constantly been personally attacked and vilified in such a manner will not be too happily disposed towards his detractors, which in this case were Christian missionaries, and doubly so when the guru whom he has dedicated his life to is also abused in the same way. But Vivekananda had to face much worse from Christian missionaries and orthodox Christians. He was the victim of a campaign of active persecution, lies and slander by the latter during his initial years in America. The campaign was aimed at derailing his mission in the West and it almost succeeded. Nonetheless, Vivekananda seemed to have retained no ill-feelings towards the missionaries in particular, or Christians in general.

Vivekananda's success in the World's Parliament of Religions in Chicago was blazoned in the American press. As his popularity grew, it raised the hackles of the orthodox Christian clergy. What followed was an insidious but consistent campaign to discredit Vivekananda in the eyes of those who had welcomed him into American society. The attack was two-pronged. A series of articles appeared in prominent Protestant and Protestant-leaning newspapers and journals claiming that Vivekananda was a charlatan, and no monk. These articles alleged that Vivekananda had no credentials to represent Hinduism and that his pretensions to being a sanyasi were not accepted by his own fellow countrymen. These reports mainly quoted American or British missionaries from India to support their claims.

Anonymous letters were sent to people who were to host Vivekananda containing all kinds of calumnies against his character and alleging that he was a fraud. The slander worked enough that on occasions Vivekananda was disinvited or turned away by his alarmed hosts.[73] The press and whisper campaign imputed disreputable traits to Vivekananda's character with the aim of showing that he was unfit to be welcome at any decent American home. This played at a particularly susceptible point: the middle-class Victorian morality. As a foreigner, and that too an Asian with no known connections or credentials, Vivekananda was at particular risk of social ostracism. Vivekananda stayed at the home of Mr and Mrs Hale in Chicago. Reportedly, Mr Hale one day received a scandal-filled letter about Vivekananda, warning him not to let his daughters associate with him; Mr Hale threw it into the fireplace.[74]

Over the course of a year or more, the orthodox section in America attacked Vivekananda not only from the pulpit and through newspaper articles, but by spreading rumours about him. This included rumours of sexual promiscuity and of flouting the monastic vow of chastity. While Indian newspapers dutifully reported Vivekananda's successes in America, none of these reports reached America. And Vivekananda could offer no reassurance to his friends, supporters, and well-wishers that he was a genuine representative of Hinduism and that he was accepted by his countrymen as such. Meanwhile, the attacks on Vivekananda's character and credentials appearing in the Indian missionary press were regularly printed in orthodox Protestant newspapers in America.[75]

The orthodox clergy was enabled in their campaign not only by Christian missionaries who sent defamatory reports of Vivekananda's previous life in India, but also, strangely enough, by a section of the Brahmo Samaj reform society. Pratap Chandra Mazoomdar of the Brahmo Samaj, who was also an attendee at the Parliament of Religions, was an expounder of a Christianized form of the Brahmo faith and the author of the *Oriental Christ*, which had been well received in intellectual circles in Bengal and certain British Christian groups and press interested in India. Mazoomdar and Vivekananda were known to each other from the days of Vivekananda's association with the Brahmo Samaj. But it seems Vivekananda's success at the Parliament made Mazoomdar jealous and, with the help of the orthodox clergy of Chicago, he went about denouncing Vivekananda as a layabout who had just donned the sanyasi's garb in America.

Mazoomdar worked further mischief on his return to India. When Vivekananda was lecturing in Boston, the *Boston Daily Advertiser* of 16 May 1894 published reports quoting an article on Vivekananda from the publication of the Brahmo Samaj sect of which Mazoomdar was a leader. The original report read:

The Indian Mirror has published several long leaders in praise of the Neo-Hindu BABU NORENDRANATH DUTT alias VIVEKHANANDA in some of its late issues. We have no objection to the publication of such panegyrics on the sanyasi (monk), but since the time he came to us to act on the stage of the Nava-Vrindavan Theatre or sang hymns in one of the Brahmo Samajs of this city we knew him well that no amount of newspaper writing could throw any new light on our estimate of his character. We are glad our old friend lately created a good impression in America by his speeches, but we are aware that the Neo-Hinduism of which our friend is a representative is not orthodox Hinduism. The last thing the latter would do is to cross the Kalapani (ocean), partake of the Mleccha food (food of foreigners and other religionists) and smoke endless cigars and the like. Any follower of modern Hinduism cannot command that respect from us which we entertain for a genuine orthodox Hindu. Our contemporary may try to do his best to promote the reputation of VIVEKHANANDA, but we cannot have patience with him when he publishes glaring nonsense.[76]

The insinuations were crystal clear. What Vivekananda preached in America was not genuine Hinduism, but his own invention. He was not a genuine Hindu because he broke all the rules of conduct of orthodox Hinduism. Though he styled himself Swami Vivekananda, he was just really Babu Narendranath Dutta of Calcutta, who was a singer and an actor and by implication a bohemian rather than an ascetic.

Mazoomdar apparently continued to spread rumours about Vivekananda in Calcutta, this time about the life he was leading in America. Vivekananda wrote to Mary Hale in a letter dated 18 March 1894, 'Mazoomdar has gone back to Calcutta and is preaching that Vivekananda is committing every sin under the sun in America—especially *"unchastity"* of the most degraded type!!! Lord bless his soul.'[77] Elsewhere, Vivekananda expressed his anguish at the thought of the pain his old mother would be going through if she had heard these stories.

For a long time, Vivekananda ignored the attacks and the slander. But by March 1894, the campaign had started to take effect. The suspicion gained ground in many quarters in American society that Vivekananda might actually be a fraud. Vivekananda started feeling that even some of his staunchest friends and allies could start doubting him. Things had come to such a pass that it looked as if Vivekananda's mission in America would be doomed. His frustration and misery are apparent in a letter he wrote to a disciple in Madras during this period.

Now as to my prospects here—it is well-nigh zero.... Your letters say again and again how I am being praised in India. But that is between you and me, for I never saw a single Indian paper writing about me, except the three square inches sent to me by Alasinga. On the other hand everything that is said by the Christians in India is sedulously gathered by the missionaries and regularly published, and they go from door to door to make my friends give me up. They have succeeded only too well, for there is not one word about me from India. Indian Hindu papers may laud me to the skies, but not a word of that came to America, so that many people in this country think me a fraud. In the face of the missionaries and the Hindu herd to back them, I have not a word to say.... I came here without credentials. How else to show that I am not a fraud in the face of the missionaries and the Brahmo Samaj? Now I thought nothing so easy as to spend a few words; I thought nothing would be so easy as to hold a meeting of some respectable persons in Madras and Calcutta and pass a resolution thanking me and the American people for being so kind to me and sending it over officially.... Now after all I found that it is too terrible a task for India to undertake. There has not been one voice for me in one year and everyone against me.... Every moment I expected something from India. No, it never came. Last two months I was especially in torture at every moment. No, not even a newspaper from India! My friends waited—waited month after month; nothing came, not a voice. Many consequently grew cold and at last gave me up.[78]

The situation was eventually remedied after large public meetings were held in Calcutta, Madras, and many places in India, and attended by prominent personalities. Vivekananda's success was commemorated, and formal addresses were sent to American organizations and published in American newspapers. The campaign against Vivekananda soon lost steam. But it would be reasonable to assume that even the most broadminded of people would bear some animus towards those who relentlessly subjected them to persecution and their religion to abuse. But apart from the one interview to *Prabuddha Bharata*, there is no other instance where Vivekananda expresses ill-feelings or antagonism towards Christian missionaries or any section of Christians. As mentioned in an earlier chapter, when the American clergyman Dr Barrows wished to come to India to spread the message of Christianity, Vivekananda arranged a grand reception for him in Calcutta. (Of course, Barrows was not an orthodox clergyman and believed in pluralism, but he was nonetheless convinced that Christianity was the one true faith and that India would eventually become Christian). To be so completely free of negative feelings towards those who have abused all you hold dear and have actively tried to harm you is, by the standards of ordinary human nature, quite an extraordinary achievement. Even with Pratap

Chandra Mazoomdar, Vivekananda forgave his vicious slander to the extent of continuing to call him his friend. For instance, in a letter written during the peak of the missionary–Brahmo campaign against him, he writes: 'the fever of jealousy which attacked Mazoomdar gave me a terrible shock, and I pray that he would know better—for he is a great and good man who has tried all his life to do good.'[79]

Vivekananda's comments to *Prabuddha Bharata* have to be understood in the context of the history of the missionary attacks on Hinduism and its efforts to seek the conversion of India through violently abusing Hinduism and trying to actively hinder attempts of Hindus to revive their religion. New converts to Christianity in India were co-opted into this belligerent religious project, which also had powerful imperialistic overtones then. Vivekananda would have considered that his comments would have been read in the context of the universalist message of the Ramakrishna Mission and by the few thousand subscribers that *Prabuddha Bharata* had. Vivekananda was no doubt a visionary, but unless his alleged psychic powers were not only true but made him omniscient about the future, it is difficult to see how he could predict the uses his words would be put to in the twentieth century and later. He had no way of knowing that these words would come to be read by millions of people, or that they would be widely read nearly 120 years after his death. Nor could he have imagined a future where the power dynamics between a colonized Hinduism and an imperialistic Christianity would be turned on its head into the dynamic of a Hindu majoritarianism and a Christian minority. And he certainly couldn't have imagined that his words would be hijacked and used to promote hatred by Hindu nationalism. Let alone Hindu nationalism, Indian nationalism itself did not exist in a significant form in Vivekananda's lifetime.

Nevertheless, knowing Vivekananda, he would have deeply regretted uttering these words if he knew what evil they would go out in the world to do. The hatred and violence generated by those casually uttered remarks would have pained him deeply. He would have seen it not only as an error of judgment on his part, but by the extraordinarily high standards he set for himself, as a moral failure. For by the spiritual principles he believed in, tried to live by, and preached, there is no occasion at all when one should speak of another human being with anything except love.

VIVEKANANDA'S HINDUISM VS THE SANGH PARIVAR'S HINDUISM

'I am a monk,' he said, as he sat in the parlors of La Salette Academy which is his home while in Memphis, 'and not a priest. When at home I travel from place to place, teaching the people of the villages and towns through which I pass. I am dependent upon them for my sustenance, as I am not allowed to touch money.'...

There was a touch of pathos in the speaker's voice and a murmur of sympathy ran around the group of listeners. Kananda (American reporters generally spelt his name as Vive Kananda in those days) knocked the ashes from his cigar and was silent for a space.

Presently someone asked: 'If your religion is all that you claim it is, if it is the only true faith, how is it that your people are not more advanced in civilisation than we are? Why has it not elevated them among the nations of the world?'

'Because that is not the sphere of any religion,' replied the Hindu gravely. 'My people are the most moral in the world, or quite as much as any other race.... No religion has ever advanced the thought or inspiration of a nation or people. In fact, no great achievement has ever been attained in the history of the world that religion has not retarded....

'But, in pursuing the spiritual, you lost sight of the demands of the present,' said some one. 'Your doctrine does not help men to live.'

'It helps them to die,' was the answer....

'The aim of the ideal religion should be to help one to live and to prepare one to die at the same time.'

'Exactly,' said the Hindu, quickly, 'and it is that which we are seeking to attain. I believe that the Hindu faith has developed the spiritual in its devotees at the expense of the material, and I think that in the Western world the contrary is true. By uniting the materialism of the West with the spiritualism of the East I believe much can be accomplished. It may be that in the attempt the Hindu faith will lose much of its individuality.'

'Would not the entire social system of India have to be revolutionised to do what you hope to do?'

'Yes, probably, still the religion would remain unimpaired.'[1]

This brief portrait of an informal conversation between Vivekananda and an American audience, published in the newspaper *Appeal Avalanche*, on 21 January 1894 contains many elements of the fundamental opposition between Vivekananda's thinking on Hinduism and his way of life and what the Sangh Parivar espouses. Vivekananda did not consider Hinduism a static entity which had remained unchanged since the Vedic age. Vivekananda believed that Hinduism had certain fundamental spiritual truths discovered by its saints and prophets, but its religious and social forms have always kept on changing and will keep changing, even to the point that what was believed and practised in different historical epochs would be completely dissimilar and even contradictory. The Sangh Parivar on the other hand is obsessed with maintaining a Hindu ethos which they claim has existed with unbroken continuity since the Vedic ages. Vivekananda thought that Hinduism, (in the extended sense of a religious culture and affiliated social institutions) had much to learn from other countries; especially from Western materialism.[*] And Hinduism also had unique spiritual wealth to give other nations, especially the West, where material power was concentrated. When Vivekananda contrasted the materialism of the West and the spirituality of the East, he was not creating a binary between the Abrahamic faiths and Hinduism. The binary was between Europe and America, and Asia. In defending Asia's contribution to the religious thought of the world, Vivekananda told Western audiences that Jesus was from the Orient and pointed out that all the great religions of the world including Christianity, Judaism, and Islam had originated in Asia.

Vivekananda in the above quoted conversation talks about the possibility that Hinduism would in the process of cross-cultural contact with the West, lose much of its individuality, that is, its particular forms of religious and social expression, and concomitant forms of social life. Now these concrete peculiarities are what differentiate one religion from the other at the plane of lived reality. It is thus the basis of religio-ethnic identity. It is this identity

---

*Vivekananda in his work uses 'materialism' in two senses of the word. When he used it in a positive sense, he used it to refer to the conquest of the physical world achieved by the Western nations through science and technology and the political and social organizations they had built. When he used it in a negative sense, he meant the concentration of economic power in the hands of a few in the West, the ruthlessness of military conquests, and a competitive culture that valued the acquisition of wealth above all else.

which the Sangh Parivar mobilizes and which makes its politics of Hindutva possible by creating an 'other': the Muslim and Christian who do not share in this religio-ethnic identity. Vivekananda not only sees such an identity as dispensable, but sometimes, as in the preceding conversation, anticipated a future where what he here called 'the individuality of Hinduism', that is, its distinctive social and religio-cultural features, would become highly diluted as it became more and more permeable to ideas and modes of life from other cultures and civilizations. At the same time, he envisioned that Hindu spiritual ideas would also spread over the globe influencing and enriching other religions and creating a revolution in spiritual thought. The corollary of such a vision would naturally be that in the future there would be no very distinct Hindu ethos to preserve, even if one were so minded. The long-term historical direction of development Vivekananda envisaged for Hinduism and Hindu society, (as well as all religions in the world), was a progression towards a universal spirituality, where individual differences of theology, mythology, ritual, and social practices would be considered secondary, non-essential matters. In other words, in Vivekananda's vision, the conditions of possibility of religio-ethnic identity, the very basis of the Sangh Parivar's Hindutva project, would be progressively negated.

There are two lines of thought at work here. One was Vivekananda's conviction that the contact between the West and India, and the working of the forces of economic and cultural modernity would eventually affect a tremendous transformation which would change Indian society and world civilization. The second was his belief that the same universal spiritual truths lay at the heart of every religion, and his hope that as human civilization advanced and people became increasingly more rational, this truth would be recognized. Vivekananda once planned to build a universal temple with a section devoted to the mode of worship of every religion in the world.

As Vivekananda said to an American audience '[I]f one religion is true, all the others must be true. Thus the Hindu religion is your property as well as mine.'[2] Vivekananda considered the advent of Sri Ramakrishna as setting in motion a new age of spirituality that would obliterate all caste and religious distinctions. Sri Ramakrishna in his spiritual quest had practised both Christianity and Islam. Sri Ramakrishna claimed that he had identical mystical experiences at the culmination of his practices of Islam, Christianity, and various forms of Hinduism. Vivekananda's philosophy that all religions were true was based on Sri Ramakrishna's putative spiritual experiences. Vivekananda said, 'My master used to say that these names, as Hindu, Christian etc., stand as great bars to all brotherly feelings between man and man. We must try to break them down first. They have lost all their good powers and now stand as only baneful influences under whose black magic even the best of us behave like demons. Well, we will have to work hard and succeed.'[3]

Vivekananda's very mode of living was antithetical to the Sangh's prescription for being a good Hindu. As per the RSS and the Sangh Parivar's model, a good Hindu is someone who is a vegetarian, does yoga exercises (hatha yoga) with pride, doesn't drink, and does not use addictive substances like tobacco. The cigar smoking monk hardly fits into this category, and the Sangh's idea of the good Hindu wouldn't fly with Vivekananda.

Vivekananda was a regular smoker. He started smoking the hookah as a college student[4] (if not before) and found no reason to drop the habit when he undertook sanyas; this is mentioned in *Vivekananda: A Biography* and volume one of *The Life of Swami Vivekananda*. Apparently, he could go months without smoking, and live for days without food (when he lived as a wanderer in India), by force of will. But he saw no need to forgo the pleasure when it was available. He felt it did not impede him on his spiritual path. On the other hand, he followed celibacy strictly and insisted it was essential for higher spiritual realization, just like his guru Sri Ramakrishna did. (Yet, he did not view abstinence from sex as a moral virtue; it was only considered instrumental to attaining mystical meditative states, like Buddhist monks do.) When he landed in America, he took to smoking cigars and cigarettes; though, according to the fifth volume of *The Complete Works of Swami Vivekananda*, it would seem he preferred the former.[5] Not only did Vivekananda see no moral value to be obtained from not smoking, he considered anti-smoking campaigners to be fanatics. Vivekananda went out of his way to puncture the hypocritical holier than thou attitudes behind moral judgements on smoking, whether in the West or in India.

In late Victorian America and England, it was not considered polite to smoke when ladies were present. Vivekananda happily broke this decorum, scattering ashes about the house and, as a future woman disciple complained, 'blowing the cigarette smoke deliberately into one's face'.[6] The Sangh's idea of Hinduism and virtue consists in obedience to rules. Golwalkar wrote: 'Let us thus mould our life with an attitude of discipline throughout the day, from morning till night. A Hindu is born to be trained in a life-long course of discipline and self-restraint, which purify and strengthen him to reach the Supreme Goal in life.'[7] Vivekananda was a born rebel, and a senseless rule was to him merely an obstacle that society placed in the individual's path. A man named Frank Rhodehamel, who knew Vivekananda when he was in California, wrote in an article recollecting the time he spent there.

> Once while crossing the bay between San Francisco and Oakland, he took the notion to smoke. He was seated with some ladies on the upper deck of the ferry where smoking was prohibited. Drawing a pack of cigarettes from his pocket, he lit one and blew the smoke in playful defiance at the prohibitive sign, 'No Smoking.' One of his companions quickly warned him, 'Swami! Swami! You can't smoke here!... Here comes the officer! Quick—put it out!' 'Why should I put it out?' he drawled in exasperating coolness. The officer in question caught sight of the offender, and started for him. Swami continued to puff until the officer came up to him. Then he laughingly threw the half-smoked cigarette overboard. The officer looked at him a moment and slowly passed on.[8]

The ethics of disregarding civic authority can perhaps be debated, but what is certain from this account is that Vivekananda certainly does not fit into the Sangh's mould of the 'Sanskari Hindu'.

Vegetarianism has been pushed on the nation with renewed energy since the BJP came to power in 2014.[9] Yoga gurus, mystics, and bringers of spiritual peace have all been overtly or covertly pushing vegetarianism as the panacea for all health problems. Vegetarianism is also supposed to make you sattvic, or spiritual. Except for Brahmin castes (and there are exceptions among them too, like Kashmiri and Bengali Brahmins),[10] Hindus have historically never been vegetarians uniformly. Nonetheless, there is a definitive association of vegetarianism with spirituality in the Hindu tradition, just as there is within Buddhism and Jainism.* Vivekananda happened to be a renegade in this matter. In *The Monk as Man*, Sankar notes that he not only ate meat but enjoyed treating his friends to spicy mutton dishes he cooked himself, and most significantly, he advised Hindus to eat meat.[11]

In the Hindu religious discourse of the day, (we find these basic ideas in the Bhagavad Gita) all things in nature, including humans, were believed to have one of three qualities (gunas). Tamas is the lowest quality, representing dullness and inertia. Next in order came rajas, the quality of activity and passion. The highest quality was sattva, of calmness and moral purity. Sattva was considered a prerequisite to attaining spirituality. Meat was believed to increase the quality of rajas or passion in people. The scientific knowledge

---

*The exception is Tantra, whose ritual practices include the taking of meat and alcohol.

of the time also advanced the proposition that the consumption of animal proteins made one stronger.

Vivekananda wrote a long essay in Bengali in *Udbodhan* titled 'The East and the West'. After discussing the question of differing food habits and the different arguments put forward by meat eaters and vegetarians, he wrote, 'Whatever one or the other may say, the real fact, however, is that the nations who take animal food are always, as a rule, notably brave, heroic and thoughtful. The nations who take animal food also assert that in those days when the smoke from Yajnas used to rise in the Indian sky and the Hindus used to take the meat of animals sacrificed, then only great religious geniuses and intellectual giants were born among them; but since the drifting of the Hindus into the Babaji's vegetarianism, not one great, original man arose midst them.'[12] Vivekananda's final conclusion was that vegetarianism is better because it does not entail killing, but he acknowledged that in a world where there is competition among people, the strength provided by animal food was absolutely necessary.

A disciple's account of his conversation with Vivekananda at Belur Math is a good example of Vivekananda's views on the relationship between spirituality and vegetarianism, particularly in the Indian context.

> Disciple: It is the fashion here nowadays to give up fish and meat as soon as one takes to religion.... How, do you think, such notions came into existence?
>
> Swamiji: What's the use of your knowing how they came, when you see clearly, do you not, that such notions are working ruin to our country and our society? Just see—the people of East Bengal eat much fish, meat, and turtle, and they are much healthier than those of this part of Bengal...
>
> ...Yes, take as much of that as you can, without fearing criticism. The country has been flooded with dyspetic Babajis living on vegetables only. That is no sign of Sattva, but of deep Tamas—the shadow of death....
>
> Disciple: But do not fish and meat increase Rajas in man?
>
> Swamiji: That is what I want you to have. Rajas is badly needed just now! More than ninety per cent of those whom you now take to be men with the Sattva quality are only steeped in the deepest Tamas.... So, I say, eat large quantities of fish and meat, my boy![13]

Vivekananda continued: 'All liking for fish and meat disappears when pure Sattva is highly developed, and these are the signs of its manifestation in a soul: sacrifice of everything for others, perfect non-attachment to lust and wealth, want of pride and egotism.... And where such indications are absent, and yet you find men siding with the non-killing party, know it for a certainty that herein, there is either hypocrisy or a show of religion.'[14] In other words, to imagine that just by becoming vegetarian one could become more spiritual is like believing that if you wear trainer shoes you would become an athlete.

Vivekananda also had diametrically opposite attitudes towards many ideas and notions that the Sangh Parivar has made part of the mainstream discourse today. They are too many to enumerate fully, so I will mention just two. The first is the celebration of yoga exercises as a great part of India's ancient heritage. The second is the tendency to give pseudo-scientific explanations for all kinds of Hindu religious beliefs.

What Vivekananda taught in America and Great Britain was what he termed raja yoga, an eight-limbed system of yoga[*], taking Patanjali's *Yoga Sutra* as its founding text. It did not contain any of the physical exercises of hatha yoga (simply called yoga today) and according to their biographers, neither Vivekananda nor Sri Ramakrishna ever learned this system. From this point onwards, the term yoga when used without any qualifiers refers to raja yoga.

The Indian government has made a huge push to introduce hatha yoga into schools and into public discourse as not only the best form of exercise from the point of view of health and physical well-being, but also as an integral part of India's ancient wisdom. The government's greatest achievement on this front was to get the UN General Assembly to declare 21 July as 'International Yoga Day' in 2015.[15] While Vivekananda believed India's past held wonderous spiritual treasures for the world, hatha yoga did not figure among them. On the contrary, he held hatha yoga to be quite unspiritual. In his first published book *Raja Yoga*, Vivekananda wrote:

> Hatha-Yoga…deals entirely with the physical body, its aim being to make the physical body very strong. We have nothing to do with it here, because its practices are very difficult, and cannot be learned in a day, and, after all, do not lead to much spiritual growth. Many of these practices you will find in Delsarte (French physical educationalist) and other teachers, such as placing the body in different postures, but the object in these is physical, not psychological…. The result of this branch of Yoga is to make men live long; health is the chief idea, the one goal of the Hatha-Yogi. He is determined not to fall sick, and he never does…. A banyan tree

---

[*]The eight limbs are yama (moral imperatives), niyama (moral regulations), asana (posture), pranayama (control of prana through breath control), pratyahara (detaching the mind from sense objects), dharana (concentration), dhyana (meditation), and Samadhi (superconsciousnesss).

lives sometimes 5000 years, but it is a banyan tree and nothing more. So, if a man lives long, he is only a healthy animal.[16]

In a letter to his brother disciple Akhandananda written from Ghazipur in March 1890 and included in the sixth volume of his *Complete Works*, he referred to hatha yoga as 'nothing but a kind of gymnastics'.[17]

Vivekananda held science in high regard, much more so than most of his Indian contemporaries. In fact, like so many nineteenth century Western intellectuals, scientific knowledge was for him the paradigmatic case of knowledge, because it is completely evidence based.* Hence, he demanded that even religion should be scientific; in the sense that it should offer proportionate evidence for its claims. However, the Spirit is not something that can be demonstrated in a laboratory, any more than an atom can be expected to answer prayers. While Vivekananda held that people who asked for material evidence for spiritual truths were intellectually confused, people who gave 'scientific' explanations for their religious beliefs, met with his derision. This applied even more to Hinduism, for as a Hindu he was especially concerned with keeping Hindu thought free of irrationality and preserve its rational and philosophical character. He remarked of those among his contemporaries who took the aid of pseudoscience to explain Hindu customs: 'There is another class of men among us who are intent upon giving some slippery scientific explanations for any and every Hindu custom, rite, etc., and who are always talking of electricity, magnetism, air vibration, and all that sort of thing. Who knows but they will perhaps some day define God Himself as nothing but a mass of electric vibrations!'[18] One can scarcely imagine what Vivekananda would have said if he had heard of Ganesha being given an elephant head transplant through plastic surgery, gaushalas administering cow urine based mixtures to cure Covid-19, parliamentarians claiming that cow urine cured them of cancer, or high court judges who say cows inhale and exhale oxygen.[19] We have probably missed out on some delightful rapier-sharp thrusts of Vivekananda's sarcasm, and the rationalist monk has been spared the torture of the theatre of the absurd which Indians live in today.

But Vivekananda did have to live with that particular variety of Hindu

---

*This, however, does not mean Vivekananda believed in a kind of scientism or that other fields of human endeavour should follow the lead of science. In fact, from a philosophical perspective, Vivekananda considered scientific knowledge to be always uncertain, while spiritual knowledge was certain. The idea that the certainity of scientific knowledge is provisional has become a dominant position in the philosophy of science over the past half decade or so. The main reasons are that present scientific theories can always be replaced by future theories and because of what is called 'the underdetermination of theory' by empirical data.

whom we encounter increasingly, who claim that almost every scientific invention, discovery, or theory known to mankind is in the Vedas or was known to the ancient rishis. Today, this species of imagination is running amok with people presenting 'scientific' papers, writing blogs, and creating memes about how knowledge of modern science and technology from aeroplanes, Wi-Fi, nuclear weapons, and spacecrafts, to Einstein's theory of relativity and quantum mechanics, are all to be found in the Vedas and Puranas.

In an article titled 'Knowledge: Its Source and Acquirement', written in Bengali for *Udbodhan* in 1899, Vivekananda addressed Brahmins who claimed modern scientific knowledge were contained in Hindu scriptures. "'Well, the moderns are making many new and original discoveries in the field of science and arts, which neither you dreamt of, nor is there any proof that your forefathers ever had knowledge of. What do you say to that?" "Why certainly our forefathers knew all these things, the knowledge of which is now unfortunately lost to us. Do you want a proof? I can show you one. Look! Here is the Sanskrit verse...." Needless to add that the modern party, who believes in direct evidence only, never attaches any seriousness to such replies and proofs.'[20]

RELIGION AND HINDUISM ACCORDING TO VIVEKANANDA

To make sense of the positions Vivekananda took on various aspects of Hinduism, we need to understand Vivekananda's exposition of Hinduism as well as his personal situatedness within that religious tradition. In a colonial context, where Hinduism was constantly attacked, Vivekananda defended the worth of Hinduism vociferously, and tried to instil a sense of pride in India's past among deracinated Hindus, especially young educated men, who were starting to develop nationalist aspirations. Vivekananda was proud to be a Hindu and he personally considered Hinduism to be the grandest religion in the world. But the last statement has to be understood with several caveats, and would be completely misleading if understood as stating a position of religious supremacy. While Vivekananda preached to Indians to be proud of the achievements of their ancestors, especially the spiritual truths they discovered, he was careful that restoring civilizational confidence should not descend into bigotry. Thus, we never find Vivekananda preaching that Hinduism was an inherently superior religion. Based on his speeches and writings, it is highly unlikely that he believed in the inherent superiority of his religion. He did not think that Hinduism possessed spiritual truths that were its exclusive property. His opinion that Hinduism was the grandest religion in the world was the opinion of a religious figure who had surveyed, read, and engaged with most of the major religious traditions of the world. His assessment was based on certain specialized criteria which are internal to religious discourse, one of which was that Hinduism had manifested a greater range of spiritually relevant phenomena. It was not an opinion he expressed often even in private, for he considered religious traditions to be means to spirituality rather than ends. But it increased his reverence and admiration for Hinduism to an extremely high degree.

Vivekananda's greatest contribution to the Hindu tradition was that he was able to bring the various quarrelling sects and interpretations of scriptures present in his day under the conceptual framework of Vedanta, so that one could speak of Hinduism as a single religion without loss of coherence. Here, I will give an extremely brief summary of the most central features of Vivekananda's exposition of Hinduism. These relate to scriptural authority, the centrality of the Advaitic philosophy, and the nature of spiritual knowledge. 1) The primary scriptures of the Hindus are the Upanishads and the Bhagavad Gita. The other scriptures, including the Puranas, are acceptable only in so far as their teachings agreed with the primary scriptures. In taking this view, Vivekananda was not saying something new. This hermeneutical hierarchy is followed by every Vedantic school and goes back as far as Shankaracharya (eighth century CE), and can be traced further back in antiquity.[21] While Vivekananda did not innovate on the principle as such, his contribution was to elucidate its application in the modern world in relation to the values of modernity and in a form that was radical in spirit. He showed how to apply it in the most general manner on the basis of philosophical principles, without any need for reference to scriptures or any punditry. 2) There are mainly three schools of thought in contemporary Hinduism. Advaita or absolute monism whose greatest exponent was Shankara, Vishistadvaita or qualified monism, first promulgated by Ramanuja, and Dvaita or dualism. Advaita takes the ultimate reality or Brahman of the Vedas to be identical with the individual Self (Atman). Vishistadvaita makes the individual Self (jivatma) a part of the Universal Self (Brahman or Ishvara), while Dvaita makes God and the individual souls qualitatively and quantitatively different. Vivekananda, like Sri Ramakrishna before him and Ramana Maharshi, Swami Sivananda, Swami Chinmayananada, and other Hindu spiritual figures after him, was an Advaitist. Advaita holds that the ultimate reality of the Upanishads, the Brahman, is an impersonal infinite Absolute that transcends space, time, and causality. The personal God or ishvara is the impersonal Absolute that appears to the individual ego through the prism of space, time, and causality, all of which are the categories through which our mind synthesizes experience. The yogi tries to go beyond even the direct knowledge of the personal God, through a complete cessation of mentation; revealing the impersonal Brahman as the true nature of reality, which is identical with her own real Self. This is revealed in Upanishadic statements such as 'Tatvam Asi' (Thou art that (Brahman)), 'Aham Brahmasmi' (I am Brahman) etc., which are referred to as the mahavakyas (Great Statements). 3) The goal of Hinduism was the realization and knowledge of God through direct perception in mystical states of consciousness. This can be accomplished through meditative contemplation, devotion, or unattached work, but all the paraphernalia of religion were only preparatory aids to reach this state. The destiny of every soul was the attainment of a state of union with the ultimate reality, whether conceived as the impersonal Absolute or as a personal God.

The aim of this chapter is to place Vivekananda's teachings on Hinduism beside the Sangh Parivar's view of Hinduism. Vivekananda's exposition of Hinduism is considered definitive and authoritative by millions of Hindus. The Sangh has never directly made pronouncements on theological matters, but its edicts and interventions in the practice of Hinduism has direct implications for what it considers Hinduism to be. To define Hinduism is also to define what it means to be a Hindu. In Chapter 2, I had remarked that Hindutva as a political project as well as a concept, is parasitic upon Hinduism the religion. The RSS talks about preserving the Hindu ethos and way of life. The elements that they want to preserve overlap with the spiritual praxis of Hinduism, so that in both its social and religious activities the Sangh invariably constructs and imparts a view of Hinduism. The ethos of a religious community can never be completely divorced from its religious beliefs. The former flows out of the latter at least nominally, and to the extent to which the community's ethos expresses the spirit of its religion, it is successful in implementing its religious ideals. While the Sangh pays lip service to the universal philosophy of the primary Hindu scriptures, the ethos it promotes is exclusive, insular, and parochial. And in so far as we can take Vivekananda to represent the Hindu tradition, the 'Hindu ethos' the Sangh wants to preserve is in direct conflict with the spiritual principles he preached and the vision of Hinduism he articulated.

What is this Hindu ethos that the Sangh wants Hindus to adhere to? Savarkar, the originator of Hindutva ideology, had called this ethos 'Sanskriti', and it was one of the three criteria that he identified as that which a person should possess to be a Hindu. (The other two being that his ancestors should have been Hindu and that he should belong to the Hindu nation). Based on these criteria, Savarkar defines a Hindu thus: 'A Hindu then is he who...has inherited and claims as his own the Hindu Sanskriti, the Hindu civilization, as represented in a common history, common heroes, a common literature, common art, a common law and a common jurisprudence, common fairs and festivals, rites and rituals, ceremonies and sacraments.'* What Savarkar calls the Hindu Sanskriti can loosely be identified with the Hindu ethos or way of life that the Sangh Parivar wants to preserve and which, in different terminological iterations, we find being used by all the Sangh ideologues down to the present day. For Golwalkar, it was the Hindu Samskaras that needed to be preserved, while for Deendayal Upadhyaya, it was Bharatiya culture,[22] which had to be maintained. Savarkar returned to the theme of Hindu Sanskriti several times in his essay 'Hindutva: Who is a Hindu?' 'We have feasts and festivals in common. We have rites and rituals in common. The Dasara and the Divali, the Rakhibandhan and the Holi are welcomed wherever a Hindu breathes.... The Rathayatra festival at Jagannath, the Vaishakhi at Amritsar, the Kumbha and Ardhakumbha—all these great gatherings had been the real and living congress of our people.... The quaint customs and ceremonies and sacraments they involve...impress upon each individual that he can live best only through the common and corporate life of the Hindu race. These then in short... constitute the essence of our civilization and mark us out a cultural unit.'[23]

This assertion that the cultural and ritualistic aspects of Hinduism are the defining feature of what it means to be Hindu, is a line of thinking that the Sangh has continued to this day and it is reflected in their actions. Customs and traditions that were part of the social fabric of Hindus are all endowed with a quasi-religious meaning as forming the Hindu samskars. Golwalkar wrote:

> We pride ourselves upon our spiritual tradition. But how are we actually living? What are our daily samskars? Is there any place for God in all our daily routine? Is there at least some place in our homes where we can contemplate upon Him? Once an acquaintance of mine invited me to visit his newly built house. It was a well-furnished and in every sense a 'modern' house. When he had finished showing me its special features, I just asked him, 'Well, where is the devagriha? Have you no family deity, which your forefathers had worshipped and handed down to you?' My question came as a surprise to him. He replied apologetically, 'Yes, yes, but I had forgotten all about it.[24]

---

*See Chapter 2, 'What is Hindutva?', p. 55.

The Sangh is not trying to deceitfully foster a cultural conservatism cloaked as preservation of religion. The ideologues of the Sangh Parivar, and their followers, genuinely believe that the customs, traditions, and rituals they want to freeze in time and which they want Hindus to follow in perpetuity, are linked to Hindu spirituality. It is a reflection of their understanding of Hinduism itself. Throughout Golwalkar's *Bunch of Thoughts*, there are appeals and impassioned pleas to preserve Hindu samskar. Even the most quotidian custom or habit of life can be elevated to a spiritual principle by the thinkers of the Sangh. Thus Golwalkar writes:

> One of our ancient customs is to get up early in the morning before sunrise. Once a sadhu described to me his early childhood, how his mother used to get up early in the morning and, while doing the normal household duties, would be reciting in her melodious voice various hymns describing the glory of the Divine Mother of the Universe, and how she would awaken him with words invoking Her holy blessings. The Sadhu said, 'Those holy words which I used to hear immediately after I woke up from my sleep went deep into my being, purified me, gave me faith and strength to resist all worldly temptations and devote myself to the service of the Mother.' This is Hindu samskar.... But, unfortunately what do we see at present? All such benevolent customs and codes of conduct are ridiculed as superstition.[25]

For the Sangh, markers of ethno-religious identity have to be adhered to and performed, so that every Hindu may identify deeply with the notion of being a Hindu. This is also important to set them apart from other communities, to define a very strong Hindu identity through promoting the idea of difference. But the raison d'être for being Hindu is always linked to Hinduism's great spiritual heritage. Golwalkar writes, '...our young men must be made to feel proud of being born in the great lineage of Rishis and Yogis. If we have to live up to their legacy, we must live as Hindus, we must appear as Hindus and also we must make ourselves felt by the whole world as Hindus. It is only when we learn to respect ourselves, our national customs and manners that we can hope to command respect from the outside world also.'[26]

Sangh thinkers hardly ever discuss Hindu theology or philosophy. For the most part, they seem completely ignorant of it. Rituals, customs, traditions, festivals, mythical objects of worship, and other markers of ethno-religious identity are considered as genuine expressions of the spirituality preached by Hinduism as well as necessary pathways for the community to access that spirituality.

When Mohan Bhagwat said, 'Gau mata and Ram form the basis of the Hindu culture',[27] he was not only making a political statement, but also expressing his understanding of Hinduism. Golwalkar, in a typical mixing of religion and culture, recounts how he had instructed that youngsters belonging to the ABVP on a visit to Pune, should not be put up in 'westernised' homes, but ones in which Hindu traditions are followed. 'They must reside in homes where the light is lit before the deity every morning and evening, where our festivals and customs are very much alive, and where they can imbibe our cultural norms.'[28]

Cultural change is seen as tantamount to a loss of religion. For the RSS, Hinduisim is defined by ethno-religious and cultural parameters, and it is partly because of this that the Sangh treats Hinduism as an ahistorical monolith which has remained essentially unchanged in its pristine purity since Vedic times. There are thus three major components of the Sangh's Hindutva project. One is that of achieving communitarian hegemony presented as nationalism, the second is that of cultural conservatism, and the third is religious. The second and third especially flow into each other. For the Sangh, it is only by obeying religio-cultural rules, codes of conducts, and norms that Hindu spirituality can be preserved and manifested. Referring to the Indian diaspora in the West, Golwalkar writes how they should preserve the spirituality of Hinduism by preserving their identity, which is to be done through following certain practices.

> Those who go over there seem to lose their identity altogether. Their habits of food, daily customs and traditions all get changed.... It is necessary, therefore, that our Hindu brethren there, who have imbibed the right samskars here, should meet regularly with a view to rekindling among all our people there the spirit of national pride.... Apart from their regular assemblage, there should be daily singing of bhajans and shlokas at home. Especially the children should be taught to recite the same with due devotion and earnestness. And wherever there are our temples the Hindus should cultivate the habit of congregating on certain holy occasions and conduct programmes like satsangs and havans.'[29] Talking about converting Christians and Muslims to Hinduism, Golwalkar identifies the same kind of cultural and religious elements as constituting the matrix of being a Hindu. 'This is a call for all those brothers to take their original place in our national life.... This is only a call and request to them to understand things properly and come back and identify themselves with their ancestral Hindu way of life in dress, customs, performing marriage ceremonies and funeral rites and such other things.[30]

The Sangh Parivar continues to practice the same kind of religio-cultural conservatism today. The essence of Hinduism is seen as tied to customs like Raksha Bandhan, kumbh mela, temples, pilgrimages, and various Hindu social customs. For example, the RSS mouthpiece *Organiser* recently ran a story which was an extract from a book titled *Tales of Bharat* that discussed the Vat Savitri Vrat. The ritual has been criticized as patriarchal and in an attempt to rationalize it, the article follows the same pattern of mixing social structure (in this case the family) and the spiritual.

> On this day, women in many parts of Bharat tie a thread around the Vat Vruksh (pipal tree) and pray for the long life of their husband. Many 'modern' people wonder why the wife has to keep fasts and pray for the husband. Why don't husbands do this? Actually, the husband has no choice but pass on his accrued blessings to his wife. As per our Shastras, half of the blessings (punya) got when a husband does a Puja, pilgrimage, mediation or any good deed, goes to the wife. No question asked, no option given! But the blessings received by a wife are not split between the husband and the wife.
>
> Now, how can the wife show her gratitude to her husband? She prays for him and keeps a fast for his long and happy life…. It is silly and derogatory to call this 'patriarchal abuse of women', like some are calling it these days.[31]

As usual in such rationalizations by the Sangh and those sympathetic to its cultural and religious aims, a vague appeal is made to 'our scriptures'. This hardly gives the impression of a serious theological statement. Which scripture? What verse? What is the status of this scripture in the Hindu canon? What about those scriptures that say the opposite thing? Of course, there is no dearth of Hindu scriptures and it is quite possible one many find ideas corresponding to these in one or the other, but the vagueness makes one suspect that either half-baked knowledge based on folklore or a fertile imagination is at play here.

In the second chapter, we saw Vivekananda's derision for those who were obsessed with ritualism and how he thought Hinduism was being degraded by ritualism. But it can be argued that Vivekananda's criticism was directed at the orthodoxy of his time; that he objected to degenerated practices that were popular in his day and that the customs, traditions, and rituals that are now championed by the Sangh are genuine expressions of Hindu spirituality. Before we look at Vivekananda's views in this regard, a few lines are required to address what kind of religious discourse Vivekananda preached. This question arises because Vivekananda preached both about universal religion and Vedanta. Vedanta literally means the end of the Vedas and refers to the last section of the Vedas, the knowledge portion, or the Upanishads. Vedanta also refers to the most famous philosophical school of classical Hinduism, and the only one which has survived into the present day. Hence, for all practical purposes, it can be considered the philosophical core of Hinduism.

Vivekananda delivered speeches and lectures both on universal religion and Vedanta. It is often difficult to separate the two in his discourses, the reason being that Vivekananda's idea of universal religion as well as of Vedanta grew out of the putative mystical experiences of his guru Sri Ramakrishna, as well as his own. They were cut of the same cloth. But we can make a distinction in principle. When Vivekananda talked of religion or spirituality without reference to Vedanta, he was talking about what he took to be the common essence shared by all the great religious traditions. In that sense, what he said automatically applied to Hinduism also. When he talked about Vedanta, he was either addressing Hinduism directly, or his words had direct implications for Hinduism.

For Vivekananda, the goal of religion was the realization of the divine or the transcendental. While some religions like Hinduism, Buddhism, and Jainism recognized this explicitly in their philosophy and theology, this knowledge was bound up with esoteric mystical traditions within other religions, especially the Abrahamic faiths. Each religion oriented itself towards the transcendental, and what it asked of its adherents are different ways towards this ultimate goal. As far as Hinduism was concerned, Vivekananda was categorical in what the religion demanded of its followers. 'Hinduism indicates one duty, only one, for the human soul. It is to seek to realize the permanent amidst the evanescent. No one presumes to point out any one way in which this may be done. Marriage or non-marriage, good or evil, learning or ignorance, any of these is justified, if it leads to the goal,' Vivekananda said.[32] There could hardly be a more radically opposite view to that of all the rules of conduct of living that the Sangh believes the Hindu owes to her religion.

The most consistent and recurrent theme in Vivekananda's discourses on religion, which is repeated again and again, is that religion consists of an essential and non-essential part. When asked in an interview by an American reporter what exactly about religion it was that he was teaching, Vivekananda replied:

It is really the philosophy of religion, the kernel of all its outward forms. All forms of religion have an essential and a non-essential part. If we strip from them the latter, there remains the real basis of all religion, which all forms of religion possess in common. Unity is behind them all. We may call it God, Allah, Jehovah, the Spirit, Love; it is the same unity that animates all life, from its lowest form to its noblest manifestation in man. It is on this unity that we need to lay stress, whereas in the West, and indeed everywhere, it is on the non-essential that men are apt to lay stress. They will fight and kill each other for these forms, to make their fellows conform. Seeing that the essential is love of God and love of man, this is curious, to say the least.[33]

The kernel or essential part of religion is spiritual knowledge, whose acme is direct knowledge of the divine or the Absolute. Then there are the outward forms in which this knowledge is expressed. Men confuse these forms, which are concrete and particular, for the abstract knowledge that is expressed through them. They fight and kill each other over these outward forms. What does Vivekananda mean by 'outward forms'? For Vivekananda, outward forms consisted of rituals, customs, traditions, mythology, and symbols—in other words, the very paraphernalia of Hindu religion that the Sangh Parivar has caught hold of and elevates as the 'Hindu way of life'. Vivekananda's view makes it crystal clear that Savarkar's Sanskriti of 'feasts and festivals', 'rites and rituals', or Golwalkar's 'samskars' have no part to play in Hindu religion. Vivekananda said, 'Ceremonials and symbols etc. have no place in our religion which is the doctrine of the Upanishads, pure and simple. Many people think the ceremonial etc. help them in realising religion. I have no objection.'[34]

According to Vivekananda, the essence of Hinduism was the direct perception of Ishvara (personal God) or Brahman (the Absolute) in mystical experience, in an altered state of consciousness that Vivekananda termed 'superconsciousness'. All concrete forms of religion, whether rituals, festivals, or ceremonials, were symbolisms through which the mind tries to grasp the abstract principle. They are all optional aids, available for those who want to take their help. According to Vivekananda, the more highly evolved a person is spiritually, the less she had needs of rituals and customs. Vivekananda understood well enough that most people need religious symbols in order to visualize the divine, which is not only abstract but beyond conceptualization. He did not expect every Hindu to turn into a yogi or mystic overnight. But he was acutely aware of the danger that the symbol could get mistaken for the object of symbolism and that this would lead to a regress of religion. He said:

Religion is not going to church, or putting marks on the forehead, or dressing in a peculiar fashion; you may paint yourselves in all the colours of the rainbow, but if the heart has not been opened, if you have not realized God, it is all vain. If one has the colour of the heart, he does not want any external colour. That is the true religious realization. We must not forget that colours and all these things are good so far as they help; so far they are all welcome. But they are apt to degenerate and instead of helping they retard, and a man identifies religion with externalities. Going to the temple becomes tantamount to spiritual life. Giving something to a priest becomes tantamount to religious life.[35]

The phrase 'identifying religion with externalities' can serve today as the most apt definition of the religious aspect of the RSS and the Sangh Parivar's Hindutva project.

It is important that we do not misunderstand Vivekananda as the kind of mystic or ascetic who was completely isolated from the popular forms of Hindu religious life. Totapuri, the wandering ascetic who taught Advaita to Sri Ramakrishna, was such a figure and many such existed in the India of that time. But both Ramakrishna, who was the priest at the Kali temple at Dakshineshwar, and Vivekananda, were both very much part of the current of mainstream Hindu religious life. After establishing the Ramakrishna Math at Belur, Calcutta, Vivekananda conducted yearly Durga Pujas on a grand scale. He himself occasionally worshipped Hindu deities through pujas, but as symbolic worship, not in its ritualistic form with a set of rules choreographing its conduct according to shastric instructions. Vivekananda did not expect the Hindu community to live a religious life devoid of ritualistic celebrations and sacred symbols. Several contemporary Hindu reform societies like Brahmo Samaj or the Arya Samaj attempted radical reforms to Hindu religion and practice, including the abolition of idol worship. Vivekananda's reform programme was more modest, seeking to root out what he believed to be superstitious rituals which were the product of Brahminical priestcraft and were antithetical to the spirit of Hinduism as expressed in its primary scriptures viz. the Vedas, Upanishads, and Bhagavad Gita. The reformation of Hinduism Vivekananda worked towards has been carried through only very partially even to this day. But even if it were fully implemented, it would leave most of the structure of Hindu practices, excepting its orthodox ritualism, intact. How these practices are viewed and understood, however, would change tremendously.

What Vivekananda wanted Hindus to understand, and this flowed directly from the philosophy of the Upanishads and Gita, was that all traditions, customs, rites, and even the various forms of deities, were only a means to a spiritual end and not an end in themselves. For almost a century, the RSS has promoted the values of Hinduism as living in accordance with its ancient heritage; their watchwords have been discipline and conformity. For an extraordinary individualist like Vivekananda, nothing could be more abhorrent than a life lived according to external rules, whether in the secular or religious domain. He said, 'If living by rule alone ensures excellence, if it be virtue to follow strictly the rules and customs handed down through generations, say then, who is more virtuous than a tree, who is a greater devotee, a holier saint, than a railway train?'[36]

If one mines Vivekananda's work extensively enough, one would probably find a few statements that promote some custom or particular kind of worship in a specific context. The problem of the public debate about Vivekananda is that those who profess different interpretations of him can provide at least a few quotes, which seem to support their reading. It is impossible for someone who has not read Vivekananda herself to know whether such quotes are representative of the monk's thinking or whether they are anomalous strands, aberrations, or context-dependent statements. One objective metric of how the Hinduism that Vivekananda discoursed on has almost nothing in common with the kind of Hinduism the Sangh talks about, is the frequency with which the elements that the latter values as constitutive of Hinduism occur in Vivekananda's work. In the nine volumes of Vivekananda's *The Complete Works*, there is not a single mention of Holi, Diwali, Dussehra, Raksha Bandhan, or the various holy days. There is just a single passing reference to the Kumbh Mela in a letter he sent. In his speeches to the Hindu public, Vivekananda never tried to talk about what customs or traditions Hindus should follow. What he preached was a return to the philosophy of the Vedas, which he specified meant a return to the Vedanta. 'Vedanta means the end of the Vedas, the third section or Upanishads, containing the ripened ideas which we find more as germs in the earlier portion,' Vivekananda clarified.[37] The progressive development of metaphysical ideas from the earlier ritualistic parts of the Vedas, to the 'ripened ideas' in the Upanishads is elaborated by the late scholar of Indian philosophy, T. M. P. Mahadevan: 'The Upanisads are usually concluding sections of the Brahmanas (a section of a Veda that concludes the ritualistic portion),* and the transition from Bhrahmana to Upanisad is effected through what is known as Aranyaka. The Brahmanas lay down rules and directions concerning the performance of rituals. The Upanisads contain the teachings about the ultimate Reality. In the Aranyakas, the rituals are given allegorical interpretations and certain meditations are prescribed, which

---

*My insertion.

pave the way for the philosophy of the Upanisads.'[38]

Every major religious tradition has a scriptural canon and an established view, or set of competing views, on how to interpret this canon. The RSS makes all kinds of claims about Hinduism, but without any theological backing, or any reference to the more than two millennia-long hermeneutical tradition of Hinduism. Thus, regional and local customs are elevated into being the very essence of Hinduism; the taboo on eating beef is an example of this. Beef was consumed by large sections of Hindus for a long part of India's history, especially in ancient India. 'Beef eating remained a fairly common practice for a long time in India...scholars have drawn attention to the textual evidence on the subject, which, in fact starts to become available in the oldest Indian religious text, *Rgveda*,' writes D. N. Jha.[39] The consumption of beef by Hindus is not geographically or demographically uniform throughout present-day India.* In other words, the Sangh wants to make a local dietary custom an integral component of Hindu theology. Vivekananda derided such tendencies to universalize local customs in his own time, more than once. For instance, he said, 'The Brahmin of Southern India, for instance, would shrink in horror at the sight of another Brahmin eating meat; a Brahmin in the North thinks it a most glorious and holy thing to do—he kills goats by the hundreds in sacrifice. If you put forward your custom, they are equally ready with theirs. Various are the customs all over India, but they are local. The greatest mistake made is that ignorant people always think that this local custom is the essence of our religion.'[40]

How was Vivekananda's own exposition of Hinduism grounded in the Hindu tradition? And what exactly did he teach about essential Hindu practices and beliefs that clarified them in a new light? The principle Vivekananda uses to abstract the core of Hindu philosophical beliefs (and how these beliefs inform practice) is the ancient hermeneutical principle of dividing Hindu scriptures into Shruti and Smriti, which is accepted almost universally in Hindu scriptural literature and the six schools of Hindu philosophy.[41] Shruti is that which is heard, that is, divinely revealed, while Smriti, is that which is remembered. The four Vedas are considered to be Shruti; the Smritis consist of the Puranas, and the Dharmashastras and other shastras. The Shruti is considered the ultimate authority for knowledge and the Smritis are considered to be a secondary

---

*There is no prohibition on eating beef for Hindus in the state of Kerala, and among many castes in Tamil Nadu. Assam, West Bengal, and Meghalaya consume the most beef. According to the National Sample Survey (NSS) data, 71 percent of the Hindus who consume beef are SC/STs, while only 7 percent are upper castes. See Roshan Kishore and Ishan Anand, 'Who are the beef eaters in India?', *Mint*, 20 October 2015.

source of knowledge, which base their knowledge on the Shrutis. Whenever a conflict is found between Shruti and Smriti on some issue, it is the view of the Shruti that prevails. This hermeneutical rule perhaps finds its earliest articulation in the Purva Mimamsa Sutra (300–200 BCE),[42] is reflected in the Bhagavad Gita, and is pervasive throughout Hindu scriptural literature. Most of the Smritis, including the Puranas, and the two great epics Ramayana and Mahabharata, cite Shruti as the ultimate source of knowledge.

But saying that Shruti is the primary authority does not in itself get one very far. By the end of the classical age of Hinduism (200–500 CE), the stories of the Puranas or the codes of conduct of the Dharmashastras, were much easier to understand than the Shrutis (the Vedas), with their ancient hymns and poetic philosophical speculations and abstruse and almost cryptic metaphysics. The Shruti required systematic philosophical interpretation. The first attempt to do this took the shape of the Brahmasutras, traditionally attributed to Vyasa, which seek to interpret the metaphysics and ethics of the Upanishads. As different philosophical systems arose, they interpreted the metaphysics of the Vedas differently, but they followed the principle of the subordination of Smriti to Shruti. This accounts for the primacy that is still given to the Vedas in contemporary Hindu imagination, even though they are hardly read any more, and religious practices and beliefs revolve around later scriptures, many produced during the medieval period or later.

As the second half of the nineteenth century progressed, Vedanta became the only extant philosophical system, with Hindus of various sects, at least indirectly, seeking support from the various schools of Vedanta. This made the philosophical unification of Hinduism an easier task for Vivekananda compared to his predecessors in the sixteenth and seventeenth centuries, like Vijnanabhikshu who had to show the underlying unity of all the philosophical systems.[43] In fact, Vivekananda suggested that the Hindus stop calling themselves Hindus. 'The word Hindu, by which it is the fashion nowadays to style ourselves, has lost all its meaning, for this word merely meant those who lived on the other side of the river Indus (in Sanskrit, Sindhu). This name was murdered into Hindu by the ancient Persians, and all people living on the other side of the river Sindhu were called by them Hindus. Thus this word has come down to us; and during the Mohammedan rule we took up the word ourselves. There may not be any harm in using the word of course; but, as I have said, it has lost its significance.... I therefore, would not use the word Hindu. What word should we use then? The other words which alone we can use are either the Vaidikas, followers of the Vedas, or better still, the Vedantists, followers of the Vedanta.'[44]

The Shruti/Smriti distinction, though ubiquitous in the Hindu scriptural tradition finds a very formal articulation in the words of the first great Vedanta philosopher, in fact, the first known Hindu philosopher to build a complete and comprehensive metaphysical system, Shankara (eighth century CE). Shankara also introduces a sharp distinction within the category of Shruti. By virtue of chronology as well as subject matter, he argues that the Jnana Kanda, that is, the Upanishads, are the sole source of spiritual knowledge. The Karma Kanda, the ritualistic portion, is delimited to the realm of secular matters, and Shankara states unequivocally that no ritual can conduce to spirituality. Despite the fact that the Advaita (non-dual)* philosophy of Shankara has never reached the majority of the Hindus, it has retained its place as the most influential philosophical interpretation of Hinduism, because most of the principal Upanishads,† propound an impersonal Brahman and proclaim or indicate the identity of the individual Self (Atman) with Brahman, lending itself most naturally, to a non-dual interpretation. There are several nuanced explanations that are needed to substantiate this statement, but such a philosophical discussion is beyond the scope of this book.

All the schools of Vedanta are based on the Upanishads and hence accord them supremacy over the Karma Kanda of the Vedas.‡ The majority of the Upanishads deny that rituals lead to any spiritual upliftment, at best interpreting them as allegories for practices of meditation and enquiry into the nature of the Self. But many Upanishads deny the use of rituals categorically, while some harshly deride them. 'The spirit of the Upaniṣads by its very nature is opposed to ritual. In the Brihadaranyaka (an Upanishad) he who worships a divinity other than the self is described as a domestic animal of the gods, and it is also stated that while Yama, the god of death has his abode in (ritual) sacrifice, sacrifice has its basis in the fees paid to the priests. Parodying the priestly procession in a sacrifice, the Chandogya (Upanishad) describes a procession of dogs chanting "Om! Let us eat. Om! Let us drink...",' writes T. M. P. Mahadevan in *History of Philosophy Eastern and Western*.[45] Vivekananda put it thus, 'The ideal of the first part of the Vedas is entirely different from the ideal of the other part, the Upanishads. The ideal of the first part coincides with [that of] all other religions of the world except the Vedanta. The ideal is

---

*Refer to p. 208 in this chapter.
†Called the Mukhya Upanishads, they are thirteen in number.
‡The only exception is Ramanuja's Vishishtadvaita school. For Ramanuja, along with Shruti, the Pancharatna and the saying of the Alvar saints had primary authority. But Smriti remained dependent on Shruti for authority.

enjoyment here and hereafter—man and wife, husband and children. Pay your dollar, and the priest will give you a certificate, and you will have a happy time afterwards in heaven.... Side by side, there was the other system. The Upanishads are diametrically opposite in all their conclusions...the Upanishads condemn all the sacrifices and say that it is mummery.'[46]

The Vedantic tradition from Shankara onwards builds on a set of canonical texts called the Prasthanatrayi (the three axioms), mentioned here in the order of decreasing epistemic authority. They are the Upanishads (the Shruti Prasthana or text of revelation), the Bhagavad Gita (the Sadhana Prasthana or practical text), and the Brahma Sutras (the Nyaya Prasthana or the logical texts). As mentioned before, the Brahmasutras are the first commentary to be composed that tried to create a philosophical system out of the mystical philosophy and poetry of the Upanishads. Technically, the Bhagavad Gita is Smriti, belonging to the Bhishma Parva of the Mahabharata. But the Gita has been traditionally given an epistemic status on par with the Upanishads, and is treated as Shruti, and is often termed the Gitopanishad.

Vivekananda, who is probably the most original, and definitely the most influential expositor of Advaita after Shankara, focused his discourses only on the Upanishads and the Gita, completely eschewing any reference to the more philosophically technical, but dry, text of the Brahmasutra. This was in part, because of the nature of the audience he spoke to. But it was also because Brahmasutras, not being Shruti, did not have the scriptural authority of the Upanishads and the Gita. Vivekananda wanted to categorically clarify what the sources of scriptural authority in Hinduism are, in opposition to the orthodox Brahminical and priestly section who wanted to claim scriptural authority for all kinds of ritualistic texts and various books of social law, including the *Manusmriti*.

Keeping in mind that he's an Advaitist, how did Vivekananda modify the Hindu tradition? When we answer this question, we must remember that all major spiritual figures in Hinduism, whether it is Shankara, Ramanuja, Madhva, Chaitanya, Kabir, Mira Bai and the Bhakti poets, the Alwars and Nayanars, and countless others, all modified the existing tradition, sometimes in radical ways. No religion is a static monolith through history but rather remains in a dynamic process of change and continuity, and no religious tradition is as heterogenous and seemingly contradictory as Hinduism or has undergone the same extent of historical change.* Shankara was not the first Advaitin, but his theory of

---

*This can perhaps also be said of Buddhist doctrine which has undergone extreme transformations in historical time and geographic space, but as a practised religion Buddhism still displays a comparatively higher level of homogeneity.

maya, of which we can find only the faintest shadows in the Upanishads, revolutionized Hindu philosophical thought. Shankara was responding to a crisis in Hindu thought brought about by the Buddhist philosophical challenge. The Madhyamika school of Buddhism, especially in the work of the great philosopher Nagarjuna, attacked the notion of essences (svabhava); that is, the idea that something has an inherent nature that defines its existence. This was aimed primarily at the Buddhist school of Sarvastivada, which believed that there were eternally existing cosmic principles (dharmas). It was also aimed at the Upanishadic notion of Brahman/Atman which assumes a permanent unchanging nature. Shankara's genius lay in developing a conception of Brahman that while retaining the idea of permanence, could dispense with the notion of essence. Ironically in doing so, he borrowed a lot from Madhyamika Buddhist philosophy, including the concept of maya, though he modified it considerably.

In the same way, Vivekananda's exposition of Hinduism was a response to the intellectual challenge posed to the religion by science and intellectual modernity and a zeitgeist that viewed knowledge as subject to the demands of evidence-based reason. So, one significant way in which Vivekananda shifted the terms of the Hindu philosophical discourse was by making the scriptures subject to reason. This allowed Hinduism to meet the challenge of modernity by formalizing in the philosophical discourse what has been inherent as an implicit principle in a substantial part of its tradition: that any man or even woman was allowed to disagree with scriptural statements on religion without inviting charges of heterodoxy, or blasphemy.* Even in Shankara, who is at pains to establish the authority of the Vedas when it comes to his philosophical discussions, though the Vedas, that is, the Upanishads, are considered one of the sources of knowledge of Brahman, it reads like a purely strategic move. In fact, this is necessarily so, because Shankara declares again and again (for example in his famous commentary on the Brahmasutras, the Brahmasutra Bhasya), that Brahman cannot be reached by language or thought. As such the Vedas cannot give any positive knowledge of Brahman, but only orient the seeker after spiritual truth towards the path to follow in their search for truth. But most significantly, Vivekananda's rejection of scriptures as a final authority was a return to the epistemology of the Vedas itself. The Upanishads declare that reading the scriptures will not give you knowledge of Brahman. As Mahadevan notes, 'The Upanishads make a distinction between two kinds of knowledge,

---

*It is only the rejection of the value of the Vedas as valid scriptures in toto, like the Buddhists and Jains, that made someone heterodox.

the higher (para) and lower (a-para). The lower knowledge consists of all the empirical sciences and arts as also of such sacred knowledge as related to things and enjoyments that perish. It is interesting to know that even the four Vedas are included in the category of lower knowledge.'[47] Vivekananda was also speaking from the authority of his putative mystical experiences and was drawing from the esoteric ascetic tradition. Rather than philosophy or reading of scriptures, it has been the sanyasis and their accounts of encountering the transcendental which have always been the basis for popular piety in India, much like how Sufi pirs were for Islam till the decline of Sufism in the nineteenth century. Mystical traditions, and particularly Hindu ones, have emphasized practice and spiritual realization over reading scriptures.

In a lecture delivered in the West, titled 'Soul, God and Religion', Vivekananda gave expression to this perspective through an analogy.

> Many years ago, I visited a great sage of our own country, a very holy man.* We talked of our revealed book, the Vedas, of your Bible, of the Koran, and of revealed books in general. At the close of our talk, this good man asked me to go to the table and take up a book; it was a book which, among other things, contained a forecast of the rainfall during the year. The sage said, 'Read that.' And I read out the quantity of rain that was to fall. He said, 'Now take the book and squeeze it.' I did so and he said, 'Why, my boy, not a drop of water comes out. Until the water comes out, it is all book, book. So until your religion makes you realize God, it is useless.'[48]

The Vedas are almost talismanic in the Sangh's consciousness and its understanding of Hinduism. For RSS thinkers and Sangh idealogues, the Vedas are the repository of all wisdom. Vivekananda drew inspiration from the Upanishads, asked Hindus to read them, and considered them the most sublime spiritual texts in the world. That said, however, it was only a book. Vivekananda said, 'Personally I take as much of the Vedas as agrees with reason. Parts of the Vedas are apparently contradictory.'[49] When asked about the nature of the Vedas during a discussion in a club in Boston, Vivekananda answered, 'One peculiarity of the Vedas is that they are the only scriptures that again and again declare that you must go beyond them. The Vedas say that they were written just for the child mind; and when you have grown, you must go beyond them.'[50] The metaphor of the spiritual journey is millennia old and

---

*The unnamed sage seems to have been Sri Ramakrishna Paramahamsa.

occurs in almost every religion. In mature mystical traditions like Yoga, Islamic Sufism, and the Jewish Kabbalah, the various stages of the journey are named and classified. For Vivekananda and for Sri Ramakrishna,[51] the scriptures of all religions, including the Vedas, did not even provide a rough map of the terrain to be travelled in the search for spiritual truth. It is only the guru who has already travelled through that terrain who can guide the disciple in his journey. (The master–disciple relationship and the initiation ritual are also a common feature of most mystical traditions, though there are exceptions.) All that the scriptures do is point the way; they are like the wayposts at the beginning of a traveller's journey. But those who deify their scriptures are like travellers who keep standing at the waypost and read the directions over and over again as if they can make the journey just by repeatedly reading the directions; or worse, imagine that the waypost is the destination. It is, as Vivekananda said, a case of identifying 'externalities' with religion.

Vivekananda gave Hindus a sense of pride and faith in their religious heritage when their native belief was being undermined through the delegitimization of Hinduism by colonial forces. So, there are a few instances of him talking about how a smattering of education has made Hindus think that their scriptures are worthless. This can be and is conveniently read as being the same kind of religious conservatism that prompts the Sangh to bemoan the loss of respect for the Vedas and Hindu tradition because of Westernization. Not only are the historical contexts completely different, but even when faced with the undermining of Hinduism by British imperialism Vivekananda never demanded or wanted Hindus to respect and revere the Vedas as an obligation. What he wanted of them—that is, the English educated Hindu youth mainly—was to give the same epistemic primacy to Indian thought as to Western philosophy, as possible sources of knowledge. But whether reading the Upanishads or the philosophy of a Locke or a Bishop Berkeley (familiar reading material for Indian graduates then), Vivekananda wanted Hindus to approach them in the spirit of critical enquiry, not reverence. Vivekananda sometimes remarked that the atheist was closer to discovering God because he thought for himself, while those who believed in religion blindly had not even begun the search for spiritual truth.*

In fact, for Vivekananda, even when you had accepted a religious tradition, it was important to view it from a critical standpoint if one were to find the true sources of wisdom in that tradition. 'The man who discovers a spiritual

---

*See Chapter 10, p. 332.

law is inspired, and what he brings is revelation; but revelation too is eternal, not to be crystallised as final and then blindly followed,' he said.[52] In his view, all religious traditions, Hinduism included, contained much that was dross, irrelevant, irrational, misleading, erroneous, or just superfluous. He told a Western audience: 'The Hindus have been criticized so many years by their conquerors that they (the Hindus) dare to criticize their religion themselves, and this makes them free. ...Nor have they any artificial respect for prophets or books, or for hypocritical piety.'[53] In the nineteenth century and earlier, before the nationalist phase started, the statement about Hindus often criticizing things in their own religion was quite true, as attested to by many contemporary accounts by both Indians and Europeans.

Vivekananda himself had no artificial respect for the prophets and books of Hinduism. That is, while he considered them great sources of spirituality in general, he did not consider them above critical scrutiny or criticism. He often remarked that all Indian philosophers, many of whom are considered saints, resorted to text torturing of the scriptures to prove their point. Vivekananda's own spiritual ideal, what he called his 'ishta deva', was the Buddha; he even favoured Buddha over Shankara. 'Shankara sometimes resorts to sophistry in order to prove that the ideas in the books go to uphold his philosophy. Buddha was more brave and sincere than any teacher. He said: "Believe no book; the Vedas are all humbug. If they agree with me, so much the better for the books. I am the greatest book; sacrifice and prayer are useless." Buddha was the first human being to give to the world a complete system of morality. He was good for good's sake, he loved for love's sake.'[54]

Though in several speeches and lectures, Vivekananda spoke of the spirituality manifested in Shankara, over time he started entertaining doubts about his Advaitic predecessor. He was troubled by Shankara's lack of concern with the sufferings of humankind and also a few passages in his most famous work, the commentary on the Brahmasutras (Bhrahmasutra Bhashya) which restricted Shudras to the reading of Puranas (Smriti) and prohibited them from reading Vedas (Shruti). In a letter written to a friend in 1897, Vivekananda writes: 'Ramanuja*, Shankara etc., seem to have been mere Pundits with much narrowness of heart. Where is that love, that weeping heart at the sorrow of others?—Dry pedantry of the Pundit—and the feeling of only oneself getting to salvation hurry—scurry! But is that going to be possible, sir? Was it ever

---

*This comment on Ramanuja is an anamolus one. Vivekananda generally spoke of Ramanuja as large-hearted and his movement as one which tried to include the lower castes.

likely or will it ever be so? Can anything be attained with any shred of "I" left anyhow?'[55]

'Hurting Hindu sentiments' is a favourite rallying cry for the Sangh Parivar to organize agitations, file cases, and even get people arrested for perceived slights to Hindu deities, symbols, myths, etc. It could be anything from a comedian's quip to a song on an OTT platform.[56] An instance of the extent to which Vivekananda did not care to pay mindless obeisance to what the Sangh considers the holy cows of the Hindu tradition can be seen in a letter he wrote to the scholar Paramadas Mitra. Written three years after Sri Ramakrishna's death almost to the day, a young Vivekananda wrote out a list of doubts he had to the scholar. 'Vyasa makes out in the Vedanta-Sutras that it is wrong to worship the tetrad of divine manifestation, Vasudeva, Sankarshana, etc., and again that very Vyasa expatiates on the great merits of that worship in the Bhagavata! *Is this Vyasa a madman?*'[57]

By the Sangh's lights, if they had been around to comment at that time, it is likely that the twenty-six-year-old Narendranath would be deemed to have fallen and lost his Hindu Sanskriti in the worst way possible. Perhaps the only question is whether they would have attributed it to his Western education or his habit of smoking. Maybe mutton curry?

✓

The RSS has had a close relationship with Brahmin orthodoxy since Independence. There have not been enough sociological studies done on this front, so one can only surmise on the exact nature of the relationship. Since the eighties, the Sangh Parivar's work of playing an increasingly active role in community religious activities of Hindus has brought them in alliance with priests and Brahmin subcastes that follow an extremely ritualistic form of Hinduism. With no ethnographic studies available, and with the complicated factor of regional variation added in, it is extremely difficult to tell what scriptures form the basis for the rituals. In the majority of the cases, going by anecdotal evidence, what is being followed are not the rituals prescribed in the Vedas. Most of the ritualistic practices that claim Shastric authority today are probably Puranic or Tantric in origin, and often derived from regional religious literature rather than Sanskrit texts. At the other end, since the time of the Ram Janmabhoomi movement, the VHP and other Sangh affiliates have created simplified rituals which they have increasingly introduced at a pan-India level with the tacit approval of the priestly class.[58]

During the 2021 Durga Puja celebrations, an article published in *Organiser* alleged Hindu sentiments had been hurt by the way artists decorated certain pooja pandals in West Bengal. The article says, 'The liberty of Hindus has been taken for granted for so long that today we see a whole lot of puppetry with the excuse of theme pujas. The Shastras do not give the leeway that some puja committees end up with, in effect hurting Hindu sentiments in the name of artistic license which works as a proxy for political beliefs.'[59] Two days later, on Vijayadashami, RSS chief Mohan Bhagwat delivered a speech which further added to the list of insults supposedly delivered to Hindu religion. This included changes in rituals introduced by temple authorities. 'Specific ceremonial guidelines and guiding texts apply to each temple and the deity residing therein. Instances of interference and meddling with those ceremonial matters have also been reported.... It is apparent for all that many decisions regarding the religious code of conduct of the temples are whimsically made without any consultation with the scholars and spiritual teachers and with indifference towards the sensitivities of the Hindu community.'[60]

The motivation for both statements is political rather than religious. But the political potency of these statements depends on convincing Hindus that they deal with a religious matter; this is how the RSS constructs a certain idea of Hinduism. This notion of Hinduism is that religiosity in Hinduism consists of ritualistic observations and worship in accordance with prescribed rules laid down in scriptures.

Vivekananda understood the history of Hinduism starting from the composition of the earliest Upanishads to his own time, as a fight between ritualism, represented by Brahmins, and real spirituality as represented by sanyasins. It was a battle that the sanyasins had won in theory, but in practice Hinduism always remained ritualistic and in the hands of the priests. And just like the Brihadaranyaka Upanishad linked the foundations of ritual sacrifices (yajna) to the priests' interest in money making, Vivekananda saw ritualism as the product of the greed of Brahmin priests. According to Vivekananda, Brahmins had invented all kinds of superstitious rituals which they foisted on to Hinduism to increase their own social power and attain wealth through the performance of rituals. Vivekananda described the historical dynamic between the priests who perverted Hinduism and the ascetic sages who rose to clarify the spiritual truths of Hinduism again and again:

> The priests in India, the Brahmins, possessed great intellectual and psychic powers. It was they who began the spiritual development of India, and they accomplished wonderful things. But the time came when the free spirit of development that had at first actuated the Brahmins disappeared.

They began to arrogate powers and privileges to themselves. If a Brahmin killed a man, he would not be punished. The Brahmin, by his very birth, is the lord of the universe! Even the most wicked Brahmin must be worshipped! But while the priests were flourishing, there existed also the poet-prophets called Sannyasins.... The Sannyasins have nothing to do with the two thousand ceremonies that the priests have invented: Pronounce certain words—ten syllables, twenty syllables, and so on—all these things are nonsense. So, these poet-prophets of ancient India repudiated the ways of the priest and declared the pure truth. They tried to break the power of the priests, and they succeeded a little. But in two generations their disciples went back to the superstitious, roundabout ways of the priests—became priests themselves: 'You can get truth only through us!' Truth became crystallised again, and again prophets came to break the encrustations and free the truth, and so it went on. Yes, there must be all the time the man, the prophet, or else humanity will die.[61]

And again, he says 'If all desires can be accomplished by the mere utterance of some meaningless syllables, then who will exert himself and go through difficulties to work out the fulfilment of his desires? If this malady enters into the entire body of any social system, then that society becomes slothful and indisposed to any exertion, and soon hastens to its ruin.'[62]

Vedic religion in its earliest form, as found in the Rig Veda, was poetic and philosophically speculative, and consisted of hymns. Later, as the Karma Kanda or the ceremonial portion developed, involving complex and elaborate sacrifices to the various Vedic gods like Indra, Varuna, and Agni, the religious life of the Aryans came to be ritual-centric. Following in the intellectual footsteps of canonical Hindu spiritual teachers and philosophers like Shankara, Gaudapada, Ramanuja, Madhva, Chaitanya, Vallabhacharya, Nimbarka, Bhaskara, and others,[63] Vivekananda located the emergence of the foundational spiritual ideas of Hinduism in the Jnana Kanda of the Vedas, i.e., the Upanishads. But he added a sociological dimension to the radical shift in the spiritual life of the Aryans. Many of the composers of the Upanishads are known to be Kshatriyas[64] and Vivekananda speculated that the ascetic rishis of the Upanishads were kings who renounced the world of sensual enjoyment in the search for truth. Vivekananda saw ritualism and priesthood as an unholy, mutually dependent, pair that had historically aided in the degeneration of Hinduism.

It was therefore in the interests of the priests that the ceremonial portion of the Vedas should be preserved. By it they had their living.

They consequently did all in their power to preserve that portion intact. Many of these ceremonials were very complicated, and it took years to perform some of them. The knowledge portion came afterwards and was promulgated exclusively by kings. It was called the Knowledge of Kings. The great kings had no use for the work portion with all its frauds and superstitions and did all in their power to destroy it. This knowledge consisted of knowledge of God, the soul, the universe, etc. These kings had no use for the ceremonials of the priests, their magical works, etc. They pronounced it all humbug.[65]

In a lecture delivered in the West on 'Vedic religious ideals', Vivekananda traced the growth of ritualism during pre-Buddhistic times and bemoaned its continuance in India.

As those spiritual ideas progressed in arithmetical progression, so the ritualistic ideas progressed in geometrical progression. The old superstitions had by this time developed into a tremendous mass of rituals, which grew and grew till it almost killed the Hindu life. And it is still there, it has got hold of and permeated every portion of our life and made us born slaves. Yet, at the same time, we find a fight against this advance of ritual from the very earliest days. The one objection raised there is this, that love for ceremonials, dressing at certain times, eating in a certain way, and shows and mummeries of religion like these are only external religion, because you are satisfied with the senses and do not want to go beyond them.[66]

Vivekananda's goal in life was to create a spiritual revolution in India and across the world. He saw his role as setting in motion the work by preaching the broadest, most universal yet intense spiritual ideas. He saw the spiritual revolution as happening gradually over several centuries. He often urged Indians, especially young Indians, to carry his work forward. Part of that process was dislodging the Brahmin priests' stranglehold on Hindu religion. He wrote to his disciples in Madras from the ship carrying him to Japan, from whence he would travel to Canada and then America. 'Come, be men! Kick out the priests who are always against progress, because they would never mend, their hearts would never become big. They are the offspring of centuries of superstition and tyranny. Root out priest craft first.'[67]

What did Vivekananda mean by ritualism? This is an important thing to get right, both to understand Vivekananda's thoughts on Hinduism and its relevance for contemporary Hindu religious practice. Formally, the word ritual denotes a series of actions, which if done in a particular sequence would produce a certain material effect. This could be doing certain things, like saying certain words, etc. This definition of ritual is wide enough to take in ritual practices from pagan sacrifices to the Catholic transubstantiation. For instance, take the case of saying a holy word a certain number of times with the idea that doing so changes something in the world—for example, it would increase a person's lifespan. This is a ritual in that it is purely performative; that is, the mental state of the agent is of no account here. What is important is that the words are spoken in the right order and the correct number of times. The idea behind a ritual, in all religions where rituals in this sense have a place, is that a mechanical execution of certain acts or utterances in the correct manner and order will result in a certain external effect.

Vivekananda, who could draw upon the insights provided by science unlike his Vedantic predecessors, could now reject rituals in the above-mentioned sense on the basis of rational principle. Vivekananda called rituals 'nonsense'[68] because in rituals there was no rational connection between cause and effect, that is, between the ritual actions performed and the results that they are supposed to produce. It is as good as saying 'Abracadabra' and expecting what you intended to happen. It is a form of magical thinking.

But the word ritual is used in a looser sense for any form of worship that follows a certain fixed pattern. In the context of Hinduism, this would cover everything from offering flowers, incense, and doing 'aarti' of a deity's idol daily, to complex temple rituals where the idol is bathed, clothed, fed, etc. By the definition of ritual that we have employed, these are not rituals because they are not merely performative. Vivekananda sometimes did perform this kind of worship (like when he worshipped the daughter of his Muslim boatsman as the Devi), and the idea behind it as Vivekananda and others (like Swami Sivananda and Chinmayananda) have elucidated, is that of symbolic visualization. We have already seen Vivekananda's explanation of image worship.[*] The abstract pure spirit cannot be visualized, and it is not easy to meditate on it without associating it with an image. So, a concrete expression is given through an idol, painting, or some other kind of representation, so that by psychological association the idea of the transcendental Spirit is brought to the mind of the worshipper and she directs her mind towards it via the medium of representation.

Now, the rites of worship can get more elaborate under two different

---

*See p. 203.

types of situations and with two different types of results. One is in the devotional tradition where the devotee intensifies the imaginative act by making the representation more detailed and concrete. The devotee imagines bathing, feeding, dressing, and serving the deity in various ways so that the relationship with the personal God becomes more intimate. The devotee by her power of imagination experiences herself as serving God rather than an idol. The other type is when this mode of worship in a temple or organized setting starts out as a number of religious people practising this mode of worship as a community, selecting a priest to carry out the mechanisms of the worship. The ideal is that the onlookers participate mentally in the imaginative construction of symbolic worship carried out by the priest. But often, perhaps in most cases, though to varying degrees, the ideal is lost sight of and as the worship becomes more elaborate, it becomes an end in itself and takes on the form of a custom. The patterns of worship then become reified and performative; the psychological attitude that motivated their rationale in the first place is forgotten and the process becomes a ritualized custom. Following the custom exactly is expected to please God, but there is no rhyme or reason why the worship should be done one way rather than another. While Vivekananda considered the first kind of worship a legitimate spiritual exercise, the second, as ritual, was mere superstition.

Vivekananda was a rationalist, and a great believer in the method of modern science, but he did not deny the existence of what are often called 'occult powers', which form a minor, but nonetheless integral part of the system of raja yoga. According to Vivekananda, there was nothing supernatural about such alleged phenomena. His definition of natural phenomena was phenomena where there was a rational connection between cause and effect which could explain the totality of the phenomena; without invoking any external agency (like God, angels, spirits, and so on), outside the causal network where the phenomena in question is the final effect. Such an explanation is tied to the metaphysics of Vedanta, and the basic idea is that mind and matter are not two completely separate entities, but degrees of manifestation of the absolute reality within the spatio-temporal and causal frame of phenomenal reality. Matter and mind are not separate entities, but subtler and grosser forms of each other respectively, which is why they can influence each other.

This is of particular significance when it comes to prayer. Prayer as communion with the divine is easily understood but what about the theistic belief that petitionary prayers are answered and can create real change in people's lives? Vivekananda gave an explanation for this in the preface to *Raja Yoga*.

Since the dawn of history, various extraordinary phenomena have been recorded as happening amongst human beings. Witnesses are not wanting in modern times to attest to the fact of such events, even in societies living under the full blaze of modern science. The vast mass of such evidence is unreliable, as coming from ignorant, superstitious, or fraudulent persons. In many instances the so-called miracles are imitations. But what do they imitate? It is not the sign of a candid and scientific mind to throw overboard anything without proper investigation. Surface scientists, unable to explain the various extraordinary mental phenomena, strive to ignore their very existence. They are, therefore, more culpable than those who think that their prayers are answered by a being, or beings, above the clouds, or than those who believe that their petitions will make such beings change the course of the universe. The latter have the excuse of ignorance, or at least of a defective system of education, which has taught them dependence upon such beings. The former have no such excuse. For thousands of years such phenomena have been studied, investigated, and generalised, the whole ground of the religious faculties of man has been analysed, and the practical result is the science of Raja Yoga. Raja Yoga does not, after the unpardonable manner of some modern scientists, deny the existence of facts which are difficult to explain; on the other hand, it gently yet in no uncertain terms tells the superstitious that miracles, and answers to prayers, and powers of faith, though true as facts, are not rendered comprehensible through the superstitious explanation of attributing them to the agency of a being, or beings, above the clouds. It declares that each man is only a conduit for the infinite ocean of knowledge and power that lies behind mankind. It teaches that desires and wants are in man, that the power of supply is also in man; and that wherever and whenever a desire, a want, a prayer has been fulfilled, it was out of this infinite magazine that the supply came, and not from any supernatural being. The idea of supernatural beings may rouse to a certain extent the power of action in man, but it also brings spiritual decay. It brings dependence; it brings fear; it brings superstition. It degenerates into a horrible belief in the natural weakness of man. There is no supernatural, says the Yogi, but there are in nature gross manifestations and subtle manifestations. The subtle are the causes, the gross the effects. The gross can be easily perceived by the senses; not so the subtle. The practice of Raja Yoga will lead to the acquisition of the more subtle perceptions.[69]

Vivekananda is not denying the existence of a personal God here. In Advaita, the personal God or Ishvara is the impersonal absolute reality of Brahman perceived through the limitations of the human mind. The direct mystical experience of the personal God is the penultimate step in spiritual realization, while the final one of enlightenment (Nirvana) is when the mind is completely merged in the absolute reality of Brahman. This seems to have been Shankara's position as well. What Vivekananda refers to as superstition and fearful dependence is the belief that one's prayer is answered by an anthropomorphic being, who as it were, sits in heaven 'above the clouds' and changes his plan for the world arbitrarily, depending on the supplication he receives from various devotees. When Vivekananda says that 'each man is only a conduit for the infinite ocean of knowledge and power that lies behind mankind…it was out of this infinite magazine that the supply came, and not from any supernatural being,' what he means is that there is no strict separation between God and man; they are part of a continuum. It is not erroneous or superstitious for a devotee to imagine that a personal God answers his prayers, as long as she is aware that God is an infinite extension of her own being. The question of God changing his will arbitrarily or of a degenerating dependence does not arise because no sharp division can be drawn between the will of the devotee focused in prayer and the will of God.

There is a final matter to take into consideration regarding Vivekananda's teachings on Hindu religious practice, to do with homas and yajnas. There is not much on these topics in Vivekananda's oeuvre, but it is reasonable to suppose that he must have talked about it to people who did not record them. But we know enough about Vivekananda's philosophy of religion in the context of Hinduism, to apply those principles to these practices. According to Vivekananda's views on rituals and prayer, traditional puja or homa, if performed with the expectation that merely executing its various components would produce a result, would be utterly useless. However, when a group of people gathered together to perform the puja, focus their minds on a desired end, the effect can be produced. But in such a case, the cause is not the elements of a puja, but the collective will power of the people, for which the elements of the puja are merely an external catalyst. But given Vivekananda's general indifference to pujas, homas, yajnas, and other practices, and from his views expressed in various places, I believe his position would have been that everything and more that can be achieved via such ceremonies can be achieved directly by prayer. Pujas, homas, and yajnas are an indirect and cumbersome way of doing something that can be achieved in a far more direct way through the power of personal devotion; and carry the ever-present danger of degenerating into superstition besides. In any case, Vivekananda was derisive towards the entire idea of attaining desires, whether through pujas or prayer. There was nothing spiritual about it, and such desires made religion a transactional, 'shopkeeper's religion'.[70] True religion begins only when you love God for God's own sake, without expecting anything in return.

٭

'Mandir politics' refers to the phase in the mid-1980s to 1992, where the Bharatiya Janata Party harvested electoral success from the Ram Janmabhoomi movement which swept north India and culminated in the destruction of the Babri Masjid by a mob of Hindutva activists, led by members of the Vishwa Hindu Parishad (VHP) and the Bajrang Dal. The political benefits may have been reaped by the BJP but the Ram Janmabhoomi movement was conceived, organized and executed by VHP cadre under the tutelage of the Rashtriya Swayam Sevak Sangh (RSS).[71] With the building of a Ram Mandir in Ayodhya under the order of the Supreme Court of India, Mandir politics has a short lease now as a national political plank for the BJP. But the same cannot be said of the Sangh Parivar organizations. Mandir politics, first forged in the Ram Janmabhoomi movement, has now become a template for the religio-cultural politics of the Sangh, and a source of local electoral gain for the BJP.[72] After the demolition of the Babri Masjid, the next spot of worship that became a focus for the Sangh Parivar, was the Baba Budan Giri cave in Chikmagalur, Karnataka.[73] Now, the cause extends to Krishna Janmabhoomi in Mathura and the Gyanvapi mosque.[74]

In all these instances, the template of the narrative is the same as with the Ram Mandir movement. A particular place is claimed to have a historical association with a mythical figure in Hindu lore. In the case of the Ram Janmabhoomi movement, Ayodhya is claimed to be the birthplace of Ram, who is considered a historical figure. Now, the first problem is that no serious historian has ever found any more evidence that a figure by the name of Ram ruled a dynasty in Ayodhya, than there is any evidence that the Grecian mythical hero Hercules existed. All ancient societies build myths. The Greeks created the Homeric myths, the Sumerians created the myth of King Gilgamesh, the Chinese of the Three Sovereigns and Five Emperors, the Jews the myth of Moses, and so on. In all such cases, the heroes of these myths either did not exist or grand myths were formed around some actual historical figure. The mythical character thus created bore no resemblance to the historical character who may have been the initial peg on which these myths were hoisted. And the events described in the myth are for the most part, entirely imaginary, though again, some historical event sometimes served as an inspiration for the myth building.

The second element is the claim that the alleged historical association of the place of worship with a divine figure in the Puranas, is somehow deeply essential for the practice of Hinduism. So, Ayodhya and the Krishna Janmabhoomi at Mathura, is elevated in popular consciousness to the kind of sacred status that the land of Israel holds for Judaism and Mecca holds for Islam. And in all these cases a Muslim shrine or mosque occupies part of the claimed land, and that structure has to be destroyed because of the Hindu claim to religious eminence. Needless, to say this combination of myth masquerading as history, religious fervour, and communal antagonism is a potent cocktail for communal polarization resulting in the consolidation of Hindu votes. The demolition of the Babri Masjid was the end result of a carefully orchestrated propaganda campaign that lasted several years through the 1980s.[75] The crowning piece of the propaganda effort to mobilize Hindu religious sentiments was a 'rath yatra', undertaken by the BJP leader L. K. Advani. The yatra was to start from Somnath temple in Gujarat and after travelling through several Indian states, finish in Ayodhya. Starting on 25 September, the yatra lasted almost a month and sparked off a series of Hindu–Muslim riots. The noted historian K. N. Panikkar estimates that 116 riots took place between 1 September and 20 November 1991, in which 554 people were killed.[76] Panikkar writes, 'Just before the yatra, the volunteers of the Bajrang Dal and the VHP, specially trained for the purpose, undertook an intense campaign to disseminate the Ayodhya message. They splashed the yatra route with saffron, pasted posters of the proposed mandir and circulated handbills about the treachery of Muslims. In the public meetings...VHP demagogues deploring the impotence the Hindus had shown in the past, extolled them to be aggressive at least now. Thus in each locality the Rathyatra entered into a surcharged atmosphere of Hindu militancy and hatred against the Muslims....'[77]

Advani imagined the Ayodhya issue as 'a controversy between Ram and Babur' and the construction of the temple an assertion of national pride. No Hindu, he averred, would live in peace unless the mandir at Ayodhya is completed. Ayodhya thus became a site for re-enacting the mythical fight, with Babur and his supposed descendants replacing Ravana and his troops.[78] As the yatra progressed, the stature of Ram steadily grew to be 'India's greatest national hero'.[79] On 6 December 1992, a group of VHP activists demolished the mosque in violation of court orders. This was followed by months of Hindu–Muslim riots, resulting in an estimated 2,000 deaths in the next two months.[80]

We have already seen in this chapter how Vivekananda did not believe in religio-ethnic identities. In fact, he saw such identities as hindrances to spiritual progress and antithetical to the universal spiritual message that Hinduism taught. He saw religion as a double-edged sword, which could deliver the greatest peace and solace to man, but could also degenerate easily into bloodshed and fanaticism. Vivekananda abhorred violence and his greatest pride in Hinduism came from the fact that, as far as was known in his time, Hindus had never persecuted others on the basis of religion. The Sangh Parivar's central narrative surrounding Hindu–Muslim enmity is focused on the need for Hindus to assert themselves against centuries of Muslim invasions and Islamic rule, and take revenge. Vivekananda was also quite aware of the destruction imposed by the conquests of Muslim invaders like Mohammad of Ghazni and the widespread destruction and looting of Hindu temples which took place. He even refers to the destruction of Somnath in one of his speeches. But the lesson he draws from it is that even if hundreds of conquests roll over India, India will regenerate itself, for he believed that spirituality was the keynote of India's national existence. Far from exhorting Hindus to resent either the British or the Muslims, he preached to them to vivify the world with the spiritual ideas of forbearance and love. First to love every Indian, then the whole of humanity, not as your brother, but your own Self. Hindu–Muslim riots were not unknown in nineteenth century India. As we saw in the second chapter, a series of Hindu–Muslim riots occurred during Vivekananda's Chicago speeches. But these were, comparatively speaking, a rare occurrence and Vivekananda does not anywhere address the question of what attitude Hindus should take when confronted with communal violence. But we get a sense of his attitude from a story he told over and over in his speeches. This was the story of a Hindu sanyasi, whom he held up as an exemplar of the Vedantic attitude. Vivekananda once called him his ideal. He said in an interview to the *Sunday Times* in London in 1896, 'I call to mind an incident of the Indian Mutiny. A Swami, who for years had fulfilled a vow of eternal silence, was stabbed by a Mohammedan. They dragged the murderer before his victim and cried out, "Speak the word, Swami, and he shall die." After many years of silence, he broke it to say with his last breath: "My children, you are all mistaken. That man is God Himself." The great lesson is, that unity is behind all.'[81]

But, putting aside the cynical politics aimed at communal polarization, what would Vivekananda have to say about the religious basis of the Ram Janmabhoomi movement? How would Vivekananda have responded to the idea that, to use Advani's words, no Hindu can live in peace without the Ram Mandir in Ayodhya being built? What significance would Vivekananda have attached to the religious claim that the figure of Ram is integral to Hinduism? And to the historical claim that Ram was a real king who ruled in Ayodhya?

The first thing to be said is it would scarcely matter to Vivekananda which temple or which deity was being claimed as central to Hinduism. While talking to some American disciples about his guru Ramakrishna Paramahansa, Vivekananda said: 'Temples have no hold on the Hindu religion; if they were all destroyed, religion would not be affected a grain.'[82] Here, Vivekananda, who worshipped at temples himself, meant to say that temples were not essential to Hinduism any more than monasteries were essential to Christianity. Temples were among those things Vivekananda considered 'external religion'. They were aids to spiritual realization, their value being purely symbolic, as in the case of idols. To think there was something special about the temple itself was to confuse means for ends to get stuck in the externals of religion. As Vivekananda said in a lecture on Bhakti:

> Throughout the history of the world, we find that man is trying to grasp the abstract through thought-forms, or symbols. All the external manifestations of religion—bells, music, rituals, books, and images—come under that head. Anything that appeals to the senses, anything that helps man to form a concrete image of the abstract, is taken hold of, and worshipped…. The spirit is the goal, and not matter. Forms, images, bells, candles, books, churches, temples, and all holy symbols are very good, very helpful to the growing plant of spirituality, but thus far and no farther. In the vast majority of cases, we find that the plant does not grow. It is very good to be born in a church, but it is very bad to die in a church. It is very good to be born within the limits of certain forms that help the little plant of spirituality, but if a man dies within the bounds of these forms, it shows that he has not grown, that there has been no development of the soul. If, therefore, any one says that symbols, rituals, and forms are to be kept for ever, he is wrong; but if he says, that these symbols and rituals are a help to the growth of the soul, in its low and undeveloped state, he is right.[83]

From the higher Advaitic viewpoint expressed in the Upanishads, the Self of the human being is identical to God or the ultimate reality. The goal of human existence in Hinduism was to realize this ultimate unity; to realize that what you called God and thought was external to you, was your true Self all along. The delusion was that you thought it was something different, something apart from you. Vivekananda says, 'Vedanta has been in India always, but India is full of these temples—and not only temples, but also caves containing carved images. "The fool, dwelling on the bank of the Ganga, digs a well for water!" Such are we! Living in the midst of God—we must go and make images. We project Him in the form of the image, while all the time He exists in the temple of our body. We are lunatics, and this is the great delusion.' And again, 'The Vedanta says, there is nothing that is not God. It may frighten many of you, but you will understand it by degrees. The living God is within you, and yet you are building churches and temples and believing all sorts of imaginary nonsense. The only God to worship is the human soul in the human body.'[84]

In the Upanishads, which are the foundational texts of Vedanta, there is little emphasis on devotion or bhakti. The impersonal Brahman, which is beyond all qualities and conceptions of the mind, cannot be worshipped. It can only be experienced. This is mukti or nirvana, the ultimate goal enjoined by Hinduism on its followers. The first primary scripture (Shruti), to introduce the idea of devotion is the Bhagavad Gita.[*] We saw how in his youth Narendranath was an ardent Advaitist who refused to accept the idea of a personal God, in spite of Ramakrishna's preachings. But once Vivekananda accepted that the idea of a personal God was not incompatible with the idea of the impersonal Brahman as the absolute reality, devotion to Kali became an integral part of his spiritual life. But nonetheless, Vivekananda's conflicting nature could not be content to rest with one perspective; and the more passionately he embraced a certain perspective, the more intense would be the moments of recoil towards the opposite perspective. Thus, there was always a part of Vivekananda which bridled at the idea that human beings should depend upon anything outside themselves, even an omnipotent God. In spite of his personal devotion, he always retained an element of discomfiture at the ideal of a personal God at the societal level. There was always the danger that it would degenerate into fanaticism and superstition and more often than not Hindu temples, just as is the case with the places of worship of other religions, end up being in an unholy nexus with priests who manipulated people for their own gain. During a lecture on 'Practical Vedanta' delivered in London in 1896, Vivekananda said:

---

[*]I am differentiating here between the kind of devotion to be found in the Karma Kanda of the Vedas and that in the Gita. The nature of devotion in Hinduism since the post-Vedic age has been of the latter kind, and similar to what is found in most monotheistic religions.

'Of course the impersonal idea is very destructive, it takes away all trade from the priests, churches, and temples. In India there is a famine now, but there are temples in each one of which there are jewels worth a king's ransom! If the priests taught this Impersonal idea to the people, their occupation would be gone. Yet we have to teach it unselfishly, without priestcraft. You are God and so am I; who obeys whom? Who worships whom? You are the highest temple of God; I would rather worship you than any temple, image, or Bible.'[85]

How did Vivekananda regard the various Gods of the Hindu pantheon? Vivekananda was personally devoted not only to Kali, but also Krishna and Shiva. We find frequent allusions and expressions of spiritual feelings towards 'Mother' (Kali), Krishna, and Shiva in Vivekananda's correspondence and in his informal conversations. Hindu theology and metaphysics speak of the unmanifest impersonal Brahman as the absolute reality. However, in its manifested personal aspect it is called Ishvara, or a personal cosmic God. The personal God is infinite and pervades the whole universe. Each deity of the Hindu pantheon is an anthropomorphic conception of a set of divine attributes. Since God has infinite attributes, no human conception of God can express all of them. It does not matter which name or form one worshipped God in, as long as it instantiated divine qualities. Hence, God with form is both imagined and real, on different planes of reality.

With Ram, Krishna, and other incarnations of God, Vivekananda did not take the mythical stories of the Puranas literally. In an interview given in Madurai to *The Hindu* in 1897, Vivekananda was asked about the historical status of the various Puranas. Vivekananda said:

Take the Ramayana, for illustration, and for viewing it as an authority on building character, it is not even necessary that one like Rama should have ever lived. The sublimity of the law propounded by Ramayana or Bharata does not depend upon the truth of any personality like Rama or Krishna, and one can even hold that such personages never lived, and at the same time take those writings as high authorities in respect of the grand ideas which they place before mankind. Our philosophy does not depend upon any personality for its truth. Thus Krishna did not teach anything new or original to the world, nor does Ramayana profess anything which is not contained in the Scriptures (Vedas).[86]

In fact, Vivekananda considered it one of the greatest advantages of Hinduism over other religions that it did not have a prophet or historical personality as its basis. In what reads almost as an anticipation of the Ram Janmabhoomi movement and its violence, Vivekananda talks about how a fixation with religious personalities can lead to peace and goodness, the very essence of religion, being lost.

In Vedanta the chief advantage is that it was not the work of one single man; and therefore, naturally, unlike Buddhism, or Christianity, or Mohammedanism, the prophet or teacher did not entirely swallow up or overshadow the principles. The principles live, and the prophets, as it were, form a secondary group, unknown to Vedanta. The Upanishads speak of no particular prophet, but they speak of various prophets and prophetesses. The old Hebrews had something of that idea.... Of course I do not mean that it is bad that these prophets should take religious hold of a nation; but it certainly is very injurious if the whole field of principles is lost sight of. We can very much agree as to principles, but not very much as to persons. The persons appeal to our emotions; and the principles, to something higher, to our calm judgment. Principles must conquer in the long run, for that is the manhood of man. Emotions many times. drag us down to the level of animals. Emotions have more connection with the senses than with the faculty of reason; and, therefore, when principles are entirely lost sight of and emotions prevail, religions degenerate into fanaticism and sectarianism. They are no better than party politics and such things. The most horribly ignorant notions will be taken up, and for these ideas thousands will be ready to cut the throats of their brethren. This is the reason that, though these great personalities and prophets are tremendous motive powers for good, at the same time their lives are altogether dangerous when they lead to the disregard of the principles they represent. That has always led to fanaticism, and has deluged the world in blood. Vedanta can avoid this difficulty, because it has not one special prophet. It has many Seers, who are called Rishis or sages. Seers—that is the literal translation—those who see these truths, the Mantras.[87]

While we do not have any comments from Vivekananda on the historicity of Ram, he discussed the historicity of Krishna several times. According to Hindu mythology, Krishna lived an epoch after Ram. Thus Krishna, if he existed, would be far closer to us in historical time than Ram. The Krishna Janmabhoomi movement that the Sangh is backing claims that a complex of temples in Mathura, mark the spot where Krishna was born.[88] Both the Mahabharata and the Bhagavata narrate that Krishna was born in Mathura. A temple, which was part of the complex, was destroyed by the Mughal emperor

Aurangzeb in 1670 and the Shahi Eidgah mosque built in its place. The Sangh now demands that the mosque be handed over to the temple trust, which would presumably raze it.[89] The rationale for this demand is that the god Krishna is a historical figure and that the Puranas give accurate details about his life, including his place of birth.

During a discussion about prophets and their role in religion, Vivekananda commented on the historicity of Krishna and other prophets. 'Two (of the prophets of different religions) are very historical: one, the most ancient, Buddha, and the other, Mohammed, because both friends and foes are agreed about them. So we are perfectly sure that there were such persons. As for the other persons, we have only to take for granted what the disciples say—nothing more. Our Krishna—you know, the Hindu prophet—he is very mythological. A good deal of his life, and everything about him, is written only by his disciples; and then there seem to be, sometimes, three or four men, who all loom into one.'[90]

The emergence of modernity is at the intellectual level a journey of society from a world view framed by religion to one framed, at least in principle, by rational modes of thought. This is not to say that religion is irrational. But a religious world view has its foundation in revelation recorded in sacred literature, various spiritual experiences or mysticism; usually a combination of all these. Such a foundation cannot be taken as authoritative for society as a whole, since most of its members are excluded from such religious experiences and cannot verify them. When a society is committed to a rational world view, it has to confine itself to that which everyone can experience and deliberate upon. Within such a world view, often called 'secular' for purely historical reasons, religion is one of the many domains within its diverse fields of activity; not a domain that constitutes the world view itself. No single domain can be allowed to influence, let alone constitute the world view held by society, if it is to be truly rational; including science. Rationality is autonomous and every domain can only be an element within its deliberative field; including religion and science.

There are certainly resonances in Vivekananda's thought with such a view; especially with the emphasis he placed on reason. Vivekananda did not think that reason was the highest faculty for knowledge that humans possessed. He thought the higher faculties were intuition and super sensuous perception through which spiritual truths beyond sense perception were attained. Yoga was the science of cultivating these higher faculties. But reason was the faculty everyone possessed in common and it had to be the starting point for all enquiry into truth. Not only that, reason was non-negotiable for Vivekananda.

While he proclaimed in no uncertain terms that there was an imperceptible domain of spiritual truths accessible to man's higher faculties, which was more real than the world of ordinary experience, he would have nothing to do with mystery mongering. He insisted that any claim to spiritual truth should not be in conflict with the knowledge we have already gained through reason, empirical enquiry, etc.

Thus, Vivekananda sharply distinguished between mythology which was accepted on the basis of authority, and history which is based on evidence. In a speech he gave to trainee sanyasis in Calcutta in 1897, Vivekananda lectured upon the Gita. It was a lecture meant to introduce the young monks to the philosophical and spiritual truths of the Gita. But Vivekananda started the lecture with a historical enquiry into the Gita. He says that one cannot understand the Gita properly without first answering some historical questions. Vivekananda said, 'The book known as the Gita forms a part of the Mahabharata. To understand the Gita properly, several things are very important to know. First, whether it formed a part of the Mahabharata, i.e., whether the authorship attributed to Veda-Vyasa was true, or if it was merely interpolated within the great epic; secondly, whether there was any historical personality of the name of Krishna; thirdly, whether the great war of Kurukshetra as mentioned in the Gita actually took place; and fourthly, whether Arjuna and others were real historical persons....'[91]

About the authorship of the Mahabharata, Vivekananda says that the literature shows that there were several writers who used the name Veda Vyasa. The main among them was Badrayana Vyasa and Dvaipayana Vyasa. He concludes that Vyasa was only a title, which many writers took to give scriptural authority to their writings. Vivekananda then moves on to the question of the existence of Krishna and the truth of the Kurukshetra war.

[M]uch doubt exists about the personality of Krishna. In one place in the Chandogya Upanishad we find mention of Krishna, the son of Devaki, who received spiritual instructions from one Ghora, a Yogi. In the Mahabharata, Krishna is the king of Dwaraka; and in the Vishnu Purana we find a description of Krishna playing with the gopis. Again, in the Bhagavata, the account of his rasalila is detailed at length. In very ancient times in our country, there was in vogue a festival called Madanotsava (celebration in honour of Cupid). That very thing was transformed into Dola (sic) and thrust upon the shoulders of Krishna. Who can be so bold as to assert that the rasalila and other things connected with him were not similarly fastened upon him? In ancient times, there was very little tendency in our country to find out truths by historical research. So, anyone could say what he thought best without substantiating it with proper facts and evidence…. In ancient times they had no knowledge whatever of geography; imagination ran riot. And so we meet with such fantastic creations of the brain as sweet—ocean, milk—ocean, clarified—butter—ocean, curd—ocean, etc.! In the Puranas, we find one living ten thousand years, another a hundred thousand years!

…It is human nature to build round the real character of a great man all sorts of imaginary superhuman attributes. As regards Krishna the same must have happened, but it seems quite probable that he was a king. Quite probable I say, because it was chiefly the kings who exerted themselves most in the preaching of Brahma-Jnana.

Now to the third point, bearing on the subject of the Kurukshetra War, no special evidence in support of it can be adduced.[92]

The non-historicity of Ram, Krishna, and other personages in the Hindu Puranas as well as the events described in them, rests on many sources of historical information. This includes archaeology, the linguistic dating of scriptures, stylistic analysis, accounts by foreign travellers, and other corroborative historical sources. The Sangh Parivar dismisses all this scholarly work as leftist or Western, and implicitly biased, without ever engaging or refuting the evidence they present. The bulk of this historical scholarship was not available in Vivekananda's time. The alternative histories promoted by right-wing historians merely put a historical patina on mythological narratives, which are uncritically accepted as facts. Thus, what is truly interesting about Vivekananda's historical analysis of Hindu mythology, is that Vivekananda based his analysis mainly on ancient Sanskrit scriptures rather than the work of historians.

Thus, Vivekananda answered the fourth question, about the Pandavas using this method. 'About the fourth point, there is enough ground of doubt as regards the historicity of Arjuna and others, and it is this: Shatapatha Brahmana is a very ancient book. In it are mentioned somewhere all the names of those who were the performers of the Ashvamedha Yajna: but in those places there is not only no mention, but no hint even of the names of Arjuna and others, though it speaks of Janamejaya, the son of Parikshit who was a grandson of Arjuna. Yet in the Mahabharata and other books it is stated that Yudhishthira, Arjuna, and others celebrated the Ashvamedha sacrifice.'[93]

Pre-modern societies with a religious world view see history primarily through the lens of religion. In Europe, before the Enlightenment, the historical process was seen by most historians as an unfoldment of God's divine plan.

Completely natural accounts of history in terms of historical cause and effect started becoming popular only in the eighteenth century. This was the result of the emergence of a sphere of critical rationality. Along with the writing of natural history, advanced methods of historical analysis were developed which demanded evidence and proof for establishing historical facts. This allowed for a critical examination of religious myths, which were so far accepted only on authority. This dismantling of religious myths eventually led to the disintegration of the religious world view which formed European consciousness. What replaced it is what we call 'secular modernity' and in its intellectual dimension, it aligns itself with rationality. The Sangh Parivar, whose ideological tendencies are atavistic, now tries to historicize myth by reversing this process; instead of taking myth as true on authority, dubious and fantastical historical evidence is appealed to, for establishing the truth of myths. Again, we find that Vivekananda's attitude is the exact opposite. He valued historical research precisely because it dispelled the 'superstitions' of myth, which people took to be real.

Before starting the spiritual part of his discourse, on the Gita, he says, 'One thing should be especially remembered here, that there is no connection between these historical researches and our real aim, which is the knowledge that leads to the acquirement of Dharma. Even if the historicity of the whole thing is proved to be absolutely false today, it will not in the least be any loss to us.'[94] In other words, whether Krishna was real or not, whether the Kurukshetra war happened or not, does not affect Hinduism; only the spiritual principles enshrined in the Gita are essential to Hinduism. The same goes for Krishna. Krishna is the personification of the Godhead through which a devotee who is attracted to that particular form can approach God. Vivekananda preached that whether one followed the path of yoga or devotion, it is the personal effort and agency of the spiritual aspirant that resulted in spiritual realization. Whether Krishna actually existed on earth or not, made no difference, and neither did locating the place he was allegedly born in. There was nothing inherently sacred about a place or any holy artefact. It was only symbolism, and in Vivekananda's view, it was only a gross form of materialism to invest material objects with sanctity. Can Spirit be a property of matter? Is spirituality a material force like electricity for it to be transmitted through brick and stone or some ethereal substance to keep hovering around in the air for centuries? Such notions are just materialism dressed in the garb of spirituality, an effort to seek God in physical nature than within oneself.

Such an attitude, which Ramakrishna also held, could result in indifference to historical questions. Since it did not matter one way or the other, one would expect a spiritual preacher to focus on the all-important goal of spiritual realization. But Vivekananda insisted on the importance of historical research for its own sake. If spirituality was a search after the ultimate truth, the human being had to extend that unrelenting search for truth into all domains. While reason was essential to guide one in one's spiritual quest, it was the central principal to attain the truth in most other areas of human endeavour. In seeking to determine historical facts, it was evidence that mattered, not the authority of tradition.

> Then what is the use of so much historical research, you may ask. It has its use, because we have to get at the truth; it will not do for us to remain bound by wrong ideas born of ignorance. In this country people think very little of the importance of such inquiries. Many of the sects believe that in order to preach a good thing which may be beneficial to many, there is no harm in telling an untruth, if that helps such preaching, or in other words, the end justifies the means. Hence we find many of our Tantras beginning with, 'Mahadeva said to Parvati'. But our duty should be to convince ourselves of the truth, to believe in truth only. Such is the power of superstition, or faith in old traditions without inquiry into its truth, that it keeps men bound hand and foot, so much so, that even Jesus the Christ, Mohammed, and other great men believed in many such superstitions and could not shake them off. You have to keep your eye always fixed on truth only and shun all superstitions completely.[95]

The Sangh Parivar's political project of a Hindu Rashtra and its ideology of Hindutva is predicated upon Hindus deeply identifying as culturally Hindu. As we have seen, Vivekananda's very understanding of Hinduism was such that to achieve the spiritual goals of Hinduism, one had to transcend the very elements that constitute Hindu identity in the Sangh's conception. If the majority of Hindus were to understand and accept Vivekananda's exposition of their religion, it would negate the very possibility of the Hindutva project. For Vivekananda, in the final analysis, what religion one followed was a matter of complete irrelevance. The only exclusive property Vivekananda claimed for Hinduism is that it recognized explicitly the oneness of all religious faith. God is infinite and can be worshipped or contemplated through an infinite variety of forms and modes. Vivekananda delivered a paper on Hinduism at the Parliament of Religions in Chicago in which he said:

> To the Hindu, man is not traveling from error to truth, but from truth to truth, from lower to higher truth. To him all the religions from the lowest fetishism to the highest absolutism, mean so many attempts of the human soul to grasp and realize the Infinite, each determined by the conditions of its birth and association, and each of these marks a stage of progress.... It (religion) places before society only one coat which must fit Jack and John and Henry, all alike. If it does not fit John or Henry he must go without a coat to cover his body. The Hindus have discovered that the absolute can only be realized, or thought of, or stated through the relative, and the images, crosses, and crescents are simply so many symbols—so many pegs to hang spiritual ideas on.[96]

Seen from the higher standpoint, the purpose of religion was the pursuit of spiritual realization. What path one took was irrelevant as long as it served one's purpose. For all of his life-long efforts at revitalizing Hinduism, at the deepest level of his personality, Vivekananda did not identify with either Hinduism or India. Indeed, he could not. As an Advaitin, Vivekananda's philosophy was to identify his own Self with the impersonal Absolute (God). One could not say in the same breath that one is the Brahman or the Absolute Spirit, and also a Hindu, Christian, or Jew; it would be blatant self-contradiction. Vivekananda repeated again and again that what was important was to find the path to spiritual realization, it mattered not in the least which religion that path lay through. For instance, he said, 'The farthest that all religions can see is the existence of a spiritual entity. So no religion can teach beyond this point. In every religion there is the essential truth and nonessential casket in which this jewel lies. The believing in the Jewish book or the Hindoo (sic) book is non-essential. Circumstances change, the receptacle is different; but the central truth remains.'[97]

To both the claims of national and religious identity, Vivekananda was immune. In a letter sent to a disciple from America, who had probably entreated Vivekananda to return to India, Vivekananda exclaimed 'As for me, mind you, I stand at nobody's dictation. I know my mission in life, and no chauvinism about me; I belong as much to India as to the world, no humbug about that. I have helped you all I could. You must now help yourselves. What country has any special claim on me? Am I any nation's slave?'[98] In a lecture, Vivekananda remarked upon the fact that religious identity ultimately proceeds from a sense of egotic identity, rather than true spiritual instinct. 'So this is the goal towards which we are going—the supreme Bhakti —and all that leads up to this is but preparation. But it is necessary. It prepares the infinite Soul to come out of this bondage of books and sects and forms; these [ultimately] fly away and leave but the Soul of man. These are superstitions of an infinite amount of time. This "my father's religion", "my country's religion", or "my book", or my this and that, are but the superstition of ages; they vanish.'[99]

THE INDIVIDUAL AND SOCIETY: VIVEKANANDA AND THE RSS

We saw in the last chapter that Vivekananda's and the RSS's understanding of Hinduism stand in almost complete opposition to each other. I have remarked that Vivekananda's valorization of Hinduism forms the tenuous basis for the RSS's appropriation of him. But there is another factor that allows the RSS to portray the iconoclastic monk as aligned to their sociopolitical agenda. This is the concept of seva (service), which is an integral element of the thought of both Vivekananda and the ideological stalwarts of the RSS. Other than a shared admiration (or in the case of the RSS, reverence) for Hinduism, the idea of service is the only thing that Vivekananda and the RSS have in common.* In both cases the idea of service includes the idea of self-sacrifice.

Both Vivekananda and the RSS hold that the proper ethical attitude to have towards others is that of service. This is a more important link than we might otherwise realize. People often hold extremely different or opposing belief systems, but might act in similar ways. The importance of an ethical ideal lies in the fact that it determines how one presents oneself towards the world: towards other human beings, towards society, towards the nation, towards different classes and communities. That is, to a large extent it determines how one is to live and conduct oneself in the world. I think it will come as no surprise to the reader that Vivekananda's idea of service varies in many crucial ways from the RSS's. Nonetheless, service (to humankind for Vivekananda and to society and nation for the RSS) forms the basis of their respective programmes of reform.

The RSS agenda is to mould Indian society along the principles of Hindutva, eventually creating a Hindu Rashtra. While the RSS has been accused of being a fascist or totalitarian organization by many critics,† the RSS ideologues

---

*Nationalism is another element that Vivekananda and the RSS have in common. But this is to say almost nothing as nationalism as an ideology was something in which several generations of Indian freedom fighters believed. The crucial difference here is that the nationalism of the independence movement was not based on a religio-ethnic identity.

†For example, see *The RSS: A Menace to India* by A. G. Noorani and *The Hindu Nationalist*

differ from the ideologues of European fascism or Soviet style totalitarianism in a significant aspect. The State and the Party are paramount in the politics of classical fascism and totalitarianism, exercising absolute authority over the people. At least in the written work of the major thinkers of the RSS, the State or a political party embodying Hindutva, is not a central concern. Writing in 1963, Donald Eugene Smith, a political scientist who specialized in studying the development of Indian democracy, made the same point:

> Nehru once remarked that Hindu communalism was the Indian version of fascism and, in the case of the RSS, it is not difficult to perceive certain similarities. The leader principle, the stress on militarism, the doctrine of racial-cultural superiority, ultra-nationalism infused with religious idealism, the use of symbols of past greatness, the emphasis on national solidarity, the exclusion of religious or ethnic minorities from the nation-concept—all of these features of the RSS are highly reminiscent of fascist movements in Europe. Fascism, however, is associated with a concept of state worship, the state as the all-absorbing reality in which the individual loses himself and in so doing finds ultimate meaning. This conception has no counterpart in RSS ideology; in fact, the Sangh explicitly rejects the notion that its objectives could be attained through the power of the state. Its aim is the regeneration of Hindu society, which must come from within. However, it is impossible to say how the RSS would respond if political power ever came within reach, either directly or through the Jana Sangh.[1]

The central focus and theoretical basis for the project of a Hindu Rashtra, is society. It is through a sustained programme of social engineering that RSS envisages bringing about a structural transformation of the Indian polity into one which is based on the ideology of Hindutva.

This naturally raises the question of the relationship between the individual and society. Thinkers throughout history have occupied themselves with this question, both in the East and West. While the approaches and conclusions reached vary widely, in effect, it is a question of boundaries. Where does the individual's autonomy end? Rather, where are the boundaries drawn by society where the individual is free to exercise her agency in an unconditional manner? Within the range of social philosophies offered by various thinkers and the different kind of societies that have existed throughout the ages, the answers to the question of social boundaries lie along a spectrum. At one end of the

---

Movement in India by Christophe Jaffrelot.

spectrum is totalitarianism and at the other end lies anarchism. Democracy tries to position itself somewhere between these two extremes. The debate between the leftists, centrists, and rightists within a democracy, or between liberals and conservatives, is, in part, a debate about exactly where to position democracy between these two extremes. When the boundaries are drawn too narrowly, so that the autonomy of the individual in a substantial sense is almost nullified, the result is a totalitarian society. When the boundary is so wide that it is almost non-existent, it leads to a violent, anarchic society.

We will look at the ideological view of the RSS and Vivekananda on the question of the individual and society. As far as the RSS is concerned, I will examine only Golwalkar's views on the matter. This is a choice made for the sake of brevity and simplicity. We can safely assume that Golwalkar's view is representative of the RSS in that he is considered the supreme ideological preceptor of the organization, honorifically addressed as 'Guruji' by RSS members. He is also the longest serving Sarsanghchalak (leader) of the RSS, heading the organization in its crucial formative period from 1939 until his death in 1973. There is another reason to choose Golwalkar. The fundamental tropes in Golwalkar's thinking are present in most RSS idealogues. But they might be diffused (as with the thought of Deendayal Upadhyaya) or become exaggerated and irrational as in the case of some others. Golwalkar expresses the fundamental philosophical and ideological ideas that animate the Sangh, powerfully and concretely, and in a rational mode of discourse.

First published two years after the death of India's first prime minister, Jawaharlal Nehru, the book *Bunch of Thoughts* by Golwalkar is the most important book in the RSS's ideological canon. It was published at a significant juncture in independent India's history. When the Indian republic was born, the makers of its Constitution enshrined a certain vision for the nation; India was envisaged as a secular liberal democracy.* With Nehru gone, the future direction of the Indian republic was suddenly uncertain. While Nehru had used his stature and authority to steer the country in the direction of a liberal democracy, the conversation about nation building was highly contested. Major discontent came from the communist and radical socialists on the left and from conservatives and the Hindu right wing on the other side. While committed to secularism, the communist parties espoused a revolutionary ideology, which envisioned a class revolution in society against the bourgeois state. Hindu

---

*For a reading of the Indian Constitution as a socially transformative document, see *The Transformative Constitution: A Radical Biography in Nine Acts* by Gautam Bhatia.

conservatives and the right wing (the major players being the RSS, the Hindu Mahasabha, and the Jan Sangh) not only opposed secularism, but also the vision of a liberal society embedded in Nehru's idea of Indian democracy.* What was common to both communists and the RSS is that their vision of society clashed with what the Indian Constitution envisaged, and both, for different reasons, despised the ideology of liberalism that undergirded Indian constitutionality. Under Nehru's stewardship, the nation building project largely followed along lines implied by the Constitution's philosophy, which implicitly construed the relationship between the individual and society along the lines of classical liberalism. After Nehru's death there was great anxiety regarding the continuation of India's experiment with democracy, with many Western commentators and India correspondents predicting its imminent death.†

While such dire predictions proved untimely, the political vacuum created by Nehru's death and the sudden demise of his political successor Lal Bahadur Shastri, opened up new possibilities of action to political actors dissatisfied with the present system. In 1967, a peasant revolt that broke out in Naxalbari in West Bengal, led to the beginning of the Maoist movement which seeks to wrest control of the Indian state from the civilian government through force of arms. On the right, 1966 saw a sustained push of ethno-religious mobilization led by the newly formed VHP, and the RSS, around the demand for a law banning cow slaughter. This resulted in a violent storming of the Parliament House, which was in session, on 7 November by a mob consisting of lakhs of people demanding a ban on cow slaughter. Contemporary newspaper reports and later historical accounts report that the violent mob was organized by Hindutva groups, including the Jan Sangh, the political party which was the predecessor of the present BJP.[2]

Whatever maybe the causal relationships and correlations between such movements questioning the State's authority in the post-Nehruvian years of the sixties and the ideologies of the extreme left and right; at the level of public discourse, there existed an expanded scope for questioning the nature of the social contract which the Nehruvian democratic project was trying to establish in India. Golwalkar's *Bunch of Thoughts*, appearing in 1966, was definitely speaking to its times. Among other things, the Hindutva ideology Golwalkar preached as a roadmap for the RSS to follow included a definite social philosophy. In the backdrop of the political project of creating a Hindu Rashtra, Golwalkar

---

*The main Muslim organization which denied the Constitution and demanded an Islamic state was the Jamaat-e-Islami, but it was not even a minor political player.

†For example the British journalist Don Taylor, who was otherwise a sympathetic observer of India.

lays down the central tenets of what the RSS envisions the individual Indian's relationship with the collective, to society and nation, should be.

In the Cold War era, the United States and the Soviet Union offered two differing models for developing nations to aspire to. In its economic policies as well as foreign policy alignment, India was closer to the U.S.S.R. Democracy is both a political and social project. Thus, in the civic and political values India was trying to realize through her democratic aspirations, she was nearer to the United States and Western Europe. By giving the Indian people the fundamental rights to freedom of expression, personal liberty, and life, the Constitution had put the power of the state behind the idea of an open society. Due to immigration to the West, especially the United States, the Anglo-American world continued to exert a cultural influence on India. As evolving liberal democracies, the societies of post-World War II United States and the European democracies, showed the possible trajectories that Indian society could take if it continued to be steered by the constitutional vision of an open society. There was a lot of hand-wringing among traditionalists over the loss of social values this entailed for India. As I argued before, when the RSS and the Sangh Parivar talk about preserving 'traditional Indian values', it is a cloak for preserving the social status quo, or even for restoring a social order that existed centuries back, and for imposing traditional patriarchal, semi-feudal, and authoritarian social values on the individual. It is ultimately about controlling the individual and the kind and extent of liberty an individual is entitled to enjoy is a central and recurrent concern for Golwalkar:

> There are some nations in the world, which pride themselves on being 'progressive modern societies.' It would be instructive to examine how far the dominant note of their life—which is the pursuit of material happiness—is conducive to the real progress and happiness of man. The first aspect of this pursuit of pleasure is the process of never-ending competition. ...The second aspect is what is nowadays described as the 'permissive society'. We shall start with the second aspect. In simple words, 'permissiveness' means, the individual is left free to indulge in whatever way he chooses to enjoy himself. There is no restraint of any kind on him. It is unbridled licentious behaviour with respect to sex, food, drinks, family life, social intercourse and all such aspects. This is also reflected in their talk, writing and thinking as well. Will this type of 'permissiveness' be conducive to the real happiness of man?
>
> The first and foremost effect of this trend would be the destruction of social fabric.... And it requires not much of intelligence to guess what

kind of fate awaits the pursuit of happiness by the individual where the society has disintegrated.[3]

In other words, for Golwalkar, if the individual is permitted to exercise their choice in regards to what we now consider their personal life; how to eat, drink, and dress; how or with whom to have social intercourse; what kind of life to lead in family and society; the result will be social disintegration. One needs to hardly comment that this is the polar opposite of what the Constitution of India says. The basic structure of the Constitution, as elaborated in later Supreme Court judgements, include the fundamental right to freedom of speech, expression, life (how to lead one's life), and privacy.[*] Thus, it is hardly surprising that the RSS rejected the Constitution when it was enacted, saying that the Constitution should be based on the *Manusmriti*.[4] Since the first NDA government under Atal Bihari Vajpayee came to power, the RSS has periodically demanded that the Indian Constitution should be changed to bring it in line with what it calls Indian values.[5]

Golwalkar expounds his views on the place of the individual at several places in *Bunch of Thoughts*. Giving individuals the freedom to follow their own will in deciding their lives was, for Golwalkar, an invitation to social nihilism. And for him, the source of these ideas of individual agency was modernization. 'It is the undigested modern ideas like "freedom of thought" and "freedom of speech" that are playing havoc in the minds of our young men who look upon freedom as licence and self-restraint as mental regimentation!' Golwalkar exclaimed during one of his discourses.[6]

According to Golwalkar, the two fundamental driving impulses of individuals when allowed to exercise their own will were the accumulation of wealth and the satisfaction of sensual desires. Without authority checking them, men and women would only pursue their desires; there would be no national life. Golwalkar's homilies and edicts were directed at young people (a demographic to which Vivekananda also appealed). According to Golwalkar, the root of the evil that beset the youth of the post-Independence generation was a slavish imitation of their departed colonial masters and the culture of Western nations.

This attitude of base imitation had a disastrous effect on our national life. It changed our very life attitudes. As we know, imitation implies a

---

*The basic structure doctrine of the Constitution was formulated in the Supreme Court Decision in *Keshavananda Bharati vs State of Kerala*.

complete absence of one's inherent genius and originality in one's outlook of life. Firstly, it resulted in our forsaking the noble ideals of self-sacrifice and self-restraint in a mad rush to embrace the Western life pattern of enjoyment and satiation of pleasures of the flesh. Western life is, after all, extrovert. Earthly enjoyment is its highest ideal. Their concept of individual freedom lies in allowing the senses full licence to have an unbridled sway over the mind, thereby making a slave of oneself to the brute instinct. We also, in our wild-goose chase of the white man's ideals, echoed his slogan of 'raising the standard of life', which simply means increasing our slavery to material things in life or, in other words, increasing slavery of man to the brute.... The youth of today is getting infatuated with but one dream in life—of maximum pleasures and enjoyment.[7]

I think any reasonable person will admit that it is difficult for us to imagine a hedonistic generation of youngsters in the sixties when, except the elite, a life of consumption was closed off for everyone. The Indian economy was four decades away from becoming a consumerist society even for its middle class. But what had changed drastically since Independence was that a British economic imperialism which drained India of its wealth was replaced by economic policies of a sovereign Indian government. The immediate task which faced the Indian government was to end the endemic poverty in the country for which industrialization, infrastructure-building, and generating wealth was necessary. The First Planning Commission, headed by Nehru, set as its top priority the raising of the standard of living, so that all Indians could be provided with a minimum level of comfort and dignity of life. A nascent middle class of professionals reaped the benefits of these massive economic changes, and started aspiring to a kind of life and to creature comforts which had not been available to them before. While the idealism of the independence movement (which called for self-sacrifice from Indians for national freedom) had not dissipated, its form had changed. It was now channelled into the nation building project. While citizens were exhorted to help in building the Indian nation, the pursuit of individual happiness and well-being, of self-interest, was seen as complimentary to the project of national progress. Golwalkar says, 'Our educated young men hanker after easy jobs and easier money. They are after cheap careers, which are the very antithesis of self-respect and self-reliance. The same low mentality is the reason for hankering after Government jobs. Guaranteed regular monthly income, little exertion, very little responsibility, and pension after retirement—well, this line of least resistance appeals to many. They hanker after this simplest of short-cuts to ease and comfort. How despicable is this idle "career" for filling one's belly!'[8]

In another section of *Bunch of Thoughts*, he says about his younger contemporaries: 'Since, their concept of happiness centres entirely round the satisfaction of the desires of senses, the term "raising the standards of living" has only come to mean more and more amassing of the objects of physical enjoyment, which becomes the major preoccupation of the individual to the exclusion of all other thoughts and aspirations. In order to procure the objects of physical pleasures, accumulation of wealth follows.'[9]

'The experience of millennia of our national life in this country says that the craze for unlimited sensual enjoyment and competitive rage to satiate the same would never lead to happiness. It has taught us to cultivate self-restraint—a requisite as much necessary to the preservation of social fabric as to the development of the individuals.... And that arrangement envisages duties and obligations for the individual on both the planes—personal and social. Rules of behaviour—Dharma—conducive to achieving the supreme happiness of man will guide and control all the material aspects of life.'[10]

What is the remedy that Golwalkar and the RSS proposes? To catch them young. And in a phrase that Vivekananda used frequently and is an integral element of his thought, the RSS aims at a 'man-making education'. When Vivekananda used the phrase 'man-making education' he meant by the word man, the human being, whom he conceived of in Renaissance fashion as being potentially divine. (The difference was that Vivekananda meant it literally, while the Renaissance humanist thinkers were speaking metaphorically. Even for the most ardent Renaissance neo-Platonist, the idea that man is God would be incomprehensible.) While the RSS discourse does not stress masculinity as such, the fact that the RSS is a men-only organization does speak to the Sangh's idea of man-making education. Golwalkar says about the education that should be imparted to young people: 'From the very beginning the emphasis should be on duty in all relationships. Absolute sense of duty is most desirable but if in the present atmosphere of pampering the self it seems impracticable, the truth that duty is supreme and the individual's or group's rights are only co-related to it and must be considered as subordinate to it, must be persistently impressed upon the minds of the young in their formative years.'[11]

What Golwalkar had in mind, was a form of social engineering. And though it was gradual, slow patient work, it was eventually supposed to assume monumental proportions, so as to reorder Hindu and Indian society itself. These ideas originated with Dr Hedgewar, the founder of the RSS, who exerted a formative personal influence on the young Golwalkar.[12] Golwalkar says 'Doctorji concluded that a total revolution in the mental attitude of the people was the vital need of the hour.... He was aware that the task of bringing about a total transformation in the attitudes and thought-processes and behaviour of the whole people by taking individual after individual and moulding him for an organized national life, demanded a perseverant, silent and single-minded approach free from all public fanfare and propaganda.'[13]

The idea at work here is that the individual should be in harmony with society. And that the society itself should be organized according to certain normative principles. These organizing principles derive from the matrix of cultural and socio-religious forms of traditional Hindu society. Golwalkar elaborates, 'The ultimate vision of our work, which has been a living inspiration for all our organizational efforts, is a perfectly organized state of our society wherein each individual has been moulded into a model of ideal Hindu manhood....'[14] Such an organized Hindu society, which would engulf other religions within its sociocultural matrix, would constitute a Hindu Rashtra. Golwalkar propounds what he designates an organic view of society; one in which the individual and society should be in harmony with each other. 'Our view of the relation between individual and society has always been not one of conflict but of harmony and co-operation born out of the consciousness of a single Reality running through all the individuals. The individual is a living limb of the corporate social personality. The individual and the society supplement and complement each other with the result that both get strengthened and benefited,'[15] he says.

On the face of it this statement, while not wholly unobjectionable, could be interpreted as at least a partly benign doctrine. But when we unpack the construction, a fundamental asymmetry of power is revealed. For Golwalkar, every person in society should individuate the essential nature of the collective, and variation from this essence is permitted only so far as these ordering principles of society are not disrupted. This seems to be what Golwalkar means when he talks about the individual being in harmony with society. In a slightly different context, he says, 'For this purpose some restraints will have to be placed on the individual. The concept of personal freedom cannot be so narrowly construed as to harm the interests of the community at large.'[16]

We have seen that the RSS view, as espoused by Golwalkar (and the actions of the Sangh Parivar), involves placing certain restrictions on the individual's liberty. How exactly could such restrictions be placed? One way of course is through legal means. We have seen, for example, multiple BJP-ruled states have implemented laws that basically aim at stopping citizens from eating beef. But legal means are a last resort. The boundaries a polity places on the individual are usually through authority exercised via social institutions, traditions, customs, and norms. For the RSS, this authority rests in what it claims to be the essence of Hinduism; its customs, traditions, rituals, samsakaras, and so on.

Living at the end of the nineteenth century, Vivekananda addressed the question of the relationship between the individual and society in the terms it posed itself, in the conditions of late nineteenth century India. These conditions were basically strict social laws which Indian society, particularly Hindu society, imposed on individuals. The authority of these social laws, codes, and norms was taken by many to issue from the Hindu religion and scriptures. Vivekananda wrote: 'Rishi, Muni, or God—none has power to force an institution on society. When the needs of the times press hard on it, society adopts certain customs for self-preservation.... As a man often resorts even to such means as are good for immediate self-protection but which are very injurious in the future, similarly society also not unfrequently saves itself for the time being, but these immediate means which contributed to its preservation turn out to be terrible in the long run....'[17]

That is, certain social laws or institutions are adopted by a society when it faces external or internal threats and pressures that threaten its survival. For example, in Europe during the medieval ages, society was ruled by feudal lords who exercised arbitrary power over people within their fiefdom. This necessitated the creation of centralized monarchies where the King or Queen exercised absolute authority and hence could rein in the feudal lords. Establishing that authority required recourse to social and cultural myths as well as sources of religious authority like the church. But when the need for such absolute power was no longer required, kings continued to exercise these powers not only through direct force but by appealing to divine authority. Thus, laws curtailing the individual's freedom were kept in place. Vivekananda said, 'Social laws were created by economic conditions under the sanction of religion. The terrible mistake of religion was to interfere in social matters.'[18]

Vivekananda considered the personal liberty of the individual to be inviolable, and this led him to deliberate on the nature of authority exercised by society on the individual and the nature and limits of human liberty. His fundamental conclusion was that whatever rationale, intellectual, emotional, or religious, was given for social laws and institutions that circumscribed individual liberty, it was merely a disguise for those in power to maintain their influence and authority. Vivekananda discusses the question of social control and individual liberty in a letter he wrote to Mrinalini Bose, 'Now the question is: Is it for the good of the public at large that social rules are framed or society is formed? ...Some men, being comparatively powerful, slowly bring all others under their control and by stratagem, force, or adroitness gain their own objects. If this be true, what can be the meaning of the statement that there is danger in giving liberty to the ignorant? What, again, is the meaning of liberty?'[19]

Was Vivekananda a social anarchist? Many of his statements would seem to suggest that he envisaged no boundaries on individual liberty. But this would be a misreading. Vivekananda distinguished between an ethical exercise of individual liberty and an unethical one. The only legitimate restriction society could place on the individual is that she does not use her liberty of expression and action to harm other individuals. Vivekananda defines liberty in the same letter. 'Liberty does not certainly mean the absence of obstacles in the path of misappropriation of wealth etc. by you and me, but it is our natural right to be allowed to use our own body, intelligence, or wealth according to our will, without doing any harm to others; and all the members of a society ought to have the same opportunity for obtaining wealth, education, or knowledge.'[20]

Vivekananda did not simply stop at saying that the liberty of thought, action, and speech was a natural right of all individuals. For Vivekananda it was both the necessary condition of the evolution of the human being, as well as the final destiny of existence. We find Vivekananda saying again and again: 'You must remember that freedom is the first condition of growth'.[21] The goal of Hindu philosophy and theology is mukti (liberation) of the individual Self from the cycle of birth and rebirth. At the Advaitic level of analysis though, it is freedom from maya, or the illusory nature of existence. To be under illusion, was to be in existential bondage. And to reach the truth, whether understood as God, the Spirit, the impersonal Absolute, or as the true nature of one's own Self, was absolute or infinite freedom. But freedom was not something to be achieved on purely a spiritual plane, isolated from all the other dimensions of man's Being. Vivekananda said, 'one should raise the self by the self', then continued: 'Let each one work out one's own salvation. Freedom in all matters, i.e. advance towards Mukti is the worthiest gain of man. To advance oneself towards freedom—physical, mental, and spiritual—and help others to do so, is the supreme prize of man. Those social rules which stand in the way of the unfoldment of this freedom are injurious, and steps should be taken to destroy them speedily. Those institutions should be encouraged by which men advance in the path of freedom.'[22]

Vivekananda's views on 'modern' concepts like 'freedom of speech' and 'freedom of thought', which according to Golwalkar led the youth astray and created a 'permissive society', the bogeyman against which the the Sangh's conservative reactionism is focused, is the extreme opposite of those held by Golwalkar and his ideological successors in the RSS. Vivekananda was categorical about his position on individual liberty. 'Caste or no caste, creed or no creed, any man, or class, or caste, or nation, or institution which bars the power of free thought and action of an individual—even so long as that power does not injure others—is devilish and must go down.'[23]

Writing to his disciple and friend Sringavelu Mudaliar in Madras, Vivekananda discoursed on the criteria for admission into the movement of spiritual revival he was trying to create. 'We preach neither social equality nor inequality, but that every being has the same rights, and insist upon freedom of thought and action in every way. We reject none, neither theist, nor pantheist, monist, polytheist, agnostic, nor atheist; the only condition of being a disciple is modelling a character at once the broadest and the most intense. Nor do we insist upon particular codes of morality as to conduct, or character, or eating and drinking, except so far as it injures others.'[24]

The extent to which Vivekananda took the idea that only independent action can pave the way to spiritual realization, can be seen from an incident from his life he referred to several times in his perorations. One of these occasions was when he addressed an audience in San Francisco in 1900, during his second visit to the West. He said 'Once I was in an Indian city, and an old man came to me. He said, "Swami, teach me the way." I saw that that man was as dead as this table before me. Mentally and spiritually he was really dead. I said, "Will you do what I ask you to do? Can you steal? Can you drink wine? Can you eat meat?" The man [exclaimed], "What are you teaching!" I said to him, "Did this wall ever steal? Did the wall ever drink wine?" "No, sir." Man steals, and he drinks wine, and becomes God. "I know you are not the wall, my friend. Do something! Do something!" I saw that if that man stole, his soul would be on the way to salvation.'[25]

We have seen that the RSS's view of the individual is as a unit of society. The individual can achieve meaning only through his subordination to a larger structure such as society, nation, or a religious community. Golwalkar talked of how the individual can be in harmony with society only when he becomes a 'limb of the corporate society'. He said, 'It is only when the society is looked upon as a living corporate body of which the individual is a limb that the real unifying social consciousness will be ingrained in him. Then alone will he be able to restrain his erratic impulses and harmonise them with the interests of the society. And this is exactly what the Hindu philosophy propounds.'[26] It is both interesting and pertinent to note that regarding the liberty of the individual Golwalkar and Vivekananda base themselves on Hindu philosophy. A crucial difference here is that Golwalkar only gestures towards Hindu philosophy, at least in his works whose translations are available in English. Golwalkar never touches on the Hindu philosophical tradition; in fact, he does not even use the most key terms associated with that tradition. Vivekananda on the other hand preached and expounded Hindu metaphysics and philosophy and his notion of freedom of the individual is explicitly derived from the Vedantic tradition, especially its Advaitic variant.

For the Sangh, the individual is not only subordinate to society, but is, ultimately, expendable. His only purpose is to advance the cause of the society or the nation. Golwalkar says: 'The Sangh has therefore evolved a course of samskars wherein the mind, intellect, and body of an individual are trained so as to make him a living limb of the great corporate body of society. In a human body, for instance, there are so many limbs and in each limb, millions of cells. Each cell feels its identity with the entire body and is ever ready to sacrifice itself for the sake of the health and growth of the body. In fact, it is the self immolation (sic) of millions of such cells that release the energy for every bodily activity.'[27]

Such a utilitarian view of the worth of the human being is the polar opposite of the potential that Vivekananda saw in each individual being, let alone human being. The human being was, for Vivekananda, God in human form and when he talked of service, he meant service to human beings, not to society. In a letter to his brother disciple, Swami Brahmananda written in 1895, while laying out the plan for future action, he says:

If Ramakrishna Paramahamsa be true, you also are true. But you must show it. ...In you all there is tremendous power. The atheist has nothing but rubbish in him. Those who are believers are heroes. They will manifest tremendous power. The world will be swept before them. 'Sympathy and help to the poor'; 'Man is God, he is Nârâyana'; 'In Atman there is no distinction of male or female, of Brahmin or Kshatriya, and the like'; 'All is Narayana from the Creator down to a clump of grass.' The worm is less manifested, the Creator more manifested. Every action that helps a being manifest its divine nature more and more is good, every action that retards it is evil. The only way of getting our divine nature manifested is by helping others to do the same.[28]

These are conclusions that Vivekananda derived from the Vedanta.

The individual being for Golwalkar (and for the core of the Sangh's ideological thought) is an impermanent, evanescent entity. Though Golwalkar talks about the latent divinity of the individual, it amounts to mere lip service. What was permanent and hence metaphysically valuable, was the nation or an ethnic society, which if preserved against external threats and internal strife, stretched through millennia in history. Golwalkar said, 'Individuals come and go. …Drops of water come, stay for a while and evaporate; but the flow of the Ganga goes on ceaselessly. So is the eternal flow of our national life. We, the individuals, appear on the surface like bubbles or drops for a moment, and disappear. …The "permanent"…is the national life. The "impermanent" is the individual. The ideal arrangement would therefore be to transform the impermanent-the individual-into a means to attain the permanent—the social good—which would at the same time enable the individual to enrich and bring to blossom his latent divinity.'[29]

Vivekananda did not care a whit about society. In fact, as we have seen here and in Chapter 3,[*] he tended to see society as a permanently oppressive structure, where the powerful enacted laws, customs, and norms designed to keep the individual in check, so that she would not question the rationale of the social power hierarchy. The nation, however, was a slightly different matter. Vivekananda was no doubt a patriot and as he himself once said, he loved India with all his heart. But what is it about India that he loved? Was it—its traditions, culture (in its non-normative sense), architecture, geography, art? Vivekananda did value all these things, but then he loved the same things about many other countries, including many European ones. Was it what he, and many others after him, both Indians and non-Indians thought of as the spiritual wealth of the land? There is a case to be made that the object of Vivekananda's love for India was its spiritual tradition, of Vedanta, Buddhism, Jainism, and Sufi Islam, which have imperceptibly mingled with and shaped its social and cultural evolution. But this would only be a very partial answer. What Vivekananda loved, as he avers again and again, were the people of India, especially the poor, the oppressed, and the marginalized.

In the last year of Vivekananda's life (1902), when staying at the Belur Math, Vivekananda struck up a friendship with a group of Santhal labourers. He convinced some of the Santhals to come and take food at the math. A conversation recorded by his disciple Sharat Chandra Chakravarthy who was

---

*See Vivekanada's letter to Mary Hale, Chapter 2, p. 71.

present at the occasion, narrates the event and the conversation that followed.

Feeding them sumptuously, Swamiji said, 'You are Nârâyanas, God manifest; today I have offered food to Narayana.'... After their meal, the Santals went for rest, and Swamiji, addressing the disciple, said, 'I found them the veritable embodiment of God—such simplicity, such sincere guileless love I have seen nowhere else.' Then, addressing the Sannyasins of the Math, he said, 'See how simple they are. Can you mitigate their misery a little? Otherwise, of what good is the wearing of the Gerua robe? Sacrifice of everything for the good of others is real Sannyasa. They have never enjoyed any good thing in life. Sometimes I feel a desire to sell the Math and everything, and distribute the money to the poor and destitute.... Alas! the people of the country cannot get anything to eat, and how can we have the heart to raise food to our mouths?... Seeing the poor people of our country starving for food, a desire comes to me to overthrow all ceremonial worship and learning, and go round from village to village collecting money from the rich by convincing them through force of character and Sadhana, and to spend the whole life in serving the poor.

Alas! Nobody thinks of the poor of this land. They are the backbone of the country, who by their labour are producing food—these poor people, the sweepers and labourers, who if they stop work for one day will create a panic in the town. But there is none to sympathise with them, none to console them in their misery. Just see, for want of sympathy from the Hindus, thousands of Pariahs in Madras are turning Christians. Don't think this is simply due to the pinch of hunger; it is because they do not get any sympathy from us. We are day and night calling out to them, "Don't touch us! Don't touch us!" Is there any compassion or kindliness of heart in the country? Only a class of "Don't-touchists...".

...I see clear as daylight that there is the one Brahman in all, in them and in me—one Shakti dwells in all. The only difference is of manifestation.... You are all intelligent boys, and have been coming here for a long time. Say, what have you done? Couldn't you give one life for the service of others? In the next life you may read Vedanta and other philosophies. Give this life for the service of others, then I shall know that your coming here has not been in vain.'

Saying these words, Swamiji sat silent, wrapt in deep thought. After some time, he added, 'After so much austerity, I have understood this as the real truth—God is present in every Jiva; there is no other God besides that. 'Who serves Jiva, serves God indeed'. After some pause Swamiji, addressing the disciple, said, 'What I have told you today, inscribe in your heart. See that you do not forget it.'[30]

It is only in relationship to Vivekananda's love for the people, the human beings, the individuals, who populated India that his love for Indian spirituality assumes any meaning. All Vivekananda's talk about service to the nation means only this—the upliftment of the poor and the oppressed, educationally, intellectually, culturally, and spiritually. The nation could make an ethical demand of an individual that she should help in the cause of national progress, precisely because it is for the welfare of the many. (Their standard of living, if you will.) But an ethical demand is a call an individual can choose to heed or ignore. What no nation could do, in Vivekananda's view, was to demand obedience from an individual. We saw earlier how Vivekananda rejected with scorn the constant demands that he should return to India with the words 'Am I any nation's slave?'* Vivekananda was the broadest of humanists, his love for the world both embracing and superseding his love for any one country or community.

This leads us to the question of what Vivekananda took the individual to be. For Golwalkar and the Sangh, the individual is evanescent and ultimately derives meaning from what is permanent: the community imagined as race, nation, or society. For Vivekananda, it was the opposite. Vivekananda said 'Religion is the manifestation of the divinity already in man.'[31] The individual is the expression of what is permanent; the involution of the infinite in a finite human body and mind. Society was merely an evanescent, derivative epiphenomenon, both the setting and the obstacle to the unfoldment of the divine in man. This idea of the human being followed from the Advaita philosophy, which held that true Self of man was identical with Brahman, God, or the ultimate reality. Thus, for Vivekananda, what was permanent was not society or the nation, which was mutable and perishable in time, but the true Self of man, which was timeless, unbound, and infinite. We get a sense of what the human Self meant for Vivekananda in the following description of a lecture given by Vivekananda in America, by Swami Nikhilananda, one of the earlier biographers of Vivekananda. Nikhilananda writes: 'How like a thunderbolt the words fell upon the ears of his audience when one day he exclaimed: "Christ, Buddha, and Krishna are but waves in the Ocean of Infinite Consciousness that I am!"'[32]

---

*Chapter 6, p. 233.

The illusion was that the soul thought that it was limited, that it was a little body occupying a finite amount of space, leading an existence bound by the temporal limits of origin and destruction. This was the great delusion, the metaphysical ignorance—maya. Vivekananda expressed it thus:

> We believe that every being is divine, is God. Every soul is a sun covered over with clouds of ignorance, the difference between soul and soul is owing to the difference in density of these layers of clouds.... We believe that this is the very essence of the Vedas. We believe that it is the duty of every soul to treat, think of, and behave to other souls as such, i.e. as Gods, and not hate or despise, or vilify, or try to injure them by any manner or means. This is the duty not only of the Sannyasin, but of all men and women. The soul has neither sex, nor caste, nor imperfection.[33]

The infinite is that which is not limited; that which is free. To manifest the divine is thus to be limited by no law but the ethical; whose ground is your own Self and not something external. The individual is the site for the manifestation of the infinite, which is every person's true Self, and what is spoken of as God, or to be more precise, Brahman. The infinite can never be fully manifested within the finite limits of a body and mind–ego complex. But there are gradations of manifestations, which is what separates the evil doer from the virtuous man and the virtuous man from the enlightened man. The difference is in degree, not kind. That which is infinite and unlimited, cannot be guided and limited by law. This does not mean the spiritual person would not live by any social norms. But she accepts normative rules, institutions, and structures in so far as they benefit (in the most extended sense) her fellow beings. She does not obey them out of fear, superstition, or social conditioning. According to Vivekananda, 'Wherever in any society there are too many laws, it is a sure sign that that society will soon die. If you study the characteristics of India, you will find that no nation possesses so many laws as the Hindus, and national death is the result. But the Hindus had one peculiar idea—they never made any doctrines or dogmas in religion; and the latter has had the greatest growth.'[34]

For Vivekananda, the West had achieved social progress because it had freed society. But religious dogmas and the control exercised by priests and other religious authorities over religious thought had held back the genuine development of spirituality in the West. India on the other hand had regulated society, and as a result had not socially progressed. But in order to ensure complete freedom in spiritual pursuits, the institution of the sanyasa had come about. The sanyasi went out of the pale of society, giving up his caste and all the associated regulations and rules. There, she could live and act with the greatest freedom, a condition essential for the pursuit of spiritual realization. Vivekananda said:

> Here was a society which had almost no vitality, its members pressed down by iron chains of law.... There, one was under regulations [that were] tremendous: regulations even how to breathe; how to wash face and hands; how to bathe; how to brush the teeth; and so on, to the moment of death. And beyond these regulations was the wonderful individualism of the Sannyasin. There he was. And every day a new sect was rising amongst these strong, individualistic men and women. The ancient Sanskrit books tell about their standing out—of one woman who was a very quaint, queer old thing; sometimes [she was] criticized, but always people were afraid of her, obeying her quietly.[35]

Individualism was thus of paramount importance to Vivekananda. This followed not only from his humanistic convictions gained from philosophers like John Locke and John Stuart Mill, but from his understanding of the Advaita philosophy. What he sought was the creation of a new civilization which would combine the social individualism of the West with the spiritual individualism of the East.

> In every country, real greatness of the soul means extraordinary individuality, and that individuality you cannot get in society. It frets and fumes and wants to burst society. If society wants to keep it down, that soul wants to burst society into pieces. These men, being very individualistic, they are always trying new theories and plans.... They must think something new; they cannot run in the old groove. Others are all trying to make us run in the old groove, forcing us all to think alike.... Supposing they succeeded in making us all think in the same groove, there we would be no more thought to think; we would die.[36]

The RSS on the other hand, wants to impose a uniformity of thought on all individuals so that they live according to the same principles, resulting in a society organized by a set of immutable rules. Golwalkar says:

> The training that is imparted every day in the Shakha in a strictly regulated fashion imparts that spirit of identification and well-concerted action. It gives the individual the necessary incentive to rub away his angularities, to behave in a spirit of oneness with the rest of the brethren in society and fall in line with the organized and disciplined way of life by adjusting himself to the varied outlooks of other minds. The persons assembling

there learn to obey a single command. Discipline enters their blood. More important than the discipline of the body is the discipline of the mind. They learn to direct their individual emotions and impulses towards the great national cause.[37]

Perhaps a more opposite vision of the development of the individual cannot be imagined as that exists between Golwalkar's vision of the training RSS imparts and Vivekananda's vision of education. Vivekananda said, 'All must struggle to be individuals—strong, standing on your own feet, thinking your own thoughts, realising your own Self. No use swallowing doctrines others pass on—standing up together like soldiers in jail, sitting down together, all eating the same food, all nodding their heads at the same time. Variation is the sign of life. Sameness is the sign of death.'[38]

It is not external discipline that Vivekananda wanted in his idea of a man-making education. For Vivekananda, discipline meant disciplining the mind—learning how to concentrate the powers of the mind. Instead of thinking with the herd, he wanted people to question received understandings, and come up with their own answers. Even in spirituality, realization comes to the person who questions. This was Narendranath's own journey into spirituality. He was not willing to take the existence of God on anyone's authority, however wise or knowledgeable society considered them. He wanted evidence; he wouldn't be satisfied if he did not perceive directly. Even when he accepted Sri Ramakrishna as his guru, he did not allow Ramakrishna to 'train' him without question. Vivekananda said to some of his Western pupils, 'Let none regret that they were difficult to convince! I fought my Master for six years with the result that I know every inch of the way! Every inch of the way!'[39]

The RSS way of life is to 'mould' the individual. The individual is thus conceived of as something without complete shape, something malleable that can, and should, be given shape from the outside. For Vivekananda, the individual was the infinite Spirit involuted. Education was not about imparting training, values, or knowledge to the individual, but consisted in removing the obstacles for the manifestation of her inner potential. Vivekananda said, 'You cannot teach a child any more than you can grow a plant. All you can do is on the negative side—you can only help. It is a manifestation from within; it develops its own nature—you can only take away obstructions.'[40]

He says again, 'Therefore the only duty of the teacher...is to remove all obstructions from the way. Hands off! as I always say, and everything will be right. That is, our duty is to clear the way.'[41]

The RSS believes in an extreme form of social collectivism. As Golwalkar explained, 'individuals, though imperfect, when merged into a corporate whole, can give rise to a perfect society. And therefore, the superficial difference born out of the imperfections of the individuals are only indicative of the diverse manifestations of the one great and perfect and mighty reality—the society.'[42] The individual is no more than a cog in the wheel of the social or national life.

The idea of a perfect society would be incomprehensible to Vivekananda. By his lights, there can be no such thing. For Vivekananda, perfection could only be found in the human being. Unlike the German idealist philosophers associated with the Romantic movement, or the Romantic poet Percy Bysshe Shelley, who believed in the progress of man to a state of perfection, Vivekananda did not believe that man would evolve to be perfect. Man was already perfect. It was only ignorance of her true nature that hid awareness of this from herself. Vivekananda defined education thus: 'Education is the manifestation of the perfection already in man.'[43]

One wonders what Vivekananda would think of the RSS project of training young minds with the right samskars, so that 'discipline enters their blood'[44] and of restructuring Hindu society through such education. Of course, it is impossible to say. Vivekananda did not live to see the Indian independence movement or the rise of Hindu nationalism. However, it is not as if Vivekananda did not encounter people who assumed for themselves the power of deciding what society should be and how other people should ideally think. Vivekananda said, 'What you do not make free, will never grow. The idea that you can make others grow and help their growth, that you can direct and guide them, always retaining for yourself the freedom of the teacher, is nonsense, a dangerous lie which has retarded the growth of millions and millions of human beings in this world. Let men have the light of liberty. That is the only condition of growth.'[45]

The RSS prizes uniformity of thought and aims to create a homogeneous community. The angularities and the variations of the individual are to be rubbed out. Golwalkar says, 'Then, that people should not be just a mass of men, just a juxtaposition of heterogeneous individuals. They should have evolved a definite way of life moulded by community of life-ideals, of culture, of feelings, sentiments, faith and traditions.'[46] Vivekananda on the other hand valued variety and considered individualism the most essential condition for growth. Speaking to an audience in San Francisco in 1900, he exhorted them to shake off their conformity, and become true individuals. Vivekananda said, 'How do I know that you are individuals—all saying the same thing, all standing up and sitting down together? That is the road to death! Do something for your souls! Do wrong if you please, but do something! You will understand me by and by, if you do not just now.'[47]

The very idea of training an individual how to think would have been deeply abhorrent to Vivekananda. In a lecture delivered on the theme of 'Practical Vedanta' in London in 1896, Vivekananda spoke of the importance of independent reasoning for secular as well as spiritual truth.

> We should, therefore, follow reason and also sympathise with those who do not come to any sort of belief, following reason. For it is better that mankind should become atheist by following reason than blindly believe in two hundred millions of gods on the authority of anybody. What we want is progress, development, realisation.... The only power is in realization, and that lies in ourselves and comes from thinking. Let men think.... The glory of man is that he is a thinking being. It is the nature of man to think and therein he differs from animals. I believe in reason and follow reason having seen enough of the evils of authority, for I was born in a country where they have gone to the extreme of authority.[48]

Vivekananda was discontent with the nature of education in the late Victorian age. He complained that it only taught people to uncritically believe in theories and doctrines, without questioning anything and seeking knowledge on their own terms. In the San Francisco lecture referred to earlier, he told his audience to think for themselves rather than believing theories and doctrines which were attached to important thinkers.

> All my life I am repeating what Jack said and John said, and never say anything myself. What glory is it that you know what John said twenty-five years ago and what Jack said five years ago? Tell me what you have to say.... You all talk [about] and get distracted over losing your 'individuality'. You are losing it every moment of your lives by this eternal swallowing. If any one of you believes what I teach, I will be sorry. I will only be too glad if I can excite in you the power of thinking for yourselves. ... My ambition is to talk to men and women, not to sheep. By men and women, I mean individuals. You are not little babies to drag all the filthy rags from the street and bind them up into a doll![49]

Vivekananda then extended his criticism to university education.

> This is a place for learning! That man is placed in the university! He knows all about what Mr. Blank said! But Mr. Blank said nothing! If I

had the choice, I would...say to the professor, 'Get out! You are nobody!' Remember this individualism at any cost! Think wrong if you will, no matter whether you get truth or not. The whole point is to discipline the mind. That truth which you swallow from others will not be yours. You cannot teach truth from my mouth; neither can you learn truth from my mouth. None can teach another. You have to realize truth and work it out for yourself according to your own nature....[50]

Vivekananda was, after all, a sanyasi, and a prophet of renunciation. He held that spiritual growth was not possible without renouncing the world. It can be done externally as the sanyasi does, or it can be done internally. That is, one can continue to live and work in the world, but by mentally renouncing all selfish desires and desiring only the good of others. Vivekananda's idea of service is, as in most ascetic traditions, based on self-denial. The RSS derives its ideas of self-sacrificing service from the same Hindu ascetic tradition as Vivekananda. Then how is there such an extreme stress on individual liberty and freedom? The riddle of how Vivekananda reconciles self-restraint with liberty needs examination.

Vivekananda's point was that self-restraint and self-sacrifice cannot be forced on anyone. If it is brought about by the compulsion of society, not only is it artificial, it only supresses the individual's desire. The result would not be moral or spiritual evolution, but a stupefaction of the individual's ability to think and feel. Vivekananda said:

Is not self-sacrifice, then, a virtue? Is it not the most virtuous deed to sacrifice the happiness of one, the welfare of one, for the sake of the many? Exactly, but as the Bengali adage goes, 'Can beauty be manufactured by rubbing and scrubbing? Can love be generated by effort and compulsion?' What glory is there in the renunciation of an eternal beggar? What virtue is there in the sense control of one devoid of sense power? What again is the self-sacrifice of one devoid of idea, devoid of heart, devoid of high ambition, and devoid of the conception of what constitutes society?... I say, liberate, undo the shackles of people as much as you can. Can dirt be washed by dirt? Can bondage by removed by bondage? Where is the instance? When you would be able to sacrifice all desire for happiness for the sake of society, then you would be the Buddha, then you would be free: that is far off.[51]

In his own time, Vivekananda recognized the structural oppression in Indian society of individual liberties through the force of tradition and its rationalization in the name of self-sacrifice. His thought was also keen enough to recognize that those who gave these rationalizations of self-sacrifice, virtue, and religion, were the ones who were at the top of the power pyramid and had the most to gain by retaining the status quo.

> Again, do you think the way to do it lies through oppression?... But as to the men, the masters of the situation, there is no need of self-denial for them! Is there a virtue higher than serving others? But the same does not apply to Brahmins—you others do it! The truth is that in this country parents and relatives can ruthlessly sacrifice the best interests of their children and others for their selfish ends to save themselves by compromise to society; and the teaching of generations rendering the mind callous has made it perfectly easy. He, the brave alone, can deny self.... It is action with desire that leads to action without desire. Is the renunciation of desire possible if desire did not exist in the beginning? And what could it mean? Can light have any meaning if there is no darkness?[52]

This brings us to the question of what kind of society, or societal process, Vivekananda envisaged. Was he a naive libertarian? Was it that his belief in the divine potential of man blinded him to the reality that in a society where everyone pursues their self-interest, the end result would be oppression?[*] The answer lies in Vivekananda's metaphysics of involution of Spirit and his Advaita philosophy.

The Upanishads state that the Self of man (Atman) is identical to the impersonal cosmic reality called Brahman. Brahman is the impersonal aspect of God or Ishvara, according to the Bhagavad Gita. Vivekananda uses the Spirit, Absolute, Infinite, all terms derived from German idealist philosophy, interchangeably with Brahman. Shankara's exposition of Advaita, explains the world as maya, or illusion. The world is a projection of the human mind, which it superimposes on Brahman. Vivekananda identifies 'maya' as the network of space, time, and causality which are the categories through which consciousness synthesizes all experience. Vivekananda further innovated on Shankara's theory by introducing degrees of manifestation of the infinite Brahman in the finite world, through each sentient being. Thus the amoeba is Brahman involuted to the highest degree and manifested the least. The human being is a higher stage of manifestation (what is usually called evolution is strictly speaking lesser

---

*This is the critique of liberalism by socialist and communist thinkers. Conservative and right-wing thinkers in both the West and East objected to liberalism on the basis that it will create disorder. The order that they wanted to maintain however, was a hierarchical structure where they occupied the apex.

involution), while God or Ishvara is the highest degree of manifestation of the Absolute (the least degree of involution).

Vivekananda said: '"A good world", "a happy world", and "social progress", are all terms equally as intelligible as "hot ice" or "dark light". If it were good, it would not be the world. The soul foolishly thinks of manifesting the Infinite in finite matter, Intelligence through gross particles; but at last it finds out its error and tries to escape. This going-back is the beginning of religion, and its method, destruction of self, that is, love. Not love for wife or child or anybody else, but love for everything else except this little self.'[53]

Vivekananda explains in greater detail, when he says:

Perfection is always infinite. We are this infinite already, and we are trying to manifest that infinity. You and I, and all beings, are trying to manifest it. So far it is all right. But from this fact some German philosophers* have started a peculiar theory—that this manifestation will become higher and higher until we attain perfect manifestation, until we have become perfect beings. What is meant by perfect manifestation? Perfection means infinity, and manifestation means limit, and so it means that we shall become unlimited limiteds, which is self-contradictory.... But we shall never be able entirely to manifest the Infinite here. We shall struggle hard, but there will come a time when we shall find that it is impossible to be perfect here, while we are bound by the senses. And then the march back to our original state of Infinity will be sounded. This is renunciation. We shall have to get out of the difficulty by reversing the process by which we got in, and then morality and charity will begin. What is the watchword of all ethical codes? 'Not I, but thou', and this 'I' is the outcome of the Infinite behind, trying to manifest Itself on the outside world. This little 'I' is the result, and it will have to go back and join the Infinite, its own nature. Every time you say, 'Not I, my brother, but thou', you are trying to go back.[54]

---

*The philosophers referred to by Vivekananda are mainly Johann Gottlieb Fichte, Friedrich Wilhelm Schelling, and George Wilhelm Hegel.

VIVEKANANDA AND THE WEST

The RSS and the Sangh Parivar construct an Indian culture of deep moral values and in opposition to 'Western culture'. This was a reaction to the modernization that happened as an effect of British colonialism and, after Independence, the programme of secular and progressive modernization implemented by the government. The Indian Constitution, enacted in 1950, drew upon several constitutions of the world, and the tradition of Western liberal humanism. As mentioned earlier, the RSS objected to the Constitution and wanted it to be based on the *Manusmriti*. It was also severely opposed to the Hindu code bills, which among other things, gave more equitable property and marital rights to women. The objections to Western culture and its progressive values, is articulated in a coherent fashion in the works of RSS ideologues like Hedgewar, Golwalkar, and Deendayal Upadhayaya. These days, however, tirades against Westernization from the Sangh Parivar take absurd and ludicrous forms. The Sangh Parivar has blamed various social problems on everything from women wearing jeans and scantily clad window mannequins[1] to celebrating Valentine's Day.[2] The extent to which the Sangh Parivar seeks to uproot what it believes to be the 'corrupting' influence of Western culture is extreme. According to newspaper reports, in 2015, the RSS held a meeting with senior Cabinet ministers to implement a nationwide programme to purge the country of Western culture. Then Union Culture Minister Mahesh Sharma said, 'We will cleanse every area of public discourse that has been westernised and where Indian culture and civilization need to be restored—be it the history we read or our cultural heritage or our institutes that have been polluted over years.'[3]

What was Vivekananda's attitude towards Western countries, their society and civilization? We have seen earlier that Vivekananda critiqued America and Europe, just as he had India. While today, Vivekananda's praise for Hinduism and the achievements of ancient India is blazoned, and his sharp critiques hidden, the opposite is true about his views on the West. His adverse comments on Western materialism (by which he meant the valorization of wealth and power and the inhumane competition of capitalism) and their need for spirituality have been given much publicity; almost nothing has been said about his frank and open admiration for the West. Even less is said about the role he envisaged that progressive Western ideas would play in the future of India.

Vivekananda admired the Western nations for their organizational ability, their energy and dynamism. He felt that these qualities were almost completely absent in India. He often compared India with a lifeless mass or a dead body and frequently bewailed how it was shrouded in dark tamas (inertia). He admired the spirit of adventure and enterprise that the Western nations displayed, their scientific knowledge, their sincerity in work, the boldness of thought and action, and their fierce spirit of independence. Whether he realized it or not, these were qualities that he himself possessed in abundance and which set him apart from any sanyasi modern India had seen up to that point.

Vivekananda had no qualms about saying that however sublime and lofty the heights the Indians had scaled in philosophy and religious thought in ancient times, contemporaneous India was intellectually backward, narrow minded, and bigoted—'a mine of stupidity', as he is quoted as saying in the fourth volume of his *Complete Works*.[4] In America, he found a highly intellectual culture which was remarkably open to new ideas. In a letter written in 1894 to one of his brother disciples, he wrote, 'Nowhere in the world have I come across such "frogs-in-the-well" as we are. Let anything new come from some foreign country, and America will be the first to accept it. But we?—oh, there are none like us in the world, we men of Aryan blood!! Where that heredity really expresses itself, I do not see. ...Yet they are descendants of the Aryans?'[5] In fact, one of the reasons some of Vivekananda's friends in India urged him to go to the Parliament of Religions was because they felt people in India could not appreciate or accept his radical ideas and bold interpretation of Hindu philosophy.

In a letter (*The Complete Works of Swami Vivekananda, Volume VIII*) written towards the end of the same year to the diwan of an unknown princely state, Vivekananda wrote:

I am the same here as in India, only here in this highly cultural land there is an appreciation, a sympathy which our ignorant fools never dream of. There our people grudge us monks a crumb of bread, here they are ready to pay one thousand rupees a lecture and remain grateful for the instructions for ever. I am appreciated by these strangers more than I was ever in India. I can, if I will, live here all my life in the greatest luxury; but I am a Sannyasin, and 'India, with all thy faults I love thee still'. ...I am ashamed of my own nation when I compare their beggarly, selfish, unappreciative, ignorant ungratefulness with the help, hospitality, sympathy, and respect which the Americans have shown to me, a representative of a foreign religion. Therefore come out of the country, see others, and compare.[6]

One might dismiss this as merely the emotional reaction of a young monk who found himself suddenly appreciated in a foreign land. But that is not the case. This is one of a set of themes about the Western world that recurs consistently in Vivekananda's speeches and writing throughout his career. These themes include: the need for Indians to acquire the power of intense activity and independence of thought the West had, to create the splendid social organization and social liberty of the West within the framework of India's own social evolution, for India to learn from the West material and political science, and for India in return to give back to the West a spirituality based on mysticism understood through the philosophy of Vedanta.

Comparing India and Great Britain, Vivekananda said to an English audience:

In India the bondage of superstition is a social one; here in the West society is very free. Social matters in India are very strict, but religious opinion is free. In England a man may dress any way he likes, or eat what he likes—no one objects; but if he misses attending church, then Mrs. Grundy is down on him. He has to conform first to what society says on religion, and then he may think of the truth. In India, on the other hand, if a man dines with one who does not belong to his own caste, down comes society with all its terrible powers and crushes him then and there. If he wants to dress a little differently from the way in which his ancestor dressed ages ago, he is done for.[7]

Vivekananda presents this contrast between India and the West in the areas of religion and society consistently in his work. Again and again, he repeated one of the cornerstones of his belief system, that liberty alone could lead to growth. In Europe, as Christianity became the official state religion under Emperor Constantine, the nature of Christianity, which was until then a sect persecuted by the Roman authorities, changed.[8] The Church laid down doctrines and dogmas which regulated what people could believe. Deviation in belief led to charges of heresy and even as late as the post-Reformation seventeenth century, people were burnt at the stake or executed for heresy. The growth of Protestantism eventually gave greater freedom of religious thought, but religious belief was still policed by the community of believers. All this not only restricted the growth of religious thought in Christian Europe, (the immediate contrast in historical time and geographical proximity lies with the flourishing of religious thought and philosophy in Islamic countries) but also arrested the growth of mysticism, or wherever it existed, drove it underground. Hinduism on the other hand allowed complete freedom in matters of religious speculation. As Wendy Doniger writes, 'Heresy is not really a Hindu idea at all. People have been killed in India because they did or did not sacrifice animals, or had sex with the wrong women, or disregarded the Vedas, or even made use of the wrong sacred texts, but no one was impaled (the Hindu equivalent of burning at the stake) for saying that god was like this rather than like that.'[9] The result of such absolute liberty in religious thought was that there was a proliferation of religious philosophy; and mysticism flourished in India to a degree and extent unparalleled in any other civilization.[10]

Vivekananda saw the same principle of liberty and growth operating in the social sphere in the West. With the start of the Enlightenment in Europe, political and social thought were liberated from the control of the kings and priests. As modern technicalist societies took birth in Europe, institutions that regulated social conduct lost power. In turn, the free association of people and ideas led to tremendous development in social and political organization, mass education, and the spread of social egalitarianism. While no one could have predicted the end of European monarchies and the rise of modern democracies within a few short decades, in the longer term, Vivekananda seems to have believed that Europe would see some kind of democratic government, as already existed in America. The result was overall emancipation and increasing opportunity for each individual regardless of religion, sex, or class to pursue their own happiness and well-being.

Vivekananda said over and over that the social freedom of Western societies is what allowed them to progress materially. He told an English audience:

Let men have the light of liberty. That is the only condition of growth. We, in India, allowed liberty in spiritual matters, and we have a tremendous spiritual power in religious thought even today. You grant the same liberty in social matters, and so have a splendid social organization. We have not given any freedom to the expansion of social matters, and ours is a cramped society. You have never given any freedom in religious matters but with fire and sword have enforced your beliefs, and the result is that religion is a stunted, degenerated growth in the European mind. In India, we have to take off the shackles from society; in Europe, the chains must be taken from the feet of spiritual progress. Then will come a wonderful growth and development of man.[11]

In Vivekananda's mind, social freedom and the empowerment of the masses, were interlinked phenomena. He wrote to a disciple from America that the fate of a nation depended upon the condition of the masses. He wrote: 'Can you raise them? Can you give them back their lost individuality without making them lose their innate spiritual nature? Can you become an occidental of occidentals in your spirit of equality, freedom, work, and energy, and at the same time a Hindu to the very backbone in religious culture and instincts?'[12] To another disciple he wrote: 'Can you make a European society with India's religion? I believe it is possible, and must be.'[13]

Vivekananda's admiration for the West is obscured in the popular imagining of the monk because his liberal admirers have chosen to ignore this aspect while the conservatives have used Vivekananda's warnings against imitating the West to paint him as a narrow-minded, anti-Western nationalist. It is true enough that on several instances Vivekananda warned Indians against imitating the West. But what he meant by that was not a rejection of the civilizational influence or thought currents that flowed from the West into India. What he objected to, was a facile and mindless imitation of Western civilization with its hegemonizing aspects.

This is extremely different from the Sangh's wholesale hostility to everything Western, especially since Vivekananda's comments against Westernization have to be seen in the colonial context existent in India before the national movement began. A few days before Vivekananda's speech at Kumbakonam in Tamil Nadu in 1897, where he blamed India's degradation solely on the upper castes of India,* he delivered a speech at nearby Ramnad where he said:

> There are two great obstacles on our path in India, the Scylla of old orthodoxy and the Charybdis of modern European civilisation. Of these two, I vote for the old orthodoxy, and not for the Europeanised system; for the old orthodox man may be ignorant, he may be crude, but he is a man, he has a faith, he has strength, he stands on his own feet; while the Europeanised man has no backbone, he is a mass of heterogeneous ideas picked up at random from every source—and these ideas are unassimilated, undigested, unharmonised. He does not stand on his own feet, and his head is turning round and round. Where is the motive power of his work?—in a few patronizing pats from the English people. His schemes of reforms, his vehement vituperations against the evils of certain social customs, have, as the mainspring, some European patronage. Why are

---

*See Chapter 2, p. 62.

some of our customs called evils? Because the Europeans say so. That is about the reason he gives. I would not submit to that. Stand and die in your own strength.[14]

Within a short time, he was in Madurai, where he told the audience:

In the first place, we cannot become Western; therefore imitating the Westerns is useless. Suppose you can imitate the Westerns, that moment you will die, you will have no more life in you. In the second place, it is impossible. A stream is taking its rise, away beyond where time began, flowing through millions of ages of human history; do you mean to get hold of that stream and push it back to its source, to a Himalayan glacier? Even if that were practicable, it would not be possible for you to be Europeanised. If you find it is impossible for the European to throw off the few centuries of culture which there is in the West, do you think it is possible for you to throw off the culture of shining scores of centuries? It cannot be.[15]

How does one reconcile comments of this kind with Vivekananda's admiration for the West and the need to replicate aspects of its social freedom and ethos of work and organization in India?

While it is true that the Bengal Renaissance created the social and intellectual conditions of modernity within which the national movement took root, the attitude of the leaders of both these movements towards the British colonial administration differed greatly from each other. From Ram Mohan Roy to Debendranath Tagore, Henry Louis Vivian Derozio, Ishwar Chandra Vidyasagar, and Keshub Chandra Sen, the intellectual and cultural leaders of the early and middle periods of the Bengal Renaissance saw the British rule of India mainly as a benign force that would bring reform, progress, and prosperity to India. It was a vast improvement on the rule of feudal princes. However, towards the latter period of the Bengal Renaissance, this opinion started changing. As the historian Anil Seal writes:

During the 1870s and 1880s came the beginnings of a mutation in Indian politics which was to convert many of the western educated from collaborators into critics of the regime. This change was not dramatic or indeed irreversible. In the 1870s some Indians were experimenting with new methods of public expression which soon incurred the candid dislike of government; after 1880 they were groping for some form of all-India organization; and towards the end of the decade, the nature and the implications of their demands were edging some of them into a certain detachment from British purposes. This slow, this reluctant, this portentous recognition of a division of interest first became apparent during the viceroyalties of Lytton, Ripon and Dufferin [1876–88].[16]

This divergence of interests between the colonial rulers and the indigenous elite led to a rupture, creating a new social space, which could be occupied by men eager to take advantage of the patronage networks provided by the British. The word 'collaborator' is often used by nationalist or postcolonial historians to characterize this new class of men, seen as complicit in the perpetuation of imperialism.* It is pertinent to note in this context that no thinker of note emerged from the Westernized reformers of the 1870s to 1900, while influential nationalistic thinkers emerged from those who rejected Westernization as the model for future progress. What this testifies to, is a lack of originality in the section sympathetic to Western rule, unlike earlier thinkers who were deeply inspired by Western ideas, like Ram Mohan Roy or Derozio. What this eventually translated to was hegemony of the conqueror's civilizational forms of life, which presented themselves to members of the subjected people as the only possibility for future lines of action. Such a superficial imitation of Western patterns of life and thought, rather than a critical assimilation of Western ideas into the Indian body politic is what Vivekananda warned against.

His warning that India should not try to become Western should be understood in the same light. The operative word is 'imitate'. Vivekananda welcomed the ideas of political and social liberty and rationalist thought that Western education was inadvertently spreading in the country. What he wanted of Indians was to weigh the many different kinds of ideas flowing in from the West carefully, accept what was true and useful, and then work out those principles within the sociocultural institutions of the country. He wanted what he called 'life-giving' principles from all civilizations of the world to enter India through the channels of communication that British imperialism had created. What he warned against was a Westernization that attempted to deliberately model Indian society on the life patterns of the West. Growth must be organic, from inside out.

Vivekananda's position on the matter of India's relationship to Western

---

*This seems to me to be too harsh a judgment, and one based on the political requirements of nationalist historiography and the theoretical assumptions of postcolonialism respectively. While opportunism and materialistic concerns might have played a role, I think it is fairer to see these men largely as people who were less thoughtful, less critical, and insufficiently committed to the project of nation building, compared to their predecessors who had broken ranks with the British.

ideas, thought, and values is succinctly expressed in the formulation he gave to the matter in an article titled 'The Problem of Modern India and its Solution' published in *Udbodhan*.

> [W]e must always keep the wealth of our own home before our eyes, so that every one down to the masses may always know and see what his own ancestral property is. We must exert ourselves to do that; and side by side, we should be brave to open our doors to receive all available light from outside. Let rays of light come in, in sharp-driving showers from the four quarters of the earth; let the intense flood of light flow in from the West—what of that? Whatever is weak and corrupt is liable to die—what are we to do with it? If it goes, let it go, what harm does it do to us? What is strong and invigorating is immortal. Who can destroy that?[17]

Vivekananda attributed two central reasons for the decline of Indian civilization, which he dated as beginning around 200 years before conquest by Muslim rulers, around the tenth century CE. One reason was, as we have seen, the oppression of the masses by the elite upper classes and castes, by the kings and the priests. The second reason that Vivekananda gives is that Indians withdrew into themselves, became intellectually insular, and stopped travelling to foreign countries; from exchanging ideas with other nations and keeping up with the growth of knowledge. By this, Vivekananda did not mean that there was no trade contact between Indians and the wider world. But the trade was carried out by the merchant classes. The intelligentsia, who were found among the higher castes, stopped being intellectually curious and confined themselves to refining the existing corpus of thought and practices. Eventually, even within that domain, they started clinging to outward forms rather than allowing for a continuation of the original impulses of creativity that animated the tradition. This inwardness found its most extreme manifestation in the social sanction against crossing the seas at the penalty of losing caste.

Speaking at the Triplicane Literary Society of Madras in 1897, Vivekananda said:

> We cannot do without the world outside India; it was our foolishness that we thought we could, and we have paid the penalty by about a thousand years of slavery. That we did not go out to compare things with other nations, did not mark the workings that have been all around us, has been the one great cause of this degradation of the Indian mind. We have paid the penalty; let us do it no more. All such foolish ideas that Indians must not go out of India are childish. They must be knocked

on the head; the more you go out and travel among the nations of the world, the better for you and for your country. If you had done that for hundreds of years past, you would not be here today at the feet of every nation that wants to rule India. The first manifest effect of life is expansion. You must expand if you want to live. The moment you have ceased to expand, death is upon you, danger is ahead. I went to America and Europe...I have to, because that is the first sign of the revival of national life, expansion.[18]

Vivekananda remarked that prohibitions against upper castes travelling overseas and other such customs also had a political purpose. After the decline of Buddhism in India, the rulers and Brahmin priests wanted to shield Hinduism from further influences or challenges from Buddhistic countries spread across Asia. He said, 'To my mind, the one great cause of the downfall and the degeneration of India was the building of a wall of custom—whose foundation was hatred of others—round the nation, and the real aim of which in ancient times was to prevent the Hindus from coming in contact with the surrounding Buddhistic nations.' It is not that Vivekananda looked on the influence of the West alone as beneficial to India. He wanted Indians to learn from all the different nations on the earth. Among Asian countries, he particularly marked out the patriotism of the Japanese as something Indians could study and profit from. He said in the same speech, 'Expansion is life, contraction is death. Love is life, and hatred is death. We commenced to die the day we began to hate other races; and nothing can prevent our death unless we come back to expansion, which is life. We must mix, therefore, with all the races of the earth. And every Hindu that goes out to travel in foreign parts renders more benefit to his country than hundreds of men who are bundles of superstitions and selfishness, and whose one aim in life seems to be like that of the dog in the manger.'[19]

In the late Victorian age, Vivekananda aptly remarked that a 'great upheaval' was going on in the world, in the world of ideas, technology, and politics. As a student of history, Vivekananda knew that though conquests were violent affairs involving mass deaths and human misery on a vast scale, it had a collateral effect that was in the long run beneficiary. Whether they were the conquests of Alexander of Macedonia, the Roman conquests, the Arab conquests, or the Mongol conquests, they brought together large geographical areas which were both politically and culturally disunited, under a centralized administration. Even when these empires did not prove durable, as in the case of Alexander and the Mongolians, they created the material channels through which ideas and culture could be transmitted between distant parts of the world. All the above-mentioned conquests led to an eventual flowering of arts, culture, philosophy, and religious thought, and civilizational growth.

This is what Vivekananda believed that British imperialism, with all its iniquities and evil, was paving the way for. He was right, in the sense that the globalization that we are witnessing now was made possible by European, especially, British imperialism. It is important to note that Vivekananda was by no means a supporter of British rule in India, let alone global British colonialism. In this, he differed from most of his predecessors in the Bengal Renaissance who welcomed the influx of modern ideas from the West, like Debendranath Tagore or Keshub Chandra Sen. These men saw British rule as mainly beneficial for India. Before his speech at the Parliament of Religions, Vivekananda discoursed to an informal gathering in a house in or near Boston. From notes taken by Mrs Wright, wife of Henry Wright who has been mentioned earlier, we have an account of Vivekananda's comments on the British occupation of India.

> You look about India, what has the Hindu left? Wonderful temples, everywhere. What has the Mohammedan left? Beautiful palaces. What has the Englishman left? Nothing but mounds of broken brandy bottles! And God has had no mercy upon my people because they had no mercy. By their cruelty they degraded the populace; and when they needed them, the common people had no strength to give for their aid. If man cannot believe in the Vengeance of God, he certainly cannot deny the Vengeance of History. And it will come upon the English; they have their heels on our necks, they have sucked the last drop of our blood for their own pleasures, they have carried away with them millions of our money, while our people have starved by villages and provinces.[20]

But at the same time, Vivekananda did not take the nationalist position that the rule of the British was nothing but an unmitigated evil. Evil it certainly was, but it unintentionally brought along with it things that made it something of a blessing as well. What it brought was Western education and progressive ideas, along with the forces of capitalistic economic competition. The first was a catalyst for social reformation, while the second disrupted the economic conditions which made the oppressive structure of Indian society, which Vivekananda called 'diabolical',* possible. Though Vivekananda never used these terms, what he characterized as the tyranny of the kings and priests,

---

*See Chapter 2, p. 70.

is what we would now characterize as a feudal, casteist social system. Such a social system can only be sustained by a non-industrialized economic structure where trade was controlled by duties, tariffs, and monopolies which enriched only the mercantile and ruling classes. From Vivekananda's comment about how modern-day competition would one day destroy caste (it is important to remember, however, that Vivekananda usually talked of historical developments in terms of centuries, not decades) as well as other similar remarks, we can infer that he believed that the economic basis of feudalism and casteism would be undermined by the incipient industrial capitalism the British were introducing into India.

It is possible that he came to this conclusion from his experience of the transformation happening in Western society, and by studying the history of Europe that led to that transformation. Free market capitalism, while developing its own type of social and economic exploitation, destroyed feudalism and the guild system, which tied the peasant to the land and the artisan class to particular jobs. The structural logic of such an economic arrangement was the control of movement and migration, geographical, professional, and social. Free market, however, requires maximum labour participation. Thus, social and legal restrictions in the West on particular classes of individuals which were characteristic of medieval feudal society, were pried apart by the economic forces generated by industrial capitalism. The ideas that Western education brought to India, included the liberal ideas of the European Enlightenment, which envisaged a society which stressed legal, social, and civil liberty for the individual in society. Vivekananda remarked in a conversation, 'There is such pain in this country! Such pain! Some, of course, there must always have been. But now the sight of Europeans with their different customs has increased it. Society knows that there is another way!'[21]

This, however, does not entail that Vivekananda was a votary of capitalism and that is the vision he had for the future of India. He considered capitalism the economic basis of a new phase in the development of humankind and an improvement on the despotic feudal monarchies and empires built on mercantile and similar protectionist economic systems. However, he was quite aware of the exploitative nature of capital and there are several comments on the issue in his work. He put it most pithily when he said that the West was groaning under the tyranny of Shylocks while the East was groaning under the tyranny of priests.[22] Another point to note is that when Vivekananda says that in the long-term, economic competition will destroy caste, he is not reducing the category of caste to that of class as in the orthodox Marxist analysis of caste.

This will be discussed in greater detail in Chapter 13.

The problem in ascertaining Vivekananda's views on any subject, as we saw before, is that there are very few instances when he gives what can be described as categorical expositions of his position. When dealing with speeches delivered in multiple and highly contested social settings, it is easy for a commentator on Vivekananda to cherry-pick statements and attribute ideological positions to the monk that he never held or even those which are the opposite of what he maintained. Fortunately, on the subject of India's relationship to the West and the role it was to play in the country's future, we have a written account from Vivekananda whose stated aim is to make his position explicit in the article 'The Problem of Modern India and its Solution'. Originally written in Bengali, it was contributed by Vivekananda to the magazine *Udbodhan* and partly functions as a kind of mission statement for it. The first half of the article addresses what Vivekananda believes is the history of India and its current state. The second sets out the direction in which Indian society should move, if it were to solve those problems. In the following paragraphs, I will quote only parts of the first section, but I will reproduce the second section of the article almost in toto, making only minor omissions for ease of reading and to avoid repetition of sections I have already quoted.

THE PROBLEM OF MODERN INDIA

Though the article was titled 'The Problem of Modern India and its Solution', it began not with contemporary India, but with the migration of the Indo-Aryan race from their original homeland and their colonization of ancient India and Greece.[23] Vivekananda's historical thought gave a central place to India (Aryans in Sanskrit) and Greece (Yavannas in Sanskrit) in the shaping of world history. It is not that he ignored the contributions of other civilizations, for he spoke often of the Arabic and Chinese civilizations. But in his thinking, these two branches of the Indo-Aryan race formed a kind of central axis, around whose activities, much of the development of classical civilizations into the early Middle Ages took place. Vivekananda's theory of history was one in which each race, each nation, each individual, was trying to manifest an ideal within material conditions, which resisted them. Political and military events, economic factors and so on were for him only the outer pages in the story of man's historical development, just as the physical body was only the outer covering of man's mental and spiritual core, which was his truer self. Though less immediate and tangible, and even perhaps with far less determinative power in directing history compared to material forces, the unfolding of the human spirit behind the outward march of historical events represented for Vivekananda, the real story of man's development.

The Greeks living in the pleasant climate of the Mediterranean, turned their energies outwards towards the study and conquest of external nature, while the Aryans living in the snow-capped Himalayas or the heat of the Gangetic belt, turned their attention inwards, to the study and conquest of man's inner psychological and spiritual nature. Each represented a certain kind of man, the development of a certain phase of the human spirit.

Thus, Vivekananda taught that each race or nation was consciously or unconsciously working out an ideal in its national life, a certain phase of the human spirit. He saw England and America as working out the ideal of political liberty and the Western nations as manifesting the power of the conquest of external nature. However, it has been India's special destiny to manifest the spiritual side of man. The life of the Aryan civilization was steeped in mysticism, asceticism, and the philosophical search for a transcendental reality beyond the world of senses. (This was an assessment of India with which many Indologists of the age, like Paul Duessen, and many of the German Romantic writers and philosophers of the nineteenth century, agreed, to a lesser or greater extent). This way of understanding history may seem to our contemporary intellectual sensibilities as simplistic, crude, or even odd. But to think of Vivekananda being any of these would be to ignore his intellectual context. In his historical thinking Vivekananda was one of the last representatives of a historical tradition that began in the late Enlightenment in Germany with the philosopher Johann Gottfried von Herder. According to Herder's system, 'Each nation has its own history and line of development, prefigured in its natural endowments and in its relationship to its natural environment. At the same time the different lines of development form one pattern, one great harmony; and the whole process of evolution is the manifestation or working-out of divine providence.'[24] This description of Herder's theory of history comes close to being one of Vivekananda's modes of historical thinking, with the difference that Vivekananda did not give any role for divine providence or God in the historical process.

> Wherever and in whatever nation there has been, or is, any advance made in earthly science up to the present day—such as social, martial, political, sculptural, etc.—there the shadow of ancient Greece has fallen. Let us leave apart the consideration of ancient times, for even in this modern age, we, the Bengalis, think ourselves proud and enlightened simply by following the footmarks of these Yavana Gurus for these last fifty years,

illumining our homes with what light of theirs is reaching us through the European literature.

The whole of Europe nowadays is, in every respect, the disciple of ancient Greece, and her proper inheritor; so much so that a wise man of England had said, 'Whatever nature has not created, that is the creation of the Greek mind.'[25]

Here, Vivekananda identifies the intellectual achievements of modern Europe as the inheritance of ancient Greece. When he talks about Bengalis thinking themselves enlightened by following the footsteps of the Yavanas, he is talking about the liberal Western education the bhadralok intelligentsia were exposed to in colleges set up by the British. Vivekananda's attitude towards the educational institutions of his day had two opposing aspects. He opposed the delegitimization of Indian history and civilization by the British imperial pedagogy imposed on Indians. Such utterances from Vivekananda are particularly useful for the Sangh Parivar as they colour the secular history and liberal civic values that are taught in India today as history written by Westerners that obliterates India's cultural heritage. Of course, in reality, the history curriculum for Indian schools draws largely on the work of Indian nationalist historians, not British colonial historians.

What Vivekananda objected to was the historical education imparted in the nineteenth century, where British historians aligned themselves with Britain's imperialist agenda and portrayed an India which was in continuous decline since the Vedic ages, with no stable empires. It is important to remember that in their agenda to show that Indians did not have a history of self-rule, the Mughal empire was portrayed as an inefficient, foreign presence. The study of European literature, philosophy, and political science on the other hand, Vivekananda considered to be of utmost importance to India. In fact, the contact with European thought, which catalysed the Bengal Renaissance and various social reformation movements was essential in Vivekananda's view, for India's national regeneration.

Vivekananda's identification of Europe as the disciple of ancient Greece and the political and technological developments of modern Europe as an expression of the Grecian spirit needs both context and clarification. The dominant story about the genesis of European modernity traces it back to the artistic, intellectual, and cultural movement called the Renaissance that started in Italy in the fourteenth century and spread across Western Europe, lasting till the early to mid-seventeenth century. This Renaissance started with the rediscovery of classical Greek texts including the work of Aristotle and Greek literature and sculpture. The impetus these new ideas gave Europe, propelled it out of the relative intellectual stagnation of the Middle Ages[*] and eventually to the eighteenth-century movement towards critical reason called Enlightenment. Even the Enlightenment, which broke the stranglehold of Christianity over European thought and created the intellectual crucible of secular modernity, drew its inspiration from Greek thinkers, through the work of Roman writers.[26] Vivekananda's historical knowledge of Europe was both vast and detailed, and the reduction of this extremely complex process of historical evolution to the spirit of ancient Greece was not the result of a lack of knowledge.

At the basic level, in this article and other speeches dealing with the West where Vivekananda spoke to an educated Indian audience, the derivation of everything European from the Greek intellectual lineage, was primarily a necessary simplification for the sake of communication. Few of his readers or audience would have understood a reference to the Renaissance and Enlightenment. The first book dealing exclusively with that period and identifying it as a key cultural turning point was Jacob Burckhardt's *The Civilisation of the Renaissance in Italy*, which was published in 1860. Though the book caused a sensation, it would still take decades before European historiography fully integrated the paradigm of the Renaissance into the history of early modern Europe.

But Vivekananda spoke of these developments in terms of the 'spirit of Greece', also because of the historical paradigm he used, which has been referred to earlier. This was historical thinking of the kind that the German Romantic Movement with its concept of the 'zeitgeist', or the 'spirit of the times' would have found congenial. While Vivekananda was certainly exposed to that intellectual movement, it is difficult to talk with certainty about direct influence; though we do find definite traces of Hegel's historical thinking in Vivekananda. But it is difficult for us today to understand history as a movement of either the human or the universal Spirit, because these terms lack the analytical precision that modern history demands. Additionally, a wealth of economic, sociological, anthropological, and other kinds of historical data has become available after Vivekananda's time. Meta-categories like 'spirit', 'essence', 'energy', etc., so common to historical thinking in the nineteenth century, (even assuming they were theoretically valid) are almost impossible to apply across such massive amounts of information.

---

[*]One can no longer call them the dark ages without risking being attacked by a mob of irate medieval historians.

These two gigantic rivers (Aryans and Yavanas), issuing from far-away and different mountains (India and Greece), occasionally come in contact with each other, and whenever such confluence takes place, a tremendous intellectual or spiritual tide, rising in human societies, greatly expands the range of civilization and confirms the bond of universal brotherhood among men.

Once in far remote antiquity, the Indian philosophy, coming in contact with Greek energy, led to the rise of the Persian, the Roman, and other great nations. After the invasion of Alexander the Great, these two great waterfalls colliding with each other, deluged nearly half of the globe with spiritual tides, such as Christianity. Again, a similar commingling, resulting in the improvement and prosperity of Arabia, laid the foundation of modern European civilization. And perhaps, in our own day, such a time for the conjunction of these two gigantic forces has presented itself again. This time their centre is India....

In this age, both these types of mankind are extinct, only their physical and mental children, their works and thoughts are existing.

Europe and America are the advanced children of the Yavanas, a glory to their forefathers; but the modern inhabitants of the land of Bharata are not the glory of the ancient Aryas. But, as fire remains intact under cover of ashes, so the ancestral fire still remains latent in these modern Indians. Through the grace of the Almighty Power, it is sure to manifest itself in time.[27]

Vivekananda assumed, like most leaders of the later Bengal Renaissance, that India's future would come through a revival of her ancient civilizational heritage, in a manner analogous to how the European Renaissance came about through the revival of Greek thought, philosophy, and culture. But, according to him, such growth could only occur through the contemporary conditions, namely the British presence in India and the influence of Western civilization and thought.

In the essay, Vivekananda goes on to ask a series of questions regarding India's future. What would the socio-polity of the India of the future look like when such growth occurs? What customs would be followed? Will caste remain? If so, in what form? By virtue of birth or by virtue of aptitude? Would the restrictions on taking of food from different kinds of people remain or be done away with? Vivekananda tells his readers that these questions do not admit any ready answer because of the sheer scale of the ethnic, linguistic, and cultural variations present in India. At this point in history, it was impossible to imagine India as a united polity marked by any homogeneous characteristics.

If there was no way to imagine a model to steer the present Indian society towards, what should India aspire to? As always, Vivekananda preferred to answer the question in terms of abstract principles and values rather than offer a normative solution.

> Then what is to be? What we should have is what we have not, perhaps what our forefathers even had not—that which the Yavanas (Greeks) had; that, impelled by the life-vibration of which, is issuing forth in rapid succession from the great dynamo of Europe, the electric flow of that tremendous power vivifying the whole world. We want that. We want that energy, that love of independence, that spirit of self-reliance, that immovable fortitude, that dexterity in action, that bond of unity of purpose, that thirst for improvement. Checking a little the constant looking back to the past, we want that expansive vision infinitely projected forward; and we want—that intense spirit of activity (Rajas) which will flow through our every vein, from head to foot.[28]

As the West met with the East on the soil of India, Vivekananda desired a confluence of the positive ideas and ideals of both these civilizations to be the basis of India's future growth as well as the major influence on the future development of humankind. Vivekananda declares that the one aim of *Udbodhan* magazine was to further this fusion of civilizational values of the East and West.

As discussed earlier, Vivekananda utilized the concept of the gunas—rajas, sattva, tamas—to communicate his vision of what India should be. This triad of qualities originated with the Samkhya philosophy but was integrated into the philosophy of the Bhagavad Gita. It was subsequently popularized in Hindu religious discourse to the point that a significant section of upper-caste men was familiar with these terms and the values they advocated. These qualities not only characterized persons but were considered inherent in the universe itself. The entire purpose of earthly existence from the Hindu point of view was to become sattvic, thus attaining spiritual qualities and preparing oneself to reach moksha, or the ultimate stage of liberation from the cycle of birth, death, and rebirth.

> What can be a greater giver of peace than renunciation? A little ephemeral worldly good is nothing in comparison with eternal good; no doubt of that. What can bring greater strength than Sattva Guna (absolute purity of mind)? It is indeed true that all other kinds of knowledge are but non-knowledge in comparison with Self-knowledge. But I ask: How many are there in the world fortunate enough to gain that Sattva Guna? How

many in this land of Bharata? How many have that noble heroism which can renounce all, shaking off the idea of 'I and mine'? How many are blessed enough to possess that far-sight of wisdom which makes the earthly pleasures appear to be but vanity of vanities? Where is that broadhearted man who is apt to forget even his own body in meditating over the beauty and glory of the Divine? Those who are such are but a handful in comparison to the population of the whole of India; and in order that these men may attain to their salvation, will the millions and millions of men and women of India have to be crushed under the wheel of the present day society and religion?

And what good can come out of such a crushing?

Do you not see—talking up this plea of Sattva, the country has been slowly and slowly drowned in the ocean of Tamas or dark ignorance? Where the most dull want to hide their stupidity by covering it with a false desire for the highest knowledge which is beyond all activities…where one, born and bred in lifelong laziness, wants to throw the veil of renunciation over his own unfitness for work; where the most diabolical try to make their cruelty appear, under the cloak of austerity, as a part of religion…where knowledge consists only in getting some books by heart, genius consists in chewing the cud of others' thoughts, and the highest glory consists in taking the name of ancestors: do we require any other proof to show that that country is being day by day drowned in utter Tamas?

Therefore Sattva or absolute purity is now far away from us. Those amongst us who are not yet fit, but who hope to be fit, to reach to that absolutely pure Paramahamsa state—for them the acquirement of Rajas or intense activity is what is most beneficial now. Unless a man passes through Rajas, can he ever attain to that perfect Sattvika state? How can one expect Yoga or union with God, unless one has previously finished with his thirst for Bhoga or enjoyment? How can renunciation come where there is no Vairagya or dispassion for all the charms of enjoyment?…

In India, the quality of Rajas is almost absent: the same is the case with Sattva in the West. It is certain, therefore, that the real life of the Western world depends upon the influx, from India, of the current of Sattva or transcendentalism; and it is also certain that unless we overpower and submerge our Tamas by the opposite tide of Rajas, we shall never gain any worldly good or welfare in this life; and it is also equally certain that we shall meet many formidable obstacles in the path of realization of those noble aspirations and ideals connected with our after-life. The one

end and aim of the Udbodhan is to help the union and intermingling of these two forces, as far as it lies in its power.[29]

It is important to note that while Vivekananda is talking about the need for the influx of rajas, the spirit of activity and dynamism from the West, he is not merely talking about an imitation of a mode of life, any more than when he wants India to spread the currents of sattva or transcendentalism in the West; rather, he is talking about an attitude of mind. In both these cases, he was talking about the exchange of ideas and their cultural bearers; political, social, and scientific ideas from the West and spiritual, mystical, and philosophical ideas from India. As he said many times over, India should be willing to sit at the feet of any nation and learn what she has to offer. Of the two causes of the civilizational degeneration of India Vivekananda identified, one was how India had cut herself off from the rest of the world and the thought currents flowing from different countries and culture. This is the reason why in spite of the evils of British colonial rule, Vivekananda saw in it India's possible salvation. In the Anglobalization that British colonialism was creating, ideas were pouring into India not only from the West, but from several other nations and civilizations. What Vivekananda wanted for Indians was maximum exposure to such foreign cultural and intellectual influences.

Especially in the case of the West, what Vivekananda vehemently objected to was Westernization in its vulgar sense, where convinced of the superiority of Western civilization, Indians and many other colonized Asian people imitated Western modes of thought, living slavishly, without taking the trouble to understand the ideas and ideals which expressed themselves in these life patterns and evaluating those ideas in the light of independent reasoning. Far from being against the progressive, liberal, and individualistic ideas introduced by Western education, Vivekananda welcomed them wholeheartedly and saw in them the true application of the Vedantic ideals he wanted to resuscitate within Hinduism and in India. Towards the end of the *Udbodhan* article, Vivekananda muses that whatever customs and traditions were disappearing from India by the onslaught of Western ideas and economic competition were probably rotten in the first place. For what is true and strong always sustains, it is that which is non-essential and weak that dies.

> How many gushing springs and roaring cataracts, how many icy rivulets and everflowing streamlets, issuing from the eternal snow-capped peaks of the Himalayas, combine and flow together to form the gigantic river of the gods, the Ganga, and rush impetuously towards the ocean! So what

a variety of thoughts and ideas, how many currents of forces, issuing from innumerable saintly hearts, and from brains of geniuses of various lands have already enveloped India, the land of Karma, the arena for the display of higher human activities!

Look! how under the dominion of the English, in these days of electricity, railroad, and steamboat, various sentiments, manners, customs, and morals are spreading all over the land with lightning speed. Nectar is coming, and along with it, also poison; good is coming, as well as evil. There has been enough of angry opposition and bloodshed; the power of stemming this tide is not in Hindu society. Everything, from water filtered by machinery and drawn from hydrants, down to sugar purified with bone-ash, is being quietly and freely taken by almost every one, in spite of much show of verbal protest. Slowly and slowly, by the strong dint of law, many of our most cherished customs are falling off day by day—we have no power to withstand that. And why is there no power? Is truth really powerless? 'Truth alone conquers and not falsehood.'—Is this Divine Vedic saying false? Or who knows but that those very customs which are being swept away by the deluge of the power of Western sovereignty or of Western education were not real Acharas, but were Anacharas after all....

'For the good of the many, as well as for the happiness of the many'—in an unselfish manner, with a heart filled with love and reverence, the *Udbodhana* invites all wise and large-hearted men who love their motherland to discuss these points and solve these problems.[30]

What exactly did Vivekananda foresee as the ultimate direction in which the influx of progressive ideas from the West would take India? Was it merely moderate reform, the casting off of old superstitions and cumbersome rituals from Hindu society that Vivekananda had in mind? Would Hindu society retain its essential character after assimilating advantageous ideas of modernization from the West? Or did Vivekananda envisage a reformed Hinduism providing a religious umbrella for the secular and democratic institutions of the West? A position of this kind is often attributed to Islamic modernizers of the nineteenth century like Muhammad Abduh and Jamal al-Din al-Afghani, who had to contend with the pressures of the contact of Islamic civilization with technicalistic modern Western civilization. Because of Vivekananda's insistence that he would not lay down prescriptive and particular solutions for society to follow, and the difficulty of evaluating his utterances in varied contexts whose social dynamic is hidden from us, it is possible to read Vivekananda as leaning towards both viewpoints.

But a careful and sustained reading of Vivekananda which focuses on this issue can reveal that what Vivekananda had in mind was a transformation far more drastic than either moderate reform or religiously backed modernization of political, legal, and civic institutions. Vivekananda did not see the contact with the emerging modernity of the West as a challenge that confronted traditional Hindu society and which it had to engage with. As we have seen, for Vivekananda, India's state of crisis was bound to the endemic poverty of the masses and the exploitative structure of Indian society with its rigid caste hierarchy, untouchability, and despotic concentration of power in the hands of the kings, nobility, and priests. While British rule exacerbated the economic situation and increased poverty in the short term; in the long term, Vivekananda saw the salvation of India as coming through mass education and the corrosion of oppressive social structures through Western thought combined with the economic forces unleashed by industrial capitalism. To this, he wanted to conjoin a confidence and pride in India's past civilizational achievements which had been undermined by colonialism; and the dissemination of Vedantic ideals with their immense potential for egalitarianism and individual emancipation. How necessary and indispensable he considered the part played by the presence of Western thought and institutions in India's national regeneration can be seen from several comments he made.

For example, in an informal interview he gave to the American newspaper, the *San Francisco Chronicle* in 1900, he discoursed on a variety of topics for almost two hours. The interviewer wrote: 'Then he talked long of ancient Russian history, and of the wandering tribes of Tartary, and of the Moorish rule in Spain, and displaying an astonishing memory and research.' But the reporter's attempt to get him to talk about politics was met with a firm refusal. When asked about the ongoing Boer War, between Great Britain and the white Boer settlers in South Africa, Vivekananda lamented the bloodshed but replied, 'I do not wish to discuss politics.' This was something Vivekananda did on principle, however strong his political opinions might be. When asked his opinion about the British rule in India, he replied

> Tell you about the English in India? But I do not wish to talk of politics. But from the higher standpoint, it is true that but for the English rule I could not be here. We natives know that it is through the intermixture of English blood and ideas that the salvation of India will come. Fifty years ago, all the literature and religion of the race were locked up in the Sanskrit language; today the drama and the novel are written in the

vernacular, and the literature of religion is being translated. That is the work of the English,* and it is unnecessary, in America, to descant upon the value of the education of the masses.[31]

What exactly did Vivekananda see as the end result of the historical process set into motion by the 'intermixture' of English ideas? In an interview he gave to a London newspaper in 1896, he replied to a question of that import, couched in the reporter's phrase 'Where will it end?' Vivekananda replied: 'It will certainly end in the working out of India's homogeneity, in her acquiring what we may call democratic ideas. Intelligence must not remain the monopoly of the cultured few; it will be disseminated from higher to lower classes. Education is coming, and compulsory education will follow. The immense power of our people for work must be utilised. India's potentialities are great and will be called forth.'[32]

How transformative this process was in Vivekananda's mind can be seen by the fact that he considered the age, which was contemporaneous with the second industrial revolution and led by Great Britain, the beginning of a new epoch in human civilization. Vivekananda theorized that human history developed in four phases. The first phase was dominated by priests and the power of religion, the second by the power of kings, the third by the power of the merchant class, and the fourth which was yet in the distant future, by that of the average person. Vivekananda expounds this theory only a few times. When addressing an Indian audience, he called the four epochs, the age of the Brahmin, the age of the Kshatriya, the age of the Vaishya, and the age of the Shudra. Each age had its defects as well as good points compared to other ages. But social equality and the democratization of knowledge increased as one epoch transitioned to the next. Thus, in the final age of the masses, equality among the populace would be at its highest.

Certain distinctions have to be made here to avoid misinterpreting the relationship of Vivekananda's historical thinking with various political ideologies. Vivekananda's positive evaluation of the third epoch, of capitalistic modernity, as tending to break up the feudal system built on exclusion was the opposite of conservative and right-wing thinkers across the world. It agreed with both the liberals and Karl Marx's views on this aspect of industrial modernity. His

---

*Vivekananda is referring to the work of British Oriental Scholars who translated Sanskrit texts including the Vedas, into English and regional languages. This directly catalysed the intellectual ferment that led to the Bengal Renaissance. See *British Orientalism and the Bengal Renaissance* by David Kopf for a detailed study.

insight that the project of European liberal republicanism was compromised by the power exercised over the people and the state by the emerging capitalist class, ran parallel to the Marxist analysis. For example, Vivekananda says of the European countries, 'The wealth and power of a country are in the hands of a few men who do not work but manipulate the work of millions of human beings. By this power they can deluge the whole earth with blood.'[33]

However, the fourth epoch controlled by the masses Vivekananda envisaged was not the same as the rule of the proletariat that communism envisaged. Vivekananda did not expect it to arise in the foreseeable future, unlike the socialists; neither did he see it arising as a result of the internal contradictions of capitalism (through peaceful means or a revolution). What he seems to have thought instead, if we were to go by his analyses of the transition between previous epochs, is that internal developments within the material conditions and internal structure of the new economic system would eventually give rise to a different set of socio-economic conditions which would replace it. The new socio-economic conditions would make the dissemination of power among the masses possible. So, to read Vivekananda as a socialist on the basis of his four-stage theory of history would be erroneous.

Vivekananda gave no historical examples, which would allow us to map these epochs to historical periods with any significant degree of confidence. But given certain features of his general description of each age and related historical references in other parts of his work, we can make some guesses. What seems certain is that these epochs did not begin or end simultaneously across the world but varied by geographical area. We can be reasonably sure that the priestly epoch started with the early agrarian states, followed by the agrarian civilizations of Mesopotamia, Egypt, India, Nubia, China, and other later ones. The shift from hunter–gatherer societies which existed for at least a hundred thousand years to settled agriculture is the greatest revolution to have occurred in the course of the history of humankind, barring the development of language. Though ruled by kings with absolute sovereignty, religion was the most important aspect of these societies. The priests who conducted magical rites and rituals and mediated between the people and the gods, held the highest power as a class, framing the horizons of life possibilities for entire populations.

It is extremely difficult to say when Vivekananda thought the second phase, when power passed from the priests to the kings, began. Based on certain comments he made suggesting that the authors of the Upanishads were mainly Kshatriyas and connections he made with the passing on of spiritual knowledge from Brahmins to Kshatriyas, it is possible that he believed the epoch of the kings start around the Axial Age (eighth to third century BCE), at least in India.* This period roughly corresponds to the period of composition of the principal Upanishads. It is also possible that in Vivekananda's mind the epoch of the kings started several centuries earlier when centralized empires began appearing. The temptation to associate the second epoch with the Axial Age comes also from the fact that the Axial Age is the only period of extraordinary civilizational transformation that lies between the agrarian revolution and the industrial revolution. Nonetheless, this dating remains highly speculative.

The third epoch, that was dominated by the Vaishyas or merchants is the period that starts with the beginning of industrial capitalism in Britain. That he considered the emergence of Anglobalization, based on Great Britain's rise and the dominance of capital, a third epoch in human history, is a testament to the fact that he thought of the consequences of this new phase as more far reaching than the term 'modernization' broadly suggested. Modernization is the prism through which liberal leaders of the national movement viewed the process. Vivekananda considered the great advantage of the new age, to be the global dissemination of knowledge through commerce that linked the world together. This would eventually produce greater social equality. This aspect of it enthused Vivekananda, especially in its potential impact on India. At the same time, he saw the drawback of the era as the exploitation of labour by the moneyed class, as well as the domination of the instruments of the state, like the legislature and an independent executive, by those in whose hands wealth was concentrated. But Vivekananda indicates that in being open to these forces of change, Indian society in the long run would be transformed in radical ways. The form of this transformation would be as difficult to predict as it would have been to predict the civilizational form of agrarian empires at the beginning of the agrarian revolution.

Vivekananda states this in his 1899 article 'Modern India', in which he wrote on the theme of the impact of the British conquest on India and what it portends for India's future.

> But at the end of this Mohammedan period, another entirely new power made its appearance on the arena and slowly began to assert its prowess in the affairs of the Indian world. This power is so new, its nature and workings are so foreign to the Indian mind, its rise so inconceivable, and its vigour so insuperable that though it wields the suzerain power up till now, only a handful of Indians understand what this power is. We are

---

*The concept of an Axial Age was proposed by the German thinker Karl Jaspers.

talking of the occupation of India by England.... But that a handful of Vaishyas (traders) who, despite their great wealth, have ever crouched awestricken not only before the king but also before any member of the royal family, would unite, cross for purposes of business rivers and seas, would, solely by virtue of their intelligence and wealth, by degrees make puppets of the long-established Hindu and Mohammedan dynasties; not only so, but that they would buy as well the services of the ruling powers of their own country and use their valour and learning as powerful instruments for the influx of their own riches—this is a spectacle entirely novel to the Indians, as also the spectacle that the descendants of the mighty nobility of a country (England)...would, in no distant future, consider it the zenith of human ambition to be sent to India as obedient servants of a body of merchants, called The East India Company—such a sight was, indeed, a novelty unseen by India before!

Therefore the conquest of India by England is not a conquest by Jesus or the Bible as we are often asked to believe. Neither is it like the conquest of India by the Moguls and the Pathans. But behind the name of the Lord Jesus, the Bible, the magnificent palaces, the heavy tramp of the feet of armies...behind all these, there is always the virtual presence of England—that England whose war flag is the factory chimney, whose troops are the merchantmen, whose battlefields are the market-places of the world, and whose Empress is the shining Goddess of Fortune herself! It is on this account I have said before that it is indeed an unseen novelty, this conquest of India by England. What new revolution will be effected in India by her clash with the new giant power, and as the result of that revolution what new transformation is in store for future India, cannot be inferred from her past history.[34]

It naturally follows from Vivekananda's views that the Sangh Parivar's project of seeking continuity with dead forms of the Hindu past can only be viewed as a kind of destructive atavism that tries to forcefully swim in the opposite direction of history. Trying to keep out the liberal thought currents pouring in from the West, would for Vivekananda be a national disaster. He said repeatedly in so many words, that learning from the West was necessary for the salvation of India; not only to meet India's material needs, but to create a more equal and democratic society. While the direction of transformation was apparent, the outcome was by no means certain. It required the efforts of Indians to build up a nation and society based on a combination of ideals drawn from India's own ancient philosophical and spiritual heritage and modern ideals of social and political organization of the West.

A conversation recorded by a disciple is illuminating of what Vivekananda visualized and desired as the future of India. Vivekananda was descanting on the need to educate India's masses, and what he had in mind was primarily a secular education with an emphasis on science, though it would also contain a spiritual component. When Vivekananda talked about a new order of things, the disciple asked: 'Do you think Hindu society can successfully adopt European social laws?' Vivekananda answered briefly:

> No, not wholly. I would say, the combination of the Greek mind represented by the external European energy added to the Hindu spirituality would be an ideal society for India.... India has to learn from Europe the conquest of external nature, and Europe has to learn from India the conquest of internal nature. Then there will be neither Hindus nor Europeans—there will be the ideal humanity which has conquered both the natures, the external and the internal. We have developed one phase of humanity, and they another. It is the union of the two that is wanted. The word freedom which is the watchword of our religion really means freedom physically, mentally, and spiritually.[35]

One reason the Sangh has been able to portray Vivekananda as a Hindu supremacist is because of his repeated call to Indians to spread India's spirituality in the West. Such appropriations make it sound like Vivekananda went to preach Hinduism to a West which was thirsting for spirituality; Hindu religion and society was glorious and Vivekananda sounded a triumphant call to Indians to become the spiritual teachers of the West. However, the truth as always was quite different. Vivekananda asked Indians to contribute to world civilization by sending forth teachers of spirituality, primarily for their own upliftment. The West did need Indian spirituality, by which Vivekananda meant not Hindu religious beliefs and customs, but the combined spiritual wisdom of Hinduism, Buddhism, and Jainism, all of which originated in ancient India around the same time. (The first Upanishads were written just two or three centuries before Buddha's advent and Mahavira is believed to be an older contemporary of the Buddha.) But the most important reason Vivekananda asked Indians to go to the West and teach spirituality is because India could take her place among the nations of the world only by giving back something for the knowledge of science, technology, and social and political organization that she was receiving from other countries. This is a far cry from the narcissistic, not to mention risible, image of the 'Vishwaguru' that the government projects for India.[36]

Vivekananda told an Indian audience in an exhortation which was very typical of his appeals to disseminate spirituality.

> One of the great causes of India's misery and downfall has been that she narrowed herself, went into her shell as the oyster does.... [E]very one of you knows that that little stir, the little life that you see in India, begins from the day when Raja Ram Mohan Roy broke through the walls of that exclusiveness. (Ram Mohan Roy travelled to England to lecture). Since that day, history in India has taken another turn, and now it is growing with accelerated motion. If we have had little rivulets in the past, deluges are coming, and none can resist them. Therefore we must go out, and the secret of life is to give and take. Are we to take always, to sit at the feet of the Westerners to learn everything, even religion? We can learn mechanism from them. We can learn many other things. But we have to teach them something, and that is our religion, that is our spirituality. For a complete civilisation the world is waiting, waiting for the treasures to come out of India, waiting for the marvellous spiritual inheritance of the race, which, through decades of degradation and misery, the nation has still clutched to her breast.[37]

Vivekananda created a storm at the Parliament of Religions by preaching that all religions were true. And he continued to preach that throughout his time in the West. Why then did he think the predominantly Christian nations of the West needed spirituality from India? Did Vivekananda mean that Indian religions were truer than the others? This is the position that even moderate Christian speakers took at the Parliament of Religions—that Christianity possesses spiritual truth in full measure and that other religions were true in so far as it approximated Christianity. This was, however, not what Vivekananda had in mind. When talking about the truth of religions, Vivekananda was not talking about theology. As far as Vivekananda was concerned, whether you believed in Holy Trinity or Vedanta or Sunyata was irrelevant. True religion for him consisted in direct experience of spiritual truths in meditation or higher states of devotion, in what is today called mysticism, though Vivekananda did not himself usually use that word because of the pejorative connotations it had in his time. Jesus the Christ was a prophet because he said he saw the personal God, saw him whom he called the Father in heaven. The Buddha was a prophet because he said he experienced the ultimate reality in the state of nirvana. Sri Ramakrishna Paramahamsa was a prophet because he said he experienced both the personal God and the impersonal Absolute reality. Every religion has its mystics who, Vivekananda held, transcended the world given through the senses, and directly experienced the transcendental. What was unique about the Indian religions is that they made a systematic study of mysticism, of its methods and procedures and made it a systematic discipline based on fundamental principles. 'Throwing broadcast'[38] these spiritual ideas from India into the thought currents that were shaping the modern world, would mean that spiritual truths would no longer remain esoteric and only meant for the already mystically oriented. It would make available to every person the methods for the attainment of mystical experience, which was for Vivekananda, the essence of spirituality.

If India's part in the collection of nations was in the sphere of spirituality, it naturally followed that she had the most important task. This allowed her to stake a claim in the community of nations on equal terms, in spite of her politically enslaved and economically impoverished condition. But even then, when Indian nationalism, let alone Hindu nationalism, had not emerged, Vivekananda laid down caveats that prevented his audience from mistaking his message for one of Hindu superiority. To requote from the *Udbodhan* article 'The Problem of Modern India': 'Europe and America are the advanced children of the Yavanas, a glory to their forefathers; but the modern inhabitants of the land of Bharata are not the glory of the ancient Aryas. But, as fire remains intact under cover of ashes, so the ancestral fire still remains latent in these modern Indians.'* India might produce any number of mystics and saints, but the majority of people remained sunk in ignorance, superstition, and a ritualistic form of religion devoid of any empathy for humanity. The spiritually great India Vivekananda often talked of so evocatively, was the India of at least a thousand years ago. It was an India where a long line of mystical movements from the ascetic Shramana movements of the Upanishads, Buddhism and Jainism, up to (possibly) the devotional movement of Ramanuja, acted in their own periods as the nuclei of a wider field of a transcendental oriented mode of life in which a wider section of society could participate. Of his own times, Vivekananda said: 'The present Hinduism is a degradation.'† If he called upon his fellow Indians to take up the task of spiritualizing the entire world, he made it clear that the work had to begin at home.

While Asia and especially India, had developed systems of mystical spirituality, Vivekananda did not think that they would retain a monopoly

---

*See p. 273.
†See p. 79.

on it. He often said that the West being in a state of rajas, was just one step away from attaining the state of sattva. For example, he told an Indian audience: 'The Americans are fast becoming liberal. Judge them not by the specimens of hard-shelled Christians (it is their own phrase) that you see in India. There are those here too, but their number is decreasing rapidly, and this great nation is progressing fast towards that spirituality which is the standard boast of the Hindu.'[39]

Vivekananda's greatest formal departure from the ideas of his Advaitic or Vedantic predecessors was his idea of practical Vedanta—that the universal egalitarianism implied in the idea that every human's Self is identical with Brahman or the ultimate cosmic principle must be made practical; that it should be applied to life to form both a practical ethics and build an egalitarian society. Viewed from a different angle, practical Vedanta was also about empowering the individual. Once an individual believes in the idea that her true Self is potentially divine, she attains a powerful self-conception that allows her to actualize all her latent potentialities. But it works the other way also. Only a person who has come into her true individuality can hope to progress towards spiritual perfection. Vivekananda told an American audience that while the sanyasins of India were tremendous individualists, they had to go out of society to be so and pursue the spiritual path. Inside Indian society, the life of an individual was tied down by all kinds of rules and regulations. For Vivekananda, the true meaning of spirituality was freedom, and this meant not only metaphysical freedom, but going beyond all limiting norms in every aspect of man's being. This was almost impossible within such a society that repressed the scope for individual unfoldment. On the other hand, Vivekananda told an Indian audience that by empowering the individual American society was ahead of Indians on the path of practical Vedanta:

Ay, you may be astonished to hear that as practical Vedantists the Americans are better than we are. I used to stand on the seashore at New York and look at the emigrants coming from different countries—crushed, downtrodden, hopeless, unable to look a man in the face, with a little bundle of clothes as all their possession, and these all-in rags; if they saw a policeman they were afraid and tried to get to the other side of the foot-path. And, mark you, in six months those very men were walking erect, well clothed, looking everybody in the face; and what made this wonderful difference? Say, this man comes from Armenia or somewhere else where he was crushed down beyond all recognition, where everybody told him he was a born slave and born to remain in a low state all his life, and where at the least move on his part he was trodden upon. There everything told him, as it were, 'Slave! You are a slave, remain so. Hopeless you were born, hopeless you must remain.' Even the very air murmured round him, as it were, 'There is no hope for you; hopeless and a slave you must remain', while the strong man crushed the life out of him. And when he landed in the streets of New York, he found a gentleman, well-dressed, shaking him by the hand; it made no difference that the one was in rags and the other well-clad. He went a step further and saw a restaurant, that there were gentlemen dining at a table, and he was asked to take a seat at the corner of the same table. He went about and found a new life, that there was a place where he was a man among men. Perhaps he went to Washington, shook hands with the President of the United States, and perhaps there he saw men coming from distant villages, peasants, and ill clad, all shaking hands with the President. Then the veil of Maya slipped away from him. He is Brahman, he who has been hypnotised into slavery and weakness is once more awake, and he rises up and finds himself a man in a world of men.[40]

We shall conclude this chapter by taking a look at Vivekananda's views on what seemingly frightens the RSS and the Sangh Parivar the most about the West: its culture of enjoyment and pleasure, and its sexual permissiveness. Vivekananda perhaps differed from most spiritual figures in that while believing that spiritual enlightenment was the ultimate aim of human life, he did not view human existence solely through that lens. His immensely curious mind was interested in almost everything, and he recognized that every phase of human existence required development. While he considered renunciation as the sine quo non of spirituality, with intellectual detachment he could argue for the development of its opposite for those who wanted it; the cultivation of sense pleasure. In a long essay written in Bengali titled 'East and West', Vivekananda made the case that the contempt with which Westerners held India, and the horror with which most orthodox Indians regarded the culture of the West, were stereotypes born of mutual misunderstanding. Each nation, each culture had to be studied and judged by its own standards if it is to be understood, and not by the values of an alien civilization. Vivekananda's comments about Paris, which was considered by Indians as a den of sensual vice (many contemporary Europeans too held a more moderate, but nonetheless similarly judgemental attitude), are illuminating: 'What nation in the world has not the longing to enjoy and live a life of pleasure? Otherwise, why should those who get rich hasten to Paris of all places? Why do kings and emperors, assuming other names come to Paris and live incognito and feel themselves happy by bathing in this whirlpool of sense-enjoyment? The longing is in all countries, and no pains are spared to satisfy it; the only difference is the French have perfected it as a science, they know how to enjoy, they have risen to the highest rung of the ladder of enjoyment.'[41]

He writes later:

It should lie noted here that their dances may appear improper to our eyes, but not so with them, they being accustomed to them. The girl may, at a dance, appear in a dress showing the neck and shoulders, and that is not taken as improper; and the English and Americans would not object to attending such dances, but on going home, might not refrain from condemning tile French customs! Again, the idea is the same everywhere regarding the chastity; of women, whose deviation from it is fraught with danger, but in the case of men it does not matter so much. The Frenchman is, no doubt, a little freer in this respect, and like the rich men of other countries cares not for criticism. Generally speaking, in Europe, the majority of men do not regard a little lax conduct as so very bad, and in the West, the same is the case with bachelors. The parents of young students consider it rather a drawback if the latter fight shy of women, lest they become effeminate.

...The object of my speaking of these things is to impress upon you the fact that the life of each nation has a moral purpose of its own, and the manners and customs of a nation must be judged from the standpoint of that purpose. The Westerners should be seen through their eyes; to see them through our eyes, and for them to see us with theirs—both these are mistakes.[42]

Vivekananda was open in his admiration for the English, even as he criticized them on other counts. On his return from his sojourn in the West to Calcutta in 1897, he was presented with a formal address of welcome. A few minutes into his speech, Vivekananda spoke about the mutual misunderstanding that rose between Westerners and Indians as they each judged the other's culture by their own values. It is only when seen through their own eyes that the true ideals and positive virtues of a civilization are revealed.

Addressing the Calcutta crowd when sentiments against the English colonial masters had started to turn sour, he said:

No one ever landed on English soil with more hatred in his heart for a race than I did for the English, and on this platform are present English friends who can bear witness to the fact; but the more I lived among them and saw how the machine was working—the English national life—and mixed with them, I found where the heartbeat of the nation was, and the more I loved them. There is none among you here present, my brothers, who loves the English people more than I do now. You have to see what is going on there, and you have to mix with them. As the philosophy, our national philosophy of the Vedanta, has summarised all misfortune, all misery, as coming from that one cause, ignorance, herein also we must understand that the difficulties that arise between us and the English people are mostly due to that ignorance; we do not know them, they do not know us…. We have also similarly, patiently to study the social institutions of the West and not rush into mad judgments about them, their intermingling of the sexes, their different customs their manners, have all their meaning, have all their grand sides, if you have the patience to study them.[43]

PART III

Vivekananda's Philosophy

VIVEKANANDA'S PHILOSOPHY OF FREEDOM: THE METAPHYSICAL ASPECT

To understand Vivekananda's views on most matters, even sociopolitical ones, one has to understand the philosophical background against which he expounded his views. This is particularly so since for Vivekananda, his metaphysical system was not merely an intellectual theory he believed in, but the source of life-orientational principles that he held could both guide and transform human beings. We are talking here of Advaita, which was the philosophy he was most associated with (the other being Yoga), and which is the core of the spiritual message he sought to teach the world. Here, we have to understand two interconnected but separate aspects. The first is to understand briefly what the Advaita system is, within the tradition of Hindu philosophy. The second is to understand how Vivekananda presented it and the particular lines of emphasis in his exposition.

Ancient Indian philosophy has traditionally been understood to consist of six schools or darshanas. They are Vedanta, Mimamsa, Samkhya, Yoga, Nyaya, and Vaisheshika.* Advaita is the most important sub-school of the Vedanta school. Modern Hinduism, in its philosophical beliefs, at least when they are explicitly expressed, gives allegiance to only the Vedanta school. Modern Hinduism is thus pretty much Vedantic, at least when it comes to its philosophical commitments. All the six orthodox schools of Indian philosophy used the Vedas as scriptural authority. The Vedanta differs from the other schools in basing its philosophy exclusively on one specific portion of the Vedas viz. the Upanishads: the end of the Vedas. That is how the system gets its name: Ved- and anta- meaning the end of the Vedas.

Every religious tradition evolves historically, and there are periods of sharp shifts in the meaning and practices of the tradition. But usually, there is a continuity of basic originatory elements that are preserved in these shifts, though the meaning of these elements is often re-interpreted. Hinduism is

---

*For a brief and accessible, yet comprehensive discussion of the various schools and its important philosophers, see *The Sacred Thread: A Short Introduction to Hinduism* by J. L. Brockington.

probably unique in that many of these shifts are actually radical departures whose discontinuous nature would normally have led to a rupture in the tradition.* But perhaps because of the inherent plurality and heterodoxy of the religion,† these extreme departures have been accommodated within the overall continuity of the Hindu tradition. The most drastic of these departures is the Upanishads or the Vedanta.

The Vedas are divided into two portions. The Karma Kanda and the Jnana Kanda, the ritualistic and knowledge portions respectively. The Karma Kanda which comes first, was composed mainly in the early Vedic age and consists of hymns to gods and goddesses and rituals meant for the propitiation of deities and for obtaining particular results. The Jnana Kanda, which includes the Upanishads, inherently critiques the ritual portion that precedes it. It does not generally deny the efficacy of the rituals but deny that they have any spiritual value. Rituals are thus effectively banished from the scene of Hindu soteriology and theology.‡ This is extremely important because the philosophy of the Upanishads is the predominant philosophical influence on post-Vedic Hinduism,§ being the foundation of the philosophy of the Bhagavad Gita, *Brahma Sutra*, and much of what is found in the philosophical portions of the Mahabharata, Ramayana, Bhagavata, and other important texts such as the Avadhuta Gita, the Yoga Vasishta, etc. The most popular contemporary theoretical understanding of Hinduism is that it is Upanishadic in essence. But such an understanding actually goes a long way back, stretching at least as far back as the Srimad Bhagavata, and finding definitive expression with Shankara (800 CE).[1]

Vivekananda preached Advaita¶ as a universal philosophy, shorn of its

---

*Like the rupture which occurred in Christianity during the Reformation and split Christendom into catholics and Protestants.

†For an excellent and accessible discussion of the plurality of the Indian philosophical tradition see *The Argumentative Indian* by Amartya Sen. The plurality of the Hindu tradition, with its lack of fixed religious authority, has led to questions about whether 'Hinduism' is a coherent category of description.

‡The Purva Mimamsa school would disagree as it bases itself on the Karma Kanda. But this school faces the difficulty of explaining away the Jnana Kanda and its dismissal of rituals. It is a difficult task as the Jnana Kanda is chronologically posterior to the Karma Kanda and enjoys a hermeneutic privilege of the kind the New Testament of the Bible has over the Old Testament.

§The other lesser, but by no means insignificant one, being Tantra.

¶Vivekananda often used the term Advaita interchangeably with Vedanta, which reflected current Hindu practice. Though formally both Advaita, which believed in a non-personal God, and the other Upanishadic sects, which believed in a personal God, fell under the rubric of the Vedanta philosophical school, in practice, the term Vedanta, or Vedantist had become more and more

Hindu robes. He taught it as both philosophy and mysticism i.e., as an intellectual theory which sought to explain reality, and a spiritual vision which was to be consummated in direct experience of that reality. In presenting Advaita as a philosophical theory, Vivekananda translated it into terms of the Western philosophical discourse current in the nineteenth century. He drew principally upon German Idealism, British empiricism, and the work of Herbert Spencer, though he borrowed no more than conceptual elements from these philosophies. Some important aspects of his presentation of Advaita seem Kantian, though it is not easy to say whether it was a matter of direct influence or whether Vivekananda arrived at it independently through his reading of the Advaita tradition (which is what he himself believed).* When considering Vivekananda's philosophical contribution, it is important to realize the difficulty of such a philosophical translation across two vast and robust traditions which are radically different and both of which stretch back at least two millennia. It is not a mechanical task, nor even a process comparable in creativity to translating across two different languages. It necessarily involves a level of independent thinking which both in philosophical rigour and ideational creativity is comparable to building independent metaphysical systems, the traditional summit of philosophical achievement. At any rate, it is a formidable intellectual achievement, all the more impressive because Vivekananda did it by the age of thirty.

A related matter here is that Vivekananda has been described, and sometimes accused, of creating a Neo-Vedanta which is different from the original Vedantic system. While it will be a digression to go into the various problematic aspects of this claim, one is worth mentioning in this connection. Any project of translating a metaphysical system from one philosophical tradition to another would involve a certain distortion. This is because the various descriptive categories that belong to the two traditions cannot be perfectly calibrated with each other. By putting the Advaita into the discursive language of Western philosophy, Vivekananda ipso facto changed many conceptual features of that system. To expect a replication of Advaita within the terms of Western philosophy that would not differ at all from the traditional Vedanta in this sense, is to be quite naive.

The Vedanta school is further split into three major sub-schools: Advaita (monism), Vishistadvaita (qualified monism), and Dvaita (dualism). What

---

exclusively associated with the Advaitin in Vivekananda's time.
*Shankara defines maya as 'Desha Kala Nimitta' (space, time, cause) in his commentary on the Upanishads. Vivekananda frequently used this formulation, but without referring to Shanakara's text.

then is the Advaita system? We have a clue from the meaning of the word 'Advaita' itself. The word splits into a-dvaita, meaning not-dual. Broadly, the Advaita can be considered monistic while the other two Vedantic systems can be considered dualistic. A monistic philosophical system is one in which the entirety of reality consists of one single kind of entity. For example, a majority of philosophers today are adherents of materialism, or what is more properly called 'physicalism'. Physicalism is an example of a monistic system. It tries to dissolve the traditional mind–matter dichotomy by positing that the universe is completely composed of matter.* Mind or consciousness is somehow reducible to matter; to the neurochemical activity of various brain states. Another monism of a completely different kind is that of the seventeenth century Dutch philosopher Baruch Spinoza. Spinoza argued that all reality was made of one single substance, which can be called God or nature. Mind and matter are not separate entities, but the same substance conceived in two different ways.

Advaita bases its monism on the 'Brahman' or impersonal God of the Vedas. The only true reality is Brahman according to Advaita. Nothing exists apart from Brahman. How then does Advaita account for the fact that the world we experience instead appears to be composed of a multiplicity of entities? If true reality is Brahman, how is that we do not see it and instead see the world? Here, 'world' refers to the totality of all mental and physical phenomena, not just the physical universe. In the Advaita system, both the anger I feel inside when I get stuck in a traffic jam and the tree I see in front of me when I take a stroll are part of the 'world' (prakriti).

This is where the concept of maya comes in. Advaita explains the world as an appearance, which we mistake for the real, using the concept of maya. The classical analogy, given by Shankara, is that of a man seeing a rope in the dark and mistaking it for a snake. In such an instance of misperception, the form of the snake has been superimposed on the rope. In the same way, Advaita argues, the sentient Self has superimposed the appearance of the world on the reality of Brahman. Vivekananda defines maya as space, time, and causality, which are categories through which the mind makes sense of the world. Brahman is the reality which is beyond the network of space, time, and causality created by the mind. The term maya has been often translated as 'illusion'. This, however, is a mischaracterization of its meaning. 'Misperception' would be a relatively more accurate rendering. Misperception as a species of

---

*Matter here encompasses what physics calls matter and energy, which are in any case inter-convertible entities in modern physics.

perception, consists of an object of perception and subject that perceives. The object of perception is the phenomenal world. What then is the perceiving subject? The subject of perception in Advaita is the Self of the sentient being. Misperception or miscognition by the Self is the cause that produces the effect of the phenomenal world as the object of perception. The Self is called Atman in Vedanta and can be equated to the soul in Western theology. However, the Self is not the mind or the psyche. It is the unchanging sub-stratum lying behind the flux of the mind and bearing witness to all events.

The aim of human life, according to Advaita, is to go beyond the appearance of the world and grasp the reality, Brahman, behind that appearance. But what is Brahman? What is its nature? Advaita's point of departure from other theistic philosophies lies precisely in the answer to this question. All theistic conceptions of God are personal, in that God has a personhood. And associated with this personhood are various attributes like kindness, love, mercy, goodness, and so on. The theologies of many religions also attribute the qualities of omniscience, omnipotence, and omnipresence to the godhead. Advaita does not deny the existence of a personal God. This is the God who brings forth the universe* and controls it. This is God with qualities or attributes, Saguna Brahman (Brahman with qualities), in Vedanta. But such a God is not the ultimate reality within the Advaita system. The Advaitin argues that if God is perfect and infinite, then even attributing the greatest qualities like love and goodness is to limit God. The possession of a particular attribute limits God to a finite mode of being. The personal God is Brahman seen through the limitations of the mind. The real nature of Brahman is limitless and without attributes and it is called Nirguna Brahman, Brahman without qualities. The personal God is only a stepping stone to the ultimate reality of Brahman—infinite, devoid of limiting qualities and indescribable.

Brahman, thus understood as the unqualified Absolute, is beyond all mental conceptions or descriptions of language. It is beyond the grasp of not only discursive knowledge, but of any kind of mentation. Its existence can only be affirmed by negation, that is by saying what it is not. Thus, it is described as being neither good nor evil, without any attributable form, unnameable, not subject to change, not the senses, not the body, not the mind, not the intellect, not the ego, not even consciousness (at least not as it is ordinarily understood). As the only reality, it is without any parts or duality. It stands in relation to

---

*In Indian philosophy, God does not create the world out of nothing, i.e., ex-nihilo. The idea of something arising from nothing is considered incoherent. Instead, God evolves the universe out of himself. God is both the material and efficient cause of the universe.

no other entity, has no internal structures and cannot be characterized by any kind of part–whole relationship. Because it is beyond all duality as the only true existence, it is also beyond the subject–object duality of ordinary existence. The Advaita allows only one positive characterization of Brahman: as Sat-Chit-Ananda, infinite being, pure consciousness, and unbounded bliss.

But unlike Spinoza's God that we mentioned before, the Brahman of Advaita is not just a self-existing substance of which we are particular modes of being. Like other orthodox Indian philosophical systems, Advaita posits a permanent inner Self for every creature, which stands behind the changing mental phenomena of the individual psyche, as its witness. The Self is the unchanging backdrop against which all mental phenomena appear and interact.* This Self is manifest as awareness, as consciousness. What transmutes the Advaita from a purely philosophical system into a spiritual system is that it purports to show humans both the way to comprehend the true nature of the Self and the way out of ordinary existence, which is transitory and finite, to eternal and infinite existence. This maps on to the theological concept of salvation, of achieving liberation (mukti, moksha, nirvana, kaivalya) from the cycle of births and rebirths, which all ancient Indian religious systems have in common.

The human Self is the site of access to the Absolute. The Advaita advocates a radical form of enquiry into the nature of the Self. This is to be achieved by progressively stripping away the identification of the Self with the unreal phenomena of the world: with objects of the senses, the body, the mind, the intellect, and personal selfhood. This process of sustained mental negation of everything that is not the true Self is supposed to finally result in pure Self-awareness. This Self-awareness results in the knowledge that the individual Self is identical to Brahman or the Absolute. This is encapsulated in the Upanishadic statements 'Tatvam Asi' (Thou art that [Brahman]) and 'Aham Brahmasmi' (I am Brahman), which are referred to as the mahavakyas (great statements).

The final Advaitist position collapses the triad of God, sentient animate beings, and physical nature, of traditional philosophy into one single reality without modes or distinctions. From the discursive vantage point of each of these three categories, non-Advaitist philosophers have often described Advaita as being theistic, solipsistic, and pantheistic respectively. Such descriptions can only be partially true and are sometimes mischaracterizations. This is because, whether one considers the philosophical project of Advaita as successful or not,

---

*The central disagreement with Advaita and Madhyamika Buddhism is that Buddhism denies there is a permanent Self behind the mental activity of sentient beings.

when the internal logic of the system is considered correctly, the meaning of all categories of human thought, including that of God, Self, and existence, break down when applied to the ultimate reality of Brahman. This is one of the reasons Hindu critics of Shankara accused him of being a crypto-Buddhist.[*] The Brahman of Shankara's Advaita, they alleged, cannot in any meaningful way be distinguished from the Shunyata (emptiness) of the Buddhists.[†] Advaitins, of course, do not accept this.

Out of this abstruse and technical metaphysics, Vivekananda evolved a powerful life-philosophy while remaining true to the formal theoretical commitments of the Advaita. It was a philosophy that was meant to arouse and inspire people and strengthen their spirit, even as it aimed to provide an answer to the most fundamental existential dilemma of the human condition. Vivekananda's work did not consist only of transposing the Advaita system into a Western philosophical framework. Out of the dry bones of formal reasoning, he evoked a living and breathing philosophy which resonated with the power of the human spirit and which sought to transmute the human into the divine. Or rather, to use his words, manifest the divine which is already in man. But these very qualities of his work make it impossible to give a summary of Vivekananda's thought without eviscerating it of its élan vital. Not only that, but any such attempt is likely to render his thought meaningless and sterile; for the logical structure of his thinking is too bound to the form of expression he gave it. To serve as the vehicle of his thought, he used a rich reticulation of strikingly original aphorisms, powerful rhetoric, allusions, and metaphors, which makes content inseparable from form. Readers who have tried to read the work of the philosopher Frederick Nietzsche would be able to relate to the discursive phenomenon I am trying to describe. Nietzsche eschewed systematic philosophy in favour of a highly original and idiosyncratic style of writing which closely fused form and content. No one can get a sense of Nietzsche's philosophy from a second-hand account, however penetrating or insightful such an account might be. Only Nietzsche's original words can convey the sense of what he was about. Something similar can be said about Vivekananda. (This is not to suggest that Vivekananda and Nietzsche shared any stylistic elements.) Unfortunately, there simply is no substitute to reading

---

[*]Most contemporary scholars of Indian philosophy do not maintain the view that the Advaita and Madhyamika systems are identical. However, Shankara was indebted to Buddhist philosophy for several key concepts he borrowed from it. See *Shankara and Indian Philosophy* by Natalia Isayeva.
[†]Just like with maya and illusion, the conventional translation of Shunyata as emptiness is a distortion. Shunyata may be better characterized as being devoid of essences.

Vivekananda himself to understand the originality of his ideas or to form even a rough picture of the direction of his intellectual efforts. All that is possible for a report of Vivekananda's thought, is to highlight certain crucial ideas and important points of departure. This is what I will attempt to do.

Two fundamental ideas that Vivekananda brings to the Advaitic tradition is freedom and perfectibility. Freedom is perhaps Vivekananda's most central concern, the one thing that threads together the multifarious aspects of his thought. The conceptual basis for Vivekananda's idea of freedom in Indian philosophy is 'mukti'. Common to all the six orthodox schools of Indian philosophy, mukti is traditionally used to mean liberation from the cycle of birth and rebirth in which each human soul is supposed to be trapped. Vivekananda particularly drew from the conceptions of the Samkhya and Advaita schools. In Samkhya, liberation is when the soul (purusha) realizes its absolute independence from the bondage of nature (prakriti), while in Advaita, it is freedom from ignorance. But Vivekananda expanded the notion of freedom beyond the range of anything to be found in traditional Indian philosophy, or for that matter, perhaps in any philosophical system. For Vivekananda, every thing was attempting to escape the limits of its environment and reach freedom. The entire movement of the universe was towards greater freedom and though in a much more limited sense, even human history showed a distinctive drift towards freedom. Vivekananda wrote in his treatise on Karma Yoga:

> Everything that we perceive around us is struggling towards freedom, from the atom to the man, from the insentient, lifeless particle of matter to the highest existence on earth, the human soul. The whole universe is in fact the result of this struggle for freedom. In all combinations every particle is trying to go on its own way, to fly from the other particles; but the others are holding it in check. Our earth is trying to fly away from the sun, and the moon from the earth. Everything has a tendency to infinite dispersion.* ...[I]t is under the impulse of this tendency that the saint prays, and the robber robs. When the line of action taken is not a proper one, we call it evil; and when the manifestation of it is proper and high, we call it good. But the impulse is the same, the struggle towards freedom. The saint is oppressed with the knowledge of his condition of bondage, and he wants to get rid of it; so he worships God. The thief is oppressed with the idea that he does not possess certain things,

---

*It would seem here that Vivekananda is not wholly wrong; the Second Law of Thermodynamics implies that disorder in the universe will continue to increase over time.

and he tries to get rid of that want, to obtain freedom from it; so he steals. Freedom is the one goal of all nature, sentient or insentient; and consciously or unconsciously, everything is struggling towards that goal. The freedom which the saint seeks is very different from that which the robber seeks; the freedom loved by the saint leads him to the enjoyment of infinite, unspeakable bliss, while that on which the robber has set his heart only forges other bonds for his soul.[2]

The freedom that Vivekananda saw as the destiny of each human, was absolute freedom from all limitations. That is, from all limitations imposed on her by her apparent being. The freedom that Vivekananda envisioned as the ultimate purpose of existence, thus flows from the Advaitic conception of what a human's real being is. To say that it is identical to Brahman or the Absolute, as classical Advaita does, does not take us far; for nothing positive can be said of Brahman. But in the sense that freedom is always freedom from something, Vivekananda is able to convey a lot about the real nature of a person, in describing the movement away from the limiting conditions of her apparent nature. The nature or being of man has been a perennial subject in philosophy, sometimes becoming the central focus of philosophical enquiry at certain points in history. In the early twentieth century, man's being became the theme of renewed philosophical attention for the existentialist movement, and their analysis is an interesting point of contrast. Martin Heidegger, in particular, concerned himself with the being of man as a fundamental existential question. For Heidegger, in his very existential constitution, man was embedded in the world. Temporality forms the horizon of man's existence and is in a certain sense fundamental to his very being. Temporality and spatiality, for Heidegger, are the very conditions of possibility for man's being.

But for Vivekananda, spatiality and temporality, along with causality, were only the defining conditions of man's apparent being. The mistake was that man took these conditions to be real. 'If you think you are free, you are free. If you think you are bound, you are bound,'[3] Vivekananda said again and again. Man found himself embedded in the world in a way where his Self and the world seem to interpenetrate each other. Vivekananda used the word 'nature' for the world. But by nature, he did not merely mean only the physical world studied by science. He meant the entire network of mental and physical phenomena that was bound by cause and effect, and which presented itself to our consciousness as objects, both physical and mental.[*] Thus, thoughts,

---

*Heidegger disputed the common notion that the things of the world are properly understood

emotions, feelings, and sensations were all as much part of nature, as rocks, trees, and atoms.

The condition of possibility of this world (or nature) was the condition of bondage of the Self. The Self in identifying itself with the conditional existence of the world, was limited by those conditions viz. time, space, and causality. The human impulse to freedom culminates in a spiritual quest where we are not seeking freedom from this or that thing, but from the very conditions that make the existence of things possible. Real freedom is absolute existence, existence that is not dependent on external conditions. According to Vivekananda:

All things in nature work according to law. Nothing is excepted. The mind as well as everything in external nature is governed and controlled by law. Internal and external nature, mind and matter, are in time and space, and are bound by the law of causation. The freedom of the mind is a delusion. How can the mind be free when it is controlled and bound by law? The law of Karma is the law of causation. We must become free. We are free; the work is to know it. We must give up all slavery, all bondage of whatever kind. We must not only give up our bondage to earth and everything and everybody on earth, but also to all ideas of heaven and happiness. We are bound to earth by desire and also to God, heaven, and the angels. A slave is a slave whether to man, to God, or to angels. The idea of heaven must pass away. The idea of heaven after death where the good live a life of eternal happiness is a vain dream, without a particle of meaning or sense in it. Wherever there is happiness there must follow unhappiness sometime. Wherever there is pleasure there must be pain. This is absolutely certain, every action has its reaction somehow. The idea of freedom is the only true idea of salvation—freedom from everything, the senses, whether of pleasure or pain, from good as well as evil.

More than this even, we must be free from death; and to be free from death, we must be free from life. Life is but a dream of death. Where

as objects which appear to a subject or Self. In Heidegger's analysis, things are primarily things-at-hand for the human being to relate to in various ways. The theoretical attitude of carving the world into different objects as presented to a subject, he argued, was a secondary and derivative ontology. Since we referred to Heidegger's analysis as a point of contrast, it is worth noting that for Vivekananda, nature consisted of things that are objects for consciousness. Though Vivekananda uses the language of subject/object in his discourse about the world; whether the proper philosophical apprehension of the world should be through such a polarity, or along the alternative lines proposed by Heidegger and his followers, is beside the point for Vivekananda's philosophical project. His fundamental concern is about how the Self can escape the world, not how the world should be correctly described.

there is life, there will be death; so get away from life if you would be rid of death. We are ever free if we would only believe it, only have faith enough. You are the soul, free and eternal, ever free, ever blessed. Have faith enough and you will be free in a minute.

Everything in time, space, and causation is bound. The soul is beyond all time, all space, all causation. That which is bound is nature, not the soul. Therefore proclaim your freedom and be what you are—ever free, ever blessed.[4]

If man's fundamental existential dilemma is bondage, then the search for freedom underlies all of man's struggles. But how does this metaphysical idea of freedom manifest itself in the field of human action? On all planes of existence, the spiritual, the ethical, the social, the intellectual, and the political, Vivekananda saw the quest for freedom as the breaking of law. At the deepest level of analysis, humans did not come into their authentic being by following the path of least resistance and obeying the laws of nature, society, family, or polity.

I disagree with the idea that freedom is obedience to the laws of nature. I do not understand what it means. According to the history of human progress, it is disobedience to nature that has constituted that progress. It may be said that the conquest of lower laws was through the higher. But even there, the conquering mind was only trying to be free; and as soon as it found that the struggle was also through law, it wanted to conquer that also. So the ideal was freedom in every case. The trees never disobey law. I never saw a cow steal. An oyster never told a lie. Yet they are not greater than man. This life is a tremendous assertion of freedom; and this obedience to law, carried far enough, would make us simply matter—either in society, or in politics, or in religion.[5]

It was in his very nature for man to rebel against the conditions in which he found himself. 'The very word "Sannyasin" means the divine outlaw and since it is freedom alone that is desirable...it is not law that we want but ability to break law. We want to be outlaws,'[6] he declared. Religion or spirituality for Vivekananda was not obeying a set of customs or rules, but a search that would break through every limitation till it reached the truth. He once remarked to a Western audience that the only character he found worthy of admiration in Milton's *Paradise Lost*, was the figure of the devil. 'Even hells stand out with this miraculous fact that we are born rebels. And the first fact of life—the inrushing of life itself—against this we rebel and cry out, "No law for us." As long as we obey the laws we are like machines, and the universe goes on and we cannot break it. Laws as laws, becomes man's nature. The first inkling of life on a higher level is in seeing this struggle within us to break the bounds of nature and to be free. "Freedom, oh freedom! Freedom, oh, freedom!" is the song of the soul.[7]

This was not moral nihilism or social anarchism. It was rather the deep-seated conviction that man comes into his authentic being only through acting freely, not under compulsion. It is not that Vivekananda did not recognize moral laws. The fundamental moral law for Vivekananda was the principle that we do not harm another human being except in order to prevent a greater harm. This was the moral law that was applicable to human action under all circumstances. But this principle regulated only what man should not do. The higher moral life was expressed in positive terms: unbounded love for fellow beings, the negation of the ego, the worship of the God in human beings through service to others. But none of these ideals were meaningful or genuine if they were enacted under the habit of dead custom or tradition. A genuine life, which consisted of striving for freedom, was not possible in any area, including the moral, through following a set of external norms. The legitimacy of moral principles did not issue from anything outside man: from God, from social institutions, or ethical codes of conduct. Their legitimacy derived from man's own conscience; the Self of man was the ground for ethics. The same applied to human action in the social, political, and intellectual planes. When a person acted on her conscience alone, she was not bound by any external law but was acting from her own free will. If in the struggle to break out of normative ethics, humans blundered and committed moral errors, that was a necessary price to pay for moral and spiritual evolution.

As Vivekananda explained: 'The huge steamer, the mighty railway engine—they are non-intelligent; they move, turn, and run, but they are without intelligence. And yonder tiny worm which moved away from the railway line to save its life, why is it intelligent? There is no manifestation of will in the machine, the machine never wishes to transgress law; the worm wants to oppose law—rises against law whether it succeeds or not; therefore it is intelligent…. It is more blessed, in my opinion, even to go wrong, impelled by one's free will and intelligence than to be good as an automaton.'[8]

Another important idea Vivekananda introduced into the interpretation of Advaita and the Vedanta, was that of the perfection of the human being; closely allied to this was the idea of spiritual evolution. The idea of evolution to a state of perfection, is not as such present in Vedanta or the other schools of Indian philosophy. In pursuing this line of interpreting Vedanta, Vivekananda was influenced by Western humanism, with which he came into contact as a philosophy student. His ideas of evolution owe something to Herbert Spencer and the German Idealists, but he transmogrified them into something completely different in the framework of Advaita. The idea of salvation within all Indian philosophical systems,* has been connected with the idea of reincarnation. The soul (jivatma) is caught in a seemingly endless cycle of birth and rebirth in the phenomenal world (samsara). Salvation (mukti) consists of coming out of this repetitive cycle. Human life then is seen as an endless and ultimately meaningless repetition, where souls are trapped in a network of karmic cause and effect they cannot escape. Vivekananda introduced an evolutionary perspective through which to view this schema, where the human soul is seen as progressively manifesting its latent potentialities, till it reaches a stage of expression of its inherent perfection. The state of perfection consists in the manifestation of the real being of man, which is infinite knowledge, infinite existence, and infinite bliss. The various experiences that the soul has in its journey are neither inherently meaningful or meaningless: they form the context for the unfolding of the real Self.

While Vivekananda personally believed in the theory of reincarnation, he wasn't dogmatically committed to it as a philosopher. His philosophy of the Advaita can operate independently of the theological framework of reincarnation. He once remarked to an American audience that the Hindus believed in the theory of reincarnation because it seemed the best model to explain the spiritual facts they have discovered. The Hindus, he said, would be willing to exchange it for a better theory if there was one; but he hadn't found any. The essential point for Vivekananda was the real nature of the soul and its necessary implications for man's spiritual quest. Vivekananda's core argument on this point is that if there was a spiritual essence to man's being that does not change even as the body undergoes changes and which was supposed to be immortal, such an entity had to have a simple nature. Such an entity could not be composed of parts; for any combination is subject to change and to ultimate dissolution into its constituent components. It further follows that a truly simple entity cannot have a beginning in time, because there cannot be an originatory event of its formation.† The soul has no beginning in time; it always existed.

---

*Except the Charvaka school, which was a materialistic school which denied the existence of the soul.
†The idea of something being formed presupposes the idea that it is formed from something that is not itself. Strictly speaking, all change is only a rearrangement and it follows that a simple entity cannot be formed from another simple entity, because no rearrangement would change one simple entity into another. So the formation of any entity in time can come about only by combining multiple entities, and since the soul is not a combination, it cannot have been formed.

This has direct implications for the idea of God. If the soul has no beginning in time, it means that the idea of a God who creates human beings is not logically tenable. In so far as one can speak of a God who created the universe; creation can only mean manifestation of the already existent. But where did the soul exist before creation? The answer that the Vedanta provides is that it existed in God.

God is the ground of all phenomenal reality and God's act of creation comprises of manifesting the individual soul within the temporal phenomenal universe. It is this manifested soul (jivatma) to which the experiences of birth, death, and reincarnation can be attributed. The real nature of the soul is beyond spatiality, temporality, and causality; and the central philosophical claim of Advaita is that in its real nature, the soul is identical to Brahman, or God.

The idea of a soul created by God is incoherent, Vivekananda says, for another reason as well. If God is the efficient cause of the created soul and the soul has no other antecedent material cause, God would have to create the soul out of nothing. But, repeating an argument from classical Indian philosophy, Vivekananda says that something cannot come out of nothing. The idea of existence arising out of non-existence, is fundamentally incoherent. This means that the idea of God creating sentient beings from nothing; creation ex-nihilo is not tenable according to reason. God is the efficient cause of both physical nature and sentient beings, whom God manifests in the spatio-temporal horizon of the phenomenal world. God is also the material cause of all beings and nature, who already exist in God before creation.

This is the overall metaphysical framework within which Vivekananda addressed his spiritual discourses. The idea of evolution and perfection was something Vivekananda emphasized often in his teachings. Life presented human beings with the opportunity to evolve intellectually, mentally, morally, and spiritually. Whether one believed in the theory of reincarnation or not, the essential point was to have faith in one's true nature as Spirit, not matter. As the infinite Spirit, all power, potentialities, and possibilities are already present in man. The goal was to manifest them and attain moral and spiritual perfection. The aim of existence was progressive evolution towards perfect Being. But it was evolution only in an apparent sense for man was already perfect. The goal was to unfold it. 'If it be true that man is the evolution of a mollusc, the mollusc individual is the same as the man, only it has to become expanded a great deal. From mollusc to man, it has been a continuous expansion towards infinity. Therefore, the limited soul can be styled an individual which is continuously expanding towards the Infinite Individual. Perfect individuality will only be reached when it has reached the Infinite, but on this side of the Infinite it is a continuously changing, growing personality,'[9] Vivekananda said during one of his talks.

UNIVERSAL RELIGION

Perhaps, Vivekananda's greatest contribution to religious thought was his theory of a universal religion and his greatest appeal to audiences in his own time was also his presentation of this. He preached vigorously, that all religions are true in their essence and were various paths to realizing God and our own divine nature. This was a tremendous contribution, both morally and intellectually. In a global religious discourse where most religious leaders took extremely partisan positions, those arguing for religious pluralism were in a minority, and even the pluralists usually stopped short of complete universalism, instead upholding the spiritual superiority of their own religion even as they genuinely appreciated the spiritual worth of other religions. True universalists like Vivekananda, who declared that all religions were true, and it was immaterial which religion you pursued your spiritual path through, were rare. It was not merely a question of prejudice. To be a universalist about all religions was not an intellectually easy task; it risked the problem of intellectual inconsistency. Today, it is easy to take a universalist stand regarding religion, because pluralism being the intellectual norm, one is required only to pay intellectual lip service to the idea. Intra-religious theological debate is today confined to interfaith conferences and the like and does not occur in the larger public sphere. In Vivekananda's time, however, both partisan and pluralistic theological debates were a major part of the public discourse. In such an atmosphere, to claim that all religions were true was to invite sharp theological and philosophical questioning, for, on the face of it, such a claim looks incoherent.

An illuminating contrast can be drawn with the views of a figure who attended the Parliament of Religions, but unfortunately did not draw the kind of attention Vivekananda or the Buddhist monk Dharmapala did. This was the Zen priest Shaku Soen, another religious pluralist and the master of D. T. Suzuki, who is famous for introducing Zen Buddhism to the Western world. Shaku Soen, who visited America again in the early 1900s, taught a small number of Americans the technique of Zen Buddhism. What is interesting about Soen, was that his exposition of Zen philosophy was remarkably similar in several respects to Vivekananda's exposition of Vedanta. In a loose sense of the term, his exposition of Zen was monist, like Advaita. He was welcoming of all religions and often drew upon the Christian tradition as he preached to Americans. But he could not make the move towards complete universalism because he was faced with the vexed question of a personal God and an immortal soul in Christianity. Both are denied by various schools of Buddhism while most religions in the world are committed to the doctrine of a soul. Soen says in a lecture:

> However, the followers of Buddhism usually avoid the term God, for it savors so much of Christianity, whose spirit is not always exactly in accord with the Buddhist interpretation of religious experience.... In this world of relativity, or nanatva as Buddhists call it, subject and object, thought and nature, are separate and distinct.... But the very constitution of the mind demands a unifying principle which is an indispensable hypothesis for our conception of phenomenality; and this hypothesis is called 'the gate of sameness,' samata, in contradistinction to 'the gate of difference,' nanatva; and Buddhism declares that no philosophy or religion is satisfactory which does not recognize these two gates.[10]

While Soen's spiritual message was extremely universal in spirit, these theological problems pushed him to take a pluralist position where Buddhism occupied a privileged place.

Vivekananda, on the other hand, took the position that all religions lead equally to the ultimate truth. But what does this mean philosophically? After all, all religions are in disagreement about theological questions. They disagree vehemently on the nature of God, of salvation, the nature of the soul and other fundamental religious issues. They follow different and often conflicting rituals, customs, taboos, rules, and regulations. They follow completely different mythologies. In what sense then, can they all be said to be true?

Vivekananda's answer is that they all express the same truth in different ways. God is infinite existence and has infinite aspects. It is beyond the capability of the human mind to grasp infinity in its totality. Each religion is an attempt, carried on through centuries, to grasp and express one or more aspects of the godhead. Vivekananda often used a parable to illustrate what he meant.

> I will tell you a story of five blind men. There was a procession in a village in India, and all the people turned out to see the procession, and specially the gaily caparisoned elephant. The people were delighted, and as the five blind men could not see, they determined to touch the elephant that they might acquaint themselves with its form. They were given the privilege, and after the procession had passed, they returned home together with

the people, and they began to talk about the elephant. 'It was just like a wall,' said one. 'No it wasn't,' said another, 'it was like a piece of rope.' 'You are mistaken,' said a third, 'I felt him and it was just a serpent.' The discussion grew excited, and the fourth declared the elephant was like a pillow. The argument soon broke into more angry expressions, and the five blind men took to fighting. Along came a man with two eyes, and he said, 'My friends, what is the matter?' The disputation was explained, whereupon the new-comer said, 'Men, you are all right: the trouble is you touched the elephant at different points. The wall was the side, the rope was the tail, the serpent was the trunk, and the toes were the pillow. Stop your quarrelling; you are all right, only you have been viewing the elephant from different standpoints.'[11]

In the parable, the elephant stands for God and the five blind men for the different religions quarrelling over the nature of God.

Vivekananda contended that theology was irrelevant to spirituality. Being spiritual was not about assenting to one or the other set of religious beliefs, but a matter of direct experience of truths that transcended the senses and the mind. Within every religious tradition, there have always been prophets and mystics who claimed to have directly perceived a transcendental and immutable spiritual entity, whether they termed it God, the soul, the One or something else. It is the experience of these mystics that formed the spiritual core of a religion. These experiences found expression in various ways: through mythology, rituals, ceremonials, philosophy, and spiritual practices. But all these things were merely the external trappings of religion, concrete forms that helped the novice grasp abstract truths. But the seeker attained spiritual truth only when in her spiritual quest she realized these abstract truths in her own consciousness. In doing that she did away with all the external aids of ceremonials, mythologies, and customary observances. They were like a ladder which was to be thrown away after being used to climb to the roof. All these entry points, which constitute the differences between various religious traditions, can equally serve as paths to the central truth, which is the experience of God, soul, or the Spirit.

'The furthest that all religions can see is the existence of a spiritual entity. So no religion can teach beyond that point. In every religion there is the essential truth and the nonessential casket in which this jewel lies. Believing in the Jewish book or in the Hindu book is non-essential. Circumstances change; the receptacle is different; but the central truth remains,'[12] Vivekananda said. In other words, in pursuing the idea of a universal religion, Vivekananda's philosophical strategy is to de-emphasize theology and centre the essence of religion on mysticism. In doing this he was drawing upon the teachings of his own guru, Sri Ramakrishna Paramahamsa. Ramakrishna had in turn, practised Advaita, Shaktism, Vaishnavism, Christianity, and Islam, and claimed that the practices of all these religious traditions culminated in the same unitive mystical experience.

However, a theoretical problem still remained that Vivekananda had to resolve if his philosophy of the universality of spiritual truths was to be coherent. There were a variety of mystical experiences, not only between various religions, but within the same religion itself. While some of these experiences agreed on essential points, others were flatly contradictory. Vivekananda offered a unique solution to the problem. A solution which was not only original, but one which has not been taken up by his successors in the field of comparative religion, and as such, it deserves renewed attention. Vivekananda broadly classified all mystical experiences of God as falling into three broad categories. The first and the most common is the experience of God as transcendent to yourself and the world. This corresponds to dualistic philosophies and theologies. For example, orthodox Christianity and Islam, and the dvaita school of Vedanta expounded by Madhva fall into this class. The second category of mystical experience is when the devotee experiences himself as a part of the divine entity. The most well-known philosophical counterpart to this kind of mystical experience is the qualified monism (Vishishtadvaita) school of Vedanta founded by Ramanuja. The third category of mystical experience is the kind where all distinction between the devotee and God vanishes, and there is only the experience of a single undifferentiated reality. Monistic philosophical systems such as the Advaita correspond to the mystical experience of unqualified unity.

One can question whether the wide range of mystical experiences reported in all the religious traditions of the world can fit neatly into these categories. However, what interests us here is that, assuming that Vivekananda's three-fold classification holds, how does he reconcile these three varieties of spiritual experiences and their conflicting claims of spiritual truth? For the dualist, God and the devotee are eternally separate, and their relationship is that of mutual love. For the qualified monist, the soul partakes of God's divinity; it is of the same nature as God. For the monist, God and the soul, the worshipped and the worshipper are the same entities; their distinction being an illusion. Vivekananda's answer is that none of these positions are completely wrong. The different types of mystical experiences do not actually contradict each other but are supplementary. They are all experiences of the same spiritual entity, but from different standpoints. Vivekananda explained it thus:

It is too often believed that a person in his progress towards perfection passes from error to truth; that when he passes on from one thought to another, he must necessarily reject the first. But no error can lead to truth. The soul passing through its different stages goes from truth to truth, and each stage is true; it goes from lower truth to higher truth. This point may be illustrated in the following way. A man is journeying towards the sun and takes a photograph at each step. How different would be the first photograph from the second and still more from the third or the last, when he reaches the real sun! But all these, though differing so widely from each other, are true, only they are made to appear different by the changing conditions of time and space. It is the recognition of this truth, which has enabled the Hindus to perceive the universal truth of all religions.[13]

Vivekananda thus introduces a hierarchy of mystical experiences. The first stage of experience is the dualistic one, where God is an object of one's experience. At a higher state, the subject–object distinction becomes blurred, and the individual Self experiences itself as part of a cosmic divine consciousness. The final and ultimate state is that of realizing the complete identity of the individual and divine self, where all traces of the individual ego disappear, and the individual merges into the divine. This is the Advaitic experience. This was not merely a theoretical schema Vivekananda came up with to solve an intellectual problem. He was drawing upon the putative mystical experiences of his guru, Sri Ramakrishna Paramahamsa. During a lifetime of single-minded spiritual practice, Sri Ramakrishna claimed to pass through successive stages of the three types of experience. He first realized God in the form of the Goddess Kali. Later, he had experiences of the whole world as interpenetrated by God. Finally, under the guidance of an Advaitist ascetic named Totapuri, Ramakrishna claimed to experience the nirvikalpa samadhi, union with the unconditioned and undifferentiated Absolute or Brahman.[14]

Recent scholarship has, however, thrown suspicion on the genuineness of Vivekananda's claim of belief in the universality of all religions. To varying degrees, academics such as Ashis Nandy, Sumit Sarkar, Narasimha Sil, and A. Raghuramraju have concluded that Vivekananda's philosophy of religious universalism, while apparently inclusive, smuggles in the superiority of Hinduism. A lot of this criticism is derived by focusing on Vivekananda's statements about the greatness of Hinduism, with no reference at all to the concrete historical facts about the colonial context of his work. As discussed in Chapter 5, this is historical anachronism at its worst. Of the above-mentioned scholars, Raghuramraju comes closest to recognizing the problem when he speculates that Vivekananda's colonial context can explain why he chose to make claims to Hindu superiority.[15] It is worth noting that there are no utterances in *The Complete Works of Swami Vivekananda* that categorically proclaim the superiority of the Hindu religion over others. The statements of chauvinism attributed to him hang on interpreting the intention of indirect statements that valorize some aspect of Hinduism.

There is, however, another strand to this critique of Hindu superiority that deals with the theoretical structure of Vivekananda's thought. Probably first stated by Asish Nandy, it claims that Vivekananda introduced a hierarchy into Hindu metaphysics which did not exist. This hierarchy has Advaita at the apex. Ashish Nandy writes that Vivekananda and those whose thoughts were similar 'introduced the concept of hierarchy into Hindu metaphysics…the non-Hindu's fear of being engulfed or of being fitted into the Hindu hierarchy became an indicator of his metaphysical poverty.'[16] Raghuramaraju concurs with this idea: 'Vivekananda postulates a metaphysical hierarchy wherein Hinduism, and more particularly, Advaita…is placed at the top; and this has estranged him from his teacher's construal of the equality of all religions. Here, it is relevant to note that Hegel postulated a hierarchy amongst the various religions in their march through history, in which Christianity is placed at the top. Like Hegel, Vivekananda too seems to have claimed higher status, though in his case it is for Hinduism.'[17] The reader will readily recognize this hierarchy as Vivekananda's theory of universal religion which has been sketched above.

Though on first sight one strongly suspects that at the heart of such critique is profound intellectual confusion about what equality of religions amounts to, it is difficult to refute because it is usually too vaguely stated and is not argued for with specificity. This is remedied (if one can use that word in such a context) by Jyotirmaya Sharma in *Cosmic Love and Human Apathy: Swami Vivekananda's Restatement of Religion*. Sharma sets out an explicit argument about how Vivekananda's theory of universal religion implies the inferiority of non-Hindu faiths, especially Christianity and Islam, at a purely conceptual level. The argument is simple enough. Advaita or non-dualism is a uniquely Hindu philosophy. Islam and Christianity are dualistic religions. Positing the non-dual mystical experience as the ultimate and final one and assigning a lower place in the ladder of progressive mystical experiences is to make Christianity and Islam inferior and marginalize them. Sharma writes that Vivekananda converts Ramakrishna's model of tolerance 'into a hierarchy of aspirants and an evolutionary schema conspicuously absent in his master'.[18]

To unpack the extent of intellectual confusion involved here, we have to look at what the equality of religions means in epistemological terms for Sharma. According to Sharma, to accept all religions as equal and hence to hold an appropriately tolerant religious world view, such a world view should not privilege the claims of any religion. Let us try to understand exactly what Sharma is demanding of Vivekananda. The necessary condition of an acceptably tolerant religious world view in *Cosmic Love* is that it should be non-hierarchical and accept the truth claims of all systems as equally valid. This includes the theologies of Catholics, Protestants, and dozens of other Christian denominations, the various schools of Hinduism and Buddhism, the Shias, Sunnis, Ahmadis, and so on. Such a tolerant system would then need to affirm the truth of all the following propositions at the same time.

A. Christ died on the cross to expatiate the sins of mankind.
B. Christ did not die on the cross to expatiate the sins of mankind.
C. Christ is the son of God.
D. Christ is not the son of God.
E. The Eucharist is the actual blood and flesh of Jesus Christ.
F. The Eucharist is not the actual blood and flesh of Jesus Christ.
G. God and the universe are separate.
H. God is identical with the universe.
I. God created the universe out of nothing, ex-nihilo.
J. God is the material and efficient cause of the universe.
K. Reality is infinite existence.
L. Reality is emptiness or Void (Shunyata).
M. God and the individual soul are identical.
N. God and the individual soul are not identical.

This list can be expanded ad infinitum.

In other words, Sharma's understanding of what constitutes a universal theory of religion would need to hold that P is Q and P is not Q at the same time. Such a theory would violate one of the most important laws of logic, the law of non-contradiction, in a truly spectacular way. Why, of all the philosophers in history, should Vivekananda alone shoulder the extraordinary epistemological burden of building such a theory is not explained. To put it bluntly, Sharma's argument is nonsensical.

The other problem with this position is its serious implications for minority rights. To claim a religious fact is true is ipso facto to claim that its opposite is not true. By this logic, the very act of theology becomes a crime. What position would the act of proselytizing occupy within such an ethical framework? A Christian or Muslim who wants to convert someone to her religion has absolutely no ethical justification for such an act if Sharma's position is accepted. How, then, do we defend such proselytization against a right-wing discourse that seeks to criminalize this?*

In *Swami Vivekananda and Non-Hindu Traditions: A Universal Advaita*, the religious studies scholar Stephen E. Gregg explored the precise question of how Vivekananda's universal philosophy of religion based on Advaita related to non-Hindu religious traditions. 'Vivekananda was no simplistic pluralist, as portrayed in hagiographical texts, nor narrow exclusivist, as portrayed by some modern Hindu nationalists, but a thoughtful, complex inclusivist. His was a position which necessitated interaction with, rather than damnation of, the non-Hindu, and empathy for the universal human religious condition, rather than sympathy for individual traditions per se.'[19] Gregg analysed Vivekananda's universal philosophy of religion and concluded that the hierarchy in the schema was inclusive of non-Hindu religions, not exclusive.

> Vivekananda formulated a hierarchical and inclusivistic framework of Hinduism, based upon his interpretations of a fourfold system of yoga. This framework valorised Advaita...and devalued aspects of Hinduism that were associated with what Vivekananda perceived to be 'low levels' of spiritual awareness, such as Gauni Bhakti (theistic devotion). ...Vivekananda understood his formulation of Vedanta to be universal, applying it freely to non-Hindu traditions. ...[H]is engagement with non-Hindu traditions is therefore essential to a full understanding of his 'Hindu' framework. In light of this...Vivekananda was consistently critical of 'low-level' spirituality, not only in non-Hindu traditions but also within Hinduism, thus refuting claims in some recent scholarship that Vivekananda was a Hindu chauvinist.... Vivekananda is best understood within the context of 'Advaitic primacy' rather than 'Hindu chauvinism'.... Vivekananda's inclusivism was not chauvinistically hierarchical, but universal in its valorising of 'higher-level spirituality' and devaluing of 'lower-level spirituality' both within Hinduism and with respect to wider religious traditions.[20]

---

*The last four paragraphs have been reproduced from 'Hindu not Hindutva'.

The idea that Vivekananda's valorization of non-dual Advaita as the ultimate spiritual truth is a claim of Hindu supremacy is not only logically nonsensical, it also arises only because the critics concerned seem ignorant about the history of the world's religions. As Gregg suggests, what Vivekananda preached to the world-at-large was not the Hindu Advaitic tradition with its various Sanskrit texts, commentaries, technical philosophy, and foundational centring in the Upanishads. What he taught was the philosophical and mystical kernel, which we can call either non-dualism or monism. While Advaita is usually considered the purest and most elaborately articulated form of spiritual monism, it is a misconception that spiritual monism is an exclusively Hindu affair. (I shall use the terms non-dualism and monism interchangeably from here on.) As anyone familiar with this history of world religions would know, almost every major religion has both monistic and dualistic mystical traditions within it. In promoting a monistic mysticism, Vivekananda could appeal to authentic monistic elements within each religion, which is precisely what made his idea of universal religion truly universal and of use to those situated in very different religious contexts. As Vivekananda told an audience in the West:

> Do I wish that the Christian would become Hindu? God forbid. Do I wish that the Hindu or Buddhist would become Christian? God forbid. The seed is put in the ground, and earth and air and water are placed around it. Does the seed become the earth, or the air, or the water? No. It becomes a plant, it develops after the law of its own growth, assimilates the air, the earth, and the water, converts them into plant substance, and grows into a plant. Similar is the case with religion. The Christian is not to become a Hindu or a Buddhist, nor a Hindu or a Buddhist to become a Christian. But each must assimilate the spirit of the others and yet preserve his individuality and grow according to his own law of growth.[21]

What Vivekananda expected his teachings to do was re-orient the listener or reader in the direction of a mystical search for spiritual truth, with which she could then approach the religious tradition in which she was located. The Advaitic primacy of the mysticism he taught did not require that the spiritual seeker Hinduize her quest. She could engage her religious tradition through a monistic philosophy free of any Hindu referents, and if needed turn to the monistic part of her own religious tradition for the resources to do that.

Monistic mysticism and philosophy are found in Christianity, Islam,

Buddhism, Judaism, and Taoism to varying degrees. It has even been claimed, and that too very often, that the summit of all mystical experience in all religions tends towards monism. In his influential study of spiritual experiences, *The Varieties of Religious Experience*, William James writes: 'In spite of their repudiation of articulate self-description, mystical states in general assert a pretty distinct theoretic drift. It is possible to give the outcome of the majority of them in terms that point in definite philosophical directions. One of these directions is optimism, and the other is monism.... It is on the whole pantheistic.'[22] Similar conclusions that unitive mystical experiences of the monistic type occur in every culture and is the culmination of all mystical experience, has been also made by the British philosopher Walter Stace and the Scottish religious studies scholar Ninian Smart.[23]

In Buddhism, the earliest non-dualistic philosophy is the Yogachara school which originated in India with two Buddhist monks who taught in the ancient Nalanda University.[*] Tibetan Buddhism was influenced by Yogachara while East Asian Buddhism is also predominantly monistic.[†] Zen Buddhism is, in so far as philosophical categories can be applied to it, non-dualistic. Certain forms of Kabbalah in Judaism are non-dual. Vivekananda's Advaitic primacy is accused of sidelining Christianity and Islam since the orthodox theologies of both religions are dualistic, believing in a monotheistic God who is utterly different from his creation. But monism is not alien to either of these traditions either.

In Christianity, monistic mysticism is associated with the Rhineland mystics, a group of monks active in Germany in the thirteenth and fourteenth centuries. Some form of monistic mysticism is attributed to Meister Eckhart, his disciples Johannes Tauler and Henry Suso as well as others of the Rhineland school. Monism in a pantheistic form was preached by the French theologian Amalric of Bena (twelfth century), while a Neoplatonist monism had been part of Christianity in its early stages for centuries. But the paragon of the oneness of the soul with God is Meister Eckhart, one of the most important mystics in the history of Christianity. His description of the Christian godhead in his sermons reads as if it were written about the undifferentiated Brahman by an Advaitin like Vivekananda. Eckhart declares about the godhead that it is 'absolute bare unity...the abyss, without a mode and without form, of the silent and waste divinity...where never was seen difference, neither Father, Son, nor

---

[*]Vasabandhu and Asanga (c. fourth century BCE).
[†]For example, the Tendai school in Japan.

Holy Ghost, where there is no one at home, yet where the spark of the soul is more at peace than within itself.'[24]

Many scholars have over the years drawn comparisons between Eckhart's thought and Vedanta. Rudolf Otto, the famous German theologian wrote in a comparative study of Eastern and Western mysticism that in many respects Eckhart and Shankara were almost indistinguishable. 'It would be possible to treat Eckhart just as here we have dealt with Shankara. Expressions from his writings could be gathered together, which were exactly, or almost exactly equivalent to those quoted above [from Shankara]. Sentences could be taken unchanged from his works...exactly corresponding to those of Shankara. An almost identical metaphysic could be built up from them in this way.'[25] Eckhart's philosophy is marked by three central tenets. One is that the ultimate mystical experience is not of the personal God of the Christian Trinity, but of a godhead that stands above the trinity and is impersonal and beyond description. The second is that the individual soul is one with this godhead. The third principle he preached was that there is something within the human soul which is uncreated. The third one is particularly interesting because it is a theological innovation which reads the creation mentioned in the Bible as God manifesting the uncreated soul in a body, unlike the orthodox interpretation that creation means creating souls out of nothing. Taken together, these three tenets come very close to the Advaita philosophy.

There is nothing better than Eckhart's own words which can report the powerful, vivid sense of directly experiencing the undifferentiated Absolute he conveyed through his words:

'He is purely One without admission even in thought of anything quantitative or differentiated, *above everything that suffers* even in thought or name the *faintest shadow of difference,** in whom all delimitation and qualification is lost.'[26]

'God is in every way and in every respect One, so that in Him no multiplicity can be found, either in the intellect or outside the intellect. For whoever sees duality or distinction does not see God, since God is One outside all number and above all number....'[27]

'For in God there is not this nor that we can subtract from Him or which we could isolate and retain by differentiation. There is nothing in Him but One, He himself.'[28]

'God is neither good nor better nor best. When I call God good I speak as falsely as if I were to call white black.'[29]

---

*Italics mine.

We can even find passages that suggest that Eckhart held a view similar to that of the theory of maya; that the reality of the Absolute is obscured by ignorance of the soul, by its identification with the body and the false perception of multiplicity. Eckhart says in one of his sermons, 'It is hidden from the soul as the Prophet says "Lord, thou art a hidden God." This treasure of the Kingdom of God has been hidden by time and multiplicity or by the soul's own works or briefly by its creaturely nature. But in the measure that the soul can separate itself from this multiplicity, to that extent it reveals in itself the Kingdom of God. Here the soul and the Godhead are one.'[30]

As the last sentence indicates, the identity of the soul and godhead, the central theme of Advaita (Tatvamasi), is something one frequently encounters in Eckhart's sermons and sometimes even in his written work. Eckhart stands out from other monistic mystics in the Abrahamic religious traditions in how explicitly he formulated the idea of the oneness of the soul and God. In the book of Genesis in the Bible, man is said to have been made in God's image. In this sense, both orthodox Christianity and Judaism (unlike orthodox Islam) have always admitted a similarity between the human soul and the divine. Eckhart takes care to differentiate his own position from the orthodox position and insist on identity against even the greatest degree of similarity. 'Where they (the soul and God) are one in essence, they are not equal, for equality coexists always with difference. Therefore the soul must put off equality with God in order to realize identity with God.'[31] Just like Shankara, Eckhart insisted that the experience of the godhead was beyond the subject–object duality of ordinary experience. 'So long as something is still the object of our attention we are not yet with the One. For where there is nothing but the One, nothing is seen,' he says in a sermon.[32] In another one, he describes the collapse of the subject–object polarity in the ultimate experience of union with the Godhead. 'The Knower and the Known are one! Simple people imagine that they should see God, as if He stood there and he Here. That is not so! God and I, we are one in knowledge.'[33]

After Hinduism, monistic mysticism finds its widest range of expression in Sufism. Monism in Hinduism was almost exclusively associated with asceticism, while devotional mysticism held largely to dualism. (Though there are important crossovers in both cases, particularly between asceticism and theistic dualism.) Neither was monistic devotion unknown in Sufism, however, both monism and dualism manifested almost completely in a devotional way. (Again, this statement has to be qualified by noting that asceticism in Islam, while rare, was not unknown either.) A continuing misperception about Sufism, even among those familiar with the Islamic tradition, is that Sufism was a heterodox sect, tolerated by the orthodoxy, but removed from the main currents of Islamic piety. This misperception arose because Sufism underwent a rapid decline in the nineteenth century as the Islamic world was encountering technicalistic Western modernity.[34] But throughout the largest part of the history of Islam, Sufism was the dominant impulse in Islamic spiritual life.

Sufism originated in the Classical period of Islam, probably a century or two after the death of Muhammad.[35] By the eleventh century, Sufism was well settled in the Islamic lands between the Nile and the Amu Darya. But it remained one of the many branches of Islam, with a select following but without greatly impacting the more popular currents of religious life. However, after the decline of the Abbasid Caliphate, as an international Islamic social order emerged with several power centres, there was a concomitant shift in the forms of religious consciousness. 'The time of the formation of the international society was the formative age for a new popular Sufism also. Earlier than most of the ulama scholars, large numbers of people came to accept the Sufi Pirs, master holy men, as their guides in matters spiritual.'[36] By the twelfth century, Sufism started to become institutionalized in various Sufi orders, called tariqahs. Each tariqah had its own preferred spiritual practices. It had a master Pir (holy master) who was part of a long line of succession through discipleship, a small group of initiates and a larger lay group of devotees. The parallel to the panths in Hinduism and Jainism is worth noting. Over time, the headquarters of the Sufi sects where the holy men lived (khaniqas) became the centres of popular piety, with the mosques being used for the Salat worship and community matters. 'Thus gradually, Sufism from being one form of piety among others, and by no means the most accepted one…came to dominate religious life…. It can seem paradoxical…that the most personal and esoteric form of piety was the most popular.'[37]

Unlike the common notion today of Sufism as peripheral to the main body of Islamic life and thought, it was an integral, if not central, part of the religious life of ordinary Muslims for most of the second millennium. While the scholarly religious establishment concentrated on the sharia and the life of the community, the inner spiritual life was tended to by Sufi tariqahs. Of course, Sufism had an outward and an esoteric side. This necessarily had to be so to avoid conflict with the sharia-minded ulama. The mystical was confined to the esoteric, and the more radical doctrines restricted to an inner circle. Sufi literature did express these doctrines, but with much symbolism, evasions, and ambiguity so that charges of heresy from the orthodox ulama could plausibly be denied. This at least partly accounts for the loss of knowledge about the Sufi tradition the world has suffered after the tariqahs declined, in spite of the existence of a vast Sufi literature in Arabic and Persian. Though Sufism is much associated with monism, the esoteric nature of the tradition means that we have fewer systematic accounts to work with than with monism in Hinduism or Buddhism. This makes it difficult to pin down the extent to which Sufi masters took their monism and their positions on various metaphysical questions. Nonetheless, we still have enough explicit formulations of doctrines over the centuries by Sufi saints to be able to outline a broadly unitive mystical tradition that identified the cosmos and the human soul with God.

'In Sufism the tendency is from theism, that is, a mysticism of love, towards what amounts to monism in that, in the states called fana (annihilation) and infirad (isolation), it is claimed that there is no consciousness of anything but God, man thereby realising himself as God,' writes the late British scholar of Eastern religions, Robert Zaehner.[38] The earliest expositor of an explicitly monistic Sufism, is considered to be Abu-Yazid-al-Bistami, an Iranian who lived during the ninth century BCE. Al-Bistami is famous for reportedly making a statement equivalent to the Tatvamasi (I am He) of the Upanishads. He is reported as declaring 'I sloughed off myself as a snake sloughs off its skin, and I looked into my essence and saw that "I am He".'[39] Bistami was an exponent of the state the Sufis called fana, where the self of the devotee is annihilated in God. The greatest, certainly the boldest, proponent of the absolute identity of the human soul and God is usually considered to be Al-Hallaj the Persian mystic, who lived a few decades after Al-Bistami.[*] He preached in public that 'I am the Absolute Truth' (ana'l-Haqq). He wrote in one of his poems:

I saw my Lord with the eye of my heart
I said: 'Who are you?' He said: 'You!'
But for You, 'where' cannot have a place
And there is no 'where' when it concerns You.
The mind has no image of your existence in time
Which would permit the mind to know where you are.
You are the one who encompasses every 'where'
Up to the point of no-where
So where are you?[40]

---

*Al-Hallaj paid the price for his boldness when he was executed on charges of heresy. He thus became a martyr for Sufism whose fame spread throughout the Islamic world.

The knowledge of the Sufi tradition in the world of English and European letters was very rudimentary in the nineteenth century. Nonetheless Vivekananda knew enough of it to recognize that the Sufi mystical experience paralleled the Advaita he preached. Thus, during a lecture that touched on Bhakti delivered at the Triplicane Literary Society in Madras, Vivekananda explores both the dualistic and non-dualistic aspects of the Hindu Bhakti tradition. He draws out the similarities in the Krishna–Gopi devotional literature and a Sufi poem as an example of the universality of the devotional mysticism that culminated in the experience of non-duality.

> [During spiritual inspiration] the human soul transcends all limitations, and then and then alone flashes into the human soul the conception of monism: I and the whole universe are one; I and Brahman are one. And this conclusion you will find has not only been reached through knowledge and philosophy, but parts of it through the power of love. You read in the Bhagavata, when Krishna disappeared and the Gopis bewailed his disappearance, that at last the thought of Krishna became so prominent in their minds that each one forgot her own body and thought she was Krishna, and began to decorate herself and to play as he did. We understand, therefore, that this identity comes even through love. There was an ancient Persian Sufi poet, and one of his poems says, 'I came to the Beloved and beheld the door was closed; I knocked at the door and from inside a voice came, 'Who is there?' I replied, 'I am'. The door did not open. A second time I came and knocked at the door and the same voice asked, 'Who is there?' 'I am so-and-so.' The door did not open. A third time I came and the same voice asked, 'Who is there?' 'I am Thyself, my Love', and the door opened.[41]

Scholars are divided on what exactly Al-Hallaj meant with his statements of identity. While many maintain he was a pure monist, several others give a different interpretation;[*] along the lines that Hallaj was referring only to the knowledge conferred by God in virtue of which a human could say that he was one with God's truth. But for generations of monistic Sufis who followed, Hallaj became an inspiration for their metaphysics of unity. Another Persian who was inspired by Bistami and Hallaj's teachings was Abu Sa'id ibn Abi'l-Khayr. One of the founding figures of Sufi Persian poetry and a contemporary of the famous philosopher Ibn Sina (Avicenna), Abi'l-Khayr is known for giving Sufi

---

*For example, the German Orientalist and scholar of Sufism, Annemarie Schimmel.

monism a pantheistic expression. For example, in one of his famous quatrains he writes of God pervading the universe thus:

> The personality absolute, manifest in all creation fine,
> If thou desire to know of His pervading the universe, the reality and sign;
> Go! And on the surface of wine observe the bubble, see how
> The wine is within the bubble and the bubble within the wine.[42]

Sufism in general, and monistic Sufism in particular received systematic exposition under Ibn-Arabi (thirteenth century), who is referred to in Sufi lore as the 'great master' (al-Shayk-al-Akbar) and is often considered the greatest Sufi mystic in history. He is widely interpreted as having professed a pure form of monism where God is all that exists. Like most Sufis, he affirmed that what he was teaching did not conflict with the Islamic tradition. He based his teachings on close exegesis of the Quran where he tried to bring out the inward esoteric meaning of the text expressed in symbolism and allegories. Ibn-Arabi's central doctrine which was later to become highly influential in Sufism down the centuries, was what came to be called Wahdat-al-Wajud or the oneness of all Being. 'To call Real Being "one" is to speak of the unity of the Essence. In other terms, it is to say that Being...is nondelimited, that is, infinite and absolute, undefined and indefinable, indistinct and indistinguishable.... The Real is incomparable and transcendent, but it discloses itself in all things, so it is also similar and immanent.'[43]

The idea that God is one with the human Self and the universe is a theme Arabi returns to again and again. He writes in the work *Kitab-al-Ajwiba*:

> He is and there is with Him no before or after, nor above nor below, nor far nor near, nor union nor division, nor how nor where nor place. He is now as He was, He is the One without oneness and the Single without singleness...he is not other than God, but you do not know Him and do not understand that you are seeing Him. He is still Ruler as well as ruled, and Creator as well as created.... When the mystery-of realizing that the mystic is one with the Divine-is revealed to you, you will understand that you are no other than God and that you have continued and will continue without when and without times. Then you will see all your actions to be His actions and all your attributes to be His attributes and your essence to be His essence.... He who knows himself sees his whole existence to be the Divine existence.... For when you know yourself, your 'I-ness' vanishes and you know that you and God are one and the same.[44]

In his *Bezels of Wisdom* (Fusus-Al-Hakim), Arabi writes on the theme that all that exists is only God and his attributes. 'He is the First, the Last, the Outward, the Inward; He is the substance of what is manifested and the substance of what remains latent at the time of manifestation; none sees Him but Himself, and none is hidden from Him, since He is manifested to Himself and hidden from Himself.'[45] Just like in Advaita, Ibn Arabi's conception of God or the Absolute is beyond the duality of the object and subject. As Rom Landau, the late scholar of Islamic culture writes, in Ibn Arabi's conception of God, 'Since the Divine essence is the knower, the known and the knowing, there exists complete unity of the subject, the object and the function that establishes a relationship'[46] between them.

Ibn-Arabi's works, even as they generated controversy, created a philosophical system and terminology that Sufis down the centuries could adopt for their metaphysical needs. A unitive metaphysics that stressed the oneness of all existence became the predominant theme of Sufi thought. Those Sufis who were inclined to theoretical speculation, tried to work out the philosophical implications of their experience of oneness.

> Philosophically inclined mystics, with their ecstatic experiences of feeling at one with all, have had pressing reasons even more than other philosophers for conceiving all existence as fundamentally one...for insisting that the multiplicity and change that we see about us is somehow illusory.... Nothing is real except what can be identified as divine.... When it has been pointed out in the Quran that 'everything is perishing except his face', this has suggested to them not mere transience of things otherwise perfectly real, but some far fetching falsity in our perceiving them as if they endured at all. Only God's face, His essence, is not subject to this falsity.[47]

Several times, we see Vivekananda put forward the argument that if one religion is true, all the other religions must be true also. 'My religion is to learn. I read my Bible better in the light of your Bible and the dark prophecies of my religion become brighter when compared with those of your prophets. Truth has always been universal.... If one creed alone were to be true and all the others untrue, you would have a right to say that that religion was diseased; if one religion is true, all the others must be true. Thus, the Hindu religion is your property as well as mine.'[48] The proof of any religion, he argued, lies in the truth of the others. At first glance, this is counterintuitive. But what he seems to have meant is that if there are core spiritual truths available to direct mystical perception, the claims for their universal validity are diminished if they have only been discovered by one religion, nation, or race alone. Like all areas of human knowledge such as science, literature, or arts, spirituality can be considered a genuine phenomenon only if its truths are trans-cultural. Vivekananda's point is that the claim that a single religion enjoys an exclusive access to a certain domain of spiritual truth discredits that claim itself.

As the two strongest monistic religious traditions, Sufism and Hinduism present an intriguing study not only in regards to the similarity of their doctrines, but in their spiritual practices. Though there has been speculation about cross-influence,[49] they are traditions that largely evolved independently. There are a surprising number of mystical practices that are very similar in Hinduism and Sufism and seem to have developed as part of their independent evolutionary arc. This lends support to Vivekananda's claim that mysticism is a phenomenon that is universal and follows its own inner laws of evolution relatively independent of the sociocultural soil in which it finds itself. This compels us to take mysticism seriously as a phenomenon worthy of study with its own distinct characteristics. This does not mean that there is any external evidence that mystical states correspond to reality, but it does require us to give careful attention to mysticism if we are to arrive at an informed understanding of the religious enterprise.

THE EPISTEMOLOGICAL:
REASON AND RELIGION

In 1896, Vivekananda lived in London for several months, sharing a house with an Englishman named Goodwin, who was his disciple. It was his second tour to England, and he delivered a large number of lectures, most of which have not been recorded. But among those that have been taken down is one he delivered on the topic of 'Religion and Reason'.

> The physical sciences are better equipped now than formerly, and religions have become less and less equipped. The foundations have been all undermined, and the modern man, whatever he may say in public, knows in the privacy of his heart that he can no more 'believe'. Believing certain things because an organized body of priests tells him to believe, believing because it is written in certain books, believing because his people like him to believe, the modern man knows to be impossible for him. There are, of course, a number of people who seem to acquiesce in the so-called popular faith, but we also know for certain that they do not think. Their idea of belief may be better translated as 'not-thinking-carelessness'....
>
> The question is: Is there a way out? To put it in a more concrete form: Is religion to justify itself by the discoveries of reason, through which every other science justifies itself? Are the same methods of investigation, which we apply to sciences and knowledge outside, to be applied to the science of Religion? In my opinion this must be so, and I am also of opinion that the sooner it is done the better. If a religion is destroyed by such investigations, it was then all the time useless, unworthy superstition; and the sooner it goes the better. I am thoroughly convinced that its destruction would be the best thing that could happen. All that is dross will be taken off, no doubt, but the essential parts of religion will emerge triumphant out of this investigation.[1]

This is a very clearly expressed instance of something that is central to Vivekananda's thinking. Vivekananda was, of course, speaking at a time when the balance in the alleged conflict between science and religion had not shifted decisively in favour of science. But the momentum, as Vivekananda says here, was clearly swinging in the direction of the latter. We, however, live in a time where public opinion seems split mainly into two, those who consider religion a dubious enterprise in the light of modern scientific discoveries, and the religious who think religion is based primarily on faith. There is also a section, among scientists, academics, public intellectuals, and laypeople, both agnostic and religious, who think science and religion are compatible but are two totally different areas of enquiry having little to do with each other. But this position, while quite sound, finds minimal expression in the public sphere with the result that not much fruitful intellectual activity is generated from this perspective and the discourse is far more sharply polarized between those who invoke reason against religion and those who invoke faith to defend it. What both these opposite positions share in common however, is an underlying assumption that reason has no active role to play in the religious enterprise. At a more general level, the question is not so much about science vs religion but reason and religion. Vivekananda was using science as it was understood in the nineteenth century sense, where it could be used to refer to any discipline that followed rational protocols of investigation. In that sense, not only the physical sciences, but disciplines like law and history were sciences. The question then is of the relationship between rationality and religion. It is of particular significance for our times, and it is in regard to this question perhaps, that Vivekananda's thought assumes most interest for us. But before we come to the question of rationality and religion, let us take a brief look at the relationship between rationality and democracy.

Globally, from India to Eastern Europe to America, secular democracies are facing increasing threats from a populist right wing. While there are many facets to these threats, one of them is the spread of the irrational. Democracy assumes at its core that its citizens have the ability, at some times at any rate, to deliberate rationally and arrive at public consensus regarding issues that concern the polity. Right-wing populism has recruited irrational impulses like xenophobia, jingoism, and group identities based on religion, race, and sexuality, to craft narratives that smother the citizens' ability to critically interrogate the authoritarianism that is pushed under their cover. But the ascendancy of the right wing internationally, has in reality not brought up a fresh problem, but only sharply accentuated the ever present problematic of myth and critical rationality in democracy. We can see this problematic in its purest form in the small clutch of fully developed democracies in Europe, and to a lesser extent (given the high levels of income inequality there), in the US. In a relatively homogeneous field of wealth distribution,* the democratic guarantee of fundamental rights and equal political power for each citizen through universal franchise, should ideally result in a radical dilution of power asymmetries, and the achievement of social justice and individual freedom. But this does not happen. There has been progress, but it is often glacial and incremental.

Among the several complex factors that account for the present state of democracy, is the preponderance of the mythical in society. Myth here does not mean mythical stories and legends. Rather it means social, cultural, and political narratives that are unquestioned and collectively constitute public consciousness. These myths undergird dominant power structures whether of the state, corporates, or other powerful interest groups. As an example, let us look at how the question of police reform and law and order has played out in the West. Whenever there has been a push from liberals for reforming the police to make it humane and more efficient, conservative leaders have raised the cry of how any reform would lead to an increase in crime and a breakdown of law and order. If we think about it rationally, we can see that 'getting tough on crime' and checking illegal police brutality and guaranteeing the constitutional rights of those suspected of a crime are not mutually exclusive ideas. In the 1970s, US President Richard Nixon launched a 'War on Drugs' programme on the top of hysteric rhetoric about how liberal reforms were going soft on crime, leading to the streets of urban America being filled with drug powered criminals (implied to be mostly African American).[2] Nixon's success in implementing the programme and its continuance to date is a classic instance where public rationality failed to see through a myth based on the emotional fear of personal safety and racial prejudice. An urban, white middle class flocked behind the War on Drugs without rationally examining the dubious assumptions behind its policy objectives; nearly forty years down the line, the policy has turned out to be catastrophic for America, with the militarization of the police leading to rampant human rights abuses, especially against black Americans.[3] America now incarcerates about one in one hundred of its people,[4] the highest in the world.[5]

Even what are termed 'mature democracies' or 'full democracies' are thus incipient political projects, not finished enterprises. A trajectory of future progress which involves a deepening of democracy and a flattening of socio-economic power structures, depends among other things on citizens' ability to

---

*By 'relatively homogeneous', I don't mean to deny the class inequality that exists even in mature democracies. What I am referring to is the relative lack of steep class divides that causes severe deprivation in the quality of life for those placed at the bottom.

free themselves of political and sociocultural myths by examining them rationally. There is thus an essential antagonism between critical rationality and social myths at the core of the democratic project. And there are few myths as powerful as religion. In fact, religious identity and beliefs have been a big part of the right-wing global onslaught on democracy in a major way. Religious identity, beliefs, markers, and customs have all been mobilized on the rise of right-wing authoritarianism in Europe, Turkey, Israel, Indonesia, India, and USA.

By saying that religion is a very powerful myth, I do not mean to say that the religious enterprise is invalid or that it has no relationship to truth. But any set of truth claims, once they gain social legitimacy, inevitably become the nucleus of institutional networks, political and sociocultural meta-narratives, and even economic structures. But the ideological forms that these entities take have no bearing on the validity of the original truth claims. A classic example would be the narrative around freedom and liberty in the United States. Freedom and liberty are foundational concepts of political liberalism and the United States had a historical claim to being the land of political liberty during the eighteenth and nineteenth century. While European countries smarted under the restrictions imposed by monarchical and feudal regimes, America was a country free of feudal privileges, and later, of monarchy itself. As the first major modern democracy, America inspired millions across the world, from figures as varied as William Blake, the English poet, to Mohandas Karamchand Gandhi.

Thus, America as the 'land of freedom' is part of the foundational myths of the United States. In the twentieth century, this myth was deployed as part of an aggressive American foreign policy to intervene militarily in the Middle East (the US-led invasion of Iraq was codenamed 'Operation Iraqi Freedom'),[6] and in a number of regressive domestic measures including state surveillance and support for white nationalism.[7] Many left-wing critics of American foreign policy used their critique of American aggression to question the validity of 'freedom' as a political concept itself. With the rise of an authoritarian right wing across Europe and America, the concept of freedom seems suddenly back in vogue, and left critics who had questioned its legitimacy, seem to have tacitly dropped such critiques. Irrespective of such changes in intellectual fashion, it should have been self-evident from the outset that the truth of a concept like freedom, has nothing to do with its political fortunes. At the other end of the political spectrum, certain liberal writers who lay the atrocities and totalitarianism of Soviet Russia at Karl Marx's door, commit the same category mistake. Marx's economic theories and his theory of history are things whose correctness or error, have to be judged on their own intellectual merits, not by the trajectory of political events his ideas inspired, even when, in this case, they resulted in genocide.

Religious beliefs can prove dangerous to the progress of liberal democracy in a number of ways. The most obvious is when a religious dogma comes into conflict with a scientific belief or with civic and human rights. The evolution denial movement in the US and attempts by Christian groups to stop the teaching of biological evolution in schools are a case in point, as is the anti-abortion movement. In India of course, such conflicts are now taking on fantastical and absurd forms. Cow urine is claimed to cure everything from cancer to AIDS (and presumably thirst),[8] and scientific departments in universities are researching the uses of cow urine.[9] Religious dogma becomes even more dangerous when it takes the form of fanaticism that tries to curtail the rights of others who do not share the same beliefs or fall foul of the belief through some action or other. Same-sex couples are denied marriage and other civil rights in many parts of the world based on religious beliefs that the way they live and love is a sin or is not sanctioned by God. In many countries homosexuality is criminalized; certain Islamic nations even sentence people engaging in same-sex relations to death on religious grounds.[10] Similarly horrific is the belief of many conservative Hindus that because they consider the eating of beef taboo, its consumption should be banned, putting the livelihoods of tens of thousands of cattle traders at risk and indirectly encouraging and condoning the lynching of Muslims who are suspected of cattle slaughter.

The US Supreme Court pronounced an important judgment in 2018 regarding a baker named Jack Phillips in Colorado who had refused to provide a cake for a gay couple's wedding on the grounds that as a Christian, he believed that gay marriage violated his religious beliefs.[11] The state of Colorado has laws against discrimination based on gender, race, religion, and sexual orientation. The baker argued in the Supreme Court that it was lawful for him to refuse gay customers because he was exercising his constitutionally guaranteed freedom of religion. The Supreme Court ruled in favour of the baker reasoning that the State of Colorado had not maintained neutrality while deciding the case against the baker and that the State officials' bias in conducting the enquiry prejudiced their decision. The court took cognizance of a statement by an official: 'Phillips can believe "what he wants to believe," but cannot act on his religious beliefs "if he decides to do business in the state."' The Supreme Court ruled that the officials' 'treatment of his (the baker's) case has some elements of a clear and impermissible hostility toward the sincere religious beliefs that motivated his objection.'

What emerges from the reasoning of the judgment is a curious value construction in regard to the attitude that democratic institutions and, by extension citizens, in some situations at least, should hold towards religious beliefs. Notice that in the court's opinion, what mandates respect, or at least lack of hostility towards the baker's religious beliefs, is not the content of the belief but the sincerity with which that belief is held. What the court gestured towards was faith. In a philosophically sophisticated context, faith can be distinguished from mere belief, as the existentialist philosopher Sorén Kierkegaard, among others, has argued. But in the kind of legal, social, and political contexts that we are concerned with, faith is only a form of a strongly held religious belief. What distinguishes it structurally from other kinds of beliefs is the unique feature that faith, unlike other kinds of beliefs, refuses correction or modification by any epistemic elements outside its own narrowly defined religious domain. We are not here dealing with fanaticism, for fanaticism of the worst kind, whether political, racial, or religious is at least theoretically open to correction when presented with contrary facts, evidence, or reasoning.

The man or (woman) of faith, however, adopts a very different attitude towards rationality, facts, and evidence. If these things go against a dogmatically held belief on an issue, the strategy is not to dismiss or avoid engaging with the evidence or counter reasoning, but it is to declare that the issue is a matter of religious faith and hence immune to the operations of reason. In fact, the more forceful the counter evidence presented, the assertion of faith becomes deeper and hence more valuable within the logic of its circular premise.[*] We are presented with the greatest problems when from such a defensive stance such claims become the basis of social or legal onslaught on the rights of others. Here a universality is claimed for a particular religious belief (say the Quranic prohibition on drinking alcohol). In many Middle-Eastern countries, the consumption of alcohol is penalized, even when the person is a non-Muslim. Here, the idea is that certain elements of the faith of a religion deserve respect from even those who do not subscribe to it precisely because it is a matter of faith. The category of faith here then surreptitiously acquires a sacrosanct dimension outside its original narrow religious domain.

The conflict is far more violent when a religious belief acquires connotations of the sacrosanct in a secular and democratic public domain. India has seen a

---

[*]Faith here refers to only strongly held religious beliefs for which some kind of immunity is claimed. I am not referring to what is meant when we talk about someone's faith in God, or even faith in the existence of God. Such faith is an existential commitment to the divine on the part of a worshipper, not a set of religious beliefs.

raft of cases since at least the noughties where colonial era legislation (Section 153(a) and 295(a) of the IPC)* has been misused to arrest, prosecute, and harass people seen as offending or showing lese-majesty to religious symbols, icons, and markers. Such cases have been filed by members of almost all religions. While earlier such cases were mere tools of harassment, today many courts go along with the misapplication of the law, allowing arrests, denying bail, and giving permission for prosecution. In 2020, a case was filed in Uttar Pradesh against the making of the OTT series *Tandav* for hurting the religious sentiments of Hindus. The Allahabad High Court when denying anticipatory bail to the filmmakers noted, 'Western filmmakers have refrained from ridiculing Lord Jesus or the Prophet but Hindi filmmakers have done this repeatedly and are still doing this most unabashedly with Hindu gods and goddesses.'[12] The court went on to list movies 'which have used the name of Hindu gods and goddesses and shown them in disrespectful manner', such as *Ram Teri Ganga Maili, Satyam Shivam Sundaram, PK,* and *Oh My God.*[13] The Supreme Court overruled the High Court order.

It is true that in most cases, such exhibitions of religious extremism come from a minority fringe group. The majority of the religious denominations may not sympathize or may even actively disagree with such actions. However, they lack the intellectual tools and the discursive language to directly confront the conceptual basis of such religious policing. This is because a significant section of religious moderates shares the same assumption with the extremists—that faith is an autonomous and valid source of truth, and that its claims cannot be tested by external means, including reason. The problem of the role of religion in a secular democracy is precisely why Vivekananda's views on the relationship between reason and religion assume great importance. To reiterate, Vivekananda's view is that religion should justify itself by the discoveries of reason and should be open to investigation by reason. But what exactly does this mean?

There are two important ways in which Vivekananda visualized the application of reason to religion. These distinctions are not precise categorizations, but only a rough guide for the reader. Vivekananda demanded of religions that they meet the test of philosophical reason, of rational practice, and of the burden of evidence for their claims. First, in so far as every religion offers a picture

---

*Section 153(a) punishes 'Promoting enmity between different groups on grounds of religion, race, place of birth, residence, language, etc., and doing acts prejudicial to maintenance of harmony.' Section 295 penalizes 'Deliberate and malicious acts, intended to outrage religious feelings of any class by insulting its religion or religious beliefs.'

of the cosmos and reality, however crude or sophisticated, it is also offering a philosophical theory, even though the means followed to arrive at these claims are not themselves philosophical. The sources of these claims are usually revelation through a book or prophet, divine inspiration, intuition, or similar means. The first demand of reason Vivekananda introduces is that as in other rational disciplines, there can be no appeal to authority in religion. If we take science as the paradigmatic example of rational investigation, it is of absolutely no consequence to say that matter and energy are inter-convertible because the great physicist Albert Einstein said so in 1905. It is the mathematical and empirical proof he produced in support of this proposition that is of consequence. Tomorrow, if someone else produces a better proof showing that Einstein's proof is flawed, it would have to be corrected. That a holy book, whether the Vedas, the Quran, or the Bible, says that something is true is no proof of anything. In fact, all holy books contain contradictions and absurdities. To think that such books are the infallible word of God is, according to Vivekananda, a kind of irrational magical thinking. Like all books, in all fields, religious books, however great their inherent spiritual worth may be, are products of the human search after truth, and as such, while they may contain truth, they are fallible. Vivekananda said of his own approach to the Vedas, 'Personally I take as much of the Vedas as agrees with reason. Parts of the Vedas are apparently contradictory. They are not considered as inspired in the Western sense of the word.'*

Holy books are spiritual guides, containing the results of the enquiries of the human mind into the domain of spirituality. While they contain much truth, they also contain errors, absurdities, and distortions. It is essential that the seeker of spirituality be able to discriminate between them by the use of her own reason and intuition. The problem with any book claiming to be a special revelation is that it can give no substantial evidence for such a claim. It is mere self-certification and, hence, groundless. According to Vivekananda, one of the surest ways a man could go to his ruin is to try to live his life by blindly obeying the dictates of a holy book. 'I would rather see every one of you rank atheists than superstitious fools, for the atheist is alive and you can make something out of him. But if superstition enters, the brain is gone, the brain is softening, degradation has seized upon the life,' he told his fellow Indians.[14] Vivekananda considered spirituality to be a form of enquiry into the truth like any other scientific discipline. In fact, it was the ultimate enquiry,

---

*See Chapter 6, p. 210.

because what it sought was the nature of absolute reality itself. Any enquiry into the truth starts with questioning. Such questioning often begins, as it did with Vivekananda's own spiritual quest, with a dissatisfaction with received answers and traditionally accepted ideas. It is when a person is no longer satisfied by books and sacred formulas and wants to directly experience and verify spiritual truth for herself that she starts to become spiritual. Questioning and independent thinking are essential in the struggle of attaining the goal of truth, as much with spirituality as with anything else. 'There is some hope for the atheists, because though they differ from others, they think for themselves. The people who never think anything for themselves are not yet born into the world of religion; they have a mere jellyfish existence. They will not think; they do not care for religion. But the disbeliever, the atheist, cares, and he is struggling. So think something! Struggle Godward!'[15]

By dislodging appeals to sacred or scriptural authority, Vivekananda brings religious claims squarely within the domain of rationality. What Vivekananda demands of religious thought is that it presents a coherent system which does not conflict with the knowledge we have gained through reason and other faculties. 'In India the attempt has been made from the earliest times to reach a science of religion and philosophy, for the Hindus do not separate these as is customary in Western countries. We regard religion and philosophy as but two aspects of one thing which must equally be grounded in reason and scientific truth,'[16] he said. In other words, religious systems have to conform to reason both internally and externally, like all philosophical systems. At the internal level, in the main, they have to be conceptually coherent, non-contradictory, and be free from logical fallacies. To take an example, Vivekananda argued that the theological idea of a God creating the universe out of nothing goes against reason. The very idea of something coming out of nothing is incoherent at a fundamental level. As I have mentioned before, only a small portion of Vivekananda's intellectual output has been documented. He held several philosophical and theological debates with Christian ministers of various denominations. But we have no record of the arguments presented in support of the various conflicting positions.

However, it is not very difficult to reconstruct the argument against God creating the universe ex-nihilo. In such a case, we have an extra-cosmic God who at the beginning of time, brought the universe into existence. Now remember that this is a personal God, and it is God's agency which is the cause and the universe which is the result. But in what sense does God have agency? If the model followed is that of personhood, a person exercises her agency through her will. The will, as Vivekananda says is a compound of desire and purpose. So, God's will is part of God's being. When scriptures say God willed the universe, what sense can possibly be attached to that statement except that God's will is transformed into the universe? Unlike in any other case, the will here cannot act on anything external (like when we use our will to push a car), because before the universe existed, God was the only being and there was no other entity for God's will to act on. An advocate of creation-out-of-nothing may deny this reasoning based on causality, and still want to say God created the universe. Then all she is doing is postulating an entity called God and then postulating that the universe appeared next to God in an instance. Once she denies the causal relationship, she can give no coherent sense to her proposition that God created the universe.

If one wants to bring God into the question of the origin of the universe, Vivekananda argues, the only position that reason leads to is that God has to be both the material and the efficient cause of the universe. God cannot be something completely outside the universe, though the exact relationship of identity between God and the universe is a matter of further philosophical reasoning.

Now let us take a look at the external aspect of what reason demands from theoretical systems—religious or otherwise. This means that even if a set of claims are internally coherent and logical, they should conform to knowledge that we have independently attained apart from that theory. Take for example, the Ptolemaic theory of the universe that Copernicus and Galileo replaced with the modern heliocentric cosmology. Ptolemaic cosmology was perfectly internally coherent and logical. However, it did not agree with external experimental observations of astronomy and had to be abandoned for modern cosmology. Similar is the case with religion. Vivekananda argued, for example, against the idea of eternal hell in orthodox Christianity. His argument proceeded from what we know independently of the nature of causality. A finite cause cannot produce an infinite effect. Take the case of Newton's law of motion. It states that a body at rest or in uniform motion would continue in that state unless acted upon by a force. That is, the force will cause that body to accelerate, that is, the speed (or technically the velocity), to increase. But the speed of the body would not keep increasing forever. For how long the body accelerates depends on the amount of force applied. Examples of cause and effect can be drawn from several domains including history, but the basic principle is clear that the magnitude of the effect is proportional to the magnitude of the cause. Hence a finite cause cannot produce an infinite effect. The sins committed by man in his temporally limited life on earth are finite, and hence it cannot produce the effect of a hell that lasts infinitely through time. In similar fashion, Vivekananda advanced his own arguments against dualistic and qualified monistic schools of Vedanta philosophy as well as the non-self (anatta) schools of Madhyamika Buddhism.

It is important to emphasize a few things here in order to prevent any misunderstandings. The first is that Vivekananda is not saying that spirituality or religion is a predominantly rational activity. Reason merely prepares the intellectual grounds of the enquiry. The way to spiritual truth is through intuition, prayers, spiritual practices, and meditative experiences. What Vivekananda is saying is that what is presented as a set of spiritual or religious beliefs on the discursive plane, has to be congruent with reason. The other significant point is that Vivekananda never insisted as an absolute fact that the Advaitic philosophical system he arrived at through reasoning was the only rational religious position spiritual people could hold. Though he claimed that relentless reasoning led one to non-dualism, he did not therefore imply that theistic philosophical systems were not rational. In this sense, he was no different from philosophers throughout history who championed their own systems as the ultimate theory but acknowledged much truth and even intellectual debt to rival systems. Vivekananda also did not insist that adopting a rational approach to religion and reasoning it all the way through always meant reaching his own position. After all, he could be mistaken in his intellectual conclusions. What is required of a person enquiring rigorously into spiritual truth through reasoning, is that she follows it all the way through without compromise and arrives at conclusions that satisfied her own reason.

The second and most important component of Vivekananda's epistemology of religion is evidence or proof. To be a true science, that is, a truly rational discipline, it is not enough that a religion presents a world view that is internally coherent and does not conflict with our scientific, philosophical, historical, and other kinds of knowledge. Just because something is coherent and does not contradict what we know, that does not mean it is true. This was the philosopher and militant atheist Bertrand Russell's objection to the rationally constructed Christian theologies defended by Christian philosophers and theologians of his time. Sure, some theological systems were internally consistent and did not make false scientific claims like denying biological evolution or the Big Bang. But where, a spirited Russell asked, was even a shred of evidence that God existed? Religious systems are unable to provide any rational arguments, facts, or experimental proof that prove the existence of a God, soul, Spirit, or any such spiritual entity. Russell made use of a famous analogy to make his point. Suppose, he said, someone claims that there is a teapot orbiting between Mars and the Earth. Our telescopes and other instruments of astronomical observation are not precise enough to spot a tiny teacup at inter-planetary distances. In other words, not only is the proposition coherent, it cannot be disproved. But anyone who believes seriously that there is a teapot orbiting between Mars and Earth because it cannot be falsified, would make herself a candidate for the lunatic asylum. In this analogy, the teapot obviously represents God. Rational argumentation can neither prove nor disprove the existence of God. But just because something can't be disproved is no positive evidence that it exists. The crux of the matter for Russell is evidence, as it is for Vivekananda.[*]

While Vivekananda had absolutely no doubt that the domain of the spiritual is valid, he was sharply conscious of the risks attendant on basing truth on the purely private experiences of people. Any person can claim that she is divinely inspired or that God talked to her. Even assuming such phenomena are possible, it is an open invitation to every charlatan, opportunist, and fraud in the world. Even if one were to encounter an honest holy man, what evidence is there that he isn't deluded or that any of the experiences he claims to have had correspond to anything real? Vivekananda says in this connection:

> Any man may say he is inspired; many times they say that. Where is the test? ...Sometimes fraudulent people try to impose themselves upon mankind. In these days it is becoming all too prevalent.... Sometimes I find persons perfectly wanting in logical analysis of anything. A man comes and says, 'I have a message from such and such a god,' and asks, 'Can you deny it? Is it not possible that there will be such and such a god, and that he will give such a message?' And 90 per cent of fools will swallow it. They think that that is reason enough. But one thing you ought to know, that it is possible for anything to happen—quite possible that the earth may come into contact with the Dog Star in the next year and go to pieces. But if I advance this proposition, you have the right to stand up and ask me to prove it to you. What the lawyers call the onus probandi is on the man who made the proposition. It is not your duty to prove that I got my inspiration from a certain god, but mine,

---

[*]A famous incident about Bertrand Russell shows how belief in God appears from the point of view of the atheist or agnostic committed to rationality. Russell was once asked what he would say if the Christian story turned out to be true and he was confronted with God after death. Russell reportedly said: 'I probably would ask, "Sir, why did you not give me better evidence?"' See Leo Rosten, 'Bertrand Russell and God: A Memoir', *The Saturday Review*, 23 February 1974, pp. 25–26.

because I produced the proposition to you. If I cannot prove it, I should better hold my tongue.[17]

The only real evidence that God exists, says Vivekananda, is direct perception. The knowledge that God exists can come only from directly perceiving God in the same way that we see everyday objects and are able to testify to their reality. In fact, God has to be seen in a far more intense way than we see the world, for we can be mistaken in our perception of physical objects. But the knowledge of God given in mystical experience is supposed to be indubitable. This is one of the main reasons why Vivekananda's exposition of spiritual knowledge depended so much on the yoga system or the path of knowledge. It is not that he thought that devotional mysticism was of inferior spiritual worth or prowess, but that the yoga system allowed him to put the matter of spiritual knowledge within a framework of observation, experiment, and verification. This framework was of course inspired by the physical sciences; by the last quarter of the nineteenth century, physical science had become the paradigm for objective knowledge.

The idea of a spiritual entity, of a transcendental reality is something that we find in human history from almost the very beginning, expressing itself not only in religion, but in myth, art, and other forms of cultural life. What is common to these notions, especially in relation to the idea of a soul, is that the spiritual is something above and beyond the material world that we perceive through the senses. Mysticisms as well as theologies have developed this idea extensively from the time of the Axial Age onwards. This world view has expressed itself in innumerable historical developments from the metaphysical texts of the Upanishads to the Greek mystery cults, from the writings of the Gnostics to the philosophy of St Augustine, and from that of Ibn-Arabi to the poetry of Rumi. In this world view, the material world is only one domain of existence within an immeasurably larger plenitude of being.

Here, we have to understand a very important distinction that Vivekananda makes. Religion is rational, in the sense that its truths don't contradict reason and that rational methods of enquiry are part of the religious quest. However, religion is not primarily a matter of reason. In the same way that our normal reality is a matter of perception, spiritual reality for Vivekananda is a matter of direct perception and experience. It is a 'primitive given' just as the physical reality we experience. Ancient scientific theories and philosophies failed to explain the physical world because they tried to arrive at scientific laws through abstract reasoning alone. It is only when science started to perform experiments and make contact with experience that facts about nature could be unearthed.

For Vivekananda, spirituality consists in experiencing and understanding the structure of reality beyond the world given in sense perception. Vivekananda calls such perception 'supersensuous' perception and the state of such experience 'superconsciousness'.

'The proof, therefore, of the Vedas [and God] is just the same as the proof of this table before me, Pratyaksha, direct perception. This I see with the senses, and the truths of spirituality we also see in a superconscious state of the human soul,' Vivekananda said.[18] In a lecture to a class delivered in America, he says:

> The field of religion is beyond our senses, beyond even our consciousness. We cannot sense God. Nobody has seen God with his eyes or ever will see; nobody has God in his consciousness.... Where is God? Where is the field of religion? It is beyond the senses, beyond consciousness. Consciousness is only one of the many planes in which we work; you will have to transcend the field of consciousness, to go beyond the senses, approach nearer and nearer to your own centre, and as you do that, you will approach nearer and nearer to God. What is the proof of God? Direct perception, Pratyaksha. The proof of this wall is that I perceive it. God has been perceived that way by thousands before, and will be perceived by all who want to perceive Him. But this perception is no sense-perception at all; it is supersensuous, superconscious, and all this [yoga] training is needed to take us beyond the senses.[19]

Here three questions immediately suggest themselves. Firstly, what does superconsciousness actually mean? Second, what is the logic behind the claim that yogic practices like meditation and concentration give access to a kind of consciousness beyond the ordinary? And finally, even assuming that a mystic perceives the soul or God in meditation, what is the proof that the experience is not a subjective hallucination? What guarantees its objectivity? We will examine these questions one by one.

WHAT IS SUPERCONSCIOUSNESS?

No clear account can be given of the state of superconsciousness, if such a state exists. This is because much of such experience is indescribable in words. However, we can say minimally that superconsciousness is consciousness of both phenomena that lie beyond the range of sense experience as such, and those that lie beyond the spatio-temporal limitations of our embodied cognition. We have already touched upon the first kind of phenomena. These are supposed to be domains of existence of which the physical world is but a limited part. Experience of such regions of being are for the major part indescribable as language itself has evolved to describe only our everyday world of sense perception. This is what makes mysticism inherently esoteric and private, even when it is at the core of the religious enterprise. If mystical experiences indeed correspond to existents indescribable by the concepts that have evolved from our ordinary experience, then it explains why the spiritual truths discovered by mystics in various religions have been so difficult to translate into those religions' public forms and have only been expressed through symbols and metaphors.

The second type of phenomena that is the object of superconsciousness are the ordinary objects of perception which lie beyond the spatial and temporal limitations of our bodily perception. For example, using my eyes, I cannot see a tree located a thousand kilometres away, or the Marina Trench, while sitting at home. Vivekananda, following the yogic tradition, claims that a person can experience things outside the spatial range of her senses in a state of superconsciousness. Similar claims have been made in Sufi, Jain, and Buddhist traditions. In the same way, it is claimed past and future events become accessible in certain states of superconciousness.*

However, Vivekananda emphasizes that just like with any other field of enquiry, experience cannot contradict reason. We need to use reason to negotiate the interpretation of mystical experience. Vivekananda says:

> To get any reason out of the mass of incongruity we call human life, we have to transcend our reason, but we must do it scientifically, slowly, by regular practice, and we must cast off all superstition. We must take up the study of the superconscious state just as any other science. On reason we must have to lay our foundation, we must follow reason as far as it leads, and when reason fails, reason itself will show us the way to the highest plane. When you hear a man say, 'I am inspired,' and then talk irrationally, reject it. Why? Because these three states—instinct, reason, and superconsciousness, or the unconscious, conscious, and superconscious states—belong to one and the same mind. There are not three minds in

---

*There is a long tradition of philosophy, both Eastern and Western, called eternalism, where the past, present, and future events are equally real, and the flow of time is an illusion. Eternalism has received support with the discovery of Einstein's Special Theory of Relativity, which envisages what is called a block universe: the universe as a finite block of space-time points. The debate, however, is far from settled. There are both physicists and philosophers who deny that the theory of relativity forces us to accept a block universe and eternalism.

one man, but one state of it develops into the others. Instinct develops into reason, and reason into the transcendental consciousness; therefore, not one of the states contradicts the others. Real inspiration never contradicts reason but fulfils it. Just as you find the great prophets saying, 'I come not to destroy but to fulfil,' so inspiration always comes to fulfil reason, and is in harmony with it. All the different steps in Yoga are intended to bring us scientifically to the superconscious state, or Samadhi. Furthermore, this is a most vital point to understand, that inspiration is as much in every man's nature as it was in that of the ancient prophets. These prophets were not unique; they were men as you or I. They were great Yogis. They had gained this superconsciousness, and you and I can get the same. They were not peculiar people. The very fact that one man ever reached that state, proves that it is possible for every man to do so.[20]

However, the notion of superconsciousness itself requires a theoretical framework that makes the concept coherent, if it is to be rational. Ordinarily, our consciousness of the world comes through our instruments of perception, which bring sensations through contact with physical objects. These sensations, which are carried through nerve currents, are processed in the brain centres and in some as yet unknown way give rise to conscious experiences which correspond to the physical objects. The brain being the locus of normal consciousness, the idea of our field of consciousness extending in a freewheeling fashion across space and time would appear bizarre within our normal understanding of how consciousness functions. The philosophical framework Vivekananda used to explain superconsciousness drew mainly from the Samkhya philosophy, but he blended it with elements from the Vedanta. The root notion is that 'I', the sense of ego of the soul, has become identified with the body. As long as this identification exists, the body remains the locus of conscious perceptions. As the ego, which is the site of immediate awareness (what analytic philosophers term 'access consciousness'), detaches itself from the body, it gains access to the deeper recesses of the soul's being, which are not confined to the physical world. But it doesn't stop there. The soul, with its associated field of supersensuous consciousness is itself only an individuated localization in space and time of a cosmic consciousness. This cosmic consciousness is usually identified with Ishvara or God. Thus, in principle, as part of the cosmic consciousness, the individual ego can perceive the entire range of phenomenal existence across all space and time.

Now, let us take up the second question we raised earlier. Even if we grant that superconscious states of perception are possible, why should yogic practices give access to them? Vivekananda advocated forcefully for meditation as the means of inner self-reflection that leads to spiritual truth.

> This is the first principle of Vedanta, that realization is religion, and he who realizes is the religious man.... In this realization, again, we shall be helped very much by these books, not only as guides, but as giving instructions and exercises; for every science has its own particular method of investigation. You will find many persons in this world who will say, 'I wanted to become religious, I wanted to realize these things, but I have not been able, so I do not believe anything.' ...Suppose a man is a chemist, a great scientific man. He comes and tells you this. If you say to him, 'I do not believe anything about chemistry, because I have all my life tried to become a chemist and do not find anything in it', he will ask, 'When did you try?' 'When I went to bed, I repeated, "O chemistry, come to me', and it never came."' That is the very same thing. The chemist laughs at you and says, 'Oh, that is not the way. Why did you not go to the laboratory and get all the acids and alkalis and burn your hands from time to time? That alone would have taught you.' Do you take the same trouble with religion? Every science has its own method of learning, and religion is to be learnt the same way. It has its own methods, and here is something we can learn, and must learn, from all the ancient prophets of the world, everyone who has found something, who has realized religion. They will give us the methods, the particular methods, through which alone we shall be able to realize the truths of religion. They struggled all their lives, discovered particular methods of mental culture, bringing the mind to a certain state, the finest perception, and through that they perceived the truths of religion. To become religious, to perceive religion, feel it, to become a prophet, we have to take these methods and practice them; and then if we find nothing, we shall have the right to say, 'There is nothing in religion, for I have tried and failed.'[21]

This is perfectly sound in principle, but there has to be more to it. It is true enough that the methods of investigation of different disciplines are specific and peculiar to themselves. However, the methods are not arbitrary. The method should have a rational correspondence to the domain of which we seek knowledge, or else it becomes a pseudoscience or the occult. There is a kind of isomorphic relation, loosely speaking, between the experimental and theoretical investigations of science and the objects of its enquiry, whether they are chemicals and molecules or subatomic particles. What is the methodological justification Vivekananda offers for meditation and other mystical practices as appropriate methods that can lead to knowledge of the soul and God?

In his exposition of yoga in *Raja Yoga*, Vivekananda deals extensively with the meditative practices of yoga and their application. What follows is a brief summary of that explication and its logic. The two main themes that Vivekananda speaks of as the core components of yoga, are concentration and the cessation of thought. We have seen how within the framework of Samkhya and Vedanta, a self-contemplative enquiry into consciousness leads naturally to a knowledge of the soul, God, and all of reality. Vivekananda conceived of meditation as a presupposition-less investigation based purely on observation and verification, on lines similar to the physical sciences. Unlike the scientist who investigates the external world, the yogi investigates the internal world through observation. However, unlike the physical sciences where nature is studied through technical instruments, an introspective enquiry into the nature of the Self cannot use any instrument except the mind itself. Both the object of investigation and the instrument of investigation is the mind.

Then how is it to be done? According to the raja yoga system, the way to attain superconsciousness is to gain complete control of the mind. This is done through the practice of concentration. But to understand the claims that the yoga system makes, we have to understand a little bit of the Samkhya theory. According to Vivekananda, 'matter' and 'thought' are not two completely different entities. Vivekananda calls the body and matter 'objectified thought'; thought is a subtler, finer form of matter which, however, doesn't exist in physical space and time. Pure subjective awareness and physical matter are two extremities of a pole whose constitution gets finer or grosser depending on whether you are moving up or down the pole. While the gross form is the body, in its subtler form it appears as the mind. The stuff of which the mind is made is called chitta in the yoga system. Vivekananda uses the metaphor of a lake to explain what he means. The chitta is the water. When there is a stimulus through the senses, the mind reacts. Vivekananda compares the stimulus to a stone being thrown into the water. Ripples spread across the surface of the lake. These are our conscious thoughts and sensations. Just like how the ripples created by the stone on the surface of the lake also creates ripples under the surface of the lake, our conscious reactions and thoughts leave subconscious impressions.

These impressions created in the chitta are called 'vrittis'. The deeper you go into the unconscious, the finer are these impressions of past experiences stored there from past lives. A bundle of similar impressions are called samskars. In the depths of the mind or chitta, these samskars exist in a fine form and act upon the conscious mind without our knowledge. At the first stage, through concentrating on a single idea, sacred symbol, or mantra, the yogi suppresses all conscious thoughts and sensations. But then as her concentration gets deeper and deeper, the unconscious bundles of past impressions (samskars) rise up in the mind preventing her from accessing the non-physical superconscious states of her being. Vivekananda writes:

> [T]he only way of attaining to that superconsciousness is by concentration, and we have also seen that what hinders the mind from concentration are the past Samskaras, impressions. All of you have observed that, when you are trying to concentrate your mind, your thoughts wander. When you are trying to think of God, that is the very time these Samskaras appear. At other times they are not so active; but when you want them not, they are sure to be there, trying their best to crowd in your mind. Why should that be so? Why should they be much more potent at the time of concentration? It is because you are repressing them, and they react with all their force. At other times they do not react.... These have to be suppressed that the one idea which we want may arise, to the exclusion of the others. Instead, they are all struggling to come up at the same time.[22]

By preventing the subconsciously stored impressions from rising up, the yogi's awareness is able to reach the superconscious state which is beyond the subconscious. The yoga system describes various states of superconsciousness to be attained by various methods of concentration. At the penultimate state of superconsciousness, the entire mind is concentrated on a single idea to the exclusion of everything else. And finally, even that idea is given up, resulting in enlightenment or knowledge of the Self, the Atman. Vivekananda explains it thus: 'The bottom of a lake we cannot see, because its surface is covered with ripples. It is only possible for us to catch a glimpse of the bottom, when the ripples have subsided, and the water is calm. If the water is muddy or is agitated all the time, the bottom will not be seen. If it is clear, and there are no waves, we shall see the bottom. The bottom of the lake is our own true Self; the lake is the Chitta and the waves the Vrittis.'[23]

The third question we raised was about the basis of Vivekananda's claim that mystical or superconscious states of perception have evidentiary value. The sceptic could ask how we know that they are not simply hallucinations. As purely subjective experiences, how can they lay claim to objectivity? Vivekananda's answer to that question, which we have already mentioned, is that everyone can verify such experiences by following the same method. This might sound too simple though, for even if that is the case, these experiences are subjective and private. But there is more to what Vivekananda is saying here. This can be understood from the background of Kantian and post-Kantian German philosophy which framed many of Vivekananda's arguments. That at least some people in his audiences recognized this philosophical framework, can be seen from a report of one his speeches on Vedanta in *The Standard*: 'The opening passages of the lecture were a review of the rise of the grosser form of Materialism in the beginning of the present century, and the later development of the various forms of metaphysical thought, which for a time swept materialism away. From this he passed on to discuss the origin and nature of knowledge. In some respects, his views on this point were almost a statement of pure Fichteism,* but they were expressed in language, and they embodied illustrations, and made admissions which no German transcendentalist would have used.'[24] However, Vivekananda's statements are too fragmentary in nature to give a clear picture of the deeper philosophical considerations behind his position on objectivity.

However, further developments in Western philosophy after Vivekananda's time, can help illumine the real epistemological significance of Vivekananda's arguments about the objectivity of mystical experiences. The insights provided by the work of German philosopher Edmund Husserl (1859–1938), who was interested in the question of objectivity, are particularly useful here. Husserl was one of the most influential philosophers of the twentieth century, being the founder of the branch of philosophy called phenomenology. Phenomenology tries to study the structure and contents of consciousness from a first-person perspective, in the way it appears to us human subjects in experience. Thus, it is an approach to consciousness different from both empirical psychology and neurobiology. Husserl's phenomenology supplies us with the notion of intersubjectivity, which is a concept we can use to ground Vivekananda's ideas

---

*Johann Gottlieb Fichte was the first major post-Kantian philosopher, who inaugurated German idealism in philosophy.

about evidence and objectivity. 'Intersubjective' refers to objects of experience that all subjects share in common.

Rather than going deeper into what phenomenology is, we will take a tangential route to the problem of objectivity which does not involve technical metaphysics in an effort to keep things as simple as possible. Nonetheless, what follows does involve a certain amount of technicality, which readers who are not familiar with the tradition of Western philosophy may find challenging to follow. But it is my hope that the tenacious and persistent reader is able to comprehend the metaphysical view that is being presented. This is important because if one wants to truly understand Vivekananda the philosopher, as opposed to Vivekananda the spiritual thinker, one has to understand what he brought to the table of technical philosophy; what was original about it and what problems it purportedly succeeded in solving. But the reader who may, understandably, not be interested in these issues, can skip this section without any cost and move on to the next chapter.

Generally, what do we mean when we say something is objective? We use it as a binary in contrast to what is subjective, or a matter of opinion. For example, the fact that Leonardo da Vinci painted the Mona Lisa is a fact which is true regardless of what people think or feel about it. But whether Leonardo da Vinci was a better painter than Michelangelo is usually considered a matter of taste, or personal preference. Thus, when we know something to be the case, regardless of what people might believe about it, we call it an objective truth.

But there is a more significant sense in which we use the words objective and subjective. This is in the sense of existence, of what is real. We often talk about an objective vs subjective reality, with the notion that the former is real in some concrete way while the latter is ultimately illusory. Thus, the feeling of pain doesn't exist with the same kind of reality as a mountain or a lake. Emotions, thoughts, imagined objects, etc., always exist as part of the experiential field of a conscious subject. Their very existence is grounded in subjectivity, of being part of the existence of a sentient subject. In contrast, physical objects like clouds, atoms, cars, planets, and stars exist whether anyone sees them or not. This is called objective existence, which is supposedly independent and real. (This argument has been put forth by the contemporary philosopher John Searle regarding the concepts of objectivity and subjectivity.) This is the sense in which perceiving God is alleged to be a subjective experience. Even taking mystical experience for a real occurrence, the sceptic would argue that while there might be something to experiencing God, there is no entity called God which corresponds to that experience and exists by itself independently. This, of course, is not a conclusive argument against Vivekananda's claim that proof of God is possible through verification through experience. However, it can weaken the force of Vivekananda's argument by undermining the strength of the very concept of evidence he uses in support of the reality of spiritual truths.

But this entire picture of a real objectivity vs a not-real subjectivity is dependent on what one may call the 'natural' attitude, or our everyday experience of the world. It is one of the surprising facts of existence, that our experience doesn't accord with reason. This gap between experience and reason is what makes philosophy possible, and indeed necessary. On analysis, several problems emerge with our common-sense view of the world. Philosophically, the 'natural' attitude that there is a world of physical objects within which we are situated is broadly termed realism. Materialism, the philosophy that the reality of the world consists only of that which is physical, is a branch of realism. From the period of ancient philosophy onwards, both in the Western and Eastern tradition, realism has been challenged on several grounds. Its coherence has been called into question and it has been pointed out that if a world of material objects exists outside our minds, it is in principle unknowable and that its existence cannot ever be proven. Some of these critiques were quite well known in the nineteenth century and on the occasions that Vivekananda made references to Western metaphysics as a background for presenting his theory of Advaita and religion, this was the vantage point he often spoke from.* This is a matter of great importance because there is really no universally neutral concept of evidence and hence of objectivity. The concept of what constitutes evidence is crucially dependent on the metaphysical framework one assumes. The idea espoused by philosophers like John Searle, that things that exist by themselves are what are objectively real, is a concept of objectivity that assumes the metaphysics of realism. Vivekananda's concept of the individual's direct perception of God or soul as constituting evidence for its existence, draws philosophical sustenance from metaphysical positions which are critiques of realism. These critiques are too broad and wide-ranging, so we will focus only on the critique of the realist theory of perception, and that too only one strand of it. It will serve as an example of the several problems that face realism and our view of the world. But more importantly, it bears directly on the issue at hand—the evidentiary value of private and existentially subjective perception.

---

*Vivekananda often spoke from a Kantian position and more rarely from a non-materialist position like Bishop Berkeley's.

When we reflect on the experience of perception, it becomes obvious that we do not perceive the objects of the world directly. The proportions and profile of physical objects change according to how our sense organs, for example the eyes in the case of vision, are aligned with the object of perception. This realization led many ancient philosophers to come up with various theories of perception, especially of vision. Plato for example, believed that light rays emitted from the eyes allowed us to see objects. The first person to come up with the modern theory of vision, where light reflects off objects and falls on the eyes, was the medieval Islamic thinker Al Hazen. However, this came with its own set of philosophical implications. If light reflected off the surface of objects causes us to see the objects, we have to conclude that we do not see objects directly. We do not ever see the world as it is, but only representations of it. The modern theory of vision offered by physics and neurobiology is proved to be true beyond a doubt experimentally. However, these two fields of study do not provide a metaphysical explanation. Properly speaking, a scientific explanation for a phenomenon is restricted to describing how a set of events occurring under certain conditions will always be followed by another set of events, which will be followed by another set of events, and so on. A metaphysical explanation seeks a fuller explanation for what is happening.

Central to the realist story is the causal theory of perception, which explains how the brain gains sensory information and creates internal representations of the physical world. Let us take up the anti-realist critique of the causal theory of perception with regard to vision. Suppose a man sees a table in front of him. In the realist account, both the man and the table are located in physical space in a definite spatial relationship. Light waves which hit the table are reflected off various points on its surface and travel towards the man, reaching his eyes. The rays of light are focused on the retina, from where they are converted into electrical impulses by light sensitive nerve cells. These electrical impulses travel through the optic nerve and reach the visual cortex in the brain, where an image corresponding to the table is produced along with its spatial relation to its surroundings. The explanatory capacity of the account rests on the following: a) the spatial relations between the object of vision, its surroundings, and the eye; b) the physiological connections between the eye and the brain; c) the physiology of the brain; and d) the electrochemical changes taking place in the entire visual system, starting with the eye and terminating in the visual cortex.

The causal theory requires that all these components are physical entities located in a physical space. Central to the theory is the role of the brain in producing the mental image of the physical object. Now suppose a scientist is observing a person's brain during a brain surgery procedure. She is also monitoring the neural activity that occurs in the brain using an fMRI. Now these electrochemical changes can be correlated with events occurring in the patient's consciousness. But the scientist does not actually, at any point, see the physical brain. What she sees is the percept of a brain in her own mind. In other words, the image of the brain we have is an object given in consciousness. All the structures within the brain that the realist invokes to explain the origin of visual experience are actually part of a mental picture that is within consciousness. The entire network stretching from the object of perception to the eye, the optic nerves, and the brain exists not in physical space but in the perceptual space of an observer's mind. This is not to say that one cannot talk of the brain objectively. There is epistemic objectivity regarding the brain as a phenomenon since it is a public object of intersubjectivity, not just a private perception. When the scientist is observing the patient's brain, any person who is similarly cognitively situated will observe the same. But in terms of its existence, the allegedly physical brain the realist talks about as the starting point of her theory of perception, is actually an object that is part of intersubjective consciousness. Once this circularity is recognized, the causal theory of perception collapses upon itself.[25]

Vivekananda understood this philosophical problem of perception well. He used it as part of a wider argument that consciousness cannot be reduced to the activity in the brain.

> The mind cannot be analysed by any external machine. Supposing you could look into my brain while I am thinking, you would only see certain molecules interchanged. You could not see thought, consciousness, ideas, images. You would simply see the mass of vibrations—chemical and physical changes. From this example we see that this sort of analysis would not do....
>
> External analysis will go to the brain and find physical and chemical changes. It would never succeed [in answering the question]: What is the consciousness? What is your imagination? Where does this vast mass of ideas you have come from, and where do they go? We cannot deny them. They are facts. I never saw my own brain. I have to take for granted I have one. But man can never deny his own conscious imagination.[26]

Now what is the situation we are faced with in terms of realism? No rival metaphysical system has been able to provide a completely satisfactory theory of perception that explains the correlation between perception and the set consisting of stimulus, the sense organs, and electrochemical changes in areas of the brain responsible for perception. However, whatever the nature of the correlation might be, it cannot be coherently explained within the metaphysics of realism. How damaging this is to the philosophy of realism itself is a separate debate, but realism is far more crucially dependent on the causal theory of perception than other metaphysical views such as anti-realism. This is because it is fundamental for realism to explain how the objects we see in our subjective consciousness are real only if they correspond to real objects in the physical world outside our consciousness. When it fails to do that, other philosophical challenges to realism gain further strength. Even assuming there is a world of physical objects outside our minds which somehow act on our sense organs to create a representational image in our mind, how do we know that these images give us any knowledge about the objects that produced them? If there is a world of objects outside our minds, in principle, we can never know that the knowledge we think we have about them is true. All these questions remain live philosophical debates.

But what is clear is that the criteria for objectivity cannot be that something is objective if it exists in-and-of-itself independently of anyone's experience. This is one of the points of departure for the German philosopher Edmund Husserl that took him to phenomenology. Phenomenology brackets the question of the existence of the external world and concentrates instead on studying the features of phenomena given to us in consciousness from a first-person point of view. Vivekananda also consistently held the view that we can only know our own minds.

You are the only sentient being; mind is only the instrument through which you catch the external world. Take this book; as a book it does not exist outside, what exists outside is unknown and unknowable. The unknowable furnishes the suggestion that gives a blow to the mind, and the mind gives out the reaction in the form of a book, in the same manner as when a stone is thrown into the water, the water is thrown against it in the form of waves. The real universe is the occasion of the reaction of the mind. A book form, or an elephant form, or a man form, is not outside; all that we know is our mental reaction from the outer suggestion. 'Matter is the permanent possibility of sensations,' said John Stuart Mill. It is only the suggestion that is outside. Take an oyster for example. You know how pearls are made. A parasite gets inside the shell and causes irritation, and the oyster throws a sort of enameling round it, and this makes the pearl. The universe of experience is our own enamel, so to say, and the real universe is the parasite serving as nucleus.[27]

When Vivekananda talks about the 'real universe', he is not talking about the world of everyday objects or the cosmos with its stars and galaxy clusters. He is adopting the description 'real', only so that his audience can understand what he is referring to. As he says in the beginning, a reality outside the mind is completely unknowable, a blankness that can only be posited.*

This, however, still leaves us the question of how to distinguish the objective and real from the imagined and the illusory. It is to deal with this question that Husserl evolved the concept of intersubjectivity. The only meaningful criteria we can have for something that is real as opposed to imaginary or a purely private experience, is that the object in question appears to all sentient subjects under the right cognitive conditions. If we see a pink elephant, we know that it is a hallucination because other people do not see it there. But usually, everything we take for physical everyday objects—chairs, tables, cutlery—are all real because other people with the same cognitive abilities as us perceive them in the same manner. Thus, the idea that the objectively real is that which exists independently of any subject's perception, is untenable. It is in fact, the reverse. What is objectively real is that which is perceivable by all subjects. As long as the status of a material world outside our consciousness remains an empty theoretical postulation devoid of substantial content, it cannot furnish philosophical support to the notion of reality. What exists objectively are those objects and existents that exist in the domain of intersubjectivity. What we call 'objectivity' is, in fact, intersubjectivity.

This is why Vivekananda's claim that mystical experiences are available and thus verifiable by anyone who follows the right methods has more philosophical weight than may seem likely at first. What his claim amounts to is that mystical experiences are not arbitrary inspirations that holy people or saints have and whose reality will always remain doubtful. His body of arguments, especially in *Raja Yoga* with its commentary on Patanjali's *Yoga Sutra*, present mystical experiences not as random phenomena that appear without any explanation to a special class of prophets and seers, but as experiences open to rational methods of investigation. Vivekananda's philosophical claim is that mystical experiences are reproducible under systematically specified epistemic and cognitive conditions. This is what Vivekananda meant when he claimed that

---

*Vivekananda seems to be following Kant here, echoing the German philosopher's distinction between what really exists (the nouemenon) and the reality our mind perceives (the phenomenon).

religion required and could furnish scientific proof. A given set of conditions, whose method of preparation can be specified (in this case, states of mind), will always produce a certain phenomenon and this can be verified by reproducing these conditions multiple times, by multiple people in multiple situations. Thus, mystical phenomena exist in the intersubjective domain of existence. This is the basis for their claim to objectivity. Another basis, though Vivekananda never argues for this explicitly, is that various mystical phenomena reveal an ordering pattern and inner structural connections, revealing them to be parts of a totality, which constitutes a real domain of existence.

We started the discussion about religion and rationality in relation to the realm of democracy. Here, great care should be taken not to misunderstand what Vivekananda says about the evidence for religion. While he says that those who say there is no truth to religion do not have a rational basis for their claim, he equally says that those who consider themselves religious without trying to seek out the evidence for spiritual truths are believing thoughtlessly and have claim to neither genuine spirituality nor rationality. How exactly are we to interpret such a position in terms of the role religion plays in society today? Vivekananda clearly states again and again that any inspiration or dogma that contradicts reason and scientific fact should be rejected. While Vivekananda wants to put mystical experiences on an epistemologically secure foundation, he insists that whatever is erected on that foundation cannot run counter to the knowledge we have already acquired by reason and other means. So, any religious belief, whether based on scripture, dogma, or alleged mystical experience, cannot justify excluding LGBTQ+ people, denying biological evolution, or believing without any historical evidence that a king called Ram ruled in Ayodhya. Only rational beliefs should have a place in the public mind and, by extension, in the deliberative sphere of a democracy.

Vivekananda was a spiritual preacher who preached that God/Brahman existed, that he had perceived it and could show people who were interested, the way to perceive it for themselves. He also believed with conviction that the whole of humanity could be revolutionized by the spread of spirituality and by making people aware of their own divinity; of the fact that they themselves were God. So, what would he have to say about the status of spiritual belief itself? What status should belief in God, soul, or any other transcendental entity occupy within the public institutions of a democracy and that part of the public sphere which is coterminous with these institutions? It is a very pertinent question for the democracies of our own time. This question never posed itself in Vivekananda's time because liberal democracies were still almost half a century away, even in America. So, we do not find Vivekananda addressing this question, even indirectly. But given his views on all the issues discussed here, I would speculate that his position would be similar to the one I myself have espoused elsewhere. 'Even the most self-consistent, coherent, and rational of religious knowledge claims cannot be given a normative status within the public sphere. The latter's rationality is anchored in the examination of what is publicly available; that is, in the common world of intersubjectivity. Any claim to kinds of experiences that are not commonly available has not only to be treated with caution, but is forever unverifiable within the bounds of the public sphere. While one can be open to its possibility, the structure of the public sphere has always to be agnostic about the truth of religious experiences.'[28] I would imagine that Vivekananda would agree with this not only for the good of democracy, but also of spirituality. For once a religious truth, even if true, becomes publicly normative, it quickly becomes a dogma, and for Vivekananda, dogma was the death of spirituality.

ETHICS: ADVAITA AND DEMOCRACY

It may well be that Brahma is unknowable. But all the same this theory of Brahma has certain social implications which have a tremendous value as a foundation for Democracy. If all persons are parts of Brahma then all are equal and all must enjoy the same liberty which is what Democracy means. Looked at from this point of view Brahma may be unknowable. But there cannot be slightest doubt that no doctrine could furnish a stronger foundation for Democracy than the doctrine of Brahma.

To support Democracy because we are all children of God is a very weak foundation for Democracy to rest on. That is why Democracy is so shaky wherever it made to rest on such a foundation. But to recognize and realize that you and I are parts of the same cosmic principle leaves room for no other theory of associated life except democracy. It does not merely preach Democracy. It makes democracy an obligation of one and all.

Western students of Democracy have spread the belief that Democracy has stemmed either from Christianity or from Plato and that there is no other source of inspiration for democracy. If they had known that India too had developed the doctrine of Brahmaism which furnishes a better foundation for Democracy they would not have been so dogmatic. India too must be admitted to have a contribution towards a theoretical foundation for Democracy.[1]

This analysis of the implications of the Upanishadic monism of Brahman for democracy is to be found in B. R. Ambedkar's 'Riddle No. 22: Brahma is not Dharma. What good is Brahma?', *Riddles in Hinduism*. The book, which he wrote towards the end of his life and which was published two years after his death, is a dissection of Hinduism, and what Ambedkar believed were its internal contradictions and socially oppressive nature. Since 2014, the Hindutva right wing has been trying to appropriate Ambedkar.[2] To anyone who is in the least familiar with Ambedkar's writings, the attempt is absurd. Ambedkar was, throughout his career, an implacable critic of Hinduism and Hindu society. Ambedkar said 'If Hindu Raj does become a fact, it will, no doubt be the greatest calamity for this country. No matter what the Hindus say, Hinduism is a menace to liberty, equality and fraternity. It is incompatible with democracy. Hindu Raj must be prevented at any cost.'[3] He indicted Hinduism for caste oppression, for domination by the priestly Brahmins, and what he considered its lack of humanism.

Therefore, the above comments have to be placed in context. The praise for 'Brahmaism' occurs right after Ambedkar criticizes Hinduism for what he considers its inherently undemocratic character. The Hindu religion, Ambedkar states, believes in the division of society into various castes, forever separated by a social hierarchy and notions of ritual pollution. Such a society can never cultivate a spirit of fraternity, which is the most fundamental basis of democracy. Then Ambedkar proceeds to comment:

> From this it would appear that the doctrine of fraternity was unknown to the Hindu Religious and Philosophic thought. But such a conclusion would not be warranted by the facts of history. The Hindu Religious and Philosophic thought gave rise to an idea which had greater potentialities for producing social democracy than the idea of fraternity. It is the doctrine of Brahmaism [have borrowed this word from Prof. Hopkin's—The Epics of India].
>
> It would not be surprising if someone asked what is this Brahmaism? It is something new even to Hindus. The Hindus are familiar with Vedanta. They are familiar with Brahmanism. But they are certainly not familiar with Brahmaism.[4]

Ambedkar's thinking here is important because it runs parallel to Vivekananda's thinking on the ethical implications and potential of Advaita. While Ambedkar says that what he calls Brahmaism is different from the traditional Vedanta (which includes Advaita), it is clear that his Brahmaism is more or less the same as what Vivekananda calls Advaita. Let us recall what Ambedkar says: 'If all persons are parts of Brahma then all are equal and all must enjoy the same liberty which is what Democracy means.... [T]o recognize and realize that you and I are parts of the same cosmic principle leaves room for no other theory of associated life except democracy.'[5] That all creatures are part of the cosmic principle called Brahman and have the same rights, that it is an obligation for us to love others as ourselves, is the quintessence of the Advaita Vivekananda taught, which he called practical Vedanta. However, he did not couch it in terms of democracy, but social life. But democracy was not completely absent from Vivekananda's thought and we should be able to make the requisite connections if we draw them out carefully.

Coming from as harsh a critic of Hinduism as Ambedkar, the idea that Upanishadic monism (I am picking a neutral term to avoid the dispute involved in preferring either of the labels 'Brahmaism' and 'Advaita') has unsurpassed ethical potential lends credibility to Vivekananda's similar claim. This is more so since Ambedkar arrived at it independently. But that is not the only reason to use Ambedkar as a point of departure for discussing Vivekananda's ethics built on Advaita. Ambedkar was perhaps the person who thought most deeply and painstakingly about Indian democracy. His views on democracy, as we can see from the use of the term 'associated life', were heavily influenced by the theory of democracy developed by his former teacher and mentor at Columbia University, the philosopher John Dewey.

As we have noted before, Vivekananda's social and political views regarding both India and Europe were expressed at a time when there was very little reason to think that global European colonialism or monarchical political systems would collapse and give way to independent nations in the colonies, and liberal democracies in Western Europe. As a democracy, America stood in splendid isolation. So, while Vivekananda expounded on the ethical and social implications of the Advaita philosophy, he did not quite work it out in terms of democracy. Ambedkar's analysis of Indian democracy and the connections he makes with Upanishadic monism, allow us to extend Vivekananda's ideas about Advaita to contemporary Indian democracy and see what relevance it has.

Before we proceed, however, we have to first take note of the fact that there exist a series of interesting convergences between a) Vivekananda and Ambedkar's ideas of Hinduism and Hindu society and b) their ideas on the fundamental basis of a just political order. At the same time, there is also deep divergence between Vivekananda and Ambedkar. While Vivekananda saw Hinduism as a religion preaching the broadest possible universalism, Ambedkar saw it as a religion that preached social division and inequality and was mainly the product of the power machinations of the priestly Brahminical class.

AMBEDKAR AND VIVEKANANDA ON DEMOCRACY

Let us first look at how the two thinkers' ideas that pertain directly or indirectly to democracy converge. For Ambedkar, writing in the middle of the twentieth century, liberal democracy had established itself as the only form of government that could aim to give citizens liberty, equality, and justice. Historically, the nation as a civilizational and political unit had emerged as the condition of possibility of democratic government. Ambedkar was not a nationalist in the usual sense of the word, but in terms of his political philosophy he was committed to the idea of the nation state as the only possible political structure capable of implementing democracy. Theories of liberal democracies were being developed in the West, especially in America, to guide the development of a more just and equitable democracy. Even to the present day, these theories have focused on evolving the political institutions of democracy. However, as early as the beginning of the twentieth century, Ambedkar's mentor and the pragmatist philosopher, John Dewey, took a different approach. He laid emphasis not on institutions but on the way individual citizens and social groups took part in the democratic process. However, Dewey's approach was not built upon in later academic work on 'developing democracies'. The focus was on building political and administrative institutions, improving socio-economic conditions, building various kinds of functional models of governance, etc.

Drawing on Dewey's ideas, Ambedkar analysed the fundamental challenge facing Indian democracy more sharply and clearly than perhaps any other thinker. When Ambedkar famously said during the Constituent Assembly debates that, 'Democracy in India is only a top dressing on an Indian soil, which is essentially undemocratic',[6] he was not merely being cynical or critical of Indian society.[*] He was articulating an insight that is still woefully missing from public discussions about democracy in India, which focus almost exclusively on institutional reforms. What Ambedkar is saying is that the mechanisms of democracy that include free and fair elections, the separation of powers between the executive, legislature, and judiciary, a just Constitution, a free press, etc., are by themselves not sufficient to ensure democratic government or the rule of law. He is pointing out the fact that a country needs to build a democratic culture, one where each person respects the other's right to liberty and equality. It is only such a culture that can nourish the formal institutions of democratic government. Otherwise, these institutions would just ossify or get distorted, and the aims of social justice, rule of law, and liberty and equality would fail or be fatally compromised.

---

*'It follows that it is only where people are saturated with Constitutional morality…that one can take the risk of omitting from the Constitution details of administration and leaving it for the Legislature to prescribe them. The question is, can we presume such a diffusion of Constitutional morality? Constitutional morality is not a natural sentiment. It has to be cultivated. We must realize that our people have yet to learn it. Democracy in India is only a top-dressing on an Indian soil, which is essentially undemocratic.' See 'Draft Constitution—Discussion Motion re Draft Constitution', *Dr. Babasaheb Ambedkar Writings and Speeches, Volume No.: 13*, Vasant Moon (ed.), New Delhi: Dr. Ambedkar Foundation, 2019, p. 60, available at baws.in.

Ambedkar writes in 'Riddle No. 22' before he writes about Brahmaism as the surest foundation for democracy: 'There cannot be democratic Government unless the society for which it functions is democratic in its form and structure.... Government is not something which is distinct and separate from Society. Government is one of the many institutions which Society rears and to which it assigns the function of carrying out some of the duties which are necessary for collective social life...[if] a Government is to reflect the ultimate purposes, aims, objects and wishes of society and this can happen only where the society in which the Government is rooted is democratic. If society is not democratic, Government can never be.'[7] Arguing against the view that a democratic form of government is sufficient for a democracy to function, Ambedkar further says:

> Whether the Democratic form of Government will result in good will depend upon the disposition of the individuals composing society. If the mental disposition of the individuals is democratic then the democratic form of Government can be expected to result in good Government. If not, democratic form of Government may easily become a dangerous form of Government. If the individuals in a society are separated into classes and the classes are isolated from one another and each individual feels that his loyalty to his class must come before his loyalty to everything else and living in class compartments he becomes class conscious and bound to place the interests of his class above the interests of others... what can a democratic Government do?... A Government for the people can be had only where the attitude of each individual is democratic which means that each individual is prepared to treat every other individual as his equal and is prepared to give him the same liberty which he claims for himself. This democratic attitude of mind is the result of socialization of the individual in a democratic society. Democratic society is therefore a prerequisite of a democratic Government. That Democratic Governments have toppled down is largely due to the fact that the society for which they were set up was not democratic.[8]

In other words, the prerequisite for a democracy to function properly is the creation of a democratic culture in society. What does a democratic culture consist of? As Ambedkar's words indicate, it consists of, among other things, the ability of a nation's citizenry to rise above sectarian identities like class, caste, and gender and place the legitimate interests of all individuals on the same plane. As John Dewey argued, democracy is an ethical form of social life.[9] Once we recognize this, then the question becomes about the basis on which such an ethical life can be erected. Ambedkar puts the matter succinctly when he says: 'Some equate Democracy with equality and liberty. Equality and liberty are no doubt the deepest concern of Democracy. But the more important question is what sustains equality and liberty? Some would say that it is the law of the state which sustains equality and liberty. This is not a true answer. What sustains equality and liberty is fellow feeling. What the French Revolutionists called fraternity. The word fraternity is not an adequate expression. The proper term is what the Buddha called, Maitree. Without Fraternity, Liberty would destroy equality and equality would destroy liberty.'[10]

But fraternity requires a foundation to sustain it and it is not obvious what that could be. The two major candidates offered up by political theorists in Ambedkar's time were religion and the theory of natural law. The former appeals to people's fellow-feeling on the basis that they are all created by the same God. Natural law appeals to the supposedly intrinsic rights of equality and liberty every human being possesses by virtue of the fact of being human. Both theories have their shortcomings. Ambedkar preferred religion over natural rights on pragmatic grounds, writing:

> Religion is a social force. [It] stands for a scheme of divine governance. The scheme becomes an ideal for society to follow. The ideal may be non-existent in the sense that it is something which is constructed. But although non-existent, it is real. For an ideal it has full operative force which is inherent in every ideal. Those who deny the importance of religion not only forget this, they also fail to realize how great is the potency and sanction that lies behind a religious ideal as compared with that of a purely secular ideal.... But the relative potency of the two ideals is to be measured by another test—namely their power to override the practical instincts of man. The ideal is concerned with something that is remote. The practical instincts of man are concerned with the immediate present. Now placed as against the force of the practical instincts of man the two ideals show their difference in an unmistaken manner. The practical instincts of man do yield to the prescriptions of a religious ideal however much the two are opposed to each other. The practical instincts of man do not on the other hand yield to the secular ideal if the two are in conflict. This means that a religious ideal has a hold on mankind, irrespective of an earthly gain. This can never be said of a purely secular ideal.[11]

But he was, as we saw, not completely satisfied with religion as the basis for fraternity, opining that the idea that all are children of God is a weak basis for democracy. This is why he says so confidently that there cannot be the slightest doubt that Upanishadic monism provides the surest foundation for democracy; one which goes beyond fraternity. Fraternity has to assume difference as its starting point because democracy has to postulate a collection of atomic individuals free from the demands of any social collectivity and who each constitute a citizen of the State. Fraternity is the bridging of the difference of self-interest between each individual, and whatever principle is invoked as its ground, it can never completely annihilate that difference, because ultimately each individual is a monad. This is why Ambedkar says Upanishadic monism is a surer foundation of democracy than the concept of fraternity. While Upanishadic monism recognizes each individual as a monad completely differentiated from the rest of humanity in its concept of Atman or the Self, this differentiation is only apparent. As each Atman is identical with or is part of the same cosmic principle of Brahman, each individual is forced to recognize in the other, not his brother, but his own self, thus annihilating any possibility of divergent selfish interests.

Vivekananda fulfilled several roles at once in his short career. The exact relationship between these roles has always been a matter of confusion to many who read Vivekananda. Rather than view these roles externally, if one were to take a psychological approach, the matter becomes clearer far more easily. Instead of looking at the time or effort Vivekananda expended in fulfilling these different roles as a sign of their respective importance, one should look at how the monk related psychologically to these roles, as revealed through his correspondence, conversations, and the accounts from people who knew him. From this material, a complex, but clear picture emerges.

First and foremost, he was a monk who personally trained or preached to disciples or followers on the way to obtain spiritual illumination. This was the most fundamental plane of psychological reality from which Vivekananda thought and acted. For Vivekananda, at this level of reality, the whole world was maya and the entire goal of human existence was to find a way out of illusory life into truth which may be called the Absolute, God, Spirit, or soul. At a secondary level, or psychologically speaking, superimposed on this fundamental level, was Vivekananda's role as a preacher of spirituality. Here, he moved in the world of ideas rather than mysticism. He preached Vedanta philosophy and his spiritual ideas to a wide audience across the West and, less frequently, in India. It is at a third level, psychologically most peripheral from his fundamental identity and world view, that Vivekananda concerned himself with sociopolitical questions of patriotism, the regeneration of India, spreading education, eliminating poverty, ending caste oppression, reviving the true spirit of Hinduism, religious reform, etc. But what unified all these levels by running like a thread through their diverse domains of activity and thought, was the philosophy of Upanishadic monism.

Vivekananda hardly ever directly discussed democracy. In fact, in an often-quoted remark, he referred to himself as a socialist, saying 'I am a socialist not because I think it is a perfect system, but half a loaf is better than no bread.'[12] This remark, combined with a few others on socialism, has led many historians, especially of a socialist bend, to read Vivekananda as a socialist. But in my reading of Vivekananda, in so far as he was willing to commit to any political system, he saw democracy as the way forward. It would be a mistake to take Vivekananda's brief comments sympathetic to socialism as indicating any support of the state socialism that emerged after the Russian revolution, or even the idea of a socialist revolution. For one, Marx's exact ideas were comparatively unknown in the English-speaking world, with the first English translation of Das Kapital by Samuel Moore appearing only in 1887. In both America and Britain, trade unions had greater freedom than continental Europe and wanted to participate in the political process of capitalistic democracies to secure greater rights for workers. This made the incremental socialism of the Fabian socialists and the evolutionary democratic socialism of Eduard Bernstein more popular in Britain and America where Vivekananda operated from. Such socialist systems sought to achieve a socialist society through gradual reforms within the framework of capitalistic democracy.

As a political system of governance, there is much evidence to show that Vivekananda was in favour of democracy. For one, he repeatedly praised American democracy. He believed America, unlike her monarchical counterparts in Europe, had succeeded in giving freedom to the masses. Though he decried the materialistic mentality of American society, of the singular focus on accumulating wealth (this can be considered a social critique of laissez-faire capitalism), he hailed America as the land of liberty and equality. For instance, he wrote 'The Americans have their faults too, and what nation has not? But this is my summing up: Asia laid the germs of civilization, Europe developed man, and America is developing the woman and the masses. It is the paradise of the woman and the labourer. Now contrast the American masses and women with ours, and you get the idea at once.'[13] While he expressed sympathy for socialism, he also ultimately warned that the subjugation of the individual to the collective that socialism demanded would lead to tyranny. 'And you are trying today what you call socialism! Good things will come; but in the long run you will be a [blight] upon the race. Freedom is the watchword,' he told an English audience.[14] Freedom, with its concomitant values of personal liberty and equality, were the cornerstone of Vivekananda's philosophy. And these resonated with the core political values of liberal democracy. If Vivekananda was not an enthusiastic public champion of democracy, it is not something to be surprised about. He stated explicitly that he would not get directly involved in political and social causes; he felt it would dilute his spiritual message. As a sanyasi, he felt he had no right to dictate to society the course it should take. His role, as he saw it, was to preach the spiritual and ethical principles society should apply to solve particular political and social problems. This is exemplified in his attitude towards Indian nationalism. Though he aggressively attacked the slavery that the British had imposed on the Indians, he refused to make any public statements supporting Indian political nationalism. He felt that to do so ran the danger of politicizing his spiritual message.

Of all the various social problems that plagued nineteenth century India, the one that most deeply concerned Vivekananda was the enormous poverty in which the majority of India's population of 300 million was sunk. Though he partly blamed the British, the majority of his blame was reserved for the upper classes and castes of India. Nearly a millennium of caste and feudal tyranny by the elites had rendered Indian society 'diabolical'.* Even the upper classes, unlike the aristocracy in many nations, were divided along rigid caste lines and could not work together to achieve any common purpose. Vivekananda believed that India had a mission in the world, a spiritual message to preach. This message consisted of the Vedantic doctrine that each soul is potentially divine, combined with the yogic teachings that it is possible to directly experience spiritual truths about God, soul, and the universe, rather than believe in it as a matter of faith. But before India could do that, or at least concurrently with that process, she had the greater mission of regenerating herself. And the key to that for Vivekananda, was the material, educational, and spiritual uplift of the masses of India. How this was to be accomplished was a question he struggled with for most of his short life.

He had several plans, including enlisting monetary help from reform-minded Indian princes and getting technological and financial aid from America. He even envisaged enlisting the thousands of sanyasis in India to form a band and go from village to village, teaching villagers the basic facts of science and geography using maps and magic lanterns (an early form of

---

*See Chapter 2, p. 70.

an image projector). None of these however, came to fruition, mainly because the sections he appealed to for assistance did not respond with sufficient enthusiasm. Vivekananda lived through the close of the Bengal Renaissance, the socio-religious reform movement which started with Raja Ram Mohan Roy and later became a pan-India movement. Vivekananda admired Roy and generally appreciated the reform movement down to Keshub Chandra Sen. But for a number of reasons, he was critical of the direction and methods of contemporary upper class reform societies. His main reason was that the reforms they were advocating, of widow re-marriage, ending child marriage, freedom of choice in marriage, inter-caste dining, and so on, while desirable reforms, were those that were intended to benefit only their own class. He said, 'Most of the reforms that have been agitated for during the past century have been ornamental. Every one of these reforms only touches the first two castes, and no other. The question of widow marriage would not touch seventy per cent of the Indian women, and all such questions only reach the higher castes of Indian people who are educated, mark you, at the expense of the masses. Every effort has been spent in cleaning their own houses. But that is no reformation. You must go down to the basis of the thing, to the very root of the matter. That is what I call radical reform.'[15] He found that these reform societies were completely apathetic to the state of the masses who were at the bottom of the class–caste hierarchy and who were mired in starvation deaths, deprivation, and lack of education. Vivekananda blamed India's fall from one of the world's foremost civilizations to a land synonymous with poverty and superstition on the Indian elite's neglect and caste hatred of the masses. On the other hand, he attributed Europe and America's phenomenal rise in the rank of world's civilizations to its material and educational upliftment of the masses. Vivekananda wrote to his disciples in Madras after his success in America: 'Remember that the nation lives in the cottage. But, alas! nobody ever did anything for them. Our modern reformers are very busy about widow remarriage. Of course, I am a sympathiser in every reform, but the fate of a nation does not depend upon the number of husbands their widows get, but upon the condition of the masses. Can you raise them?'[16]

How was this goal to be achieved? On the basis of Indian nationhood, imagined as a community of all Indians, with a common civilizational history. The British conquest had provided the centralized administration that combined the various regional powers of India into a single political unit. The idea of a nation, and of a single people, provided the combinatorial possibilities for combined action for common goals, a prerequisite if poverty, deprivation, illiteracy, and caste oppression were to be alleviated. While Vivekananda believed that Indian interests should be represented in the British government of the day and that the form of the government itself should evolve towards one committed to the rule of law and the ideals of liberty and equality, he saw the immediate task at hand as that of nation formation. During an interview with a journalist from an English newspaper Vivekananda was asked if he had given much attention to the Indian National Congress. He replied: 'I cannot claim to have given much; my work is in another part of the field. But I regard the movement as significant, and heartily wish it success. A nation is being made out of India's different races. I sometimes think they are no less various than the different peoples of Europe.'[17] The last line is particularly important. The formation of nation states in Europe followed a pattern where members of different classes, and ethnic, regional, and religious communities started shifting their identity from that of members of relatively self-enclosed communities to that of denizens of a larger imagined community that constituted the nation. This necessitated a fellow-feeling with people living in distant places, belonging to different communities, and living very different kinds of lives.

Just as Ambedkar did, Vivekananda felt that the while the form of government and various political institutions should be such as to ensure liberty and justice, the more fundamental issue was that of the attitude and dispositions of the individuals who made up the polity. For Vivekananda, the issue was fundamentally spiritual. In an interview given to the *Sunday Times* in London, Vivekananda said, 'But the basis of all systems, social or political, rests upon the goodness of men. No nation is great or good because Parliament enacts this or that, but because its men are great and good. I have visited China which had the most admirable organization of all nations. Yet today China is like a disorganized mob, because her men are not equal to the system contrived in the olden days. Religion goes to the root of the matter. If it is right, all is right.'[18] Here, Vivekananda is using the world religion as a synonym for spirituality, as he often did.

For Vivekananda, ethics flowed from spirituality. It is not that Vivekananda thought the atheist could not be perfectly ethical, but he believed spirituality was the fountainhead of a deeper universal sympathy whose vastness and completeness could wipe out all selfish individual interests. This is because spirituality allowed one to consider each living creature as divine, which can generate a universal love and bond between humans that exceeds the more mundane possibilities of a purely secular ethics. As he said 'There are moments when every man feels that he is one with the universe, and he rushes forth to express it, whether he knows it or not. This expression of oneness is what we call love and sympathy, and it is the basis of all our ethics and morality. This is summed up in the Vedanta philosophy by the celebrated aphorism, Tat Tvam Asi, "Thou art That".[19]

In any case, Vivekananda is of the same mind as Ambedkar and John Dewey that fraternity or some similar feeling among the polity is more fundamental to a democracy or any just order of governance than political institutions, however advanced. When Vivekananda remarked that India was becoming a nation, he realized that such an enterprise required not only political organizations but a self-sacrificing spirit of fraternity, empathy, and love that was the real basis of nationhood. To become a nation, Indians had to transcend the narrow limits of sympathy bounded by region, caste, custom, language, religion, class, and social position, and come into a more universal empathy. He noted that an expanding field of empathy and fellow feeling is what enabled the gradual transition of European countries from feudal monarchies to nation states. Addressing a large crowd in Lahore, he said:

Young men of Lahore…[y]ou may make thousands of societies, twenty thousand political assemblages, fifty thousand institutions. These will be of no use until there is that sympathy, that love, that heart that thinks for all; until Buddha's heart comes once more into India, until the words of the Lord Krishna are brought to their practical use, there is no hope for us. You go on imitating the Europeans and their societies and their assemblages, but let me tell you a story, a fact that I saw with my own eyes. A company of Burmans was taken over to London by some persons here, who turned out to be Eurasians. They exhibited these people in London, took all the money, and then took these Burmans over to the Continent, and left them there for good or evil. These poor people did not know a word of any European language, but the English Consul in Austria sent them over to London. They were helpless in London, without knowing anyone. But an English lady got to know of them, took these foreigners from Burma into her own house, gave them her own clothes, her bed, and everything, and then sent the news to the papers. And, mark you, the next day the whole nation was, as it were, roused. Money poured in, and these people were helped out and sent back to Burma. On this sort of sympathy are based all their political and other institutions; it is the rock-foundation of love, for themselves at least. They may not love the world; and the Burmans may be their enemies, but in England, it goes without saying, there is this great love for their own people, for truth and justice and charity to the stranger at the door. I should be the most ungrateful man if I did not tell you how wonderfully and how hospitably I was received in every country in the West. Where is the heart here to build upon? No sooner do we start a little joint-stock company than we try to cheat each other, and the whole thing comes down with a crash. You talk of imitating the English and building up as big a nation as they are. But where are the foundations? Ours are only sand, and, therefore, the building comes down with a crash in no time.[20]

In the philosophy of Advaita, of the oneness of all beings, Vivekananda believed he had found the basis upon which the mutual love and empathy that would undergird true nationhood could be built. India is an exceedingly religious country even today. It was far more so in Vivekananda's day. With Hinduism as the dominant religion and its social structures like caste influencing even Muslim and Christian communities, Vivekananda believed that a spiritual revolution in Hinduism could lay the foundations for the mutual empathy required to uplift the masses. The basis of this revolution was the popularization of the Advaita philosophy among the masses of India. By the spreading of Advaita, Vivekananda meant not the popularization of Sanskrit scripture, but the philosophical kernel of a spiritual monism that taught each man that his Self was divine and that he had infinite power within him. Vivekananda was not claiming that he had discovered something new in the old Upanishadic philosophy. In his view, the doctrine of Advaita, with its unavoidable conclusion of the perfect equality of all human beings, was known to the Hindu upper class and castes. But they deliberately chose to ignore the social and ethical implications of the spiritual philosophy in order to maintain the oppressive social system they dominated and the privileges that system granted them. The priests even invented the doctrine of 'lokachara', meaning worldly custom to justify this. Lokachara maintained that spiritual principles laid down in the scriptures, while authoritative and valid in the spiritual realm, should not interfere with the customs established in society. Vivekananda called this, the 'national sin' in the speech quoted above. In the same speech, Vivekananda said:

The nation is sinking, the curse of unnumbered millions is on our heads— those to whom we have been giving ditch-water to drink when they have been dying of thirst and while the perennial river of water was flowing past, the unnumbered millions whom we have allowed to starve in sight of plenty, the unnumbered millions to whom we have talked of Advaita and whom we have hated with all our strength, the unnumbered millions for whom we have invented the doctrine of Lokachara (usage), to whom we have talked theoretically that we are all the same and all are one with the same Lord, without even an ounce of practice. 'Yet, my friends, it must be only in the mind and never in practice!' Wipe off this blot. 'Arise and awake.' ...Arise and awake and be perfectly sincere. Our insincerity in India is awful; what we want is character, that steadiness and character that make a man cling on to a thing like grim death.[21]

Vivekananda exhorted his countrymen that India had a special mission among the nations. While it was the destiny of America and Europe to bring material prosperity and scientific knowledge to the world, it was India's destiny to spread the light of spirituality. He often referred to the fact that India had done so several times previously in her history, the two major occasions being the diffusion of Indian spiritual ideas to Europe after the conquest of the Macedonian King Alexander, and the spread of Buddhism throughout Asia in the centuries following the Buddha's death. The world was once again being globalized through European imperialism, and Vivekananda called upon Indians to rise as a nation and take her place among the countries of the world as its spiritual teacher. This has lent itself to a Hindu supremacist reading by the Sangh Parivar, which takes Vivekananda to have championed the export of Hinduism across the globe. What Vivekananda had in mind, however, was the propagation of the philosophy of Vedanta and its ideals of the divinity of man and oneness of all being. By preaching these ideas, they would be assimilated into the thought currents of the world and could be adopted by any culture and expressed in forms suitable for its own context, thus making them its own. It did not matter to Vivekananda that these ideas should carry a Hindu tag or even a Vedantic one. It is important to understand that for Vivekananda spirituality was not a domain closed off from the social and material. He expected the idea of Upanishadic monism to contribute to both the social and material upliftment of humankind by generating an ethic of universal empathy with anyone who suffers. If you recognize your own Self in those who suffer or are oppressed, helping them is no longer an obligation, but an imperative as powerful as helping yourself.

Therefore, arise, awake, with your hands stretched out to protect the spirituality of the world. And first of all, work it out for your own country. What we want is not so much spirituality as a little of the bringing down of the Advaita into the material world. First bread and then religion. We stuff them too much with religion, when the poor fellows have been starving. No dogmas will satisfy the cravings of hunger. There are two curses here: first our weakness, secondly, our hatred, our dried-up hearts. You may talk doctrines by the millions, you may have sects by the hundreds of millions; ay, but it is nothing until you have the heart to feel. Feel for them as your Veda teaches you, till you find they are parts of your own bodies, till you realize that you and they, the poor and the rich, the saint and the sinner, are all parts of One Infinite Whole, which you call Brahman.[22]

The idea that each man's Self was identical with the universal Spirit, was not only supposed to generate a spirit of universal sympathy. Vivekananda believed that Advaita would empower each individual to manifest their latent potential by giving them faith in themselves. A person who believes in the Advaita philosophy and seeks to realize it will cease to think of themselves as a limited human being but as infinite Spirit, capable of accomplishing anything they set their minds to. Vivekananda's idea of the implication of the Vedanta ideal for the individual comes through powerfully and clearly when he says:

The Vedanta teaches men to have faith in themselves first. As certain religions of the world say that a man who does not believe in a personal God outside of himself is an atheist, so the Vedanta says, a man who does not believe in himself is an atheist. Not believing in the glory of our own soul is what the Vedanta calls atheism. To many this is, no doubt, a terrible idea; and most of us think that this ideal can never be reached; but the Vedanta insists that it can be realized by everyone. There is neither man nor woman or child, nor difference of race or sex, nor anything that stands as a bar to the realization of the ideal, because Vedanta shows that it is realized already, it is already there. All the powers in the universe are already ours. It is we who have put our hands before our eyes and cry that it is dark. Know that there is no darkness around us. Take the hands away and there is the light which was from the beginning. Darkness never existed, weakness never existed. We who are fools cry that we are weak; we who are fools cry that we are impure.... As soon as you say, 'I am a little mortal being,' you are saying something which is not true.... The Vedanta recognizes no sin, it only recognizes error. And the greatest error, says the Vedanta, is to say that you are weak, that you are a sinner, a miserable creature, and that you have no power and you cannot do this and that. Every time you think in that way, you, as it were, rivet one more link in the chain that binds you down, you add one more layer of hypnotism on to your own soul. Therefore, whosoever thinks he is weak is wrong, whosoever thinks he is impure is wrong, and is throwing a bad thought into the world.... No man becomes purer and purer, it is a matter of greater manifestation. The veil drops away, and the native purity of the soul begins to manifest itself. Everything is ours already—infinite purity, freedom, love, and power.[23]

Integral to such a project of Vedantic empowerment of humankind, was the recognition of the individual as a self-contained category. Vivekananda was an individualist to the core, refusing to admit that society or any other individual had the right to dictate what any individual should do. This directly flows from Vivekananda's understanding of Advaita. The originality of Vivekananda's thought here lies in how he interprets Advaita Vedanta by emphasizing the individual Self as the site of all reality. Man is literally God and from the Advaitic point of view, it is man who creates God in his image, rather than the other way around. Vivekananda synthesized Western humanism and Advaita to preach the glory of man in a strain loftier than even the highest flights of European Romanticism. Vivekananda's idea of man was of a being who is potentially perfect, divine, and unlimited. The individual requires absolute freedom to realize and manifest her real nature. Vivekananda clearly recognized that this meant not only spiritual freedom but concomitant liberties in the social, political, and cultural dimensions of man's existence.

This has very direct consequences for Indian democracy. While we have come a long way from Independence in building up a liberal democracy, we are still to substantially redeem the promise of fundamental rights guaranteed under the Constitution to each individual citizen. In the constitutional framework of a liberal democracy like India, the individual is the legal locus of all political and civil rights. Over the better part of a decade we have seen an escalation in attacks on fundamental rights, and the emergence of a political culture that suppresses the individual's right to dissent. But the fundamental challenge to the expansion of the space for freedom of expression, life, liberty, and other rights in India, has always been the lack of the necessary cultural soil. Among the many factors (not the least among them being socio-economic) that has prevented India's transformation into a constitutional democracy that works on the ground, has been the inability to translate the centrality of the individual as an autonomous category within our constitutional framework, to a centrality for the individual and her self-expression in our social and cultural life. The attempt to create a culture of modernity in which the autonomy of the individual is recognized has always met entrenched resistance from India's traditional society.

The very notion of individual autonomy has been viewed with suspicion and hostility, as a Western import which goes against Indian culture. When we speak of traditional Indian society, it consists of all religious denominations, but the dominant section that forms that society, and preponderates its ethos, are upper-caste Hindus. For this section, traditional Indian values favour collectivity and stand in contrast to individualism, which they see as a Western intrusion tied to a colonial past; colonialism is equated in their mind with their own loss of power in society. It is difficult to make precise generalizations here, because of the lack of any reliable sociological study or empirical data, but one does not incur much risk of error in supposing that a significant section of upper-caste Hindus see Indian cultural values as coterminous with, or at least significantly overlapping with, Hinduism. It is to this section that the RSS and Sangh Parivar cater, and which it tries to mobilize by blurring the distinction between Hinduism and conservative cultural values as much as possible. With its violent moral policing and cultural edicts against western values, the Sangh Parivar has been at the forefront of an assault on individual rights and values in the name of Hindu culture.

Vivekananda on the other hand, says the exact opposite, that Vedanta, the fountain head of Hinduism, insists on the absolute autonomy of the individual. Indian society's decay over a millennium was because the great truths of the Upanishads, with its concomitant individualism have been kept away from the masses by the priests who invented all sorts of social regulations in order to uphold their own privileges and the power of the upper castes. A non-democratic government is, as Ambedkar says, always the product of a non-democratic, that is autocratic, society. We have seen how both Ambedkar and Vivekananda thought that the necessary pre-requisite for a just form of government was fraternity or mutual empathy. A citizenry that is divided along sectarian identities and cannot rise above narrow self-interests, will produce an ineffective, partisan, or even majoritarian government. But even an effective government which is democratic in form can be tyrannical. It is the age old question of 'who will guard the guardians'? A democratic government can remain democratic only if its actions are continuously monitored by the citizenry. But in order to do that the citizens should be empowered both economically and as individuals, where they can develop their individuality and latent facilities fully. The previous chapter discussed how social myths shape the individual's self-identity in such a way as to keep in check her critical faculties. This ensures that the citizen never comes into her own as an independent being capable of interrogating the social structures that form her and the associated narratives which allows the state to abuse the power it has been entrusted with by the people and use it for the benefit of the few. In an ideal democracy, of course, this should not happen. Vivekananda makes the connection between democracy and individual freedom in a speech he delivered in San Francisco in 1900. The speech addresses the question of whether Vedanta could be the future religion of humankind. In passing, Vivekananda mentions that because America is a democracy there is a chance that Vedanta can become the religion of America, but that it cannot (one assumes he means in the near future) become the religion of India.

> You have a government, but the government is impersonal. Yours is not an autocratic government, and yet it is more powerful than any monarchy in the world.... There is no king. I see everybody equally the same. I have not to take off my hat and bow low to anyone. Yet there is a tremendous power in each man. Vedanta is just that. Its God is not the monarch sitting on a throne, entirely apart. There are those who like their God that way—a God to be feared and propitiated. ...The king is gone from this country at least. Where is the king of heaven now? Just where the earthly king is. In this country the king has entered every one of you. You are all kings in this country. So with the religion of Vedanta. You are all Gods. ...This makes Vedanta very difficult. It does not teach the old idea of God at all. In place of that God who sat above the clouds and managed the affairs of the world without asking our permission, who created us out of nothing just because He liked it and made us undergo all this misery just because He liked it, Vedanta teaches the God that is in everyone, has become everyone and everything. His majesty the king has gone from this country; the Kingdom of Heaven went from Vedanta hundreds of years ago. India cannot give up his majesty the king of the earth—that is why Vedanta cannot become the religion of India. There is a chance of Vedanta becoming the religion of your country because of democracy. But it can become so only if you can and do clearly understand it, if you become real men and women, not people with vague ideas and superstitions in your brains, and if you want to be truly spiritual, since Vedanta is concerned only with spirituality.[24]

AMBEDKAR AND VIVEKANANDA'S DIFFERENCES ON ADVAITA

This chapter began by expounding on the connection between democracy and Advaita using some of Ambedkar's observations and then goes on to show the parallels with Vivekananda's views. There are interesting convergences as well as divergences between Ambedkar and Vivekananda's views on Hinduism as a religion. The divergences are important in the matter of how Advaita links up with Hinduism. This section will take a wider look at Vivekananda and Ambedkar's diametrically opposed views on the topic and try to untangle the issues involved.

In relation to democracy and social life, what Ambedkar and Vivekananda agree on is that the Upanishads preach the identity of the individual soul and Brahman and that such a principle is an invaluable foundation for fraternity and mutual empathy within a political unit. But Ambedkar further claims that 1) Upanishadic monism or (what he calls) Brahmaism is unknown to the Hindus though it is present in Hindu philosophical thought; 2) Upanishadic monism is different from the Vedanta Hindus know and which considers the world an illusion. This refers to the Vedanta school of philosophy, specially, Shankara's Advaita Vedanta and its concept of maya. Vivekananda would disagree with both these contentions.

Ambedkar defines what he calls Brahmaism thus.

'The essence of Brahmaism is summed up in a dogma which is stated in three different forms.

They are:

(i) *Sarvam Khalvidam Brahma*—All this is Brahma.
(ii) *Aham Brahmasmi*—Atmana (Self) is the same as Brahma. Therefore I am Brahma.
(iii) *Tattvamasi*—Atmana (Self) is the same as Brahma. Therefore thou art also Brahma

They are called Mahavakyas which means Great Sayings and they sum up the essence of Brahmaism.'[25]

The three mahavakyas are from the Chandogya Upanishad 3.14.1 (Sama Veda), Brihadaryanaka Upanishad 1.4.10 (Yajur Veda), and Chandogya Upanishad 6.8.7 (Sama Veda) respectively.[26] Together they constitute the essence of the monism of the Upanishads. The first mahavakya, 'All this is Brahman' proclaims the identity of the world with Brahman, or the ultimate reality. The second and third mahavakya declare the oneness of the individual Self and Brahman. This is fundamentally the monism found in the Upanishads. This is also the metaphysics that Vivekananda taught. Vivekananda makes repeated use of the sayings 'Aham Brahmasmi' and 'Tattvamasi' as the cornerstone of his philosophy of Advaita. While he does not use the phrase 'Sarvam Khalvidam

Brahma' (All this is Brahma), he talks of Brahman as the reality behind the world, or as God 'objectified'. But Vivekananda identifies this philosophy with Vedanta, specifically, the Advaitic school and not as an esoteric doctrine unknown to mainstream Hinduism.

While Ambedkar says that the Hindus are unfamiliar with what he terms Brahmaism, he says what they are familiar with is the Vedanta.

Ambedkar defines Vedanta thus:

'The following are the dogmas which sum up the teachings of Vedant (sic)—

I.   Brahma is the only reality.
II. The world is maya or unreal.
III. Jiva and Brahma are—

(i)   according to one school identical;
(ii) according to another not identical but are elements of him and not separate from him;
(iii) according to the third school they are distinct and separate.'[27]

In the classification Ambedkar gives above, Vedanta refers to the philosophical school which starts with Shankara. (i) refers to the Advaita school of non-dualism, (ii) refers to the Vishishtadvaitic school of qualified non-dualism, and (iii) refers to the Dvaita school of dualism.

The important point for Ambedkar here concerning Vedanta is II, that the world is maya or unreal. It is on this that Ambedkar bases his differentiation between Vedanta and what he calls Brahmaism, or the monism of the Upanishads, which is what Vivekananda also preached. Why is this crucial? Ambedkar and Vivekananda's claims about Upanishadic monism being the surest foundation of democracy hangs on the identity of each individual self with the cosmic principle or ultimate reality called Brahman. If people actually accepted the meaning of the mahavakyas and practised the same, they would see themselves in the other person, and would be as committed to protecting the rights of others as their own.

But all this obtains only if the world and the sentient creatures in it are real. According to Advaita as expounded by Shankara, the world is maya and only Brahman is real. Ambedkar, like many others who have commented on the Advaita Vedanta philosophy, understands this to mean that the world is unreal. If the world is unreal, then individual souls are just illusions, and ethics have no importance. The only duty of every individual then becomes that of securing his liberation (moksha) and things that maintain the social status quo, including the caste system, are no longer objectionable because they belong to the realm of unreal maya. Throughout the nineteenth and early twentieth centuries, many Western scholars who were sympathetic to Hinduism, (as well as polemical Christian missionaries) blamed Hinduism's supposed belief in the unreality of the world for its lack of initiative regarding social reform and doing social good.

We need to keep the history of Hindu thought in mind to understand the context of the disagreement. Most of the Upanishads, which occur at the end of the Vedas, express an absolute monism where the real self (Atman) of all sentient beings and the physical universe is declared as identical to the Absolute cosmic principle (Brahman). The Mukhya Upanishads or Principal Upanishads, which are thirteen in number, were composed somewhere beginning between 800 and 600 BCE and ending in the early centuries of the first millennium CE. During this time, several heterodox sects like Buddhists, Jains, and Ajivikas arose which denied the authority of the Vedas and some of which became separate religions. The Mukhya Upanishads* composed before the common era, mainly present monism or non-dualism as discoveries of mystical experiences. As Indian philosophical systems started to take shape over the centuries of the first millennium CE, and various kinds of debates between Buddhistic and Hindu philosophical schools like Nyaya and Vaisheshika took place, the monism of the Upanishads received only a skeletal philosophical treatment in the *Brahmasutras*, a commentary on the Upanishads (400 CE). It was not until the emergence of Shankara in the eighth century CE, that the monism of the Upanishads was built into a complete metaphysical system. It acquired the name of Vedanta.[†] Its central doctrine was Advaita or non-duality, and subsequent schools based on the Vedanta named themselves Vishistadvaita, Dvaita, Shuddhadvaita, etc., to differentiate themselves from Shankara's Advaitic position, against which all of them were arguing. By Vivekananda's time and probably even in Ambedkar's, Vedanta came to be used as a synonym for Advaita and the theory of maya. Presenting a truth at an intuitive or mystical level as the Upanishads do, is an entirely different business from constructing a rational philosophical system that can reconcile intuitive truth with reality

---

*In the later Upanishads too, while there is philosophical argumentation against opponents, there is no attempt at systematic philosophizing.

†The Advaitic system did not originate with Shankara, though he was the one who gave it a decisive form. There was an earlier Advaitic tradition about whose protagonists not much is known. Shankara's immediate predecessor in this philosophic tradition was Gaudapada, who composed an Advaitic treatise called the Manduka Karyaka.

as we know it, without inviting contradictions or logical errors. As spiritual texts, it was enough for the writers of the Upanishads to declare what they claimed they had realized in mystical experience; that the true reality is non-dual and undifferentiated Brahman and that world too is Brahman. But as a philosopher, Shankara was faced with the thorny problem of how to reconcile the non-dual Brahman with the world of multiplicity. It is in order to explain away the perception of multiplicity, that Shankara deploys the concept of maya, which he borrows from the Buddhists and modifies. Though many orthodox Hindus certainly read some of the Upanishads, they understood it through the prism of Shankara's philosophical system. It was a prevalent idea among many sections that maya meant that the world was unreal. But this is almost certainly a misconception.

As the late Hendrick Vroom, a scholar of the philosophy of religion wrote, 'The term Maya has been translated as "illusion," but then it does not concern normal illusion. Here "illusion" does not mean that the world is not real and simply a figment of the human imagination. Maya means that the world is not as it seems; the world that one experiences is misleading as far as its true nature is concerned.'[28] Commenting on the Vedantic world view, Wendy Doniger writes: 'To say that the universe is an illusion (maya) is not to say that it is unreal; it is to say, instead, that it is not what it seems to be, that it is something constantly being made. Maya not only deceives people about the things they think they know; more basically, it limits their knowledge to things that are epistemologically and ontologically second-rate.'[29] Apart from the purely philosophical, even at the level of lived religion, Ambedkar's claim that the Hindus did not know the idea that the world and every creature is one with God, does not seem warranted by the facts. Though it is difficult to trace its definite contours back through history, a mysticism with a unitive world view seems to have been very much a part of the Hindu tradition, finding its more recent representatives in mystics like Sri Ramakrishna.

In Ramakrishna's words, taken down by his disciple Mahendranath Gupta, 'God alone has become everything. All that we perceive is so many forms of God. Narendra (Vivekananda) used to make fun of me and say: Yes, God has become all! Then a pot is God, a cup is God! …I used to worship the Deity in the Kali temple. It was suddenly revealed to me that everything is Pure Spirit. The utensils of worship, the altar, the door-frame—all pure spirit. Men, animals and other living beings—all Pure Spirit.'[30] In Ambedkar's own time, we have for example the Bengali saint Anandamayi Ma (1896–1982) whose preaching also expressed the fundamental unity of all existence. She saw the whole universe, including human beings as a manifestation of the divine. She says in one of her recorded conversations about the relationship between Brahman and the world:

> Some people call him arupa (formless) and anama (nameless), which is the subject of Advaita philosophy. If He is said to be nameless and formless, then, what is He? He is nirakara Brahman (the formless supreme). He is the Supreme Spirit, the Supreme Atman. This idea is akin to the idea of water and ice. What is ice? Water only. And what is water? Ice only. The water is ice and the ice is water. The ice is the name of the special formation of the water. Similarly, this jagat (world) is akin to the ice. Just like the ice is nothing but water, even so this world is nothing but Hari (an epithet of Vishnu) alone. One should see Hari in the world as he sees water in ice. This world is the vigraha (individual form or image) of that Eternal Formless Brahman.[31]

While Vivekananda would not agree with Ambedkar's assessment that Hindus themselves did not know the central message of the Upanishads, he would agree with him that the message was kept from Hindu society at large. The doctrine of Advaita, of the identity of Atman and Brahman, remained an esoteric doctrine confined to sanyasins who led a life of renunciation and cut themselves off from society. Thus, these ideas with their potential for egalitarianism and the empowerment of the individual never became common currency in society. In some places, Vivekananda seemed to take the view that this was deliberately done to maintain the social hierarchy. The core of Vivekananda' message to India was what he called 'Practical Vedanta' wherein the Advaitic ideals would be broadcast to the nation and be worked out not only on the spiritual plane but also in social life.

In a speech on the application of Vedanta, he said:

> What can we not do? Everything can be done by us; we all have the same glorious soul, let us believe in it. Have faith, as Nachiketa…. This is the strength that you get from the Upanishads, this is the faith that you get from there. Ay, but it was only for the Sannyasin! Rahasya (esoteric)! The Upanishads were in the hands of the Sannyasin; he went into the forest! Shankara was a little kind and said even Grihasthas (householders) may study the Upanishads, it will do them good; it will not hurt them. But still the idea is that the Upanishads talked only of the forest life of the recluse. As I told you the other day, the only commentary, the authoritative commentary on the Vedas, has been made once and for all by Him who

inspired the Vedas—by Krishna in the Gita. It is there for every one in every occupation of life. These conceptions of the Vedanta must come out, must remain not only in the forest, not only in the cave, but they must come out to work at the bar and the bench, in the pulpit, and in the cottage of the poor man, with the fishermen that are catching fish, and with the students that are studying. They call to every man, woman, and child whatever be their occupation, wherever they may be.[32]

THE POLITICAL: GENDER

American women! A hundred lives would not be sufficient to pay my deep debt of gratitude to you!... 'The Oriental hyperbole' alone expresses the depth of Oriental gratitude—'If the Indian Ocean were an inkstand, the highest mountain of the Himalaya the pen, the earth the scroll and time itself the writer' still it will not express my gratitude to you!... And then the modern American women—I admire their broad and liberal minds.

—Letter to Maharaja of Khetri, 1894[1]

We can see the same kind of ahistorical analysis, indifference to social context, and the free play of historical anachronism, which we have talked about before, operating in contemporary critiques of Vivekananda attitude towards women. It would be superfluous and tedious to demonstrate how these intellectual failures account for the negative judgements about Vivekananda and gender put forward by many present-day academics. Vivekananda was, by the standards of his time especially, not a misogynist. Any sexism that has been evidenced in his writings or speeches has more to do with the language available in the discourse at the time rather than his own personal feelings. This chapter will be confined to locating Vivekananda's views on women within the gender discourse of his own day. Compared to the prevalent views on women's inherent value, their equality with men, and the role women were to play in society, Vivekananda's views are extraordinarily enlightened for a man belonging to the late Victorian age. I hope to show the reader how absurd it is to read Vivekananda as sexist, let alone as the originator of a version of Hinduism entwined with ideological masculinity.[*]

What set apart the stretch of time between roughly the 1850s and the 1920s in the Western world, and the ages that preceded it, was the emergence at the broadest levels of a discourse on women's rights. The advance of industrial capitalism was redefining women's roles in the workforce, society, public letters,

---

[*]See for example, Jyotirmaya Sharma's *Human Love and Cosmic Apathy* and Indira Chowdhury's 'Spiritual Masculinity and Swami Vivekananda' in *Debating Vivekananda*.

and even politics. While earlier, the idea of women's biological, intellectual, and even spiritual inferiority was accepted as a matter of course, now, those who held such opinions were forced to offer arguments in support of their view. The conversation on women's rights thus encompassed a spectrum of positions from patriarchal reactionism, moderate reform, and liberal positions to radical emancipation. Hardly any public figure could hold off from taking some kind of a position on the issue at some point in their careers. As the historian Kathleen Canning writes: 'The "woman question" was articulated in the arena of both high and low politics and attempts to resolve it crisscrossed disparate political and cultural milieus and transcended boundaries of class, ethnicity, region and religion. At some point in the history of the nineteenth century, each nation and each social group addressed a "woman question" and sought resolutions according to its own capacities and ideologies.'[2]

Many prominent thinkers, writers, and public figures of this time are recognized to have held views that were misogynist, sexist, and patriarchal even relative to the normative standards of the age. Prominent examples from the time include the Germans philosophers Friedrich Nietzsche and Arthur Schopenhauer, Soren Kierkegaard, the founder of existentialist philosophy; and Charles Darwin, who discovered the theory of evolution. But Victorian writers and thinkers who are not generally considered sexist took positions on the 'woman question' and brought to bear upon it ideas of gender roles, which from our vantage point will sound decidedly regressive. For example, Leo Tolstoy wrote in his diary, 'For seventy years I have been steadily lowering and lowering my opinion of women, and I must still lower it more and more. The woman question!—How could there not be a woman question! Only not about how women should control life, but how they should stop ruining it.'[3] Friedrich Engels, along with Karl Marx, constructed the Marxist analysis of how women are oppressed by the capitalist system and function as property within the family system. Engels's analysis would influence succeeding generations of feminists. Nonetheless, Engels proved susceptible to the kind of patriarchal stereotypes that we now know to be instruments to control female independence and sexuality. In his classic study of the industrial working class of England, Engels examined the effects of the employment of women in factories.

> The employment of the wife dissolves the family utterly and of necessity, and this dissolution, in our present society, which is based upon the family, brings the most demoralising consequences for parents as well as children. A mother who has no time to trouble herself about her child, to perform the most ordinary loving services for it during its first year,

who scarcely indeed sees it, can be no real mother to the child…. In many cases the family is not wholly dissolved by the employment of the wife, but turned upside down. The wife supports the family, the husband sits at home, tends the children, sweeps the room and cooks…. [T]his condition…degrades, in the most shameful way, both sexes, and, through them, Humanity.

[A] girl who has worked in a mill from her ninth year is in no position to understand domestic work…. The moral consequences of the employment of women in factories are even worse. The collecting of persons of both sexes and all ages in a single work-room, the inevitable contact…is not calculated for the favourable development of the female character. A witness in Leicester said that he would rather let his daughter beg than go into a factory…. Another, in Manchester, 'did not hesitate to assert that three-fourths of the young factory employees, from fourteen to twenty years of age, were unchaste'…. And Dr. Hawkins says: 'An estimate of sexual morality is scarcely possible to be reduced into figures; but…a most discouraging view of the influence of the factory life upon the morality of female youth obtrudes itself.'[4]

In India, the woman question came into prominence because of the socio-economic and intellectual changes brought on by British colonialism. The terms of the debate were different in India, but much of the substance was the same. A figure with one of the broadest and most universal outlooks among the intellectuals of the late Bengal Renaissance was the poet Rabindranath Tagore. A true cosmopolitan and humanist, he stood aside as a voice of reason when nationalist sentiments engulfed the country in the early twentieth century. Although a great supporter and admirer of Gandhi and the independence movement, he urged the spread of internationalism as a counterweight to neutralize the dangers inherent in nationalism. Tagore promoted the education of girls, especially at Shantiniketan, the school his father Debendranath Tagore had founded, and he was a fierce critic of the oppression of women caused by the unequal power dynamic between the genders. He wanted women to play a more active role in social life. Nonetheless, Tagore was unable to conceptualize equality for women beyond a deified role. Women in their goodness and moral purity were to encourage and help men overcome their brutish tendencies and create a spirit of harmony at home and in society where human endeavours would flourish. Tagore could accept the spiritual equality of men and women, placing woman on a higher pedestal. But he could not accept the intellectual equality of women or consider them capable of the same skill as men. Consequently, he considered it undesirable for women to be active in many areas of traditional male endeavours, especially thinking and entrepreneurship.

In 1922, twenty years after Vivekananda's death, Tagore wrote an essay called 'Women and Home':

> Creative expressions attain their perfect form through emotions modulated. Woman has that expression natural to her.... She has been an inspiration to man, guiding, most often unconsciously, his restless energy into an immense variety of creations in literature, art, music and religion. This is why, in India, woman has been described as the symbol of Shakti, the creative power.... But if woman begins to believe that, though biologically her function is different from that of man, psychologically she is identical with him; if the human world in its mentality becomes exclusively male, then before long it will be reduced to utter inanity. For life finds its truth and beauty, not in any exaggeration of sameness, but in harmony.... [W]hen woman refuses to acknowledge the distinction between her life and that of man, she does not convince us of its truth, but only proves to us that she is suffering. ...In the present case, the wrong is in woman's lack of freedom in her relationship with man, which compels her to turn her disabilities into attractions, and to use untruths as her allies in the battle of life, while she is suffering from the precariousness of her position. From the beginning of our society, women have naturally accepted the training which imparts to their life and to their home a spirit of harmony. It is their instinct to perform their services in such a manner that these, through beauty, might be raised from the domain of slavery to the realm of grace.... Thus the Eastern woman, who is deeply aware in her heart of the sacredness of her mission, is a constant education to man.... Woman has to be ready to suffer. ...Women of India, like women everywhere, have their share of suffering, but it radiates through the ideal, and becomes, like sunlight, a creative force in their world....
>
> Our women know by heart the legends of the great women of the epic age—Savitri who by the power of love conquered death, and Sita who had no other reward for her life of sacrifice but the sacred majesty of sorrow.
>
> ...[T]heir activity is not for money-making, or organizing power, or intellectually probing the mystery of existence, but for establishing and maintaining human relationships requiring the highest moral qualities.[5]

Vivekananda, on the other hand believed in the complete equality of men and women in their mental, intellectual, and spiritual capabilities as far back as 1893. We have Vivekananda's correspondence only from 1887 onwards, and it would seem that his experiences in America radicalized his ideas of women's capabilities and their place in society. A letter written to Indumati Mitra in May 1893, a few months before he sailed for America, shows that Vivekananda retained traditional ideas of gender roles, in spite of his doctrine of the fundamental spiritual unity of all souls. He wrote in passing: 'Please be careful not to become impure even in thought, as also in speech and action; always try to do good to others as far as in you lies. And remember that the paramount duty of a woman is to serve her husband by thought, word, and deed.'[6] This was not particularly surprising for a young Indian man in the 1890s. Vivekananda did not have the advantage of studying in a coeducational college (there were none in India at that time) and all his interactions with women until his college days were within the traditional confines of Hindu homes. He hardly came into contact with women in the years after he took up sanyas and had no significant interaction with independent-minded Indian women or with the nascent discourse of gender equality in India. But his contact with American women, more educated, independent, and cultured than in any country at the end of the nineteenth century, speedily brought him to the conclusion that gender difference was merely biological and women were in every other respect equal to men.

On 22 September 1893, Vivekananda delivered a lecture on the women of India at the Parliament of Religions in Chicago. He remarked inter alia that the 'best thermometer to the progress of a nation is its treatment of women' and the 'idea of perfect womanhood is perfect independence'.[7] Three days later, in a letter written to his brother disciples, he wrote that he would die in peace if he could raise a thousand women in India who had the spirit of the American women whom he had met and admired. He went on to declare, 'I shall not rest till I root out this distinction of sex. Is there any sex-distinction in the Atman (Self)? Out with the differentiation between man and woman.'[*] Afterwards, he told an American friend that women could do everything that man could do. Later, when he was touring the Eastern United States, he said in a talk, 'Women in statesmanship, managing territories, governing countries, even making war, have proved themselves equal to men, if not superior. In India, I have no doubt of that. Whenever they have had the opportunity they have proved that they have as much ability as men.'[8]

The oppressed condition of women became a central concern for

---

*See Chapter 4, p. 136.

Vivekananda. He was especially appalled by the condition of Indian women who were illiterate (except for an elite minority), and had no access to public life, professions, or economic independence. Vivekananda was a vocal proponent of women's education, of stopping child marriage and increasing the age of marriage for girls. He planned to start a math for women, something unknown in India since Buddhist times. Though his plans were not realized in his lifetime, the Ramakrishna Mission eventually established maths for women. There were many social reformers in India at that time, especially in Bengal, who took similar stands on these obstacles that kept Indian women suppressed; some likely had more progressive ideas on how to change women's conditions in India than Vivekananda. But Vivekananda stood out among the Indian intelligentsia of his time for having a well-developed view about the universal condition of women as oppressed by a male dominated society. Though his travels in the West opened him up to the superlative freedom, education, and culture Western women possessed in relation to Indian women, it was clear to him that everywhere in the world, including the West, women were still dominated by male society. He recognized that the nature of female oppression in society was structural. In a letter written from America to his brother disciple Swami Ramakrishnananda, he wrote: "There is no chance for the welfare of the world unless the condition of women is improved. It is not possible for a bird to fly on only one wing."[9]

Vivekananda's commitment to women's equality was absolute, at least at the philosophical level. This proceeded from his Advaitic convictions, which as we saw in the previous chapter, imply the spiritual identity and equality of all beings. For Vivekananda, man was the highest manifestation of the divine; all differentiations, whether of religion, creed, caste, or gender, were illusory impositions of the mind. Human beings differed only in the goodness of their nature, in the degree to which they had been able to manifest the divinity within them. In the Western intellectual tradition, starting from Plato, what set human beings apart and above animals, was their rational faculty. For Vivekananda, it seems that what made humans special from other living creatures was not rationality, but the possibility of ethical choice, of possessing a moral conscience.[*] This line of thinking is very much present in classical Indian philosophy, though it is more often articulated in salvific terms. But Vivekananda took the special status of human beings to be more expansive than

---

[*]Vivekananda does not, to my knowledge, state this explicitly. But it can be inferred from his moral philosophy.

merely the manifestation of goodness. Each soul was the manifestation within material conditions of the infinite Absolute and the aim of life was to manifest the soul's inherent divinity and potentialities. Vivekananda said, 'Everything that is strong, and good, and powerful in human nature is the outcome of that divinity, and though potential in many, there is no difference between man and man essentially, all being alike divine. There is, as it were, an infinite ocean behind, and you and I are so many waves, coming out of that infinite ocean; and each one of us is trying his best to manifest that infinite outside. So, potentially, each one of us has that infinite ocean of Existence, Knowledge, and Bliss as our birthright, our real nature.'[10] The word 'man' here is used in its non-gendered generic sense to mean human being. From this doctrine of the universal equality of human potential, the principle of the absolute equality of the sexes, follows inevitably. The Advaitic doctrine as Vivekananda expressed it, did not admit of the slightest room of differentiation between human beings in terms of their potentials and capabilities on the basis of sex or race.

Vivekananda pointed this out repeatedly to his brother disciples, disciples, and admirers, all of whom were at least nominally Advaitists. Within the Hindu philosophical tradition, spiritual bondage and maya arises from the soul's erroneous identification with the body. He appealed to this very tradition to change social attitudes that held women as unequal to men. Vivekananda first pointed out that the true spiritual Self of human beings is beyond gender differentiations. 'The soul is also sexless; we cannot say of the Atman that it is a man or a woman. Sex belongs to the body alone. All such ideas, therefore, as man or woman, are a delusion when spoken with regard to the Self, and are only proper when spoken of the body.'[11] Next, he would go on to emphasize that sexual difference exists only on the relative plane of earthly existence and that as one grows more and more spiritual and recognizes the essential Self of human beings, the idea that men and women have essentially different natures, vanishes. 'In the highest reality of the Parabrahman, there is no distinction of sex. We notice this only in the relative plane. And the more the mind becomes introspective, the more that idea of difference vanishes.... Therefore do I say that though outwardly there may be difference between men and women, in their real nature there is none.'[12] The idea of women's freedom was linked to Western ideas and formed the basis of rejection or suspicion among many sections in India based on either xenophobia or just resentment of the colonial cultural hegemony. Vivekananda strived to show that the idea of the equality of the sexes was inherently present in the Indian spiritual tradition and that it was important to do away with the idea of gender differences in human ability if one were to enter the world of true spirituality. He said, 'The great Aryans, Buddha among the rest, have always put woman in an equal position with man. For them sex in religion did not exist. In the Vedas and Upanishads, women taught the highest truths and received the same veneration as men.'[13]

One of the reasons that Vivekananda's extremely enlightened position on women, which was far ahead of his times, has not been sufficiently appreciated, is due to his refusal to categorically affirm the freedom of women in many areas which were marginal discussions in his time, but have assumed centrality in our own. These have to do with things like the relation between the sexes, the extent of women's sexual freedom, and questions of whether women would 'unsex' themselves by throwing off all restraints and making 'masculine' activities their own. But as we saw earlier, this was part of Vivekananda's general attitude to all sociopolitical issues; even those which he championed passionately. He considered that as far as was practical, he had no right to dictate to society what course of action it should take, but rather illumine the issues in light of what he believed were the right moral and spiritual principles to be applied in these cases. People had to work out its application on their own by making these principles their own, for all true growth, he was convinced, came from within and could not be achieved with people following prescriptions laid down by others.

This was particularly so in the case of women whose destinies and roles have been determined by men for millennia. It is important to understand that on the finer aspects of the women's question, where Vivekananda maintained an agnostic (at least outwardly) stand, the debate was not just between conservative men and emancipated women, but also within the emerging women's rights movements. Vivekananda considered that it was not the place of a man to advocate what women should or should not do in the cause of their emancipation. Their duty was to remove social and economic obstacles from women's paths and provide the cultural and educational resources they required to raise themselves. He told Indians: 'Educate your women first and leave them to themselves; then they will tell you what reforms are necessary for them. In matters concerning them, who are you?'[14] He was confident that the so-called 'women's question' was something that women themselves were capable of answering on their own terms. 'Women will work out their destinies—much better, too, than men can ever do for them. All the mischief to women has come because men undertook to shape the destiny of women.'[15]

There are passages and speeches in Vivekananda's oeuvre where themes such as the ideal of women's motherhood and of the ideal of women's chastity as the centre of the Hindu household, are descanted upon. But again, these must be understood in their context; as delivered to American audiences who were embedded in a racist discourse that stereotyped Hindu women as sexually licentious and prone to infanticide (see Chapter 5). To say that Vivekananda's views on women's freedom were much ahead of his time is not, however, to say that he was a twentieth century feminist in nineteenth century clothing. However, egalitarian his vision was, he was bound by the ignorance of his age, by the horizons of possibility that hemmed in conceptions of gender and historical distance from the feminist movement which would not break out into the public sphere until a decade or two after his death. In other words, he was mortal. He held out the all-renouncing Sita as the ideal for Indian women. He sometimes used language that if used today would be clearly sexist. Like many reformers throughout history who preached freedom, he seemed to have worried that freedom could lead to anarchy. We find him at places cautioning Indian women against losing their spirituality by running after new ideas of materialism.

The fact is that it would be truly difficult, to locate men or women who held feminist views as we understand them today, in the late Victorian age, except for some exceptional feminists. Even women who dedicated their lives to the cause of women's rights were circumscribed in the conception of gender roles that they aspired for women. Perhaps nothing illustrates how truly egalitarian and ahead of his times Vivekananda's views as a man on gender were, as much as his views on women's suffrage. Vivekananda categorically supported the enfranchisement of women in the 1890s.

The demand for women to be given the right to vote had been voiced in both Britain and America since the mid-nineteenth century. But the limited franchise given to men based on class, and the overall economic condition, did not favour a mass movement in favour of the women's vote. By the last decades of the nineteenth century though, from being regarded as a fringe issue raised only by 'disreputable' women, women's suffrage became a part of public discussions. In 1884, when the British government introduced the Third Reform Act, an amendment was actually introduced in the male-only house to grant women the vote. The amendment was defeated as only one-third of the members of parliament voted in favour of it.[16] At the same time, an anti-women's rights reaction was growing in both Britain and America. In the first decade of the twentieth century, things came to a head when some suffragettes in Britain adopted tactics like boycotting, picketing, and even bombing public property. The police arrested the women and treated them brutally. A similar process played out in the USA. After World War I ended, British women gained the right to vote in 1918 and American women in 1920. A major reason was that the labour participation of women in the war had drastically altered traditional views about the propriety of women participating in public life.

It was not merely that in the first decade of the twentieth century voting rights for women had insufficient support among the majority of the public (both men and women). The idea of women taking part in representative politics was such a tectonic shift in the moral and social conception of womanhood, that it split the women's rights movement itself into those who supported and opposed voting rights. It would be difficult, if not actually silly, to judge women who had defied Victorian patriarchy and dedicated themselves to the upliftment of women of being sexist or being co-opted by patriarchy for being anti-suffrage. The surprising stance of those who were anti-suffrage points to how complex gender issues appeared in a period of unprecedented historical transition, how difficult it was to achieve intellectual clarity as fundamental concepts of identity underwent change, and how commitment to egalitarian principles by themselves could not often break the stranglehold of the past on one's political imagination.

One of the most prominent women to oppose women's voting rights during the suffragette movement was the famous Beatrice Webb. Though not known to the public at large today, Beatrice Webb has an important place in British intellectual history. A sociologist and economist, she coined the now well-known concept of 'collective bargaining'. A socialist, she, along with her husband Sydney Webb, was the central influence on the Fabian Society, a society dedicated to bringing about socialism by peaceful means and whose members included Bernard Shaw, H. G. Wells, and Bertrand Russell. She was one of the founders of the London School of Economics, whose early institutional thought was very much influenced by Beatrice Webb's economic theories. She was also a social reformer who studied the condition of women in factories and argued for equal pay for women.

Beatrice Webb opposed women's suffrage initially. In 1908, Mary Ward, one of the most popular novelists of her time and a promoter of female education, founded the Women's National Anti-Suffrage League. Next year she prepared a petition against giving women the vote which garnered 250,000 signatures and to which Webb added her name. Webb, who years later changed her stance on women's suffrage, wrote about her motives for opposing it. Firstly, Webb had an aversion to women speaking in public. She said this of women speaking in public: 'It is not womanly, to thrust yourself before the world. A woman, in all relations, should be sought.'[17] In spite of her extraordinary intellectual achievements as well as her work to alleviate the poverty of women, Beatrice Webb was still discomfitted by the idea that women would 'unsex' themselves by taking part in political activity. She would later write in her autobiography: 'But at the root of my anti-feminism lay the fact that I had never myself experienced the disabilities assumed to arise from my sex. Quite the contrary.... In the craft I had chosen a woman was privileged.... A competent female writer on economic questions had, to an enterprising editor, actually a scarcity value.'[18]

Mary Ward's motives are debated. But her objections stemmed at least partly from the same ones of women unsexing themselves. She probably also subscribed to what then was considered an ultra-feminine position: that women had to set a higher moral standard for men. In this view, the wild brutality of men's nature could only be channelled into civilized behaviour by women setting a higher example. The National Women's Anti-Suffragette League had several women who had pursued independent and successful careers in traditionally male domains. The most outstanding member in this respect was probably Gertrude Bell. Gertrude Bell was the first woman to be awarded a degree at Oxford, the first woman to be employed by the British intelligence, and the first British woman to write a government white paper. She was also a writer, traveller, and archaeologist, and influenced British foreign policy in the Middle East and played a significant role in establishing the modern state of Iraq. Yet Bell not only did not think women should have the vote, but actively campaigned against it. The reasons had to do partly with British party politics, and the fear that since a majority of the women were less literate, giving them a say in representative government would affect Great Britain negatively, as well as her idiosyncratic and rather inconsistent views on the importance of motherhood. Whatever they might be, these views clouded her judgement on the question of women's suffrage. Bell eventually changed her mind on women's voting rights, years after women gained the vote in Britain.

Another important campaigner against women's suffrage was Violet Markham, a social reformer who made important contributions to education, including the education of girls, which was a lesser priority for governments in the nineteenth century. She also worked on alleviating the effects of unemployment and poverty on women. In a speech at an anti-suffrage meeting held in London in 1912, she said: 'We believe that men and women are different—not similar—beings, with talents that are complementary, not identical, and that they therefore ought to have different shares in the management of the State, that they severally compose. We do not depreciate by one jot or tittle women's work and mission. We are concerned to find proper channels of expression for that work. We seek a fruitful diversity of political function, not a stultifying uniformity.'[19] Markham too eventually changed her mind on suffrage, to the extent that she stood for elections and became the first female mayor of Chesterfield in 1927.

There were, of course, men in America and Britain who were not part of the socialist movement but supported women's suffrage. But they, like Mark Twain and the English writer Lytton Strachey, were intimately involved in political circles. Vivekananda on the other hand, operating exclusively in the domain of religion in the West, was completely isolated from the more liberal political voices for women's suffrage. Indeed, we do not seem to have any record of him interacting with a suffragist. (In the 1890s, radical suffragism had not begun and female suffragist voices were not given much press coverage.) In an interview given to an American newspaper in 1894, Vivekananda spoke on current political issues, something he rarely did as a rule, confining his opinions to private correspondence. After criticizing the American government's xenophobic ban on Chinese immigration, Vivekananda spoke on the problems facing Indian and American women. 'There is no such thing as divorce in India,' he said; 'our law does not allow it. Our women are more limited in their sphere than the women of America. Some of them are as highly educated. They are entering the medical profession to some extent now. I see no reason why American women should not vote.'[20] It is then to Vivekananda's immense credit that his belief in the inherent equality of sexes gave him the intellectual clarity to see that there was no sound basis to deny women the right to vote. On the suffrage issue, he also managed to free himself from the pull of conceptions of female identity and women's role in political life stemming from the existing patriarchal structure of Western society; a rock on which even several women who had passionately dedicated their lives to the feminist cause, floundered.

What is the basis then, of the various critiques of Vivekananda as promoting a patriarchal or masculine identity? They play upon Vivekananda's frequent exhortations to people to manliness and strength. This, together with Vivekananda's philosophy of a 'man-making education', have been interpreted as promoting masculinity and, in various permutations and combinations with elements like nationalism and Hinduism, have produced readings that his thinking endorses some kind of ideological masculinity. Some readings link this supposed ideology of masculinity with the puritanical masculinity of RSS thought through their shared valorization of Hinduism; thus rendering Vivekananda a Hindu nationalist. In other words, these critiques affirm the position of the RSS on Vivekananda.

On the whole, these critiques proceed to analyse Vivekananda's ideology as patriarchal either without any reference to his innumerable statements on the absolute equality of men and women; or by glossing over them. To put things in perspective, in *The Complete Works of Vivekananda*, which runs over 4,500 pages, there are exactly sixteen times where Vivekananda uses the word 'manliness' and twelve times he uses the word 'manly'. One would think that a person who wants to construct an ideology of masculinity would at least use it with a modicum of regularity. Apart from this, if one reads the contexts in which Vivekananda defines 'manliness' as a virtue, it is clear that he uses the word primarily in a non-gendered sense, to refer to both the male sex and to the human being in general. It is only after the 1960s that feminists pointed out the structural sexism of conceptualizing all humanity as male.

Vivekananda used manliness to refer to strength and the quality of being heroic. It is true that manliness as a traditional virtue exemplifying strength and heroism has been understood as a masculine virtue. But Vivekananda elicits these qualities by referring to the biological male as the referent of the word, only to abstract these qualities from their gendered setting and re-ground them in the referent of manliness as being human. Since for Vivekananda, the human was potentially divine, he used manliness mainly to refer to a spiritual quality. Within the domain of spirituality, strength and heroism denoted a host of qualities most of which are different, and many are opposite to the qualities associated with traditional masculinity. The sense with which Vivekananda used the words manliness and manly, can be easily gleaned by examining a few instances of their utterance.

To a disciple vexed that he was unable to attain spiritual realization, Vivekananda said:

> What fear? If there is sincerity of spirit, I tell you, for a certainty, you will attain it in this very life. But manly endeavour is wanted. Do you know what it is? 'I shall certainly attain Self-knowledge. Whatever obstacles may come, I shall certainly overcome them'—a firm determination like this is Purushakara. 'Whether my mother, father, friends, brothers, wife, and children live or die, whether this body remains or goes, I shall never turn back till I attain to the vision of the Atman'—this resolute endeavour to advance towards one's goal, setting at naught all other considerations, is termed manly endeavour…. If you follow the common run of people in the world and float with the general current, where then is your manliness?[21]

Here Vivekananda is using the word manliness to mean determination and individuality. Vivekananda did not consider that either of these qualities belonged only to the male sex. This is clear in a letter he writes to Mary

Hale, where he pleads with her to inculcate the quality of manliness, by which he seems to mean individuality and determination. Individuality has never been considered one of the traditional male virtues; this is something Vivekananda derives from his conception of what it means to manifest the latent potentialities of the human being. 'My instincts may be very feminine, but what I am exercised with just this moment is, that you get a little bit of manliness about you. Oh! Mary, your brain, health, beauty, everything is going to waste just for lack of that one essential—assertion of individuality. Your haughtiness, spirit, etc., are all nonsense, only mockery.... This is very harsh, very brutal; but I can't help it. I love you, Mary, sincerely, genuinely; I can't cheat you with namby-pamby sugar candies. Nor do they ever come to me. Then again, I am a dying man; I have no time to fool in. Wake up, girl.'[22]

It was true enough that in Vivekananda's time especially, being feminine and being manly were associated with the two genders along with an associated set of qualities. The positive qualities were tenderness, kindness, self-sacrifice etc., in the case of women, and courage, emotional control, and strength in the case of men. But in many places in Vivekananda's discourse, we can find statements pointing to the fact that he did not believe that the qualities of femininity and masculinity, in so far as they were applicable, said anything about the essential nature of men and women. We have seen before Vivekananda categorically asserting that gender difference was only biological and there was no difference in the internal (mental or intellectual) nature of men and women. The 'feminine' and 'masculine' qualities that both the sexes displayed, Vivekananda understood, were a product of historical circumstances. Women developed the qualities they displayed, both positive and negative, within the circumstances of male-dominated oppression, while men developed their corresponding characteristics in the plenitude of opportunity available to them and in relation to the power and dominance they enjoyed in various domains. Vivekananda envisaged a far distant future where women would gain equal opportunities as men. While he did not conceptualize an erasure of gender roles in such a future, he seemed to believe that both genders will be able to manifest any set of human potentialities they wished to.

Vivekananda's idea of spiritual strength and manliness consisted mainly of qualities that were the exact opposite of those associated with masculinity in the popular imagination: non-violence in thought, speech, and action, love, self-sacrifice, surrender, non-assertiveness, selflessness, and so on. Vivekananda associated these qualities with strength rather than meekness. What is outwardly manifested as meekness or pacifism can proceed only from an immense strength of character which is able to completely bring one's mind under control. The classic example is how one reacts to violence directed at oneself. Vivekananda's thought here has similarities with Gandhi's pronouncements of non-violent satyagraha. Gandhi held that it took the greatest strength of character not to react to violence. Vivekananda took all moral failings including greed, violence, and the need for power, to be weakness. True strength consisted in transcending these, of annihilating the bondage to desire. A conversation with Vivekananda recorded by a disciple shows how the monk used the concepts of manliness, and of the hero, in opposite senses to the patriarchal construct of masculinity.

> Vivekananda: Can anyone, my dear friend, have faith or resignation in the Lord, unless he himself is a hero? Never can hatred and malice vanish from one's heart unless one becomes a hero, and unless one is free from these, how can one become truly civilised? Where in this country is that sturdy manliness, that spirit of heroism? Alas, nowhere. Often have I looked for that, and I found only one instance of it, and only one.
>
> Disciple: In whom have you found it, Swamiji?
>
> Vivekananda: In G.C [Babu Girish Chandra Ghosh] alone I have seen that true resignation—that true spirit of a servant of the Lord…he was ever ready to sacrifice himself…. What a unique spirit of resignation to the Lord! I have not met his parallel. From him have I learnt the lesson of self-surrender.[23]

Girish Chandra Ghosh was a writer and dramatist, who was a lay disciple of Sri Ramakrishna. A bohemian and an alcoholic when he met Ramakrishna, Girish took to the path of spirituality gradually through the method of surrendering his will completely to God.

To give another instance of how Vivekananda associated the term manliness with the spirit of love and self-sacrifice is seen in a letter he wrote to Sister Nivedita (Margaret Noble). It concerned the actions of his brother disciple Ramakrishnananda.

> Dear Margo, (Margot),
>
> …Ramakrishnananda came a few weeks before I came away, and the first thing he did was to lay down at my feet 400 Rs. he had collected in so many years of hard work!!! It was the first time such a thing has happened in my life. I can scarcely suppress my tears. Oh, Mother!! Mother! There is not all gratitude, all love, all manliness dead!![24]

THE POLITICAL: CASTE

On 19 July 1897, barely a month after the magnificent diamond jubilee celebrations of Queen Victoria's ascension to the British throne and two days before the Tate Gallery opened in London, the House of Commons of the British Parliament was in session after a two-day break. During the session, Lord George Hamilton, the India Secretary (the cabinet minister responsible for the department that governed Britain's Indian empire), received a rather unusual question from the Opposition benches. The Liberal MP, a Welshman by the name of Herbert Roberts, asked Lord Hamilton about an untouchable caste in the tiny kingdom of Travancore, on the southern tip of India.

The record of proceedings reads thus:

Mr. Herbert Roberts:

I beg to ask the Secretary of State for India (1) whether a class known as the Elavas (Ezhavas) are excluded from all appointments in the State of Travancore on the ground that they belong to a low caste, although they form over 16 per cent. of the population of the State, and contribute largely to its revenues; (2) whether they are denied admission to most of the Government schools in the State, and whether two graduates of the Madras University (of this class) have recently been compelled to take service under the Madras and Mysore Governments because they were denied positions in their own State; and (3) whether any, and, if so, what, steps have been taken by the Madras Government, through the Political Agent, to remedy this state of things in Travancore?

Lord George Hamilton:

I have no precise information as to the first Question. As to the second, I find from the latest report I have received that 9,517 Elava boys and 1,368 Elava girls were under instruction in Travancore, representing eight per cent of the total number of pupils. I have no information as to the two graduates referred to, and I must observe that in the internal administration of education and patronage in the Native states of India the British Government does not actively interfere. I have no objection, however, to calling the attention of the Madras Government to the Question asked by the hon. Member.[1]

The genesis of the question lay in the efforts of a lawyer, who travelled from Travancore to Britain on train and ship, to meet an Irish woman, carrying a letter written by Swami Vivekananda. The letter read:

DARJEELING,
3rd April 1897

DEAR MISS NOBLE,

I have just found a bit of important work for you to do on behalf of the downtrodden masses of India. The gentleman I take the liberty of introducing to you is in England on behalf of the Tiyas (Ezhavas), a plebeian caste in the native State of Malabar. You will realize from this gentleman what an amount of tyranny there is over these poor people, simply because of their caste. The Indian Government has refused to interfere on grounds of non-interference in the internal administration of a native State. The only hope of these people is the English Parliament. Do kindly everything in your power to help this matter [in] being brought before the British Public,

Ever yours in the truth,
VIVEKANANDA[2]

Miss Noble was Margaret Noble, who would later become Vivekananda's disciple and take the monastic name of Sister Nivedita. After receiving this letter, she would initiate contact with Herbert Roberts, who was known to be sympathetic to the Indian cause, and persuade him to place the plight of the Ezhavas before the British Parliament. But the originator of the effort to enlist Vivekananda's help was a remarkable man named Dr Padmanabhan Palpu. Palpu was one of the two graduates referred to by Herbert Roberts in his parliamentary question, who had to take employment in Mysore state, because he was denied employment in Travancore due to his caste. A revolutionary anti-caste reformer as well as public health doctor, he would play a pivotal role in India's first mass anti-caste movement. Later, Palpu would arrive in London and get Dadabhai Naoroji to present the case directly to the India Secretary, Lord George Hamilton. According to many historical accounts, the combined effect of these efforts was pressure from the British Resident on the

Travancore government to start making its policy regarding government jobs inclusive of Ezhavas.[3]

The Ezhava movement was the only non-party mass mobilization by an untouchable caste in Indian history, against caste discrimination. It was also one of first anti-caste movements in India, beginning towards the end of the nineteenth century and continuing till the 1940s. There were many historical and social reasons why the Ezhava community (also called Thiyyas in north Kerala), was able to organize and agitate against the discrimination and oppression they faced. The Ezhavas, a large section of whom were toddy tappers, were a dominant caste which was demoted to untouchable status centuries ago. Sections of the Ezhavas continued to maintain cultural links to the Sanskrit tradition.[4] Though rare, some Ezhavas were wealthy and titled landowners. A small section acted as physicians because of traditional knowledge of medicinal plants and herbs. The economic situation of the Ezhavas also improved substantially with the emergence of a cash economy. All these factors together placed the Ezhavas in a unique position compared to most untouchable castes in India, possessing just enough dispersed cultural and economic capital to challenge the system on untouchability, prohibition from government jobs, public schools, and colleges, from temples and their vicinity, and various other obstructions to living a dignified life. The Ezhava movement was led by Sri Narayana Guru, a sanyasi who belonged to the Ezhava caste, but was a Vedantist and a Sanskrit scholar. In 1903, Palpu established an organization to fight for the rights of Ezhavas called the Sree Narayana Dharma Paripalana Yogam (SNDP). Other than Narayana Guru and Palpu, the most influential figure in the Ezhava movement was probably Kumaran Asan, the legendary Malayalam poet who introduced romanticism into Malayalam poetry.

Though Vivekananda's views on caste have been the subject of revisionist history, his own contemporaries, both friend and foe, considered him an anti-caste reformer. This was mainly due to several speeches he delivered to massive audiences where he called for an end to caste privileges and to untouchability, and rebuked Brahmins for priestcraft and their oppression of the masses. The orthodox section of Hindu society repudiated his attacks on the caste system and disputed his assertion that Hinduism did not sanction caste and that it was simply a social custom which had received the sacerdotal backing of priests intent on preserving their privileges. The most tangible effects of Vivekananda's discourses and actions were on the Ezhava movement.

When Vivekananda visited Mysore in 1892 before his journey to America, he met Palpu, who was working as a doctor for the Mysore government.

Palpu appraised Vivekananda of the rampant caste discrimination that pervaded Kerala and the problems faced by the Ezhavas. Vivekananda advised Palpu not to look for help from the upper castes. Vivekananda's view, which he would later expound in public, was that no social reform movement would succeed in India, except through the vehicle of religion. Vivekananda instructed Palpu to find a spiritual master of his own caste and build a movement under his leadership. Palpu was convinced and, four years later, he had his fateful meeting with Sri Narayana Guru. Narayana Guru had already started establishing temples for Ezhavas. With Palpu providing financial help and organizational leadership, Narayana Guru's spiritual movement became an umbrella for Ezhava consolidation and social and caste reforms. Robbin Jeffrey, a historian who specializes in the social history of modern Kerala, writes: 'Shortly after Palpu took up service in Mysore, Vivekananda visited the state. Palpu appears to have got to know him well, and many of Vivekananda's teachings were to find their way into the Ezhava movement as it developed at the turn of the century. Palpu became receptive to the idea of Hindu revivalism and reformation.'5

When Vivekananda landed in India in 1897 after his success in the West, he delivered a dozen speeches in various places in Tamil Nadu, including several at Madras. By several contemporary and later accounts, they created a perfect firestorm in the collective consciousness of English educated Hindus in the south. Vivekananda used these occasions to powerfully preach for creating a fraternal national consciousness, for a Hindu spiritual revival, reforming Hinduism and for the equality of all castes. The Ezhava leader most inspired by Vivekananda's thought and whose own writings acted as a channel for the monk's ideas into the Ezhava movement, was Sri Narayana Guru's protégé Kumaran Asan. Asan, who served as the general secretary of the SNDP since its formation in 1903, for seventeen years, was also the editor of the SNDP's journal. The journal was named *Vivekodayam* in tribute to Vivekananda. Kumaran Asan translated Vivekananda's poem 'And Let Shyama Dance There' from Bengali to Malayalam; it appeared in two issues of *Vivekodayam*. Kumaran Asan later translated Vivekananda's seminal book *Raja Yoga* into Malayalam.

The great agitations and triumphs of the Ezhava movement and the SNDP came in the three decades after Vivekananda's death. Even before Independence, untouchability was banished from public spaces and people from the lower castes gained representation in government jobs as well as political representation, and the right to enter temples. Next to Sri Narayana Guru's own preaching, Vivekananda's thought seems to have remained an integral component of the SNDP's spiritual and social outlook. Writing in the post-Independence era,

P. Sugatan, an early Ezhava trade unionist leader and later communist party member who had been part of the SNDP wrote, 'It was Swami Vivekananda who made us aware of our slavery and inspired us for national freedom. The wonder of it was that he did it through his religious and spiritual talks and lectures. It was Swami Vivekananda who first loudly proclaimed that without the removal of caste, poverty and ignorance of the masses, Indian freedom is an impossibility.'[6]

Vivekananda has been lately criticized as being sympathetic to the caste system or even lending support to it, and as an upholder of upper-caste hegemony. I think one thing we can be certain about is that if any of these are true, then Vivekananda must have been a fantastically poor communicator of his ideas.

⌒

In the several areas in which Vivekananda has been the object of criticism, the only subject regarding which his exact views would appear to have a certain amount of ambiguity at first blush, is that of caste. In and of itself, there is nothing exceptional in such ambiguity. With any thinker there are always issues which belong to the periphery of their main thought, and hence would not have been considered at length and given theoretical elucidation. Just like caste, there are several subjects like nationalism, the question of India's political independence, patriotism, democracy, socialism, the idea of historical progress etc., where Vivekananda's views are not easy to ascertain exactly. This issue occurs with most thinkers. But in Vivekananda's case, there is, I suspect, a tendency to underestimate the need to analytically extract his theoretical position on peripheral subjects because of the sheer simplicity, crispness, and concise nature of his language. This often gives the erroneous impression that a simple view of a matter is being presented briefly. In the case of caste and certain other subjects especially, brief and scattered remarks are only the surface of deeper and more complex views.

Vivekananda never gave a speech on the caste system or wrote an essay or article on it, unlike a number of national figures in the late nineteenth and early twentieth century. We have to reconstruct his views on the caste system from passages that are interspersed among his speeches on other subjects, his correspondence, and conversations recorded by disciples and friends. But there are certain obstacles that make this task difficult. The first problem is that the sources we have for Vivekananda's views on several subjects including caste are not vehicles he chose to convey his thought to the public at large, but arbitrary and local sources. At the risk of repetition, Vivekananda's writings, in the form of books and essays, form a very small part of his oeuvre. These can be taken as expressing the considered opinion of the writer on the topics he has addressed, at least at the time of writing. However, the largest part of Vivekananda's corpus comes from speeches and lectures which while not unreliable, have to be approached with the understanding that he is tailoring his message to communicate with an audience's localized set of beliefs, knowledge, attitudes, prejudices, expectations, aspirations, and so on. Now, we do not have a full record of the speeches Vivekananda gave. Moreover, on many topics, especially those unconnected with religion, like nationalism, gender, politics, and caste, we can find only passing comments in his speeches. Sometimes, these opinions are accompanied by an argumentation that validates its rationale. Oftentimes, they are not. In such cases, we have to resort to Vivekananda's conversations recorded by various people, where we might find him speaking more on the issue.* However, in a number of cases, these conversations, (which have been preserved for history according to the individual whim of listeners rather than due to any topical significance), may not contain enough material on the issue to shed sufficient light on Vivekananda's thinking on the matter.

On the whole, however, I believe it is possible to trace and reconstruct Vivekananda's views on the caste system accurately along its main lines. Some parts have to be constructed by joining the dots and by inferring the best explanation and necessarily introduce an element of speculation. Some questions raised by his views may forever remain unanswered because of the lack of enough relevant information in the Vivekananda corpus. Nonetheless, I think a meticulous scrutiny of his various comments on the caste system, scattered through the body of his work, can provide us with a very accurate picture of the main dimensions of his understanding of the caste problem and what he proposed as a solution. We can also be reasonably confident that unlike most caste reformers of the Indian Renaissance, Vivekananda desired not merely to extinguish untouchability and caste inequalities but believed that the caste system itself had to be annihilated eventually. He seemed to believe that in a matter of a few centuries, caste would disappear from India.

Now, the first thing to be said is that the solution Vivekananda proposed for the caste problem is dated and is not relevant to us today, except for reasons of historical interest. The second thing of note is that in spite of wide travels through India, Vivekananda's understanding of caste oppression

---

*To a lesser extent, newspaper interviews are another source that come in useful for the same purpose.

was limited by the upper-caste vantage point from which he saw it. This was of course, the only vantage point available to him. It was a top–down view of the oppression of caste. But though Vivekananda pushed against the boundaries of this perspective, it was impossible for him, or any upper-caste person of that time, to break through those boundaries and obtain a bottom–up perspective of caste oppression as experienced by lower-caste people. There were no Dalit or lower-caste voices which articulated the subjective experience of caste oppression and critiqued the caste system on that basis. The only exception was the Maharashtrian reformer Jyotiba Phule, but his movement was not widely known, and it is almost certain that Vivekananda had no contact with Phule's writings on caste, which in any case, were available only in Marathi during Vivekananda's time. Except for Christian missionaries and Western critics, whose motives were mixed, hardly any noted caste reformer other than Phule, whether from the upper or lower castes, seems to have demanded the dismantling of caste as an organizational structure of society.

What most of them, including the leaders of the Ezhava movement in Kerala, demanded was equality between the castes. Yet, even this proved a difficult demand to put into practice through political action. Dr Palpu found to his bitter disappointment that people from his caste, while willing to fight for equal rights for Ezhavas, were not prepared to give up on their superiority over castes lower than them in the hierarchy. When Palpu famously arranged an inter-dining event between Ezhavas and the lower Dalit castes, the Ezhavas not only objected but actually beat him up. While some of the more radical Bengali intelligentsia, did write about the evils of the caste system and the need to get rid of it, it remained within the discourse of a mainly Brahmin elite, with absolutely no connection to even the middle castes, let alone lower castes. The attack on the caste system was articulated with no reference to or understanding of the oppression or social conditions of the lower castes. It presented no systematic programme of how to bring about the abolition of caste and was devoid of any intellectual attempt to conceptualize a model of society in India free from caste groupings.[*]

Narayana Guru, who played the most significant part in the Ezhava revolution, demanded political, social, and economic equality for all castes, but did not demand, nor seems to have envisaged, a society which was arranged without caste groupings. This came from a lack of availability in the thought of

---

*For an explication of the self-contained Brahmin milieu of the reformers of the Indian Renaissance, see *A Critique of Colonial India* by Sumit Sarkar.

the day of alternative social models. Socialism did not serve as a model because socialist thought had only a sliver of following in India in the late nineteenth century. Even M. N. Roy, one of the tallest and earliest communist leaders in India, did not become a Marxist till after World War I. Western capitalistic societies did not offer themselves as a model, partly because their impact was felt through colonialism, and partly because it was doubtful whether the socio-economic conditions necessary for industrialization and the creation of a technicalistic society existed in India. So, when we look at the caste discourse of the period, we need to make a conceptual differentiation between criticism of the evils of the caste system as a form of social structuralization, and the egalitarian idea of a society where caste still served as the basic social unit, but without the vertical hierarchy of status, power, and attendant oppression.

Between Jyotiba Phule, who was mainly active in the 1870s and 1880s, and B. R. Ambedkar, active from the 1920 onwards, both of whom systematically attacked the caste system and sought its abolition, even radical low-caste reformers like Narayana Guru, worked towards and conceptualized an equitable society without caste privileges; but one whose model of organization implicitly remained based on caste groupings. While intermarriage between castes was promoted by reformers in the nineteenth century, they saw this as a fight against superstitious social taboos rather than as a systematic programme that would eventually break down the endogamous nature of castes and eradicate the caste system as Ambedkar advocated later.[7]

In the late nineteenth century, though there were several caste reformers, it was not at all the case that liberal thought aligned automatically with the cause of caste reform. While there was overlap, there was more often, significant divergence. As an example, let us look at the views of Rabindranath Tagore on caste during the period roughly parallel to Vivekananda's public career. From the 1920s onward, Tagore was one of the harshest critics of untouchability and also of the oppression upper castes visited on the peasant castes. Despite his liberal outlook from the beginning of his career, Tagore's views on caste evolved over time from an initially conservative position. In the period we are dealing with, the turn of the nineteenth century, when Vivekananda was active, Tagore's views on caste were very different from those he eventually came to hold. I had alluded in the first chapter to the fact that from roughly the 1870s onwards, there was a breach between the interests of the pro-Western reformist intelligentsia of Bengal and the British authorities. This led to the emergence of nationalist feelings and a looking back into India's own cultural and civilizational past for a source of values which could be a basis for political action, without feeding off of the values of the conquering race.

Rajarshi Chunder, a researcher on Tagore's political ideas, writes:

The development of Tagore's ideas on caste can be divided into several phases. The first phase corresponds to the period between 1899 and 1905. It started with the foundation of a school at Shantiniketan on a supposedly Vedic model—Brahmacharyashram. Students were required to lead a life of celibacy, abiding by caste regulations that involved living with their preceptors and practising a simple and austere life.... Between 1899 and 1905, Tagore was fascinated by ancient Vedic customs and social prerogatives.... Tagore located the basis of social progress in the system of caste distinctions as they were prevalent in Vedic times or so he thought. For Tagore, it was both a rational and humane system of division of duties among individuals because it put a check on mutual conflict which could lead to the destruction of the weak and culturally inferior groups by the superior....

Tagore thought that far from being a system of stratification, caste in ancient India brought different antagonistic groups under an umbrella of unity. This was exactly the opposite of European history, where antagonistic and 'inferior' groups and races had been destroyed by conquerors in order to establish the political supremacy of the superior group. Indian caste, in contrast, achieved a peaceful integration of various mutually opposed groups.

At the Shantiniketan Ashram, caste distinctions were introduced. In his very first address to the students, Tagore extolled hierarchy....

The address may have been the exposition of an ideal and imagined social order, reworked in a colonial milieu, but Tagore was not averse to practical segregation. Hence Brahman students dined separately from non-Brahmans. They were also not supposed to touch the feet of non-Brahmans, even if the latter were teachers. This practice prevailed till as late as 1915.[8]

If Tagore had died at the age of forty-four in 1905, history would have judged him as a liberal thinker who was conservative on the issue of caste. But unlike Vivekananda, whose life was cut short at thirty-nine, Tagore lived to see the tremendous transformations in Indian society brought about by the national movement. This exposed the dynamics of caste relations and the oppressive nature of its stratification to Tagore, for whom the tyranny practised by the upper castes (including Brahmins) became obvious. Tagore went on to become a strident crusader against untouchability and caste distinctions till the end of his life in 1941.

I chose to examine Tagore's views on caste at length here, only as a roughly representative example of the kind of views on caste current among liberal thinkers of Vivekananda's time. The point is that to judge Vivekananda's moral complicity, or lack thereof, in the practice of an oppressive caste ideology, one has to understand the discursive background that he is speaking against. To illustrate what I mean, take the issue of casual racism against African Americans in the US. Today, the preferred epithet is 'black', as a term that confers dignity to them. To address a black person using the word 'negro' for example is considered highly insulting and those who use that term can be justifiably accused of racism. But wind the tape back to the fifties and you would find the term 'negro' being used as a moniker of self-respect by black people, including community leaders and civil rights leaders. The appellation 'black', on the other hand evoked different reactions, oftentimes unfavourable. After the liberation of black Americans from slavery in 1865, black organizations discussed the name with which they should identify as a community. The term 'black' was then rejected as racist and disparaging because it was used previously by slave owners. So, in effect, whether the use of the term 'negro' or 'black' is a reflection of racism or an acknowledgment of racial dignity depends on the historical period in which that statement has been uttered. 'Caste' by itself, stripped of its hierarchical stratification and considered only as communities, was not yet a bad word in the nineteenth century among the progressive Indian intelligentsia; not even among lower-caste reformers. This was partly because inter-caste violence of the kind seen in later years rarely occurred in the nineteenth century and the word did not carry the association with violence and oppression it has acquired in the twentieth and twenty-first centuries due to thousands of incidents of caste atrocities.

Roughly since the nineties, there have been charges, mostly by academics, that suggest Vivekananda was a conservative on caste. But what has had more impact on the public perception of Vivekananda, I believe, is how Vivekananda's views on caste have been presented on the internet and social media discourse. For example, on Vivekananda's birth anniversary in 2022, a Twitter user posted a tweet which became widely shared on social media. The tweet said: 'Vivekananda was just another typical Dwija personality who made all the possible attempts to preserve the Varnashrama Dharma. That's it. Just an episode in the history, that too, unworthy.'

This was followed by a series of quotes from Vivekananda, which began with the user writing: 'Why I hate Vivekananda – 6 (out of hundreds) Casteist Quotes of Vivekananda.' He proceeded to give the following quotes in order.

1) I do not propose any leveling of castes. Caste is a very good thing. Caste is the plan we want to follow.
2) Indian caste is better than the caste which prevails in Europe or America.
3) Caste should not go; but should only be readjusted occasionally. Within the old structure is to be found life enough for the building of two hundred thousand new ones. It is sheer nonsense to desire the abolition of caste.
4) The Brahminhood is the ideal of humanity in India, as wonderfully put forward by Shankaracharya at the beginning of his commentary on the Gita, where he speaks about the reason for Krishna's coming as a preacher for the preservation of Brahminhood, of Brahminness.
5) This Brahmin, the man of God, he who has known Brahman, the ideal man, the perfect man, must remain; he must not go.
6) As Manu says, all these privileges and honours are given to the Brahmin, because 'with him is the treasury of virtue'. He must open that treasury and distribute its valuables to the world.... It is true that he was the earliest preacher to the Indian races, he was the first to renounce everything in order to attain to the higher realization of life before others could reach to the idea. It was not his fault that he marched ahead of the other castes.

Read together, all these quotes paint a pretty damning picture. To our modern sensibilities, they appear shocking, almost medieval. The first thing to note about these quotes, however, is that they are standalone quotes, extracted from the speeches or conversations within which they were made; the context is, hence, completely missing. The second is that they are a curation of the most egregious sounding quotes on caste from Vivekananda's work gathered together in one place. I find it strange that someone could come across all the instances of Vivekananda apparently praising the caste system, while completely missing the far more numerous instances when he criticizes it hammer and tongs. But then, the internet is a strange place.

All the above quotes are drawn from two sources. The first two are from an interview Vivekananda gave to *The Hindu* in February 1897, when travelling by train from Chennai to Chengalpattu. The rest are from the speech 'The Future of India'. I would like to add one more quote to the list given above, from the speech 'Vedanta in its application to Indian Life'.

We believe in Indian caste as one of the greatest social institutions that the Lord gave to man. We also believe that through the unavoidable defects, foreign persecutions, and, above all, the monumental ignorance and pride of many Brahmins who do not deserve the name, have thwarted, in many ways, the legitimate fructification of this most glorious Indian institution, it has already worked wonders for the land of Bharata and is destined to lead Indian humanity to its goal. We earnestly entreat the Brahmins of the South not to forget the ideal of India—the production of a universe of Brahmins, pure as purity, good as God Himself: this was at the beginning, says the Mahabharata, and so will it be in the end.[9]

To my knowledge, this last speech completes the sources for statements from Vivekananda's work that on the face of it look like he is extending support to the caste system. There are not, in fact, hundreds of quotes like this. There are, however, other quotes where Vivekananda says something positive about some aspect of the caste system. The caste system in the sense that was explained earlier—as the natural coming together of people who do a particular trade or job. Very loosely, it can be compared to the trade guilds that dominated European life in the Middle Ages. The second sense of the caste system is a modification on the basic template of the first. The key feature that sustains the caste system in the second sense is enforced endogamy within castes and rituals of discrimination and separation between castes based on a social hierarchy of increasing privileges where Brahmins occupy the top. This is the sense in which we today talk about the caste system.

At no point in his work, does Vivekananda say anything positive about caste in the second sense. Vivekananda's work contains both statements that attack the caste system (understood in both senses) as well as statements which seem to say positive things about it in the first sense. But in the entire corpus of his work, stringent criticism of caste far outweighs statements that cast it in a positive light. By my count, in *The Complete Works of Swami Vivekananda* there are 185 instances where Vivekananda attacks or says something negative about caste in both the senses of the word. There are sixty-four instances where he says something positive about the caste system in the first sense.[*] There are absolutely no instances where he says anything positive about the hierarchy between castes, or the privileges claimed by castes higher up in the hierarchy.

---

*When it comes to certain statements, there is an element of subjectivity involved in determining whether a quote is a positive/negative comment or a value-free reference. Nonetheless, I think any reasonable method of tabulation would arrive at approximately the same figures.

To counterbalance the portrait created by the above quotes, let us look at comments by Vivekananda where he criticizes the caste system itself, where his criticism is aimed at the caste system in the first sense, as a grouping of people, even when devoid of its hierarchical, endogamous, and exclusive nature.

1. 'In spite of all the ravings of the priests, caste is simply a crystallised social institution, which after doing its service is now filling the atmosphere of India with its stench.'[10]

2. 'With the introduction of modern competition, see how caste is disappearing fast! No religion is necessary to kill it. The Brahmana shopkeeper, shoemaker and wine-distiller are common in northern India. And why? Because of competition. No man is prohibited from doing anything he pleases for his livelihood under the present Government, and the result is neck and neck competition, and thus thousands are seeking and finding the highest level they are born for, instead of vegetating at the bottom.'[11]

3. 'Modern caste distinction is a barrier to India's progress. It narrows, restricts, separates. It will crumble before the advance of ideas.'[12]

4. 'The Caste system is opposed to the religion of Vedanta. Caste is a social custom, and all our great preachers have tried to break it down…. Caste is simply the outgrowth of the political institutions of India…. Trade competition with Europe has broken caste more than any teaching.'[13]

5. 'Krishna had opened the gates of spiritual knowledge and attainment to all irrespective of sex or caste, but he left undisturbed the same problem on the social side. This again has come down to our days, in spite of the gigantic struggle of the Buddhists, Vaishnavas etc., to attain social equality for all.'[14]

6. 'I have no doubt that according to the ancient view in this country, caste was hereditary, and it cannot be doubted sometimes that the Shudras used to be oppressed more than the helots among the Spartans and the negroes among the Americans!'[15]

7. 'Moreover, these distinctions of caste and the like have been the invention of our modern sapient Brahmins. Who is a servant, and to whom?'[16]

8. 'The conviction is daily growing on my mind that the idea of caste is the greatest dividing factor and the root of Maya; all caste either on the principle of birth or merit is bondage. Some friends advise, "True,

lay all that at heart, but outside, in the world of relative experience, distinctions like caste must be maintained." ...The idea of oneness at heart (with a craven impotence of effort, that is to say) and outside, the hell dance of demons—oppression and persecution, ay, the dealer of death to the poor.'[17]

9. 'It is in the books written by priests that madness like that of caste are to be found, and not in the books revealed from God.'[18]

10. 'Buddha was the only great Indian philosopher who would not recognize caste, and not one of his followers remain in India. All the other philosophers pandered more or less to social prejudices; no matter how high they soared, still a bit of the vulture remained in them. As my master used to say, "The vulture soars high out of sight in the sky, but his eye is ever on a bit of carrion on the earth."'[19]

11. 'Caste is a social organization and not a religious one.... It was found necessary and convenient at one time.... It is useless now. It may be dispensed with.'[20]

12. 'Buddha's summary of misery as the outcome of "ignorance and caste" has been adopted by the Vedantists, because it is the best ever made.'[21]

A first-time reader who is confronted with this diametrically opposed set of quotes may well ask of Vivekananda, what the monk once asked of Vyasa when confronted with his statements which were in polar opposition.* But these statements are not as contradictory as they appear at first glance, for in the six quotes included earlier, the words 'caste' and 'Brahman' have completely different meanings from what is usually meant by these two words. This becomes explicit if the complete speeches in which these statements occur are read in their entirety. In them, Vivekananda goes on to offer a redefinition of these terms and what he means by them. The next section will attempt to reconstruct Vivekananda's views on the caste question, in terms of how he viewed the institution, the solution he proposed to eliminate the oppression and inequality of the caste system, and the context and reasons which explain the intellectual route that took him to his views. But before we do that, we will need a very short propaedeutic on the reading of historical texts. Ours is an age which seems to have completely set aside historical consciousness, and from intellectually fashionable academicians to purveyors of cancel culture on the internet, there is a tendency to treat texts without either historical or hermeneutic context.

As an exercise in the reading of historical texts, here is an experiment in

---

*'Is this Vyasa a madman?' quoted in Chapter 6.

the dangers of making assumptions based on standalone quotes like the ones on Twitter on Vivekananda and caste. Here are four quotes whose authors are not identified. The reader can try and guess who may have said them.

1. 'From the commencement of the titanic American strife (Civil War), the workingmen of Europe felt instinctively that the star-spangled banner (the American flag) carried the destiny of their class.'

2. 'The idea underlying sangathan is to remove from the mind of the Hindu that timidity and cowardice which so painfully mark him off from the Mahomedan and the Sikh.... From where does the Sikh or the Mahomedan derive his strength, which makes him brave and fearless?... It is due to the strength arising out of the feeling that all Sikhs will come to the rescue of a Sikh when he is in danger, and that all Mahomedans will rush to save a Muslim if he is attacked.

   The Hindu can derive no such strength. He cannot feel assured that his fellows will come to his help. Being one and fated to be alone, he remains powerless, develops timidity and cowardice, and in a fight surrenders or runs away. The Sikh as well as the Muslim stands fearless and gives battle, because he knows that though one he will not be alone.'

3. 'The so-called Negroes must be truly civilised, and the right civilised man has not performed his duty until this is accomplished.'

4. 'The chimera of equality is the most dangerous of all beliefs in a civilised society. To preach this system to the people is not to recall its rights, it is to invite the people to murder and pillage; it is to unchain domestic animals and transform them into wild beasts.'

The first quote was written by Karl Marx.[22]

The second is from B. R. Ambedkar's *Annihilation of Caste*.[23]

The third is from an essay on education by Mohammad Elijah, who was a mentor to civil rights leader Malcom X.[24]

The last belongs to Denis Diderot, the French philosopher, who after Voltaire, Rosseau, and Montesquieu, is usually considered the figure most instrumental in bringing about the French Revolution. The most famous quote attributed to Diderot is, 'Man will never be free until the last king is strangled with the entrails of the last priest.'[25]

I don't think one needs to make the case that Karl Marx was not an admirer of American international hegemony, that Ambedkar did not have an iota of sympathy for Hindutva, that Mohammad Elijah was not a racist, and that Diderot was not a class elitist opposed to equality. What I hope is that this exercise demonstrates to the reader the complete distortion in meaning that can occur when you take a few lines that are part of a much larger text, of the body of a person's thinking and from a specific historical context and present it without these referents. It is precisely this phenomenon that is at work in the supposedly casteist quotes curated from Vivekananda's work.

Vivekananda's statements that appear to be supportive of the caste system have a radically altered meaning when considered in the context of the speeches where he delivered them. It was mentioned earlier that there are sixty-four instances of Vivekananda saying something positive about some aspect of caste as a social arrangement (not caste hierarchy). Most of these instances are in speeches and interviews given in America and Great Britain. As we saw in Chapters 4 and 5, Vivekananda in the West was continuously confronted with tropes created by Western imperialism and missionary Christianity that indicted Indian civilization as inherently inferior to the West on the basis of social evils like sati, child marriage, the conditions of widows, the caste system, etc. The combative Vivekananda when put on the defensive, would counterattack, usually pointing to the flaws in Western civilization. This allowed him not to cede ground in an unequal cultural power dynamic. It is in such contexts, that Vivekananda made statements defending caste as a social institution, which had positive characteristics, or was neccessitated by the evolution of society, but had degenerated to its present form of untouchability, hereditary privilege, exclusion, and hierarchy. When Vivekananda found himself talking to a Western interlocutor he judged as being more neutral and receptive, Vivekananda often described the terrible conditions in India in reference to social evils like the condition of women, child marriage, and the caste system. In fact, many of the statements we read earlier attacking the caste system in toto, were made in the West.

While this issue has been discussed before in the book, the problem is that such Western cultural assumptions always remain in the background of speeches and interviews Vivekananda gave in the West. We are able to infer them from historical record and from some places where these assumptions break into the foreground. The following is one of those rare interviews where Western cultural assumptions about India and the East come to the surface. This was a friendly interview given to the *San Francisco Chronicle* in 1900, where the reporter, Blanche Partington, returned impressed with Vivekananda. This interview deviated from the usual style of American newspaper journalism then, of articles with a series of questions and answers written in a crisp, almost terse style. The reporter chose a more impressionistic style of writing, and her own thoughts and impressions which thread through the substance of the interview, give us a window into the cultural stereotypes through which Vivekananda was often viewed and the unbridgeable gap of communication it opened up between Vivekananda and his Western audiences. A part of the interview is reproduced below with important phrases in bold:

Bowing very low in **Eastern fashion** on his entrance to the room, then holding out his hand in good American style, **the dusky philosopher** from the banks of the Ganges gave friendly greeting to the representative of that **thoroughly Occidental institution**, the daily press. I asked for a picture to illustrate this article, and when someone handed me a certain 'cut' which has been extensively used in lecture advertisements here, he uttered a mild protest against its use. 'But that does not look like you', said I. 'No, it is as if I wished to kill someone,' he said smiling, 'like—like—' **'Othello', I inserted rashly**…. He was pacing up and down the room most of the time during our talk…it was a chill morning for **this child of the sun**—and doing with grace and freedom whatever occurred to him, even, at length, smoking a little.

'You, yourself, have not yet attained supreme control over all desires', I ventured. The Swami's frankness is infectious. 'No, madam', and he smiled the broad and brilliant smile of a child; 'Do I look it?' But the Swami, from **the land of hasheesh and dreams**, doubtless did not connect my query with its smoky origin.

But for English rule I could not be here now', said the monk, 'though your lowest freeborn American Negro holds higher position in India politically than is mine. Brahmin and coolie, we are all 'natives'. But it is all right, in spite of the misunderstanding and oppression. England is the Tharma [Karma?] of India, attracted inevitably by some inherent weakness, past mistakes, but from her blood and fibre will come the new national hope for my countrymen….

'I must go', I said. 'I have to catch a train'. 'That is like all Americans', smiled the Swami, and I had a glimpse of all eternity in his utter restfulness. 'You must catch this car or that train always. Is there not another, later?' But I did not attempt to explain the **Occidental conception of the value of time** to this **child of the Orient**, realizing its utter hopelessness and my own **renegade sympathy**. It must be delightful beyond measure to live in the land of 'time enough'. In the Orient there seems time to breathe, time to think, time to live; as the Swami says, what have we in exchange? We live in time; they in eternity.[26]

By any standard, this interview can only be characterized as warm and sympathetic. Yet, there is a cultural chasm between Vivekananda and the reporter that makes it difficult for Vivekananda's spiritual message as well as his representation of India to be communicated to the reporter in an undistorted way. The words and phrases highlighted in bold, show the recurrent themes in the reporter's mind that constructed the very conceptual frame through which she viewed Vivekananda and what he represented. This is not to say that the reporter was racist or personally complicit in Western imperialism or anything of that sort. It is merely that in her cultural milieu, and in spite of her sincere efforts, she was incapable of encountering Vivekananda as he was. At the beginning of the interview, Vivekananda's very act of greeting her generates a cultural gap. She instantly identifies it as in the 'Eastern fashion', generalizing from what is indeed a detail of cultural difference of journalistic interest, to a sweeping civilizational stereotype of the East and the West. This difference, where the East is the 'other' to the West and a source of racial identity, is magnified, when she notes the difference in skin colour and goes on to give Vivekananda the epithet of the 'dusky philosopher' and again when she makes the 'rash' suggestion that Vivekananda's portrait looks like Othello, the jealous African moor, who is the protagonist of Shakespeare's play of the same name.

Another civilizational binary that sets the tone for the interview is that of the 'Occident' vs the 'Orient'. The opening line itself characterizes the interview as an encounter, not between a reporter and a philosopher, but between the representatives of two quintessentially different civilizations, of two different ways of being. Daily newspapers are a 'thoroughly Occidental institution', and by implication thoroughly alien to the East. (There were of course several daily newspapers in India by this time). It is important to note that the reporter, Blanche Partington, was no wide-eyed American woman with no experience of Eastern cultures. Partington, who would go on to become a celebrated literary and art journalist, was already mentoring the Japanese poet Yone Noguchi. She had editorially assisted in the publication of Noguchi's novel *The American Diary of a Japanese girl*, the first English language novel published by a Japanese writer.

Nonetheless, Oriental tropes exoticizing and thus inadvertently 'othering' Vivekananda appear frequently in the interview. Vivekananda is called a 'child of the sun' and India 'the land of hasheesh and dreams'. When Vivekananda comments that 'That is like all Americans. You must catch this car or that train always. Is there not another, later?', it is interpreted as the Oriental's inability to comprehend the occidental concept of time. The fact, however, is that the comment Vivekananda makes is about Americans; he is not talking about the West. The notion of Americans as energetic hustlers was a notion widespread among European nations with their more traditional societies, as well. Vivekananda had not landed in California right off the shores of the Ganga. He was an experienced international traveller quite acquainted with European culture. But Partington's response is to imagine an uncrossable civilizational bridge across which no understanding was possible. It is revealing that even her sympathy for the timeless Orient is described, though casually, as 'renegade', as a kind of betrayal of her fellow occidentals.

If Vivekananda could be seen through such a lens even by a sympathetic journalist who had some experience of Asia, one can imagine the insurmountable obstacles he would have faced in being understood by audiences who were thoroughly ignorant of India, many of whom were fed an information diet of missionary propaganda about the need to save souls being crushed under the oppressive society of a heathen and superstitious religion. Any discussion of sati, child marriage, caste, etc., in such a context would be distorted within the gravitational fields of Orientalism, Western assumptions of civilizational superiority, and Protestant missionary constructions of Hinduism. If Vivekananda was interrogated about caste in such situations, it would not be a neutral questioning about a social evil, but a civilizational indictment by members of a hegemonizing civilization over the hegemonized. It is when Vivekananda was confronted with such a social context, or what he judged to be such a social context, that he made statements defending some aspects of the caste system. That is, what he called the original caste system, which was a grouping of people of mutual interests and professions, before it had degenerated to its present form of exclusion, hereditary privilege, and hierarchy.

A rigorous and thorough exploration of Vivekananda's views on caste would require a small book and so, what is on offer here are only the salient themes, not an exhaustive explication. With that caveat in mind, Vivekananda's fundamental thesis about caste was that it was not a religious, but a social institution. He may have been the first major public intellectual to make that argument in the nineteenth century. (Narayana Guru seems to have arrived at similar views parallelly, though he did not quite state it in the same terms.) After Vivekananda, and to an extent due to his influence, this became the liberal Hindu position articulated by scholars like Sarvepalli Radhakrishnan. This view has a long lineage in the Hindu tradition, especially among the Bhakti cults, but had become seemingly weakened a few centuries before the British conquest of India. According to Vivekananda, caste, or the earlier varnashrama dharma, had nothing to do with Hinduism the religion, where religion is understood as the doctrines of metaphysics, theology, and ethics. This is the spiritual core of Hinduism and is to be found in the Upanishads and the Bhagavad Gita. They are also to be found partially in the three great epics (Ramayana, Mahabharata, and Srimad Bhagavata) and other devotional literature. The idea of varnas, and the rules regulating their conduct are mainly found in texts of social legislation, viz., the Dharmashastras which include texts like the *Manusmriti*. These texts have nothing to do with religion in the sense that they do not usually discuss metaphysical and theological matters at all. Neither the philosophical nor mystical tradition of Hinduism gives the dharmashastras any authority in spiritual matters. Caste, Vivekananda says, is a crystallized social institution that received quasi-religious sanctions through the work of priests.

The mistake that reformers from Ram Mohan Roy onwards and up to Keshub Chandra Sen and Swami Dayanand Saraswati had made, according to Vivekananda, was that they had taken caste to be a religious institution. They had thus to either attempt a theological amputation of Hinduism, consequently rejecting important parts of it as a degradation or superstition. (Dayanand Saraswati, who tried to build a Hinduism based on only the Vedas, had to reject idol worship and elements of temple worship because they were not found in the Vedas.) Or, they had to go outside Hindu society, as the members of Young Bengal had done and criticize Hindu religion wholescale. The problem with both these approaches was that these reformers preached to a very small minority and could not mobilize larger public opinion. Asked to change their religion, moderate Hindus who were not extremely orthodox, and who might have formed a broader constituency for social reforms, dug their heels in, and refused to engage with the reform programmes. Vivekananda's view (which was essentially the same as his guru Sri Ramakrishna Paramahamsa's) was that the Hindu did not have to change his religion to get rid of caste discrimination, he only needed to understand it better. That is, if Hindus understood what was the true nature of their religion, and what is sanctioned by their holy books, they would recognize that caste is not part of its philosophy, theology, or the fundamental structure of its beliefs and praxis. But as a social institution, caste was an unmitigated evil—not only did it crush underfoot millions of the lower castes, but it had for thousands of years held back India's progress as a nation.

But if caste was a social problem, it demanded a solution on the social side. To understand how Vivekananda approached caste, we need to understand the various lens through which Vivekananda viewed the issue. These were that of nationalism, modernity, and colonialism. All these three interacted in a definite but unpredictable way. Another decisive factor was his own position in relation to Hindu and Indian society after his return from America in 1897 as a national celebrity. Vivekananda maintained from the beginning, even before the commencement of his public career in America, that the days of caste distinctions in India were numbered. The changes brought about by the British conquest, Vivekananda believed, were not only too powerful for Indian society to resist, but that they were fundamentally destructive for the structure of the caste system. Despite the political oppression British colonialism brought, economic competition would force people to seek jobs outside their traditional caste trades as well as their domiciles. Vivekananda here was talking in the long term, of a process that might take two or three centuries perhaps, to play out. But he considered the building of a technicalistic economic modernity imperative for India's national progress. His primary reason for going to America was to try and get help in importing modern technical education and investment in industrialization in India. However, within a few months of being in America, he realized that such a plan would find few backers there. This meant that the process of destruction of caste and related social ills through gradual economic modernization could not be accelerated as he had hoped.

Let us overview what we already know of Vivekananda's views on caste. He considered that class and caste oppression by the Brahmins and Kshatriyas were responsible for India's national downfall, which commenced presumably around the tenth century CE. This is something he not only expressed in private but spoke about in his speeches both in India and abroad. He especially criticized the Brahmins for the oppression of the masses and for untouchability and caste separationism. He attacked caste privileges and demanded the equality of all castes in the speeches he gave when he arrived in India after his success in America. He denounced the Brahmins in public, even as he asked them to come forward and cure the mischief they themselves had created. At the same time, he did not call for the destruction of caste. This by itself would not have been surprising, given that almost no prominent reformer, whether upper-caste or untouchable, did. But on a small number of occasions, he positively states that it was foolishness to desire the abolition of caste, and generally that caste was the plan that India needed to follow.

These are glaringly contradictory positions. We have to keep in mind that these latter are brief statements with only a few lines offered in explanation and sometimes none. This is why the need for interpretation arises. The first explanation that springs to mind would be that Vivekananda took a position close to that of Gandhi, who wanted to remove caste inequality, but wanted to preserve the varnashrama dharma—the division of social duties according to the caste one is born into. (In later life, he revised this position and seemed to have come close to desiring a casteless society.)[27] As Gandhi wrote:

> If the members of the [human] body had the power of expression and each of them were to say that it was higher and better than the rest, the body would go to pieces. ...It is this canker that is at the root of the various ills of our time, especially class and civil strife. It should not be difficult for even the meanest understanding to see that these wars and strifes could not be ended except by the observance of the law of varna. For it ordains that everyone shall fulfill the law of one's being by doing in a spirit of duty and service that to which one is born.[28]

But this explanation does not work for several reasons. For one, Vivekananda uses the term 'varnashrama' only eight times in his entire corpus of work. The word Varna appears only six times and in none of these instances does he suggest that it should be given any importance, let alone be followed. He considered the concept completely alien to Hinduism because it is not present in the Shruti, i.e., the Upanishads and has only a passing mention in the Bhagavad Gita. In the latter, in the verse where Krishna refers to it, varna is defined as an individual's inherent nature, rather than a social order. The other reason that this is an erroneous explanation is that any intellectual allegiance to the traditional concept of varnashrama dharma, would need to imagine a society where there is no significant social mobility. Each member of a caste would stick to the hereditary profession. But this is exactly the opposite of what Vivekananda envisaged for India, as seen in the following quote supporting the annihilation of caste mentioned earlier. The quote begins with the monk exclaiming: 'With the introduction of modern competition, see how caste is disappearing fast!'* Vivekananda starts with the sociological observation that Brahmins who only performed priestly or scholarly duties were taking up professions which were not only exclusive to other castes but were considered as menial or even ritually polluting for Brahmins. Then he gives an economic explanation for the fact, which is modern economic competition. But what does this mean? The political dislocation caused by the British rule in India had destroyed traditional patronage structures dependent on Hindu royalty and

---

*Quote 2, p. 404.

nobility, pushing the upper castes to seek English education for employment with the East India Company and later the British government. Those who did not or could not take this route, had to enter commerce. The commercial scene had itself undergone a severe economic dislocation as a result of British trade.

Earlier, while commerce was by no means static, its ebbs and flows were controlled within a certain range by the hereditary caste system, which checked the free play of market forces. A person belonging to the merchant class, or who provided a certain kind of commercial service did not have to fear that a cheaper or more efficient product or service would put him out of business. Any innovation in production, distribution, or marketing that could happen would happen within his own caste grouping and would soon be assimilated into the traditional business practices or professional techniques of the caste. But as Britain introduced cheap mass-produced goods into the Indian market, traditional artisan guilds collapsed, unable to compete in terms of price. If one leaves aside the question of social dislocation, the economic result was that Indians started adopting competitive free market practices which attracted those with aptitude to trades and professions whose very natures were altered now. With the British government applying no legal restrictions linking caste and profession, migration across caste lines into all kinds of professions and trades became possible. And the social consequence Vivekananda draws from this is that every man can eventually find the position in life that is most suitable to his capabilities, rather than be held down by the caste hierarchy of professions—the very spirit of capitalistic competition is destructive to the caste system.

So, if Vivekananda wanted a society where castes existed perpetually, but there was no hierarchy and no caste privileges but there was social mobility which continually eroded the caste system, such a position is simply incoherent. The answer to the conundrum is that Vivekananda is using caste in a completely different meaning when he says that caste should remain, or caste is the plan to follow or that it is sheer nonsense to desire the abolition of caste. This becomes obvious in the speeches themselves. Vivekananda uses the word caste on these occasions in two different senses. The first sense, which is not really essential to explain Vivekananda's proposed solution to the caste problem, is however, easier to understand. Here, Vivekananda uses the word 'caste', in its original meaning in English. It was still used in that sense quite popularly during the nineteenth century. On encountering the 'jati' system in India, the British used the word 'caste' to describe it, which was the nearest equivalent in the English language. Caste in the original sense, meant 'a division of society based on differences of wealth, inherited rank or privilege, profession, occupation, or race'.[29] (Today, the word is used in this sense usually only in academic contexts.) Vivekananda mentions a number of times that by caste he means a coming together of people who share the same profession or the same interests. In his speech 'Vedanta in its application to Indian Life', Vivekananda talks of how the egalitarianism of Vedanta, would empower every individual regardless of their station in life.

> If the fisherman thinks that he is the Spirit, he will be a better fisherman; if the student thinks he is the Spirit, he will be a better student. If the lawyer thinks that he is the Spirit, he will be a better lawyer, and so on, and the result will be that the castes will remain for ever. It is in the nature of society to form itself into groups; and what will go will be these privileges. Caste is a natural order; I can perform one duty in social life, and you another; you can govern a country, and I can mend a pair of old shoes, but that is no reason why you are greater than I, for can you mend my shoes? Can I govern the country? I am clever in mending shoes, you are clever in reading Vedas, but that is no reason why you should trample on my head. Why if one commits murder should he be praised, and if another steals an apple why should he be hanged? This will have to go. Caste is good. That is the only natural way of solving life. Men must form themselves into groups, and you cannot get rid of that. Wherever you go, there will be caste. But that does not mean that there should be these privileges. They should be knocked on the head.[30]

If we examine this passage carefully, we can see that Vivekananda is using caste in the sense of a grouping of people who are engaged in a particular profession, or activity. Being a student or lawyer is not a hereditary caste. If all privileges are removed, and caste stops being a hereditary activity, in what sense of the word is Vivekananda using it when he says, 'Caste is good. That is the only natural way of solving life'? It cannot be in the sense of jati, or varna, because what characterizes the varna and jati systems are precisely a hierarchy of privilege and its hereditary nature. It is clear that Vivekananda means here by caste, the formation of humans into groups based on professions, mutual class or political interests, or ethnicities. What he says immediately after saying caste is the only natural way of solving life, makes it clear. 'Men must form themselves into groups, and you cannot get rid of that. Wherever you go, there will be caste. But that does not mean that there should be these privileges.'

So, what Vivekananda seems to be saying is that caste, or rather, community groupings based on professions, trades, ethnicity, or mutual interest is a natural ordering of society. It would be reasonable to assume that this is what he meant when he said that it was sheer nonsense to desire the abolition of caste. But there is, as there is inevitably bound to be when we are dealing with fragments of speeches, a total lack of clarity as to what point of view Vivekananda is countering here. What is the alternative model of society, without community groupings (what Vivekananda refers to as caste), that Vivekananda is refuting? Who has staked out such a position? The thing is that in India, no well-known thinker had yet put forward a model of on what principle a post-jati, post-varna (caste in the hereditary privileged sense) Indian society would be organized. In so far as the critique against the jati–varna society came from Christian missionaries and many western inspired reformers, the assumption was that the capitalistic modern society of Britain, Western Europe, and America was the automatic option as a social model for India.

As late as 1916, Tagore was still defending the jati–varna system as he imagined it originally existed in a pristine form in the Vedic age, because he rejected the Western model. Varna was, he said, India's solution to harmonious co-existence of different groups, while avoiding strife and competition. In 1920, in *Young India*, Gandhi argued that the varna system could be 'offered to the world as a leaven and as the best remedy against heartless competition and social disintegration born of avarice and greed.'[31] The two key themes here are competition and social disintegration. What was common to both Tagore and Gandhi was their direct experience of Western society and its social institutions. While the solution that Tagore and Gandhi offered were bad ones and at the very least, myopic, they were responding to legitimate concerns about modernity which were being raised in the West in the early twentieth century. Social structures like family, church, and ethnicity were being destabilized by the intellectual, economic, and technicalistic aspects of modernity. Modern society was becoming fragmented and atomistic; the individual often found herself isolated socially, ethically, and existentially. Apart from those who dreamt of a socialist revolution which would replace capitalistic society, the problematic of the modern condition haunted many thinkers, artists, and writers. The anxiety of the fragmentation of society elicited a wide range of responses from the western intelligentsia.

While conservatives like the German historian Oswald Spengler saw in the modern condition a decline of Western civilization, thinkers like Theodor Adorno responded by subjecting the political and social structures of capitalist society to sociological analysis. Fragmentation became a dominant theme explored by the Modernist movement in Western visual arts (like cubism) and in literature. It was also commented upon by a number of popular writers. The adaptation of the western social model thus seemed unpromising to men like Tagore and Gandhi in the early twentieth century and they offered some kind of modernized and modified form of the varna system as an alternative model that would keep the organicity of society intact and control the destabilizing forces of modern capitalism.

Now the difference between Tagore and Gandhi's views and Vivekananda's views on the organization of society, expressed twenty years earlier, was that the latter lent no support to the varna system. He supported, instead, a path of social evolution that would have communities of people (which he calls 'caste') who organize along non-hereditary and non-hierarchical lines of mutual ethnic, professional, commercial, or intellectual interests (students for example), while allowing full scope for the development of the individual. Of Vivekananda's thoughts about how this was to be accomplished, we have no information other than that this was partly to be achieved through spreading the egalitarian Vedantic idea of infinite human potential and perfect equality among India's masses. We can be sure about what Vivekananda meant when he said that caste is good, but we cannot be sure about what alternate views of social organization prompted his statement. While it is unproblematic to assume that in the case of Tagore and Gandhi's support for the varna system, the intellectual reasons were the problems of capitalistic modernity, one cannot assume that Vivekananda was also responding to the same, with certainty. It is at best, one among several reasonable explanations.

This is because the fragmentation and atomization of Western society was not part of the larger thought currents of the late nineteenth century. However, it was not entirely unknown. A handful of thinkers had already articulated the problem, including the French social thinker Georges Sorel, the French sociologist Emile Durkheim, and possibly the German sociologist Max Weber. But what we can call the 'problematic of the modern condition', was confined to academic circles. It is almost a certainty that Vivekananda did not read any of these thinkers, though it is certainly possible that the gist of such ideas could have reached him through his intellectual contacts with William James and other members of the philosophical department at Harvard. Other possible conduits for such ideas were his contacts with the Fabian Society and social democrats in London.

The other possibility is that the intellectual catalyst for Vivekananda's aforementioned statements on caste came from the far left: from communism or anarchism. While Vivekananda almost certainly did not read communist literature, he must have had some idea of the theories that proposed a classless society where the only social bond was membership in the universal community of workers.* Vivekananda met and exchanged ideas with the influential anarchist thinker Peter Kropotkin in Paris. Kropotkin theorized on creating a society where all existing social structures would be dismantled. Such a view could very well elicit a dialectical response where one thinks that social groups aligning along certain unique identities are essential for society. However, the meeting took place in 1900, while the speeches we are concerned with were delivered in 1897. But anarchist views of this kind could have reached the intellectually curious Vivekananda through other channels. The socialist poet Edward Carpenter, who according to Vivekananda, visited him on many occasions in London in 1896, remains a possibility.[32] Though not an anarchist himself, Carpenter, who was an early advocate for gay rights, used to be a member of the Socialist League, which had a sizeable anarchist membership. Marie Louise, (not to be confused with Vivekananda's biographer Marie Louise Burke), who was reportedly an anarchist, met Vivekananda in New York and converted by Vivekananda's ideas, became his disciple. While it is uncertain whether she really held anarchist views, she was a close friend of Emma Goldman, the most prominent female anarchist in the Anglo-American world. On the whole, unless previously unknown material on Vivekananda comes to light, this question will remain a matter of speculation.

Now let us look at the third sense in which caste is used by Vivekananda by examining two speeches ('The Future of India' and 'Vedanta in its application to Indian life') and an interview given in 1897. Vivekananda's health had not started deteriorating yet, and he had no idea that he would die within five and a half years. Like any other normal person, he too would have imagined several decades of life ahead. These were to be years of intense work, where he planned to move beyond just delivering speeches and lecturing, and undertake mass education drives in the country and build institutions capable of taking on that task. Vivekananda was not a revolutionary; he believed that social change had to be brought about by gradual evolution. Vivekananda gave a brief sketch of the initial phase of work he had in mind in the lecture 'My Plan of Campaign', delivered in Madras a few days before the two speeches

---

*For Vivekananda, variety was the sign of life. A homogeneous communist society without any of the cultural variation produced by group identities, would have appeared to him a lifeless society.

we are concerned with. But from other conversations and correspondence, we can glean that what he had in mind was a programme that had many areas of activity and would take a lifetime to accomplish. It would require both great manpower and substantial finance. The Ramakrishna Mission would be the nucleus of this effort, but it was to be a widespread and diffused movement. In most of his speeches, he exhorted young men to join him in his cause, looking for recruits. None of this, of course, came to bear fruit. Vivekananda had hardly four years of active public life left; he would die on 4 July 1902.

Thus, for Vivekananda, many of the things that he said relating to political and social issues, were only opening statements of what he would have imagined were long years of spreading his ideas and bringing about changes in attitudes among Indians. When he states his opinion about many things, including caste, there is little effort to present a fully formed picture. He often made brief categorical statements, without sufficient explanation of the rationale, or even the exact meaning. This is not particularly unknown among orators, especially those who spoke extempore without a written speech that would present their views in a more systematic fashion. In the case of such orators, their views on particular subjects often crystallized in the public sphere over a long period of time, over repeated perorations on the same subject. This is precisely what did not happen in Vivekananda's case due to his early death.

This particularly affects our ability to understand his views on caste, since the solution that Vivekananda offered to the caste problem was addressed exclusively to Indian audiences and he spoke in India for only four years. Many public figures who used oratory as a vehicle for political or social change, especially leftist thinkers, would periodically write more theoretical expositions of their positions to give clarity and coherence to what they said in public. Vivekananda did have plans for writing books, and it is quite possible that had he lived on, he would have written clarifications of views presented only imperfectly through his speeches. This would have helped avoid misunderstandings about his views in many areas as well as cleared up confusing expressions of his thought. With caste, the confusion is intricate because at times we see Vivekananda using the term caste in three different senses in the same paragraph without distinguishing them. All this notwithstanding, by giving meticulous attention to what Vivekananda says about caste and cross-referencing it across his oeuvre with expressions of the same ideas, we can arrive at a broad-brush understanding of his view. We are helped in this by the great simplicity and clarity of Vivekananda's language, so that, unlike with many thinkers, we do not face additional interpretative difficulties which are linguistic.

Let us look at some of the allegedly pro-caste quotes posted by the Twitter user and referenced earlier in their full textual context. In the interview Vivekananda gave to *The Hindu* in February 1897, he said: 'I do not propose any levelling of castes. Caste is a very good thing. Caste is the plan we want to follow. What caste really is, not one in a million understands. There is no country in the world without caste. In India, from caste we reach to the point where there is no caste. Caste is based throughout on that principle.'[33]

To say that 'not one in a million understands' what caste really is, is to say that there is an apparent caste and a real caste. We know what is apparent as caste; it is the jati and varna system. What then does Vivekananda mean by real caste? While Vivekananda alludes to what he calls the real meaning of caste on at least three occasions, the clearest exposition of what he means is given in a letter he wrote to Justice Subramania Iyer in January 1895 from America. Iyer, who would go on to become the first Indian Chief Justice of the Madras High Court, would later co-found the Home Rule Movement for Indian self-rule. The letter Vivekananda wrote appears to be meant as an address to the people of Madras to be presented at some forum. Vivekananda wrote:

I fully agree with the educated classes in India that a thorough overhauling of society is necessary. But how to do it? The destructive plans of reformers have failed.... Now, take the case of caste—in Sanskrit, Jati, i.e. species. Now, this is the first idea of creation. Variation (Vichitrata), that is to say Jati, means creation. 'I am One, I become many' (various Vedas). Unity is before creation, diversity is creation. Now if this diversity stops, creation will be destroyed. So long as any species is vigorous and active, it must throw out varieties. When it ceases or is stopped from breeding varieties, it dies. Now the original idea of Jati was this freedom of the individual to express his nature, his Prakriti, his Jati, his caste; and so it remained for thousands of years. Not even in the latest books is inter-dining prohibited; nor in any of the older books is inter-marriage forbidden. Then what was the cause of India's downfall?—the giving up of this idea of caste. As Gita says, with the extinction of caste the world will be destroyed.* Now does it seem true that with the stoppage of these variations the world will be destroyed? The present caste is not the real Jati, but a hindrance to its progress. It really has prevented the free action of Jati, i.e., caste or variation. Any crystallized custom or privilege or hereditary class in any shape really prevents caste (Jati) from having its full sway; and whenever

---

*This is said by Arjuna in the Gita when he refuses to fight.

any nation ceases to produce this immense variety, it must die. Therefore what I have to tell you, my countrymen, is this, that India fell because you prevented and abolished caste. Every frozen aristocracy or privileged class is a blow to caste and is not-caste. Let Jati have its sway; break down every barrier in the way of caste, and we shall rise. Now look at Europe. When it succeeded in giving free scope to caste and took away most of the barriers that stood in the way of individuals, each developing his caste—Europe rose. In America, there is the best scope for caste (real Jati) to develop, and so the people are great. Every Hindu knows that astrologers try to fix the caste of every boy or girl as soon as he or she is born. That is the real caste—the individuality.... And we can only rise by giving it full sway again. This variety does not mean inequality, nor any special privilege. This is my method—to show the Hindus that they have to give up nothing, but only to move on in the line laid down by the sages and shake off their inertia....[34]

This passage makes clear what Vivekananda means by 'real caste', which should be preserved. He takes the etymological meaning of the word 'jati', which he says means species in Sanskrit. Vivekananda here seems to be drawing on the terminology of the Nyaya school of philosophy. By reading species as 'own nature', i.e., the inherent nature of something, Vivekananda equates it to the individuality of a person—the particular way in which they vary from the rest of humanity and which constitutes their individuality. Vivekananda essentially turns caste on its head here. The essence of the jati system, which is the social reality of India, is the suppression of individuality. A person's jati decides what she can and cannot do, where she can and cannot live, who she can touch or not touch, what privileges she enjoys or does not. The jati system brutally crushes out the freedom of the individual with the whole force of society. Vivekananda is here drawing upon the Hindu tradition itself to invert the meaning of caste. The hereditary and privilege-based jati system can be eliminated if Hindus are told that they are not following the real jati dharma which they should be following.

The result of such a revolution in Hindu thinking, if Vivekananda were able to accomplish it, would be the annihilation of the caste system. The vast majority of Hindus believed that their religion sanctioned jati. (Vivekananda disagreed). But Vivekananda seemed to think that instead of condemning the institution downright as not belonging to Hinduism, which people like Ram Mohan Roy and Dayanand Saraswati had largely tried and failed, it would be more practical to take the opposite tack. Such condemnation and its demand for theological reformation was too close in tone to the Western liberal and missionary condemnation of caste. It came from a standpoint located outside the Hindu tradition. Instead, Vivekananda is attempting to work from within that tradition and instead of attacking the idea of varna and jati, which too many Hindus considered part of their religion, he wanted to redefine the meaning of jati into its opposite, to be accomplished on the strength of the spiritual revival he was attempting.

That the hereditary jati as a social structure is the exact opposite of the jati he wants Hindus to follow, is something he makes explicit when he says: 'The present caste is not the real Jati, but a hindrance to its progress. It really has prevented the free action of Jati, i.e. caste or variation. Any crystallized custom or privilege or hereditary class in any shape really prevents caste (Jati) from having its full sway.'[35] Historically, in all religions, spiritual revivals have often led to social change, while theological reformations have accomplished little in that area. In fact, the scope of the reform Vivekananda seemed to have been aiming at by claiming that authentic jati according to the rishis referred to individuality, went beyond caste. Asking Hindus to bring back the real jati, which is to allow each person to manifest their individuality, is the demand to give individuals liberty and freedom. Most social evils proceed from the attempt of society to control and determine the scope of the individual's action under the guise of tradition, custom, and authority. When Vivekananda refers to 'caste' in the context of Europe and America in the above quote that, 'When it (Europe) succeeded in giving free scope to caste and took away most of the barriers that stood in the way of individuals, each developing his caste—Europe rose. In America, there is the best scope for caste (real Jati) to develop, and so the people are great,' he is referring to the liberal revolution in the West which started with the Renaissance and increasingly loosened society's control over the individual's agency.

Interestingly, Narayana Guru in Kerala, took a decidedly similar approach to the caste question. He coined the slogan: 'One caste, one religion, one God for mankind', which was a demand for equality and equal treatment of all people regardless of faith or caste. But he did not directly attack the caste system; that is the ordering of society into caste groupings. Narayana Guru wrote two critiques of the caste system in poetic form called *Jati Nirnayam* and *Jati Lakshanam*. It was common at the time in Malayalam literature to present philosophical theses through the poetic form. As such Narayana Guru is far clearer than Vivekananda is on the issue. To be fair to Vivekananda though, Narayana Guru wrote *Jati Nirnayam* in the mature phase of his life, in 1914—an age Vivekananda would never see. Narayan Guru too tried to redefine 'Jati' and take away its deployment in casteist discoruse. He too locates the etymological meaning of jati as species. Narayana Guru gives the meaning of species as that which is universal: the 'nature' present in all beings. Thus, he says that the true meaning of jati is that of the universal human nature. It is a unifying principle, not a principle that supports caste divisions and exclusive privileges. Narayana Guru's definition is closer to the meaning of jati as used in Nyaya logic; both Vivekananda and Narayana Guru seem to have drawn from common Nyaya sources. Vivekananda's reading of species as individuality is a further interpretational innovation on the concept.

The last four quotes in the tweet on p. 402 all come from the speech 'The Future of India', which was delivered by Vivekananda on 14 February 1897 at the Harmston Circus Pavilion in Madras.[36] The third quote also uses caste in the sense of a mutual grouping and its meaning follows the same logic as we have seen. The fourth to sixth quotes all deal with the Brahmin.

The speech, titled 'The Future of India', starts with praising the greatness of the ancient rishis and the sublime spirituality that was attained by India before any nation did. India has a great civilizational past and Vivekananda asks the audience to take pride in it, to gaze upon it till they feel confidence in themselves as the descendants of ancient India. But having done that, he asks them to go forward and build a future India and not get stuck in the past. The first problem that is taken up as the goal to be accomplished, is raising the lower castes. Two themes dominate the early discussion, and they continue to shape the speech till the end, though other themes are discussed. The first is the concern that there be no more inter-fighting between the various castes. The second is Vivekananda's idea for a practical plan of action which would be a solution to the caste problem, that is the problem of inequality and oppression created by hereditary and endogamous castes grouped in a hierarchy of increasing privilege, with Brahmins at the top.

While Vivekananda blamed the Brahmins and their priestcraft for India's national degeneration, in some of his public speeches in India while blaming the Brahmins squarely, he also tried to offset that criticism with what few positive things he could find to say about the Brahmins: namely that they had initiated India's spiritual growth and that they deserved credit for preserving the scriptures through the millennia. (It is difficult to find any positive statements at all about the Brahmins in Vivekananda's discourse and correspondence with friends, disciples, and the Western press and his criticism of them was at times almost vituperative.) Vivekananda's primary concern was nation building. While it can be debated whether he was ideologically right or not, along with an entire generation of men who would shortly inaugurate the nationalist phase of Indian history, he saw the nation as the very horizon of political possibility for any widespread emancipatory action even in social matters, whether it was the education of the masses, female literacy or the destruction of caste oppression.

As he said in this speech:

Why is it that organizations are so powerful? Do not say organization is material. Why is it, to take a case in point, that forty millions of Englishmen rule three hundred millions of people here? What is the psychological explanation? These forty millions put their wills together and that means infinite power, and you three hundred millions have a will each separate from the other. Therefore to make a great future India, the whole secret lies in organization, accumulation of power, co-ordination of wills…. And the more you go on fighting and quarrelling about all trivialities such as 'Dravidian' and 'Aryan', and the question of Brahmins and non-Brahmins and all that, the further you are off from that accumulation of energy and power which is going to make the future India. For mark you, the future India depends entirely upon that. That is the secret—accumulation of will-power, co-ordination, bringing them all, as it here, into one focus. Each Chinaman thinks in his own way, and a handful of Japanese all think in the same way, and you know the result. That is how it goes throughout the history of the world. You find in every case, compact little nations always governing and ruling huge unwieldy nations, and this is natural, because it is easier for the little compact nations to bring their ideas into the same focus, and thus they become developed. And the bigger the nation, the more unwieldy it is. Born, as it were, a disorganized mob, they cannot combine. All these dissensions must stop.[37]

One of Vivekananda's concerns here is that blaming Brahmins for India's social problems and national condition, as thoroughly merited as it might be, would lead to resentment and hatred of Brahmins as a caste. This was already happening in the Madras Presidency. He would want to avoid that both on spiritual grounds and on the grounds of nation building. These had nothing to do with any personal sympathy for Brahmins as a class. Vivekananda's personal contempt for the orthodox Brahmin class and their caste taboos almost exceeded the limits of expression. His conversations, correspondence, and talks with disciples are peppered with the denunciation of Brahmin orthodoxy and their culpability in India's ruined condition. As an example, we find a particularly scathing and passionate denunciation of Brahmin priestcraft and exploitation in a letter he sent to a brother disciple in 1895.

Well, tell Shashi (Sanyal) to go to Malabar. The Raja there has taken his subjects' land and offered it at the feet of Brahmins. There are big monasteries in every village where sumptuous dinners are given, supplemented by presents in cash.... There is no harm in touching the non-Brahmin classes when it serves one's purpose; and when you have done with it, you bathe, for the non-Brahmins are as a class unholy and must never be touched on other occasions! Monks and Sannyasins and Brahmins of a certain type have thrown the country into ruin. Intent all the while on theft and wickedness, these pose as preachers of religion! They will take gifts from the people and at the same time cry, 'Don't touch me!' And what great things they have been doing!—'If a potato happens to touch a brinjal, how long will the universe last before it is deluged?' 'If they do not apply earth a dozen times to clean their hands, will fourteen generations of ancestors go to hell, or twenty-four?'—For intricate problems like these they have been finding out scientific explanations for the last two thousand years—while one fourth of the people are starving. A girl of eight is married to a man of thirty, and the parents are jubilant over it.... And if anyone protests against it, the plea is put forward, 'Our religion is being overturned.' What sort of religion have they who want to see their girls becoming mothers before they attain puberty even and offer scientific explanations for it? Many, again, lay the blame at the door of the Mohammedans. They are to blame, indeed! Just read the Grihya-Sutras through and see what is given as the marriageable age of a girl. ...There it is expressly stated that a girl must be married before attaining puberty. The entire Grihya-Sutras enjoin this. ...All the Brahmanas mention them, and all the commentators admit them to be true. How can you deny them?[38]

The ideological antagonism was mutual. The main opposition to Vivekananda and his ideas on Hinduism came from the orthodox Hindu Brahmins and Christian missionaries. Orthodox Brahmin priests denied Vivekananda entry to temples on many occasions because he had crossed the seas and because he associated freely with Westerners (who were considered mlecchas and hence untouchables). Brahmin orthodoxy also reacted against the ideas of Hinduism that Vivekananda was spreading, especially his dismissal of rituals, rites, traditions, and caste privileges. Conservative Hindu newspapers and publications carried many articles criticizing Vivekananda's liberal and universal interpretation of Hinduism. They questioned his understanding of scripture and Vedanta, said he was not a proper sanyasi since he was not part of a guru parampara, and claimed that the Kayasthas were Shudras, and hence, as a Kayastha, Vivekananda had no right to become a sanyasi, let alone preach Vedanta. As far as the reform of Hinduism was concerned, Hindu orthodoxy was the most implacable opponent Vivekananda faced. That said, in the short term at least, they could do little to dent Vivekananda's immense popularity, especially among young educated Hindus.

On the grounds of nation building, there were two reasons for Vivekananda's reservations that ideological anti-Brahminism would turn into anti-Brahmin caste feelings. One was that, as he put it, India was already a divided nation, and caste antagonisms would further divide the country and prevent India from coming together as a nation, which was essential for regenerating India and improving the condition of the masses. (Vivekananda was not thinking in terms of political nationalism). The second reason is that it was from the upper castes, the Brahmins and the Kshatriyas, that Vivekananda expected to find recruits to build his movement to spread mass secular education and universal spiritual ideas in India. He expected Brahmins especially, to play a role, since they were the caste that had taken most to modern education. So, even as he admonished Brahmins, he asked them to atone for the past mistakes of their ancestors by dedicating their lives to uplift the downtrodden lower classes and castes. He says in the speech that, 'The first task must be to break open the cells that hide the wonderful treasures which our common ancestors accumulated; bring them out and give them to everybody and the Brahmin must be the first to do it. There is an old superstition in Bengal that if the cobra that bites, sucks out his own poison from the patient, the man must survive. Well then, the Brahmin must suck out his own poison.'[39]

But why did Vivekananda place his expectations mainly on the Brahmins? Pragmatically, it was the only course open to him. The leaders of the Bengal Renaissance, from Ram Mohan Roy onwards, almost all hailed from Brahmin castes. This is because, given their cultural capital, they were the ones most able to access modern Western education and reap the benefits offered by the nascent modernity British colonialism was introducing into India. They formed an overwhelming majority of the Indian intelligentsia. It might seem paradoxical that Vivekananda wanted those at the apex of the oppressive caste hierarchy to initiate reforms that would include the dismantling of the system. But if one studies the history of emancipatory movements, whether it is the

French Revolution, the emancipation of slaves in the United States, or even the communist movement, the initial impulse usually came from a small band of enlightened people acting against their own class or ethnic interests.

The significant role of Brahmins in the success or failure of caste reforms within Hindu society, was argued for by Ambedkar in *Annihilation of Caste*. In that written speech which was never delivered, Ambedkar says that he had decided to leave the Hindu fold because he had no hope left that caste could be destroyed from within Hinduism itself. According to him, the principal reason why the destruction of caste is not possible for Hindu society, is the reluctance of the Brahmin castes. Though the task appears to him to be hopeless, Ambedkar says that the only way for Hindu society to eliminate caste is for the Brahmins to come forward and take the lead in the elimination of caste. He writes: 'The Brahmins form the vanguard of the movement for political reform, and in some cases also of economic reform. But they are not to be found even as camp-followers in the army raised to break down the barricades of caste. Is there any hope of the Brahmins ever taking up a lead in the future in this matter? I say no.'[40] Then he goes on to outline the logic of why caste reform within Hinduism, has to be led by the Brahmins if it were to be successful.

> Some of you will say that it is a matter of small concern whether the Brahmins come forward to lead the movement against caste or whether they do not. To take this view is, in my judgement, to ignore the part played by the intellectual class in the community. Whether you accept the theory of the great man as the maker of history or whether you do not, this much you will have to concede: that in every country the intellectual class is the most influential class, if not the governing class. The intellectual class is the class which can foresee, it is the class which can advise and give the lead. In no country does the mass of the people live the life of intelligent thought and action. It is largely imitative, and follows the intellectual class. When such an intellectual class, which holds the rest of the community in its grip, is opposed to the reform of caste, the chances of success in a movement for the break-up of the caste system appear to me very, very remote.[41]

Ambedkar's solution was for the Dalits, the untouchable castes to convert to Buddhism. But as far as it was at least theoretically possible for Hindus to reform and eliminate caste from within their ranks, Ambedkar argued that the lead had to be taken by the Brahmins.

Vivekananda's speech 'The Future of India' is probably unique in his oeuvre, for laying out in one place the essential details of Vivekananda's analysis of the caste problem and his proposed solution. What Vivekananda intended was both a spiritual and social revolution at the national scale, to be worked out through the generations. These two were not separate movements, but inextricably intertwined, both informing the other. Thus, the spiritual renaissance would be hollow if it did not result in social change and the removal of human suffering, while social change could not be affected without the inspiration of spiritual upliftment. For reasons that will be examined, the term Brahmin comes to have a central importance in this programme, and it is used in different times in the speech in two different senses: one to indicate the spiritual meaning of the word and the other to refer to the social caste of Brahmins respectively. One needs to differentiate the two usages and meanings of the word to avoid misunderstanding, and to make sense of Vivekananda's proposed reform plan.

The word Brahmin in Hindu philosophical and religious thought originally meant 'The knower of Brahman'. That is, any person, who had obtained knowledge of the ultimate reality of the non-dual Brahman, the impersonal God proclaimed by the Upanishads. Such a person is morally perfect and pure, above all material entanglements. That person could be of any sex, caste, or even religion. The Brahmins as a caste, appropriated power and privilege for themselves in the late Vedic age, by virtue of such spiritual knowledge they claimed to possess as a group devoted only to religious rites and the study of the scriptures. In the Hindu philosophical and theological tradition, there has been a consistent effort to differentiate Brahmin as the knower of Brahman and the possessor of a spiritual nature (sattvic), from the Brahmin caste. For instance, in the Bhagavad Gita, Krishna defines the varnashrama as based on the inherent quality of a person, rather than their birth (Chapter 4, Verse 13).[42] Yudhishthira does the same in the Mahabharata and so on.[43] The spiritual tradition of Hinduism was associated in the popular mind with the Brahmins to a large extent (though taking a backseat to sanyasis and spiritual mendicants who remained the primary authority), and part of the reason Brahmins could command respect from other castes and quell resentment, was the association of piety with Brahmins. Vivekananda's concern here seems to be that the continuous criticism of Brahmins would, because of the association of Brahmins with spirituality in the popular mind, result in the abandonment of Hindu spirituality itself.

Such apprehensions were rooted in the experience of the reformation movements in Bengal. Reform societies like the Brahmo Samaj and its various offshoots and later the Arya Samaj, were both religious and social reform movements. In the case of both movements, especially the Brahmo Samaj, most of its leaders and members were drawn from the Brahmin caste, even as it positioned itself against the Hindu orthodoxy led by Brahmins. In Vivekananda's view, both these movements failed to generate any genuine spiritual empowerment because in their reformist zeal they cut themselves off not only from Brahminism, as they should have, but also the sources of the Hindu spiritual tradition. In the 1870s, Keshub Chandra Sen came under the influence of Sri Ramakrishna Paramahamsa. This contributed to a schism in the Brahmo Samaj group he led, and eventually to a dissident group splitting away.* In the reformist Brahmo Samaj's eyes, Ramakrishna was everything which represented the retrograde Hinduism they were trying to break free from. He was the Brahmin priest of a Kali temple, followed ritualistic worship, prayed to an idol, and claimed to have supersensuous visions of the various deities of the Hindu pantheon. This went against the Brahmo Samaj's general reformist convictions of monotheism, the meaninglessness of idol worship, and ritualistic devotional practices. The sources of the spiritual/mystical tradition overlapped and permeated institutionalized forms of religion. And the Brahmins remained the custodians of the Sanskrit literature and the institutions of religion. In Vivekananda's mind, the spirit of religion and priestcraft were essentially opposed. But that said, he found it counter-productive to continuously blame Brahmins in public. He thought the anti-Brahmin feelings it produced would result in the tarring of the Sanskrit scriptural tradition with the same brush as the oppressive Brahmins.

He says in 'Future of India':

> The solution of the caste problem in India, therefore, assumes this form, not to degrade the higher castes, not to crush out the Brahmin. The Brahminhood is the ideal of humanity in India, as wonderfully put forward by Shankaracharya at the beginning of his commentary on the Gita, where he speaks about the reason for Krishna's coming as a preacher for the preservation of Brahminhood, of Brahminness. That was the great end. This Brahmin, the man of God, he who has known Brahman, the ideal man, the perfect man, must remain; he must not go. And with all the defects of the caste now, we know that we must all be ready to give to

---

*The immediate catalyst for the split was Sen's decision to marry off his daughter though she was underage, which looked like rank hypocrisy from someone who had opposed child-marriage all his life. But the tension had been building up for some time, mainly over Sen's increasing attraction to traditional Hindu devotional practices.

the Brahmins this credit, that from them have come more men with real Brahminness in them than from all the other castes. That is true. That is the credit due to them from all the other castes. We must be bold enough, must be brave enough to speak of their defects, but at the same time we must give the credit that is due to them. Remember the old English proverb, 'Give every man his due'. Therefore, my friends, it is no use fighting among the castes. What good will it do? It will divide us all the more, weaken us all the more, degrade us all the more. The days of exclusive privileges and exclusive claims are gone, gone for ever from the soil of India, and it is one of the great blessings of the British Rule in India. Even to the Mohammedan Rule we owe that great blessing, the destruction of exclusive privilege…. There ought to be no more fight between the castes.[44]

In the speech itself, Vivekananda does not explicitly differentiate between Brahminhood as a spiritual quality and the Brahmin caste. He does not need to. It was a distinction that an educated Hindu crowd understood. Nonetheless, the distinction is implicit in his words. When he says that 'Brahminhood is the ideal of humanity in India', it is clear that it is not the ideal a particular caste can appeal to, but all of humanity. He then goes on to define a true Brahmin as 'the man of God, he who has known Brahman, the ideal man, the perfect man'. Even the most dogmatic Brahmin cannot claim that all members of the Brahmin caste had seen God. When Vivekananda says that the Brahmin caste has furnished 'more men with true Brahminness' in them than other castes, the necessary logical implication is that true Brahmins have come from other castes also and that true 'Brahminness' is an inherent quality of an individual, not a property that accrues from being a member of the Brahmin caste.

This is clearly seen if we look at other portions of Vivekananda's work. Take for example, this conversation between Vivekananda and a disciple named Priya Nath Sinha, recorded by the latter.

Vivekananda: The Brahmin caste and the Brahmanya qualities are two distinct things. In India, one is held to be a Brahmin by one's caste, but in the West, one should be known as such by one's Brahmanya qualities. As there are three Gunas—Sattva, Rajas, and Tamas—so there are Gunas which show a man to be a Brahmin, Kshatriya, Vaishya or Shudra….

Disciple: Then you call those Brahmins who are Sattvika by nature.

Swamiji: Quite so. As there are Sattva, Rajas, and Tamas—one or other of these Gunas more or less—in every man, so the qualities which make a Brahmin, Kshatriya, Vaishya, or Shudra are inherent in every man, more or less.[45]

'That is why in the Vedas the term Rishi means "the seer of the truth of the Mantras", and not any Brahmin with the holy thread hanging down the neck. The division of society into castes came about later on.'[46]

A pertinent question to ask here is why did Vivekananda want to promote the usage of a term like Brahmin which was so linked to the hereditary and endogamous caste hierarchy. Wouldn't it only end up giving legitimacy to the Brahmin caste? In the conditions prevailing in nineteenth century India under the British government, the short answer is no. Outside the princely states, as per my reading, it is at a more advanced stage of economic modernity and political independence from the British (roughly from the 1920s, as Indians gradually gained political representation) that the Brahmin caste came to wield more direct power over the middle and lower castes. Within nineteenth century British India, it was the zamindari castes who wielded direct power in rural areas. In terms of centralized administration, however, though Brahmins were extraordinarily overrepresented, the administrative roles the British granted Indians were very restricted, and Indians had no legislative roles. To a large extent then, the power Brahmins exercised came from the cultural power of religion. Vivekananda might have been able to convince a highly educated audience that within the high tradition of Hindu philosophy and mysticism, the priests had no authority whatsoever. But at the level of popular religion, both the jati system and the privilege Brahmins drew from it was too embedded in most areas of Hindu religious consciousness for it to be displaced by a frontal attack. Like many religious and social reformers before him, Vivekananda thought that it was more pragmatic to modify the popular tradition in an egalitarian direction by redefining its terms of reference and drawing it closer to the high tradition.

Vivekananda was not attempting something new. During several tides of spiritual reform in India, the attempt had been made to inject egalitarianism into the popular idea of varna, by redefining the meaning of the varnas as inherent individual qualities, rather than birth. Such attempts had particularly focused on defining the Brahmana as it is found in the Upanishad and the Gita, as a knower of Brahman. The existence of such a long tradition made Vivekananda's attempts at least theoretically more viable. This is in contrast to someone like Dayanand Saraswati, who in his reformist zeal had to create a completely new tradition based on his own idiosyncratic and allegorical interpretation of the Vedas. Such a tradition could not take root among already well-entrenched traditions and the Arya Samaj that Dayanand Saraswati created, eventually became engulfed within the currents of popular Hinduism. But the tradition Vivekananda was appealing to in defining Brahminhood as a spiritual state rather than a caste, went back to the later Vedic age. It goes without saying that such attempts in the past at redefining the popular conception of varna, met only partial and temporary success. But this does not necessarily mean the idea was unsound. One of the texts in that tradition which attest to the pragmatic value of such an intervention, as perhaps the best among available options, is the Dhammapada.

Buddhism in both philosophy and practice, completely eschewed caste and represents the most powerful movement in Indian history to attempt to break caste. Nonetheless, in engaging with the lay population outside the Sangha, Buddha adopted similar tactics to the ones the Hindu high tradition and its nineteenth century representative, Vivekananda attempted. The twenty-sixth chapter of the Dhammapada titled 'The Brahman' is a conversation between Buddha and two Brahmins over whether one is a Brahmin by birth or qualities. It is interesting to note here that the terms in which the Dhammapada defines the Brahmin is extremely similar to the ones Vivekananda uses two-and-a-half millennia later: as the knower of the ultimate reality, morally pure, spiritual, and glorious. A selected extract is given below for the reader to examine the similarities.

> 383. 'Having striven, cut off the stream!
> Dispel sensualities, O brahmana,
> Having known the dissolution of the samkharas,
> A knower of the Unmade (the ultimate reality) are you, O brahmana.
> 386. The one meditating, free of dirt, quietly sitting,
> Tasks done, free of intoxicants,
> Who has obtained the goal supreme,
> That one I call a brahmana.
> 387. A brahmana would not attack a brahman
> Or let loose [wrath] upon him.
> Shame on one who strikes a brahmana,
> And greater shame [on one] who lets loose [wrath] upon him.
> 393. Not by matted hair, nor by clan,
> Nor by birth does one become a brahman
> In whom is truth and dhamma,
> He is the pure one, and he is the brahman
> 396. And I do not call one a brahmana

Merely by being born from a brahmana womb,
Sprung from a brahmana mother.
He is merely a 'bho-sayer'
If he is a possessor of things.
One who has nothing and takes nothing,
That one I call a brahmana.
403. One having profound insight, wise,
Proficient as to path and non-path,
Who has attained the highest goal,
That one I call a brahmana.
413. Who, like the moon, is spotless, pure,
Serene, unagitated,
In whom is extinct the desire for existence,
That one I call a brahmana.
418. Who, having abandoned attachment and aversion,
Who has become cool, free from substrates,
A hero overcoming the entire world—
That one I call a brahmana.
422. A bull, splendid, heroic,
A great sage, a victor,
Passionless, who has bathed, awakened,
That one I call a brahmana.[47]

Vivekananda's plan to get rid of caste too, was conceived in the same pattern of working from within the traditional religious and social structure, and for similar reasons. The plan, Vivekananda told the Madras crowd, would take generation upon generation to work out. Though of its success there was no surety, it should still be attempted. A beginning should be made and questions as to where the money for the cause would come from would take care of themselves. Vivekananda's plan for regenerating India and eventually eliminating caste, as he laid it out in the speech, was three pronged. One was to gradually elevate every caste to the social status of Brahmins. The end aim was an India were everyone was a Brahmin and caste would be meaningless. This is what Vivekananda meant in his remark in the interview given to *The Hindu* that in India 'from caste we reach to the point where there is no caste'. The second part was the spread of the spiritual ideas of Vedanta, along with a secular education. The third was the dissemination of Sanskrit literature. All three had to go together.

For various reasons, Vivekananda disagreed with the dominant theories put forward by Western historians to explain the origins of caste divisions. His theory was that originally there was only a single group which, as labour specialization developed in Aryan society, split into different castes. In many places, he referred to this explanation as it is found in the Mahabharata. He said in the speech, 'The only explanation is to be found in the Mahabharata, which says that in the beginning of the Satya Yuga there was one caste, the Brahmins, and then by difference of occupations they went on dividing themselves into different castes, and that is the only true and rational explanation that has been given. And in the coming Satya Yuga all the other castes will have to go back to the same condition.'[48] The idea of a new Satya Yuga was not there in Hindu Puranic literature. But Vivekananda had a deep, almost mystical conviction that the advent of Sri Ramakrishna was to be the dawn of a new golden age for India, both spiritually and in material prosperity. It was by taking Ramakrishna's name implicitly that Vivekananda tried to inspire the Hindu crowds that he spoke to, that India had an even greater future ahead of it than her ancient past.

Vivekananda then raised the problem of caste:

The solution is not by bringing down the higher, but by raising the lower up to the level of the higher. And that is the line of work that is found in all our books, in spite of what you may hear from some people whose knowledge of their own scriptures and whose capacity to understand the mighty plans of the ancients are only zero. They do not understand, but those do that have brains, that have the intellect to grasp the whole scope of the work. They stand aside and follow the wonderful procession of national life through the ages. They can trace it step by step through all the books, ancient and modern. What is the plan? The ideal at one end is the Brahmin and the ideal at the other end is the Chandala, and the whole work is to raise the Chandala up to the Brahmin.... I have no time to place before you all these workings, nor how they can be traced in detail; but coming to plain facts, we find that all the castes are to rise slowly and slowly. There are thousands of castes, and some are even getting admission into Brahminhood, for what prevents any caste from declaring they are Brahmins? Thus caste, with all its rigour, has been created in that manner. Let us suppose that there are castes here with ten thousand people in each. If these put their heads together and say, we will call ourselves Brahmins, nothing can stop them; I have seen it in my own life. Some castes become strong, and as soon as they all agree, who is to say nay? Because whatever it was, each caste was exclusive of the other. It did not meddle with others' affairs; even the several divisions of one caste did not meddle with the other divisions, and those powerful epoch-makers, Shankaracharya and others, were the great caste-makers. I cannot tell you all the wonderful things they fabricated, and some of you may resent what I have to say. But in my travels and experiences I have traced them out, and have arrived at most wonderful results. They would sometimes get hordes of Baluchis and at once make them Kshatriyas, also get hold of hordes of fishermen and make them Brahmins forthwith.[49]

What does this mean? Vivekananda is referring to the fact that over the centuries, caste in India has shown a lot of fluidity, and castes have risen and fallen in the caste hierarchy. Caste is not reducible to class. Caste markers, and identity and discrimination on the basis of caste can continue to exist even when a person belonging to a lower caste rises to wealth. But nonetheless, the lower social status of an entire caste or subcaste remains within the gravitational field of its position in the class hierarchy and can never be completely uncoupled from it. When a caste rises in wealth and power and retains that position over a long period of time, they usually take the position of a jati higher to them in the caste hierarchy. Unfortunately, even today, we do not have a skeletal, let alone comprehensive account of the history of caste formation and change in India. But in the patches that historical evidence becomes available, there is definite evidence of migration of caste positions, both up and down the caste ladder. Many Shudra castes became powerful enough to rule kingdoms and became Kshatriyas (often fabricating lineages with the help of Brahmins in exchange for wealth), while there are several instances of lower castes, including Shudras attaining Brahminhood. The acclaimed sociologist M. N. Srinivas writes:

> The historian K. M. Panikkar has maintained that there has been no such caste as the Kshatriya during the last two thousand years of history. The Nandas were the last 'true' Kshatriyas and they disappeared in the fifth century B.C. Since then every known royal family has come from non-Kshatriya castes, including the famous Rajput dynasties of medieval India. Panikkar also points out that 'the Shudras seem to have produced an unusually large number of royal families even in more recent times. The Palas of Bengal belonged undoubtedly to that caste. The great Maratha Royal House…could hardly sustain their genealogical pretensions connecting them with Rajput descent.'[50] (One of the most important

functions of genealogists and bardic castes was to legitimise mobility from the ranks of lower castes to the Kshatriya by providing suitable lineage and myth.)

There are good reasons why Vivekananda announces this as a discovery. Western, or rather mainly British historians studying India, held the view that socially, India was what was called a static society. This was partly because the eighteenth and nineteenth centuries were broadly a period of social stagnation, but there was a good deal of race superiority behind such theoretical assumptions. The net effect this had was that modern history in Vivekananda's time considered the present caste order to have more or less continued in the same form from ancient times. Vivekananda had to resort to ancient Sanskrit texts, usually of a scriptural nature, to unearth a different and truer account of the historical nature of caste. But this method had its own severe limitations. Apart from the obvious lack of time Vivekananda faced, a historical picture cannot be built from scriptural literature alone, but needs corrections, additions, and collaboration from other sources of historical information. Such historical research is of recent origin and still in a nascent stage. So, while Vivekananda was on the right track in recognizing that mobility existed within the caste system, the picture he could form from the limited resources available to him, was incomplete. This could explain why he doesn't talk about downward mobility. It could also be a strategic move on his part to create the ideological basis to inspire a programme of social action.

Vivekananda's plan then, is to take advantage of the changing economic fortunes of caste groups which have been catalysed by the economic competition introduced by British imperialism and give them all Brahmin status as soon as they are able to achieve enough social status to lay claim to it. This would, as he explains later in the speech, bring about the levelling of caste. Other partial accounts and fragments detailing his plans for the reformation of caste can be found in many other places. In the interview Vivekananda gave to *The Hindu* quoted earlier, he said, 'The plan in India is to make everybody a Brahmin, the Brahmin being the ideal of humanity. If you read the history of India, you will find that attempts have always been made to raise the lower classes. Many are the classes that have been raised. Many more will follow till the whole will become Brahmin. That is the plan. We have only to raise them without bringing down anybody. And this has mostly to be done by the Brahmins themselves, because it is the duty of every aristocracy to dig its own grave; and the sooner it does so, the better for all. No time should be lost.'[51]

Such a state of affairs, if realized, would be equivalent to the annihilation of caste. For in a country where everyone is a Brahmin, the term Brahmin cannot be used as a term of social differentiation. The situation would be parallel to what happened in the West to the term 'gentleman'. In Europe, till the nineteenth century, class (which is what Vivekananda calls the caste of the West) had to do with social status that was inherited, with its accompanying privileges and power. The walls of class were rigid and exclusive, with intermarriage and unregulated mixing between the classes prohibited. In the Middle Ages, the term came to signify classes above the peasant and yeoman, including the nobility. The term was always associated with the Christian ideals of chivalry, honour, and good conduct. But as traditional class started becoming porous after the transformation brought about by industrial capitalism, 'gentleman' as a social term came to mean a man hailing from a family of good social standing and of whom a certain standard of conduct can be expected. With the hereditary class system completely dissolved, in the twentieth century, 'gentleman' became a generic term of address for any man.

Vivekananda tried to carry out his plans in practical ways. The next year in 1898, exactly a year and four days from when he delivered the 'Future of India' speech, Vivekananda handed out sacred threads to non-Brahmins including Shudras at the Belur Math in Calcutta. It was on the occasion of the celebrations of Sri Ramakrishna's birthday. The sacred thread is usually worn exclusively by Brahmins and was deeply intertwined with their exclusive claims to spiritual superiority. Fifty to sixty devotees from all castes, including Shudras, who came to pray at Sri Ramakrishna's shrine were initiated with the Gayatri mantra and invested with the sacred thread. The conversation which transpired was written down by the devotee who was asked to perform the ceremony. (It is probably not a verbatim account as it was clearly written from memory.)

Disciple: I have collected, Sir, quite a good number of holy threads according to your instructions, and after the worship I shall with your permission invest the Bhaktas with them.

Swamiji: To the Bhaktas who are not Brahmins, give this Mantra of Gayatri....* By degrees all the people of the land have to be lifted to the position of Brahmins, not to speak of the Bhaktas of Shri Ramakrishna. Each Hindu, I say, is a brother of every other, and it is we who have degraded them by our outcry, 'Don't touch, don't touch!' And so the whole country has been plunged to the utmost depths of meanness, cowardice, and ignorance. These men have to be uplifted; words of hope and faith

*The Brahmins would already know the Gayatri mantra, so there was no need to instruct them in it.

have to be proclaimed to them. We have to tell them, 'You are men like us, and you have all the rights that we have.' Do you understand?

Disciple: Yes, sir, it should be so.[52]

The reason we have a record of this incident is because of the several dozens of people there, this particular disciple considered the conversation worth recording. We do not know if Vivekananda made other efforts in this direction between 1897 and 1900, when he left for the West again. He engaged in little public activity in India after his return in 1901.

In his speech 'The Future of India', Vivekananda says that the plan of the ancient rishis (mystics) was to eventually raise every caste to Brahmin status. From his various discourses on history, we can see that Vivekananda subscribed partially, and in a conditioned manner, to the great man theory of history which was still popular in the Victorian age. Historians who subscribed to this theory saw history as being shaped by the actions and decisions of a few powerful men and occasionally women. So, it would make sense within the pattern of Vivekananda's thinking, to consider the mobility of jatis within the caste system as part of a plan by the ancient spiritual guardians of society to evolve an egalitarian culture gradually out of a divided and barbaric one. However, even on the basis of the great man theory of history, this is credulous as a historical theory, and Vivekananda was not a credulous man. It is more plausible that Vivekananda believed there was a nugget of truth to the idea but exaggerated its scope for strategic reasons in service of his plan for India's regeneration.

While the economic competition of British-ruled India created favourable conditions for upward caste mobility, that was hardly enough in and of itself. His experiences in America had taught him that industrialization of India was not possible in the near future. To raise the lower castes to the status of Brahminhood required both empowering the lower castes and mitigating the resentment and obstruction from the upper castes. Whether conceived of as a gradual evolutionary movement, as Vivekananda did, or a revolution, such a gigantic restructuring of millennia long social structures towards equality needed a powerful ethical and intellectual impulse. This was to be supplied by the Vedanta philosophy. Among the upper and lower castes, a spiritual, moral, and intellectual transformation was to be affected by the spread of the ideals of the Upanishads, the Gita, and other Vedantic scriptures. Its fundamental principles were the divinity and perfectibility of each human, their infinite potential and ultimate identity, and equality with every living creature. This Vivekananda believed, would empower each individual, who would find the strength within to work out her own destiny. While it will empower the lower classes and give them self-confidence and awareness of their rights, it would make the upper castes realize their oneness with the rest of humanity and banish ideas of high and low. To put it another way, Vivekananda wanted to spread humanistic ideals through the length and breadth of a caste-bound, feudal, and patriarchal India through the vehicle of religion.

In Europe, even when technology and industrialization changed the landscape of lived reality, the transition from a feudalist and theocratic society to a liberal one was achieved by a series of political and social revolutions, broadly inspired by Enlightenment ideals of humanism. Vivekananda wanted to transform the casteist and feudal society of India through a spiritual revolution of humanist ethics. He said in the Madras speech:

> My idea is first of all to bring out the gems of spirituality that are stored up in our books and in the possession of a few only, hidden, as it were, in monasteries and in forests—to bring them out; to bring the knowledge out of them, not only from the hands where it is hidden, but from the still more inaccessible chest, the language in which it is preserved, the incrustation of centuries of Sanskrit words. In one word, I want to make them popular. I want to bring out these ideas and let them be the common property of all, of every man in India, whether he knows the Sanskrit language or not.[53]

Vivekananda's plans for the removal of caste by raising every caste to Brahmin status may appear extraordinarily naive to us today, but we have the advantage of more than a century of historical hindsight. The India Vivekananda and the people he talked to inhabited was an India before World War I, before Indian nationalism, before the introduction of democratic representative politics in the country through the Minto–Morley Reforms of 1909. The political and economic changes that occurred in India in the first half of the twentieth century revealed the faultlines of caste in India and the structural violence built into the caste hierarchy. The idea of Brahminizing people from the lower castes in order to emancipate them, could have a certain logical appeal within the social conditions of the late nineteenth century, where none of this had happened. Almost two decades after Vivekananda's speech in Madras, the great Tamil poet Subramania Bharati, followed a similar line of thinking and invested a Dalit man with the sacred thread as a means of fighting caste.[54]

That said, Vivekananda's sociological analysis of caste mobility was correct. The process of castes rising up the hierarchy when their social circumstances changed was studied in post-Independence India by the sociologist M. N. Srinivas, who focused his fieldwork on the erstwhile Mysore state. He writes, 'Certainty of position in the ranked order of castes is not, however, a characteristic of caste at the existential level.... Thus the position of castes in the hierarchy as it actually exists is liable to change, whereas in the varna model the position of each varna is fixed for all time.... What is more noticeable, however, is the fact that the possession of secular power by a caste is either reflected in its ritual ranking or leads, sooner or later, to an improvement of its position.'[55] He termed this process of upward caste mobility, Sanskritization.

'Sanskritisation is the process by which a "low" Hindu caste, or tribal or other group, changes its customs, ritual, ideology and way of life in the direction of a high, and frequently "twice-born" caste. Generally, such changes are followed by a claim to a higher position in the caste hierarchy than that traditionally conceded to the claimant caste by the local community. The claim is usually made over a period of time, in fact, a generation or two, before the "arrival" is conceded,' Srinivas writes.[56] Srinivas lists several castes which had moved up the caste ladder in modern times. The Patidars, originally called Kunbis, who were a peasant caste in Gujarat, had become wealthy by the end of the Mughal rule in the eighteenth century. As the Rajput power and prestige also declined, the Patidars started claiming kshatriya status by adopting 'kingly customs and manners'. During the era of Rajput dominance over Gujarat (tenth to thirteenth century CE), the Kolis, who are classified as a Scheduled Caste today, were the largest ethnic group in Gujarat. In tribal areas, Koli tribal chieftains served as the links with the Rajput administration. As Rajput men started marrying from the lineages of the Koli tribal chieftains, many of these clans used this connection with Rajputs to climb into the Rajput caste. (Bardic Brahmin castes were happy to oblige by fabricating genealogies of descent from ancient Rajput kings.) In north Kerala, from the sixteenth century onwards, a fluid political situation ensured that several aristocratic Nair (a martial caste) clans acquired control over patches of territory and became kings. In post-Independence India, Marathas, Reddys, and Padayachis laid claim to Kshatriya status.[57]

What Vivekananda seems to have missed, is that while there was great social mobility among castes in some regions and periods witnessing political flux, the overall power asymmetry within the caste system never changed significantly. As some castes rose in the hierarchy, others fell. As Srinivas writes, 'It is necessary to stress that the mobility characteristic of caste in the traditional period resulted only in positional changes for particular castes or sections of castes and did not lead up to a structural change. That is, while individual castes moved up or down, the structure remained the same. It is only in the literature of the Bhakti movement that the idea of inequality was challenged. A few sects even recruited followers from several castes in their early evangelical phase, but gradually either the sect became an endogamous unit, or endogamy continued to be an attribute of each caste within the sect.'[58] Or perhaps, he did not miss it after all.

Though Vivekananda claimed that the plan of ancient spiritual figures was to lift up all castes, it was plain that if there were indeed such an attempt, it was a failure. Vivekananda acknowledges this and draws conclusions that are important to his reform programme. He said in his Madras speech:

> The attempts of the great Ramanuja and of Chaitanya and of Kabir to raise the lower classes of India show that marvellous results were attained during the lifetime of those great prophets; yet the later failures have to be explained, and cause shown why the effect of their teachings stopped almost within a century of the passing away of these great Masters. The secret is here. They raised the lower classes; they had all the wish that these should come up, but they did not apply their energies to the spreading of the Sanskrit language among the masses. Even the great Buddha made one false step when he stopped the Sanskrit language from being studied by the masses. He wanted rapid and immediate results, and translated and preached in the language of the day, Pali. That was grand; he spoke in the language of the people, and the people understood him. That was great; it spread the ideas quickly and made them reach far and wide. But along with that, Sanskrit ought to have spread. Knowledge came, but the prestige was not there, culture was not there.... Teach the masses in the vernaculars, give them ideas; they will get information, but something more is necessary; give them culture. Until you give them that, there can be no permanence in the raised condition of the masses. There will be another caste created, having the advantage of the Sanskrit language, which will quickly get above the rest and rule them all the same. The only safety, I tell you men who belong to the lower castes, the only way to raise your condition is to study Sanskrit.... The only way to bring about the levelling of caste is to appropriate the culture, the education which is the strength of the higher castes. That done, you have what you want.[59]

What Vivekananda is advocating here may seem the same as what Srinivas has termed Sanskritization. But they are very different. Knowledge of the sacred

Sanskrit literature was reserved for the upper castes, mainly Brahmins. From the apex of the caste pyramid, the knowledge of the sacred literature and the cultural power that came from it trickled down to the bottom. This knowledge was associated with manners, customs, rites, and rituals and it is these secondary and tertiary religio-cultural aspects which a caste imitated when it tried to lay claim to the status of the caste next to it in the caste hierarchy. As long as Brahmins monopolized the scriptures, the mobility of individual castes within the caste structure would not challenge the structure itself. What Vivekananda wanted to do it seems, was to make this Sanskrit literature available to everyone. In the nineteenth century, the work of the British Orientalist scholars who recorded the Hindu scriptures in a written form, combined with the printing press, made the mass dissemination of scriptures possible. If the monopoly of the Brahmins and other upper castes Hindu religion and culture could be broken, it would become the property of all. The cultural, (though not economic) domination exercised by the upper castes would no longer have a foundation because that culture would have become universal. This is what Vivekananda means when he says, 'The only way to bring about the levelling of caste is to appropriate the culture, the education which is the strength of the higher castes.'

There is, ultimately, a certain coherence to Vivekananda's ideas of caste, though they appear completely contradictory at first glance. The solution to eliminating caste that Vivekananda proposed might have appeared feasible at a certain point in historical time, but the tectonic shifts in India's political and economic life that followed, make it irrelevant. For us today, it is only of historical interest. But it is not of historical interest only in relation to the figure of Vivekananda. It reveals how caste appeared to nineteenth century observers, both Indian and Western. There has been no attempt, to the best of my knowledge, to write a history of caste violence in India, and it is quite possible that the source material for such a historical investigation may not exist. But we do know that through the nineteenth and eighteenth centuries, there was no significant inter-caste violence. This reinforced the belief of Westerners— historians, missionaries, and administrators—that a) India was a static society whose structure has continued significantly unaltered since the Vedic age and b) caste was a product of belief in Hindu theology which enjoins a four-fold varna system with different duties for each varna. Thus, caste was seen as a religious superstition and hence of a more benign character than oppression enforced by violent means.

It seems to be the case that one belonging to an upper caste would tolerate the rise of one lower in the hierarchy, only as long as it did not undermine the former's position and status within the overall caste system. As incidents from the twentieth century demonstrate, while upward mobility by lower castes over several generations was acceptable, efforts to assume a higher caste status immediately were met with opposition, recrimination, and violence from upper castes—usually from the one on the next rung of the caste ladder. Srinivas notes a few incidents from the 1920s and 1930s where lower castes making a concerted effort to claim higher caste status met opposition and mild violence. From the 1980s on, caste massacres started occurring regularly in India. In our own time, thousands of Dalits and other people from the lower castes have been subject to murder, beatings, and inhumane torture by dominant castes for transgressing caste boundaries.[60]

When large scale socio-economic changes lead to lower caste assertion in a way that challenges the power distribution within the caste system, the structural violence inherent in the system manifests as physical violence. But an almost opposite picture presented itself to most nineteenth century observers, including Vivekananda. The iron walls of untouchability, prohibitions on inter-dining and other types of fraternal mixing, made each caste look like an isolated compartment, and this was essential to Vivekananda's reasoning that a caste, which could unite all its sub-castes into a cohesive unit, could just declare themselves Brahmins. As he said in the Madras speech (see p. 434), 'Let us suppose that there are castes here with ten thousand people in each. If these put their heads together and say, we will call ourselves Brahmins, nothing can stop them.... Because whatever it was, each caste was exclusive of the other. It did not meddle with others affairs; even the several divisions of one caste did not meddle with the other divisions.'

The idea that one caste would not meddle in the affairs of another caste was a complete misunderstanding of the latent structural violence that held the caste system together. Even if historical changes which followed upon the nineteenth century had taken a different course than they did, this misunderstanding more than anything else, would make Vivekananda's solution to the caste problem unworkable. Though this is squarely in the domain of the hypothetical, it can be said with reasonable certainty that if Vivekananda had known of the extent of violence that the upper castes were capable of visiting on the Dalits and other lower castes, or even if he had come into contact with someone like Jyotiba Phule who articulated a cogent critique of the caste system from the vantage point of those who were crushed at the bottom of it, Vivekananda would have taken a different view of the solution to caste.

IS THE HINDU RELIGION CASTEIST?

The roots of Indian modernity are intimately connected to religion. They can be traced back to the Bengal Renaissance and the overhaul of Hindu society undertaken by reformers starting with Raja Ram Mohan Roy and ending with Rabindranath Tagore. Faced with the challenge of modernity and rationality, most of these reformers rejected the caste system, at least in theory, if not always in social practice. In rejecting caste, sati, child marriage, and other social ills prevalent in Hindu society, these reformers of the Bengal Renaissance, took their lead from British Orientalist scholars of Sanskrit literature, and posited a golden age of Hinduism in the Vedic age. Contemporary and post-Vedic Hinduism was seen as the result of the corruption that had beset the religion after the Vedic age. Orthodox Hindu thinkers, while welcoming change on certain fronts, on the whole, rejected the reforms including legislation introduced by the British to abolish sati and child marriage. They held that these practices as well as caste regulations were an integral part of Hinduism. Many reformers went outside Hinduism, rejecting the authority of the scriptures and embracing Christianity, deism, the rationalist and syncretic religion of the Brahmo Samaj, and occasionally even atheism.

When Vivekananda entered public life in the late 1880s, he staked out a position on Hinduism and social customs that was different from the orthodox, reformist, or atheistic positions. Like the orthodox thinkers, he embraced the entirety of the Hindu tradition, including post-Vedic developments such as the Bhakti movement, idol worship, and temples. But unlike them, he rejected the notion that child marriage, caste differentiations, and other customs were sanctioned by the scriptures. Like the freethinker and atheist, he considered reason supreme, bringing even the scriptures under its jurisdiction, but unlike them he accepted the spiritual claims proclaimed in the Hindu scriptures; especially the Upanishads and the Bhagavad Gita. Vivekananda thus defined Hinduism for his contemporaries and for generations of liberal Hindu thinkers who followed, including the philosopher Sarvepalli Radhakrishnan, who was the first of a new generation of Hindu philosophers to give a technically elaborate treatment to Hindu philosophical systems.

In regard to the issue of caste, Vivekananda, as we have seen, held that caste had nothing to do with the Hindu religion and was merely a social institution. Though Vivekananda seems to be the first major figure to articulate this view, it was developed independently and articulated in the early twentieth century by Sri Narayana Guru, a Vedantist and the leader of the anti-caste Ezhava movement, in present day Kerala. The exact opposite position was taken by Dr B. R. Ambedkar, whose views on caste have been more influential on various post-Independence anti-caste movements than any other figure. Ambedkar held that caste discrimination and oppression was built into the essential structure of Hinduism. As he notes in *Annihilation of Caste*, 'Caste may be bad. Caste may lead to conduct so gross as to be called man's inhumanity to man. All the same, it must be recognized that the Hindus observe Caste not because they are inhuman or wrong headed. They observe Caste because they are deeply religious. People are not wrong in observing Caste. In my view, what is wrong is their religion, which has inculcated this notion of Caste. If this is correct, then obviously the enemy, you must grapple with, is not the people who observe Caste, but the Shastras which teach them this religion of Caste.'[61]

For two thinkers who held such opposing positions on an issue that was fundamental to both, there are a number of interesting convergences between the views of Ambedkar and Vivekananda on several questions relating to Indian society and polity, the Hindu religion and caste. Both Vivekananda and Ambedkar held that Indian society would eventually have to democratize and overcome or abolish caste. Both of them argued that caste, or at least its exclusionary, restrictive, and hierarchical character was invented by Brahmins who wanted to arrogate social power to themselves. They held upper caste Hindu society squarely responsible for the caste oppression perpetuated through millennia. At the same time, as we have seen in this chapter, both of them called on Brahmins, as the educated and intellectual class, to take the lead in the social cause of emancipating the lower castes. (This was Ambedkar's position till the 1930s when he still thought that caste could be eradicated by the Hindus through internal reform. In his undelivered speech, 'The Annihilation of Caste', he declared that he had no hope that this was possible and that he was leaving Hinduism. Ambedkar would later embrace Buddhism, in which he found an egalitarian religion that could transcend the divisions of caste.) Ambedkar and Vivekananda saw caste as responsible for the lack of fraternity among Hindus, the exclusionary nature of the institution to be in tension with the industrialization India required and caste to be injurious to the liberty of the individual. Both the thinkers viewed education as the most important means for emancipating the lower castes.

In the context of colonial India, Ambedkar famously questioned the nationalists' decision to prioritize political independence over social reform. He strongly believed that a government composed of upper caste Hindus would only perpetuate the oppression of the lower castes. Vivekananda died three years before the beginning of the Swadeshi Movement. Though it is highly unlikely that he would not have supported the nationalist demand for political independence once it gathered momentum among the people, he did show a certain apathy towards the Congress movement during his lifetime that was grounded in concerns similar to Ambedkar's. He criticized the demand for political independence in his own day as premature because Hindu society wasn't fraternal enough to form a nation yet. He thought that if Indians were to get political power immediately, the elite and powerful, consisting of the upper castes, could use the political power to oppress the masses.

Ambedkar condemned the *Manusmriti* and other Dharmashastras as irredeemably casteist. Vivekananda rejected the authority of the Dharmashastras including *Manusmriti*, holding that they were not religious texts but texts of social legislation. Vivekananda saw in the monism of the Upanishads the source of a universal ethics of unrivalled potential. As we saw in Chapter 11, even as he condemned Hinduism, Ambedkar independently came to the same conclusion in 'Riddles in Hinduism', stating that Upanishadic monism, which he termed 'Brahmaism', was the surest foundation possible for a democratic society. And while Ambedkar stressed that this egalitarian metaphysics remained mere theoretical speculation that had no influence on Hindu society, Vivekananda too recognized this. He spoke often of how the metaphysics of the Upanishads had remained the monopoly of renunciates and its lessons were never applied to Hindu society.

But in spite of these significant converges in their analysis of the nature of Hindu society, Brahminism, and caste, there is a sharp divergence in opposite directions between the two on the question of the relationship between Hinduism and caste. Vivekananda held that the varna and jati system were unrelated to Hindu philosophy and theology, and Ambedkar came to the conclusion that it was the essence of Hinduism. How could two perspicacious thinkers of extreme intellectual integrity whose analyses of Hinduism, caste, and society were in sympathy on so many points, come to such startlingly opposite views on the matter?

At first glance, the difference may appear to stem from definitional issues regarding the Hindu religious canon. Vivekananda does not consider the *Manusmriti*, the Dharmashastras, the Grihya Sutras, etc., as religious texts. These texts are not metaphysical and theological texts, but rather texts framing social conduct. Orthodox Hindus in Vivekananda's, and later Ambedkar's, time did not deny this. These texts were never used for religious instruction. However, they claimed that these and other texts of social legislation drew their authority from the Vedas. They were expansions and elaborations of the themes already present in the Vedas. Vivekananda on the other hand claimed that the Vedas categorically did not have a place for normative social functions, including caste.

Who was right in the debate between Vivekananda and orthodox Hindu thinkers? The four Vedas (Veda Samhitas)—Rig Veda, Sama Veda, Yajur Veda, Atharva Veda—contain more than 21,000 verses.[62] Of this entire corpus, the word 'Shudra' appears only eighteen times in the Vedas: once in the Rig Veda, twelve times in the Yajur Veda, and five times in the Atharva Veda. Some of these eighteen instances are degradatory, while almost an equal number are laudatory. Thus, of the former kind we have this verse from the Purusha Sukta of the Rig Veda:

'The Brahman was his mouth, of both his arms was the Rajanya made. His thighs became the Vaisya, from his feet the Sudra was produced.'[63]
And of the latter this verse from the Yajur Veda:
'Homage to the Shudra and the charitably disposed.'[64]

While the *Manusmriti* prohibits the reading of the Vedas in the hearing of Shudras, the Yajur Veda seems to suggest that it is a sin to prevent Shudras from carrying out religious acts. A hymn seeking expiation from God for sin says:

Each fault in forest or in village,
In society or mind,
Each sinful act we have done to Sudra or Vaisya,
Or in preventing anybody from religious performances,
Even of that sin,
O God, Thou art the expiation.[65]

The view of Vivekananda and Narayana Guru, that the Vedas do not sanction caste discrimination, is on the whole borne out. Apart from its extremely minimal presence, even the verses that talk about the Shudras do not prescribe any mandatory rules or penalties, let alone endogamy, untouchability, or ritual purification. The reason why the debate between Vivekananda and orthodox Hindus on caste remained alive in the late nineteenth century was that the Vedas were difficult to access. While there were English translations by Western scholars, they were not widely available and most people did not know the archaic Sanskrit in which the Vedas were composed. This situation started to change as the twentieth century progressed, and English translations became more widely available, including those by Indian scholars.

In 'The Philosophy of Hinduism', Ambedkar writes that the *Manusmriti* 'must be regarded as the Bible of the Hindus and containing the philosophy of Hinduism.'[66] For Ambedkar's purposes, whether the text's casteist schema finds support in the Vedas or not is irrelevant, for he is using entirely different criteria to ascertain what counts as sacred literature. But nonetheless, Ambedkar's position that the *Manusmriti* is sacred literature, on the face of it, aligns him more with the time's orthodox Hindu thinkers than with Vivekananda or Narayana Guru. But this does not make much sense, for Ambedkar demanded reform in Hinduism and the rejection of the Shastras that support caste.

One could imagine that such a disparity exists only because a conversation between Ambedkar and those who adopted Vivekananda's position, such as Radakrishnan, did not take place. Or that in debating Gandhi, who was religiously conservative and held varnashrama to be essential to Hinduism, Ambedkar was operating with a misunderstanding of the Hindu tradition. But to think this would be very naive. Ambedkar, who had studied Sanskrit, was a scholar of Hinduism and intimately acquainted with the Vedas, Upanishads, and the epics, as primary texts. The answer lies somewhere else. In the imaginary scenario where Vivekananda and Ambedkar were to talk on the question of Hinduism and caste, they would talk past each other, not just because their understanding of what constituted Hinduism was different, but more fundamentally because their understanding of the very category of religion was different. While it is true that Ambedkar claimed that Hindu philosophy was essentially casteist, his position does not make sense unless we understand how Ambedkar conceptualizes religion.

In 'The Philosophy of Hinduism', Ambedkar discusses his conception of the philosophy of religion and the criteria by which it is to be judged. It would be too much of a digression here to reconstruct Ambedkar's arguments which are drawn from the history of religion, but he concludes that the norm to judge the philosophy of religion in modern society is justice, by which he means the principles of equality, fraternity, and liberty. Ambedkar writes about what he means by religion: 'I take Religion to mean the propounding of an ideal scheme of divine governance the aim and object of which is to make the social order in which men live a moral order. This is what I understand by Religion and this is the sense in which I shall be using the term Religion in this discussion.'[67]

There are two things to be noted immediately. The first point is that such a conception of religion, as that of a scheme of divine governance, if applied to Hinduism, leads naturally to the *Manusmriti*, the Dharmashastras, and the Grihya Sutras, and judged by any egalitarian principle, these books are mired in bigotry and prejudice of every kind. The second is that this is an extremely non-standard definition of religion. No noted philosopher or scholar of religion, at least of recent times, would subscribe to such a view. One of the implications of equating religion with a divinely prescribed form of governance would be that the philosophy of Islam is to be found in the Sharia and Judaism in the Halakah.

This, of course, does not say anything about the validity of Ambedkar's definition. It does, however, explain the confusion inherent in contemporary discussions about Hinduism and caste. It would not do to merely say that Ambedkar said that Hinduism is casteist. To make such a claim without elucidating the conception of religion Ambedkar is operating with can only create confusion and misunderstanding. This is because in no register, theological, sociological, phenomenological, or philosophical, is the word religion taken to mean a divine scheme of government. The conversation today, in so far as it takes place at all, between those liberal Hindus who take the problem of caste seriously but deny that the religion is implicated in it and those who believe caste to be an essential feature of Hinduism, is doomed from the beginning because both groups are talking with completely different conceptions of religion and hence, Hinduism, in mind.

It is far beyond the scope of this book to elucidate the exact relationship between Hinduism and caste. But what I hope has emerged from the discussion in this section is that in order to tackle the question of caste in contemporary society, and inter alia the relationship between caste and the Hindu religion, there has to be a concerted effort on the part of the various interlocutors to achieve conceptual clarity about the basic terms of the discourse. It is important to understand that the issue between Ambedkar and those who would define religion differently, in terms of theology, mysticism, philosophy, or other referents, is not a definitional one, though it concerns precisely the definition of religion. That is, it is not a question of mere semantics. It is not the case that if the different parties were to redraw the contours of the concept involved, i.e., religion, there would be an agreement. There are substantive issues involved in how one defines religion. In other words, if the conversation is to move forward, it has to start with asking the question 'what is religion?' and what is meant by saying a religion has some kind of a property, whether it is one of being egalitarian, or of being regressive.

ADDENDUM

The speech 'The Future of India' (see p. 420), which Vivekananda delivered in Madras in 1897, was widely influential in the Reformation Movement in Kerala, a sociocultural reform movement which started in the late nineteenth century. In the speech Vivekananda castigated Kerala (then called Malabar) for its extremely oppressive caste regulations, and called the homes of the upper castes in Malabar 'lunatic asylums'. Recently though the speech has come under fire online due to his allegedly casteist comments.

In speaking of the quarrel between the castes, Vivekananda said, 'Why did not the other castes so understand and do as [The Brahmin] did? Why did they sit down and be lazy, and let the Brahmins win the race?'[68] And later in the speech, Vivekananda says:

> There is an old superstition in Bengal that if the cobra that bites, sucks out his own poison from the patient, the man must survive. Well then, the Brahmin must suck out his own poison. To the non-Brahmin castes I say, wait, be not in a hurry. Do not seize every opportunity of fighting the Brahmin, because, as I have shown, you are suffering from your own fault. Who told you to neglect spirituality and Sanskrit learning? What have you been doing all this time? Why have you been indifferent? Why do you now fret and fume because somebody else had more brains, more energy, more pluck and go, than you? Instead of wasting your energies in vain discussions and quarrels in the newspapers, instead of fighting and quarrelling in your own homes—which is sinful—use all your energies in acquiring the culture which the Brahmin has, and the thing is done. Why do you not become Sanskrit scholars? Why do you not spend millions to bring Sanskrit education to all the castes of India? That is the question. The moment you do these things, you are equal to the Brahmin. That is the secret of power in India.[69]

This has unsurprisingly been taken as Vivekananda preaching that people from the lower castes of India deserved their fate because they were lazy and did not learn Sanskrit. While Vivekananda may be accused of many things, whether he is ultimately guilty of them or not, insanity cannot be one of them. No man whose mind was still in working order could ask Dalits, that too in the

450

nineteenth century when they lived on subsistence agriculture and perished from famines, why they did not spend millions to bring Sanskrit education to the various castes of India. The assumption that Vivekananda was addressing lower castes in the speech is a sociological blunder, made possible only because of the almost complete lack of sociological data for the period.

But there are enough indications in the speech itself to allow us to form a correct idea about who and what Vivekananda was speaking about. The speech was delivered in English. English education was not very common among even the upper castes in the late nineteenth century. It was unheard of among lower castes, except a few castes like the Ezhavas who could boast of the very rare English educated youth. In other words, Vivekananda was addressing a crowd mostly composed of Brahmins and other non-Brahmin upper castes.

Vivekananda's reference to discussions and quarrels in the newspapers, point to what issue was vexing him. In south India, in Travancore and in the Madras and Mysore provinces, non-Brahmin upper castes were starting to rise against the Brahmins over their dominance over official appointments and their nepotism. In Travancore, where the nationalist movement never became very powerful, by the 1920s, the situation had led to different upper castes and communities waging war through newspapers they owned to put pressure on the royal administration for preference in appointments, education, and commerce. The situation has been described by a recent historian as 'competitive communalism'.

The concern which animates these statements of Vivekananda was that each caste would fight for a piece of the pie, instead of coming together to form a national community. Vivekananda said, 'And the more you go on fighting and quarrelling about all trivialities such as "Dravidian" and "Aryan", and the question of Brahmins and non-Brahmins and all that, the further you are off from that accumulation of energy and power which is going to make the future India. For mark you, the future India depends entirely upon that.'[70] The formation of a national community, where each member of the community put the interest of the imagined nation above her own caste or community, was essential to pursue common goals of national interest. For Vivekananda these national goals were the eradication of poverty and education of the masses, especially the lower castes who were the most deprived. For the succeeding generation of Indian nationalists, the goal would be political independence from the British.

The arguments that Vivekananda gave for why the Brahmins had overtaken the other upper castes, were of course, sophistry. There are far too many instances of Vivekananda dissecting how the Brahmins monopolized Sanskrit learning to think that Vivekananda actually believed what he was saying. The fact that Vivekananda never used these arguments except on this one occasion, supports the conclusion that Vivekananda was being sophistic. But it was sophistry in service of what he considered a noble cause—the creation of a national community for the regeneration of India, through educational and economic upliftment of the masses. Vivekananda seemed to have believed on this occasion, as did many later nationalists including Gandhi when faced with the clash of ethnic, class, religious, and caste interests, that the ends justified the means in service of the greater good.

ACKNOWLEDGEMENTS

This book could not have been attempted, let alone written, without the contributions of many friends and family members. My first thanks go to G. Hari Kumar, without whose generous help this book could not have been begun. And to Madhavi, without whom it would not have been completed. I am grateful to Acchan for his steady and unfailing support through the years it took me to finish the book. My brother Ambu, for lightening my intellectual burdens.

I am deeply grateful to Dr Syed Abdul Sayeed for his patient intellectual mentorship for over a decade and for several lengthy discussions that helped me get clarity on some of the thorny issues explored in the book. Dr Irfan Habib gave of his time and intellect freely, always ready to help out with historical information, which I would have been hard-pressed to find elsewhere. I can never repay Dr Shashi Tharoor for his advice, encouragement, and help, which played a crucial part in the book growing from a couple of chapters to its final form.

A lot of people read parts of the book and helped me with their feedback. I am thankful to all of them, but would like to especially mention Aarefa, Raghu, and Suresh. Aarefa, thank you for taking time from your extremely busy life, to promptly read the drafts of early chapters and assure me I was going in the right direction. Words of praise from Raghu Sheshadri, the most prodigiously talented prose writer I know, helped me get through dark hours of self-doubt and uncertainty. A special thanks to Suresh Thomas, for reading through the entire draft of the book and for his insights and sound advice.

Writing a long non-fiction book without institutional support or a peer group in the midst of a two-year pandemic was a difficult and isolating experience. It is difficult to express in words my gratitude to Sasi Ammavan, whose untiring mental support helped me keep my sanity. I am really thankful to Gayatri Devi Nair, who for almost a year, was a one-person support team over WhatsApp when dark thoughts and loneliness accompanied night vigils. And also to Shukti Sharma for her care and interest in the book. I am obliged to Dr Ashley Tellis for commiserating with my frequent writer's block and sharing his own experiences. My debt to Mahesh Natarajan is irredeemable.

My thanks to Ashok, Gokul, Devraj, and Sandeep for having my back since as far back as I can remember. And to Mathew Varghese, Ashok Ganguly, and Nikhil Varma for their help and support, and for putting up with me ever since the mad, crazy days of ACJ. Special thanks to the Hyderabad gang: Imran Khan, Harsha Vadlamani, Rahul Ramakrishna, and Rajesh Asopa, for all the love and gallows humour. And to Aswathy, for being there, as always. I am also obliged to Sree Hari Varma for going out of his way to help with my project. I am grateful to Sujatha S. for praying for me and Sarika Premkumar for her help. Gautama Polanki, for several useful philosophical discussions around the concept of God and for helping me get hold of many academic papers behind paywalls. And to Karthika Gopalakrishnan, 'for having faith'.

I want to express my thanks to Prem Kumar for unintentionally introducing me to Vivekananda during my college days. I would have been left adrift except for Rakhin, who recovered several essential files after my laptop crashed when I was writing the last portions of the book. I would also like to thank Bhavani Shankar for technical help that made the research for the book much easier. Also, Gautam Shenoy, for last minute help with reference material.

There are several others who offered help and support in various ways during the time I was working on this book and to whom I am grateful. While I may not be able recall all of them here, I would like to thank N. P. Ashley, Sabarinath (Shanku), Samrat Chakrabarthy, Pheroze Vincent, and Dipanjan Sinha.

I am deeply thankful for the editorial team at Aleph: to David Davidar, for reposing his confidence in me and the book; Aienla Ozukum, for her great patience and understanding; and Kanika Praharaj for her meticulous scrutiny of the manuscript as well as editorial wisdom.

Last, but by no means the least, my teachers to whom I will be grateful my entire life. To Sita Sharma teacher, who has been one of the most blessed presences in my life: if I have seen anyone approach the ideal of a perfect teacher, it is you. Thank you for your wisdom, inspiration, unenending love and the confidence and trust you placed in me. It has made me who I am. I will forever remain grateful to Prem Sir, not only for his love and support, but for also being an exemplar of moral idealism and values. The lessons he taught were by example, not instruction, and went beyond any subject or textbook. And to Sherin teacher who taught me that 'Beauty is Truth, Truth Beauty'.

REFERENCES

PREFACE

1   Gavin Flood, *The Blackwell Companion to Hinduism*, Hoboken: Blackwell, 2003.
2   Christophe Jaffrelot, *Modi's India: Hindu Nationalism and the Rise of Ethnic Democracy*, Chennai: Context, 2021, pp. 216–21 and 437–42.

CHAPTER 1: VIVEKANANDA: THE LIFE

1   Swami Vivekananda, *The Complete Works of Swami Vivekananda: Volume V*, 7th edn, Almora: Advaita Ashrama, 1991, p. 10.
2   Jawaharlal Nehru, *Sri Ramakrishna and Vivekananda*, Mayavati: Advaita Ashrama, 1961, p. 2.
3   Anshul Chaturvedi, 'At 15, a life turned upside down: How Vivekananda shaped Subhas', *Times of India*, 23 January 2020.
4   Tapan Raychaudhuri, *Europe Reconsidered: Perceptions of the West in Nineteenth-century Bengal*, New Delhi: Oxford University Press, 1988, pp. 222–23.
5   *The Life of Swami Vivekananda: His Eastern and Western Disciples, Volume 1*, Mayavati: Advaita Ashrama, 2001, p. 31.
6   *The Life of Swami Vivekananda, Volume 1.*
7   Ibid.
8   Rajagopal Chattopadhyaya, *Swami Vivekananda in India: A Corrective Biography*, Delhi: Motilal Banarasidass Publishers, 1999.
9   Ibid.
10   *The Life of Swami Vivekananda, Volume 1.* Rajagopal Chattopadhyaya, on the other hand, argues that the preface was written not by Narendranath, but by the co-compiler, Vaishnav Charan Basak.
11   Swarupa Gupta, *Notions of Nationhood in Bengal Perspectives on Samaj, c. 1867–1905*, Leiden, Boston: Brill, 2009.
12   *The Life of Swami Vivekananda, Volume 1.*
13   Ibid., p. 48.
14   *The Life of Swami Vivekananda, Volume 1*, p. 107 and 109.
15   Ibid., p. 60.
16   William Wordsworth, 'The Wanderer', *Excursion: A Poem*, London: Edward Moxon, 1814, p. 31.
17   *The Life of Swami Vivekananda, Volume 1*, p. 48.
18   Ibid., p. 84.
19   Ibid., p. 77; Swami Nikhilananda, *Vivekananda: A Biography*, pp. 24–25.
20   *The Life of Swami Vivekananda, Volume 1*, p. 76.
21   Ibid., p. 111.
22   *The Life of Swami Vivekananda, Volume 1*, pp. 123–24.
23   Swami Vivekananda, *The Complete Works of Swami Vivekananda, Volume VIII*, Almora: Advaita Ashrama, 2012., p. 263.

24 *The Life of Swami Vivekananda, Volume 1*.

25 Mahendranath Gupta, *The Gospel of Sri Ramakrishna*, Vol. II, tr. Swami Nikhilananda, Mayavati: Advaita Ashrama, 2009, p. 55.

26 *The Life of Swami Vivekananda, Volume 1*.

27 Ibid.

28 Ibid.

29 J. A. Baines, *Census of India, 1891: General Report*, London: Eyre and Spottiswoode, p. 7.

30 *The Complete Works of Swami Vivekananda, Volume III*, p. 477.

31 Available at www.vivekananda.net/NewspaperReports/28Jan93.html.

32 *The Life of Swami Vivekananda, Volume 1*.

33 Ibid., p. 402.

34 Swami Vivekananda, *The Complete Works of Swami Vivekananda, Volume VIII*, 9th edn, Almora: Advaita Ashrama, 1991, p. 209.

35 Marie Louise Burke, *Swami Vivekananda in the West: New Discoveries, Volume 1*, Mayavati: Advaita Ashrama, 1983, p. 63.

36 Ibid., p. 20.

37 Kate Sanborn, *Abandoning an Adopted Farm*, New York: D. Appleton and Company, 1906.

38 Ibid.

39 Ibid., pp. 8–9.

40 Ibid., pp. 10–11.

41 Ibid., p. 7.

42 Henry David Thoreau, *Walden*, Boston and New York: Houghton, Mifflin & Co., 1906, p. 328.

43 Available at www.vivekananda.net/NewspaperReports/25aug93.html.

44 *The Life of Swami Vivekananda, Volume 1*, pp. 405–406.

45 Ibid.

46 Swami Nikhilananda, *Vivekananda: A Biography*.

47 *The Life of Swami Vivekananda, Volume 1*, p. 412.

48 *The Complete Works of Swami Vivekananda, Volume VIII*, p. 445.

49 Ibid.

50 *The Complete Works of Swami Vivekananda, Volume V*, p. 21.

51 *The Life of Swami Vivekananda, Volume 1*, p. 418.

52 Burke, *Swami Vivekananda in the West: New Discoveries, Volume 1*, p. 90.

53 Ibid.

54 Ibid.

55 *The Complete Works of Swami Vivekananda, Volume V*, p. 21.

56 Burke, *Swami Vivekananda in the West: New Discoveries, Volume 1*, pp. 136–37.

57 Ibid.

58 Amiya P. Sen and Sahapedia, 'On the anniversary of Vivekananda's Chicago speeches, time to remember what he said – and didn't', *Scroll.in*, 11 September 2019.

59 Burke, *Swami Vivekananda in the West: New Discoveries, Volume 1*, p. 86.

60 Ibid.

61 Ibid., pp. 117–18.

62 *The Complete Works of Swami Vivekananda, Volume I*, p. 11.

63 Burke, *Swami Vivekananda in the West: New Discoveries, Volume 1*, p. 118.

64 *The Life of Swami Vivekananda: His Eastern and Western Disciples, Volume 2*, Almora: Advaita Ashrama, 2001.

65 Ibid.

66 Burke, *Swami Vivekananda in the West: New Discoveries, Volume 4*, p. 170.

67 Hans Rollmann, 'Deussen, Nietzsche, and Vedānta', *Journal of the History of Ideas*, Vol. 39,

No. 1, 1978, pp. 125–32.

68 *The Complete Works of Swami Vivekananda, Volume V*, p. 101.

69 *The Complete Works of Swami Vivekananda, Volume II*, pp. 28–29.

70 *The Complete Works of Swami Vivekananda, Volume V*, p. 530.

71 *The Complete Works of Swami Vivekananda, Volume VII*, p. 389.

72 *The Life of Swami Vivekananda, Volume 2*, p. 199.

73 *The Complete Works of Swami Vivekananda, Volume III*, p. 169.

74 *Reminiscences of Swami Vivekananda*, 4th edn, Mayavati: Advaita Ashrama, 2004.

75 R. K. Dasgupta, *Swami Vivekananda on Indian Philosophy and Literature*, Chennai: Sri Ramakrishna Math, 2013.

76 Eugene Taylor, *William James on Consciousness Beyond the Margin*, Princeton: Princeton University Press, 1996, p. 63.

77 Dasgupta, *Swami Vivekananda on Indian Philosophy and Literature*, p. 267.

78 Taylor, *William James*, p. 62.

79 *The Life of Swami Vivekananda, Volume 2*, p. 658.

80 *The Complete Works of Swami Vivekananda, Volume VI*, pp. 431–32.

CHAPTER 2: VIVEKANANDA AND HINDUTVA

1   *The Complete Works of Swami Vivekananda, Volume I*, p. 4.

2   Mark Doyle, *Communal Violence in the British Empire: Disturbing the Pax*, London and New York: Bloomsbury Academic, 2016.

3   *The Complete Works of Swami Vivekananda, Volume VI*, pp. 449–50.

4   Ibid., p. 251.

5   Iain Marlow, 'Cow Vigilantes in India Killed at Least 44 People, Report Finds', *Bloomberg*, 20 February 2019.

6   'The states where cow slaughter is legal in India', *Indian Express*, 8 October 2015.

7   'Violent Cow Protection in India: Vigilante Groups Attack Minorities', Humans Rights Watch, 18 February 2019, available at www.hrw.org/report/2019/02/18/violent-cow-protection-india/vigilante-groups-attack-minorities.

8   Khushboo Sandhu, 'Haryana to issue I-cards to "genuine" gau', *Indian Express*, 12 May 2017; Dehradun News, 'Uttarakhand to issue ID cards to gaurakshaks, call them "cow guardians"', *Hindustan Times*, 4 August 2018.

9   Vishva Hindu Parishad, 'Cow Protection', available at https://vhp.org/cow_protection; PTI, 'RSS organ on Dadri lynching: Vedas say kill cow murderers', *Economic Times*, 18 October 2015; 'Rajasthan minister says both sides are guilty after cow vigilantes beat Alwar man to death', *Scroll.in*, 5 April 2017.

10 *The Complete Works of Swami Vivekananda, Volume I*, p. 474.

11 Burke, *Swami Vivekananda in the West: New Discoveries, Volume 5*, p. 74.

12 D. N. Jha, *The Myth of the Holy Cow*, New Delhi: Navayana Publishing, 2009.

13 Swami Nikhilananda, *Vivekananda: A Biography*, p. 62.

14 Jha, *The Myth of the Holy Cow*, pp. 29–31.

15 *The Complete Works of Swami Vivekananda, Volume III*, p. 536.

16 Ibid., p. 174.

17 *The Complete Works of Swami Vivekananda, Volume II*, p. 43.

18 *The Complete Works of Swami Vivekananda, Volume I*, p. 13.

19 Christophe Jaffrelot, *Hindu Nationalism: A Reader*, Princeton University Press, 2007; Nilanjan Mukhopadhya, *The RSS: Icons of the Indian Right*, Delhi: Tranquebar, 2019.

20 K. N. Panikar, 'Culture and Communalism', *Social Scientist*, Vol. 21, No. 3/4, 1993, pp. 24–31.

21 Christophe Jaffrelot, *The Hindu Nationalist Movement in India*, New York City: Columbia University Press, 1996.

22 Ibid.

23 V. D. Savarkar, *Hindutva: Who is a Hindu?*, Bombay: Veer Savarkar Prakashan, 1969.

24 Wendy Doninger, *On Hinduism*, New Delhi: Aleph Book Company, 2013.

25 Savarkar, *Hindutva*, p. 99.

26 Ibid., pp. 135–36 and 140.

27 M. S. Golwalkar, *We or Our Nationhood Defined*, New Delhi: Global Vision Publishing House, 2022, p. 45.

28 Govind Krishnan V., 'No Christians Please', *Fountain Ink*, 5 March 2015.

29 Savarkar, *Hindutva*, p. 114.

30 'Muslim invasion created Dalits and tribals in India, says RSS', *India Today*, 22 September 2014.

31 Savarkar, *Hindutva*, p. 24.

32 Ibid., p. 19.

33 Ibid., p. 5.

34 Petr Charvat, *The Birth of the State: Ancient Egypt, Mesopotamia, India and China*, Daniel Morgan (tr.), Prague: Karolinum Press, 2013.

35 Upinder Singh, *A History of Ancient and Early Medieval India: From the Stone Age to the 12th Century*, Noida: Pearson, 2009, p. 274.

36 Ibid., pp. 11–12.

37 *The Complete Works of Swami Vivekananda, Volume IV*, pp. 103–105.

38 G. Parameswaran, *Vishwa Vijayi Vivekanandan* (World-conquerer Vivekananda), Thiruvananthapuram: Bharateeya Vichara Kendram, 2013, p. 12.

39 Ibid.

40 Ibid., p. 51. Author's translation from Malayalam.

41 Ibid.

42 Ibid., p. 48. Author's translation.

43 PTI, 'Ram, "Gau Mata" basis of Hindu culture: RSS chief Mohan Bhagwat', *Financial Express*, 7 February 2019.

44 'Rapes happen in India, not Bharat: RSS chief Mohan Bhagwat blames western culture for gangrapes', *India Today*, 4 January 2013.

45 Shailaja Neelakantan, 'Indian politicians' revolting comments about rape', *Times of India*, 2 August 2016.

46 'RSS leader Indresh Kumar says western culture like Valentine's Day responsible for violence against women', *Financial Express*, 3 June 2017.

47 Karnataka: 'Police to probe moral policing by Bajrang Dal in Mangaluru', *India Today*, 16 June 2016; Moral policing: Deepa Balakrishnan, 'Man thrashed, stripped allegedly by Bajrang Dal activists in Mangalore, *News 18*, 25 August 2015; Nayantara Narayanan, 'Stories of moral policing in Mangalore that you didn't hear about', *Scroll.in*, 28 August 2015.

48 PTI, 'Now, VHP blames western lifestyle for incidents of rape', *India Today*, 6 January 2013.

49 Vasudha Venugopal, 'RSS wants to set up a model school in every block of the country before 2017', *Economic Times*, 2 January 2015.

50 Jaffrelot, *The Hindu Nationalist Movement in India*.

51 Ibid.

52 Surendra Chandra, 'After Millennia a Tradition is Reborn', *IndiaFacts*, 12 June 2016.

53 Ibid.

54 'Reliving Vaidika Dharma', available at vaidikabharata.in.

55 Ibid.

56 Burke, *Swami Vivekananda in the West: New Discoveries, Volume 2*, p. 176.

57   *The Complete Works of Swami Vivekananda, Volume IV*, pp. 367–68.

58   Ibid., p. 515.

59   *The Complete Works of Swami Vivekananda, Volume V*, p. 70.

60   Ibid., p. 75.

61   *The Complete Works of Swami Vivekananda, Volume VIII*, p. 124.

62   *The Complete Works of Swami Vivekananda, Volume III*, p. 521.

63   *The Complete Works of Swami Vivekananda, Volume IV*, p. 159.

64   *The Complete Works of Swami Vivekananda, Volume V*, p. 482.

65   Ibid.

66   *The Complete Works of Swami Vivekananda, Volume VI*, p. 264.

67   *The Complete Works of Swami Vivekananda, Volume III*, p. 429.

68   *The Complete Works of Swami Vivekananda, Volume V*, pp. 126–27

69   *The Complete Works of Swami Vivekananda. Volume VIII*, p. 125.

70   *The Complete Works of Swami Vivekananda, Volume IV*, p. 328.

71   *The Complete Works of Swami Vivekananda, Volume V*, p. 52.

72   Ibid., pp. 56–57.

73   Ibid.

74   *The Complete Works of Swami Vivekananda, Volume III*, p. 167.

75   *The Complete Works of Swami Vivekananda, Volume V*, p. 93.

76   Ibid., p. 222.

77   Ibid., p. 15.

78   *The Complete Works of Swami Vivekananda, Volume VII*, p. 214.

79   *The Complete Works of Swami Vivekananda, Volume VI*, pp. 106–107.

80   *The Complete Works of Swami Vivekananda, Volume III*, pp. 192–93.

81   Jaffrelot, *Hindu Nationalism*.

82   Siddhartha Rai, 'RSS Chief Mohan Bhagwat's comments on reservation policy stirs controversy', *India Today*, 22 September 2015.

83   M. S. Golwalkar, *Bunch of Thoughts*, Bangalore: Sahitya Sindhu Prakashana, 1996, p. 108.

84   Balasaheb Deoras, 'Social Equality and Hindu Consolidation', *Arise Bharat*, 10 December 2013.

85   *The Complete Works of Swami Vivekananda, Volume III*, p. 414.

86   *The Complete Works of Swami Vivekananda, Volume IV*, p. 469.

87   *The Complete Works of Swami Vivekananda, Volume V*, p. 378.

88   *The Complete Works of Swami Vivekananda, Volume IV*, p. 458.

89   Ibid.

90   *The Complete Works of Swami Vivekananda, Volume VII*, p. 327.

91   *The Complete Works of Swami Vivekananda, Volume III*, pp. 192–93.

CHAPTER 3: CHRISTIANITY AND ISLAM

1   *The Complete Works of Swami Vivekananda, Volume VI*, p. 207.

2   *The Complete Works of Swami Vivekananda, Volume IV*, p. 198.

3   *The Complete Works of Swami Vivekananda, Volume V*, p. 122.

4   *The Complete Works of Swami Vivekananda, Volume IX*, p. 423.

5   *The Complete Works of Swami Vivekananda, Volume IV*, pp. 138–39.

6   *The Complete Works of Swami Vivekananda, Volume V*, p. 12.

7   *The Complete Works of Swami Vivekananda, Volume VIII*, pp. 159–61.

8   *The Life of Swami Vivekananda, Volume 2*.

9   Gauree Malkarnekar, 'The seminary where Swami Vivekanand got a lesson in theology', *Times of India*, 8 May 2016.

10   'Vivekananda's Chicago speech echoes 125 yrs later', *Herald Goa*, 14 September 2018.

11   *Swami Vivekananda in the West: New Discoveries, Volume 6*, p. 395.

12   *The Life of Swami Vivekananda, Volume 2*, p. 35.

13   Ibid., p. 120.

14   Ibid., pp. 155–56.

15   *The Complete Works of Swami Vivekananda, Volume IV*, p. 384.

16   *The Life of Swami Vivekananda, Volume 2.*

17   *Reminiscences of Swami Vivekananda*, p. 250.

18   Ibid., p. 193.

19   *The Complete Works of Swami Vivekananda, Volume III*, pp. 133–34.

20   *The Complete Works of Swami Vivekananda, Volume IX*, p. 377.

21   Sister Nivedita, *Notes of Some Wanderings with the Swami Vivekananda*, Swami Saradananda (ed.), Brahmachari Gonendra Nath, Udbodhan Office: Baghbazar, Calcutta, 1913, p. 121.

22   Max Weber, *The Protestant Ethic and the Spirit of Capitalism*, tr. Talcott Parsons and Anthony Giddens, London and Boston: Unwin Hyman, 1930.

23   *The Life of Swami Vivekananda, Volume 1*, p. 228.

24   Chaturvedi Badrinath, *Swami Vivekananda: The Living Vedanta*, Delhi: Penguin Books, 2006.

25   *The Life of Swami Vivekananda, Volume 1*, p. 265.

26   *Ibid.*, p. 322.

27   Ibid.

28   Ibid.

29   Ibid.

30   Ramachandra Guha, *Gandhi: The Years that Changed the World (1914–1948)*, Delhi: Penguin Books, 2018, p. 123.

31   *The Life of Swami Vivekananda, Volume 2.*

32   *Notes of Some Wanderings with the Swami Vivekananda*, p. 157.

33   *The Life of Swami Vivekananda, Volume 2*, p. 332.

34   Damini Nath, 'Akbar Road could become Maharana Pratap Marg', *The Hindu*, 18 May 2016.

35   Ankita Sinha, 'When Shivaji Stole Mughal Thunder in Maharashtra History Textbooks', *The Quint*, 9 August 2017.

36   Ishita Bhatia, 'History will be rewritten to erase Mughals: BJP MLA', *Times of India*, 17 October 2017.

37   'BJP MLA: Taj Mahal built by traitor, not part of our history', *Rediff.com*, 16 October 2017.

38   Kanchan Srivastava, 'Erasing Mughal History BJP Renames Old Cities', *Asia Times*, 16 November 2018.

39   M. S. Golwalkar, *Bunch of Thoughts*, Bangalore Sahitya Sindhu Prakashana, 1996, pp. 127–28.

40   *The Complete Works of Swami Vivekananda, Volume III*, p. 294.

41   Ibid.

42   *The Life of Swami Vivekananda, Volume 2.*

43   *The Complete Works of Swami Vivekananda, Volume IX*, p. 345.

44   *The Life of Swami Vivekananda, Volume 1*, p. 217.

45   *The Life of Swami Vivekananda, Volume 2*, p. 295.

46   Ibid., p. 339.

47   *The Complete Works of Swami Vivekananda, Volume IX*, p. 345.

48   *Reminiscences of Swami Vivekananda*, pp. 188–91.

49   *The Life of Swami Vivekananda*, Volume 2, p. 332.

50   *The Complete Works of Swami Vivekananda, Volume VI*, p. 415.

CHAPTER 4: THE WEST: HISTORICAL CONTEXT

1   Jonathan Sperber, *Europe 1850–1914: Progress, Participation and Apprehension*, London: Pearson Longman, 2009.
2   Ibid.
3   Innovation and Technology in the 19th Century, available at https://teachinghistory.org/history-content/ask-a-historian/24470.
4   *The Complete Works of Swami Vivekananda, Volume III*, p. 241.
5   A. Raghuramraju, *Debating Vivekananda: A Reader*, Oxford University Press, 2014.
6   F. M. L. Thompson, *The Rise of Respectable Society: A Social History of Victorian Britain: 1830–1900*, Cambridge: Harvard University Press, 1988.
7   Sperber, *Europe 1850–1914*.
8   Ibid.
9   Richard J. Evans, *The Pursuit of Power: Europe, 1815–1914*, New York: Penguin/Viking, 2016.
10 *Handbook to Life in America: Postwar America, 1950 to 1969*, Rodney P. Carlisle (ed.), New York: Infobase Publishing, 2009.
11 *The Complete Works of Swami Vivekananda, Volume VI*, p. 272.
12 Ibid.
13 *The Complete Works of Swami Vivekananda, Volume IV*, p. 479.
14 Thompson, *The Rise of Respectable Society*.
15 *The Complete Works of Swami Vivekananda, Volume VI*, p. 366.
16 *The Complete Works of Swami Vivekananda, Volume II*, p. 369.
17 Ibid., p. 364.
18 Ibid., p. 371.
19 Marshall G. S. Hodgson, *The Venture of Islam* (*Volume 1: The Classical Age of Islam* and *Volume 2: The Expansion of Islam in the Middle Periods*), Chicago: University of Chicago Press, 1974 and 1977.

CHAPTER 5: HINDOOS, AMERICANS, AND ENGLISHMEN

1   *The Complete Works of Swami Vivekananda, Volume I*, p. 383.
2   *The Complete Works of Swami Vivekananda, Volume VI*, p. 390.
3   Ishita Banerjee-Dube, *A History of Modern India*, Delhi: Cambridge University Press, 2014.
4   David Kopf, *British Orientalism and the Bengal Renaissance: The Dynamics of Indian Modernization 1773–1835*, Berkeley and Los Angeles, California: University of California Press, 1969.
5   Brian K. Pennington, *Was Hinduism Invented?: Britons, Indians, and the Colonial Construction of Religion*, New York: Oxford University Press, 2005, p. 3.
6   James Mill, *The History of British India: Volume 1*, London: Baldwin, Cradock and Joy, 1826, p. 214.
7   Theodore Koditschek, *Liberalism, Imperialism, and the Historical Imagination: Nineteenth-Century Visions of a Greater Britain*, 2011, p. 82.
8   James Mill, *The History of British India: Volume 2*, London: Baldwin, Cradock and Joy, 1826, p. 457.
9   Ibid., pp. 456–57.
10 Ibid., p. 194.
11 Sudhir Chandra, *Dependence and Disillusionment: Emergence of National Consciousness in Later Nineteenth Century India*, Delhi: Oxford University Press, 2011.
12 Pennington, *Was Hinduism Invented?*, p 8.

13 William Hastie, *Hindu Idolatry and English Enlightenment: Six Letters Addressed to Educated Hindus Containing a Practical Discussion of Hinduism*, Calcutta: Thacker, Spink and Co., 1883, p. 71.

14 Ibid., p. 31.

15 S. N. Balagangadhara, *The Heathen in His Blindness: Asia, the West & the Dynamic of Religion*, Leiden: Brill, 1994.

16 Pennington, *Was Hinduism Invented?*, p. 77.

17 Ibid., p. 82.

18 Ibid.

19 Ibid., p. 84.

20 Ibid., p. 93.

21 Ibid., p. 71.

22 Ibid.

23 *The Complete Works of Swami Vivekananda, Volume I*, p. 428.

24 Michael J. Altman, *Heathen, Hindoo, Hindu: American Representations of India, 1721–1893*, New York: Oxford University Press, 2017, p. 52.

25 Ibid., p. 353.

26 Ibid.

27 Ibid., p. 356.

28 Ibid.

29 Ibid.

30 Altman, *Heathen, Hindu, Hindoo*, p. 30.

31 Ibid., p. 31.

32 Ibid.

33 Ibid., p. 32.

34 Ibid.

35 Ibid.

36 Ibid., p. 34.

37 Ibid.

38 Caleb William Wright, *India and Its Inhabitants*.

39 Ibid., p. 52.

40 Ibid.

41 Ibid.

42 Ibid.

43 Ibid.

44 *The Complete Works of Swami Vivekananda, Volume V*, p. 26.

45 *The Complete Works of Swami Vivekananda, Volume VII*, p. 472.

46 Marshall G. S. Hodgson, *The Venture of Islam* (*Volume 3: The Gunpowder Empires and Modern Times*), Chicago: University of Chicago Press, 1977.

47 Hodgson, *The Venture of Islam, Volume 2*.

48 *The World's Parliament of Religions: An Illustrated and Popular Story of the World's First Parliament of Religions in Connection with the Columbian Exposition of 1893: Volume 1*, John Henry Barrows (ed.), Chicago: Chicago Publishing Company, 1893, p. 72.

49 Richard Hughes Seager, *The World's Parliament of Religions: The East/West Encounter, Chicago, 1893*, Indiana: Indiana University Press, 1995.

50 Ibid., p. 457.

51 Ibid., pp. 538–40.

52 Ibid.

53 Ibid., p. 143.

54 Asim Chaudhuri, *Swami Vivekananda in Chicago: New Findings*, Chicago: Advaita Ashrama, 2000, p. 106.

55 Ibid.
56 *The Complete Works of Swami Vivekananda, Volume VIII*, p. 214.
57 Ibid.
58 Chaudhuri, *Swami Vivekananda in Chicago*, p. 103.
59 Apurva, 'Terror probe: CBI arrests Aseemanand in Haridwar', *The Indian Express*, 2010.
60 Press Release, *The Caravan*, 5 February 2014.
61 Vijaita Singh, '"Had enough proof against Aseemanand"', *The Hindu*, 9 March 2017; Ipsita Chakravarty, 'The Daily Fix: Acquittals in Samjhauta blast case throw doubts on the NIA's credibility once again', *Scroll.in*, 22 March 2019.
62 Christophe Jaffrelot and Malvika Maheshwari, 'Paradigm Shift by the RSS? Lessons from Aseemanand's Confessions', *Economic and Political Weekly*, Vol. 46, Issue 6, 5 February 2011; Leena Raghunathan, 'The Believer Swami Aseemanand's Radical Service to the Sangh', *The Caravan*, 1 February 2014.
63 Raghunathan, 'The Believer Swami Aseemanand's Radical Service to the Sangh'.
64 *The Complete Works of Swami Vivekananda Volume V*, p. 233.
65 Ibid., p. 5.
66 Sharma, *Cosmic Love and Human Apathy*, p. 205.
67 Hastie, *Hindu Idolatry and English Enlightenment*, p. xii.
68 Ibid., pp. xiv–xv.
69 Ibid., p. xxi.
70 Ibid., p. xxii.
71 Ibid., p. 26.
72 *The Complete Works of Swami Vivekananda, Volume III*, p. 211.
73 *The Life of Swami Vivekananda, Volume 1*.
74 Ibid.
75 Ibid.; *Swami Vivekananda in the West: New Discoveries, Volume 1*.
76 *The Life of Swami Vivekananda, Volume 1*, p. 31.
77 Ibid., p. 482.
78 *The Complete Works of Swami Vivekananda, Volume VIII*, pp. 310–11.
79 *The Complete Works of Swami Vivekananda, Volume VII*, pp. 466–67.

CHAPTER 6: VIVEKANANDA'S HINDUISM VS THE SANGH PARIVAR'S HINDUISM

1   *The Complete Works of Swami Vivekananda, Volume VII*, pp. 282–83.
2   *The Complete Works of Swami Vivekananda, Volume I*, p. 329.
3   *The Complete Works of Swami Vivekananda, Volume VI*, p. 301.
4   Swami Nikhilananda, *Vivekananda: A Biography*; *The Life of Swami Vivekananda, Volume 1*.
5   *The Complete Works of Swami Vivekananda, Volume V*, p. 12.
6   *Reminiscences of Swami Vivekananda*, p. 197.
7   Golwalkar, *Bunch of Thoughts*, pp. 60–61.
8   Burke, *Swami Vivekananda in the West: New Discoveries, Volume 6*, p. 126.
9   Divya Trivedi, 'Politics of diet', *Frontline*, 18 July 2018.
10 M. N. Srinivas, *Social Change in Modern India*, New Delhi: Orient Longman, 1972.
11 Sankar, *The Monk as Man: The Unknown Life of Swami Vivekananda*, New Delhi: Penguin Books, 2011, p. 108 and 120.
12 *The Complete Works of Swami Vivekananda, Volume V*, p. 484.
13 Ibid., p. 403.
14 Ibid.

15   PTI, 'UN declares June 21 as "International Day of Yoga"', *Economic Times*, 11 December 2014.

16   *The Complete Works of Swami Vivekananda, Volume I*, p. 138.

17   *The Complete Works of Swami Vivekananda, Volume VI*, p. 233.

18   *The Complete Works of Swami Vivekananda, Volume III*, p. 450.

19   Maseeh Rahman, 'Indian prime minister claims genetic science existed in ancient times', *The Guardian*, 28 October 2014; 'Cows exhale oxygen, absorb cosmic energy, home to gods: Rajasthan HC judge', *Hindustan Times*, 19 June 2017; 'Cow urine cured my breast cancer: Sadhvi Pragya', *India Today*, 23 April 2019; Avinash Nair, 'Covid care centre inside "gaushala" with medicines from cow milk, urine', *Indian Express*, 9 May 2021.

20   *The Complete Works of Swami Vivekananda, Volume IV*, p. 433.

21   Advaita Ashrama, *Aspects of Vedanta*, Golpark: Ramakrishna Mission, 1995.

22   Deendayal Upadhyaya, *Integral Humanism: An Analysis of Some Basic Elements*, Prabhat Prakashan, 2009.

23   Savarkar, *Hindutva*, pp. 98–99.

24   Golwalkar, *Bunch of Thoughts*, p. 61.

25   Ibid., p 60.

26   Ibid., p 244.

27   PTI, 'Ram, "Gau Mata" basis of Hindu culture: Bhagwat', *Deccan Herald*, 7 February 2019.

28   Golwalkar, *Bunch of Thoughts*, pp. 244–45.

29   Ibid., pp. 345–46.

30   Ibid., p. 129.

31   'Importance of Vat Savitri Vrat and how such rituals strengthen family bond', *Organiser*, 10 June 2021.

32   *The Complete Works of Swami Vivekananda, Volume V*, page 232.

33   Ibid., p. 197.

34   *The Complete Works of Swami Vivekananda, Volume VIII*, p. 523.

35   *The Complete Works of Swami Vivekananda, Volume III*, p. 283.

36   *The Complete Works of Swami Vivekananda, Volume IV*, p. 489.

37   *The Complete Works of Swami Vivekananda, Volume V*, p. 203.

38   T. M. P. Mahadevan, 'The Upanishads', *History of Philosophy Eastern and Western: Volume 1*, Sarvepalli Radhakrishnan, Ardheshir Ruttonji Wadia, Dhirendra Mohan Datta, and Humayun Kabir, (eds.), London: George Allen & Unwin Ltd, 1952, p. 56.

39   Jha, *The Myth of the Holy Cow*, p. 21.

40   *The Complete Works of Swami Vivekananda, Volume III*, p. 173.

41   *History of Philosophy Eastern and Western: Volume 1.*

42   Sheldon Pollock, 'The Revelation of Tradition: sruti, smrti, and the Sanskrit Discourse of Power', *Boundaries, Dynamics and Construction of Traditions in South Asia*, Federico Squarcini (ed.), Delhi: Anthem Press, 2011, p. 41–62.

43   Andrew J. Nicholson, *Unifying Hinduism: Philosophy and Identity in Indian Intellectual History*, New York: Columbia University Press, 2010.

44   *The Complete Works of Swami Vivekananda, Volume III*, p. 118.

45   Mahadevan, 'The Upanishads', p. 57.

46   *The Complete Works of Swami Vivekananda, Volume I*, p. 450.

47   Mahadevan, 'The Upanishads', p. 58.

48   *The Complete Works of Swami Vivekananda, Volume I*, p. 326.

49   *The Complete Works of Swami Vivekananda, Volume V*, p. 411.

50   Ibid., p. 311.

51   Mahendranath Gupta, *The Gospel of Sri Ramakrishna*, Vol. II, tr. Swami Nikhilananda, Mayavati: Advaita Ashrama, 2010.

52   *The Complete Works of Swami Vivekananda, Volume VII*, p. 30.

53   Ibid., p. 30.

54   Ibid., p. 41.

55   *The Complete Works of Swami Vivekananda, Volume VI*, p. 394.

56   'Why comedian Munawar Faruqui was arrested: A timeline', *Hindustan Times*, 28 January 2021; Dhrendra K. Jha, 'Hindutva Groups Ordered UP Police To File Sedition Cases, And Yogi's Police Obeyed', *Article 14*, 8 February 2022; Tejas Joshi, '"Hurting Religious Sentiments": Assam Man Arrested For Dressing Up As Lord Shiva For Nukkad Play', *HW News*, 10 July 2022.

57   *The Complete Works of Swami Vivekananda, Volume VI*, p. 213.

58   Jaffrelot, *The Hindu Nationalist Movement*.

59   Arghya Jyoti Ganguly, 'West Bengal: Chappals on Pandals Contradict Durga Puja Essentials', *Organiser*, 13 October 2021.

60   'Param Poojaniya Sarsanghchalak Dr. Mohan Bhagwat Ji's Full Speech on the occasion of Sri Vijayadashami Utsav 2021 (Friday, October 15, 2021)', Rashtriya Swayamsevak Sangh, 15 October 2021.

61   *The Complete Works of Swami Vivekananda, Volume VIII*, p. 95.

62   *The Complete Works of Swami Vivekananda, Volume IV*, p. 462.

63   Advaita Ashrama, *Aspects of Vedanta*.

64   Doninger, *On Hinduism*.

65   *The Complete Works of Swami Vivekananda, Volume IX*, p. 275.

66   *The Complete Works of Swami Vivekananda, Volume I*, p. 354.

67   *The Complete Works of Swami Vivekananda, Volume V*, p. 10.

68   *The Complete Works of Swami Vivekananda, Volume VIII*, p. 95.

69   *The Complete Works of Swami Vivekananda, Volume I*, p. 121.

70   *The Complete Works of Swami Vivekananda, Volume III*, p. 392.

71   Jaffrelot, *The Hindu Nationalist Movement*, pp. 416–23.

72   'UP deputy CM stirs Hindutva pot, hints at grand temple in Mathura', *Hindustan Times*, 1 December 2021.

73   'VHP activists now want to hold rituals on Bababudangiri shrine premises', *The Hindu*, 4 December 2022.

74   'The Gyanvapi mosque case: All you need to know', *Deccan Herald*, 12 September 2022.

75   Jaffrelot, *The Hindu Nationalist Movement*, pp. 416–23.

76   K. N. Panikkar, 'Religious Symbols and Political Mobilization: The Agitation for a Mandir at Ayodhya', *Social Scientist*, Vol. 21, No. 7/8, 1993, p. 71.

77   Ibid., p. 70.

78   Ibid., p. 70–71.

79   Ibid.

80   Ramchandra Guha, *India After Gandhi: The History of the World's Largest Democracy*, New Delhi: Picador, 2008, p. 641.

81   *The Complete Works of Swami Vivekananda, Volume V*, p. 192.

82   *The Complete Works of Swami Vivekananda, Volume VII*, p. 23.

83   *The Complete Works of Swami Vivekananda, Volume II*, pp. 390–40.

84   *The Complete Works of Swami Vivekananda, Volume IV*, p. 465.

85   *The Complete Works of Swami Vivekananda, Volume II*, p. 320.

86   *The Complete Works of Swami Vivekananda, Volume V*, p. 207.

87   *The Complete Works of Swami Vivekananda Volume VI*, pp. 7–8.

88   Amrita Madhukalya, 'Krishna Janmabhoomi: Will BJP's temple trick work?', *Deccan Herald*, 5 February 2022.

89   'Explained: The Krishna Janmabhoomi case and the controversy behind it', *The Federal*, 21

May 2022.

90   *The Complete Works of Swami Vivekananda Volume III*, p. 524.
91   *The Complete Works of Swami Vivekananda Volume IV*, p. 102.
92   Ibid., pp. 103–105.
93   Ibid., pp. 105.
94   Ibid.
95   *The Complete Works of Swami Vivekananda. Volume IV*, pp. 105–106.
96   *The Complete Works of Swami Vivekananda, Volume I*, p. 17.
97   *The Complete Works of Swami Vivekananda, Volume II*, p. 483.
98   *The Complete Works of Swami Vivekananda, Volume V*, p. 95.
99   *The Complete Works of Swami Vivekananda, Volume IX*, p. 231.

CHAPTER 7: THE INDIVIDUAL AND SOCIETY: VIVEKANANDA AND THE RSS

1   D. E. Smith, *India as a Secular State*, London and Bombay: Oxford University Press, 1963, p. 468.
2   'Anti-cow slaughter mob storms Parliament', *The Hindu*, 8 November 1966, available at www.thehindu.com/archives/article16183780.ece. See also, Jaffrelot, *The Hindu Nationalist Movement in India*.
3   Golwalkar, *Bunch of Thoughts*, p. 10.
4   Ramachandra Guha, 'Which Ambedkar?', *Indian Express*, 21 April 2016.
5   A. G. Noorani, 'Is Constitution "anti-Hindu" or the RSS anti-Indian?', *Deccan Chronicle*, 29 September 2019.
6   Golwalkar, *Bunch of Thoughts*, p. 412
7   Ibid., p. 442.
8   Ibid., p. 439.
9   Ibid., p. 11.
10   Ibid., p. 16.
11   Ibid., p. 47.
12   Nilanjan Mukhopadhyay, *The RSS: Icons of the Indian Right*, New Delhi: Tranquebar, 2019.
13   Golwalkar, *Bunch of Thoughts*, pp. 391–92.
14   Ibid., p. 66.
15   Ibid., pp. 25–26.
16   Ibid., p. 32.
17   *The Complete Works of Swami Vivekananda Volume V*, p. 145.
18   *The Complete Works of Swami Vivekananda Volume IV*, p. 358.
19   *The Complete Works of Swami Vivekananda Volume V*, p. 146.
20   Ibid., p. 146.
21   *The Complete Works of Swami Vivekananda Volume II*, p. 115.
22   *The Complete Works on Swami Vivekananda Volume V*, p. 147.
23   Ibid., p. 29.
24   *The Complete Works on Swami Vivekananda Volume IV*, p. 356.
25   *The Complete Works on Swami Vivekananda Volume VI*, p. 65.
26   Golwalkar, *Bunch of Thoughts*, p. 11.
27   Ibid., p. 409.
28   *The Complete Works of Swami Vivekananda, Volume VI*, p. 319.
29   Golwalkar, *Bunch of Thoughts*, pp. 45–46.
30   *The Complete Works of Swami Vivekananda, Volume VII*, pp. 245–47.

31 *The Complete Works of Swami Vivekananda, Volume III*, p. 482.

32 Swami Nikhilananda, *Vivekananda: A Biography*, p. 74.

33 *The Complete Works of Swami Vivekananda, Volume IV*, pp. 357–58.

34 Ibid.

35 *The Complete Works of Swami Vivekananda, Volume III*, pp. 517–18.

36 Ibid.

37 Golwalkar, *Bunch of Thoughts*, p. 409.

38 *The Complete Works of Swami Vivekananda, Volume VI*, p. 65.

39 Ibid.

40 *The Complete Works of Swami Vivekananda, Volume V*, p. 410.

41 *The Complete Works of Swami Vivekananda, Volume IV*, p. 358.

42 Golwalkar, *Bunch of Thoughts*, p. 39.

43 *The Complete Works of Swami Vivekananda Volume IV*, p. 358.

44 Golwalkar, *Bunch of Thoughts*, p. 409.

45 *The Complete Works of Swami Vivekananda, Volume II*, p. 115.

46 Golwalkar, *Bunch of Thoughts*, p. 121.

47 *The Complete Works of Swami Vivekananda, Volume VI*, pp. 65–66.

48 *The Complete Works of Swami Vivekananda, Volume II*, p. 336.

49 *The Complete Works of Swami Vivekananda, Volume VI*, pp. 64–65.

50 Ibid., p. 65.

51 *The Complete Works of Swami Vivekananda, Volume IV*, pp. 490–91.

52 Ibid., pp. 490–92.

53 Ibid.

54 Ibid.

CHAPTER 8: VIVEKANANDA AND THE WEST

1   'Bajrang Dal protest lingerie ads', *NDTV*, 14 January 2010.

2   'Mangaluru: Valentine's Day celebration - Bajrang Dal warns district administration', *Daijiworld.com*, 12 February 2016; 'Foreign culture allows women to wear jeans and drink. It's good for them but not us, says MP BJP leader', *India Today*, 14 January 2013.

3   'Modi government, RSS plan to "cleanse" India of western culture, roadmap to be prepared', *DNA*, 24 September 2015.

4   *The Complete Works of Swami Vivekananda, Volume IV*, p. 490. The full quote says: 'Were good possible, then instead of being slaves for hundreds of years, we would have been the greatest nation on earth, and this soil of India, instead of being a mine of stupidity, would have been the eternal fountain-head of learning.'

5   *The Complete Works of Swami Vivekananda, Volume VI*, p. 256.

6   *The Complete Works of Swami Vivekananda, Volume VIII*, p. 327.

7   *The Complete Works of Swami Vivekananda, Volume II*, p. 114.

8   Justo L. Gonzalez, *The Story of Christianity: Volume 1: The Early Church to the Dawn of the Reformation*, New York: HarperOne, 2010.

9   Doniger, *On Hinduism*, p. 36.

10 Hodgson, *The Venture of Islam, Volume 2*.

11 *The Complete Works of Swami Vivekananda, Volume II*, p. 115.

12 *The Complete Works of Swami Vivekananda, Volume V*, p. 29.

13 *The Complete Works of Swami Vivekananda, Volume IV*, p. 368.

14 *The Complete Works of Swami Vivekananda, Volume III*, p. 151.

15 Ibid., p. 172.

16   Anil Seal, *The Emergence of Indian Nationalism*: Competition and Collaboration in the Later Nineteenth Century, Cambridge: Cambridge University Press, 1971, p. 23.

17   *The Complete Works of Swami Vivekananda, Volume IV*, p. 406.

18   *The Complete Works of Swami Vivekananda, Volume III*, p. 272.

19   *The Complete Works of Swami Vivekananda, Volume IV*, p. 365.

20   *The Complete Works of Swami Vivekananda, Volume VII*, p. 280.

21   *The Complete Works of Swami Vivekananda, Volume IX*, p. 424.

22   *The Complete Works of Swami Vivekananda, Volume III*, p. 168.

23   *The Complete Works of Swami Vivekananda, Volume IV*, pp. 399–408.

24   Frederick Copleston, S. J., *A History of Philosophy, Volume IV: Modern Philosophy: From Descartes to Leibniz*, New York: Doubleday, 1994, p. 43.

25   *The Complete Works of Swami Vivekananda, Volume IV*, p. 401.

26   Peter Gay, *The Enlightenment: An Interpretation: The Rise of Modern Paganism*, New York: Alfred A. Knopf, 1967.

27   *The Complete Works of Swami Vivekananda, Volume IV*, pp. 401–403.

28   Ibid., p. 404

29   Ibid., pp. 404–406.

30   Ibid., pp. 407–408.

31   *The Complete Works of Swami Vivekananda, Volume IX*, p. 328.

32   *The Complete Works of Swami Vivekananda, Volume V*, p. 199.

33   *The Complete Works of Swami Vivekananda, Volume III*, p. 158.

34   *The Complete Works of Swami Vivekananda, Volume IV*, p. 448.

35   *The Complete Works of Swami Vivekananda, Volume V*, p. 216.

36   Parsa Venkateshwar Rao Jr, 'India's Vishwaguru Syndrome Marks Intellectual Regression', *Deccan Herald*, 24 May 2022.

37   *The Complete Works of Swami Vivekananda, Volume III*, p. 317.

38   *The Complete Works of Swami Vivekananda, Volume I*, p. 22.

39   *The Complete Works of Swami Vivekananda, Volume V*, p. 22.

40   *The Complete Works of Swami Vivekananda, Volume III*, pp. 428–29.

41   *The Complete Works of Swami Vivekananda, Volume V*, p. 512.

42   Ibid.

43   *The Complete Works of Swami Vivekananda, Volume III*, p. 311.

CHAPTER 9: VIVEKANANDA'S PHILOSOPHY OF FREEDOM: THE METAPHYSICAL ASPECT

1   Advaita Ashrama, *Aspects of Vedanta*.

2   *The Complete Works of Swami Vivekananda, Volume I*, pp. 108–109.

3   *The Complete Works of Swami Vivekananda, Volume II*, p. 195.

4   *The Complete Works of Swami Vivekananda, Volume VI*, pp. 92–93.

5   *The Complete Works of Swami Vivekananda, Volume VIII*, p. 257.

6   *The Complete Works of Swami Vivekananda, Volume V*, p. 289.

7   *The Complete Works of Swami Vivekananda, Volume I*, p. 355.

8   *The Complete Works of Swami Vivekananda, Volume IV*, p. 489.

9   *The Complete Works of Swami Vivekananda, Volume II*, p. 346.

10   Shaku Soen, *Zen Buddhism for Americans*, tr. D. T. Suzuki, New York: Dorset Press, 1906, p. 25.

11   *The Complete Works of Swami Vivekananda, Volume VI*, p. 416.

12   *The Complete Works of Swami Vivekananda, Volume VIII*, p. 218.

13 *The Complete Works of Swami Vivekananda, Volume I*, p. 385.

14 Gupta, *The Gospel of Sri Ramakrishna, Volume I*; Swami Saradananada, *Sriramakrishna: The Great Master*, Madras: The Ramakrishna Math, 1952.

15 A. Raghuramaraju, 'Universal self, equality and hierarchy in Swami Vivekananda', *Indian Economic & Social History Review*, Vol. 52, No. 2, 2015, pp. 185–205.

16 Ashis Nandy, 'Vivekananda and Secularism: A Nineteenth Century Solution and a Twentieth Century Problem', *Debating Vivekananda: A Reader*, A. Raghuramaraju (ed.), New Delhi: Oxford University Press, 2014, p. 293.

17 Raghuramaraju, 'Universal self, equality and hierarchy in Swami Vivekananda', *Indian Economic and Social History Review*, Vol. 52, No. 2, 2015, pp. 185–205.

18 Jyotirmaya Sharma, *Cosmic Love and Human Apathy: Swami Vivekananda's Restatement Of Religion*, New Delhi: HarperCollins, 2013, p. 93.

19 Stephen E. Gregg, *Swami Vivekananda and Non-Hindu Traditions: A Universal Advaita*, Oxford and New York: Routledge, 2019, p. 1.

20 Ibid.

21 *The Complete Works of Swami Vivekananda, Volume I*, p. 24.

22 William James, *The Varieties of Religious Experience: A Study in Human Nature: Being the Gifford Lectures on Natural Religion Delivered at Edinburgh in 1901–1902*, London: Longsman Green & Co., 1945, p. 407.

23 *The Oxford Handbook of the Study of Religion*, Michael Stausberg and Steven Engler (eds.), Oxford: Oxford Unviersity Press, 2016.

24 Will Durant, *The Reformation: A History of European Civilization from Wyclif to Calvin: 1300–1564 (The Story of Civilization: Part VI)*, New York: Simon and Schuster, 1957, p. 153.

25 Rudolf Otto, *Mysticism East and West: A Comparative Analysis of the Nature of Mysticism*, tr. Bertha L. Bracey and Richenda C. Payne, London: Macmillan & Co., 1932, p. 4.

26 Ibid., p. 11.

27 *The Complete Mystical Works of Meister Eckhart*, tr. and ed. Maurice O'C. Walshe, New York: The Crossroad Publishing Company, 2009, p. 28.

28 Otto, *Mysticism East and West*, p. 11.

29 *The Complete Mystical Works of Meister Eckhart*, p. 28.

30 Otto, *Mysticism East and West*, p. 12.

31 Ibid., pp. 12–13.

32 Ibid., p. 13.

33 Ibid.

34 Hodgson, *The Venture of Islam, Volume 2*.

35 Hodgson, *The Venture of Islam, Volume 1*.

36 Hodgson, *The Venture of Islam, Volume 2*.

37 Ibid., pp. 203–204.

38 R. C. Zaehner, *Hindu and Muslim Mysticism*, London and New York: Bloomsbury Academic, 2016, p. 12.

39 Ibid., p. 98.

40 Tawasin of Mansur Al-Hallaj, 'The Tasin of the Point', tr. Aisha Abd Ar-Rahman, quoted in Steven Ashe, *Qabalah: The Complete Golden Dawn Initiative*, Glastonbury: Glastonbury Books, 2007, p. 529.

41 *The Complete Works of Swami Vivekananda, Volume III*, p. 282.

42 Zahurul Hasan Sharib, *Abu Said Abul Khair and His Rubaiyat*, London: Sharib Press, 1992.

43 'Ibn 'Arabî', *Stanford Encyclopedia of Philosophy*, 2 August 2019, available at plato.stanford. edu/entries/ibn-arabi/. (Some Arabic terms from this quote have been removed for ease of reading.)

44 Rom Landau, *The Philosophy of Ibn'Arabi*, Oxon: Routledge, 2008, p. 82.

45   Ibid., p. 69.

46   Ibid., p. 29.

47   Hodgson, *The Venture of Islam, Volume 2*, p. 232.

48   *The Complete Works of Swami Vivekananda, Volume I*, p. 329.

49   Zaehner, *Hindu and Muslim Mysticism*.

CHAPTER 10: THE EPISTEMOLOGICAL: REASON AND RELIGION

1   *The Complete Works of Swami Vivekananda, Volume I*, p. 367.

2   Rick Perlstein, *Nixonland: The Rise of a President and the Fracturing of America*, New York: Scribner, 2008.

3   'War on Drugs: Report of the Global Commission on Drug Policy', June 2011, available at www.scribd.com/document/56924096/Global-Commission-Report.

4   Peter Wagner and Wanda Bertram, '"What percent of the U.S. is incarcerated?" (And other ways to measure mass incarceration)', Prison Policy Initiative, 16 January 2020.

5   'Incarceration Rates by Country 2023', World Population Review, worldpopulationreview.com/country-rankings/incarceration-rates-by-country.

6   'Operation Iraqi Freedom', Naval History and Heritage Command, 7 November 2022.

7   Fiona MacDonald, 'The "freedom convoy" protesters are a textbook case of "aggrieved entitlement"', *The Conversation*, 16 February 2022.

8   The Hindu Bureau, 'Urine therapy can control AIDS and cancer, according to BA reference book in Karnataka, but author says "just an unscientific theory"', *The Hindu*, 19 November 2022.

9   Vasudevan Mukunth, 'Blinded By Its Cow-Urine Craze, the Government Isn't Fostering Good Research Practices', *The Wire*, 4 July 2018.

10   '#OUTLAWED "THE LOVE THAT DARE NOT SPEAK ITS NAME"', Human Rights Watch, available at internap.hrw.org/features/features/lgbt_laws/.

11   *Masterpiece Cakeshop vs Colorado Civil Rights Commission*.

12   Soumyarendra Barik, 'Tandav Case: Allahabad HC Rejects Anticipatory Bail Plea Of Amazon Prime Video India's Head Of Content', *MediaNama*, 26 February 2021.

13   'Allahabad HC rejects anticipatory bail plea by Amazon Prime Video head in Tandav case; says serial is against fundamental rights of the majority of citizens', *The Leaflet*, 25 February 2021.

14   *The Complete Works of Swami Vivekananda, Volume III*, p. 278.

15   *The Complete Works of Swami Vivekananda, Volume IV*, p. 127.

16   *The Complete Works of Swami Vivekananda, Volume III*, p. 5.

17   *The Complete Works of Swami Vivekananda, Volume IV*, p. 213.

18   *The Complete Works of Swami Vivekananda, Volume III*, p. 253.

19   *The Complete Works of Swami Vivekananda, Volume I*, pp. 415–16.

20   Ibid., pp. 184–85.

21   *The Complete Works of Swami Vivekananda, Volume VI*, pp. 14–15.

22   *The Complete Works of Swami Vivekananda, Volume I*, p. 233.

23   Ibid., p. 202.

24   *The Complete Works of Swami Vivekananda, Volume IX*, p. 516.

25   Quoted from Govind Krishnan V., 'Is Religion Rational? Science, Evidence and Objectivity', *De Natura Fidei: Rethinking religion across disciplinary boundaries, Volume 1*, New Delhi: Authorspress, 2022, pp. 69–70.

26   *The Complete Works of Swami Vivekananda, Volume VII*, pp. 431–32.

27   *The Complete Works of Swami Vivekananda, Volume I*, p. 201.

28   Govind Krishnan V., 'Is Religion Rational?', p. 84.

CHAPTER 11: ETHICS: ADVAITA AND DEMOCRACY

1   'Riddles in Hinduism: An Exposition to Enlighten the Masses', *Dr. Babasaheb Ambedkar Writings and Speeches, Volume No.: 4*, compiled by Vasant Moon, New Delhi: Dr. Ambedkar Foundation, 2019, p. 286, available at baws.in.

2   Rakhi Bose, 'Politics Of Appropriation: Why Ambedkar's Legacy Matters', *Outlook*, 18 October 2022.

3   Shivam Vij, '10 Ambedkar quotes that show why the BJP can't co-opt him', *The Print*, 12 April 2018.

4   Ibid., p. 284.

5   Ibid., p. 286.

6   'Draft Constitution—Discussion Motion re Draft Constitution', *Dr. Babasaheb Ambedkar Writings and Speeches, Volume No.: 13*, Vasant Moon (ed.), New Delhi: Dr. Ambedkar Foundation, 2019, p. 60, available at baws.in.

7   'Riddles in Hinduism', p. 282.

8   Ibid.

9   *The Cambridge Companion to Dewey*, Molly Cochran (ed.), Cambridge: Cambridge University Press, 2010.

10 'Riddles in Hinduism', p. 283.

11 'The Philosophy of Hinduism', *Dr. Babasaheb Ambedkar Writings and Speeches, Volume No.: 3*, compiled by Vasant Moon, New Delhi: Dr. Ambedkar Foundation, 2019, p. 23, available at baws.in.

12 *The Complete Works of Swami Vivekananda, Volume VI*, p. 381.

13 *The Complete Works of Swami Vivekananda, Volume V*, p. 22.

14 *The Complete Works of Swami Vivekananda, Volume III*, p. 515.

15 Ibid., p. 216.

16 *The Complete Works of Swami Vivekananda, Volume V*, p. 29.

17 Ibid., p. 199.

18 Ibid., p. 192.

19 *The Complete Works of Swami Vivekananda, Volume I*, p. 389.

20 *The Complete Works of Swami Vivekananda, Volume III*, p. 429.

21 Ibid.

22 Ibid., p. 432.

23 *The Complete Works of Swami Vivekananda, Volume II*, p. 294.

24 *The Complete Works of Swami Vivekananda, Volume VIII*, p. 125.

25 'Riddles in Hinduism', p. 284.

26 *108 Upanishads*, compiled by Richard Sheppard, International Gita Society.

27 'Riddles in Hinduism', p. 285.

28 H. M. Vroom, *No Other Gods: Christian Belief in Dialogue with Buddhism, Hinduism, and Islam*, tr. Lucy Jansen, Michigan and Cambridge: William B. Eerdmans Publishing Company, 1996, p. 57.

29 Wendy Doniger, *Dreams, Illusions and Other Realities*, Chicago and London: The University of Chicago Press, 1984, p. 119.

30 Mahendranath Gupta, *The Gospel of Sri Ramakrishna, Vol. I*, tr. Swami Nikhilananda, Mayavati: Advaita Ashrama, 2009, p. 396.

31 Lisa Lassel Halstrom, *Mother of Bliss: Anandamayi Ma (1896–1982)*, New York: Oxford University Press, 1999, p. 187.

32 *The Complete Works of Swami Vivekananda, Volume III*, p. 244.

CHAPTER 12: THE POLITICAL: GENDER

1   *The Complete Works of Swami Vivekananda, Volume VI*, pp. 248–49.
2   Kathleen Canning, 'The "Woman Question"', *A Companion to Nineteenth Century Europe 1789-1914*, Stefan Berger (ed.), Malden, Oxford, and Victoria: Blackwell Publishing, 2006, p. 193.
3   Hugh McLean, *In Quest of Tolstoy*, Brighton: Academic Studies Press, 2008, p. 105.
4   Friedrich Engels, *The Conditions of the Working-Class in England*, London: Penguin Books, 1987, pp. 168–174.
5   'Was Rabindranath Tagore a feminist? Read his essay "Woman and Home" from 1922 to find out', *Scroll.in*, 9 May 2017.
6   *The Complete Works of Swami Vivekananda, Volume VI*, p. 246.
7   *The Complete Works of Swami Vivekananda, Volume VIII*, p. 198.
8   Burke, *Swami Vivekananda in the West: New Discoveries, Volume 2*, p. 238.
9   *The Complete Works of Swami Vivekananda, Volume VI*, p. 328.
10 *The Complete Works of Swami Vivekananda, Volume I*, p. 388.
11 *The Complete Works of Swami Vivekananda, Volume III*, p. 128.
12 *The Complete Works of Swami Vivekananda, Volume VII*, p. 219.
13 *The Complete Works of Swami Vivekananda, Volume VIII*, p. 28.
14 *The Complete Works of Swami Vivekananda, Volume VI*, p. 115.
15 *The Complete Works of Swami Vivekananda, Volume VIII*, p. 91.
16 'John Stuart Mill Amendment', available at www.parliament.uk/about/living-heritage/evolutionofparliament/houseofcommons/reformacts/from-the-parliamentary-collections/collections-reform-acts/great-reform-act112/.
17 Rosalind Jones, 'Review: Anti-Suffrage "Participative Citizens"', *Government and Opposition*, Vol. 27, No. 2, 1992, p. 253.
18 Beatrice Webb, *My Apprenticeship*, London: Longmans, Green and Co., 1946, pp. 303–304.
19 Tessa Boase, *Mrs Pankhurst's Purple Feather: Fashion, Fury and Feminism – Women's Fight for Change*, London: Aurum Press, 2018, p. 178.
20 *The Complete Works of Swami Vivekananda, Volume IX*, p. 474.
21 *The Complete Works of Swami Vivekananda, Volume VII*, pp. 212–13.
22 *The Complete Works of Swami Vivekananda, Volume V*, p. 168.
23 *The Complete Works of Swami Vivekananda, Volume VII*, p. 271.
24 *The Complete Works of Swami Vivekananda, Volume IX*, pp. 180–81.

CHAPTER 13: THE POLITICAL: CASTE

1   TRAVANCORE (STATE APPOINTMENTS), HC Deb 19 July 1897 vol 51 cc400-1, available at https://api.parliament.uk/historic-hansard/commons/1897/jul/19/travancore-state-appointments.
2   *The Complete Works of Swami Vivekananda, Volume IX*, p. 95.
3   Robin Jeffrey, *The Decline of Nair Dominance: Society and Politics in Travancore 1847-1908*, New Delhi: Manohar Books, 1994.
4   Dr S. N. Sadasivan, *A Social History of India*, New Delhi: A. P. H. Publishing Corporation, 2000.
5   Jeffrey, *The Decline of Nair Dominance*, p. 189.
6   Translated and quoted in Shankari Prasad Basu, 'Swami Vivekananda and Social Reform Movements in Kerala: Kumaran Asan, Dr. Palpu, Shri Narayana Guru and the SNDP Movement', *Prabuddha Bharata*, January and February 1989, pp. 50–58 and 99–105.

7   'Annihilation of Caste', *Dr. Babasaheb Ambedkar Writings And Speeches, Volume No.: 1*, compiled by Vasant Moon, New Delhi: Dr. Ambedkar Foundation, 2019, available at baws.in.

8   Rajarshi Chunder, 'Tagore and Caste: From Brahmacharyasram to Swadeshi Movement (1901–07)', 19 September 2018, *Sahapedia*, available at www.sahapedia.org/tagore-and-caste-brahmacharyasram-swadeshi-movement-1901–07.

9   *The Complete Works of Swami Vivekananda, Volume IV*, pp. 299–300.

10   *The Complete Works of Swami Vivekananda, Volume V*, pp. 22–23.

11   Ibid., p. 23.

12   Ibid., p. 198.

13   Ibid., p. 311.

14   *The Complete Works of Swami Vivekananda, Volume VI*, p. 161.

15   Ibid., p. 210.

16   Ibid., p. 247.

17   Ibid., p. 394.

18   Ibid.

19   *The Complete Works of Swami Vivekananda, Volume VII*, pp. 39–40.

20   *The Complete Works of Swami Vivekananda, Volume IX*, p. 524.

21   *The Complete Works of Swami Vivekananda, Volume VIII*, p. 27.

22   'Address of the International Working Men's Association to Abraham Lincoln, President of the United States of America', available at www.marxists.org/archive/marx/iwma/documents/1864/lincoln-letter.htm.

23   'Annihilation of Caste', p. 55.

24   Abul Pitre, *An Introduction to Elijah Muhammad Studies: The New Educational Paradigm*, Maryland: University Press of America, 2010, p. 40.

25   *The Encyclopedia of Libertarianism*, Ronald Hamowy (ed.), Sage Publications, p. 125.

26   Marie Louise Burke, *Swami Vivekananda in the West: New Discoveries, Volume 5*, pp. 389–94.

27   Guha, *Gandhi: The Years That Changed the World, 1914–1948*.

28   Tapan Basu, 'Caste Matters: Rabindranath Tagore's Engagement with India's Ancient Social Hierarchies', *South Asia: Journal of South Asian Studies*, Vol. 35, No. 1, 2012, pp. 162–171.

29   Definition of 'caste', *Merriam Webster*.

30   *The Complete Works of Swami Vivekananda, Volume III*, p. 243.

31   Tapan Basu, 'Caste Matters: Rabindranath Tagore's Engagement with India's Ancient Social Hierarchies', *South Asia: Journal of South Asian Studies*, Vol. 35, No. 1, 2012, pp. 162–171.

32   Marie Louise Burke, *Swami Vivekananda in the West: New Discoveries, Volume 4*, Mayavati: Advaita Ashrama, 1992, p. 383.

33   *The Complete Works of Swami Vivekananda, Volume V*, p. 214.

34   *The Complete Works of Swami Vivekananda, Volume IV*, pp. 371–73.

35   Ibid., p. 372.

36   Rajagopal Chattopadhyaya, *Swami Vivekananda in India: A Corrective Biography*, Delhi: Motilal Banarsidass Publishers, 1999.

37   *The Complete Works of Swami Vivekananda, Volume III*, pp. 299–300.

38   *The Complete Works of Swami Vivekananda, Volume VI*, pp. 317–18.

39   *The Complete Works of Swami Vivekananda, Volume III*, p. 298.

40   'Annihilation of Caste', p. 70.

41   Ibid., p. 71.

42   *The Bhagavad Gita*, tr. Sarvepalli Radhakrishnan, London: George Allen & Unwin Ltd, 1948, p. 161.

43   Ibid., see 'Introduction'.

44   *The Complete Works of Swami Vivekananda, Volume III*, pp. 293–295.

45   *The Complete Works of Swami Vivekananda, Volume V*, p. 377.

46 *The Complete Works of Swami Vivekananda, Volume VI*, p. 496.
47 Chapter XXVI, 'The Brahmana', *The Dhammapada*, tr. John Ross Carter and Mahinda Palihawadana, Oxford: Oxford University Press, 2000, pp. 66–71.
48 *The Complete Works of Swami Vivekananda, Volume III*, pp. 295–96.
49 Ibid.
50 Srinivas, *Social Change in Modern India*, p. 9.
51 *The Complete Works of Swami Vivekananda, Volume V*, p. 214.
52 *The Complete Works of Swami Vivekananda, Volume VII*, pp. 107–108.
53 *The Complete Works of Swami Vivekananda, Volume III*, p. 290.
54 Aroon Raman, 'Colliding worlds of tradition and revolution', *The Hindu*, 14 December 2009.
55 Srinivas, *Social Change in Modern India*, p. 4.
56 Ibid.
57 Ibid.
58 Ibid., pp. 290–91.
59 *The Complete Works of Swami Vivekananda, Volume III*, p. 290.
60 'Over 1.3 lakh cases of crime against Dalits since 2018; UP, Bihar, Rajasthan top charts', *Economic Times*, 1 December 2021.
61 'Annihilation of Caste', p. 68.
62 *The Yajur Veda*, tr. Devi Chand, Hoshiarpur: Devi Chand, 1959, p. 2.
63 Verse 10.19.12, *The Rig Veda*, tr. Ralph T. H. Griffith, Grey Books, 2018.
64 *The Yajur Veda*, p. 172.
65 Ibid., p. 219.
66 'The Philosophy of Hinduism', p. 8.
67 Ibid., p. 6.
68 *The Complete Works of Swami Vivekananda, Volume II*, pp. 297–98.
69 Ibid., pp. 298–99.
70 Ibid., p. 299.

BIBLIOGRAPHY

BOOKS

'Annihilation of Caste', *Dr. Babasaheb Ambedkar Writings And Speeches, Volume No.: 1*, compiled by Vasant Moon, New Delhi: Dr. Ambedkar Foundation, 2019.

'Chronology of Vivekananda in the West (1893-1900)', Terrance Hohner and Carolyn Kenny (eds.), available at vedanta.org/wp-content/uploads/2016/10/Swami-Vivekananda-in-the-West-A-Chronology.pdf.

'Riddles in Hinduism: An Exposition to Enlighten the Masses', *Dr. Babasaheb Ambedkar Writings and Speeches, Volume No.: 4*, compiled by Vasant Moon, New Delhi: Dr. Ambedkar Foundation, 2019.

'The Philosophy of Hinduism', *Dr. Babasaheb Ambedkar Writings and Speeches, Volume No.: 3*, compiled by Vasant Moon, New Delhi: Dr. Ambedkar Foundation, 2019.

108 Upanishads, International Gita Society.

A Chorus of Faith as Heard in the Parliament of Religions, Chicago: The Unity Publishing Company, 1893.

A Companion to Nineteenth Century Europe, 1789–1914, Stefan Berger (ed.), Oxford: Blackwell Publishing, 2006.

Ahmed, Shahab, *What is Islam? The Importance of Being Islamic*, Princeton: Princeton University Press, 2018.

Altman, Michael J., *Heathen, Hindoo, Hindu: American Representations of India, 1721–1893*, New York: Oxford University Press, 2017.

Armstrong, Karen, *Islam: A Short History*, London: Phoenix Press, 2011.

Ashe, Steven, *Qabalah: The Complete Golden Dawn Initiative*, Glastonbury: Glastonbury Books, 2007.

Aslan, Reza, *No God but God: The Origins, Evolution, and Future of Islam*, New York: Random House, 2005.

Aspects of Vedanta, Kolkata: Ramakrishna Mission Institute of Culture, 1995.

Atlick, Richard, *Victorian People and Ideas: A Companion for the Modern Reader of Victorian Literature*, New York: W. W. Norton and Company, 1973.

Badrinath, Chaturvedi, *Swami Vivekananda: The Living Vedanta*, Gurgaon: Penguin Random House India, 2015.

Balagangadhara, S. N., *The Heathen in His Blindness: Asia, the West & the Dynamic of Religion*, Leiden: Brill, 1994.

Bayly, C. A., *The New Cambridge History of India: Indian Society and the Making of the British Empire*, Cambridge: Cambridge University Press, 1988.

Bayly, Susan, *Caste, Society and Politics in India from the Eighteenth Century to the Modern Age (The New Cambridge History of India): Volume 4*, New York: Cambridge University Press, 1999.

Blackwell Companion to Hinduism, Gavin Flood (ed.), Oxford: Blackwell, 2003.

Blom, Philipp, *The Vertigo Years: Europe, 1900–1914*, New York: Basic Books, 2008.

Boase, Tessa, *Etta Lemon: The Woman Who Saved the Birds*, London: Aurum Press, 2018. Republished as *Mrs. Pankhurst's Purple Feather: Fashion Fury and Feminism: Women's Fight for Change*, 2021.

Brahmasutra Bhasya of Sancaracarya, tr. Swami Gambhirananda, Mayavati: Advaita Ashrama, 1965.

Brahmasutra, tr. Swami Vireswarananda, Mayavati: Advaita Ashrama, 1936.

Brockington, J. L., *The Sacred Thread: A Short History of Hinduism*, New Delhi: Oxford University Press, 2000.

Burke, Mary Louise, *Swami Vivekananda in the West: New Discoveries, Volume 1 to 6*, Mayavati: Advaita Ashrama, 1994.

Calvé, Emma, *My Life*, New York: D. Appleton and Company, 1922.

Cambridge Companion to Dewey, Molly Cochren (ed.), Cambridge: Cambridge University Press, 2010.

Chandra, Bipin, Mukherjee, Aditya, Mukherjee, Mridula, Mahajan, Sucheta, and Panikkar, K. N., *India's Struggle for Independence*, New Delhi: Penguin Books, 1989.

Chandra, Sudir, *Dependency and Disillusionment: Emergence of National Consciousness in Late Nineteenth Century India*, Delhi: Oxford University Press, 2011.

Charvat, Petr, *The Birth of the State: Ancient Egypt, Mesopotamia, India and China*, tr. Daniel Morgan, Prague: Karolinum Press, 2013.

Chattopadhyaya, Rajagopal, *Swami Vivekananda in India: A Corrective Biography*, Delhi: Motilal Banarsidass Publishers, 1999.

Chaudhuri, Asim, *Swami Vivekananda in Chicago: New Findings*, Mayavati: Advaita Ashrama, 2000.

Claeys, Gregory, *Imperial Sceptics: British Critics of Empire: 1850–1920*, Cambridge: Cambridge University Press, 2010.

Constituent Assembly Debates, Book 2, Volume VII, Lok Sabha, available at https://loksabha.nic.in/writereaddata/cadebatefiles/C05111948.pdf.

Copleston S. J., Frederick, *A History of Philosophy, Volume IV: Modern Philosophy: From Descartes to Leibniz*, New York: Doubleday, 1994.

Dasgupta, R. K., *Swami Vivekananda on Indian Philosophy and Literature*, Calcutta: The Ramakrishna Mission Institute of Culture, 1996.

De Natura Fidei: Rethinking Religion Across Disciplinary Boundaries: Volume 1, Jibu Mathew George, New Delhi: Authors Press, 2021.

Debating Vivekananda: A Reader, Raghuram Raju (ed.), New Delhi: Oxford University Press, 2014.

Deutsch, Eliot, *Advaita Vedanta: A Philosophical Reconstruction*, Honolulu: East-West Center Press, 1969.

Doniger, Wendy, *Dreams, Illusions and Other Realities*, Chicago and London: The University of Chicago Press, 1984,

————*On Hinduism*, New Delhi: Aleph Book Company, 2013.

Doyle, Mark, *Communal Violence in the British Empire: Disturbing the Pax*, London: Bloomsbury Academic, 2016.

Dube, Ishita Banerjee, *A History of Modern India*, Delhi: Cambridge University Press, 2014.

Durant, Will, *The Reformation: A History of European Civilization from Wyclif to Calvin: 1300–1564 (The Story of Civilization: Part VI)*, New York: Simon and Schuster, 1957.

Eckhart, Meister, *The Complete Mystical Works of Meister Eckhart*, tr. Maurice O'C. Walshe (ed.), New York: The Crossroad Publishing Company, 2009.

Engels, Friedrich, *The Conditions of the Working Class in England*, London: Penguin Books, 1987.

Eraly, Abraham, *The First Spring: The Golden Age of India*, New Delhi: Penguin Viking, 2011.

————*The Mughal World: Life in India's Last Golden Age*, New Delhi: Penguin, 2008.

Evans, Richard J., *The Pursuit of Power: Europe 1815-1914*, Cambridge: Penguin, 2016.

Gambhirananda, Swami, *Bhagavad Gita with the Commentary of Sancaracharya*, Mayavati: Advaita Ashrama, 2000.

Gay, Peter, *The Enlightenment: An Interpretation, the Rise of Modern Paganism*, New York: Norton, 1966.

Golwalkar, M. S., *Bunch of Thoughts*, Bangalore: Sahitya Sindhu Prakashana, 1996.

————*We or Our Nationhood Defined*, Nagpur: Bharat Publications, 1939.

González, Justo L., *The Story of Christianity, Volume 1: The Early Church to the Dawn of the Reformation*, New York: HarperOne, 2010.

————*The Story of Christianity, Volume 2: The Reformation to the Present Day*, New York: HarperCollins, 1985.

Gopal, Sarvepalli, *British Policy in India (1858–1905)*, Cambridge: Cambridge University Press, 1956.

Gregg, Stephen E., *Swami Vivekananda and Non-Hindu Traditions: A Universal Advaita*, Oxon: Routledge, 2019.

Guha, Ramchandra, *Gandhi: The Years that Changed the World, 1914-1948*, Gurgaon: Penguin Allen Lane, 2018.

————*India after Gandhi: The History of the World's Greatest Democracy*, New Delhi: Picador India, 2008.

Gupta, Mahendranath, *The Gospel of Sri Ramakrishna Volume 1 and 2*, Chennai: Sri Ramakrishna Math, 2008.

Hallstrom, Lisa Lassell, *Mother of Bliss: Anandamayi Ma (1896 to 1982)*, Oxford: Oxford University Press, 1999.

Hindu Nationalism: A Reader, Christophe Jaffrelot (ed.), Princeton: Princeton University Press, 2007.

History of Philosophy Eastern and Western, Volume 1, Sarvepalli Radhakrishnan (ed.), London: George Allen & Unwin, 1952.

History, Religion and Culture: British Intellectual History, 1750–1950, Stephan Collini, Richard Whatmore, and Brian Young (eds.), Cambridge: Cambridge University Press, 2000.

Hobsbawm, Eric, *On Nationalism*, London: Little, Brown, 2021.

————*The Age of Capital: 1848–1875*, London: Abacus, 1997.

————*The Age of Empire: 1875–1914*, London: Abacus, 1994.

————*The Age of Revolution: 1789–1848*, London: Abacus, 1977.

Hodgson, Marshall H., *The Venture of Islam: Conscience in a World Religion*, Volumes 1 to 3, Chicago: University of Chicago Press, 1974.

Houghton, Walter E., *The Victorian Frame of Mind*, Yale: Yale University Press, 1975.

Husserl, Edmund, *Cartesian Meditations: An Introduction to Phenomenology*, Dordetcht: Kluwer Academic Publishers Group, 1999.

Ibn'Al'Arabi: The Bezels of Wisdom, tr. R. W. J Austin, New York: Paulist Press, 1980.

Isayeva, Natalia, *Shankara and Indian Philosophy*, New York: State University of New York Press, 1993.

Isherwood, Christopher, *Ramakrishna and His Disciples*, Mayavati: Advaita Ashrama, 1990.

Jaffrelot, Christophe, *Modi's India: Hindu Nationalism and the Rise of Ethnic Democracy*, Chennai: Context, 2021.

————*The Hindu Nationalist Movement in India: 1925 to the 1990s*, New York: Columbia University Press, 1996.

James, William, *Pragmatism*, Auckland: The Floating Press, 2010.

————*The Varieties of Religious Experience: A Study in Human Nature*, New York: Routledge, 2012.

Jeffrey, Robin, *The Decline of Nair Dominance, Society and Politics in Travancore 1847–1908*, Manohar Publishers & Distributers, 1994.

Jha, D. N., *The Myth of the Holy Cow*, New Delhi: Navayana Publications, 2009.

Katju, Manjari, *Hinduising Democracy: The Vishva Hindu Parishad in Contemporary India*, New Delhi: New Text, 2017.

Kemp, John, *The Philosophy of Kant*, Oxford: Oxford University Press, 1968.

Koditschek, Theodore, *Liberalism, Imperialism, and the Historical Imagination: Nineteenth-Century Visions of a Greater Britain*, New York: Cambridge University Press, 2011.

Kopf, David, *British Orientalism and the Bengal Renaissance: The Dynamics of Indian Modernization 1773–1835*, Berkeley: University of California Press, 1969.

————*The Brahmo Samaj and the Shaping of the Modern Indian Mind*, Princeton: Princeton University Press, 1979.

Landau, Rom, *The Philosophy of Ibn' Arabi*, Oxon: Routledge, 2008.

Lekshmi, R., *Humanism of Swami Vivekananda*, Thiruvananthapuram: Ramakrishna Sarada Mission, 2005.

Macmillan, Margaret, *The War that Ended Peace: How Europe Abandoned Peace for the First World War*, London: Profile Books, 2013.

McLean, Hugh, *In Quest of Tolstoy*, Boston: Academic Studies Press, 2008.

Metcalf, Thomas R., *The New Cambridge History of India: Ideologies of the Raj*, Cambridge: Cambridge University Press, 1995.

Mill, John, *A History of British India, Volume 1*, London: Baldwin, Cradock and Joy, 1826.

Mukhopadyay, Nilanjan, *The RSS: Icons of the Hindu Right*, Chennai: Tranquebar, 2019.

Mukhopadyaya, Santilala, *The Philosophy of Man Making: A Study in Social and Political Ideas of Swami Vivekananda*, Calcutta: Central Book Agency, 1971.

Muller, F. Max, *Ramakrishna: His Life and Sayings*, Library of Alexandria, United States, 1898.

Nehru, Jawaharlal, *Sri Ramakrishna and Vivekananda*, Calcutta: Advaita Ashrama, 1965.

Nicholson, Andrew J., *Unifying Hinduism: Philosophy and Identity in Indian Intellectual Traditions*, New York City: Columbia University Press, 2013.

Nikhilananda, Swami, *Vivekananda: A Biography*, New York: Ramakrishna Vivekananda Center, 1989.

Nivedita, Sister, *Kali the Mother*, London: Swan Sonnenschein and Co, 1900.

———*Notes of Some Wanderings with Swami Vivekananda*, Calcutta: Udbhodan, 1913.

———*The Master As I Saw Him*, London: Longmans, Green and Co, 1907.

Noorani, A. G., *RSS: A Menace to India*, New Delhi: Left Word Books, 2019.

Otto, Rudolf, *Mysticism East and West, A Comparative Analysis of the Nature of Mysticism*, tr. Bertha L. Bracey and Richenda C. Payne, London: Macmillan & Co., 1932.

Parameswaran, P., *Swami Vivekanandan Navayuga Shilpi*, Kochi: Kurukshetra Prakashan, 2012.

———*Vishwavijayi Vivekanandan*, Thiruvananthapuram: Bharateeya Vichara Kendram, 2013.

Pennington, Brian K., *Was Hinduism Invented? Britons, Indians and the Colonial Construction of Hinduism*, New York: Oxford University Press, 2005.

Perlstein, Rick, *Nixon Land: The Rise of a President and the Fracturing of America*, New York: Scribner, 2008.

Pinkard, Terry, *German Philosophy 1760–1860: The Legacy of Idealism*, Cambridge: Cambridge University Press, 2002.

Pitre, Abul, *An Introduction to Elijah Muhammad Studies: The New Educational Paradigm*, Maryland: University Press of America, 2010.

Radhakrishnan, S., *Swami Vivekananda and Kerala*, Chennai: Vivekananda Kendra Prakashan Trust, 2012.

Radhakrishnan, Sarvepalli, *Bhagavad Gita*, New Delhi: HarperCollins, 2011.

Raychoudari, Tapan, *Europe Reconsidered: Perceptions of the West in Nineteenth Century Bengal*, New Delhi: Oxford University Press, 2002.

Reminiscences of Swami Vivekananda: His Eastern and Western Admirers, 4th edn, Mayavati: Advaita Ashrama, 2004.

Richards, John F., *The New Cambridge History of India: The Mughal Empire*, Cambridge: Cambridge University Press, 1995.

Rolland, Romain, *The Life of Vivekananda, And the Universal Gospel*, Mayavati: Advaita Ashrama, 2005.

Russell, Bertrand, *An Outline of Philosophy*, London: George Allen and Unwin, 1951.

Sadasivan, S. N., *Social History of India*, New Delhi: A. P. H. Publishing Corporation, 2000.

Sadhana: Swami Sivananda, The Divine Life Society, 2005.

Sanborn, Kate, *Abandoning an Adopted Farm*, New York: D. Appleton and Company, 1891.

Sankar, *The Monk as Man: The Unknown Life of Swami Vivekananda*, Gurgaon: Penguin Random House India, 2011.

Saradananda, Swami, *Sri Ramakrishna: The Great Master*, Chennai: Sri Ramakrishna Math, 2012.

Sarkar, Sumit, *A Critique of Colonial India*, Calcutta: Papyrus, 1988.

Savarkar, V. D., *Hindutva: Who is a Hindu?*, Bombay: Veer Savarkar Prakashan, 1969.

Schimmel, Annemarie, *Mystical Dimensions of Islam*, Chapel Hill: University of North Carolina Press, 1975.

Seager, Richard Hughes, *The World's Parliament of Religions: The East/West Encounter*, Bloomington: Indiana University Press, 1995.

Searle, John, *Mind, Language and Society: Philosophy in the Real World*, New York: Basic Book, 1998.

Sen, Amartya, *The Argumentative Indian: Writings on Indian History, Culture and Identity*, New Delhi: Penguin Books, 2006.

Sen, Amiya P., *Swami Vivekananda*, New Delhi: Oxford University Press, 2013.

Sen, Gautam, *The Mind of Swami Vivekananda*, Mumbai: Jaico Publishing House, 2011.

Sengupta, Hindol, *The Modern Monk: What Vivekananda Means to Us Today*, Gurgaon: Penguin Random House India, 2016.

Seth, Anil, *The Emergence of Indian Nationalism: Competition and Collaboration in the Later Nineteenth Century*, Cambridge: Cambridge University Press, 1971.

Sharma, Jyotirmaya, *Cosmic Religion and Human Apathy: Swami Vivekananda's Restatement of Religion*, New Delhi: HarperCollins, 2013.

Sil, Narasimha, *Swami Vivekananda: A Reassessment*, Selinsgrove: Susquehanna University Press, 1997.

Singh, Upinder, *A History of Ancient and Early Medieval India: From the Stone Age to the 12th Century*, Noida: Pearson, 2009.

Smith, Donald Eugene, *India as a Secular State*, New Jersey: Princeton University Press, 1963.

Soyen, Shaku, *Zen for Americans*, Illinois: Dorset Press, 1987.

Sperber, Jonathan, *Europe 1850–1914: Progress, Participation and Apprehension*, Harlow: Pearson Education Limited, 2009.

Srinivas, M. N., *Social Change in Modern India*, Hyderabad: Orient Blackswan, 2009.

Swami Vivekananda and His Guru: With Letters From Prominent Americans on the Alleged Progress of Vedantism in the United States, Madras: The Christian Literature Society for India, 1897.

Swami Vivekanandanum Prabuddha Keralavum, P. Parameswaran (ed.), Thiruvananthapuram: Bharateeya Vichara Kendram, 2013.

Taylor, Eugene, *William James on Consciousness Beyond the Margins*, Princeton: Princeton University Press, 1996.

Thapar, Romila, *A History of India: Volume 1*, Middlesex: Penguin Books, 1966.

Tharoor, Shashi, *Why I am a Hindu*, New Delhi: Aleph Book Company, 2018.

The Al-Qaeda Reader, Raymond Ibrahim (ed.), New York: Doubleday, 2006.

The Blackwell Guide to the Philosophy of Religion, William E. Mann (ed.), Oxford: Blackwell Publishing, 2005.

The Cambridge Companion to Husserl, Barry Smith and David Woodruff Smith (eds.), Cambridge: Cambridge University Press, 2005.

The Complete Works of Swami Vivekananda, Volumes 1 to 9, Mayavati Memorial Edition, Mayavati: Advaita Ashrama, 1991. Also available in DVD form as 'Complete Works of Swami Vivekananda' in 'Swami Vivekananda: Life, Work & Research', Oceanus Creative Technologies, Kolkata: Advaita Ashrama.

The Dhammapada, Oxford: Oxford University Press, 2000.

The Hymns of the Atharva Veda, tr. by Ralph T. H. Griffith, Global Grey, 2019.

The Life of Swami Vivekananda: By his Eastern and Western Disciples, Volume 1 to 2, Mayavati: Advaita Ashrama, 1989.

The Oxford Handbook of Philosophy of Religion, William J. Wainright (ed.), Oxford: Oxford University Press, 2005.

The Rig Veda, tr. Ralph T. H. Griffith, Global Grey, 2018.

The Roaring Twenties: 1920 to 1929, Rodney. P. Carlisle (ed.), New York: Facts on File, 2009.

The Sama Veda, tr. by Bibek Debroy and Dipavali Debroy, New Delhi: Books For All.

The Teachings of Ramana Maharshi, Arthur Osborne (ed.), London: Rider, 2014.

The World's Parliament of Religions: An Illustrated and Popular Story of the World's First Parliament of Religions in Connection with the Columbian Exposition of 1893, Volume 1 to 2, John Henry

Barrows (ed.), Chicago: Chicago Publishing Company, 1893.

The Yajur Veda, tr. Devi Chand, Hoshiarpur: Devi Chand, 1959.

Thompson, F. M. L., *The Rise of Respectable Society: A Social History of Victorian Britain: 1830–1900*, Cambridge: Harvard University Press, 1988.

Thoreau, Henry David, *Walden*, Boston and New York: Houghton, Mifflin & Co.,1906.

Tola, Fernando and Dragonetti, Carmen, *Being as Consciousness: Yogacara Philosophy of Buddhism*, Delhi: Motilal Banarsidass, 2004.

Tripathi, Rakesh, *Swami Vivekananda: The Journey of a Spiritual Entrepreneur*, New Delhi: Bloomsbury, 2019.

Twells, Alison, *The Civilising Mission and the English Middle Class (1792–1850): The Heathen at Home and Overseas*, Basingstoke: Palgrave Macmillan, 2009.

Upadhyaya, Deendayal, *Integral Humanism: An Analysis of Some Basic Elements*, New Delhi: Prabhat Prakashan, 2018.

Vivekananda and the Modernisation of Hinduism, William Radice (ed.), New Delhi: Oxford University Press, 1999.

Vivekananda in Indian Newspapers, 1893–1902, Shankari Prasad Basu (ed.), Calcutta: Basu Bhattacharya and Co, 1969.

Vroom, H. M., *No Other Gods: Christian Belief in Dialogue with Buddhism, Hinduism, and Islam*, tr. Lucy Jansen, Michigan and Cambridge: William B. Eerdmans Publishing Company, 1996.

W. Hastie, *Hindu Idolatry and the European Enlightenment: Six Letters Addressed to Educated Hindus Containing a Practical Discussion of Hinduism*, London: Thacker, Spink and Co., 1883.

Webb, Beatrice, *My Apprenticeship*, London: Longmans, Green and Co., 1946.

Weber, Max, *Capitalism and the Protestant Ethic*, New York: Penguin Books, 2002.

Wordsworth, William, 'The Wanderer', *Excursion: A Poem*, London: Edward Moxon, 1814.

Wright, Caleb, *India and its Inhabitants*, Cincinnati, Ohio: J. A. Brainerd, 1858.

Zaehner, R. C., *Hindu and Muslim Mysticism*, London: Bloomsbury Academic, 2016.

JOURNAL ARTICLES

Adam, Abba Idris, 'Islamic Civilization in the Face of Modernity: The Case of Jamal Al-Din Al-Afghani and Muhammad Abduh', *International Journal of Humanities and Social Science*, Vol. 7, No. 6, June 2017.

Banerjee, D. N., 'Rabindranath and the Cult of Nationalism', *The Indian Journal of Political Science*, Vol. 6, No. 1, July–September 1944, pp. 1–10.

Basu, Shankari Prasad, 'Vivekananda and Social Reform Movements in Kerala: Kumaran Asan, Dr. Palpu, Shri Narayana Guru and the SNDP Movement', *Prabuddha Bharata*, January and February 1989.

Basu, Tapan, 'Caste Matters: Rabindranath Tagore's Engagement with India's Ancient Social Hierarchies', *South Asia: Journal of South Asian Studies*, Vol. 35, No. 1, 2012, pp. 162–71.

Chattopadhyay, Kanan Lal, '19th Century Social Reform Movement in India: A Critical Appraisal', *Proceedings of the Indian History Congress*, Vol. 57, 1996, pp. 415–39.

Dasgupta, Swarupa, 'Notions of Nationhood in Bengal: Perspectives on Samaj (1867-1905)', *Modern Asian Studies*, Vol. 40, No. 2, 2006, pp. 273–302.

Dhar, Pulak Naranyan, 'Bengal Renaissance: A Study in Social Contradictions', *Social Scientist*, Vol. 15, No. 1, January 1987, pp. 26–45.

Dhavan, Rajeev, 'Harassing Husain: Uses and Abuses of the Law of Hate Speech', *Social Scientist*, Vol. 35, No. 1/2, January–February 2007, pp. 16–60.

Gandhi, Supriya, 'The Persian Writings on Vedānta Attributed to Banwālīdās Walī', *Journal of Indian Philosophy*, Vol. 48, 2020, pp. 79–99.

Jaffrelot, Christophe and Maheshwari, Malvika, 'Paradigm Shift by the RSS? Lessons from Aseemanand's Confessions', *Economic and Political Weekly*, Vol. 6, No. 6, February 2011, pp. 5–11.

Jones, Rosalind, 'Anti-Suffrage "Participative Citizens"', *Government and Opposition*, Vol. 27, No. 2, Spring 1992, pp. 252–58.

Kennedy, Marie and Tilly, Chris, 'Socialism, Feminism and the Stillbirth of Socialist Feminism in Europe, 1890–1920', *Science & Society*, Vol. 51, No. 1, Spring 1987, pp. 6–42.

Madaio, James, 'Rethinking Neo-Vedanta: Swami Vivekananda and the Selective Historiography of Advaita Vedanta', *Religions*, Vol. 8, No. 101, 2017.

Madan, T. N., 'The Sociology of Hinduism: Reading "Backwards" from Srinivas to Weber', *Sociological Bulletin*, Vol. 55, No. 2, May–August 2006, pp. 215–36.

Nair T. P. Sankarankutty, 'Dr. Palpu—The Pioneer Ezhava Social Reformer of Kerala. (1863-1950)', *Proceedings of the Indian History Congress*, Vol. 40, 1979, pp. 841–48.

Panikkar, K. N., 'Religious Symbols and Political Mobilization: The Agitation for a Mandir at Ayodhya', *Social Scientist*, Vol. 21, No. 7/8, July–August 1993, pp. 63–78.

Pollock, Sheldon, 'The Revelation of Tradition: śruti, smrti, and the Sanskrit Discourse of Power', *Boundaries Dynamics and the Construction of Tradition in South Asia*, Federico Squarsini (ed.), Firenze University Press, 2005.

Rambachan, Anantanand, 'The Place of Reason in the Quest for Moksha: Problems in Vivekananda's Conceptualization of Jñānayoga', *Religious Studies*, Vol. 23, No. 2, June 1987, pp. 279–88.

Rambachan, Anantanand, 'Where Words Fail: The Limits of Scriptural Authority in the Hermeneutics of a Contemporary Advaitin', *Philosophy East and West*, Vol. 37, No. 4, October 1987, pp. 361–71.

Rollmann, Hans, 'Deussen, Nietzsche, and Vedānta', *Journal of the History of Ideas*, Vol. 39, No. 1, January–March 1978, pp. 125–32.

Singh, Upinder, 'Varna and Jati in Ancient India: Some Questions', *Irreverent Histories: Essays for M. G. S. Narayanan*, Keshavan Veluthat and Donald R. Davis Jr. (ed.), Delhi: Primus Books, 2019.

Stavig, Gopal, 'Congruences between Indian and Islamic Philosophy', *Annals of the Bhandarkar Oriental Research Institute*, Vol. 81, No. 1/4, 2000, pp. 213–26.

Syed, Rachelle, 'Vedānta in Muslim Dress: Revisited and Reimagined', *Journal of Dharma Studies*, 2019, pp. 83–94.

INDEX

Ward, William, 153–55
Wilberforce, William, 154
Wodeyar, Chamrajendra, 17
World War I, xv, 40, 110, 124, 132, 134, 136, 138, 385
World War II, 40, 238
World's Colombian Exposition, 133

World's Parliament of Religions, 3, 4, 17–19, 23–32, 46
Wright, John Henry, 23–25

Yoga Sutra, 192, 350
Yoga Vasishta, 294